CHARLES GRAVIER,

COMTE DE VERGENNES

CHARLES GRAVIER, COMTE DE VERGENNES

French Diplomacy in the Age of Revolution: 1719-1787

Orville T. Murphy

Department of History

State University of New York at Buffalo

State University of New York Press

ALBANY

Published by State University of New York Press, Albany

Printed in the United States of America

For information, address State University of New York Press, State University Plaza, Albany, N.Y. 12246

Library of Congress Cataloging in Publication Data

Murphy, Orville Theodore.
Charles Gravier, comte de Vergennes.

Bibliography: p. 579
Includes index.
1. Vergennes, Charles Gravier, comte de, 1719-1787. 2. Diplomats—France—Biography.
3. France—Foreign relations—1715-1793. I. Title.
DC131.9.V3M84 327.2'092'4 [B] 81-2281
ISBN 0-87395-482-3 AACR2
ISBN 0-87395-483-1 (pbk.)

Acknowledgments

For permission to use materials, with modifications and additions which have previously appeared in print, we thank the editors of the *Economic History Review*, the *Canadian Historical Review* and the University of Virginia Press.

For permission to reproduce the portrait of Charles Gravier, Comte de Vergennes on the front cover, we thank Mr. Georges Dethan and Mr. Martial de la Fournière of the French Archives of Foreign Affairs, and Mr. Pierre de Tugny of Marly le Roi, France.

This book is dedicated to
Carolyn, Lisa and Marc
who have enriched my life

Contents

Part V. The Master Juggler Performs

Part VI. Eve Of Disaster

Preface

This is an old-fashioned, narrative history. It is based on the assumption that humans, although conditioned and restricted by the complex structures of their past and present, ultimately make their own history. Charles Gravier, Comte de Vergennes, was an aristocrat, a son of provincial nobility of the robe. His life history demonstrates the values of provincial service nobility: his mode of life was not excessively luxurious, he had little artistic taste or interest, and, at Court, he stood out as an overly domestic, very serious, hardworking servant of the King. Personally, he abhorred the extravagant, dissolute lives led by many of the Court nobility.

Yet, paradoxically, his career shows a steady determination to raise himself and his family into the ranks of the court aristocracy. At his death, the family was ensconced in important diplomatic posts, his two sons were military officers, and the older had been admitted to the King's exclusive circle. The Comtesse de Vergennes, sometimes mocked because of her low origins, was, nevertheless, a prominent figure at Court. Despite the relative modesty of their fortunes and their many social inadequacies, the Vergennes family rose steadily upward during the eighteenth century.

But to see Vergennes only as an aristocrat would be to misunderstand him. He was also a professional diplomat, a career officer of the State, and a loyal and obedient servant of his King. As a high officer of the extensive bureaucracy of the French Foreign Office, Vergennes belonged to a circle and a hierarchy that generated its own set of values. In many ways, Vergennes' life confirms the idea that, for the individual who makes a career of service to the State, "The State's purposes become his private purposes."[1] He was obedient to authority and lived the "mechanisms of fixed formal activity, fixed principles, views, and traditions."[2]

But Vergennes' personal career also represents values deeply imbedded in Western society. As a diplomat, and as Secretary of State, he developed a technical skill, a devotion to duty, and a capacity for sheer hard work that have characterized an active, efficient, and energetic civilization. At the same time, he learned to use organized and institutional pugnacity to achieve policies, and skillfully to divert the resources of society into power politics, war, and aggression. Acute observers have seen this tendency as a fatal trait of Western civilization.[3] Vergennes was probably among the least aggressive of all the Secretaries of State who served France from the reign of Louis XIV to that of Louis XVI. Still, he could not resist the temptation to aggress when the aggression promised an increase in French power and prestige. He valued peace (probably more than most statesmen of his century), but he valued it only on the condition that it furthered his aim to make Louis XVI arbiter of European high politics. To achieve such a goal by means of war was honourable; not to make war, when circumstances favourable to that goal arose, he would have considered a dereliction of duty to his King. Such are the keys to the mentality of this aristocrat, career diplomat, and Minister of State.

Vergennes performed his duties and he performed them superlatively well. Using the standards of his day, (and, perhaps, even standards of today) he was a success. He rose from obscure diplomat to Secretary of State for Foreign Affairs. His family rose from provincial nobility to status at Court. Louis XVI's foreign policies, according to many French historians, were the most successful aspect of his reign. Yet Vergennes's career inevitably raises the question of whether the pursuit of international power and prestige, and the cultivation of tendencies so necessary to that pursuit, are not ultimately self-destructive, to the state, the nation as well as to the individual. For Vergennes, the pursuit meant extraordinary personal sacrifices that, many times, left him ill; for his family, the result was tragedy and exile;[4] for Louis XVI, catastrophe and the guillotine.

There is not available, in any language, a study of Vergennes' entire career. With this study, I hope to fill that need. It is both a synthesis of earlier studies and, at the same time, an attempt to create a more complete portrait of the development of an individual whose decisions and policies played a significant role in the history of eighteenth century France and, indeed, the world.

A study covering a career as long and as varied as that of Vergennes of necessity relies heavily on the scholarship of others. Vergennes and his policies have been the subjects of excellent specialized monographs in both French and English. I have studied, borrowed, and modified these earlier interpretations. Scholars familiar with the subject will easily recognize my debts to others. In my notes and bibliography I have tried to make them explicit.

Several scholars, however, deserve special mention. For John B. Wolf's friendship, intelligence and advice I am eternally grateful. To John J. Meng I owe many "thank-yous;" his earlier study of Vergennes opened the way and pointed out the need for a study of Vergennes' entire career. The scholarship, conversations, critiques and enthusiasm of young scholars Robert Crout, Marie Donaghay, Jonathan R. Dull, and Svetlana Kluge have been a valuable and unique inspiration to me; they have taught me the meaning of the term "community of scholars."

My thanks also to Marcella Brannigan and Dorothy Ward who patiently and competently typed through so many revisions of the manuscript.

Part I

THE INITIATION

CHAPTER 1

War of the Austrian Succession

Charles Gravier de Vergennes' initiation into the diplomatic service of France was an experience of sharp contrasts: tranquillity and chaos, respect and humiliation, triumph and failure. In 1739 his "uncle" Anne-Theodore Chavignard de Chavigny, Louis XV's Minister to Portugal, invited Vergennes to be his Counselor of Embassy at Lisbon. Vergennes accepted. The appointment cost his father 50,000 *livres* paid to the crown for purchase of the post. With an additional 4,000 *livres* borrowed by his father to "furnish the need of my younger son for his voyage to Paris and Portugal,"[1] the twenty-year-old left his native Dijon to begin his diplomatic career.

At Lisbon, his professional education began in relative quiet. From a remote corner of Europe, he watched the War of Austrian Succession break over the Continent. The primary responsibility of the French minister at Lisbon was to keep Portugal neutral[2] and, since she was already inclined to remain so, the task did not overtax the French Minister or his nephew. The apprentice diplomat studied commerce, war, and high politics for four years at his leisure. But late in 1743 the uncle and nephew were ordered from Lisbon to Frankfort to represent France on a special mission to the Court of the Emperor Charles VII. One of the most difficult posts in Europe,[3] it was to become the arena for a major diplomatic defeat for France.

The military campaign of 1743 had gone badly for France and her allies: Bavaria had fallen to the Austrians; the Hanoverian-English troops had pushed back the French Marshal de Noailles in Alsace; and in Germany the French soldiers had been forced to retreat to the left bank of the Rhine River. But most threatening of all was the attitude of the Emperor Charles VII, France's protégé on the throne of the Holy Roman Empire. He had grown weary of the war and obviously wanted peace. The experienced Chavigny had long ago learned to take such tribulations in stride, even though they fatigued him and made him long to "return to the beautiful climate of Lisbon..."[4] But to the young Charles Gravier de Vergennes, resignation did not come so easily; his days in Germany were dominated by an intense desire to leave.[5] No doubt he realised that Germany might be the graveyard of his diplomatic career, begun barely four years before.

With his talents and family influence, Vergennes might have chosen to become a lawyer in *Parlement,* the ancient French high court of justice, or an officer in the *Chambre des Comptes* at Dijon, one of the sovereign courts responsible for supervision of the King's finances. His older brother, Jean, had been, since 1738, a *maître des comptes* and, since 1742, Président in the *Chambre des Comptes* though he was then not yet twenty-five. As a lawyer or an officer of the *Parlement* of Burgundy, located at Dijon, Vergennes would have enjoyed, at least, the acclaim and prestige of his home city.[6] Instead, in 1743, he was abroad at a court which was damp with fear and torn by intrigue and strife, a court from which Chavigny, Minister of his Most Christian Majesty Louis XV, would depart under a heavy guard.

Since the fifteenth century, generation after generation of service as lawyers to the Crown had solidly established the Seigneurs de Vergennes as respectable *noblesse de robe* of Burgundy.[7] The Gravier family traced its origins back to Jean Gravier, Seigneur de Chavigny, and Claudine Boiteaux. Their sons, Théophile, Seigneur de Drambon, and Jean, were both lawyers. The older, Théophile, married the sister of Claude de Saumaise, the famous scholar at the court of Queen Christina of Sweden. The younger, Jean, lived at Autun, practiced law at *Parlement,* and married Madeline Thomas, whose family also had for generations provided officers to *Parlement* and the *Chambre des Comptes* at Dijon. Their son, Philibert, another lawyer at *Parlement,* married the daughter of Charles Perrault, Seigneur de Vergennes. From this union came Charles (I) Gravier, the grandfather of the young diplomat, and through this marriage the Graviers inherited the Seigneurie de Vergennes.[8]

There were three different lands bearing the name "Vergennes" by the late eighteenth century. The Seigneurie de Vergennes, in the *bailliage* of Chalon and listed in the *Nouvel Etat Général* of 1783, had been the town of Ormes and its dependencies. In 1768 Ormes contained 84 homes, probably no more than 300 people, and four villages which were its dependencies.[9] It now belonged to Jean Gravier de Vergennes, the diplomat's older brother, who had the name changed to Vergennes only in 1778.[10] The much larger Comté de Vergennes had been the Comté de Toulongeon in the *bailliage* of Montcenis. Charles (III) Gravier de Vergennes, the subject of this biography, inherited it from his uncle and protector, Chavigny, and had the name changed to Vergennes by a letter patent from Louis XVI in 1778.[11]

But neither of these possessions, both substantial, was the original Seigneurie de Vergennes. This too was located in the *bailliage* of Montcenis, in what is now the commune of Saint-Gervais-sur-Couche in the Département of Saône-et-Loire. The diminutive size of this seigneurie is easily judged by the fact that, as late as 1848, the entire commune of Saint-Gervais-sur-Couche had no more than 130 houses, a small woods, called the *Bois de Vergennes,* the ruins of an old château, and some vineyards, producing wines which the priest and scholar, Courtepré, judged "barely potable".[12] The size of this tiny original seigneurie, compared with the much greater and more valuable Vergennes possessions at the end of the eighteenth century, clearly illustrates how much the family fortunes advanced during those years.

On April 30, 1680, Vergennes' paternal grandfather, Charles (I) Gravier, married Anne Garnier, the daughter of a *Parlement* lawyer, and by 1708 had risen to the position of Treasurer of the *Chambre des Comptes* at Dijon.[13] He had four children: three daughters, of whom two became Ursuline nuns; and a son, Charles (II) who, on February 15, 1718, married Marie Francoise, daughter of Jean Chevignard de Charodon, the first President of the Bureau of Finances of Dijon. They had two sons: the older, Jean, was born on November 5, 1718, and eventually inherited the original Seigneurie of Vergennes.[14] The other, Charles (III) Gravier became the novice diplomat under his uncle Chavigny.

The records of Charles (III) Gravier de Vergennes' early life are so scanty that we know very little about his childhood. He was born at home on December 29, 1719, near the "*Coin du Miroir*", rue Saint-Jean, now rue Bossuet, in the city of Dijon. On the day of his birth, he was baptized at the parish church of Saint-Jean, just a few steps from his home.[15] Here and in the townhouse of his grandfather, the Treasurer General of *Parlement,* located not far away on the rue Charrue, and at their family country estates, he spent his childhood.

Both the Vergennes house on the rue Saint-Jean and the grandfather's house on the rue Charrue have been reconstructed since the eighteenth century,[16] making it impossible to estimate anything of their wealth from the family's homes. But the marriage contract of Vergennes' father and mother gives some evidence of their resources. On February 15, 1718, the family of Charles Gravier de Vergennes agreed to contribute to the couple's assets 80,000 *livres,* in *rentes,* inheritance, and land, including the Seigneurie du Bois de Vergennes, while the wife's dowry totalled 45,000 *livres,* of which 10,000 *livres,* were for immediate half ownership of the Chevignard house on rue Saint-Jean, 20,000 in *rentes* and the rest at the death of her father, Jean Chevignard.[17]

Other marriage contracts of Dijon in the eighteenth century indicate that the assets of Vergennes' mother and father placed them economically in the upper five per cent of Dijon.[18] Dijon had neither industry nor a great deal of commerce, and no significant class of important bourgeois or merchants. The *Parlement* nobility, therefore, were the richest in the city. In fact, the absence of a large middle class at Dijon justifies the conclusion that, in that city, the robe nobility exercised an overwhelming economic domination.[19] The Vergennes family were by no means the wealthiest family in Dijon.[20] But just how far above the "common man" the Vergennes family was is strikingly illustrated by the fact that in seventy-eight per cent of the marriages there the assets brought to the marriage totaled between 200 and 5,000 *livres*.[21]

Vergennes grew up in the neighborhood of the historic Church of Saint-Jean. He never really knew his mother. She died before he was four and his father married Bernarde Petit, widow of a Monsieur Alexandre, substitute *conseillier du roi* at the Bureau of Finances of Dijon.[22] As a boy, he no doubt watched the traditional festival, the *feu de Saint-Jean* held once a year on the feast of Saint-Jean. In the evening, before the church a huge bonfire blazed, while around it danced and chanted the townsfolk: "Squire Saint-Jean, here is your festival; Squire Saint-Jean, make merry," they sang and, having paid their respects to the Saint, proceeded to follow their own advice and make merry.[23] Only one of the old houses, the seventeenth century "*La Tourelle*" at the "*Coin du Miroir,*" stands today. And, except for the Cordeliers Square, little remains of the neighborhood where Vergennes' grandfather lived and where he himself lived between 1728 and 1734.

The school where he received his education from the Jesuits is today the Municipal Library of Dijon. The chapel where Vergennes worshipped is now the reading room. With the Jesuits Vergennes studied law, presented two theses, one on canon law and the other on civil law, and became *licencié en droit* early in 1739.[24] It was later that same year that his "uncle," Chavigny, offered him the post of Counselor of Embassy.

The "uncle," Théodore Chevignard de Chavigny was not, strictly speaking, Vergennes' uncle. And he did not emerge at the court of Louis XIV "out of the mud" as that inveterate scandalmonger, Saint-Simon, suggests.[25] Although Théodore as well as his brother Philibert habitually referred to themselves during their lifetimes as Vergennes' "uncle", their relation was, infact, more distant. Our diplomat's maternal grandfather, Jean Chevignard de Chorodon, was Théodore's first cousin. In the popular language of the day Théodore was Vergennes' uncle "*à la mode de Bretagne*". Chavigny's ancestors were notaries at Beaune, and his father was first, the king's attorney at the salt granary there, and then, secretary to the Comte Le Roy de Chavigny. Chavigny's father died before the boy and his brother Philibert, were grown, and their mother placed them under the tutelage of their maternal uncle Vinchon, who handled the business affairs of the Comte de Chavigny. He sent them to school at the Collège de Clermont in Paris.

With their uncle's connivance, they discarded the family name of Chevignard and began to pose as sons of the now-dead Grand Seigneur Chavigny. Their Jesuit teachers apparently had a hand in the deception; they recommended the boys to Louis XIV's confessor as poor sons of the illustrious house of Le Roy de Chavigny and, soon afterwards, in 1706, the young men were presented to Louis XIV under the names they had assumed. Louis offered them positions in the army. However, when Louis XIV later discovered the deception, he made them sell their positions, and they fled to Holland in disgrace.

Nevertheless, the two ingenious young men refused to accept defeat. They established a semi-professional spy service at the negotiations for the Peace of Utrecht (1712-1713) and, in this capacity, proved so valuable to France that they once again began to enjoy favor at court. After the Sun King's death, Théodore attached himself to the powerful minister, the Cardinal Dubois (Secretary of State for Foreign Affairs, and Chief Minister, 1718-1723) who launched him on his diplomatic career. During the negotiations for the Triple and Quadruple Alliances Dubois sent Chavigny to England as his secret agent.

In 1719, Chavigny served in Italy–first in Genoa, then Parma, Piacenza, and Tuscany–and in 1722, he successfully carried out a mission to Spain. For his services he was rewarded with the governorship of Beaune, an honor which brought him additional income, but few responsibilities. Then he was sent to Hanover (1723-24), and to the Diet of Ratisbon (1726), where he strove to revive the pro-French party among the Electors of the Holy Roman Empire.[26] It was there that he won Charles Albert of Bavaria to the French cause. In 1731, he was in London, where he remained until 1737, when he was transferred to Denmark. Chavigny thus had behind him a long and varied career of diplomatic service when he took his nephew under his wing in 1739. Experienced, cosmopolitan, and enjoying the respect and friendship of important people at court and in Europe, he was the ideal tutor for an aspirant to the diplomatic service. The Duc de Luynes said of him: "Without contradiction he was one of the most experienced ministers in foreign affairs and, especially, in those questions having to do with Germany."[27]

In Germany, the Holy Roman Emperor, Charles VII, the former Charles Albert, Elector of Bavaria, was one of those pathetic individuals whose ambitions "were greater than his talents."[28] Chavigny was sent to supply the imagination and intelligence that Charles lacked, but the task was impossible. Reflecting on the situation in Germany in 1743, Vergennes could see only a chain of complex negotiations, illusory victories, and costly defeats whose origins went back to a time even before his birth.

In 1719 the previous Holy Roman Emperor, Charles VI, had tried to secure the future of the Hapsburg possessions to his daughter Maria Theresa by a family law, the Pragmatic Sanction, which he spent his life trying to persuade the princes of Europe to recognize. In 1726, Charles Albert, new Elector of Bavaria, formally agreed to the Emperor's wishes. His action was a victory for Charles VI because the Elector, having married a daughter of Emperor Joseph I,[29] was one of the two male relatives of the Hapsburgs (the other was Augustus III of Saxony) who might through their wives make a claim to the inheritance. When the great powers of Europe agreed to the Pragmatic Sanction, the Hapsburg inheritance seemed secured for the Emperor's daughter, Maria Theresa.

But no sooner was Charles VI dead, than Frederick II of Prussia violated the treaties and invaded Silesia, demanding the territory from Maria Theresa, now Queen of the Hapsburg dominions of Bohemia and Hungary and Archduchess of Austria. Once the Pragmatic Sanction was violated, the Elector of Bavaria, who had always had reservations about it, advanced claims of his own, knowing that the Austrian Queen was occupied with her war with Frederick. To give his demands weight, he marched his soldiers, most of them French, for the French had by treaty agreed to help him, down the Danube toward Vienna. In December, 1741, Charles Albert was crowned king of Bohemia and, helped by French gold, within six weeks was elected to Imperial throne as Emperor Charles VII.[30]

Nevertheless, on the day of his coronation the Margravin Wilhelmine of Bayreuth noted that the "poor Emperor did not have all the satisfaction he must have expected." The French armies were now in retreat; the Austrians had invaded Bavaria, "which they devastated unmercifully;" and Charles was "terribly ill with gout."[31] That very day his capital city of Munich fell to the Austrians,[32] putting Maria Theresa in an excellent position to destroy Charles, and even to take Alsace and Lorraine from France as indemnity for France's assistance to Charles Albert. She refused to recognize Charles' claims to Bohemia or the Emperorship, and she organized a formidable anti-Bourbon coalition in the Treaty of Worms in September of 1743. Now France had cause to fear for its border provinces. Already at war with England, France declared war on Austria.[33]

By now Charles VII had grown weary of the war, and Louis XV feared that he was secretly trying to ease out of it.[34] In fact, Charles had lost confidence in France's ability to protect his hold on the Imperial Crown and to advance his demands on Austrian possessions. Charles continually complained that France never listened to his counsels nor permitted him to participate in any important decisions. He was especially piqued that the French auxiliary troops had retreated from Bavaria and allowed the Austrians to overrun his electrorate.

Chavigny's responsibilities at Charles' court[35] were primarily to assure the

Emperor that Louis XV was determined to stand by his commitments.[36] The crumbling military situation made it impossible to gain for the Emperor all the advantages that he had earlier hoped for, but Louis XV promised to help him obtain as much as possible. He further assured Charles that France would never listen to any propositions for peace without Charles' participation, a pledge that he hoped Charles would reciprocate.

The most explosive cause of distrust between Charles and Louis, however, was that of subsidies. France had paid Charles 500,000 *livres* a month to maintain an army of 35,000 men. But the army never amounted to more than 20,000 men, and part of the reduced army was financed, as France knew, from the Bavarian treasury. Thus, according to French calculations, the Emperor had gained considerable personal benefits out of the total of 6,000,000 *livres* Louis XV had paid him for his army. If the subsidies were to continue, France wanted its own commissioner present at the reviews and musters of Charles' army to insure that the soldiers on the muster lists actually existed.

Despite France's generosity, Charles' demands continued to multiply. He wanted more money to maintain the army, more to maintain his household, and more to maintain his "dignity" as Emperor. France generously agreed to higher subsidies, but she considered the sums already paid to be part of the new agreement. Charles protested that the new arrangements were *in addition* to the older subsidy. Chavigny, with Vergennes' assistance, had to make Charles recognize that French resources were not unlimited. In addition to her commitments to the Emperor, France had sent an army to Italy because Sardinia had broken her French alliance. Moreover, she had armies in northern Europe which had to be kept in a state of readiness for the next campaign. Louis XV, also, found it difficult to understand why the price of maintaining Charles' Imperial "dignity" now cost so much more than the 2,000,000 *livres* a year which had earlier proved sufficient.

The most significant result of Chavigny's first mission to Germany was his discovery of the plans of Charles and Frederick of Prussia for a union of German princes. When he reported this fact, upon his return to Versailles, his superiors immediately dispatched him back to Germany with new instructions, and with full powers to conclude alliances with the German princes concerned in the proposed union.[37] Once again in Germany Chavigny busied himself, with Frederick's active assistance, in organizing the Union of Frankfort. By this agreement, Frederick of Prussia, the Prince of Hesse-Cassel, and the Palatinate Elector promised to maintain Charles Albert's rights to his lost territories and to the Imperial throne. In addition, they all vowed to defend the constitution of the Empire and piously hoped for the return of peace to Germany.[38] Shortly afterwards, France was invited to join the Union, and did so immediately since, in the articles of the Union,

Chavigny had protected her interests.

The presence of Frederick's troops in Germany in the campaign of 1744 gave the Emperor Charles the opportunity to recover Bavaria. When he moved his court from Frankfort to Munich,[39] Chavigny and Vergennes moved with him, and lived there with everyone in constant fear of an Austrian invasion.[40] Daily the Bavarians hounded Chavigny for more French soldiers and more money to defend themselves. But far away in Versailles one had to become accustomed, to use the phrase of René Louis, Marquis d' Argenson, the Secretary of State for Foreign Affairs, to Chavigny's "demonstrations of despair"; Versailles simply sent back irritating advice,[41] but no more assistance. Suddenly, in January, 1745, Charles' agonies were brought to an abrupt close. He suffered a violent attack of the gout. The symptoms spread and two days later he died, showing in his last minutes, "the most perfect submission to Divine will."[42] Now Chavigny was left, along with the new French Ambassador to the Emperor, the Comte de Bavaria,[43] to salvage whatever could be saved of the French position in Germany. Unfortunately, this was very little.

Charles' unexpected death threatened the Union of Frankfort and reopened the question of the election of an Emperor.[44] Maria Theresa was now more than ever determined to push the candidacy of her husband, the Grand Duke Francis. When Argenson heard of her plan, he vowed that he would use the French army down to the last soldier to prevent the election of Francies.[45] This was only a bluff. He really had no alternative candidate he could advance as a serious contender for the throne.[46]

At Munich, Chavigny saw that Argenson's new policy meant the abandonment of the new Elector of Bavaria, the young Alexander-Maximilian, as France's candidate for the Imperial succession. Chavigny did not presume to support the young man's candidacy, but he took "possession of him," as the English so aptly put it, and became his spokesman.[47] Chavigny felt that France was obligated to support the new Elector's claims to Austrian possessions. He also felt that the Union of Frankfort should be held together to assure the "freedom" of election for a new Emperor, thereby at least leaving the door open for Maximilian.

Chavigny's advocacy of the young elector's cause provoked a warning from Argenson that he should be more French and less Bavarian.[48] The French Secretary of State for Foreign Affairs had no desire to revive the Union of Frankfort and he greatly resented Chavigny's uncalled-for advice.[49] Chavigny was acting, he grumbled, like a magpie "spoiling her baby." With his French auxiliary forces melting away and no reinforcements promised or in sight, Maximilian abandoned Munich and fled to Augsburg. Maria-Theresa, sensing his desperation, presented her terms for peace.[50]

Chavigny, with Vergennes, followed Maximilian to Augsburg, but there was really nothing they could do to cushion his defeat. Maximilian had no alternative but to sign for peace. In the Treaty of Füssen he renounced all claims to Hapsburg lands, pledged his vote to Francis for Emperor, and promised to remain neutral. In return, he recovered his electorate of Bavaria. The following September, despite the refusal of Prussia and the Palantinate to give the Grand Duke their votes, Francis was elelcted Emperor of the Holy Roman Empire.[51] France stood defeated on every front. At the coronation of Francis I, Maria Theresa, pregnant and content with her achievements, glowed with the satisfaction of knowing that, almost alone, she had caused the miscarriage of her enemies' designs on the Imperial throne and her possessions.

As Chavigny struggled to advance French policy in Germany, Vergennes provided whatever assistance he could. With great care, the novice read reports of troops recruited, transports contracted for, and subsidies paid out. These activities involved huge expenditure of money, and Vergennes soon learned the terrible cost of the game of high politics. France undertook to hire 6,000 troops in the name of the Holy Roman Emperor from Prince William of Hesse-Cassel. Since England had previously contracted for the use of these same troops, Prince William had a seller's market and he knew it. To facilitate the bargaining, Chavigny advanced to his Imperial Majesty letters of exchange worth over 1,000,000 *écus* of the Empire.[52]

Once subsidy agreements were concluded, Vergennes assumed the duties of payment and accounting. During the fall of 1744, for example, he sent to the French representative with the Imperial forces, a M. de Lantingshaussen, 820,000 *livres* to be used to sustain the Imperial army and to pay for horses, artillery, and pontoons. When the Emperor recruited new soldiers, France also paid for muskets and bayonets.

Accounting for these huge expenditures in time of war was next to impossible. Generals at the front did not hesitate to take money earmarked for special purposes if they needed it to pay their troops. Contractors took advantage of the fortunes of war. Louis XV agreed to pay contractors one *écu* a day for each of six hundred fifty transport horses. But Vergennes learned that sometimes only four or five hundred horses were actually in use. Conscientiously, Vergennes counted, paid,questioned, and tried to make order out of the chaos created by war and man's greed.[53]

In Germany, Vergennes also began his career as a negotiator. He was commissioned to approach Prince William of Hesse-Cassel in the fall of 1744 to persuade him to occupy the neutral city of Cologne. Vergennes carried with him to the discussion good military reasons why William should comply. Louis XV proposed to send an army to the lower Rhine, and the occupation of the city would help cover the territory of France's allies, Prussia and the Palatinate. Also, troops at Cologne could threaten Hanover, and free Prussian troops near Magdeburg to permit them to intimidate Saxony.

"But I no sooner opened my mouth," Vergennes wrote his uncle, "than they openly opposed such an undertaking." The occupation of the city of Cologne, Vergennes heard, would be "diametrically opposed" to the principles of the Union of Frankfort whose object was the maintenance of the Empire in conformity with the Treaty of Westphalia. The enemies of the Union would then have cause to arouse the fears of other states against France and her allies. Furthermore, Vergennes heard, the French army was not strong enough to risk a plan that would excite hatred and defiance and alienate those states which might be disposed to unite with her. The Union of Frankfort, Prince William reminded Vergennes, had been formed to guarantee the German states against oppression from Vienna. Violence against the neutral city of Cologne, no matter how justified militarily, would be interpreted by the German states as another form of oppression. "... The Union would cease to be legitimate," Vergennes later explained, "and this could not happen without our losing all the advantages that we wanted to draw from it: I mean popularity. That would not be an insignificant inconvenience in a country such as this." In response to Vergennes' arguments of military expediency, Prince William lectured him on public law, the constitution of Germany, and public opinion. What soldiers called military expediency, Prince William noted, others called oppression. "There, my dear Uncle," the novice ended the report of his first diplomatic failure, "is what I was told relative to the occupation of Cologne. . . ."[54]

As the French policy in Germany collapsed, manifestations of German contempt and dislike for France became fierce.[55] When Chavigny left Augsburg to return to Munich, he had to have a heavy guard.[56] Chavigny had patiently suffered the humiliations as long as there was a possibility that something could be accomplished, but when Maximilian put his signature to the Treaty of Füssen there was nothing left for him to do. And Maximilian informed Chavigny that his presence at court could no longer be tolerated.[57]

Since little could be salvaged for France from the debacle at Munich, Chavigny decided to devote his energies to helping his nephew. To the influential Prince de Conti he wrote that, if France decided later that Bavaria merited a minister to represent her, "without doubt the choice of my nephew ought to be given consideration over that of anyone else. . . ." Chavigny argued that it would be a good idea to leave behind in Germany "a token of my principles and of whatever credit I have acquired here. To tell the truth, my nephew would have no great inclination to remain here, because he has too soon learned, watching the setbacks I have experienced, the difficulty people have in achieving anything when they are as isolated as we are."[58] Nothing came of Chavigny's letter. Argenson was in no mood to reward anyone. On November 5, 1745,[59] he granted Chavigny permission to return to Versailles. As Chavigny bitterly contemplated his ill-fated experience, he hoped that Argenson would, at least, keep a promise he had earlier made to arrange his debts, pay his pension, and send him back to Lisbon.

The atmosphere at Versailles was unpleasant. Argenson was hostile, and the King, too removed from affairs to form his own opinions, took his cue from his Secretary of State in his treatment of his ex-minister to Charles VII. Outside of official circles, life was no easier. Everywhere they went, Chavigny and Vergennes were living reminders of France's diplomatic defeat in Germany. In addition, on December 12, 1745, Vergennes' father died. To the scourge of public humiliation was added the pain of personal sorrow.

Argenson kept his promise to send Chavigny back to Lisbon, but when the old diplomat and his nephew were ready to leave, their way was blocked by a dispute over etiquette. Portugal refused to receive Chavigny until he was instructed to address the Portuguese Minister of Foreign Affairs as "Your Excellency."[60] Lisbon claimed that Chavigny had already recognized the validity of the title before his mission to Germany, and further claimed that Argenson had agreed to the formula. But Argenson flatly denied he had agreed to anything.[61] When Portugal retorted that the Papal Nuncio and the Spanish Ambassador had already agreed to use the title, Argenson curtly inquired if the crown of France had to take its examples from others.[62]

Portugal was not really prepared to break relations over a point of etiquette and ultimately capitulated, but the bickering and haggling delayed the departure of Chavigny and his entourage until the fall of 1746. The precious question of etiquette finally settled, Chavigny, accompanied by Vergennes, set out once more for Lisbon.[63] They had hardly entered that city before they were confronted with another unpleasantness. King John V had been publicly insulted by the great powers of Europe, and he held France responsible.

Louis XV had agreed to support John V as mediator for settlement of the War of Austrian Succession. Perhaps the idea originated with Argenson; the evidence is not clear on this point.[64] But it was obvious to the other powers that John lacked the power and personal force to serve as a mediator. A sick and dying man, he was a religious fanatic, completely dominated by the church.[65] The reactions of the European powers to the suggestion were to be expected: they did not take the idea seriously.[66] England, Spain, and Austria, already involved in negotiations at The Hague and at Breda, brusquely declined the suggestion, making no attempt whatsoever to hide their contempt for the Portuguese monarch. Humiliated, John exploded and turned on those he believed responsible for his embarassment. His first target was France. Chavigny and Vergennes received the brunt of his wrath.

Since Chavigny disliked Argenson, he was not at all reluctant to relay John's outbursts to Versailles.[67]

The question of who had originated the idea became the main issue for dispute. Argenson insisted that the Portuguese Ambassador to France, Don Luis D'Acunha, had suggested it to him; but the Ambassador denied parenthood and stoutly argued that Argenson was the father of the plan.[68]

Vergennes once again saw his uncle in the uncomfortable position of being the medium through which a court's violent reaction to French policy was conveyed to Versailles. Chavigny told his superiors that the Portuguese could not understand how Argenson could believe that Portugal had initiated the plan for mediation.[69] Don Luis d'Acunha was not a man who would mislead anyone, the Portuguese court insisted, and Argenson's imputation was an attack on his honour. Portugal was suggesting, in other words, that Argenson was a liar. Either Louis XV had to support his Secretary of State and reveal all the documents on the negotiations to prove Argenson's veracity, or else disown him. A few weeks later Argenson was dismissed. The encounter with John V helped to precipitate his fall.[70] Neither Chavigny nor Vergennes regretted his departure.

During the remaining years of his stay in Lisbon, Vergennes watched Chavigny repair the damage which the crisis over mediation had created. In addition, Chavigny still had previously assigned orders to try to conclude a commercial treaty with Portugal. To these responsibilities they both turned, with Chavigny using all the skill and *délicatesse* which had earned him a reputation as one of Europe's most sophisticated diplomats. The work of the commercial treaty was not completed, but the ill-feeling aroused by John V's humiliation was soon dissipated. When they left Lisbon at the end of 1749 to return to France, they did so with the satisfaction of having successfully carried out a difficult assignment. Vergennes' apprenticeship in the diplomatic service thus ended with a mild triumph.

In the diplomatic service of England, D.B. Horn has noted, the higher one rose, the fewer the opportunities for further promotion because of the competition from noblemen, court favorites, and politicians.[71] The same could be said for the French diplomatic service. In the French diplomatic service, as in other high offices of the state, the nobility claimed an unquestioned right to preference. And their monarch usually agreed. Louis XIV had been especially exclusive in his selection of diplomats, preferring to appoint members of the nobility of the sword, rather than the nobility of the robe, to the important posts at Vienna, Rome, Madrid, and London. This preference for nobility of the sword lingered well into the eighteenth century.

As a son of nobility of the robe, Vergennes was very conscious of his inferiority before those who were nobles of the sword. How else can one explain his painful anxiety to please, his compulsion for work, and his unending exhibition of respect for his social and official superiors? His consciousness of his place in the social hierarchy certainly explains his determination, later in life, to start his sons in the officer ranks of the military before they launched their careers in diplomacy. For Vergennes, the diplomatic service was never the place to get rich, but for one's self and family it would be, as it was in England, "... a purgatory through which it was possible to reach high office ...."[72]

To have served his apprentice years under such a man as Chavigny was an honor that the nephew fully recognized, even though these first years were trying in the extreme. To watch France's prestige and influence in Germany disappear, to see French-supported armies collapse, and a French puppet surrender to the enemy, to experience defeat, were painful. For the diplomats these meant reprimands from Versailles, and contempt in Germany. And when the fledgling diplomat opened his first negotiations with Prince William of Hesse, he won nothing but a lecture on the realities of politics. Diplomacy, like human history, the prince noted, could not be reduced to the calculations of soldiers. What seemed to be expedient from France's point of view easily appeared to others an injustice. During these early years in Germany the young Vergennes also saw the waste, corruption and downright dishonesty bred by War. As for French attempts to place their own candidate on the Imperial throne, the obvious lesson was drawn by the Marquis d'Argenson: "... Let's leave the Empire in repose and it will do the same toward us; to create and protect an Emperor cost us more than it would ever cost us if the Empire decided to destroy us."[73] Vergennes never forgot that lesson; years later it became his policy.

CHAPTER 2

A King of the Romans

The return of Vergennes and Chavigny to France in October, 1749, brought them back once again to the Court at Versailles. What a contrast this time compared with their return from Germany! The Minister of Foreign Affairs was no longer the unfriendly Argenson who regarded Chavigny as a weak "nursemaid".[1] In his place was Chavigny's old friend, Louis Philoxen Brulart, marquis de Puysieux.[2] Instead of a return tarnished by the humiliations of a diplomatic defeat, Chavigny was recognized as having accomplished a great deal toward the rebuilding of the French influence in Portugal. Indeed, rumors were afloat that Chavigny might be the next Minister of Foreign Affairs.[3] How agreeable it was for Vergennes to enjoy the reflected glory of one whose political star was shining brightly! How satisfying to the young apprentice diplomat to find that, as a result of several reports he had written on a treaty of commerce with Portugal, Puysieux recognized his merit.[4] And how promising to know that, when Puysieux presented Chavigny to the King, the uncle now 62 years old did not forget his protégé. "Sire," Chavigny had said to Louis XV, "the young negotiator I have developed . . . no longer needs my help, and I would need his in order to continue to serve Your Majesty; it is time for me to quit and for him to begin."[5]

But Chavigny's recommendation to Louis XV had no immediate effect. Autumn passed and winter came. Chavigny was named Ambassador to Venice.[6] Vergennes received nothing. He lingered on at Versailles because (as he much later admitted) "absence is a mortal poison at court." Not until spring came did Chavigny's remark begin to bear fruit; Vergennes was appointed minister to the Elector of Trier, with an income of 12,000 *livres* a year, retroactive to January 1, 1750. In addition, he was granted extra pay for refurnishing his residence, and an "extraordinary" 3,000 to cover incidentals.[7] At last he was on his own. Almost immediately his new post became a challenge, for the complex evolution of European diplomacy produced a proposal to elect the Hapsburgs' Archduke Joseph as King of the Romans. And the opposition that developed temporarily forced the reluctant Elector of Trier out of seclusion and onto the diplomatic stage of Germany.

The Treaties of Westphalia gave France the justification to intervene in German affairs. Furthermore, by the close of the seventeenth century, France had become a Rhenish power. It was therefore possible to influence politics in Germany by exerting pressure on the small powers such as Trier, Deux-Ponts, and the Palatinate, who were within easy reach of French armies, and to do so in the name of the Imperial Constitution and the Treaties of Westphalia. Vergennes' service at Trier, Hanover, and the Palatinate during the negotiations for election of a King of the Romans gave him practical schooling in how useful it was to have small powers bordering France. Large powers were not so easily intimidated.

The close of the War of Austrian Succession had produced a new worry for the English Secretary of State, Newcastle: the danger of England's diplomatic isolation from the Continent. The peace settlement had left the principal English ally, Maria Theresa of Austria, thoroughly dissatisfied and inclined to blame Great Britain for her unhappiness. She felt the English had deserted her in the secret negotiations preceding the Treaty of Aix-la-Chapelle. At that time, British negotiators had agreed to guarantee to Frederick the Great the territory of Silesia, which he had taken by force from the Austrian Archduchess. Not only that, but the English cabinet, led by the First Lord of Treasury, Henry Pelham, was disinclined to recognize Maria Theresa's claims for £ 100,000 in subsidies which she insisted the English owed her.[8]

Concurrently, Maria Theresa stubbornly refused to negotiate a renewal of the Barrier Treaty with England's Dutch allies. The third Barrier Treaty, signed in 1715 as a deterrent to French aggression, had obligated Austria to provide three-fifths of a force of 30,000 to 35,000 troops to be stationed in the Austrian Netherlands. The treaty had also stipulated that Austria pay subsidies to the Dutch, who furnished the remaining two-fifths of the soldiers manning the Barrier fortresses. The War of Austrian Succession had virtually nullified the Barrier Treaty. Maria Theresa was reluctant to renew it because, during the war, the Dutch had surrendered some of the Barrier fortresses to the French armies with scarcely any attempt at defense. When the war was over, the Archduchess had quite willingly restored to the Dutch the fortresses they had previously garrisoned, but she refused to continue the subsidies until the Dutch agreed to help pay for reconstructing the fortresses destroyed by the French. Since a French invasion of the Netherlands was a threat to English as well as to Dutch interests, George II and his Secretary of State, the Duke of Newcastle, had every reason to desire an immediate renewal of the Barrier Treaty.

George II also needed Austrian friendship because Austrian military forces constituted part of the defense of his German possessions in Hanover, where he was the Elector. Both France and Prussia were in a position to strike at Hanover. Although Frederick the Great was George II's nephew, the English King did not trust his blood relation. He considered Frederick a "mischievous rascal, a bad friend, a bad ally, a bad relation, and a bad neighbour, . . .the most dangerous and evil-disposed prince in Europe."[9] To bolster England's uneasy position in Germany, Newcastle decided to take the initiative. The key to his plan was the election of the Archduke Joseph of Austria as the King of the Romans.

The Emperor of the Holy Roman Empire was elected, and the successor to that position, who bore the title of King of the Romans, was often elected before the throne became vacant. The Hapsburg Emperors had favored such a practice because it gave them an opportunity to select their own successors; by skillfully exploiting the Emperor's position, the Hapsburgs had gradually managed to make the Imperial crown a quasi-hereditary possession.

Yet the power of the Hapsburgs to keep the Imperial office in the family was not absolute, and the German Electors and European powers were always alert to prevent its becoming so. In 1671 the German Diet had loosened the Austrian Hapsburgs' hold on the title by declaring that an election of a King of the Romans would take place during the lifetime of the Emperor only when he was incapable of ruling, or when he found it necessary to leave Germany for an extended length of time. When Charles VI had become Holy Roman Emperor in 1711, he had been obliged to accept these conditions.

There were many possibilities for war hidden in such conditions, and they became apparent in 1740 when Charles VI died. When Charles Albert of Bavaria, backed by the military and diplomatic resources of France, was elected Charles VII, Emperor of the Holy Roman Empire, the Hapsburg hold on the throne of the Empire seemed broken. Then, after a long and desperate war, Maria Theresa once more secured the Austrian inheritance and brought the Imperial crown back into the family. It was to reduce the chances of another such war that the Duke of Newcastle and George II promoted the plan to elect the young Archduke Joseph of Austria King of the Romans.[10]

Sir Charles Hanbury Williams, Britain's newly appointed plenipotentiary to Prussia, conceived the idea in 1749. Williams proposed that the German Electoral princes be won over to England by a series of subsidy treaties, in which they would agree to vote for the Archduke Joseph as King of the Romans. The idea appealed to Newcastle; it seemed to be an ingenious way to revive England's sagging continental system.[11] Furthermore, the election of her son and heir apparent as King of the Romans might be the inducement needed to persuade Maria Theresa to renew the Barrier Treaty, the negotiations for which were being carried on in Vienna while George II and Newcastle organized the election from London and Hanover.[12] Newcastle also wanted to be sure that the crown would not fall into the hands of some one who might become a tool of France or Prussia.

His Dutch allies were also much impressed with the idea.[13] If the plan worked, it might serve as a restraint to Prussia and, should a new war break out, as a counterbalance to France. In that case, Britain's German allies could divert France's attention by a continental war, while England concentrated on exploiting her superiority at sea.

Newcastle was not really so inept as his critics made him out to be.[14] He represented "Continental School" of foreign policy which argued that active engagement in the affairs of the European continent was in England's best interest. Opposed to him, the "Blue-Water School" insisted that England should avoid entangling commitments on the continent and concentrate on strategic use of the British Navy.[15] Isolation or alliances in Europe? The question was ready-made to provoke political debate in England.[16] A major subject of the debate was peace-time subsidies to the German powers. English subsidies to European powers in time of peace were almost unprecedented, and the idea aroused hostility in members of Parliament and the Cabinet. Newcastle's own brother, Henry Pelham, interested in economy and domestic reform, at first led the resistance to the plan.Newcastle, however, finally got his brother's reluctant consent to limited subsidies by emphasizing that the policy was a way of maintaining the peace: "Quiet is what we want," Pelham insisted,[17] and Newcastle answered that the election of the King of the Romans would bring just that.[18] But speed was essential. The Archduke had to be elected before opposition was organized in Germany.

Frederick later condemned Newcastle's policy when he quipped that George II had found a "harmless time waster,"[19] but at first he could see no way to prevent its success. By the summer of 1750, two of the nine electors, Mainz and Trier, seemed securely in the Austrian camp, and it appeared that England could bring under her influence Saxony, Cologne, and Bavaria.[20] In addition, Frederick's ally, Louis XV, appeared indifferent to the outcome of the election.

Frederick decided, first, that without the backing of Louis XV he would be helpless. By dispatch, he suggested that the German allies being assembled by George II through the election and the subsidy treaties might some day be used against France. He also pointed out, shrewdly pricking French pride, that important decisions concerning German politics should not be made to the complete exclusion of France who, by the Treaty of Westphalia, was the Guarantor of German "liberties." Frederick's sly appeal fermented awhile at Versailles, and then Puysieux, as Frederick gravely put it, began to take the affair "to heart."[21] The first thing to do, Puysieux decided, was to put someone in an advantageous spot to watch affairs develop in Germany. By a happy coincidence, Vergennes was waiting in the wings. He was experienced in German politics, he was familiar with the complex structure of the German Empire, and he personally knew many German diplomats. He was also the nephew of Puysieux's friend, Chavigny. In August 1750, Vergennes, with instructions and baggage,[22] was rolling eastward towards the Rhine.[23] He was not quite thirty-one years old.

On the evening of the sixteenth he entered Coblenz, the seat of the Electorate of Trier, and had his first view of the picturesque city located at the confluence of the Moselle and Rhine Rivers. After a night's rest he addressed himself to the Archbishop-Elector's grand chamberlain to arrange an audience, saw to the unpacking of his effects, and the next day composed a short dispatch to Puysieux to report his arrival.[24] On the nineteenth he had his audience with the Archbishop-Elector, François-Georges de Schönborn. Then, he suddenly collapsed with a high fever; for nearly four days the fever raged, leaving Vergennes exhausted and weak, and unable to render account to his superiors of his audience with François-Georges.[25]

The choice of the Electorate of Trier as the spot for a French minister to watch over Empire affairs was a good one, for the Archbishop of Trier exerted a good deal of influence in German politics. He held second rank in the Electoral College of the Holy Roman Empire. He was also, alongwith the Palatinate Elector, a co-director of the Circle of the Upper Rhine. Concurrently, as a provost of Elwangen in Swabia, he was a ranking prelate of the Circle of Swabia. The French government deemed that he warranted a French minister when the Empire was agitated by English intrigues and secret negotiations.[26]

Equally important in the choice of Trier as the spot from which to observe Germany was the fact that the territorial possessions of the Archbishop were easily accessible to the French army. Several times the French had invaded and occupied the Electorate, causing François-Georges, who derived most of his revenues from the lands, woods, and vineyards of his estates, to live in constant fear of soldiers come to destroy and consume his wealth. Indeed, when Vergennes arrived in Trier, the territory was still suffering from the ravages of the French and Austrian armies who had wintered there during the War of Austrian Succession. François-Georges complained that France still owed him for 200,000 rations which hungry French soldiers had devoured in his land during the war.[27]

The French government turned a deaf ear to François-Georges' claims for the 200,000 rations, but it wanted, nevertheless, to keep the lines of communication between France and the Elector open. In addition, Vergennes was told to keep an eye on all the negotiations of the Empire, and, especially, to find out if Vienna had approached Trier concerning the Election of the Archduke. The French government was also interested in a rumor that one of the Archduke's brothers was a candidate for the office of co-adjutor to the Archbishop of Trier. If the house of Austria filled that important religious post, the influence of Vienna at Trier would, indeed, be great. Vergennes was to sound out François-Georges' intentions regarding these issues.[28]

Vergennes' instructions included some useful information about the people with whom he was to deal. The minister, Colz, was more favorable to France, but had the lesser influence with the Elector, and concerned himself solely with internal affairs. The other minister, Spangenberg, handled the Elector's Imperial and foreign relations. His opinions were decidedly influenced by the 3,000 *florins* which he received annually from Vienna.[29] Also, Spangenberg enjoyed the greater confidence of the Elector,[30] and so it was with Spangenberg that Vergennes had to negotiate.[31]

In their first meetings, each man explored the strengths and weaknesses of the other. Spangenberg immediately saw the youth of the French minister, and hastily jumped to the conclusion that he was naïve, an error which was to cost him some embarrassment later. Vergennes judged his counterpart lacking in subtlety. He noticed, too, that Spangenberg often dissembled in order to get out of difficult situations.[32] But, as he observed him more closely, Vergennes began to respect the older man. Spangenberg, Vergennes finally concluded, was a capable and untiring worker whose obligations to Vienna did not blind him to the fundamental interests of the Elector of Trier.[33] It is to Vergennes' credit—and it illustrates his realistic attitude—that he did not try to bypass Spangenberg by working through the more friendly Colz. Spangenberg was firmly ensconced in his post and well protected by Vienna. Any attempt to outmaneuver him would have failed.

In his first audience with François-Georges, Vergennes came away impressed with the Elector.[34] The Archbishop Elector was a huge man who still followed the hunt despite his seventy years and a painful permanent injury. He had a vast knowledge of the affairs of the Empire, but he was suspicious to the point of defiance. He remained aloof in his castle at Ehrenbreitstein near Coblenz, he explained to Vergennes, because he disliked having people try to influence him. The metropolitan chapter of the Archbishopric was located at Trier. There, forty canons and sixteen clerical capitularies were ever ready to give advice to their Archbishop, frustrate his plans, or even run his affairs. François-Georges preferred to follow the long-established traditions of his predecessors and live away from the intriguing and presumptuous clergymen.

François-Georges, however, was an old man, sick and somewhat careless about following the strict diet prescribed by his doctors. With his death the opinions of the forty canons and, more especially, of the sixteen capitularies would, overnight, become very important, for they would elect a new Archbishop-Elector.[35] Vergennes remained, therefore, ever alert for information about these clergymen. He wanted to know, in advance of an election, which candidates for the succession favored France and which were hostile. But the task was a delicate one, for François-Georges was a sensitive and proud man who would have been outraged to learn that the French minister at his court was already sizing up his possible successor.

Immediately after his arrival at Coblenz, Vergennes took up the matter of the proposed election of the King of the Romans. Although informed opinion, including that of Newcastle, held that his vote for the Archduke was already assured, François-Georges insisted to Vergennes that it was not.[36] When Vergennes asked Spangenberg, the latter dismissed the question, saying there was no foundation to the reports. Later, Vergennes again raised the question, and Spangenberg politely but firmly rebuffed the inquiry with the curt observation that the question was, after all, a domestic affair of the Empire.[37] In other words, it was not France's concern.

Spangenberg's response may have been part of a calculated effort to keep France in the dark to the Trier Elector's intentions, or simply a sign of the experienced Spangenberg's contempt for the younger Vergennes. It soon became very difficult, however, for the Electoral minister to continue to feign ignorance. The Imperial Minister, Count of Cobenzl's arrived at Coblenz, and for several days was closeted with François-Georges and Spangenberg in secret talks. Vergennes questioned everyone, trying to penetrate the wall of secrecy and ferret out the reason for Cobenzl's visit, but to no avail. Finally he asked Spangenberg point-blank to tell him the purpose of the visit, and Spangenberg neatly turned aside the question with the remark the Cobenzl's visit had no significance whatsoever. He had come to talk over some minor affairs of the Imperial circles, and he had extended his stay simply because he found the pleasures of Coblenz attractive.[38] Ironically, the explanation convinced Vergennes that Spangenberg was not telling the truth, since Vergennes had overheard Cobenzl complain of the dull countryside and boring society of Coblenz.[39] Spangenberg's response was obviously false, but how did one force out the truth?

The opportunity came, surprisingly, from Vienna. The Emperor informed the French Ambassador there that the election was under consideration. The French government quickly passed the news to Vergennes.[40] Spangenberg was greatly embarrassed when Vergennes told him that Austria had opened the question of the election with France. The Electoral minister's close contacts with Vienna made it impossible for him to plead ignorance: he had no recourse but to admit that he knew of the preparations for the election. He also admitted that the purpose of Cobenzl's visit had been to discuss the election. Vergennes, sensing a victory in his private campaign to force Spangenberg to be honest with him, pressed his advantage until the German agreed that, henceforth, the two diplomats would be frank with each other. In return for the promise, Vergennes agreed that, in case Spangenberg could not speak frankly, Vergennes would be satisfied if the Electoral minister simply told him so.[41]

The Archbishop-Elector readily admitted that plans for the election were underway. He maintained, however, that, up to that time, he had not taken part in the negotiations and that he was probably the only elector, during the elections of the last two Emperors, who had not sold his vote beforehand. He had informed Vienna, he said, that his sentiments concerning the election would be made known only in the Electoral College, and that he would support Vienna only if the elction were carried out according to the laws and agreements of the Empire.[42] Since France had also told Vienna that she would not hinder the election as long as the laws and constitutions of the Empire were observed, Vergennes could do no more than commend François-Georges for his "wise and...impartial" conduct, even though both of them knew that the laws and constitutions concerning the election of the King of the Romans were a breeding ground for conflicting interpretations.

The plans for the election were now public, and, therefore, could be discussed. Spangenberg's confessions and promises, and François-Georges' protests of independence, did not provide Vergennes or his superiors with any new information. But the young Frenchman undoubtedly got some personal satisfaction out of the fact that he had tactfully, but completely, exposed Spangenberg's duplicity. The achievement had no immediate effect on diplomacy, but it put Vergennes on a better footing at Coblenz; from that day on, Spangenberg treated the junior diplomat as his equal.

The use that could be made of interpretations of the laws and constitutions of the Empire became apparent when France's allies, Prussia and the Elector Palatinate, wrote to Trier in separate dispatches to learn what François-Georges thought of the proposed election. Frederick questioned whether their Imperial Majesties at Vienna were not too hasty in calling an election during a time when Europe and the Empire were enjoying peace, the Emperor was in good health, and the Archduke Joseph was still a child. Frederick insisted, also, that the preliminary question of the necessity for the election must be decided by all the Empire, according to the terms of the Peace of Westphalia. His point was a clever one: Frederick hoped to bring into the election affair the College of the Princes, every prince of the Empire, rather than simply the nine Electoral Princes, thereby vastly complicating the procedure. In addition, his insistence that the election be advanced according to the terms of the Peace of Westphalia meant that he intended to invite France into German politics, since France was the Guarantor of that Treaty.[43]

When he read the note, François-Georges exploded. He vowed that Frederick and the Palatinate Elector would have a lesson on the "true system of the Empire," which, as Spangenberg remarked, "they did not understand too well." But Vergennes observed that when two Electors as important as the King of Prussia and the Palatinate Elector thought that it was too early to elect a King of the Romans, and when they both were anxious about the laws and liberties of the Empire, the Electoral College ought not to precipitate anyhing.[44] Spangenberg and François-Georges immediately saw the implications of Vergennes' observation: France, while publicly claiming it had no objections to the election, was backing Prussia's attempts to delay it. Frederick and the Palatinate Elector never received their lesson on Imperial law. François-Georges answered their letters with a non-commital statement that he would go along with the majority of the Electors.[45]

Election negotiations soon ran into difficulties in other parts of Germany. From the beginning, Maria Theresa had given only half-hearted support to the project, because she suspected that George II was primarily interested in increasing his own influence in Germany, and she sincerely felt that there was plenty of time—after all, the Archduke was only ten years old. Most of all, she feared that the election would whet the appetites of the German princes and give them an opportunity to make costly demands on Austria.

When the bargaining for the Electoral votes had got underway in the spring and summer of 1750, Maria Theresa had found her fears justified. The German princes had been even more hungry than she had expected. The vote of the Elector of Cologne had cost Maria Theresa nothing (the subsidy treaty made in May of 1750 obligated only England and Holland to pay the yearly bill of 40,000 pounds sterling). But, in order to get the vote of the Elector of Bavaria, Maria Theresa had had to pay one fourth of an annual subsidy of 40,000 pounds sterling for four years, later changed to six.[46]

Bavaria's price was high, but now Maria Theresa saw her worst fears confirmed when the plenipotentiary of the Palatinate, Wrede, announced the price of his master's vote. The Elector not only wanted large subsidies; he also wanted Austria to surrender the county of Pleistein to the Palatinate, and to pay 2,000,000 pounds sterling which the Palatinate claimed for damages suffered at the hands of the Austrians in the late war.[47] Furious, Maria Theresa refused to pay one *pfennig*, thereby inadvertently furthering Frederick's plans to delay the election. Frederick quickly saw the value of Wrede's move and immediately rallied behind him. At the same time, Frederick threatened to call in France to guarantee the liberties of the

Empire, if the Hanoverian-Austrian group decided to elect before the Palatinate's claims were satisfied.[48]

To better coordinate his efforts, Frederick introduced France into his designs by alleging that he had no minister he could trust to negotiate a concert with the Palatinate. He requested that Tyrconnell, the French minister at Berlin, inform the Palatinate of Frederick's sentiment through France's minister at Mannheim. France proved accommodating, and the English soon noted with concern the "close union and concert that now actually subsist between the courts of Versailles and Berlin."[49]

English suspicions were well-founded. France announced that she would agree to the election only if there were unanimous consent among the Electors. Since Prussian and Palatinate opposition made unanimous consent impossible, France's stand meant the election could not go forward without the risk of antagonizing Louis XV. Thus the successful conclusion of the election, apparently so inevitable a few months before, hit a serious snag. Frederick observed, with a good deal of satisfaction, that the courts of Vienna and London no longer pressed it as enthusiastically as they had at the beginning.[50]

As German interest in the proposed election grew, so did that of Elizabeth II, Czarina of Imperial Russia. To her, the election offered an opportunity to extend her influence in German affairs and, at the same time, to settle some old accounts with her archenemy, Frederick the Great. Elizabeth's chancellor, Count Alexius Petionit Bestuzhev-Ryumin, as early as 1745, had convinced the Russian Empress that only Russian guns spoke a language that Frederick respected. But his several attempts to implement the conviction had always been hindered by the firm refusal of Britain and Austria to give him the subsidies he needed to carry out his plans.

Nevertheless, Bestuzhev would not give up his scheme to pit the Russian bear against the Great Frederick, and the diplomatic ferment over the election of the King of the Romans gave him new hope. While Hanover and Vienna sought to round up votes for the election of the Archduke Joseph, they might not object to Russian troop movements in the north to divert Frederick's attention and hinder Prussian opposition to the election.

Frederick feared that England might make use of Russian power to counter his opposition in the election affair.[51] In November, 1750 his fears were confirmed when England, with some reservations, adhered to the Russo-Austrian alliance of 1747. Frederick's earlier apprehensions about Russo-Prussian relations[52] also proved to be valid in December of 1750 when the Russian envoy, Von Gross, suddenly departed without taking leave. Frederick, in retaliation, recalled Von Warendorff from St. Petersburg.[53] Immediately, there was a Russian announcement that there would be an election of a King of the Romans, even if force had to be used to get it.[54] The crisis created by the proposed election of a King of the Romans gave substance to the fears that another war was in the offing.[55]

But Bestuzhev could do nothing without the support of his allies,[56] and they did not want the proposed election to be the occasion for war. Furthermore, on Russia's southern flank, Turkey, pushed by France, threatened Russia in case of war. Frustrated, Bestuzhev once more shelved his plans for a war; Russia once more withdrew to wait for another crisis. The war scare of the winter of 1750-51 impressed upon the powers the unsavory fact that the election issue was explosive. And no one feared war more than François-Georges. Consequently, Vergennes took pains to warn Spangenberg that the election of the King of the Romans could rekindle a war in Europe. Convinced, François-Georges wrote to Vienna that he favored an election only if it served to strengthen the peace.[57]

The war scare proved useful to Vergennes. He had reached the conclusion that politeness and gentleness were not adequate for influencing the policy of Trier. When François-Georges revealed his fears of war, he delivered into Vergennes' hands another means to move the Elector.[58] In April of 1751 when Spangenberg, obviously alarmed, questioned Vergennes concerning a rumor that Louis XV was going to assemble an army on the Rhine in the spring, Vergennes remarked that he did not know, and he doubted the validity of the rumor. "Yet," he reflected, exploiting Spangenberg's alarm, "such talk would not be hard to believe if Russia takes it into her head to invade any of France's allies."

"But what does all this have to do with us?" asked Spangenberg. "You can easily transport any aid you must furnish by sea." Laughing, Vergennes responded that the choice of military routes would not be referred to him. He observed, however, that the princes of Germany never contemplated seriously the consequences of a northern war. The Empire, he concluded, by its own indifference, prepared for itself a series of misfortunes which it would someday deplore.[59] Puysieux readily understood Vergennes' tactic and encouraged him to push the point further.[60] The vision of French troops marching once more over his rich lands made François-Georges tremble. Vergennes perceived this, and tirelessly hammered away at the idea that the election of the Archduke Joseph might explode into war.

In the spring of 1751, it appeared that the Elector of Trier might hold the deciding vote in a majority election. Spangenberg questioned Vergennes concerning France's attitude towards such an eventuality. Vergennes replied with a veiled threat: "I respect the wisdom of the Elector, your master, too much to think that he wants to be the arbiter of the situation and tip the balance."[61] The threat hit the mark. Soon Vergennes learned that the Elector had written to Vienna saying he would consent to the election only if France gave her consent.[62]

Vergennes was pleased. He now knew François-Georges would give his consent to the election of the Archduke, but only when he could do so without risking the security of Trier.[63] The opponents of the election had been successful beyond their most optimistic expectations. François-Georges, holding what might have been the decisive vote, was afraid of French retaliation if he voted with Vienna.[64] Now, more than ever, he wanted to delay the election until more general consent made his vote less crucial.

Nevertheless, George II and Newcastle worked at their project. In September of 1751, Holland and England signed the Treaty of Dresden with Saxony and got, in return for a subsidy of 48,000 pounds sterling, an engagement of 6,000 troops, and Saxony's vote for the Archduke. The treaty assured the Archduke of six votes in the Electoral College, a clear majority. Yet Newcastle hesitated to force matters to a vote. Why?

Prussia and France were, by now, completely agreed on their policy of insisting that the election be by unanimous vote. In addition, both powers argued that the laws of the Empire required that the College of German Princes, and not simply the nine Electors, must first decide on the necessity of holding the election.[65] Louis XV and Frederick also stood solidly behind the Elector Palatinate, and insisted that the Palatinate's claims be satisfied before the election could proceed. Such a formidable opposition Newcastle could not ignore.

He refused to admit the right of the College of Princes to decide on the question of necessity, but he came around to admitting some of the Palatinate's demands in the mistaken belief that Austria was willing to give some satisfaction.[66] Newcastle also had misgivings about electing the Archduke by a simple majority. A speedy election was now out of the question.

The election delayed, François-Georges was free to enjoy his favorite pastime. In October 1751, he left Coblenz for the hunt, planning to stay away until the winter cold closed the hunting season. His departure left Vergennes with no pressing responsibilities, with time on his hands and, to his annoyance, with very little to do. He occupied himself with drawing up long memoranda on the three clerical candidates for the electorate; with keeping track of Spangenberg's comings and goings; and with avoiding the angry outbursts of François-Georges when he returned to Coblenz for the winter. To Vergennes it was a barren period at a sterile court. In his January dispatch to Versailles, he began: "Absolutely nothing is happening here which merits your attention."[67]

Still, he was not forgotten in his isolation. In the French Ambassador's palace in sunny Venice, Chavigny continued to watch over and protect Vergennes. The uncle was preparing to return to Versailles for a leave of absence. Perhaps a word or two would encourage a rescue operation. The intervention was successful: "M. de Chavigny," Vergennes soon read in a dispatch from Versailles, "having requested that I accord you a leave to permit you to be here during his stay here, I grant it to you with pleasure, and you may take it when you wish after notifying the Elector."[68] Vergennes was eager to return. Less than three weeks later, leaving his secretary in charge of his affairs at Coblenz, he departed.[69]

As the first signs of spring appeared along the Rhine Valley, Vergennes sped along the roads towards Versailles and renewed association with his uncle and sponsor. He had reason to be pleased with his first independent diplomatic assignment. François-Georges, the second-ranking Elector in the Holy Roman Empire, traditionally at the beck and call of Vienna, was now in agreement with France to delay the election of a King of the Romans. Vergennes could honestly claim some measure of credit for the Elector's strong desire to put it off as long as possible. The motives behind the Elector's policy and those behind France's policy were quite different, but the results were the same.

In his assessment of his performance, Vergennes had no reason to be humble about his relations with Spangenberg, whose initial disdain had given way to sincere respect. Chavigny had been right, in 1749, when he told Louis XV that the young man he had trained was no longer in need of his uncle's help. His first assignment was almost completely free from blunder.

Almost, but not quite.

The recollection of one mistake—an obvious product of inexperience—must have nagged Vergennes as he stared out at the surrounding countryside. A certain rascal by the name of Marquin had twice destroyed a road constructed by Louis XV's engineers near his mill, close to the French-Trier border. When the Maréchal de Belle-Isle sent someone to arrest him, he took refuge in the town of Revin near Trier. Belle-Isle asked Vergennes to request from François-Georges that the criminal be extradited. Vergennes immediately obtained the extradition, and the affair seemed closed.

Unfortunately, however, Vergennes was ignorant of the fact that both Louis XV and François-Georges claimed soverignty over Revin. The dual claims were the subject of a long dispute. The French government immediately saw that Vergennes' request for extradition could be interpreted to mean that Louis XV had given up his claims, which was by no means the case. Vergennes found himself the object of severe reproaches and, finally, an official repudiation from Francois-Dominique de Barberie, Marquis de Saint-Contest, who now had replaced Puysieux as Minister of Foreign Affairs. The blunder was not a serious one, yet it had a sobering effect. If Vergennes ever entertained the notion that his diplomatic education was complete, Marquin, the "disturber of the public repose," had effectively destroyed the illusion.[70]

CHAPTER 3

The Congress at Hanover

Before Vergennes returned to Versailles in mid-March of 1752, Puysieux, who had been Secretary of State at the time of his appointment, was replaced by François-Dominique de Barbarie, Marquis de Saint-Contest, a lawyer, intendant, and diplomat, who had some reputation as a *philosophe*. Nevertheless, he seems to have had few admirers outside of Madame de Pompadour's circle. The Marquis d'Argenson, the former Minister of Foreign Affairs, who apparently liked no one, thought Saint-Contest was "only a pedant" who lacked ideas, failed to keep order in his affairs, and was full of prejudices; in short, "a mediocre and complacent man."[1] The English Ambassador at Versailles, Albemarle, summarily dismissed him as "a shuffling lawyer adorned with good manners."[2]

Vergennes' opinion of Saint-Contest is dificult to ascertain. Before his return to Versailles, Saint-Contest had assured him that "I am already aware of your application and services; you can count on my efforts . . . to make the King recognize their value."[3] Nevertheless, Vergennes must have been humiliated by Saint-Contest's official disavowal in the Revin extradition case, for already the young man was assuming the attitude of a career diplomat that a blunder was more to be feared than an immorality. Nor was Vergennes allowed to forget the mistake when he arrived at Versailles. Yet nowhere did Vergennes reveal what he thought about the reprimands he received. In subsequent correspondence with Saint-Contest, he epitomized a principle later expressed by Guizot: "Diplomats never get angry; they take notes." Vergennes' notes to his superior were always phrased with a balance and discipline which assured their impersonality.

Vergennes' stay at Versailles was brief. On the eighth of April, less than a month after his return from Trier, he received orders to leave on the twentieth for Hanover. His salary was to be 1000 *livres* a month, plus an additional 4,000 for expenses.[4] The extradition matter was recalled in his instruction; he was to pass through Coblenz, and to indicate to François-Georges that France still claimed her rights over Revin, but was willing to negotiate a settlement.

The assignment to Hanover placed Vergennes close to the focal point of German politics. The appointment of a French representative had been urged upon Louis XV by Frederick of Prussia, who, in anticipation of the arrival at Hanover of his uncle, King George II, asked for a minister "as skillful as he was honest, and as firm in his principles as he was reserved in his language."[5] Frederick regarded Hanover as "the place where the King of England always came to plot and haggle at his leisure,"[6] and Newcastle's efforts to assure the election of the Archduke Joseph forewarned of long and complicated haggling. The Duc de Mirepoix, the French Ambassador to London, was ineligible for the assignment because it was not customary for the ambassador of France to accompany the King of England on his frequent trips to Hanover. George II would have considered his presence an unwarranted intervention in German politics. Vergennes was a happy choice for the post; he not only fitted Frederick's requirements, but also was knowledgeable about the details of the complex election diplomacy.

French pressure on Trier, exerted by Vergennes during his stay there, had helped delay the election of the Archduke Joseph. Newcastle had refused to admit defeat, however, and had continued to labor at his project during the winter of 1751-1752. But a difficulty arose in the debate in Parliament on the Subsidy Treaty with Saxony, signed at Dresden on September 13, 1751, and ratified two months later.[7] When the necessary motion to grant a sum of £ 32,000 towards the subsidy required by the treaty came up, there was opposition.[8] Horatio Walpole, the younger brother of Sir Robert, led the attack in the House of Commons. Although he was ultimately to agree to vote for the subsidy, he criticized the expenditure of money for what he considered a doubtful scheme, in part because it would establish a bad precedent of paying subsidies in peace time.[9] Opposition in the House of Lords was led by the Duke of Bedford, who argued that the treaty was unnecessary, that it was too costly, and that Great Britain would not profit from it.[10]

Newcastle and his brother, Pelham, persevered in their position in support of the treaty,[11] basing their defense on the argument that the treaty was essential to the prevention of war in Europe, or, if a war proved inevitable, to the securing of allies.[12] Pelham stated that, as a result of the treaty, England now had two-thirds of the electoral college in its favor. "I hope, nay, I trust," he said, "that the Archduke Joseph will be chosen before we meet here again in a new session." Persuasively, he added that "this will be the last expense which the nation may be obliged to put itself to . . ."[13] The treaty was accepted by a vote of 236 to 54.[14]

The commitment to elect the Archduke before the next session of Parliament, coupled with the word that opponents of his candidate were meeting at Mannheim in the Palatinate, caused Newcastle to call Electoral ministers to meet in a "congress" at Hanover in June of 1752, before the convocation of the election Diet.

In a grand council, held by Newcastle and his King before their departure for Hanover, it was concluded that the most desirable plan of action was to obtain unanimous consent from all electors. If unanimity could not be achieved, however, it was decided that England should attempt to establish the principle that a majority vote was sufficient to elect a King of the Romans.[15] France, to be represented at Hanover by Vergennes, was the unknown factor in England's second line of defense, since she was the "guarantor of the liberties and and constitution of the Empire." Would France permit an election by majority?

The French attitude toward the election was the center of a web of misconceptions early in 1752.[16] The basis for these misconceptions was the assumption that there were no differences between France and England on the legality of an election carried by the majority. The consensus in England was that France was withholding its full approval of the election only because of the unsolved question of satisfaction to the Elector Palatinate, a claim which the English felt to be exorbitant, but one on which they were willing to try to get "some satisfaction."[17] Secure in his optimism, Newcastle sailed with George II on April 18, 1752, from Harwich to proceed to Hanover.[18] To gain Vienna's agreement to this plan, Newcastle decided upon a joint English-French appeal to Maria Theresa in favor of the Elector Palatinate. If Vienna were willing to co-operate, only the details of Palatinate satisfaction would be left for further negotiation.[19] The diplomatic exchange, which had given Newcastle such confidence, had disregarded the existence of the newly-chosen French minister to Hanover; but Pelham reported that there was no cause for worry. "I do not doubt your address in managing M. Vergennes when he comes to you... good words may do a great deal; I am sure they have with the Duc de Mirepoix."[20]

Vergennes' own instructions from Saint-Contest indicated that one of his most important responsibilities at Hanover was to assure George II that Louis XV wanted to conserve and strengthen the general peace re-established at Aix-la-Chapelle.[21] Saint-Contest also referred to the fact that the Ministers of England had held a conference with the Duc de Mirepoix before leaving for Hanover. He mentioned that there had been a great deal of frankness in the discussions concerning the means of conciliating all the affairs of Europe, particularly those which concerned France and England. He regretted that the orders given Vergennes did not include decisions resulting from the conference, but promised that these would arrive later.

Saint-Contest continued his instructions by stating that Louis XV would not oppose the election if it were carried out according to the laws and usages of the Empire, and if the Palatinate's demands were given a "reasonable satisfaction." He then recapitulated the Palatinate position: 500,000 *florins* from England and the Low Countries to pay the balance of back subsidies dating from 1700; assumption by these two nations of the debt, plus interest of 500,000 *florins*, that the late Elector of the Palatinate had contracted under their guarantee during the War of the Spanish Succession (1702-1713); restoration by Vienna of the fief of Pleistein and, in exchange for the huge indemnities sought earlier, the county of Falkenstein and the eventual cession and investiture of the fief of Ortenau, plus freedom from all feudal fiefs enclosed in the Duchy of Sulzbach; and accordance by Vienna to the Palatinate as well as to the Duke of Deux-Ponts (a branch of the House of the Palatinate) of the privilege of *non-appellando*; that is, exemption from being called before the courts of the Empire. The instructions closed with Saint-Contest's reaffirmation that Louis XV had agreed to the support of Palatinate demands only to the extent of a "reasonable satisfaction." The definition of "reasonable" was left open to future negotiation.

France's concern with satisfying the claims of the Palatinate, some of which dated back to the War of the Spanish Succession when the two countries had been enemies, requires some analysis. France's primary aim now was to keep her influence in Germany, and to stall the election in order to have maximum time for its exploitation. Article XVIII of the Treaty of Aix-la-Chapelle had provided for deferment of negotiations regarding the Palatinate's unsettled claims. The election of the King of the Romans now provided an opportune occasion to settle the claims since the Palatinate had bargaining power in its vote, and bargaining power in the fact that France backed its claims. France reasoned that she would get credit for whatever satisfaction the Palatinate received. In addition, her support of Palatinate claims would please France's ally, Frederick the Great, who, together with Wrede of the Palatinate, had devised the strategy. If no satisfaction were granted, the election would not occur, thus thwarting England. The danger remained that the explosive situation might lead to war, but France was putting her trust in the skill of her representative at Hanover.

Recognizing that Newcastle would be Vergennes' most formidable opponent, Saint-Contest included some comments about him. "Monsieur the Duke of Newcastle, Secretary of State of England for the Department of the North, has found the secret, by means of intrigues, for sustaining himself for thirty years in the ministry, and has at last succeeded in playing the primary role there, a role of which he is extremely jealous." Although Newcastle was described as being "polished, obliging, and more sensitive than anyone to the considerations one shows him," Vergennes was warned that in diplomatic affairs Newcastle liked to "utilize trickery," and that "he has somewhat the common fault of Englishmen that when one makes two steps forward . . . (the Englishmen) make four backwards."

The British foreign office had already supplied Newcastle with its estimate of Vergennes. Albemarle had written that Vergennes was a "sensible man, but, having been bred up by his uncle M. de Chavigny, he has a great many of his ways . . ."[22] The force of Albemarle's reference to Chavigny is evident both from the fact that British diplomats regarded him as a man of "mischievous abilities and dangerous maxims,"[23] and from Albemarle's own statement in an earlier letter to Newcastle: Vergennes "seems to be a compound of everything bad, for he is instructed by Saint-Contest, bred up by Chavigny, and now advised by him. *C'est tout dire.*"[24]

The mutual suspicions engendered by these descriptions, ascerbated by the disparity between Vergennes' instructions and Newcastle's expectations, made a clash between the two men inevitable. Newcastle, the first to reach Hanover, was impatient at Vergennes' delays, and urged his ambassador at Versailles to press for his departure with the "proper instructions."[25] On the evening of the tenth of May, Vergennes arrived. The two men met the next morning.[26]

Newcastle's treatment of Vergennes resembled that of a schoolmaster. He first read aloud to Vergennes a dispatch from the English Secretary of State, Robert D' Arcy, the Earl of Holderness which reiterated the intention of George II not to pursue the election except in close conformity with the laws and constitution of the Empire. It also stated that, even though the English ministers regarded the claims of the Elector of the Palatinate to be exorbitant, they were disposed to give him some satisfaction — perhaps the "cession" of the fief of Pleistein, with some indemnity for the county of Falkenstein. Newcastle indicated further that England wanted France to join her in assuring Vienna that Louis XV would acquiesce in the election after the Palatinate was satisfied. The next step, Newcastle said, was to request Vienna to obtain Frederick's approval; when Vienna did so, France was to join with England in supporting Vienna's proposal. At this point, Newcastle quoted Mirepoix as saying that the majority of suffrages was sufficient to elect a King of the Romans; unanimity was not necessary.

Newcastle followed his reading of Holderness' dispatch with a letter from Albemarle which implied that Saint-Contest seemed not to be opposed to joining with England in order to influence Prussia and Vienna, and had gone so far as to agree that the election could soon be decided if the English plans were carried out.[27]

Vergennes was astonished. No one had given him the slightest hint that such agreements had been made. Before he could comment, however, Newcastle began attacking him with a barrage of questions, without giving him any opportunity to reply. To the final one — whether he had instructions to concert with England on the message to be sent to Vienna and Berlin — Vergennes was able to interject a quick "No", and to explain that Mirepoix's return from England to Versailles had so immediately preceded his own departure that there had been no time to obtain his report. Newcastle countered that King George would be very surprised to learn that France had not delayed Vergennes' departure long enough to include Mirepoix's report in Vergennes' instructions. Newcastle stressed that the election had to be decided quickly, and that his candidate already had a more than necessary majority. Vergennes replied that the question of the legality of a majority election should be left to the lawyers. Newcastle grew impatient: "What *did* you come here to do?"

Vergennes had brought with him a personal letter from Louis XV to Newcastle which eulogized the Englishman's character. It provided the basis for the bland reply that Vergennes' most essential instruction was "to assure your master, the King, of the sentiments of His Majesty Louis XV, and to lose no opportunity to make him understand Louis XV's intention to affirm, encourage, and strengthen the mutual understanding which so happily exists between the two crowns . . ."

"All that is well and good," Newcastle observed, obviously irritated, "But haven't you something a little more precise on the election of the King of the Romans?"

Vergennes' inability to be more precise angered Newcastle. But when he repeated the statement that the Palatinate's claims were too high, Vergennes interjected the comment that he would not discuss these until the Palatinate ambassador, Wrede, arrived. Newcastle informed the French minister that the English had not invited Wrede to Hanover, because such an invitation would have made it appear that England accepted the Palatinate claims.[28] Newcastle then suddenly announced that he had to go and dress. He departed, leaving Vergennes with a memo he had written.

Vergennes began to read the memo, but, before he had finished the first page, Newcastle returned to announce that George II was awaiting the presence of the French minister. This early audience nonplused Vergennes, who had not brought his letters of accreditation with him. He rushed back to his lodgings to get them; but when he returned, George II was otherwise engaged. Vergennes and the agitated Newcastle waited together. The King had already been apprised of Newcastle's disappointment with the French position. The ensuing audience was frigid.[29]

The meeting of Vergennes and Newcastle left both men confused and annoyed. Vergennes was puzzled by the drift of the discussion. The divergence between Newcastle's expectations of him and what he had been able to deliver surprised him. The fear that Newcastle really knew more about Saint-Contest's line of action than he did raised the humiliating possibility that he had been sent to Hanover without the full confidence of Saint-Contest. It is small wonder that Newcastle noted that "Monsieur de Vergennes is much embarrassed."[30] Vergennes' first move was to ask Versailles for clarification.[31] While awaiting further orders, he began procedures to get Wrede to Hanover.

Vergennes' insistence on Wrede's presence disturbed Newcastle. He knew that Wrede would insist on advancing the entire list of Palatinate claims and, in the bargaining to follow, the power to limit the satisfactions might slip from England's control. Further annoyance lay in the fact that Vergennes had indicated French unwillingness to let Great Britain be the final arbiter of the question of "reasonable satisfaction."[32]

Nevertheless, Newcastle reluctantly approved the invitation to Wrede. When the Palatinate minister arrived with his list of demands, he presented them to the proper ministers, who immediately rejected them. Maria Theresa responded to the Palatinate's claims with the argument that the Palatinate really owed *her* money. Newcastle exploded when he learned that the Palatinate also insisted on pushing claims against England and the Low Countries. Most important to him, however, was the fact that the question of "reasonable satisfaction" was now wide open for negotiation. His reactions became childish; he hedged; he lost his temper; he stamped his feet; he avoided discussion; and once, in a moment of complete exasperation, he even closed himself in his room and refused to see anyone.

When he turned to Vienna, he found Maria Theresa's attitude swinging between the poles of lukewarm interest and outright anger. She had already begun to woo France away from Prussia and into an Austrian alliance, and she wanted to avoid further obligation to England. Furthermore, she was convinced that, if the Imperial throne should become vacant, her son was the most likely candidate for Emperor, anyway. Still Maria Theresa knew that the English alliance could not be destroyed until the one with France was concluded. She was willing, therefore, to permit Newcastle to push the election to a conclusion if he could, but only if the cost to her were not too dear.[33]

Newcastle's discomfort was further enhanced by Vergennes, when he explained to Newcastle that the English version of Saint-Contest's intentions was in error. Unwilling to believe this, Newcastle accused Vergennes of persuading Saint-Contest to alter his earlier declarations. Vergennes again presented the position of his King. Soon Vergennes' most important function at Hanover became that of clarifying and explaining Louis XV's policy, so that Newcastle and others involved always knew where France stood.[34]

Newcastle next tried to separate the Palatinate from France. Working with George II's Hanoverian minister, he tried insult and insinuation, and finally attempted to corrupt Wrede by offering him some "personal expediencies."[35] All of these approaches failed, and Wrede remained loyal to the Palatinate's alliance with France.

Newcastle's alternatives were now obvious: either the Palatinate must be satisified, or Newcastle must forgo the election altogether. If he forced the election without the Palatinate, he ran the risk of Prussian and French intervention. Moreover, some of the electoral princes insisted that a King of the Romans could not be elected without unanimous consent. Since Newcastle wanted the election to gain the friendship of the Electors, he was unwilling to antagonize them. The Palatinate claims had to be satisfied. If satisfaction could be arranged, possibly all the Electors, including Frederick, would agree to the election of the Archduke. He would then dispose of the constitutional problem.[36]

Newcastle sent the demands of the Palatinate to Maria Theresa, and charged a special envoy, Lord Hyndford, to go to Vienna and insist on a solution.[37] He then proposed to proceed with preparations for the election and, at the same time, to negotiate a settlement with the Palatinate. He informed the Austrian minister that, unless Austria wanted to try to elect the Archduke by a majority, she must "give a little, a very little, to the Elector Palatinate, to procure the unanimous consent of France and all the electors," and added cajolingly that England had done much for the sake of Vienna. If the latter continued stubbornly to refuse to help, "the election is at an end; and the present system with the House of Austria, dissolved." The note, which Newcastle saw as bluff, came dangerously close to being an ultimatum.[38]

In June of 1752, Maria Theresa consented to the Palatinate's demand for the restoration of Pleistein, and yielded to the extent of offering 500,000[39] *florins* instead of the territory of Falkenstein.[40] Her consort, Emperor Francis I, appeared even grateful for Newcastle's efforts. He "talked with great freedom to Lord Hyndford," and gave the impression of having "the election very much at heart.[41] To help cover the monetary claims of the Palatinate, he even offered to pay the 500,000 *florins* out of his own funds if no other source were found.[42]

Despite her apparent willingness, Maria Theresa did not really go very far to meet the Palatinate Elector. She insisted on a number of conditions; her offer of 500,000 *florins* was only half of Newcastle's suggested equivalent for Falkenstein;[43] and she wanted assurances from the Electors, as well as His Britannic Majesty and Holland, that they would assist her in case a war resulted from the election. At Francis I's insistence, she also demanded that the Imperial princes and the Electoral College agree not to use the election to force Francis I or the young Archduke to accept any further capitulations, since the Emperor's power already had been reduced to almost nothing as a result of those previously made.[44]

Encouraged by her response, Newcastle decided to arrange a conference to draw up a plan of protocol for proceeding. The conference was composed of Newcastle, two Hanoverian ministers, and Steinberg, representing George II, and the ministers of the "well-intentioned" electors, from Mainz, Bavaria, and Saxony. Not representing a "well-intentioned" elector, Wrede was excluded. Newcastle proposed that the Electoral Diet should decide if an election were necessary. Immediately he ran into difficulty. Stadion of Mainz,[45] whose master had the constitutional responsibility for convoking a Diet, assured Newcastle that Mainz would expedite the affair whenever the Emperor demanded it, but he would not sign Newcastle's proposal. His example was followed by the others, all of them alleging that they had no instructions to sign. They took the proposal *ad referendum*.[46]

Newcastle next read to them a letter he wrote to the minister from Vienna, in which he argued that "nothing could contribute more to the assurance of tranquillity, within as well as without, than some small satisfaction given to the Elector Palatinate, in settlement of its vast claims against the Court of Vienna." Once again Newcastle was unsuccessful. The minister from Mainz objected to the terms "small satisfaction" and "vast claims," thereby softening the implication that the Palatinate claims were excessive. But, even with the changes, Count de Rex of Saxony would not sign. He approved, he said, but pled lack of orders.[47]

When Newcastle came to Maria Theresa's conditions, he found the electoral ministers no more pliable. Her insistence on excluding the College of Princes from the election, and her demand for assurances of reciprocal aid in case of war, smelled of gun powder, and the electors did not like the odor. Her demands that the electors require no further concessions from the Emperor threatened the very liberties of the Diet. When Newcastle asked the ministers to agree to Maria Theresa's recommendations, Stadion refused to sign until he received orders from Mainz to do so.[48] This so angered George II that he refused henceforth to speak to Stadion.[49]

Newcastle's continued lack of success was apparent to Vergennes, who was quick to identify at least one reason for it. He noted, with some amazement, that, throughout the meeting of the ministers, Newcastle had scarcely mentioned Francis I or Maria Theresa or their interest in the election. He had based his arguments repeatedly in terms of his own and England's need for the election, and this repeated stress had weakened his position with the electors who saw in England's need an opportunity for their own gain.[50]

In his search for assistance, Newcastle turned, more and more frequently, to Vergennes. Despite their first unfortunate encounter, Newcastle approved of Vergennes. He wrote to his brother, "I like Vergennes very well; and what is more material, I think he likes me very well; though His Grace of Grafton says that I think everybody loves me."[51] He was to change his opinion, however, after almost two months of association (and of clandestinely reading the French minister's opinions of him in intercepted letters). He complained that "if Vergennes did not play the knave, we should finish this thing to all our satisfactions." After describing some of the Frenchman's "villainous" activities, the English statesman concluded that had "Mirepoix had the conduct of this negotiation, I am sure all would have gone on well; but this friend of mine, this coxcomb, Vergennes, thinks the skill of a minister consists in jealousies and suspicions."[52] Soon Vergennes joined Stadion, Wrede and Vorster, the ambassador from Vienna, on the list of those to whom George II would not speak.[53]

Suddenly, Assebourg, the Minister of Cologne, arrived at Hanover.[54] He presented Newcastle with Cologne's claims against Vienna, thereby endangering settlement of the Palatinate's demands by giving substance to Maria Theresa's fears that satisfaction of the latter would bring claims from all the other electors.[55]

Meanwhile, Frederick was doing everything in his power to obstruct the election. He busied himself trying to get the German princes to agree on a circular letter to Mainz protesting that, before one could proceed with the election of the King of the Romans, the College of Princes *and the Imperial Towns,* as well as the College of Electors, had to agree on its necessity.[56] Frederick was irritated that French policy was not equally aggressive.

Partly as the result of Frederick's urging, and partly because he had heard of Wrede's fears that Louis XV was relaxing his support of the Palatinate,[57] Vergennes increased his efforts to prevent a convocation of the Diet until the Palatinate had some assurance that her claims would be honored. He first argued the illegality of such a convocation, but, when his powers of persuasion proved inadequate, he resorted to more brutal methods. When the Hanoverian ministers agreed to admit "in principle" the need to settle with the Palatinate, yet insisted, meanwhile, that the election take place prior to the negotiation of a "reasonable satisfaction," Vergennes bluntly refused to consider the idea. Startled by his tone, the ministers fell into a silence. Vergennes interrupted the silence by telling Stadion that while Louis XV did not want a war, he was not afraid of one.[58]

As another means of delaying the election, Vergennes encouraged the demands of the Electors. Stadion had previously raised with him the question of some claims his master had against France. Vergennes' recommendation to Versailles was that these claims should be converted into a subsidy for Mainz, thereby tying the Elector to France and separating him from England.[59] He also recommended that France encourage Bavaria to "strongly insist" on a settlement with Vienna of a long-standing dispute over territorial limits.[60] Concurrently, Louis XV should also give attention to Saxony. France officially supported the Elector of Saxony as the candidate for the elective throne of Poland; but Vergennes noted that there were rumors that Austria had some anti-Saxon reservations about the succession which could be used by France to produce some "anxieties."[61]

Maria Theresa's initial concessions had pleased Newcastle, but they were insufficient. Now, angered by England's persistent badgering, Maria Theresa would not give more.[62] Moreover, Newcastle's brother urged the necessity for unanimous consent. "I am greatly afraid of a partial election," Pelham wrote to Newcastle. "I own I am; the conduct of the Court of Vienna has made that a much more dangerous measure than it would have been, had they acted otherwise."[63] Newcastle was forced to the conclusion that England must share the costs of securing the Palatinate's vote.

But how to make the additional expenditures palatable to Parliament? He presented his case in a letter, dated June 29, 1752, to Chancellor Hardwicke: "As I am afraid the subject of this letter will not be quite agreeable to my brother, I address it to your lordship, though it is for the consideration of you both. The most that I can possibly hope to bring the Court of Vienna to, would be to yield Pleistein, and to give a sum of money, of 500,000, perhaps 600,000 *florins.*" Since the least he thought he could get the Elector Palatinate to accept was 1,000,000 *florins*, "the question, therefore, is shall the election be lost, or shall we carry it with our eminent majority, and risk the consequences, for the sake of 50 or 60,000 pounds (500,000 or 600,000 *florins*)?" If the election were dropped or should miscarry, Newcastle pointed out, the honor and reputation of King George and England would be lost; if it carried by only a majority, "France and Prussia may (though I do not think they will) make such demonstrations of armies, etc., as must necessarily put us to five times the expense . . ." He suggested they try to avoid Parliament by drawing the funds from the King's Civil List; should this prove impossible he recommended an arrangement under which the Palatinate would be paid after the election had been achieved. Thus Parliament could be presented with a diplomatic victory along with the bill.[64]

Pelham had no choice but to agree. However, he made it clear that his conditions included a unanimous agreement in favor of the Archduke, plus the condition that nothing would be paid until the "whole is finished." Moreover, his promise to assist would hold only "after the Empress Queen, Maria Theresa, has done what she can be brought to do."[65]

Wrede agreed to lower all his claims against Vienna to a total of 1,000,000 *florins*. But he balanced this favor by raising anew the Palatinate's earlier claims against England and Holland, which he was willing to settle for an additional 400,000 *florins*. In desperation, Newcastle turned to Vergennes for help.

The French minister listened attentively, and finally agreed that the Palatinate ought to reduce its request to 200,000 *florins*. Furthermore, he suggested that the Palatinate combine its claims against the Maritime Powers with those against Vienna in order not to furnish Newcastle's political enemies at home with a handle to be used against him.[66] Newcastle pondered, once again, where he was going to find the money. Vienna had reluctantly agreed to pay 500,000 *florins*, and Pelham could probably manage to get 500,000 from English sources as a last resort, but where would an extra 200,000 be found? George II certainly would not hear of paying it from his Hanoverian treasury. Nevertheless, Newcastle assured Vergennes that he would do everything humanly possible to get another 100,000 out of Vienna, and he would find the balance somewhere else.[67]

But Vienna refused, the King "would not give one farthing," and Newcastle had to go begging anew to his brother. For the second time Pelham came to the rescue, but this time he warned that "the basket is shut. We can have no more demands of this sort."[68]

Wrede's tenacious refusal to go below the 200,000 *florins* suggested by Vergennes confirmed Newcastle's growing suspicion that Vergennes was the principal agent behind Palatinate maneuvers,[69] and, therefore, was the person with whom he should be negotiating. Vergennes' role at Hanover, therefore, became an increasingly prominent one. When Newcastle made a small offer to the Palatinate and requested postponement of payment until after the election, the communication went through the French minister. When Wrede's attitude hardened, Newcastle complained of Vergennes' *trop de rigueur*. He even went so far as to tell Vergennes that he knew full well that Wrede would withdraw the demand on the Maritime Powers if the Frenchman were to suggest it.[70] Vergennes was fully aware of the importance of his new position of "honest broker." His letters show an air of assurance and authority which they had hitherto lacked. In his new role, he criticized the experienced Newcastle . . . "(his) arrogance," Vergennes observed, "is insupportable; he lays down the laws rather than suggests conditions."[71]

Newcastle's ultimate defeat was near at hand. The Count de Stadion, Minister of the Elector of Mainz, drew up the plan which came to be known as the *ultimatum*.[72] It provided, in its first Article, that the Elector of the Palatinate receive, immediately *after* the unanimous election of the Archduke as King of the Romans, the sum of 600,000 *florins*. Within a year, another 300,000 would be paid, and yet another 300,000 by the end of the following year. There were no specifications as to who should actually pay the money, although the implication was that England was standing behind the proposal, an implication that Pelham immediately caught, and objected to, when he read the brief.[73]

The *ultimatum* engaged Maria Theresa to restore and cede to the Palatinate not only Pleistein, but also all the possessions enclaved in the Duchies of Newberg and Salzbach, along with freedom from all the feudal ties to Maria Theresa's crown of Bohemia. The third Article proposed that Maria Theresa grant the Palatinate, as well as the Duchy of Deux-Ponts, the privilege of *non-appellando*. Article Four provided that Maria Theresa promise the fief of Ortenau to the Palatinate, when and if there was a default in the masculine succession of the incumbent house of Baden-Baden. If, for any reason, she could not give up Ortenau, another fief of equal value and importance would be granted instead. Also, it was stipulated that this Article could not be cause for delaying the election. Article Five required that the Palatinate give up any further claims against Maria Theresa.

Had Newcastle been unaware of Vergennes' influence on Stadion and on Wrede, the reading of the first five Articles of the *ultimatum* certainly would have enlightened him. With the exception of exchanging an indemnity for Falkenstein and combining the claims against the Maritime Powers with the indemnity against Vienna (both changes later recommended by Vergennes), the Articles contained the major provisions outlined in Vergennes' instructions. Article Six, moreover, explicitly stated what the others implied concerning France's influence: the concessions would be delivered only after the "*unanimous consent of all the electors and with the approval and acquiescence of France.*" The acceptance of such a provision would deliver the Congress of Hanover, as well as the elelction, into the hands of Vergennes. No one signed the brief, but all the ministers present approved it. All parties, including France and the Palatinate, were told to respond within a month.

Stadion's *ultimatum* was quickly sent off to Vienna and London for approval with letters intended to facilitate acceptance. The letter to the English ambassador at Vienna was especially urgent. "You have now one last trial to make, after many," Newcastle told Keith, "for concluding the great affair of the election." Newcastle was convinced that there was no other way to carry the election. While he admitted that the demands were "not moderate," he thought he had convinced the Palatinate Elector that he must be reasonable. Otherwise, he would get nothing, and end up being a sacrifice to the policies of France and Prussia. If agreement could not be reached and there should be no election, Newcastle saw a black future, in which "France and Prussia will dictate to all the world."

The most difficult Article of the *ultimatum* was that of the 1,200,000 *florins*; Vienna had promised only 500,000. Newcastle's brother, presumably with the approval of King George, had agreed to make up the difference if no other resource could be found. But when Newcastle showed the plan to the King, His Majesty "fell into the strongest declarations against the making up of the 700,000 *florins*." The King had changed his mind. He even hinted that he had lost interest in the project. Newcastle was in an extremely painful situation.[74] Where was the remaining 700,000 balance to come from? Clearly Maria Theresa would not agree to pay the entire amount. So Newcastle sent Keith to the Emperor, whose opinions were known to be more favorable than those of Maria Theresa or her minister, Bartenstein. "Beg him, nay, conjure him," Newcastle entreated, to "hearken to the advice of those who are in his Imperial Majesty's own service." Above all, Keith was warned not to let Bartenstein put his "malicious and boundless pen" to the *ultimatum*.[75] As soon as the couriers were dispatched, Newcastle set out with the King for George II's palace at Lüneberg. There was nothing to do but wait.

The waiting period gave Vergennes a welcome opportunity to rest. The mission to Hanover was an arduous one. Furthermore, Vergennes—and France—had few friends. Newcastle's temper, his suspicions, his nervousness, and his manner, "always in a hurry and always behind hand," made him extremely difficult to deal with. Rex, the minister of Saxony, avoided all communication with Vergennes.[76] Haslang of Bavaria[77] had specific instruc tions to be unfriendly; and, while Stadion of Mainz often visited him, he always did so with a prudence that bespoke his basic fear of Vienna.[78] Assebourg of Cologne, who should have been an ally, was so incompetent as to be only an additional burden. Wrede's cooperation never completely overcame Vergennes' suspicions that he might underhandly seek a settlement with England. The only reliable support Vergennes had came from the Spanish envoy to Sweden, Marqués de Grimaldi, who had arrived on a special mission to support the French minister against England. Grimaldi gave Vergennes a boost by making it clear to Newcastle that there was a perfect union between the Spanish court and France on the election question.[79] Much later in their careers, Grimaldi and Vergennes would meet again.

In addition to the strains involved in negotiating, the social functions set a rigorous, torturous pace. There were elaborate dinners at which the King's daughter played hostess; there were hunts, fireworks, masked balls, theatre, and sumptuous celebrations which became courtly purgatories.[80] But of such stuff is diplomacy made, and Vergennes performed his social duties with the same diligence he exercised elsewhere.

As soon as George II and Newcastle departed, Vergennes set off for the Duchy of Brunswick with Grimaldi. Vergennes' official duty was to assure the Duke of Brunswick of Louis XV's "esteem and personal affection."[81] On September 10, 1752, Vergennes was once again at Hanover, where he awaited Vienna's answer to the *ultimatum*.[82]

The other representatives also waited. Among them was Newcastle, fully aware of the awkwardness of his position. The bits of information he received from Vienna did nothing to calm him.[83] Sometimes, he suffered the waiting with patience; but usually he could not hide his nervousness, and expressed his anxieties and agitation to Vergennes.[84] The "delay (of the messenger) is very extraordinary," he wrote his brother, "and I am afraid promises no great good when he comes."[85]

Maria Theresa had good reason to delay her reply to the *ultimatum*. She was occupied with the fruits of Frederick's earlier efforts — a declaration by the Princes of Württemberg, Cassel, Bayreuth, and Ansbach to Mainz, to the effect that the "College of Princes could not permit an election of the King of the Romans before the three Colleges had deliberated on the necessity of an election."[86]

As the days of waiting passed into weeks, Vergennes abandoned the vigil, and took advantage of the season to slip away on an autumn hunting trip. Meanwhile, Newcastle found himself fighting off a new threat to his election project: one, to his surprise, created by George II himself. King George had already objected to the English payment of 700,000 *florins* to pave the way for the election, but Newcastle had resolved to work on the assumption that, in the last analysis, the King would not refuse his consent.[87]

Newcastle now learned that the King was undermining his transactions in yet another way. Baron Vorster, the ambassador from Vienna, had told him that, after the *ultimatum* had gone to Vienna, a *pro memoria* signed by George II's Hanoverian minister, Grosvoight Münchausen, had followed. It represented to the Emperor and Maria Theresa that, since His Majesty, King George, had, on the occasion of the election, showed "his great regard for the interests of their Imperial Majesties, and as other powers were asking for fiefs, the King hoped their Imperial Majesties would give His Majesty a fief also." At the time, King George did not know of any particular fief that he wanted, but if he could find one, "he hoped then their Imperial Majesties would give it to him." "What a handle," as Newcastle so aptly exclaimed, "has the King given by this, to the Court of Vienna, against himself?" Now Vienna could refuse to grant the Palatinate the territories she demanded on the quite reasonable grounds that, if it did so, "everybody else will expect it." But what Newcastle feared most was that Vienna would refuse the Elector Palatinate and then court King George by giving him some insignificant fief "to make His Majesty easy with the miscarriage of the Election." "It is," Newcastle bemoaned, "a most terrible consideration."[88]

When Vienna's response to the *ultimatum* was finally received, Newcastle was exuberant to a degree unwarranted by its terms.[89] In addition to paying the 500,000 *florins* already agreed upon, Maria Theresa promised only another 100,000. Pleistein she was willing to grant. The privilege of *non-appellando* she would extend to the Palatinate, but not necessarily to the Duke of Deux-Ponts, who would first have to convince her of his good behavior. She refused to part with Ortenau, but offered Wildenau as an equivalent. Her major objection, however, was critical: she insisted they strike the requirement of France's consent to the election, or even to the necessity of a unanimous election.

Vergennes saw clearly now that Newcastle's plans would never succeed. He had only an inkling of King George's intrigues,[90] which had included advice to Maria Theresa not to advance more than 500,000 *florins* to satisfy the Palatinate,[91] but, even before he learned the details of the response from Vienna, he had arranged with Wrede, who had returned to Mannheim, not to come back to Hanover unless the Austrians accepted the *ultimatum* without essential alterations.

The election ground to a standstill.[92] And there it remained. The counter-project from Vienna modified the original *ultimatum* project,[93] so there was a declaration by the Palatinate on the counter-project,[94] and finally a counter-counter-project by the Hanoverian minister, Münchausen, to reconcile the counter-project and the declaration.[95] At long last, Newcastle realized that his plan for electing the Archduke Joseph as King of the Romans was dead. His own King had turned against it. His brother had accepted it only with reluctance. Vienna did not want it. The German princes were not enthusiastic. And the two most powerful nations on the Continent would accept it only if some extreme demands were fulfilled.

Newcastle's retreat began with a declaration on October 29, 1752, in which he stated that King George "observed with pleasure" the fact that the parties were beginning to "approach each other." Newcastle added that His Majesty would allow two months from the date of the declaration for the courts to make final statements regarding their respective decisions. The time limitation was a device to avoid admission of defeat; Newcastle had not been able to get the ministers of Vienna and Mannheim to sign Münchausen's latest project for conciliation.[96] His final attempt in this direction was as futile as it was foolish, and Wrede took pleasure in reporting it promptly to Vergennes. George II invited Wrede as well as Newcastle to attend a wild-boar hunt. During the course of the affair, several Hanoverian ministers appeared by design. There, in the middle of the forest, surrounded by the baying of hounds, the neighing of horses, and the general tumult of the chase, Newcastle tried to re-introduce the question of negotiation. Wrede refused to talk and returned to the hunt.[97]

Discomfited by the total failure of his electoral plans, Newcastle decided to remove himself from his proposal. He chose Vergennes as the object of his diplomatic swan-song. His recital was clearly composed to maintain both King George's prestige and his own ego. He informed Vergennes that the King had ordered him to communicate "in the most minute detail" the state of the negotiations, and to thank the French diplomat for the "amiable and confident" way he had explained France's position to the British ambassador at Versailles. Newcastle went on to say that His Britannic Majesty further hoped that the French minister not only would refrain from interfering with the happy conclusion of the business at Hanover, but also would employ himself in such a way as to confirm the "good intentions" which he had shown heretofore. Vergennes promised to send to Saint-Contest an account of Newcastle's conversation, but he was unable to offer anything further.[98] France's insistence on Article Six of the *ultimatum* and Wrede's continued allegiance to France made an election impossible unless Vienna were to capitulate. Maria Theresa's position fell far short of capitulation. Newcastle had no choice but to dissolve the Congress of Hanover.

Courtesy required Vergennes to remain at Hanover long enough to celebrate the birthday of George II and see him off to England,[99] but on the eleventh of November he was on his way to Versailles. The reception he was to receive had been anticipated in a letter from Saint-Contest: "Since the conferences at Hanover have terminated," he had written on the seventh, "and the King has given his permission for you to return here immediately, I await your arrival to discuss with you all that has just passed. At the moment, I will simply limit myself to saying in advance that the King's council seemed very satisfied with the way you conducted yourself during your stay at Hanover."[100]

But Vergennes had hardly returned to Versailles when he learned that his success at Hanover was in jeopardy. By the middle of January, 1753, he was on his way to Mannheim in the Palatinate. Secret intelligence gathered at Versailles indicated that the Palatinate was at the point of accepting a separate settlement with Vienna.[101]

By the middle of December, 1752, the differences that had separated Vienna and the Elector Palatinate were not great.[102] If the Palatinate agreed to accept what Maria Theresa had accepted in the *ultimatum*, the only major obstacle to an election, and to the Palatinate's satisfaction, was Vienna's refusal to sign the agreement (Article Six) which required that France consent to the election. Austria, with good reason, did not want to recognize that French right; France, with equally good reason, wished to confirm it.

To prevent a possible settlement between Vienna and Mannheim, Saint-Contest hurriedly dispatched a memo to the Ambassador of the Palatinate in France, M. de Wachendonc, urging the Elector to remain firm, and declaring that Maria Theresa's new offers were "inadmissable." Maria Theresa had suggested the accession of the Elector Palatinate, as well as the Duke of Deux-Ponts, to the Treaty of Füssen in exchange for eventual cession to the Palatinate of the territories it demanded. Such an exchange, Saint-Contest argued, was contrary to the Palatinate's obligations to France, and the Treaty of Füssen was an "odious treaty." Vienna, the French statesman believed, was only trying to detach the Palatinate from its allies with the bait of imaginary gains. He urged the Elector to insist on all his claims. He could then rest assured of Louis XV's support.[103]

A letter to Wrede, written by Vergennes, soon followed the memo. In it Vergennes emphasized that the memo was not simply a word of friendly advice, but an ultimatum.[104] Politely, but unmistakably, Vergennes closed the ring on the Palatinate by ordering that there be no separate settlement.

Saint-Contest was not entirely confident of his own minister at Mannheim, the Marquis de Tilly.[105] The Marquis, in his responses to Versailles, sympathetically repeated the Elector's desire to accept Vienna's offers and, by the tone of his report, indicated that he saw no objection to such a settlement. Obviously something had to be done about Tilly. The Duke of Deux-Ponts, Christian IV, had already made a suggestion: he urged that Tilly be replaced by Vergennes.[106]

Christian's motives were not disinterested. One of Maria Theresa's modifications of the *ultimatum* had been that Deux-Ponts would have to demonstrate his "compliance" before he would be granted the privilege of *non-appellando.* Maria Theresa did not indicate how such compliance could be demonstrated, but Christian IV readily saw that it probably would involve his satisfying stiff conditions. The word that the Palatinate was planning a separate settlement, Tilly's incompetence,[107] and Christian IV's recommendations explain why Vergennes departed in haste from Versailles for Mannheim on January 16, 1753.

Vergennes' instructions bade him to stress the dangers the Palatinate courted if she did not insist upon her original demands and, especially, if she made a separate settlement. Without French consent to the final resolution, there would be no one to hold Vienna to her agreements.[108]

After Vergennes arrived at Mannheim, he reported that the Palatinate was not as ready to settle as previous information had indicated.[109] Even Tilly wrote to assure the French Secretary of State that the Palatinate would do nothing without concerting with France.[110] An immediate result of Vergennes' appearance at Mannheim was that the Elector's minister, Wrede, prepared to go to Versailles.[111] Wrede was greatly disturbed when he learned that he was suspect at Versailles, and welcomed the opportunity to go there and clear himself.[112]

By the twenty-third of February, Vergennes' objectives had been achieved: the Palatinate renounced any arrangements with Vienna, except on French terms,[113] and Wrede's presence at Versailles was assured. Since Vergennes' visit to Mannheim had been announced as simply a stop-off on the way to Coblenz,[114] he should have gone on to Trier upon leaving Mannheim. Instead, he went to Strasbourg, where he secretly waited for Wrede. Together they traveled to Paris. "I will profit from the intimacy of the journey," Vergennes wrote Saint-Contest, "to get as much information as I can," and to make Wrede a "certain proposition which I have not yet had a chance to broach to him."[115]

There has been a good deal of speculation about the "certain proposition" referred to by Vergennes. There is some evidence, though it is not conclusive, that Saint-Contest was planning a system of alliances in Germany to form a federation of the Rhine.[116] Did Saint-Contest want to open the subject with Wrede in the secrecy of his cabinet? Perhaps the proposition was simply to arrange a gratification to Wrede to guarantee his loyalty to France. He did eventually receive a diamond-studded snuff-box with a portrait of Louis XV,[117] but Saint-Contest's *précis* of his conversations gives no further hints as to the details of the proposition.[118] Wrede tried to get Saint-Contest to agree that, if the Palatinate finally received nothing from Vienna, Louis XV would make up the loss, but the idea was still-born. The only definite thing known about Wrede's talks with Saint-Contest is that France made it clear, once again, that Louis XV would not accept a separate agreement between the Palatinate and Vienna.[119]

Vergennes had succeeded in fixing the Palatinate more securely in the French orbit, but to do so it had been necessary to deal rather harshly with Elector Charles Theodore. The Elector had reluctantly accepted the inevitable, but his acceptance was accompanied by a sense of humiliation and loss which he would not soon forget. Naturally, he saw Vergennes as the instrument of his frustration and he welcomed an early opportunity for revenge.

No sooner had Wrede returned to Mannheim than Tilly, no doubt piqued by the fact that so many things had been arranged without his help, demanded a leave. Saint-Contest neatly turned the request for leave into the opportunity to recall him. On hearing of the recall, Charles Theodore was instantly aggrieved. Tilly was one of his personal favorites, as well as a gracious and obliging flower of Mannheim court society. Wrede was immediately ordered to oppose the action.[120] Charles Theodore "would with the most profound displeasure," Wrede wrote to Versailles, "see the recall of M. Marquis de Tilly."[121] When Charles Theodore realized that all the pleading was in vain, Wrede's letters began to change. The new question was, who would succeed Tilly?

Charles Theodore suspected that Vergennes was in line for the appointment, and he found this idea distinctly disagreeable. He, therefore, ordered Wrede to say bluntly that, while the Elector did not in the least wish to slight Vergennes' skill and knowledge, his appointment would not be acceptable. "We are disposed to pray most earnestly to Your Majesty," he told Louis XV, "that it please him to accredit to us a person other than the said Chevalier de Vergennes."[122] Saint-Contest feigned ignorance of the cause of the Palatinate's dislike of Vergennes, but did not insist. A certain Vincent became the temporary *chargé d'affaires*,[123] and was soon relieved by the new permanent minister, the Baron de Zuckmentel.[124] While Vergennes may have been annoyed by the Elector's refusal to receive him, he unquestionably saw that the rebuff reflected credit on his abilities; it was obviously not his incompetence which decided the Elector to object to his appointment.

Vergennes returned once more to the lusterless court at Coblenz. The prospect had no appeal to him, and the summer of 1753 waned and fall was well underway before he assumed his post. He spent some leave at Versailles and then visited Chavigny, who, since May, was the French Ambassador to the Swiss Cantons, residing in the elegant embassy at Soleur. The reunion of the uncle and nephew proved to be so enjoyable that Chavigny wrote Saint-Contest requesting permission for Vergennes to give him "a few days more" than originally proposed, a request that was granted "with pleasure." Then Vergennes returned to Coblenz[125] for a fourteen-month stay in the backwash of affairs. The matter of the election of the King of the Romans was quiet, and Coblenz was even less interesting than before.

Still, the routine diplomatic chores had to be done and Vergennes, bored but dutiful, performed them all. He intervened to get the Elector of Trier to let grain, bought in Cologne and Westphalia by merchants of Metz, pass Trier without duty.[126] When the Elector received a Papal Bull authorizing him to convoke the religious chapter at Trier to deliberate on the question of an election of a co-adjutor, Vergennes paid close attention. Happily, on July 12, 1754, he could report that the more pro-French of the candidates, Baron de Wallendorf, was elected co-adjutor by unanimous vote.[127] Periodically, too, Francois-Georges brought up his claims for reimbursement for the 200,000 rations, and Vergennes went through the motions of putting the question before his superiors.[128] Such routine affairs were the brightest spots in his existence. He revealed the discouraging character of his daily life in a letter, written during his winter of boredom, 1753-54. He hoped that Saint-Contest would not think him negligent, but it was "impossible", where he was, to find out anything that would possibly interest Versailles. "This court, always loyal to its own ideas of impartiality," he wrote, "affects ignorance, as well as indifference, concerning everything that happens in Europe."[129] "My uselessness here," he complained another time to the new foreign minister Antoine Louis, Comte de Joux Rouillé, "could not be more complete nor better demonstrated. I never have anything to do and, nearly always, nothing to write."[130] Finally, his lamentations produced results; he was granted leave. With great relief he departed from Coblenz on December 13, 1754.[131] He had every reason to believe that his next post was to be that of minister to the King of Bavaria, but the intricacies of eighteenth-century European politics were to present him with a much more challenging assignment.

Germany was the school of diplomacy for Vergennes. There, from his uncle and by personal experience, he learned to negotiate, to apply various means to implement a policy or gain maximum advantage. He studied and tried out the arts of persuasion and coercion, without the use of violence, but with the threat of violence forever in the background. He grappled with the terribly complex "constitution" of the Empire; he observed the tremendous influence of money in international politics, and saw the terrible costs, both in money and personal corruption, of the political instrument of war. But he also tested the limits of what money could buy. The votes of the Electors of the Holy Roman Empire all carried price tags, but, in the last analysis, the Elector of Trier would vote according to his understanding of his own interest. But, whatever the costs or consequences, Vergennes never questioned the validity of the assumption that international politics had first claims on the financial resources of France.

The attempt to elect a King of the Romans contained another lesson for Vergennes. The war scare of 1750-51 was disturbing evidence that Russia, daily growing more powerful, would force her way onto the European stage at every opportunity. Vergennes recognized that new presence and, during the rest of his life, he never forgot to include Russia in all of his political calculations. To Vergennes, Russia had become a part of the European international system.

In Germany, Vergennes learned also to appreciate the fact that public opinion had to be taken into account in diplomacy. The failure of French relations with the Holy Roman Emperor, Charles VII, had aroused an angry public reaction against the French ministers and Louis XV, which hindered the work of Chavigny and his nephew and put them in danger of physical harm. Prince William of Hesse taught him that to lose popularity and trust was not an "insignificant inconvenience". Also, he pointed out that if one's professed role in the international system was that of upholder of public law, the role could be seriously undermined by a brutal disregard of public law. On the other hand, Vergennes saw how much Newcastle had to keep a weather eye on opinion in Parliament, and the French minister did not approve of a form of government which made it necessary to go so far as to cater to public opinion. As an aristocrat, Vergennes shared the view that only the ruling élite and the professional initiates were capable of real understanding of the complexities of international politics.

Vergennes' negotiations in Germany completed his apprenticeship and demonstrated his unusual talents as a professional diplomat. Even his enemies praised him. Newcastle, in a note to Saint-Contest, acknowledged that Vergennes' performance at Hanover had earned him the esteem of the diplomatic corps.[132] Moreover, the Englishman even wrote to Uncle Chavigny, praising the nephew whose polished manners and good disposition he recognized as the qualities of the uncle.[133] When Frederick learned that Newcastle and George II had returned to London,[134] he suspected a trick and, at the same time, evaluated the work of Vergennes. "Monsieur de Newcastle," he wrote, "flatters himself that at London he will get a better bargain out of Wrede. He (Wrede) will no longer be under the influence of a French minister as vigilant and firm as Monsieur de Vergennes."[135]

Vergennes himself was wise enough not to expect public recognition of his successful missions to Germany, but he must have been content in the knowledge that his skillful negotiations were respected by the other diplomats, and that Saint-Contest, a few ministers in the King's Council, and some of the chief clerks in the Ministry of Foreign Affairs in France recognized his achievement.

Part II

THE TURKISH EQUATION

CHAPTER 4

Constantinople

The appointment in 1755 of Charles Gravier de Vergennes to be Louis XV's diplomatic representative at Constantinople came at a dramatic turning point in France's relations with the Ottoman Empire. Traditionally, the French monarch had seen the Turks as one of the keys to his influence in Eastern Europe. The "Turkish diversion" was a classic weapon in the French diplomatic arsenal for containing, pressuring, or threatening Russia or the Hapsburg Empire. But the extraordinary rise of Russia in the eighteenth century, and the slow but steady decline of Poland and the Ottoman Empire, created the conditions for painful and violent upheaval, which would force France to reconsider her traditional policies in Eastern Europe. As Ambassador of Louis XV at Constantinople, Vergennes lived at the fault-line of these tremendous readjustments. Long before nineteenth-century diplomats came to diagnose the Ottoman Empire as the "sick man of Europe", Vergennes had taken the patient's pulse and found him feeble.

The concept of balance-of-power and equilibrium, so basic to the international politics of the Ancien Régime, suggests stability. Yet the diplomatic history of the latter half of the eighteenth century reveals very little stability, balance or equilibrium. To Vergennes, the uncertain character of the international system meant that his day-to-day activities were carried out in a tense atmosphere of suspicion, intrigue, and competition. Today's friends may be tomorrow's enemies. Your enemies today may be your allies tomorrow. Also, the personal preoccupation of monarchs with their "prestige" and "honor" created sensitivities to which the diplomats had to give special consideration. A random act, or a failure to act, could be interpreted as detracting from a monarch's prestige, or as a slight to his honor. Such an act or non-act could unexpectedly explode into an ugly crisis and a chain reaction that could shake the foundations of a longstanding relationship, for great-power relations were defined not only in terms of interests, policies, and power, but also in terms of personalities, egos, and prestige values.

Effectiveness in Ancien Régime diplomacy required a considerable technical understanding of the ways, traditions, and conditions in which international relations were carried out. How, for example, was an ambassador to go about implementing his assignment? What were the resources at his disposal, and how should he use them? How did he organize his embassy and staff to meet his responsibilities? In what ways did his own personal ambitions or anxieties condition his effectiveness? And how did he interpret and respond to the instructions and orders of his superiors, and to the communications from his host government? Such questions are especially pertinent to the study of an ambassador to Constantinople, because the problems of language, cultural and religious differences, and the distance from Versailles complicated the diplomat's task in the extreme. A prolific letter-writer and memorandist, Vergennes left behind a remarkable record of the judgments, habits, and techniques of this very competent professional diplomat.

But, above all, the records permit the reconstruction of a chapter of French diplomatic history which reveals the contradictions, the "misalliances", the fumblings, frantic heroics, and bitter setbacks suffered by the Ancien Régime French monarchy as it entered the last decades of its existence.

In 1754 the balance-of-power system of Europe operated with France and her allies on one side, and England and her allies on the other. One power whose relation to this system was rather ambiguous, but whose friendship France valued highly, was the Ottoman Empire. Although there was no formal political alliance between the two countries, there were strong commercial ties and a bond of self-interest, stemming from a common suspicion of Austria, and a common fear of an increasingly obtrusive Imperial Russia.

Eighteenth-century Europe witnessed the rise of Russia to the status of a great power, and the Russian army was prepared to support Russian political designs.[1] Russian pressure began to be felt in the Baltic, along the eastern frontier of Poland, and against the boundaries of the Ottoman Empire. Diplomats in Constantinople, Stockholm, and Warsaw watched every Russian move, and alerted each other to any evidences of Russian influence. Russian ambitions at times appeared to outrun her uneven capabilities, but she was learning her way, and the West recognized her potential.[2] In 1746, Austria had allied with Russia against Prussia, and in 1755, Maria Theresa brought her ally, George II, into a convention with the Czarina Elizabeth. King George welcomed an association with Russia. In the event of a war with France, he hoped to use his Russian and Austrian allies to keep both France and Prussia busy on the Continent, while England concentrated on the destructions of French maritime trade, and the harrassment of French overseas possessions.

Aware of England's designs, French diplomats sought a system of their own. They maintained an alliance with Prussia as a counterweight to Austria; they strengthened the pro-French forces in Poland in an attempt to seal

Russia's gateway to Europe; and they supported the anti-Russian factions in Sweden and in the Ottoman Empire, countries flanking Russia.

No listening-post was more important to France than Constantinople. The ambassador there had to be continually alert to the damaging influences of foreign agents, and to explain French policies again and again to the Sultan. Versailles was well aware of the necessity of keeping the post at Constantinople constantly and ably manned. Such was the situation when, in December, 1754, a messenger clattered into Versailles with the word that the Comte des Alleurs, the French ambassador to the Ottoman Empire, had died, thus leaving French interests unguarded.[3]

Des Alleurs' death could not have occurred at a more critical time for France. Her relations with England were deteriorating rapidly; the arena of conflict was the American wilderness. The British Secretary of State, Sir Thomas Robinson, regarded French conduct in America to be "...evidently the effect of a settled, premeditated plan to distress the English trade in those parts, and to commit the most glaring encroachments and usurpations upon His Majesty's just rights and possessions."[4] The French interpretation of the situation placed blame on the English, but their conclusion was the same: France and England were on the brink of war. The solidarity of alliances on both sides might have to be put to the test.

The loss of Des Alleurs to France had a personal significance to Louis XV. The ambassador to Constantinople had been one of the small group of diplomats who were privy to Louis' pattern of secret diplomacy, the *secret du roi*.[5] The beginnings of the *secret du roi* go back to the year 1745, and to a comparatively small episode in Poland. Augustus III was then King of the Poles. His poor health prompted a party of Polish noblemen to seek a successor. Augustus III, also the Elector of Saxony, had been elected King of Poland by a minority of Polish nobles supported by the presence of Russian and Austrian troops in Poland. The Polish noblemen wanted neither a Saxon nor a pro-Russian to succeed Augustus. Their search took them to Paris, where they invited a relative of Louis XV, Prince de Conti, to become a candidate. Louis XV, to whom Conti privately communicated the proposal, authorized him to accept, and promised financial support. King Louis stipulated, however, that the entire project must be kept secret from the French ministers. Conti organized a network of agents and arranged for the appointment of ambassadors in Eastern Europe who, on his explicit instructions, were to report to him as well as to the Ministry of Foreign Affairs. Ultimately, Conti was unsuccessful in the Polish election; but Louis XV now had at his disposal a tightly-knit and secret mechanism for interference in the formal channels of foreign affairs.[6]

The sudden death of Des Alleurs created a threat to Louis' secret diplomacy. An uninitiated embassy official might publicly discuss the dead ambassador's correspondence, thus unwittingly revealing the French King's machinations; or enemies of France might arrange for the theft of confidential documents; and there was the unknown factor of Des Alleurs' widow, who belonged to a Polish princely family.[7] She had close contacts with influential Polish aristocrats, and made no secret of her zeal in forwarding the interests of Poland. Did she know anything about the *secret du roi*?

Recognizing the dangers inherent in the situation at Constantinople, Louis XV took immediate action to place a reliable person in the Ottoman capital. He determined upon the appointment of an envoy exraordinary rather than an ambassador. There were only three precedents for sending a representative of so low a rank to treat with the Sultan,[8] but assembling a fleet, customary for the ceremonial arrival of an ambassador, would take precious time. Moreover, ceremonies were expensive and the post at Constantinople, especially under Des Alleurs, had already been an extremely expensive one.[9]

In selecting his envoy extraordinary, Louis XV did not have to look far. Present at this opportune moment was Vergennes, just returned from a successful diplomatic mission in Germany and awaiting another assignment. Present also was Vergennes' uncle, Chavigny, recently recalled from Switzerland to serve temporarily as advisor to Rouillé, the new Minister of Foreign Affairs. Chavigny was an intimate of the Prince de Conti; he knew of the *secret du roi*; he had faith in the trustworthiness of his nephew. This combination of availability and family connections proved successful. The Chevalier de Vergennes was named France's representative to the Sultan of the Ottoman Empire.[10]

"I learned, about eight days ago, of the death of M. des Alleurs . . ." the Duc de Luynes, whose wife was the French Queen's *dame d'honneur*, recorded in his journal for January 16, 1755: "M. de Vergennes, nephew of M. de Chavigny, expressed his thanks today. He has just been named minister plenipotentiary of the King to the Porte. He will bring to the post a character very different from that of M. des Alleurs. M. de Vergennes is still young; but he has a good mind, talent, and even experience. He was trained by M. de Chavigny, his uncle."[11]

In a memorandum announcing Vergennes' appointment, Rouillé urged him to depart immediately for his destination.[12] To expedite his journey, the sea route was chosen rather than either of the two land routes through Vienna or Warsaw.[13] The bad sailing season, and the possible presence of hostile British ships in the Mediterranean made the choice a risky one, but necessity favored the quickest route. The Ministry fitted out and armed a merchant ship at Marseille[14] and furnished Vergennes with letters of credit for his expenses. The date of departure from Paris was set for January 25, 1755[15] just two weeks after his appointment. Such a tight schedule assumed considerable good luck in completing the preparations; unhappily, at this point, Vergennes' luck ran out.

The schedule had allowed Vergennes only a fortnight in which to settle his affairs in France, to be fitted for the wardrobe proper to his new post, to buy furnishings for his new residence, to recruit his personnel, and to select presents for the Sultan and for the Turkish ministers and petty officials. The last task, especially, was extremely important in order to establish the relations so useful at the Turkish court. Despite the obvious fact that so much could not possibly be completed in such a short time, Vergennes set to work in high spirits and with great energy.

As the date of departure approached, however, the problems of preparation seemed to multiply rather than diminish. There was not enough money for the gifts;[16] his luggage could not be ready to leave Paris before the first of February, and would not arrive in Marseille until the seventeenth or eighteenth of that month. The government eased his financial problem by increasing his gift allowance,[17] but other preparations still lagged. In despair, he finally asked for a delay. "I beg you, Monseigneur," he wrote to Rouillé, "to permit me to stay here in Paris all next week, since I have no one to whom I can entrust the responsibility of hastening my arrangements."[18]

At this moment, word arrived that the reigning Sultan Mahmud I had sudddenly died.[19] Now, more than ever, French interests in Constantinople needed a responsible overseer. Frantically, Vergennes labored day and night. The first of February came and passed, but the young diplomat found himself still in Paris and, worse still, ill from over-fatigue, and bedridden.[20] The anxieties over new responsibilities had sapped his physical strength.

Again Chavigny intervened on behalf of his protégé, in response to the impatience in the Ministry of Foreign Affairs. "I found M. de Vergennes well advanced in his convalescence," Chavigny assured Vergennes' superior on the fifteenth of February. "A few more days ought to strengthen it even more. I plan to accompany him to Versailles next Thursday, where he will receive your final orders and then depart."[21] But the first of March passed and the nephew was still not on his feet. Chavigny, ever watchful of his nephew's interests, advised his friend, Rouillé, that "the health of M. de Vergennes is about as good as one could expect. He needs only a few more days to consolidate it solidly, and not expose himself to a disagreeable relapse." Chavigny was now certain that Vergennes would definitely leave Paris on the eighth of March.[22] This time the prediction came true. Vergennes was on his way to Marseille at dawn on the eighth.[23]

But rains and floods slowed his travel to Marseille, and a contrary wind held up the sailing after he arrived.[24] At last, in the early afternoon of April 3, 1755, the converted merchantman, renamed, ironically, *L'heureux,* raised anchor and edged out of port.[25] Two months had passed since the original date of departure, but finally, with every detail of preparation completed, the new minister to Constantinople could relax in his quarters. There was time now to get to know his subordinates, who were sailing with him;[26] and, above all, he could contemplate his future in the new assignment. As it turned out, there was more than enough time; winds from the southeast and south plagued them, and forced the ship to put in, first at Toulon,[27] and later at the Isle of Saint Pierre near Sardinia.[28] At long last, however, a favorable wind billowed their sails and they rode toward the Dardanelles.

Constantinople was a critical spot in the French diplomatic network, and it was certain to offer Vergennes a wider range of responsibilities than had his earlier assignments. One of the major interests France had in the Ottoman Empire was trade. In 1740 the French ambassador to Constantinople, Villeneuve, had reached agreements, or "capitulations," with Turkey that enlarged the French commercial relations in the Empire to the point where France enjoyed the commercial advantages of a vast empire without the administrative costs of governing one. According to one estimate, French trade with the Porte was a major source of income for perhaps as many as two million Frenchmen. The city of Marseille, and the provinces of Provence and Languedoc, greatly benefited from the trade.[29] To protect that trade, and the French subjects engaged in it, was one of the principal tasks of the French ambassador.

The death of Mahmud I in October of 1754 had brought to the throne Mahmud's brother, Osman III, and with the new Sultan came a new administration. France was in total darkness as to the character of Osman, or the changes that could be expected from him. One of the first tasks assigned to Vergennes, in his instructions, was to gather as much information as possible on the new ruler, as well as on the persons he had raised to positions of power.[30]

In addition to his duties *vis-à-vis* the Sultan's officials, Vergennes had clearly-defined responsibilities towards the diplomats of other powers. He was told to cultivate publicly the minister from Sweden, Celsing, in order to emphasize the close understanding that existed among France, Sweden, and the Ottoman Empire.[31] He was told also that he should treat with "respect" the ministers of other powers at Constantinople, even the ambassador from Russia; but those representing London and Vienna deserved whatever attention their conduct merited.[32] The King of France desired peace and concord, Vergennes was told, and no one must see in the behavior of France's ministers anything to indicate the contrary.[33]

While Vergennes was to be a man of peace at Constantinople, he was nevertheless to be alert for signs of war. If the Turks went to war, their most probable enemies would be the Russians, the Austrians, or the Persians. In

1747, the Ottoman Empire had made peace with its eastern neighbor, Persia, thus bringing to a close the long, bloody duel which had kept the two Empires at war, or preparing for war, since the sixteenth century. Peace terms, however, had been dictated by Persia after the crushing defeat of a huge Turkish army of invasion. The resultant treaty, although quite mild and imposing on the Turks no great disadvantages, was not calculated to restore their pride.[34] Only a victorious return engagement could do that. Many Turks believed that revenge could easily be theirs.

France, however, did not favor the Turks' engaging, and perhaps exhausting, themselves in another war with Persia. If the new Sultan should have "a taste for war," Vergennes was ordered to dissuade him from it.[35] Furthermore, if the Turks began to eye Russia, or Austria's possessions in Hungary, as possible objectives for attack, Vergennes was also to discourage them.[36] Moreover, he should do so in a public way, so that the Russian and Austrian ambassadors would see that France, in its liaison with the Porte, had only the "tranquillity of Europe in view."[37]

A thorny problem inherent in the French-Turkish relation was the absence of a formal political alliance between them. For many years, their association had been most intimate and their commerce flourishing. But, for several reasons, no formal defensive or offensive treaties had been contracted. Such a treaty with the infidel Turks would be "odious," Rouillé explained to Vergennes in his instructions, "and would arouse a large number of the Christian powers against France."[38] Furthermore, the Ottoman Empire was so far away that any agreement for mutual military assistance would be impossible to implement. Since France, therefore, could not sign a treaty, Vergennes was warned not to raise false hopes which, of necessity, would be disappointed. Such an unpleasant reaction might lead to the expulsion of French merchants and businessmen from the Empire, and French loss of trade with the Levant.[39]

Vergennes was to understand, however, that while France wanted to encourage a peaceful Ottoman Empire, if Russia became aggressive, France counted on the Turks to help check her. Vergennes was to pay particular attention to any Russian move against the Republic of Poland. The Turks must not "abandon the Poles to the arbitrary disposition of Russia," Rouillé insisted, and he pointed out that, if Russia controlled certain areas of Polish territory, she had an ideal strategic position for launching an attack on the Ottoman Empire.[40] Louis XV's policy of discouraging Turkish inclination to war was, therefore, conditional and subject to revision if Russia threatened the balance of power in Eastern Europe, especially if her troops set foot on Polish territory.

The political relations between France and the Ottoman Empire were complicated enough, but the embassy in Constantinople was beset with other important problems as well, some of them decidedly explosive. One such problem was a religious one. The Roman Catholic Christians in the Empire looked to the Very Christian King of France as their protector. The King of France willingly accepted the role, because he sincerely felt the honor and gravity of the responsibilities involved; also, it gave him a useful wedge for intervention in Turkish affairs.

Unhappily, however, the Christians in the Ottoman Empire did not make the position of protector an easy one. They were constantly squabbling with "infidels" or, even worse, with each other, and then calling for the aid of the protector. If such aid were not promptly rendered, or if, as sometimes happened, the King judged that the party calling for aid was in the wrong, the indignant petitioners might appeal the case to the Pope or even the Sultan. When this occurred, the King of France found himself enmeshed in a diplomatic wrangle.[41]

Another purpose of Vergennes' mission to Constantinople was to protect the integrity of Louis XV's secret diplomacy. Just before he sailed from Marseille, Vergennes was initiated into some of the intricacies of this bizarre method of carrying on diplomatic affairs.[42] In envelopes addressed to a "Monsieur Boranis" or a "Monsieur Coramin," he was to forward his secret dispatches directly to the King's first *valet de chambre,* Le Bel.[43] Whatever Vergennes' judgement and experience may have taught him regarding the diplomatic pitfalls of such an unorthodox practice, his personal ambition was undoubtedly nourished by the knowledge that the King would personally read his dispatches.[44]

Yet, what did this cautious, conventional diplomat think as he read, with his formal instructions, a second set of secret instructions from Louis XV? The secret instructions outlined the King's wishes as to the attitude the diplomat was to assume toward each of the major points of his official instructions.[45] Vergennes ought to follow completely, Louis told him, the instructions Rouillé had given him concerning the efforts to prevent Turkey from declaring war on her neighbors. On the other hand, Vergennes' predecessor had received full power from Frederick II of Prussia to negotiate a Prusso-Turkish Treaty of Commerce. Louis told Vergennes to do nothing positive to advance the treaty. Louis stressed, as did Rouillé, the necessity for keeping the Turks alert to Russian aggression. The Turks must be made to feel, Louis explained, that it was in their own interest to sustain the liberties of Poland, and to protect the tranquillity of Sweden.

So far, the secret instructions did not radically alter the official ones. But then, Louis referred Vergennes to secret orders given to Des Alleurs, and told Vergennes to continue to follow them. These orders revealed that Louis XV was opposed to Rouillé policy of avoiding a formal treaty with the Porte. His Majesty *did* want a treaty of friendship with the Sultan, and he also wanted a secret article in the treaty, in which the Turks would formally assure the "liberties" of Poland against Russian aggression. Louis' instructions indicated that the negotiations for such a treaty had been well underway at Des Alleurs' death, although the Ministry of Foreign Affairs at Versailles knew nothing of them.[46]

Thus, by putting greater stress here, reducing the emphasis there, and changing important points, Louis XV made it clear that Vergennes' public role as a minister was distinct from his secret role as King's agent. Since the points of difference between official French policy and Louis XV's secret diplomacy[47] were substantial, what would happen if Vergennes' two roles came into conflict? No doubt, he would obey his King and not the Minister of Foreign Affairs, but such a decision could easily wreck his career. Would Louis XV, wanting, above all, to protect his secret, feel obliged to protect his agent?

Other important functions also occupied the French representative at Constantinople. In the eyes of the Sultan, pomp and magnificence were equated with power and glory; and sovereigns of both great and small powers insisted that their diplomats at Constantinople create both. The Sultan held in contempt any prince whose envoys constantly and publicly pinched pennies; he even considered it a public insult to himself if a foreign diplomat at his court failed to display the customary splendor.

Before leaving France for Constantinople, Des Alleurs had spent six months and over 70,000 *livres* gathering around him a large entourage, and preparing the way for a splendid entry into Constantinople.[48] Yet his outlay was not unusual. There are numerous examples of such extravagant expenditures; facts which explain why paying the bills for such activities was a chronic problem for the foreign affairs ministeries of Europe.[49] Des Alleurs had gone deeply in debt in order to pay for his elegant furniture, the objets d'art, the luxurious cloth and other fine accoutrements. But when he arrived at the Straits of the Bosporus, escorted by a fleet of French warships with cannons blasting, roaring salutes to the Turkish pavilion, and when, in the port of the Turkish Sultan, artillery answered with crashing salvos of welcome, no one was left in doubt that a Very Important Person had arrived.[50]

But Des Alleurs' retainers, his fine furniture, and splendid display were his personal undoing; he was never able to get out from under his debts. Apparently he had hoped to make up some of his expenses from the resources his Constantinople post opened to him, as the embassy at Constantinople had a reputation for being a lucrative spot.[51] But the expected returns never materialized. In 1752, he tried speculating in Levantine grain on the market at Marseille, planning to take advantage of a bumper crop in the eastern provinces of the Ottoman Empire. His luck failed; the grain proved to be of mediocre quality, and high costs of transportation and an unfavorable rate of exchange completed the sad story. When he died, he left to his widow a debt of 50,000 *écus* in France, and additional debts amounting to 140,000 *écus* at Constantinople.[52] Needless to say, Des Alleurs' creditors, as well as his distracted widow, daily and with great eagerness watched for the arrival of the envoy from France.

On May 18, 1755, forty-five days out of Marseille, *L'heureux* trimmed her sails and made ready to enter the forty-mile stretch of the Dardanelles. Vergennes hoped to slip past the Turkish naval ships guarding the entrance, in order not to lose any precious time wining and dining with the Grand Admiral of the Turkish fleet. Rumors of plague in the Turkish Navy also made him want to avoid any intimate contacts with Turkish sailors. But the Turkish Grand Admiral had received orders to look out for him, and to render all the honors that were due a minister of the "Emperor" of France.[53] French ingenuity was put to test to find a way to evade the usual eight-day delay with the reception committee.

Just before they entered the Straits they sighted a caravelle of the Turkish Navy anchored off Tenedos on Bazcaada Island; its rig was scudding towards them. There was, on board *L'heureux,* a French army officer, a certain Tott, a veteran of the French missions in Constantinople and the Crimea.[54] Tott met the Turkish sailors at the ship's ladder and, speaking to them in their own language, won their agreement not to come aboard. But such an accord, both parties allowed, was worth some recompense. Consequently, the cabin boy was ordered below to get some bottles of good French liqueur, to reward the Turks for their compliance. Somehow the boy made a mistake and brought back six bottles of lavender water. When he realized his error, he turned to go back and exchange them; but Tott assured him that it made no difference whatsoever what kind of liqueur the Turkish sailors were given. Whereupon they delivered the bottles of lavender water to the Turkish officers who made haste to depart.

Once in his rig, and impatient to taste a product of the celebrated French vineyards, a Turkish officer uncorked a bottle and swilled it down. After a moment's pause, he made a sign to the French ship that the Frenchman's drink was indeed excellent. All but Tott aboard *L'heureux* were aghast, expecting the Turk to topple over dead. Instead, he uncorked a second botle, disposed of its contents in the same fashion, and once again signaled his whole-hearted approval as he sailed away.[55] A few minutes later *L'heureux,* unescorted, entered the Straits of the Dardanelles. Once inside, she lowered her pennant so as not to be recognized and, four days later, about noon on the twenty-second of May, she quietly dropped anchor in the Port of Constantinople.[56]

Although Vergennes had seen the busy sea ports of Portugal and France, the brilliance of Versailles, and the beauty of Paris, Constantinople must have shocked and jangled his senses. Situated at the extreme eastern tip of Europe, the port city and its magnificent suburbs presented a rich and splendid picture to the newcomer. Hundreds of small boats and ferries crossed and recrossed the port of the Golden Horn in the morning, carrying people from the suburbs to their work in the city, and in the evening, back to their homes. Daily, thousands of transports carrying food and provisions for the city crowded into the port and tied up at the docks.

Along with these activities were the operations of all those engaged in foreign commerce. The merchants who served both East and West, Jews, Armenians, Greeks, Frenchmen, Germans, Egyptians, Russians, Englishmen, Orientals, as well as Turks, each speaking his own tongue, made the city a tower of Babel and a cauldron of boiling motion.

In the city, the overhanging roofs let very little light into the narrow streets and alleyways, which were sometimes graveled, but rarely cared for, and always dirty.[57] The closeness of the buildings and the materials of construction—mostly unpainted wood — plus the frequent high winds and the greed of arsonists who hoped to create the opportunity for plunder, made the city a fire trap. The Turk, long habituated to such catastrophes, took the loss of life and property with a fatalism that stunned the European.[58]

At the extreme end of the cape which closed the Golden Horn, on the site of old Byzantium, stood the Seraglio of the "Very High, Very Powerful," etc., etc., "World Creator" and Sultan of the Ottoman Empire. Surrounded by the old walls of Byzantium and a forest of cypress trees, the peaks of the cupolas of the Seraglio, covered with lead and gold, formed a pyramid at the top of which stood the tower of the divan. There, in the inner court of the Seraglio, the Sultan deigned to hold audiences every Tuesday (unless it was a religious holiday) with the ambassadors of all the powers of the world.[59]

Constantinople, therefore, was a microcosm of the sacred, profane, and diplomatic world. Placed between two seas, the center of a network of trade routes, foreign missionaries, espionage, and intrigue, it was the ideal spot to observe the combats of empires.

Foreigners at Constantinople did not live in the city, but on the other side of the Golden Horn in Pera, today called Beyoglu. Pera was the cosmopolitan capital,[60] for it was there that all the establishments of the foreign infidels, the merchants, missionaries, and adventurers, as well as the foreign consulates and embassies, including the residences of the French representatives were located. The distance between the Seraglio and the embassies meant that most of the day-to-day communications between the two were carried on by *drogmen,* interpreter-messengers, who shuttled back and forth over the Golden Horn. When Vergennes wished to visit the Seraglio for an audience, he had to go down to the harbor, perhaps near the present location of the Galata Bridge, and cross over the Golden Horn into Constantinople by ferry. The trip ordinarily took about half an hour.

CHAPTER 5

Ceremony and Debts at the Court of the Sultan

The moment he arrived at Constantinople, Vergennes dispatched messengers to the Porte to announce his presence.[1] He was anxious to obtain an official audience quickly because the Mohammedan religious holidays, the Ramadan, were approaching, and he feared that, once they began, he would have to wait two months before an audience could be arranged. Furthermore, a few days before Vergennes' arrival, the *Grand Vizir,* or chief minister, and his principal colleagues had been disgraced, and Vergennes was anxious to make contacts with the new ministry in order to gauge its character.[2]

Several technicalities had to be overcome, however, before plans for the audience could proceed. Louis XV had furnished Vergennes with two sets of credentials: one set giving him the title of envoy extraordinary, and the other, the title of minister plenipotentiary. He was told to determine, after his arrival in Constantinople, which of the two titles would be the more useful. Vergennes sent his *drogman* to ask the *Re'îs Efendi,*[3] the Turkish Minister of Foreign Affairs, his opinion as to which title he should use.[4] The *Re'îs Efendi* in turn consulted the *Grand Vizir,* and together they decided that the title of minister plenipotentiary would carry the greater prestige. The Turkish word for "minister," they explained, was also the word for "ambassador;" thus, if he chose the title of minister plenipotentiary, Vergennes would carry a title which the Turks would translate as "ambassador plenipotentiary." Without further ado, Vergennes elected to follow this advice.[5]

Even though his title carried more prestige than he merited, he was still not certain that the Turkish government was going to give him all the honors he expected. In the reception given for the presentation of the diplomatic credentials, it was customary for representatives of the great powers to be privileged to wear a rose-colored, fur-lined robe which was reserved only for the highest dignitaries. Vergennes' predecessor had received it without question, but the last two ambassadors from Venice, Vergennes learned, had had their right to wear the robe contested. Since Vergennes did not officially have the title of ambassador, he feared that the privilege might also be denied to him.[6]

He was determined not to begin his relations with the Porte with a diminution of honors. He decided, consequently, that, in spite of his title, he would insist on the rights of an ambassador and demand to wear the robe. When he raised the question with the *Re'is Efendi,* there seemed to be no objection; he assumed, therefore, that the issue was settled in his favor.[7]

On the afternoon of the twenty-fifth of May, the *Grand Vizir's drogman* notified Vergennes that he was prepared to see him. The French minister immediately dispatched a horse to bring him to the Embassy. Soon the *drogman* appeared, followed by servants bearing gifts, flowers, and baskets of fruit. Compliments were exchanged, coffee was served; eventually the *drogman* introduced the purpose of his visit: did Vergennes wish to have an audience before the religious holidays? Vergennes assured him that he did, and the dates were settled. On the thirty-first of May he was to have his audience with the *Grand Vizir,* and on the third of June with the Sultan. When the *drogman* left, Vergennes could well be content with how easily the preliminary details of his new assignment had been settled.[8]

At the last minute, however, just forty-eight hours before the audience, the *Re'is Efendi* called in the *drogman* of the French embassy and informed him that his master would neither be accorded the privilege of wearing the fur-lined robe nor was he going to have the Chief Usher of the Council of State to lead the procession to the Divan.[9] The *Re'is Efendi's* sudden change of heart surprised Vergennes; it also sorely embarrassed him, for it was a blow to his personal price as well as to his public role. The important audience with the *Grand Vizir* was only two days away, and the essential question of protocol were still undecided.

When the ambassadors of Venice had been faced with a similar problem, they had negotiated a settlement after long, drawn-out discussions. But now there was not time for that solution. The *Re'is Efendi* might have raised the issue at this particular moment in order to have it settled favorably with a discreet bribe. Such a practice, Vergennes knew, was not uncommon, and would likely produce a quick and desirable settlement. But Vergennes disliked paying for distinctions which were his due, and he decided, therefore, to stand on principle.

He firmly, but with "suitable politeness," told the *Re'is Efendi* that he was astonished that there could be any question about customs which had heretofore been invariable; that he would be "very mortified" if some unforeseen contingency interfered with his eagerness to be admitted to the audiences with the *Grand Vizir* and the Sultan. But, before he could admit any innovations which might render him guilty of failure to defend the honor of his King, he would have to await further orders from France.[10]

When he was acquainted with Vergennes' stand, the Turkish Foreign Minister became furious. He expelled Vergennes' *drogman* from his presence and ordered the man never again to appear before him. Nevertheless, he closed his tirade with the comment that Vergennes should send someone the next day to hear his final decision. Vergennes, meanwhile, drew up a memorandum repeating his position and presented it to the *Grand Vizir*.[11]

His tactics produced a victory. The next day, everything was sweetness and light at the Turkish Ministry. Yes, Vergennes would be accompanied by the Chief of the Ushers of the Council of State; yes, he would wear the coveted robe at the moment of the audience. In addition, he would be preceded in the procession by forty-seven horses and forty-five coffee bearers, the largest escort ever accorded anyone of his rank. Satisfied, Vergennes now agreed that the audiences would take place.

On the morning of the thirty-first of May, the Chief Usher of the Divan sent a boat to bring Vergennes and his company to the boat landing at the shipping port of Constantinople.[12] There they were met by the Chief Usher and his officers, and were led to a kiosk where they were ceremoniously served coffee, sherbet, and perfumed water, while the major body of the procession was formed. When everything was ready, the French minister descended from the kiosk and mounted a richly decorated horse. The Chief Usher and his officers, magnificently uniformed and wearing splendid ceremonial hats, ranged themselves in line to his right. The slow parade to the palace of the *Grand Vizir* began.

At the palace, Vergennes dismounted and, preceded by the Ushers, climbed the broad steps and entered the great hall of audiences. There he was solemnly introduced by a *drogman* of the Porte. Immediately the *Grand Vizir*, the *Re'îs Efendi*, the Chief Usher, and several other dignitaries entered, wearing ceremonial turbans. The *Grand Vizir* seated himself with great dignity on his sofa and Vergennes, with equal dignity, took his place on a taboret reserved for him.[13]

"The Emperor of France, my august master," Vergennes, with solemn expression, began, "...has ordered me most expressly to testify to you His Imperial Majesty's constant desire to maintain and render even more close, if it is possible, the friendship which exists between the two Empires..." Vergennes then flattered the *Grand Vizir* with statements as to his merit and virtues, and expressed his "most just and most entire confidence" in the *Grand Vizir's* intention to procure for France all the advantages that the various commercial agreements between France and the Ottoman Empire assured her. He finished his statement with the respectful plea that His Highness deign to accord him his kindness and his friendship.[14]

The *Grand Vizir's* reply, Vergennes thought, was uttered with grace and facility, but the *drogman,* apparently confused, translated it into Italian, rather than French. Vergennes strained to get the meaning, but he was unable to understand the greater part of it. He did note with considerable satisfaction, however, that the gist of the statement was that the friendship between the two "Empires" was of reciprocal utility.[15]

With the formalities over, servants entered and Vergennes rose to permit the precious fur-lined robe to be placed on his shoulders. Then he once again took his place on the taboret. Coffee, sherbet, and perfumed water were again offered. In due course Vergennes took his leave, but not before noting that the ceremonial turbans worn by the *Grand Vazir* and the Chief Usher were an honor ordinarily accorded only to ambassadors.

When Vergennes reported the details of the audience to his superiors, he assured them that the occasion left nothing to be desired, and that, in fact, the honors shown him went beyond anything he had anticipated.[16] It augured well, he believed, for his audience with the Sultan.

The Sultan, Osman III, did not leave much of an impression on history. Aged fifty-three when he mounted the throne, he had spent most of his life a virtual prisoner in the palace of his brother, Sultan Mahmud I, occupying himself with the reading of the Koran, the Laws, and the Commentaries.[17] Monsieur Peyrotte, who handled the correspondence of the French embassy at Constantinople in the interim between Des Alleurs' death and Vergennes' arrival, feared that Osman was a religious fanatic, and consequently unsympathetic to the interests of Christian foreigners in the Empire.[18] Osman proved to have rigid religious views, but the consequences were a boon, rather than a hardship, to the Christians. His predecessor had insisted on receiving annual gifts from foreigners, and had actually remade the calendar in order to reduce the intervals between gifts. Osman, however, refused to accept any gifts, and ordered destroyed all the palace furniture, pictures, porcelains, statues, indeed everything which had not been made by Moslem hands. The Sultan, he claimed, should give and not receive.[19]

In the early days of his reign, he gave every indication that he was going to reform the dilapidated Turkish government. He replaced all the eunuchs with new, presumably more loyal, ones; he abolished all useless jobs and dismissed incompetents. He called in a new *Grand Vizir,* and had him assure the French, who were somewhat anxious amidst the uncertainties of a governmental housecleaning, that French commercial and political interests were safe "under the wing of the Emperor."[20] But the Sultan's enthusiasm soon cooled, *ennui* set in, and he began to change his *Vizirs* one after another.[21] He accomplished nothing of note for the rest of his reign, save to issue the first order for veiling women's faces.

More than two hundred fifty people took part in the formal procession of the Minister Plenipotentiary of France to the Seraglio of the Sultan. In order to assure enough time for assembling such a multitude, Vergennes left the embassy palace at three in the morning, descended the hill to the Golden Horn and crossed over to the kiosk where the Chief Usher of the Porte awaited him. There he mounted a horse brilliantly caparisoned in Turkish harness, and took his place in the procession, surrounded by six Turkish attendants wearing his livery. Then, caterpillar-like, the parade began crawling up the hill to the site of the acropolis of Old Byzantium where, since the fifteenth century, the Sultans of the Ottoman Empire, received ministers of foreign powers in the Topkapi Palace, or Seraglio.

At the gateway whose name diplomats also used to mean the seat of the Ottoman government, *Babi Humayun* or "Sublime Porte," the cavalcade of four hundred horses halted to permit the *Grand Vizir* to pass and precede them into the first court. Then the procession filed into the first court and, after a halt to permit the Chief Usher to dismount, they entered the second court, which, surrounded by arcades, served as the place of assembly for all public affairs. Vergennes dismounted and waited to be conducted into the *Kubbealti,* to the Divan of the *Grand Vizir*.

The Chief Usher and the Grand Master of Ceremonies soon appeared and, with great solemnity, led him into the *Kubbealti*. Stiffly lined up before him on a sofa, and decked-out in ceremonial array, were two military judges, the Chancellor, the Superintendent of Finances, and two officers of the Treasury. The French Minister stood respectfully until the *Grand Vizir* was seated on the sofa; then he sat down on a taboret to which he had been directed. The *Grand Vizir* saluted him, and the preliminary audience began.[22]

These preliminary formalities, which Vergennes called the *audience de justice,* bored the Frenchman. And so did the ceremonies which followed. One special one, the paying of the Janissaries in the palace parade grounds, was carried out with great pomp and flourish.[23] The ceremony was traditional at receptions for foreign diplomats, and it was based on the legend that the Sultan — the "World Creator" — helped keep the "world on its axis" by paying his troops.[24] The more practical intention behind the practice, however, was that of impressing foreigners with the Sultan's riches.

After the parade of the Janissaries, the Turks honored Vergennes with an elaborate ceremonial dinner, which probably consisted of no less than fifty dishes, served one after the other, by a brawny head servant who stood behind the minister. His arms bared to the elbow, he tore the fowl into pieces for the honored guest. All the time, the servant kept up an incessant commentary about the excellence of the repast.[25] Vergennes was not impressed; the Sultan's dinner offered "nothing to merit attention."[26]

The dinner completed, Vergennes prepared for the audience at the Divan of the Sultan. An infidel, and therefore unclean, Vergennes first retired to cleanse himself by washing. Next, the head attendant and steward placed the ceremonial robe on his shoulders. Only twelve members of his company, including two *drogmen* and his secretary, Monsieur de Lancey, who still carried the diplomatic credentials were allowed to accompany him into the third court. Quickly the attendants cloaked this select group in elegant caftans. Now they were ready to appear before the Sultan. They were escorted past the eunuch guards, through the Gate of Felicity, and into the vestibule outside of the Divan of the Sultan. Two head doorkeepers, both white eunuchs, stepped forward, grasped Vergennes by the arms and half-carried him into the Divan. He was then led, taking care not to show his back to the Sultan, to a given spot before the Sultan.[27] At a signal, he delivered his formal discourse greeting.[28]

While Vergennes paid his respects, the Sultan listened attentively (a "singular circumstance," Vergennes observed), and stared at the Frenchman with a "benevolent and kind gaze." Upon finishing the reading of the credentials, Vergennes had it passed from *Kapici Basi* to a *Nisanci Basi,* then to the *Grand Vizir,* who demonstrated his respect by carrying it first to his lips and then to his forehead, before placing it on the throne beside the Sultan. As the translator interpreted Louis XV's letter, the Sultan flung aside all the customs of his predecessors and responded to the compliments himself. Ordinarily, he answered only through the medium of the *Grand Vizir,* but this time, addressing himself sometimes to the *Grand Vizir* and sometimes to Vergennes, he assured the French minister that he knew the value of French friendship, and wanted to maintain the good harmony and intelligence that existed between the two Empires. To demonstrate to Vergennes that he was highly satisfied with the audience, the Sultan graciously permitted his principal officers to kiss the hem of the imperial vest.[29] Worn out by the strains of the day's ceremonies, Vergennes patiently watched the kissing ceremony. Later he sat an additional hour, astride his horse, watching a parade of the militia and officers of the Seraglio.

A little before noon, the wearisome ceremonies over, the procession re-formed and descended the hill towards the Golden Horn, under the eye, Vergennes later learned, of the Sultan himself, who watched them from behind the latticework of a kiosk. Vergennes proudly reported that the Sultan was "content with the spectacle."[30]

The effect of this astonishing audience, calculated by each sovereign to impress the other with the glories of his "Empire," cannot be measured. Certainly, Louis XV's prestige did not suffer at Constantinople on June 3, 1755. Vergennes, with the skill of a professional, had organized the resources of his embassy, of the French community at Constantinople, and even of the dead Des Alleurs, to stage an impressive show. He played his role with polish and self-discipline, despite the fact that he was overcome by fatigue long before the audience terminated. He suffered with dignity the self-effacement and humiliation required to sit on a low taboret and call his own King an Emperor in order to raise his position in the eyes of the Turks. Patiently, he played out the ritual of diplomacy. His reward for the fatigue he endured was the knowledge (and it is significant that he took the trouble to find out) that the Sultan had been "content with the spectacle." Nevertheless, he honestly confessed that he found the whole thing "infinitely painful and fatiguing."[31] But his private likes and dislikes were rapidly becoming a buried stream which rarely emerged into the public world where he lived.

One of the first persons to greet Vergennes, when he disembarked at Constantinople, was the groom of the Comtesse des Alleurs, who welcomed the new minister in the name of his mistress.[32] Vergennes found the Comtesse in a state of total distress. As if the sorrow caused by her sudden loss were not enough, the dead man's impatient creditors were knocking at her door. Had the new French minister come prepared to pay them?

The question startled Vergennes. He was so moved by the sorry plight of the widow that he immediately offered her the hospitality of the embassy palace, and promised to support her and her children and twenty servants until she returned to France. But the creditors of her dead husband? Vergennes had to tell her that he had neither authorization nor funds to pay the debts.[33] Yet the young minister could not ignore the question. Aside from the fact that he wanted personally to give what aid he could to the unhappy woman, his own position as successor to the dead man, and even the honor of France, were deeply involved. Public opinion at Constantinople held that the King of France ought to give a demonstration of his liberality.[34]

Moreover, Louis XV could not afford to alienate the Comtesse. If she really knew the secrets of the embassy, and Vergennes was convinced that she knew more than she ought to have known,[35] she could become a dangerous enemy of French secret diplomacy if provoked. Only aid from the King, Vergennes warned, would keep her content, and assure France of her discretion until she had time to forget what she knew.[36]

Meanwhile, the creditors closed in. The Comtesse had assumed responsibility for her husband's debts, as well as those for which she was personally pledged, but she had done so on the assumption that the King of France would be charitable. She was sorely disappointed by Vergennes' inability to pay. The creditors showed no sympathy whatsoever, demanding settlement to the full extent of the law. They claimed the Comte's entire assets and, when these proved insufficient, the Comtesse sold her silver.[37] She could not satisfy the voracious appetites. She auctioned her furniture and some of her Dresden porcelain. Still the receipts from these belongings were not enough.[38]

While he was in no position to save her from the insatiable creditors, Vergennes was upset by the financial ruin of the Comtesse des Alleurs. In a letter to Rouillé he became her advocate: "I cannot finish this letter, Monseigneur, without representing to you the sad condition of Madame la Comtesse des Alleurs; how much she counts on your kindness, and on the generosity of His Majesty . . . ." With the letter, he included an inventory of Des Alleurs' debts.[39]

"Although we expected a great deal of confusion in the affairs of the deceased Monsieur le Comte des Alleurs," Rouillé answered, "I never realized . . .they had reached such a point." Rouillé observed that if the Comte had paid more attention to his affairs, he would not have ended in such ruin. Yet, as he recognized, the time for reproaches was past.[40] The need now was for remedies. Vergennes' inventory indicated that the debts were of different sorts. Some of them merited consideration; others, Rouillé was certain, could very well be "deferred." Legally, Rouillé noted, Louis XV had no responsibility whatsoever for these debts, since Des Alleurs had already received from the King payment for his services. There was a danger that a precedent might be established which would lead other ambassadors to expect the King to pay their debts.

Nevertheless, it was essential to maintain the good credit of the embassy at Constantinople, to prevent the enemies of France from profiting from any misunderstanding between the Turks and the French. Rouillé, therefore, told Vergennes that he had ordered the Bureau of Finances to remit, without delay, whatever money was still due Des Alleurs for salary or allowance. This money, added to the 24,224 *piastres* made from the sale of the effects of the Comtesse des Alleurs, should be used towards payment of the debts. The first persons to be paid, Rouillé ordered, should be the Turkish creditors, to avoid ill will.[41] If the 24,000 *piastres* plus what the Bureau of Finances furnished were not enough, Vergennes was authorized to borrow from French sources in Constantinople enough to pay the rest. These French lenders, in turn, were to be reimbursed by letters of exchange drawn on Marseille.[42] Any other creditors of Des Alleurs Rouillé refused to recognize, although he did give Vergennes permission to give partial payment in cases where the debts merited recognition. On absolutely no account, however, was Vergennes to pay interest on these latter debts. "The creditors of M. des Alleurs," Rouillé believed, "ought to consider it a great favor that the King consents to repay the capital."[43] Rouillé concluded his letter with an assurance that the Comtesse would be taken care of when she reached France. Rouillé promised, "I will assiduously do everything possible to console her."[44]

With the King's official authorization and a source of funds now available,

Vergennes began to make order out of the chaotic financial affairs of his predecessor. The settlement with the creditors proved to be extremely difficult. Many of them were obviously usurers hoping to profit from Louis XV, and not all of these were Turks. Several members of the French community of Constantinople had loaned the Comte des Alleurs money, at exorbitant rates of interest, and were now counting on their King to stand behind the follies of his ambassador. Yet, at the same time, many of the claims were legitimate and arose out of loans made to Des Alleurs for the purpose of maintaining the embassy. Vergennes' task was that of deciding on the legitimacy of each individual claim. The job was a tedious one, involving investigations, negotiations, offers and counter offers. After a year of negotiation, Vergennes settled the accounts at a cost to his King of 80,000 *ećus.* When he considered that the total debts of his predecessor originally were over 140,000 *ećus,* he felt that the final settlement was a reasonably good one.[45]

Nothing Vergennes could do would have lightened the Comtesse's sorrow over the death of her husband. He was in no position to save her from the humiliation of selling her household furnishings at a public auction. He had sympathetically offered her and her household the hospitality of the embassy palace. For a bachelor, with no experience whatsoever in the trials of domestic life, the experience of having a distressed woman, her children (one of whom was only a toddler), and her twenty servants around was taxing and helps explain why, a day after she left, Vergennes, as usual after a trying experience, took to his bed with a fever.[46] He had done his best to help her. In spite of all his efforts, the Comtesse harbored a deep resentment against him, and she no sooner arrived in France than she began to express her rancor.

She was, Vergennes knew, an "impetuous" woman. But he was surprised and sharply stung when he heard that, on her return to Paris, she accused him of being a miserly man who led a niggardly and undignified life at Constantinople.[47] The Comtesse's judgment, Vergennes retorted angrily, reflected more the way of life she had been accustomed to lead at Constantinople than it did his own. "I do not pretend to glorify myself by the establishment I keep here," he wrote Rouillé, taking a back-handed slap at Des Alleurs. "It is superior to that of any other ambassador . . . .Never has the Embassy Palace been better, perhaps never so well decorated as it is now. My household is correct and numerous: I have fifty people in my service. As for my table, it is exquisitely prepared every day to serve fourteen people, and any respectable person is welcome at it."[48]

In response, Rouillé strove to calm his young minister: "I owe Mme. la Comtesse des Alleurs the justice to assure you, Monsieur, that every time she spoke to me about you, she did so in the most fitting terms, in praise of your behaviour . . . .I do not know if she has spoken differently to others; but, whatever the case, you ought not to worry about the effect any such talk will have." Rouillé closed his dispatch with assurances that he was quite satisfied with Vergennes' work.[49]

Rouillé's dispatch gave Vergennes confidence that he was doing the right things to maintain the dignity of his new post; but he had an additional anxiety. The twin spectacles of the utter confusion of Des Alleurs' finances and the pitiful condition to which his widow had been reduced, aroused in Vergennes something more than sympathy. Vergennes came from a family of means, but not of great wealth; furthermore, his own wealth was limited, for he was a younger son. Nevertheless, the costs of maintaining an embassy were enormous, and unforeseen obligations constantly threatened to exhaust the funds furnished by the King. Vergennes wrote to Rouillé in July, 1755, complaining that "the hospitality that I have given, since the third day of my arrival, to Madame l' Ambassatrice Comtesse des Alleurs and her retinue of no less than twenty people, had considerably added to my expenses, especially in a time of famine which has pushed the cost of food way beyond the usual price."[50] A series of such unexpected drains in his funds would lead Vergennes inevitably to the expedient of borrowing. The obvious question occurred to him: would the future also force him into financial ruin? Would he, too, become entangled in the webs spun by unscrupulous money lenders?

The contemplation of such an eventuality frightened him. "The frightful wreck of the affairs of M. le Comte des Alleurs," Vergennes wrote to his superior, "the almost physical experience of it which I have felt trying to deal with them, the fact that, for the most part, his debts arose out of the enormous interest he had to pay in order to procure the means of subsistence during the early part of his stay here, all this leads me to fear the same fate, if I have to resort to the assistance and credit of the French community here, or to the people of this city."[51]

Vergennes reminded Rouillé how scrupulous he had been about the costs of the preparations for the journey to the Porte. His purchases for gifts for the Sultan and his officials cost 10,000 *livres* less than Des Alleurs had spent for the same purpose. Vergennes's fixed salary as minister was set at 30,000 *livres* annually, but the additional gratifications brought the annual total to 95,000 *livres*.[52] In addition, he was given nearly 35,000 *livres* as allowance to maintain the embassy, plus 60,000 *livres* for presents and other costs of establishing himself at his new post.[53] Although both Rouillé and Vergennes agreed at the time that the money was enough, the steps taken to assure Vergennes of these funds proved to be inadequate. This money was to come from profits made from selling brevets to Turkish subjects. These brevets or *barats*, as they were called, gave the holder the legal right to place himself under the jurisdiction of French law, and outside the reach of Turkish law, and, for that reason, were valuable. But Vergennes discovered that the demand for these privileges was not as great as anticipated. In fact, he soon learned that the income from such sales would not go above 8 or 9,000 Turkish *piastres* (roughly 3,000 *livres*).[54] At the same time, the costs of the embassy were much higher than expected. His large staff, the hospitality shown to the Comtesse des Alleurs, the inflation caused by the famine, all drained his resources. "God be my witness, Monseigneur, that these details are not given with a view to asking you for favors which I do not presume to merit. Even if my situation were much worse than it is, I would be happy with it, since I owe it to your generosity and the opinion you hold of me. I did not come here with the hope of getting rich; I only want to avoid contracting debts, and to be able to dispense with the ruinous services of the people here." Vergennes then requested that instead of annual payments, his salary should be paid quarterly and his allowance biannually in order to make it possible for him to cover current expenses without resorting to loans.[55] The request was eventually granted.[56]

In addition, Vergennes pointed out that the resources of the Constantinople embassy were not nearly so great as everyone in France believed.[57] The income generated by the embassy chamber of commerce which received contributions from the French business interests in Constantinople was almost entirely absorbed by operating expenses, and what was left over was barely enough to pay the secretaries who handled the paper work. "I am ashamed," Vergennes confessed, as he neared the end of the dispatch, "to take so long discussing all of this minutia with you." No doubt he did feel a bit ashamed, but the alarm produced by the example of Des Alleurs overcame the shame.[58] He was clearly pleading for more funds.

Both Rouillé and Vergennes were happy to close the Des Alleurs affair. The creditors at Constantinople presented to the French minister a time-consuming and irritating series of problems demanding a considerable measure of firmness, tact, and patience. At the same time, Vergennes' anxieties, those of a relatively inexperienced young man for the first time in charge of managing a large embassy establishment, must have caused Rouillé several headaches. Alarmed by the prospect of ending his career burdened with debts, the overanxious diplomat abandoned his characteristic reserve and frantically pressed his superior for help. Stung by rumors that the experienced Comtesse des Alleurs did not think much of the dignity of his household, Vergennes openly begged for reassurance. Patiently and graciously, Rouillé read the pleas and tried to calm his representative, and assured him that the King was quite confident of his minister's ability to manage affairs at Constantinople.

The profession of diplomat during the Ancien Régime was not an easy road to wealth. It often demanded great economic sacrifices from an individual and sometimes led to bankruptcy. Yet the financial problems of individual diplomats only reflected in microcosm the greater problem of the costs of Ancien-Régime diplomacy; costs so enormous that the state itself ran the risk of bankruptcy to play the role of great power.

The first months of Vergennes' assignment in Constantinople reveal how difficult it was for a diplomat to divide his activities into his "serious" functions as a negotiator, his "trivial" functions as master of pomp and ceremony, and advocate of his master's esteem. Neither the ethos of the social class from which the diplomat came nor the structure of international politics allowed for such a division. Given the concept of hierarchy that pervaded the system, the concern for titles and the disputes over protocol and honor were as important to the system as the alliances and wars. A great deal of Vergennes' workday was taken up with problems of etiquette, with ceremony, with rank and prestige. He took these problems seriously because everyone in the system did. The Ancien-Régime diplomat had to be ever alert that his rank was recognized and that his prestige, and that of his master, were forever intact.

CHAPTER 6

1755—Turkish Declaration to Russia

In the spring of 1755, an alert observer of European politics could not have failed to notice an unusual increase in the tempo of comings-and-goings of diplomats, soldiers, and various unclassified agents of the great powers. As Vergennes landed at Constantinople, a new British ambassador appeared at St. Petersburg, and General Edward Braddock, the new Commander-in-Chief of the British forces in North America, assumed his duties in the British colony of Virginia. While their destinations were widely separated, the movements of these men were conditioned by the same fact: England and France were about to go to war.

In anticipation of trouble with England in America, France had sent an additional naval squadron and troop reinforcements to Canada. On the American continent, French and British soldiers along the Ohio Valley and the Great Lakes built forts and dug in. Once they consolidated their positions, only force could dislodge them, and both sides knew it. The two hostile powers, therefore, turned their attention to creating the military means necessary to assure success. An atmosphere of suspicion and suspense settled over Franco-British relations. The parliamentary elections of 1754, which brought a bellicose majority to the House of Commons, gave no hope of reducing the tensions.[1]

Far from either London or Virginia, but not unaffected by what happened in those far away places, Vergennes busily organized his staff, and restored the routine broken by Des Alleurs' death. Fortunately he had, to assist him, an exceptionally talented group of men. The Chancellor of the Embassy, Monsieur Peyrotte, was an intelligent, hardworking person who, despite a serious illness, had carried more than his share of the responsibilities of the embassy during the interim between Des Alleurs' death and Vergennes' arrival. Vergennes found him somewhat lax with the security of the secret diplomacy,[2] but he had well represented France at the coronation of Osman III, and his frequent and factual, though typically obsequious, letters to

Versailles revealed an intimate knowledge of the people with whom he had to deal.[3]

Alongside the Chancellor were the embassy interpreters, or *drogmen,* Fonton and, later, Duval. Because of the language and ceremonial difficulties of the Constantinople post, the *drogmen* were key men in every embassy. An eighteenth-century English ambassador was so impressed with their expertise and influence that he declared them to be "the absolute masters of business."[4] Neither Fonton nor Duval ever became the absolute masters of business, but as expert orientalists and translators, they provided services to Vergennes which were immeasurable.[5]

The *chargé d'affaires* of the French embassy when Vergennes arrived was Charles Peyssonel. Originally a lawyer, he had begun his diplomatic career at the age of thirty-five, as secretary to Villeneuve, the earlier French ambassador at Constantinople. For the rest of his life, he devoted his time to representing France, traveling in the Ottoman Empire, and collecting antiques and *objets d'art.* In 1747, he had been appointed French Consul at Smyrna. After Vergennes' arrival, he returned to the consulate at Smyrna and remained there until his death two years later.

His son followed in his footsteps. After completing his studies in France, the younger Peyssonel had joined his father at Smyrna, and there, under paternal tutelage, took up the study of numismatics and archeology. Later he traveled through the Ottoman Empire collecting antique medallions and inscriptions. In 1753, he became the French consul in the Crimea and four years later, the French consul on the Isle of Candia. His reports on the commerce of the Black Sea, and the politics and peoples of the Ottoman Empire, contained some of the most reliable information the French government had about these exotic peoples.[6] In 1763, he took over his father's old position as consul general at Smyrna and there he remained for the next twenty years, except for occasional official missions elsewhere.

To complete his staff, Vergennes also brought with him Monsieur Lancey, his First Secretary of the embassy. Almost immediately, however, Lancey found the climate at Constantinople unsuitable to his health, and soon begged and received a transfer to Poland, where he became secretary to the Comte de Broglie.[7] In 1756, Antoine Vivier replaced Lancey. He was the brother of the lady Vergennes would marry, and he remained with Vergennes twenty-five years; eventually he became a diplomat himself.[8]

In 1762, the French artist, Antoine de Favray, joined Vergennes' staff. A painter specializing in pictures depicting the customs of the Maltese, he traveled to Constantinople to paint there the "customs of the country."[9] A member of the French Academy, a commander in the Order of Malta, Favray produced paintings which today are scattered from Malta to Florence, southern France, and Paris.[10] It was Favray who painted the portraits of Vergennes and his wife dressed in Turkish costume which hang, today, in the country home of Monsieur Xavier d'Hauthuille at Grenay, France. Although Vergennes readily admitted that he was not a *connoisseur* of art, he was quite proud of the small collection of original Favray paintings which eventually adorned his embassy office.[11]

Unfortunately, the size of Vergennes' staff did not always serve to reduce his burdens. The unhealthy climate at Constantinople and the frequent epidemics of sickness sometimes turned the French embassy at Pera into a veritable hospital, and the harassed diplomat found himself at the head of a troupe of invalids. In May of 1767, for example, the sickness at the embassy became so widespread that nearly everyone was incapacitated. "I have twenty-five persons laid up," he wrote to his friend, the younger Baron de Tott. "The worst of all is that all my secretaries are sick." But they muddled through by helping "each other the best we can."[12]

Aside from his own personal staff, Vergennes had various contacts at Constantinople and in the Ottoman Empire, who provided him with useful information or competent assistance. Within a short while after his arrival at the Porte, he had gained the respect of the French business community there. His relations with these members of the French "nation" not only served to advance the cause of French trade, but individuals within the community helped him gather intelligence, and even served as his unofficial agents.[13] Within a month after his arrival, he also opened correspondence with the Princes of Moldavia and Wallachia. The agents of these two princes had the reputation of being among the best informed about secrets of state at Porte,[14] and Vergennes did not leave a stone unturned to gain their confidence.[15]

Among others loosely attached to his embassy were the father and son team, the two army officers, the Baron de Tott and his young son. A Hungarian by birth and a veteran of several missions to the Ottoman Empire, the older Tott it was who had gotten Vergennes' ship safely past the Turkish navy's reception, outside the straits of the Dardanelles. He was a Brigadier in the French army, about fifty years old; he spoke Turkish, Polish, Hungarian, and French, and was considered by his superiors to be intelligent and capable.[16]

The son accompanied Vergennes to Constantinople to learn the language and customs of the Turks, and to continue in the footsteps of his father.[17] Soon he, too, was to become one of France's most valuable agents in the Ottoman Empire. In 1767, he was to be named French consul in the Crimea.[18] As his father before him, he became a reliable intelligence agent, and an "adviser" to the Turkish army, helping them modernize their artillery. During the Russo-Turkish war (1769-1774) his services were used in training the Turkish army. When the Turks met with engineering difficulties, trying to build a canal uniting the Zacary River with the city of Isnak, Vergennes engaged the younger Tott to assist them.[19] Vergennes did not always approve of the younger Tott's ideas, but there is, nevertheless, no question of his competence.[20] Military "advisers" today have their prototypes in the Tott pair working under Vergennes. Like their counterparts of today, the Totts posed a special problem for the diplomat: to whom were they responsible?

Before Vergennes left for Constantinople, Versailles had learned that the Hungarians were extremely discontented with the rule of the Austrian Empress, Maria Theresa. Louis XV saw in the discontent the possibility of a rebellion. At this time, Austria was still an enemy of France, and, in case of war, the prospect of a rebellion in the Hapsburg Empire was of great interest to France.[21]

Among the points of the instructions given to the elder Tott, there was one concerning the Hungarian situation. Since the last rebellion in Hungary, Tott read, Maria Theresa had set about to despoil the country. Furthermore, she had not kept her promises to the Hungarians; promises made to them in the last war, when she needed their help so desperately. The Hungarian people were alive with discontent from the loss of their liberties and the broken promises.

The Porte had always provided refuge for those rebels who had played a role in Hungarian uprisings, and at Rodosto, near Constantinople, there was a colony of Hungarians, former rebel leaders, who lived under the protection of the Sultan. Versailles suspected that they kept up a frequent correspondence with Hungary and Transylvania. One of the most famous leaders, the Count Czaki, was still alive at Rodosto and had the confidence of the Hungarian malcontents.

After his arrival in Constantinople, Tott was to go to Rodosto to see his compatriots. He was to take great care to avoid giving any indication that he was acting in an official capacity, but since Count Czaki and his friends would no doubt discuss Hungarian politics, Tott was to listen carefully and ask questions. Which areas of Hungary and Transylvania were the most disaffected? Who were the leaders of the malcontents? How did they communicate with each other.? What did they expect from the Porte? Did all the irregular Hungarian troops who fought in Germany and Flanders in the last war return home satisfied and submissive? Again and again, Tott's instructions stressed that he be circumspect in his questioning. The name of Louis XV was never to be mentioned, except to say that His Majesty was generally interested in the fate of Hungary. Above all, Tott, was not to give the impression that Louis XV was prepared to help them.[22]

Some instinct in agents, such as Tott, compels them to try to make policy rather than simply to execute it. Tott left Constantinople for Rodosto about the middle of July, 1755,[23] and, before the month was out, Louis XV had received a letter from Count Czaki, who enthusiastically offered his assistance, and requested that Tott remain with him as his personal adjutant.[24] Rouillé knew how useful the Hungarians could be in a Franco-Austrian war. Furthermore, he knew from other reliable sources the extent of discontent in Hungary. The interrogation of Hungarian army officers, in a Hungarian regiment of the French army, indicated that many Hungarians were only waiting for a favorable opportunity to "throw off the yoke" of Maria Theresa,[25] who had done nothing to keep her promise that she would restore Hungary to its ancient "privileges and liberties." The Protestants were mistreated, and import duties of thirty per cent on Hungarian goods had destroyed commerce.

Yet Czaki's letter and Tott's report from Rodosto alarmed Rouillé. Tott had aroused unwarranted expectations, and he appeared ready to set off a rebellion. He had stayed at Rodosto forty days, he told Rouillé, and he had found Count Czaki eager to be 'useful.' Czaki reassured him that Hungary was seething with rebellion, although the chief admitted that he had not kept up a correspondence with all his friends in Hungary. If France wished, however, he would renew the correspondence. As Czaki contemplated a rebellion, his enthusiasm got the better of him. He swore not to compromise France; he promised that the Hungarians would act on their own initiative. Yet Czaki wanted to know how much the rebels could count on France. Give Vergennes the order to close his eyes and not prevent any undercover activities, he begged Rouillé, and, when the next break came, the rebels would be ready to march. Czaki was sure the Turks would march with them. Tott should also march with them, he exclaimed. He would not even have to quit the French army: "All that can be arranged." To Czaki, it seemed so easy to set off rebellion in Hungary, and Tott was obviously converted by Czaki's enthusiasm. The notion of marching in a crusade as a latter-day centurion appealed to him. He waited "with impatience" for further orders from Versailles.[26]

But the diplomats disagreed with the rebel chief and the French officer and soldier. The men at Rodosto, Vergennes judged, were old and decrepit, and had lost contact with Hungary to the extent that their group no longer even gained recruits.[27] Rouillé, when he acknowledged receipt of Tott's report praised Czaki's "sentiment of liberty," but he had grave doubts about the validity of some of Czaki's information. "Furthermore," he observed to Tott, "Monsieur le Comte de Czaki's zeal for his country went too far in the conversation he had with you." Louis XV did not intend to initiate or sustain trouble in Hungary. Tott was reminded that he was ordered only to gather intelligence. Then, *in case* Maria Theresa joined in a war on the side of France's enemies, Louis XV could then act on the intelligence. But, Rouillé insisted, the King never thought of instigating a rebellion in time of peace. In fact, Rouillé believed that, if the rebels started a rebellion, Austria would easily destroy them. Tott was told to continue to correspond with Czaki, but he was ordered not to become involved in correspondence with any other rebels. Rouillé ended his response to his agent with the intelligent command that Tott was to continue to gather information, but was to make no promises, and to precipitate nothing. And he was to be absolutely under the orders of Vergennes. To insure that Vergennes was fully cognizant of Tott's orders, Tott was told to communicate all his correspondence with Versailles to the French minister.[28] To insure Tott's subordination to Vergennes, Rouillé henceforth sent his dispatches in a cipher to which only Vergennes had the key.

As Austria began to reveal to the French her friendly intentions that were finally to develop into the Diplomatic Revolution and an alliance with Louis XV, Rouillé's fears that the Hungarian rebels might revolt, and that Tott might become involved, increased. He kept an even closer watch on his agent and continually reminded Vergennes to keep Tott within the limits of his mission. Louis XV did not want Maria Theresa to have any cause to complain of her new friend.[29]

While Vergennes organized his staff and studied his responsibilities at Constantinople, the new British ambassador to St. Petersburg made his entry at the Russian Court. Sir Charles Hanbury Williams was not a stranger to French diplomats. Out of his fertile mind had come the ideas which Newcastle transformed into the policy to organize the German Empire with subsidy treaties and an election of the King of the Romans. At Coblenz, at Hanover, and at Mannheim, Vergennes unwittingly had engaged in a long-distance diplomatic chess game with Williams, who flitted back and forth between Dresden, Warsaw, and Vienna diligently trying to check France's every move. Although the map of Europe shows St. Petersburg to be a long way from Constantinople, and the slowness of eighteenth-century communications made the two capitals even farther apart, one of the routine chores of a French minister at the Turkish capital was to be alert to any developments at the Russian capital. What Williams did at St. Petersburg was of special interest to Vergennes at Constantinople.[30]

The impending Anglo-French War compelled Englishmen to look more than ever to the upkeep of their diplomatic fences on the Continent. They knew that the next war with France, even if fought under the most favorable conditions, would strain every fiber of the Empire. But if Britain lost her continental allies, a victory in the conflict would be in doubt. Moreover, they had to take into consideration the ugly fact that Prussia would probably come to the aid of France in the event of war, thereby placing George II's Hanoverian possessions in a Franco-Prussian cross-fire.[31] When England approached Austria for a pledge of assistance in accordance with the Anglo-Austrian treaty, she received only vague assurance, coupled with the advice that England should do something to bring Russia into her continental system.

With war clouds gathering on the horizon, Vienna's suggestion received more than a polite hearing, especially since it was clear to everyone by now that Newcastle's policy of collecting allies with the election of a King of the Romans had failed. In addition, the United Provinces, equally fearful of a French-Prussian combined attack, warned Britain that they would not support her in a war unless she did ally with Austria and Russia to strengthen her continental defenses.[32] The principal object to Williams' mission to St. Petersburg, therefore, was to conclude a subsidy treaty with the Czarina Elizabeth.[33]

But the Czarina shrewdly preferred to gamble on delay. She was not averse to a treaty with England, but she was fully aware that the closer the British came to a war with France, the more desperately they would need Russian assistance, and the more willing they would be to pay a good price for it. She could, therefore, afford to bide her time while the stakes went up. At the last minute, she could cash in. She ran the risk, of course, of angering the British and getting nothing, but if she played her hand wisely, the odds were in her favor.

Vergennes would have envied Williams' reception at St. Petersburg. The Englishman arrived bearing the title of Ambassador, and since ambassadors were rare at the Russian court, he readily commanded a measure of respect that Vergennes had been able to extract at Constantinople only after stiff bargaining.[34] In addition, a rumor had preceded Williams to the effect that he had "in his train a large wagon loaded with nothing but *ducats*."[35] The rumor helped to arouse a warm interest in him, and inspired, among the corrupt and venal members of the Russian court, a desire to please the man, a desire which Williams' reputation as a person liberal with money did not diminish.

The sudden interest in the new British ambassador to St. Petersburg was shared by Rouillé at Versailles, but for very different reasons. To him Williams' arrival warned that England was about to make a major diplomatic move. The result was immediate alarm at Versailles. French statesmen considered Williams one of the "principal instruments of all of England's intrigues" in Eastern Europe.[36]

Louis XV's diplomats had not yet been able to determine precisely what Williams was up to at St. Petersburg.[37] One rumor held that he was there to negotiate a treaty for the hiring of 60,000 Russian troops to be put at the disposal of England. But where, Rouillé desired to know, were the troops going to be used? Against France? To force an election of a King of the

Romans? To attack Poland? Or to help Austria reconquer Silesia, which Prussia had taken away from Maria Theresa in the last war? Any one of these motives, even all of them at once, could conceivably lie behind Williams' assignment, and any one of them frightened Rouillé. "Whatever the object of Sir Charles Williams' mission," he wrote to Vergennes, "it involves the tranquillity of Europe and, above all, the security of Russia's neighbors."[38]

By the time Rouillé dispatch reached Vergennes, France had already begun to organize her response to England's move. The pro-French party in Poland was urged to take measures to defend Poland against Russia; the minister of Sweden had been alerted; Frederick of Prussia's press gangs were rounding up new recruits to increase the size of his army, and Louis XV had promised to render any aid his allies needed. Vergennes was instructed to alert Osman III of the possible danger, and to persuade him to make some move that would give pause to Russia.[39]

To insure that any action Turkey made had the greatest possible effect, Rouillé wanted Vergennes to recommend to the Sultan that he confront Russia with a strongly worded declaration that the Porte would not stand by and allow Russia "to violate the territory of Poland or make an attempt on its independence."[40] Rouillé also suggested that the Sultan might more effectively communicate the point of his declaration if he simultaneously ordered his troops to make conspicuous maneuvers on the Russian and Polish frontiers. If the liaison between England, Austria, and Russia were not broken up, Rouillé feared, Sweden, Poland and Prussia might succumb to the combined pressures of the alliance. Once assured of a victory over these three powers, the Czarina and Maria Theresa would have their armies free to attack the Ottoman Empire whenever a favorable opportunity arose. Vergennes had to make the Sultan understand, Rouillé insisted, that it was to his own interest to concern himself with the fate of Sweden, Poland, and Prussia, for, as long as these powers stood, Vienna and St. Petersburg would think twice before launching an attack on the Ottoman Empire.[41]

To sugar-coat this pill of diplomatic pedagogy, Rouillé told Vergennes to give "some presents" to the Turkish ministers, or to anyone who had credit at the Porte, in order "to assure the success of the operation . . . ." "Employ as much as one million *livres* or more, if it is absolutely necessary" for such presents, Rouillé authorized Vergennes.[42]

Rouillé closed his letter with the somewhat fatuous advice to "orient yourself well; know your terrain thoroughly, in order to discover the right paths and avoid those which might lead you away from your goal . . ."[43] As to how Vergennes would recognize these "right paths" when he came upon them, Rouillé offered no help. In a later dispatch, however, he did offer a bit of artful advice, which perhaps does more to illuminate Ancien Régime morality than it helped Vergennes. In the Treaty of Pruth (1711), he informed his representative, Russia and the Ottoman Empire had agreed to observe the integrity of Polish territory. But if either power did attack Poland, the attack constituted an affront against the other. Unfortunately, this treaty had been annulled and never renewed. Yet Rouillé's information indicated that many of the Turks still believed that the treaty was in force. Perhaps even Osman III, who had spent fifty three years of his life in prison before becoming Sultan, still understood it to be so. It would be wrong, Rouillé advised, for Vergennes to tell the Turks that the treaty was still in force; but he allowed that, if the Turks mistakenly believed it was, Vergennes would be wise not to disabuse them of their error. It could serve French policy.[44]

In addition to advice, Rouillé unwittingly put obstacles in Vergennes' path, by recommending that no communications with the Porte concerning this important issue be put in writing. Such a restriction, Vergennes immediately saw, imposed impossible conditions. Because he did not speak the Sultan's language, he could communicate orally only through a *drogman*, and he did not wish to trust his delicate commissions to the linguistic talents, and perhaps faulty memory, of a *drogman*. Rouillé had, in effect, Vergennes complained, forbidden the use of memoranda.[45]

The difficulties inherent in trying to execute two foreign policies, one official and the other secret, became real to Vergennes as he tried to implement Rouillé's instructions on the Turkish declaration in a way consistent with Louis XV's wishes. When Vergennes read the secret instructions given Des Alleurs before his death, he found that the French monarch wanted much more from the Turks than a strong verbal declaration. His Majesty desired to conclude a treaty of friendship with the Turks which would contain a secret article guaranteeing the integrity of Polish territory.[46]

The complex system of alliances, suggested by Louis' secret diplomacy at the Porte, grew out of an attempt to draw together France, Prussia, Sweden, Denmark, and the Porte to protect Poland from Russian aggression, and to prevent the court of Vienna from placing Prince Charles of Lorraine, the younger brother of the Emperor Francis I, on the Polish throne when it became vacant.[47] When Des Alleurs represented France at Constantinople, he worked for a treaty, either defensive or commercial, between Prussia and the Porte; a treaty of friendship between France and the Porte, with the secret article protecting the integrity of Polish territory; and a series of conventions to knit the system closer together.[48] In his personal instructions to Vergennes, Louis ordered his representative to cease assisting Frederick in the conclusion of a treaty with the Sultan,[49] but he still insisted on the pursuit of the other parts of his secret policy.

The King's instructions were difficult to reconcile with what Rouillé had ordered. Also, Vergennes recognized immediately that the Turks would be reluctant to commit themselves, in advance, to being forced into a war over violation of Polish territory, or over a contested election.[50] Despite his personal reservations, Vergennes obediently followed his King's orders and communicated to the Porte France's desire to reopen the question of a treaty of friendship.[51]

The Turks, suspicious of France's generous offers to let them "share the glory" of protecting Poland, were cautious. They did agree that, if Russia attacked Poland, the Porte should "explain itself" to the Russian minister. But, observed Vergennes, then the declaration would be too late, and would remedy nothing. Officially, he wanted a declaration and, secretly, a treaty to prevent an attack—not a protest following one.[52] Why were the English interested in negotiating with the Russians, the *drogman* asked? Vergennes confessed he did not know, but he knew that England, with all her money, was making it possible for the Russian enemies of the Turks to build up their fortifications and armies.[53]

The length and complexity of the exchange between the *drogman* and Vergennes compelled the Frenchman to end the conversations by handing the Turk a *précis* of his principal points, even though Rouillé had expressly forbidden putting anything in writing. And, along with the *précis,* he handed the *drogmen* a "present" of 100 *sequins,* "with the assurance of another present considerably bigger if the Porte accorded to Poland a protection as extensive and efficacious as the critical situation seemed to demand."[54]

To supplement his own efforts, Vergennes also contacted the Polish representative at the Porte, and discussed with him the dangers to Poland lurking in the the recent Anglo-Russian negotiations. Truly alarmed, the Pole submitted a strongly-worded message (which Vergennes helped write) to the Porte concerning the Russian threat to peace. Vergennes was so pleased, in fact, with the Polish representative's willingness to cooperate that he recommended this *très honnête homme* to Rouillé, and suggested he be rewarded with a pension from Louis XV.[55]

Vergennes' conversation with the *drogman,* the message submitted by the Pole, and Louis XV's expressed desire to reopen negotiations on a treaty soon produced results. The *Grand Vizir* began an inquiry among the foreign ambassadors at Constantinople, or, at least, among those not attached to or allied with Russia, England, or Austria, to find out what he could learn about Russia's intentions. When he approached the Swedish ambassador, who was at his country residence, the Swede begged for time, on the grounds that he had not yet had the opportunity to decipher all the dispatches from his court. He then immediately went to Vergennes for advice as to how he should respond. Vergennes wanted him to give a report to the *Grand Vizir* which would reinforce Vergennes' own story, but the Swede was afraid to go so far without orders. Vergennes then suggested an alternative response, which would second his own efforts but not compromise the Swedish minister. This was to tell the *Grand Vizir* that the dispatches from Sweden were not of recent enough date to contain any relevant confirmation, but that, for over a year, he had heard rumors of a project for a treaty between Vienna, London, and St. Petersburg.[56]

But the *Grand Vizir* was no fool. He first verified the rumors concerning the Anglo-Russian treaty, and then made a thorough study of the status of the treaty relations between Russia and the Ottoman Empire. He not only discovered that the Treaty of Pruth was not in force, but he also learned that in the Treaty of Belgrade, Russia and the Porte had promised to settle their difficulties in an amiable fashion. His study concluded, he informed Vergennes that the Porte was interested in any threat to Poland, and would be pleased to receive any news concerning the subject. He admitted, furthermore, that a treaty between England and Russia would give umbrage to Poland, and he promised to speak to the Russian minister at Constantinople, and inform him that the Porte could not remain indifferent to any violation of Polish law or liberty. He left out, significantly, any reference to a violation of Polish territory.[57]

The *Grand Vizir's* response fell far short of Vergennes' hopes. Not only was the proposed declaration weak, but there was no pledge of a secret agreement between France and the Porte to protect Polish integrity. The *Grand Vizir* knew that the conspicuous absence in the promised warning of any reference to a violation of Polish territory was enough of a hint, to an experienced diplomat, that the Turks were not inclined to risk a war with the Russians. The truth of the matter was that the *Grand Vizir* was a man of peace,[58] and did not wish to bleed the Empire for the right to "share the glory" of protecting Poland. His peaceful inclinations were not the result of idealism, but were based on the disquieting fact that the Ottoman Empire was facing a dangerous economic and political crisis at home caused by inflation, famine, riots, and rebellion.[59] It was not the time to embark on a military adventure that might bring a general collapse of the Sultan's authority. No matter how much France needed Turkish assistance to counter-act Russian aid to England — and this need became more pressing every day — the Turks could not afford to risk military and political suicide.

As Vergennes at Constantinople painted the details of the Russian threat, at St. Petersburg Sir Charles Hanbury Williams did his best to erase them. The Turkish inclinations to remain at peace were given a hearty boost by the British diplomat. Naturally the English did not wish their prospective Russian ally to tie up its armies fighting the Turks; consequently, Williams did everything in his power to ease Russian-Turkish tensions, even going to the extreme of increasing a subsidy to the Russians, if they would abandon the building at Fort Elizabeth on the Ingul River, a fort which was causing considerable friction between them and the Turks.[60] When Williams finally succeeded in negotiating a subsidy treaty with Russia, in September of 1755,* he was more than ever determined to oppose any Russian move to excite Turkey to War. The success of Williams' efforts made it difficult for Vergennes to convince the Turks of the reality of a Russian threat.

Vergennes did not give up, however. Assiduously, he labored during 1755-1756 gathering intelligence[61] and trying to cajole, flatter, or shame the Turks into taking a more aggressive stand by a strong declaration, or a treaty with France. He let no opportunity pass to create or nurture Turkish suspicions of Russia, and as the Turkish ministers fell from power, one by one — there were five ministerial changes between the spring of 1755 and March of 1756 — he patiently began the discussion anew with each succeeding minister. With each change, he presented the official demand for a Turkish declaration with one hand and the secret offer of a treaty with the other.[62]

The numerous changes of Turkish ministers were a cause for embarrassment to him and to France. Whenever a new minister replaced another, the diplomatic community at Pera was obliged to pay its respects at an audience at the Seraglio. Because Vergennes did not have the full rank of an ambassador, he was never admitted to the first audience, attended by the ambassadors of Venice, Holland, and England, but had to await the second audience for ministers of lower rank. Diplomatic conventions made such a secondary role extremely humiliating. Furthermore, the Sultan's notions of his own honor led him to conclude (with a ready assist from France's enemies) that the failure of Louis XV to send an ambassador to Constantinople was a public affront. Osman III grew to imagine, according to Vergennes, that he ceased to be a Sultan unless there was an ambassador from France at his court. The Sultan's concern about the rank of the French representative was obviously a problem which Vergennes was duty-bound to report to Versailles; yet he recognized, at the same time, that such a report could easily be misinterpreted as a manifestation of his own personal ambitions. In a dispatch dated September 14, 1755, Vergennes explained the problem to his superiors.[63]

Was the French minister angling for a promotion? No doubt he was, and no doubt but that he felt he could perform with credit as ambassador; he said so, in effect, when he wrote that he was "not persuaded that . . . an ambassador could give more activity and vigor" to affairs than he. Furthermore, he knew that Rouillé's close relations with Chavigny guaranteed that

*The treaty provided that Russia maintain 55,000 men on the Livonian frontiers as well as a fleet in the eastern Baltic in exchange for English subsidies. The agreement was to last four years. The Treaty ratifications were not exchanged, however until February of 1756.

his talent and previous service would be given sympathetic consideration, if Versailles decided that an ambassador was needed at Constantinople. At the same time, there is no reason to believe that Vergennes invented, or even exaggerated, the "prejudices" described in his letter in order to further his personal ambitions. The history of the Ottoman Empire gives more than one example of a Sultan's extreme sensitivity about his "honor", and the situation was now a real hinderance to better relations between Osman III and Louis XV. Even so, Vergennes furnished Rouillé with the appropriate and least humiliating reason for not appointing him to the rank of ambassador, if the Minister of Foreign Affairs so decided: he confessed that he did not consider himself at the stage of aspiring to such a post, which was "only the reward of long and important services."

Vergennes surely knew that Rouillé was not likely to risk a change of his representative at Constantinople at this most critical time. The truth of the matter is that Vergennes found himself in a situation where it was virtually impossible to distinguish between his personal ambition and the interests of his King. In order to perform his duties, he had simply to give full reign to his ambition. Or, to put it another way, the unusual opportunity to advance his own career inspired him to a masterful performance of his duty.

Vergennes knew that his chances of being awarded the ambassadorial rank would be improved if he could show some successes in his campaign to guide the Turks' Russian policy. So he returned to negotiations with renewed vigor. His efforts to influence the Turkish Minister of Foreign Affairs, the *Re'îs Efendi,* deserve special mention at this point, because they serve as a striking example of practices considered quite normal in eighteenth-century diplomacy. The *Re'îs Efendi's* official position made him a key target in Vergennes' plans, but the fact that he showed some ability to survive, while other ministers fell, also explains why he was singled out for special treatment. The *Re'îs Efendi* was inclined to launch a tougher policy against Russia, while the Sultan remained "impenetrable," and the *Grand Vizir* sought peace at all costs.[64] Finally, and especially important, the *Re'îs Efendi* was vulnerable: "His debts," Vergennes confided to Rouillé, "are immense."[65]

The opportunity to establish secret contacts with the *Re'îs Efendi* came unexpectedly, when a holder of French *brevet* died. The *Re'îs Efendi* approached Vergennes through a *drogman* to ask for the brevet. "I took care," Vergennes related, "not to refuse him this sacrifice; but . . . I was persuaded that he had made this request only to encourage me to make him some other, more considerable offers."[66] Consequently, Vergennes contacted a French businessman at Constantinople, a Monsieur Gautier,[67] who knew an Armenian moneychanger, a Monsieur Rafou, attached to the *Re'îs Efendi's* service, and a line of communication to the Turkish official was soon created. After brief negotiations, a date was set for an interview between Gautier and the *Re'îs Efendi*.

Gautier opened the secret interview by telling the *Re'îs Efendi* that Vergennes wished to put his confidence in him because he considered the Turkish Foreign Minister the man "most enlightened about the true interests of the Ottoman Empire, and the only man capable of re-establishing the Empire in all its splendor and glory."[68] Vergennes was certain, Gautier told the *Re'îs Efendi,* that the Turk felt the "force and truth" of the representations Vergennes had already made to the Porte concerning the Russian menace. A Russian conquest of Poland, Gautier repeated, in order to test the *Re'îs Efendi's* reaction, would open the way to a Russian attack on the Ottoman Empire.[69]

The *Re'îs Efendi* received Vergennes' advances with "great satisfaction," and charged Gautier to assure Vergennes of his esteem and friendship, and his desire to serve the French diplomat. To demonstrate that he already understood what the nature of his services might be, he added that he had read Vergennes' opinions about the Russian danger "with pleasure" and understood their value.[70] But, the *Re'îs Efendi* said, when he had communicated Vergennes' ideas to the *Grand Vizir,* the latter was unable to understand them. Furthermore, he said, a key member of the chancery, the *Khaya*, would be no help to the French diplomat because he was a "timid and irresolute" soul, who "never took one step forward without making four backward."[71] In short, the *Re'îs Efendi* was saying, although he did not put it quite so bluntly, there was only one man in the ministry who could help Vergennes: the *Re'îs Efendi*. If Vergennes wished to confide in him and submit his ideas to him, he could assure Vergennes of success. The *Re'îs Efendi* promised he would carry all the Frenchman's representations directly to the Sultan through the chief black eunuch, thereby bypassing the *Grand Vizir*. The *Re'îs Efendi* then suggested that Vergennes prepare a memorandum outlining the Ottoman Empire's interest in Polish security, and the dangers represented by Russia, and he would see to it that it got before the Sultan.[72]

With the meaty topics of the interview disposed of, the two men then turned to the dessert: Gautier handed the *Re'îs Efendi* a "beautiful watch, set in diamonds of the value of 2,600 *écus*." It was, Vergennes proudly reported, *parfaitement bien reçue*.[73] Vergennes was a little disturbed when Gautier told him that the *Re'îs Efendi* had revealed certain "prejudices" favorable to England, but all-in-all the first interview seemed promising.

Without delay, Vergennes composed the memorandum requested by the *Re'îs Efendi*. In less detail, but "without excessive alterations, and more force," he repeated all of his previous reasons why the Ottoman Empire should take some vigorous action against the Russian threat.[74] Once more,

Gautier acted as the go-between and arranged a secret meeting with the Turkish minister. When the *Re'îs Efendi* received the memo, he informed Gautier that before the Porte did anything about the Russians, it was going to wait for the arrival of the new ambassador from Poland, who could give them up-to-date information on the situation there. But Gautier,"who was prepared for this objection," told the Turk that the present crisis was so serious there was no time to wait. If the Porte needed any further evidence of Russian plans, Gautier added, they could contact the Polish representative already in Constantinople, Monsieur Malszewski. But the *Re'îs Efendi* was more willing to be corrupted by Gautier than he was willing to appear duped by him; he laughingly answered Gautier that he knew full well that Malszewski was a "tool of France."[75] If France wanted to influence the *Grand Vizir*, the *Re'îs Efendi* went on to advise, she would get someone in Poland to write to the *Grand Vizir,* describing the "sufferings" in Poland caused by Russian enterprises.[76] Then, just before the interview closed, quite neatly and almost incidentally, Vergennes reported to Versailles, the *Re'îs Efendi* "slipped in a few words" which suggested that he wanted to use the secret interviews to open negotiations for a treaty of friendship with France.[77]

It was Vergennes, and not the *Re'îs Efendi*, who "slipped in a few words" about a Franco-Turkish treaty of friendship. To Louis, Vergennes confessed and explained why: "I don's believe I would commit an indiscretion, or compromise the secret of His Majesty. . .if I present to M. Rouillé the idea of a treaty." He pointed out that he had to have the necessary official powers from the Minister of Foreign Affairs. By suggesting to Rouillé that the Turks would be more apt to make a strong declaration against Russia after the signing of a treaty with France, he hoped to get those powers. Vergennes joined with his letter to the King a summary of his request to Rouillé and meekly added: "If I have acted against the intentions of His Majesty, I very humbly beg him to pardon me."[78]

Having completed the political part of the discussion with Gautier, the *Re'îs Efendi* turned to the pecuniary negotiations. Vergennes, wary of being deceived, had given the Turk nothing beyond the diamond watch. But surprisingly, after receiving the watch, the *Rè'îs Efendi* had affected an almost superhuman disinterest, even threatening to break off the secret talks if Gautier continued to bring him such presents. Yet, when Gautier discussed the matter with the Armenian moneychanger who was close to the *Re'îs Efendi,* he heard "another language." According to the Armenian, the Turkish minister could not possibly "pull all the strings" necessary to accomplish his aims without some "advantages."[79] The *Re'îs Efendi* was trying to make clear that he wanted cash, not expensive presents, for his services. But Vergennes refused to make an offer. He feared that any offer he made would be quadrupled by the *Re'îs Efendi* and then turned into a concrete demand. Instead, when the Turk raised the question in the interview, Gautier told him that Vergennes had the "honor of serving a prince who never failed to recompense services;" consequently, the French minister was fully authorized to give recognition to anyone who rendered such services. Still, the *Re'îs Efendi* was not satisfied. He wanted a more concrete assurance of Louis XV's appreciation. Finally, in order to satisfy the Turkish foreign minister, Gautier offered himself and his own resources as security.[80] Gautier's pledge left the Turk content, but it left the French businessman, and his wealth, painfully dependent on Vergennes' word. The fact that Gautier was willing to trust the French diplomat to that extent speaks well for the respect Vergennes had earned among the French business community at Constantinople.

When Vergennes heard Gautier's report of the secret interview, he immediately recognized that the Turk had cleverly stolen the initiative and tossed the responsibility for the next move into France's lap. His suggestion that Vergennes get someone in Poland to write a letter describing Russian oppression was an obvious means of putting off any action on the part of the Turks. Yet Vergennes saw, too, that the time could be used by Rouillé to ponder the treaty of alliance, especially if the Minister of Foreign Affairs thought a Turkish declaration against Russia depended on France's willingness to negotiate a treaty with the Ottoman Empire. Vergennes was trying to get France's official policy to mesh with its secret one. Did Rouillé want a treaty?[81] If France did wish to conclude an alliance with the Sultan, Vergennes warned Rouillé, it was essential to "seize the moment" and "profit from it," for, he observed, "principles here are independent of the interest of the state," and were relative to the ministers, who changed often. A treaty, Vergennes observed, would have the advantage that, once the Turks signed it, later ministers would be bound to observe it.[82]

Rouillé responded to Vergennes' suggestion of a treaty with the reasons why he still opposed a treaty. The responses of France's enemies, to an alliance by "His Very Christian Majesty" with a non-Christian power, would be embarrassing. Furthermore, it seemed unwise to Rouillé for France to tie herself to the Turks. In case of a war, France would want to conclude a peace whenever it was to France's advantage to do so, and not be obligated to continue to fight for Turkish aims. Nevertheless, in response to Vergennes' urgings, Rouillé sent a project for a treaty to be used as the basis for negotiations if the Turks continued to insist. He admitted, however, that it committed neither side to anything.[83] Rouillé also sent Vergennes full powers to negotiate.[84]

Louis' response to Vergennes' dexterity was not so satisfying. His minister's request for powers to negotiate a treaty had profoundly disturbed him. He feared it might arouse suspicions at Versailles, and lead to a discovery of his secret. Thus, along with his powers to negotiate, Vergennes received a strong rebuke from his King. Vergennes was in the impossible position of being unable to succeed without failing.[85]

For a while it looked as though the secret talks, and promises of money, would achieve the desired results. In a sudden spasm of cruelty, the Sultan had the *Grand Vizir* strangled and beheaded, and one of the *Grand Vizir's* principal officers, the *Khaya Bey*, deposed. A former Turkish ambassador to France was given the dubious honor of replacing the *Grand Vizir*, and the *Re'îs Efendi* was promoted to *Khaya Bey*, a position which brought him even closer to the *Grand Vizir*.[86] Vergennes sent the new *Khaya Bey* his compliments through Gautier, spiced his words with a beautiful ring worth 3,200 *piastres*, and raised, once again, the question of a treaty.[87] Before long, Vergennes reported to Versailles that the Sultan seemed to be aroused over the activities of Russia. Osman III had written to the Khan of the Crimea, to get a report on new Russian fortifications there, and the *Khaya Bey* had followed the Sultan's letter with one of his own, recommending an energetic report. Soon the Sultan was closeted in mysterious meetings with his ministers. Vergennes believed that Osman III's "taste" for war had been awakened.[88]

To accelerate the evident motion towards a declaration or a treaty against Russia, Vergennes stepped up his own campaign to influence the Porte, and he knew that both aims depended on a Turkish understanding of the threat to Poland.[89] The new *Grand Vizir*, the one who had been an ambassador to France, was apparently leaning over backwards not to appear publicly partial to France, and Vergennes did not wish to do anything to interfere with the man's attempts to create an image of impartiality. Nevertheless, on the occasion of a ceremonial audience with the *Grand Vizir*, Vergennes tried to arrange a private conversation with him, to sound out his personal leanings. But the *drogman*, to whom Vergennes suggested the conversation, was horrified and refused the request, on the grounds that there was no precedent for such a privilege. At the Seraglio, one never spoke of affairs on days set aside for ceremony. Nevertheless, Vergennes continued to insist and, on the day of the audience, after the public ceremony had ended, the *Grand Vizir* dismissed the lesser officials and invited Vergennes and the French *drogman* to remain with him and a few others of the important Turkish ministers. Alone with this small circle of officials, Vergennes once again repeated his old arguments as to why the Turks must act to protect the integrity of Polish territory against the Russians. The *Grand Vizir* listened attentively and, when Vergennes finished, he assured the French ambassador of the close friendship between France and the Ottoman Empire, and promised to reread all of Vergennes' previous memoranda touching on the subject. He promised also that he would pass any further communications on the subject to Vergennes through the *Khaya Bey*. Vergennes was pleased with the *Grand Vizir's* "signs of approbation and satisfaction," and closed his statements by asking for further private conferences.

"Very well," replied the *Grand Vizir*, "we will see; I will let you know."[90]

Seeing that the conversation with the *Grand Vizir* was drawing to a close, Vergennes took advantage of a break in the discussion to approach him and say in a very low voice that, although all he had just said directly concerned the interests of only the Ottoman Empire, Louis XV would also find "doubly precious" any action taken to further the policy. "I can assure you," Vergennes whispered to the *Grand Vizir*, "that his (Louis XV's) gratitude will be proportionate." Without hesitation, the *Grand Vizir* responded: *"Pek-iyi*, that is, *très bien*." Then the *Grand Vizir* called back all of his entourage, and the conversation passed to the more public question of how many English ships were in the Mediterranean Sea.[91] A few days later, Vergennes received from the Sultan a request for a "good map of Russia." The fruit of Vergennes' labors seemed ripe for the harvest.

Then, just as a freak storm destroys in seconds the product of months of husbandry, a series of unforeseen events combined to destroy Vergennes' long hours of cultivation of the Turkish ministry. The *Khaya Bey* was "promoted" upstairs, to a position which took him out of the chancery; the new *Khaya Bey* turned out to be, at least according to Vergennes' estimate, "soft," "timid" and "uncertain."[92] The friendly Khan of the Crimea was deposed, and consequently unable to send his "energetic" report on Russian fortifications on the frontier of the Ottoman Empire.[93] England persuaded Russia to stop building the provocative fortifications and, instead, the two countries began to pour money into Constantinople. Soon the anti-war partisans had gained the Sultan's ear, and, as luck would have it, their argument that the Sultan should stay out of a foreign war found unexpected support in the news of an uprising of Janissaries in the provinces of the Ottoman Empire. Domestic problems, and not a foreign war, became the Sultan's predominant concern. Finally, to complete the rout, on April 1, 1756, the new *Grand Vizir*, the one to whom Vergennes had promised Louis XV's "gratitude," abruptly fell from office and went into exile.[94] Vergennes was convinced that if he had stayed in power all the French views on Polish liberties would have been accepted at the Porte. With full powers to negotiate a treaty of friendship and commerce with the Sultan, Vergennes watched helplessly as his friends disappeared. He was left with only the rankling anxiety that, perhaps, his very success in influencing the Turkish ministers to follow a war policy had led them to go too far too fast, and had helped produce the reaction which brought their downfall.

Whatever the case, he had no time to indulge in retracing his steps to find out what went wrong, for with very little forewarning, and not without a considerable grinding of diplomatic gears, France suddenly reversed her traditional policies and changed her major allies. As a result of the Diplomatic Revolution, Vergennes had to forget his carefully prepared arguments in favor of a Turkish action against Russia, write off the gifts intended to prepare the way for their acceptance, and reverse his diplomatic field. As he performed the intellectual and verbal acrobatics made necessary by the sudden turn of affairs at Versailles, he demonstrated that, of the many skills required of a successful ambassador, agility is not the least important.

The assignment to Constantinople provided Vergennes with his first experience in the administration of a large diplomatic bureau. Also, the distance from Versailles, and the diversity of the interests of France and Louis XV at the Porte, meant that he often had to rely on his own initiative to solve a great variety of problems. He was expected to promote and protect French trade. He had to organize and control a technical and secretarial staff, an intelligence network, and a service of military advisers. He was the protector of Christianity in the Ottoman Empire, and distributor of French money there. In addition, he had to implement the official as well as the secret and contradictory policies of Versailles and Louis XV.

The day-to-day administration of so many functions further developed his habits of self-discipline, organization, and work that many later admired and others mocked. It was at Constantinople that he learned to "work like a machine." And it was there that he trained that "organized mind" that Thomas Jefferson later so much admired.

Vergennes learned, also, at Constantinople that money "opened more doors" there than anywhere else. But he did not change his opinion that there were limits to what one could do with money, and real dangers involved in using it imprudently. Premature offers of money to an official to influence a change in policy, he believed, tended to render suspect any rational argument, no matter how convincing, that a diplomat used to encourage the policy change. Before resorting to bribes, Vergennes cautioned, let the diplomat wait until he finds some important person who already has a favorable predisposition towards the desired change. Then, and only then, was he in favor of using money to "perfect" or "hasten the effects" of the predisposition. Furthermore, he warned that the use of money towards such ends should be rigorously limited to a very few persons, for the multiplication of "confidants" by such a means was most imprudent.[95]

Louis XV's determination to form a political alliance with the Porte illustrates once again the deep contradictions between his secret diplomacy and his official policy created at Versailles. At Constantinople, these contradictions meant that Vergennes had to learn to deceive and manipulate his superiors at Versailles, in order to bring the two policies into some kind of workable arrangement. He willingly undertook the task because direct access to the King was an opportunity no ambitious aristocrat could ignore, but, in doing so, he ran the risk of personal disgrace, for he could not satisfy one set of instructions without violating the other. The dissipation of energies, the habits of mind, and the double-dealing required of the diplomat who undertook to reconcile unreconcilable orders, were themselves enough to condemn Louis XV's secret diplomacy as a wasteful, inefficient, and ridiculous way of carrying on international politics. Furthermore, Louis XV's attempt to ally with the Porte could have only ended in "misalliance" and catastrophe, for the traditional reasons why France had not allied with the Porte were still valid : an alliance would arouse the antagonism of the Christian powers of Europe, and the Ottoman Empire was too far away to allow for effective and mutual military assistance. But in 1755 and 56, there was an additional reason why the idea of an alliance between the Porte and Versailles was sheer folly. While Louis secretly pressed for a Franco-Turkish alliance, Versailles and Vienna were already officially embarked on an opposite course which would violently trouble Louis' relations with the Sultan.

Meanwhile, Vergennes' dispatch concerning the need for an ambassador at his post had long ago reached Versailles. Rouillé read the contents to the Council of State and requested a decision. The tense circumstances of the diplomatic situation, plus Vergennes' record as a servant of the King, brought the decision Vergennes hoped for: "I respond, Monsieur," Rouillé wrote November 17, 1755, "to the personal letter you took the trouble to write me on the fourteenth of September." After summarizing the reasons why Vergennes was sent to Constantinople with the lower rank, Rouillé informed his minister that "His Majesty, satisfied . . . with the zeal you have shown for his service, and the knowledge you have already acquired, as well as the liaisons that you have formed at Constantinople, has determined to award you the rank of ordinary ambassador.[96] Thus, at the age of thirty-six, sixteen years after he entered the diplomatic service as a fledgling under the wing of Chavigny, Vergennes reached the top of his profession. His recipe for success is easily formulated: the proper rank in society, a keen ambition which drove him to exploit every opportunity, an unusual skill and conscientiousness in the performance of his duties, and influential protectors in high positions.

CHAPTER 7

The Diplomatic Revolution

The Diplomatic Revolution that preceded the Seven Years' War did not cause a shift in the power relations of Europe; rather it was a belated recognition by diplomats that a shift had already occurred. There is a great deal of truth in Sir Richard Lodge's observation that "all Foreign Office bureaucrats" show an inordinate dislike for changing a system: "They want a regular groove along which their activities can proceed with the minimum both of worry and risk." Nothing causes more concern among them than a sudden break from routine or tradition.[1]

For generations, the Hapsburgs and Bourbons had considered each other bitter enemies, and the balance-of-power system of Europe adjusted itself around the fact of their quarrel. But after 1715, each of these two powers faced a new enemy who became, every year, increasingly more dangerous than the old. France, determined to grow as a colonial power, more and more frequently found England in its way, rather than Austria. And Austria, resolved to maintain its position in the German Empire, more and more found the expanding Prussian state a greater threat than France. The War of Austrian Succession (1740-1748) should have demonstrated, even to the staunchest traditionalists, that it was time to abandon their old ideas, for Prussia had exploited the Bourbon-Hapsburg feud to expand at the expense of Austria. And France, tied down on the Continent by its Austrian enemy, could not give sufficient attention to England's bid to control the seas and capture the wealth of the colonies overseas. Not for eight years after the peace settlement of 1748, however, did the diplomats break out of the well-worn rut of the "old system" and create a new one. But, when they did, the reversal of alliances went far beyond the original intentions of some of those involved.

Frederick the Great, who "had as his only principle his own interest,"[2] made the first gesture to throw aside tradition and take a new approach. After the Treaty of Breslau (1742), according to the British envoy, Hyndford, Frederick seemed to "apprehend that, sooner or later, the House of Austria will endeavour to reconquer Silesia, and for that purpose they would hereafter leave the maritime powers to join with France."[3] Frederick felt that the English and Prussians should get together and settle their differences, in order to meet the Austrian move when it came. But the idea aroused very little enthusiasm in London. George II and Newcastle detested Frederick, and there were too many irritating quarrels between the two sovereigns to make a reconciliation possible: Berlin was a center of Jacobite intrigues against George II's throne; Hanover and Prussia were in a dispute about East Friesland; Frederick was angered because of the high-handed way British men-of-war had seized Prussian ships during the war; and Englishmen were no happier about Frederick's refusal to pay both principal and interest due to British holders of a Silesian loan which Frederick had promised to pay when he took Silesia. Newcastle's attempt to elect a King of the Romans — a scheme that Frederick fought all the way — was the result of England's belief that the "old system" was her surest way of maintaining her interests in Germany.

The next step towards the Diplomatic Revolution came not from Berlin, but from Vienna. Maria Theresa's concern for perfecting old ways of doing things at home did not blind her to the value of finding fresh ways of doing things abroad. She was fortunate, too, in having the aid of Prince von Kaunitz, whose personal eccentricities in no way hindered the operation of his brilliant mind.[4] When Kaunitz studied the treaty of Aix-la-Chapelle, he saw that the only real change it brought to the European state system was the confirmation of Prussia's new position in Germany. Prussia had become, he saw, and Maria Theresa agreed, a more dangerous threat to Austrian interests than France.[5] Furthermore, Kaunitz recognized that the only way to reduce Prussian power would be to engage French assistance. The Emperor, Francis I, disagreed for dynastic reasons: he resented the fact that France had taken away from him his family inheritance, the Duchy of Lorraine. In the court and Foreign Office, he was supported by the traditionalists.

But Maria Theresa "loved her husband more than she respected his opinion;"[6] consequently, Prince Kaunitz went to France in 1750 to see what he could arrange. As a minimum, he hoped to sever the Franco-Prussian alliance. But Frenchmen turned out to be as wedded to the old ways as the Austrians, and, after two years, Kaunitz went home empty-handed. Nevertheless, he had planted the seed of new policy; quietly it germinated.

By the spring of 1755, it was clear that Great Britain and France were going to war with each other. As the tension grew, Englishmen became more and more worried about their two most vulnerable interests on the continent: the Netherlands and George II's electorate of Hanover. If Prussia, an ally of France, came into the war against England, both the Netherlands and Hanover would be dangerously exposed to attack. In order to defend themselves against the danger, English diplomats hastily drew up an alliance plan designed to offer some kind of protection to the Netherlands and Hanover.[7]

Sir Charles Hanbury Williams went to St. Petersburg to execute a principal part of the British plan. English statesmen were aware that the Czarina Elizabeth and her Chancellor, Bestuzhev, were ever ready to undertake an anti-Prussian policy, and they recognized, too, that Russia was as much a menace to Frederick's East Prussia as Prussia was to Hanover. If a Russian army threatened Frederick in the East, he would no doubt hesitate before launching an attack on the Netherlands or Hanover in the West.[8] George II had already joined (1750) the treaty of the two Empresses of Russia and Austria, and, although he had refused to accept the secret article concerning Silesia, the foundation for a closer understanding had been laid. The subsidy treaty which Williams later offered to the Russians was designed to keep a considerable Russian army on the frontier of Livonia, and a Russian fleet in the eastern Baltic as a deterrent against a Prussian attack.[9]

At the same time, English diplomats in Vienna encouraged Austria to strengthen her forces in the Austrian Netherlands. A strong army there would discourage an attack on the United Netherlands, and also be in an ideal position to launch a flank attack on any French army on its way to Hanover.

Finally, the system was to be reinforced by diverting subsidies, earmarked for the election of the Archduke Joseph as King of the Romans, to German princes who would furnish soldiers instead of votes. A treaty with William of Hesse-Cassel, signed in June of 1755, added from 8,000 to 12,000 Hessian troops to the English side, while the Russian subsidy treaty, it was hoped, would add 55,000 more soldiers to the English muster.[10]

On paper, the English system seemed to be shaping up nicely, but difficulties arose when George II looked to Vienna for the final capping of his design. Maria Theresa and Kaunitz, still determined to win the friendship of France, did not wish to strengthen Austrian forces in the Austrian Netherlands, for fear of arousing French antagonism. They could not, of course, reveal their intentions to England, so they put off an Anglo-Austrian agreement by raising impossible conditions. Consequently, as the autumn of 1755 changed into winter, and fear of war exploded into a reality, England found herself with no adequate support on the continent. George II had the Hessian soldiers, to be sure, but the final signatures on the Russian treaty were held up by wrangling over the final ratification. In the last analysis, Austria, the keystone of the entire system, had failed George II in his "hour of need": Hanover was still exposed.[11]

At this point, the idea of some kind of an English bargain with Frederick the Great once more caught the light, and this time it sparkled more than before. Lord Holderness discreetly raised the question with Frederick's brother-in-law, the Duke of Brunswick, and Frederick responded by sending full powers to his London representative Mitchell. On January 16, 1756, the two powers signed the Convention of Westminster.[12] Each party guaranteed the possessions of the other, and promised to preserve peace in Germany by joint opposition to the entry of foreign armies. From the British point of view, the convention eliminated the threat of a Prussian attack on Hanover and engaged an ally if the French attacked. Frederick, truly frightened by the Russians,[13] and more concerned about protecting his earlier acquisitions than making new ones, was also pleased with the results. He could now ask the British to calm St. Petersburg and, at the same time, remain clear of the coming war, for Britain had only asked that he stay out of it. He had much to gain and nothing to lose. Or, at least, so it seemed.

Both Great Britain and Prussia soon saw, however, that they had arrived at the Convention of Westminster by way of three miscalculations, two by Frederick and one by George II. Frederick had entered the agreement on the assumption that British influence at St. Petersburg would control the Russians, and that he could easily reconcile the convention with his treaty obligations with France. But Frederick had committed the gross error often made by political realists: he forgot that diplomats and statesmen are also creatures moved by their emotions, as well as by calculated state interest. Theoretically, two coolly rational diplomats could have reconciled the Convention of Westminster with the Franco-Prussian alliance, but Louis XV was not cool nor rational. He was furious over the Anglo-Prussian agreement, and he concluded that Frederick had treacherously betrayed him.

In addition, both George II and Frederick had failed to see that the Czarina had made the subsidy treaty with England not just because she loved subsidies, but, above all, because she hated Frederick and wanted funds to enable her armies to attack him.[14] British influence was not going to change her mind. And when Great Britain began to define the "common enemy" at St. Petersburg as France, rather than Prussia,[15] Elizabeth took exception.[16]

The miscalculations would not have been so serious if other circumstances had not simultaneously developed. Since the autumn of 1755, the Austrian envoy at Versailles, Von Starhemberg, working through Madame de Pompadour and her favorite, the Abbé de Bernis, had been offering once again an alliance with France. Furious with Frederick over the Convention of Westminster, and frightened by the specter of isolation, Louis XV was now much more agreeable to an understanding with Austria. The only serious obstacle still in the way was Louis XV's suspicion, not unfounded, that Austria was seeking the alliance in preparation for an offensive war against Prussia. With hostilities against England already underway, the

French king naturally felt that he would have enough wars to keep his military busy. But Starhemberg chipped away at French resistance, and finally toppled it with the threat that, if France continued to hold out, Austria would return to her old system of alliances, and France would be left alone in Europe to face the combined power of Russia, Prussia, Austria, and the Maritime Powers. Reluctantly, and with some of the French ministers still harboring serious reservations, the French Council finally approved the signing of a convention of neutrality and a treaty of friendship and alliance, which together formed the first Treaty of Versailles.[17]

In this revolutionary agreement with Austria, the King of France managed to stay clear of an aggressive agreement that would have, inevitably, led to war. Instead, he only gave his word not to attack or endanger any territory belonging to Maria Theresa, especially the Austrian Netherlands, and, in return, the Empress-Queen promised to remain neutral in the Anglo-French war. Both powers undertook to do everything in their power to preserve the peace between themselves and in the rest of Europe. If, however, either party were threatened or attacked, in its European possessions, by any third power, the other would first try to avert the attack with its good offices, and, if this failed, it would supply the attacked party with 18,000 infantry and 6,000 cavalry. Or, if the attacked party so chose, a fixed monthly subsidy would be paid instead of providing infantry and cavalry. The undeclared war already begun between France and Great Britain was excepted from the *casus foederis*.

There is nothing in the first Treaty of Versailles to justify the conclusion that Starhemberg had won over the French to the point of agreeing to attack Prussia.[18] The French remained adamant on this point, and the Austrians accepted the best they could get, namely, a defensive alliance. One thing which did cause Frederick some fear, however, was the possibility that, at St. Petersburg, Austrian good offices would be used to secure a Franco-Russian alliance, as they had earlier been used there to arrange Anglo-Russian treaties. But in the spring of 1756, few sensible diplomats foresaw such a bizarre turn of affairs.

At Constantinople, however, Ambassador Vergennes did foresee the possibility, and the view greatly disturbed him. After all of the French money and argument he had spent at Constantinople to induce the Turks to hate and suspect Russia, a Franco-Russian alliance would undo everything. Such an alliance could create only trouble and embarrassment for the French diplomat.[19]

Vergennes received his first news of the Diplomatic Revolution as he contemplated the significance for France of another change in ministers at the Seraglio. On April 1, 1756, the *Grand Vizir* was exiled, and a former *Grand Vizir*, Mustapha Pasha, was brought out of exile to replace him.[20]

Mustapha Pasha had two outstanding qualifications which pleased the French ambassador considerably: he hated the English; he liked the French. All of Vergennes' hopes for Turkish action against Russia, hopes which had been dashed by the previous changes of ministers, now revived—only to be neutralized by a dispatch from Versailles, informing him of the London-Berlin *rapprochement* and the resulting Convention of Westminster. As a result of this treaty, Vergennes learned, "the King of England, now more tranquil about his Electrorate of Hanover. . .will not bring into Germany the 55,000 men that Russia promised to furnish him." The English might still use the troops for a descent on the coast of France, or transport them to Canada, Rouillé informed his ambassador, although he thought such possibilities unlikely; but, in any case, "it appeared that the Russians would not pass through Poland." Rouillé indicated that France was extremely suspicious of Frederick's motives in signing the Convention with England and, at the same time, he reported that Vienna's behaviour in the new circumstances was "quite different." Rouillé concluded by warning Vergennes to be very careful in his conduct with the Prussian envoy at Constantinople, M. de Varennes, with whom Vergennes had been working to bring about a treaty of friendship between Prussia and Constantinople. Louis, however, had already ordered his diplomat to do nothing to advance the negotiations.[21] Diplomatic sands were beginning to shift.

Vergennes' reaction to the news of the Anglo-Prussian convention contrasts sharply with the reaction at Versailles, and at the Porte. "Regardless of the irregularity of the procedure of the King of Prussia in signing the convention with the King of England," he replied to Rouillé , "it is probable that he was acting in good faith when he declared that he had no intention of doing anything disagreeable to his Majesty, Louis XV, or anything contrary to his engagement with France." Frederick's future conduct would reveal, Vergennes believed, whether or not he was sincere. Nevertheless, Vergennes added, Frederick's *rapprochement* with England had wrecked Prussian chances of getting a treaty with the Porte. When the Turks heard the news of the convention, they reproached Frederick's "duplicity and perfidy."[22] According to the strict letter of the Convention of Westminster, Vergennes' wait-and-see attitude was absolutely sound, but the emotional reaction at Versailles quickly rendered irrelevant such a reasonable, common-sense response.

The day after the signing of the first Treaty of Versailles, Rouillé wrote to explain it to his ambassador at Constantinople. "Ever since the beginning of the troubles with the English," Rouillé wrote, "the Empress-Queen has appeared very disposed to cooperate in every way to keep the fires of war from igniting in Europe . . ." Several times, Rouillé continued, she made known to Louis XV the "sincerity of her inclinations." Louis XV, realizing the extent of his danger on land if England won Austria over, and "always disposed to lend himself to every means of conciliation," had "concluded a defensive treaty with the Empress-Queen." The treaty, Rouillé assured Vergennes, contained only the most innocent and simple "clauses and was only against England, and formed to keep the war from spreading to Europe." In a post-script, Rouillé recommended that, henceforth, Vergennes act in all confidence with the Austrian minister at Constantinople.[23]

Vergennes' dispatches following Rouillé's announcement of the Treaty of Versailles reveal an unusual insensitivity to the meaning of the treaty. It is difficult to believe that Vergennes was really sincere when he wrote: "I will not undertake to describe to you the sensation that His Majesty's new defense treaty with the Empress-Queen will cause at Constantinople! But it does not seem to me that we should fear any reaction contrary to our interests." He even went so far as to say that the treaty would please some Turks who wanted a *rapprochement* between the Ottoman Empire and Austria.[24] The latter statement was undoubtedly true, but it evades the very pertinent question of the attitude of those well-placed Turks — and they were not an insignificant number — who distrusted and hated Austria, and counted on France's traditional hostility to the Austrian Empire as a western counterweight to Austrian power in eastern Europe. And there was the even more delicate question of whether the defensive alliance between France and Austria required that France give Austria assistance in case of an Austrian-Turkish war.[25] Vergennes' comments to Rouillé lead one to ask if he really failed to see the far-reaching significance of the new alliance. He went out of his way to heap effusive praise on Rouillé for his "most elevated foresight."[26]

On the first of June, Rouillé signed Vergennes' new official instructions, for "now that the circumstances have changed, the application of our principles has also changed."[27] Now, one of the most important responsibilities of the French ambassador was to explain to the Porte the recent French treaty with Austria. Vergennes should explain to the Turks, Rouillé pointed out, that Louis XV's main object in making the treaty was to maintain the peace. France had never incited the Turks to attack a "Christian power" (meaning Austria), and if France had made some representations concerning the conduct of Russia (who Rouillé apparently did not consider a Christian power), they were as much in the interest of the Ottoman Empire as in the interest of Poland. Vergennes was to continue to be alert to any move on the part of the Russians that might be a threat to Poland, but if Russia began to approach France, and "there is some reason to believe that she will," England would lose her influence at St. Petersburg and Russia would no longer represent a threat. If Vergennes heard that France had an understanding with Russia, he was to say no more "against that power" and "live in friendship" with her ministers at Constantinople.

Although Rouillé protested that Louis XV's "principles" had not changed, he conceded that Vergennes' position at Constantinople had become "more delicate" because of the French treaty with Austria. In an astonishing understatement, he admitted that the defense treaty might displease the *Grand Vizir*, especially if some power, perhaps Prussia incited the Sultan to declare war on the Austrian Empire. Nevertheless, Vergennes was to explain to the Turks that the Franco-Austrian treaty contained nothing against them. Louis XV, Rouillé insisted, was motivated, in allying with Maria Theresa, only by the determination to fight England. To avoid any difficulties with the Turks over the treaty, Rouillé ordered Vergennes to be especially alert to English or Prussian agents at Constantinople who might try to sow seeds of suspicion. Rouillé then ended Vergennes' new instructions with the counsel to forget the projected treaty of friendship with the Turks if the new *Grand Vizir* did not bring it up, but, if he did, there was nothing in the new alliance between Louis XV and Maria Theresa to prohibit opening negotiations. Such a treaty might please the Sultan, and reassure the Poles that Louis XV, united with the Sultan, was still their protector. He warned Vergennes, however, not to agree to anything against Austria.[28]

Vergennes took great pains to explain to the Turks France's motives in making the treaty with Vienna, and to assure them that Louis XV had made no engagement prejudicial to the Ottoman Empire.[29] He was surprised when the Porte responded by suggesting that perhaps their failure to make a treaty with France was a cause of the Franco-Austrian treaty. Assuming that the time was ripe, Vergennes ignored, once more, Rouillé's instructions to let drop the question of a treaty with the Porte, and discussed the matter with the Turkish minister. He also wrote his king to send him money to buy the necessary presents. He could not use the money sent him by Rouillé, he explained, and he feared the consequences of borrowing too heavily at Constantinople.[30]

In the play of affairs at Constantinople, Vergennes' optimism about the effects on the Porte of the Franco-Austrian alliance could not survive long. The new *Grand Vizir* brought to his task long years of experience in government, and an unusual ability to ask the essential questions.[31] Even if the Turk had been less able, the English and Prussian agents at Constantinople were more than willing to formulate the questions for him. Since the signing of the first Treaty of Versailles, they had redoubled their efforts to stir up Turkish suspicions of the French, in order to split France and the Ottoman Empire apart.[32]

The first question the *Grand Vizir* asked was the most explosive: had France and Austria excluded the Ottoman Empire from the terms of the agreement to give each other assistance in case either power was attacked?[33] Vergennes' *drogman* had to answer that they had not, and the answer drove a wedge between Louis XV and the Sultan. According to the report of the British ambassador at Constantinople, when the French *drogman* finished his response, the *Grand Vizir* burst into a rage, insulted the *drogman,* and sent for the texts of the various treaties concluded between England and Vienna and Russia in order to show the Frenchman that the Ottoman Empire had always been excepted from the *casus foederis* when *England* made alliances with the enemies of the Turks.[34] Then the *Grand Vizir* turned on the *drogman* of Austria, who had accompanied the French *drogman*, and showed him some documents relative to France's negotiations with the Porte on issues concerning Austria and Prussia. He took great pains to point out where France had tried to encourage conflicts between the Porte and Berlin or Vienna. The *Grand Vizir* concluded his tirade, still according to the report of the British ambassador, with the statement that, since Turkey had not been expressly excepted from the terms of the treaty, the Sultan would "henceforth consider France allied with the Court of Vienna against the Ottoman Empire."

The British ambassador did not exaggerate. In Vergennes' dispatch of July 22, 1756, he confirmed that the Turkish government was thoroughly angry. "After so satisfying a debut, I would not have expected that the communication I made jointly with M. de Schwacheim (Austrian ambassador) of the act of neutrality and the defensive treaty alliance could become such a source of mistrust, suspicion, and complaints."[36] For the first time in his career, Vergennes seemed to have lost his footing. To be sure, his embarrassment was not his fault, for the Diplomatic Revolution had undermined some of the foundation of France's traditional relations with the Turks, and the English and Prussians were busily sapping the remains. But his superiors still held him responsible for keeping the Turks within the French sphere of influence and, if he failed to do so, neither Louis XV nor Rouillé was likely to accept the blame.

Vergennes did not tell Rouillé, however, that the *Grand Vizir* had also raised with him the question of the Franco-Turkish alliance. He wanted to know if the treaty of alliance prepared by France was compatible with the alliance with Austria. Vergennes quickly assured him it was. It in no way touched on the liberties of Poland, and France wanted to protect those liberties.[37]

Despite his initial outburst, the *Grand Vizir* had shown some appreciation of Vergennes' honesty in reporting the terms of the treaty to him. Even more important to Vergennes, at the moment, was the tendency among certain influential Turks to de-emphasize the importance of the first Treaty of Versailles, even though they regretted it, on the grounds that Russia, and not Austria, was now the major enemy of the Ottoman Empire. This latter point could have been very useful to the French ambassador, but almost immediately Rouillé rendered it dangerous ground to build on. He informed his ambassador that Russia was approaching France.[38]

Rouillé destroyed whatever chance Vergennes may have had to build a relation with those Turks who did not deeply resent the Franco-Austrian treaty. On June 27, 1756, the French Minister of Foreign Affairs announced that the French and Russian *rapprochement* had progressed so far that the two countries had decided to exchange ambassadors for the first time since 1748. Vergennes was ordered to cultivate the Russian minister at Constantinople as though he were a representative of a "friendly power."[39]

Rouillé could not have conceived of a more effective way to embarass his representative at Constantinople, for even the rumors of the Russian accession to the treaty with Vienna had caused great anxiety at Constantinople.[40] And it is not clear that he even appreciated the troubles he was creating. "I can imagine without any difficulty," he wrote, "the surprise of the Turks when they see occur, one after the other, the two events which they had no reason to expect." They will not be able to understand, he continued, how, "after having for several years ceaselessly excited their attention against the enterprises of the Russian Empress, His Majesty suddenly joins with her." Rouillé then concluded his observation with a comment which must have stunned his ambassador: "It will be very easy to explain this fact to them."[41]

Rouillé's explanation, although it is by no means clear why he felt it would be "very easy" to convince the Turks of its validity, was the following: for a long time England had been cultivating the Russians in order to be able to use the élite of her soldiers in a quarrel in which Russia had no real interest. But the Anglo-Prussian Treaty of Westminster had run against the Czarina Elizabeth's wishes. She had finally signed the subsidy treaty with the English (September, 1755)[42] as part of her project of attacking Prussia, and now the English were trying to use her soldiers against France. The Czarina resented the Englishmen's cavalier way of choosing her enemies for her, and, when the consequences of the diplomatic changes became clear to her, she decided that an understanding with France and Austria offered her more support for a war against Prussia than did an alliance with England who was allied with Prussia.

France, Rouillé continued, hoped to deprive England of Russian mercenaries, and to isolate England, if possible, from all her allies. Secondarily, France hoped to open up a lucrative trade with Russia and any formal treaty with the Russians, Rouillé assured Vergennes, would be only a treaty of commerce. France's recent diplomatic about-faces were, therefore, not intended to harm or alarm the Porte, but were directed only at the English.

Rouillé's explanation was not completely true. His *chargé d'affaires* at St.

Petersburg, Alexander MacKenzie Douglas, when he signed the Russian accession to the Treaty of Versailles, agreed to a secret clause committing France to aid Russia in case of an attack by the Turks. Louis XV disavowed the secret clause as soon as it arrived at Versailles, but the fact that it was the subject of serious negotiation is indicative of the haphazard way France entered into the engagements that were the by-products of the Diplomatic Revolution.[43]

Nevertheless, Rouillé was completely sincere when he insisted that France intended no harm to the Porte, and his argument would have convinced a Frenchman. But Vergennes had to present it to a Turk, not a very sympathetic Turk, and one who could easily see that a Franco-Russian alliance would leave the Turks without any substantial help against their most bitter enemy. If Elizabeth disposed of Prussia, there would be no one to keep her from turning her guns on Poland and the Ottoman Empire.

Nevertheless, Vergennes transmitted to the *Grand Vizir* Rouillé's reasons why Louis XV had been forced to seek a better understanding with Russia, and he even went beyond Rouillé's explanations to explain to the *Grand Vizir* how important to France were the treaty with Austria and the friendship with Russia in the present circumstances. England had to be isolated from her allies and deprived of Russian help. France would gain from opening with the Russians a commerce that had hitherto been monopolized by the English.[44]

The *Grand Vizir* listened politely to Vergennes' explanation, and even assumed the air of being convinced. He assured Vergennes "that the Porte had confidence in the friendship of the Emperor of France." But he also indicated doubt concerning the assurance that any treaty with Russia would be only a treaty of commerce and friendship. In fact, in a sly comment, he made it clear that he expected France to go even further in her union with Russia than Vergennes was willing to admit. ". . . [If] the circumstances later on forced the King [Louis XV] to make engagements more extensive than those of commerce and friendship," the *Grand Vizir* observed, "the Porte hoped that His Majesty would expressly except the Porte as the English did."[45]

Vergennes left the Divan, after his meeting with the *Grand Vizir*, much happier about France's interest at the Porte. "From where I see things," he wrote to Rouillé, "there will no longer be any question of a discussion of these things." He ended his dispatch to Versailles with another extravagant expression of his admiration for the "glorious epoch" in France's affairs brought about during Rouillé's ministry.[46]

His contentment lacked only one thing. "I would compliment myself," he said in his secret report to the King, "for the attitudes of those I see here, if I could consider them the advance notices of the conclusion of a treaty of friendship, with its secret article relative to Poland, which Your Majesty desires to conclude with this Empire. But no matter what cases I take to demonstrate the utility and the convenience of its conclusion, and no matter what vigor I put into my advances, I am not yet able to applaud myself for any marked progress." The *Grand Vizir,* he revealed, would not respond to the direct and indirect suggestions he had made to him through various channels. And Vergennes complained that he did not know whether the *Grand Vizir's* inaction was the result of unwillingness or impotence.[47]

Vergennes' satisfaction with the Turkish response to the Russian accession to the Austrian treaty was premature. The *Grand Vizir* had already prepared an ingenious move to keep the French ambassador in hot water. Since France made treaties with the Sultan's enemies, and claimed that there was nothing harmful to the Turks in such a practice, why should the Ottoman Empire not conclude some treaties with France's enemies, and answer any objections from France with France's own arguments? Prussia had, for a long time, been seeking closer relations with the Porte, and suddenly it appeared the proper moment to conclude treaties of friendship and commerce. The *Re'ïs Efendi* called for a French *drogman* and coyly asked him if there would be any "inconvenience" for France if the Porte signed some treaties with Denmark and Prussia. "I confess, Monsieur," Vergennes reported, "that my embarrassment was extreme." He was caught in his own web. To be consistent, Vergennes had to approve of the *Re'ïs Efendi's* idea; but he knew that, if he did, he ran the risk of arousing the suspicions of Vienna. "In this perplexity," Vergennes explained, "I had to take a middle position between a formal opposition and a formal approval." The idea, he told the *Re'ïs Efendi*, could be a good one, but at the moment Frederick's "principles" were too unstable. The Turks should wait until the Prussian King showed some consistency in his intentions. As for Denmark, "I did my best to associate that affair" with that of Prussia.

The *Re'ïs Efendi* thanked the ambassador for his counsel and the subject was closed. Nevertheless, in a little more than two weeks, a treaty with Denmark was signed, and negotiations with Frederick were opened, although the latter long faltered through mutual distrust. Frederick was determined to exploit the French embarrassment at Constantinople, and the ambassador of France had no recourse but to stand helplessly by, paralyzed by the logic of his own policy.[48]

The news of the Franco-Austrian treaty and the Franco-Russian *rapprochement* could not fail to disturb Frederick the Great. Three determined women, the Czarina Elizabeth, the Empress Maria Theresa, and the favorite Madame de Pompadour, seemed bent on destroying him. Pursued by these "Three Furies," as he called them, the Prussian monarch decided that Machiavelli was right: to master women as well as fortune, one had to conquer them by force. So, in August, 1756, he attacked Saxony to prepare the way for an invasion of Maria Theresa's kingdom of Bohemia and, in doing so, he changed the war between France and England from a colonial war into a general war involving all the great powers of the continent. The Seven Years' War began.

Frederick's attack accelerated the spinning of the web begun by the "Three Furies." In January, 1757, the prediction of the Turkish *Grand Vizir* came true: France and Russia moved closer together when the Russians adhered to the Austro-French Treaty of Versailles.[49] This time, however, but not without some fumbling, Louis XV saw to it that the Ottoman Empire was excepted from the public terms of the treaty.[50] His concern for the feelings of the Turks seemed unduly precious at St. Petersburg, but not at Constantinople. Two months later, the French in concert with the Austrians signed a Convention at Stockholm, which brought Sweden into the war against Prussia.[51] As 1757 opened, Russia and Austria had solidified their union with an offensive treaty.[52] On May 1, 1757, France and Austria negotiated an even tighter coalition in the Second Treaty of Versailles.[53] Thus the consequences of the Diplomatic Revolution unfolded in Europe. At Constantinople, amidst accumulating evidence that Prussian and English influence was daily growing more effective, Vergennes labored to piece back together the strands of Franco-Turkish relations which that revolution had frayed dangerously close to the breaking point.[54]

The experience of Vergennes at the Porte confirms the opinion that the Franco-Russian *rapprochement* which came as a by-product of the Diplomatic Revolution was indeed a "misalliance." The ties with Russia, "so cavalierly assumed," did not produce for France a workable military arrangement; they produced no commercial benefits; and they opened the way to Russian expansion in Poland.[55] To this list of failures it must be added that the *rapprochement* imperilled France's position at the Porte.

Clearly, the statesmen at Versailles entered into the Diplomatic Revolution with no clear perception of how the resulting changes would be interpreted at Constantinople. Their failure to include a clause excepting the Ottoman Empire from the provisions of the first treaty with Austria, and then fumbling over a similar clause in their negotiations with Russia, were blunders of the first order. The sudden reversal of alliances came without forewarning, and appeared at Constantinople much as the Anglo-Prussian treaty of Westminster appeared at Versailles: as a betrayal.

At first, even Vergennes apparently did not see the far-reaching consequences of the unfolding events. But the scathing session with the *Grand Vizir* quickly dispelled his complacency. He was no longer sanguine about the Porte's response to the new alliances, but he was not yet convinced that the Turks would go to war over them. Fortunately, the Porte apparently never did learn of MacKenzie Douglas' treacherous secret clause, and the same practical reasons why the Ottoman Empire was reluctant to challenge Russia held them in check against Austria. For all that, Vergennes still had several assets in his favor: the long tradition of Franco-Turkish friendship; the mutual advantages gained from their commercial ties; finally the Turks' confidence in the French ambassador himself provided Vergennes with some ground on which to begin the rebuilding of the French position.

CHAPTER 8

1761—Trade Treaties with the Porte

As the Diplomatic Revolution transformed the international system of Europe, Vergennes uneasily faced its repercussions at Constantinople. Before he had left Marseille for Constantinople he had learned from Rouillé that a Prussian, one Von Rexin, allegedly Frederick's counsellor of commerce, was on his way to Constantinople. Since Von Rexin did not go with power to negotiate treaties, Versailles had concluded that he went only to observe the government of the new Sultan. Vergennes had been advised, therefore, to give Von Rexin all the help or information he wanted. But if Vergennes were to learn that he had been sent to continue negotiations on a commercial treaty, negotiations begun earlier under the good offices of the previous French ambassador, Des Alleurs, Vergennes should inform Versailles promptly and await further orders.[1]

Von Rexin's real name was Hande. He was a Prussian army officer and his mission, as Versailles vaguely suspected, had been, among other things, to conclude either a defensive alliance or a commercial treaty with the Porte. In addition, Frederick had wanted him to find, as soon as possible, markets in the Ottoman Empire for goods, especially textiles, manufactured in his recently-acquired Duchy of Silesia. Von Rexin, or Hande, had been told also to observe the new Sultan, and forward to Frederick intelligence on the nature and capacities of the new government. Vergennes did not know then that the many encounters he would have with Von Rexin during the next few years would eventually end in one of the worst diplomatic defeats suffered by France and the French ambassador at Constantinople.[2]

The possibility that Frederick might once again be interested in concluding a commercial treaty with the Porte posed a sticky problem for the French ambassador. Earlier, as the ambassador of Prussia's ally, Des Alleurs had received from Frederick full power to negotiate a Prusso-Turkish commercial treaty.[3] As Prussia's ally, France could do no less than make the good offices of her ambassador available to the Prussian monarch. Furthermore, by assuming the role of intermediary for Frederick, France could keep abreast of, and perhaps even control, Prussian-Turkish relations. There was a somewhat similar arrangement with Denmark at the Porte, and Versailles fully recognized its advantages.

Yet, France did not wish to see either Prussia or Denmark sign a commercial treaty with the Sultan. Both official and secret diplomacy agreed on this point. "It is not in the interest of His Majesty," Rouillé explained to Vergennes, "that any power not already having a treaty with the Porte make one." Under the arrangement then prevailing, most of the nations of Europe had to trade with the markets of the Ottoman Empire in ships flying the French banner, and France, naturally, wished to continue to enjoy such advantages.[4] In his personal instructions to Vergennes, Louis XV repeated the order. Des Alleurs, Vergennes learned from Louis XV, had pursued a Prusso-Turkish treaty with "too much vigor." Louis wanted his representative to do absolutely nothing to advance a treaty unless he received orders to do so.[5]

But Louis XV knew he could not openly oppose the ambitions of his allies at the Porte. Consequently, when Vergennes informed Versailles that the Danish consul at Marseille had recommended to him a M. Galer on his way to Constantinople to conclude a Danish-Turkish commercial treaty, Rouillé faced a dilemma. The French alliance with Denmark, he said, (and he could have added Prussia) does not permit France to oppose the commercial treaty. ". . .you must appear to favor it at every point as much as you can, in such a way that he [Galer] cannot report to his court that you are more an adversary than a protector." Vergennes was to tell Galer he had orders to assist him. Yet Rouillé left it to Vergenne's "prudence and dexterity" to find ways to slow down or even prevent the conclusion of a treaty.[6]

Much to Vergennes' annoyance, however, Galer turned out to be a skillful and aggressive diplomat. Furthermore, he had had long experience in trade in the Levant, he knew the city of Constantinople, he spoke the language,[7] and enjoyed many contacts among influential Turks. In fact, he really did not need Vergennes' advice or protection. Consequently, in October of 1756, and despite the Danish King's repeated complaints that France was not doing enough to advance the commercial treaty, Galer secretly negotiated and signed a treaty of commerce with the Turks. Vergennes suspected the conclusion of a treaty was in progress, but he was completely outmaneuvered,[8] and thoroughly chagrined when the Danish minister came to announce to him that a treaty had been signed. There was nothing he could do but swallow his resentment and compliment the Dane on his success.[9] Yet he never could understand why the King of Denmark had worked so hard for a treaty that would bring no real advantages, since most of the goods Denmark had to sell, the Turks could acquire cheaply through the Black sea trade. Furthermore, the costs in bribes to the ministers at the Porte had been tremendous. Vergennes put his finger on the motive, however, when he observed that the treaty would serve as "ostentation." The King of Denmark was buying Prestige.[10]

The Danish treaty, however, did not cost Louis XV anything in prestige. When it became obvious that Galer might succeed at Constantinople, Rouillé instructed Vergennes to try as long as possible to hinder the conclusion. "You know the intentions of the King," he said. But if it appeared that Galer was going to conclude anyway, Vergennes was to demonstrate publicly his assistance to the Dane in order to merit the gratitude of the King of Denmark.[11]

Galer's success illustrated diplomacy at its most effective; Rexin's mission to Constantinople illustrated the opposite. Frederick's congenital penchant for deceit, a trait his admirers called "realism," so complicated the Rexin mission that it fell to the ground of its own weight. Instead of going as a Prussian diplomat, Rexin had posed as a Swedish army officer;[12] consequently, he had been promptly stopped at the Turkish frontier for lacking a Swedish passport. After eight days of detention and the payment of a substantial bribe, he had been allowed to continue on to Constantinople under the guidance of a Tartar guide he had hirèd along the way. He had arrived on March 22, 1755 and had immediately gone to the Swedish embassy, where he gave to the Swedish ambassador, Celsing, a letter from Frederick begging the ambassador to keep the mission secret, asking him to assist Rexin in sounding out the Turks on a commercial treaty,[13] and assuring Celsing that the request conformed with the "intentions and interests" of the Swedish government. Celsing, assuming that his government approved, and that his instructions to that effect had not yet arrived, had proceeded to put Rexin in contact with the Porte.[14]

Rexin's sudden and undiplomatic appearance had created a flurry at the Porte. He obviously had been acting without the knowledge of France, whose commercial interests would be directly affected by a treaty, and he had been obviously trying to conclude agreement with the Porte before Des Alleurs' successor arrived.[15]

His cloak-and-dagger behavior had fed the suspicions of Austrian and Russian agents at Constantinople.[16] And the fact that the Tartar guide had announced Rexin's arrival all over the foreign colony had provided grist for the public gossip mills. Had Frederick been trying to deceive his French ally? In any case, Rexin had soon learned that the Turks were not ready to make a treaty with Prussia.

At first the Porte had simply brushed off Rexin with a verbal negative to his overture, and then, with Celsing still acting as Rexin's protector, the Turks had signified their refusal with a written note. By this time, however,

Vergennes had arrived, and the facts of Frederick's duplicity were beginning to filter back to Europe. The Swedish government was furious,[17] because its ambassador had obviously been used by Frederick, and Celsing was reprimanded for his gullibility. The Porte was closed to Rexin. He left Constantinople to go on to Smyrna, and then to return to Europe.[18]

Before leaving Constantinople, however, he visited the French minister, still disguised as a Swedish army officer. Amused by the charade, Vergennes received him politely, never letting him know that he knew who he really was. Rexin left with Vergennes still puzzling over Frederick's motives. Certainly, he thought, the King of Prussia had not considered his own dignity in this affair. And if he thought that a single *"porteur des lettres"* could suddenly arrive at the Porte and influence decisions, then he was completely ignorant of the customs of the Turks. It took more than "will and effort" to succeed in diplomacy, Vergennes reflected; it also took time, and a certain respect for the occasion.[19]

Nevertheless, in spite of Frederick's maladroitness, the King of Prussia was not the King of Denmark; and opposition to his efforts at the Porte was dangerous. Still, France did not want Frederick to have freedom of action at Constantinople. When Rouillé heard of Rexin's trip, he advised Vergennes to assist him in everything he did, "but do it in such a way that he can never negotiate alone with the Turks," that he can only negotiate with the help of Louis XV. "It is extremely important," Rouillé stressed, "that the minister of the King of Prussia be always obliged to run to you for everything." In this way, even if Louis XV could not prevent a treaty, he would at least know of everything Frederick did at the Porte, and such knowledge could be of value at Versailles for influencing Frederick's conduct in Germany.[20]

Rexin's departure for Smyrna only temporarily buried the problem of Prussian influence at the Porte. The French government smugly concluded that Rexin's fiasco would teach Frederick not to try another negotiation on his own. It only vaguely saw, however, that Frederick was determined to get a treaty, with or without French help. Nor was Rexin so incompetent as Vergennes concluded he was. Like Galer, he knew Constantinople, he spoke the language, and he soon returned. In the meantime, Rouillé wrote to Vergennes that the Prussian ambassador at Paris, Knyphausen, had asked Louis XV to provide a certain Varennes with a passport to Constantinople.[21] Varennes was on his way, Vergennes learned, to continue the negotiation for a treaty, and Frederick hoped that Louis XV would extend his good offices. At the moment, trying to cement together a northern alliance of Poland, Sweden, and Prussia, Rouillé had no alternative but to order Vergennes to extend all aid possible.[22]

But the French ambassador did no such thing. He wrote Louis XV that although he had been ordered by the Minister of Foreign Affairs to extend his good offices to Varennes, he would follow the orders of his King and do nothing to assist the Prussian.[23] Varennes at Constantinople became a minor irritant, but not truly a danger to Vergennes' position. But when the Diplomatic Revolution dissolved the old relations at Constantinople, when Frederick became an enemy and looked to London for help in making a treaty with the Porte,[24] the presence of a Prussian envoy at Constantinople became a festering thorn in Vergennes' side. In addition, in the fall of 1756, Rexin slipped back into Constantinople, Varennes was recalled, and the second round between Rexin and Vergennes began.[25] This time, however, the French ambassador was on less advantageous grounds.

One of the consequences of Russian accession to the first Treaty of Versailles was that France had to allow Russian troops to cross Polish soil.[26] Now, after years of waiting, Elizabeth found the road clear to loose the Russian bear in Poland and/or send it "to dance" in East Prussia. In the next five years she did both. The Russian soldiers entered Polish territory, plundered and raided their way to East Prussia, and further prepared the weak Republic for the first partition of 1772.[27] In fact, they did everything Vergennes had warned the Turks the Russians would do if they were allowed to cross the border into Poland. But now the French ambassador was playing another tune. His new responsibility was to keep the Turks neutral, while Russia trampled Poland and fought Prussia, and he went at his new task with all the conviction he could muster under the circumstances.

After sounding out the Turkish ministry, he was convinced that the Sultan would remain neutral, and not officially object to Russian troop movements in Poland, if the passage were carried out tranquilly and without serious complaints from the Poles.[28] Vergennes worried, however, about what would happen if Poland should become the theatre of war. If that happened, he warned, "I then would not dare to answer for the Porte." He was not even certain the Porte could, under all circumstances, answer for itself. The Turkish army, he told Rouillé, is "not an easily managed being," and if it were sent to the frontiers of the Ukraine or Russia in response to a threat of war in Poland, "it would no longer lie within the power of the Porte to contain it within the limits of a simple defensive demonstration."[29] Furthermore, border difficulties between the Khan of Crimea and Russia, difficulties which Vergennes suspected both the Prussians and the English of encouraging, continually threatened to escalate into a war between the Porte and St. Petersburg.[30] Also secretly, but with little success, Vergennes now continued to press for the Franco-Turkish treaty that would guarantee the territorial integrity of Poland if the Russians failed to show restraint. But the Turks would not be convinced. The Ottoman Empire needed no alliances, the minister curtly reminded Vergennes. The force of its own "sabre" had sufficed until then to protect Turkish interests, and it would continue to do so.[31]

Vergennes' fears for the future were not allayed by the fact that Frederick the Great was now determined to use whatever influence he had at the Porte to get the Turks to come to his aid with an attack on either Russia or Austria. He still wanted the commercial treaty with the Turks, but as the Seven Years War grew more bloody, the commercial treaty became, as he frankly admitted, *ein blosser Prätext.* What he really wanted now, and he told Rexin so early in 1758, was an open break between the Porte and either Russia or Austria.[32]

Frederick's intentions disturbed Vergennes, because he knew the Porte tended to favor any power which was the enemy of Vienna or St. Petersburg. And Frederick's brilliant military successes early in the war did not help. "I totally defeated the entire Austrian army at Lissa in Silesia last December," he wrote Rexin, "they lost more than half their men. Hungary should now be empty of all troops, and the Austrians do not have enough troops to fight me and, at the same time, defend Hungary. The Porte, therefore, has a free hand."[33]

Vergennes' anxieties about Prussian attempts to make a treaty with the Porte were not diminished by the success the Danes had had in negotiating in secret. In fact, by March of 1757, he felt certain that Prussian agents with instructions to conclude a treaty were already somewhere in Constantinople and prepared to negotiate. The Porte repeatedly assured him that it would not repeat the Danish performance, but Vergennes no longer trusted the Turks. He had been duped once, and he did not wish to be duped again.[34] In order to hinder as much as possible the development of Turkish sympathy for Frederick, Vergennes recommended that whenever Frederick was defeated, the defeat be reported in detail to the Porte, in order to counteract the Turk's good opinion of the Prussian king.[35]

A diplomatic revolution as radical as the one the European state-system experienced in 1756-57 could not fail to produce some reverberations among the functionaries at the French Ministry of Foreign Affairs. Much of the groundwork for the new alliances had been laid by people working outside the Ministry. It is not surprising, therefore, that a cleavage had opened between those "inside", and officially in power, and those "outside", but unofficially making policy. Rouillé, for example, very much resented the fact that the King had given the Abbé de Bernis, who was only a diplomat in the Foreign Service, such extraordinary powers to carry out the Diplomatic Revolution and, to show his resentment, he refused to show Bernis any of the dispatches coming into the Ministry except those received from Spain, where Bernis was still, officially, the French ambassador.[36]

But by the summer of 1757, when the Diplomatic Revolution was complete, the ministerial revolution got under way. One of the first to go was

Rouillé himself, already old and in bad health. Giving his poor health as his reason for resigning, he informed Vergennes on June 29, 1757, that the King had agreed to accept his resignation.[37] As his successor the King had chosen—and few were surprised—the Abbé de Bernis.

Bernis was a perfect Ancien-Régime courtier; one who had all the talents needed to rise to the top, but not those needed to stay there. A pink, round, little abbot with cherry-red lips, he started with nothing but his wit and a family tree that boasted no misalliances since 1098, and he rose steadily in the Church, court and government of France by means of his charm, good manners, bagatelles, and poetry. As his positions and ecclesiastical benefices accumulated, so did his wealth; that is, until the French Revolution. Wherever he lived, and especially at Versailles, he cultivated intellectuals, *belles-dames*, dukes, and diplomats, gave sumptuous dinners and glowed radiantly in his circle of friends, who affectionately nicknamed him the "Little Saint," "Booby," "my Duster" and "Piglet."[38] The secret of his success was his uncanny ability to associate himself with the King's mistresses. "I could hardly fail to find myself the friend of whatever mistress the King should choose," he wrote, "because I was a very particular friend of all those who had pretensions . . ."[39]

One beauty with "pretensions" was Madame Lenormant d'Etioles, *née* Jeanne-Antoinette Poisson, and later decorated with the title of Marquise de Pompadour. She had the beauty, brains, and other equipment to hold her position as the King's mistress, but she was not familiar with the intricacies and pitfalls of the court. There was no better tutor at Versailles than the cherubic little abbé. Jeanne-Antoinette needed him and he knew that, if she succeeded, she could render him a service or two. Accordingly, the rotund abbé and the curvacious little *aspirante* allied to further their personal interests.

When Jeanne-Antoinette finally reached her goal as the polically powerful mistress to Louis XV, it seemed only fair that the abbé should also reap some rewards. And since, as he stated much later in life, he was at that time "trying to accustom people to regard me as serious and fit for public life,"[40] he asked for and received an ambassadorship. He served a while as Ambassador to Venice, then returned to Pompadour's circle at Versailles, and to further rewards which followed at decent intervals: the appointment as French Ambassador to Madrid, the King's secret negotiator of the first Treaty of Versailles, and finally the Minister of Foreign Affairs.

We do not know what Vergennes thought of the fall of Rouillé and rise of Bernis, for with bureaucratic reserve he accepted the replacements of his superiors with hardly a comment. The only opinions of Bernis which he wrote down were those he intended to send to the new Minister of Foreign Affairs. These were as embarrassingly obsequious as his earlier flatteries to

Rouillé: "the choice that His Majesty has made to fill the ministry of foreign affairs," he told Bernis, "is an outstanding testimony of his confidence in your love of the service and in the superiority of your talents and lights."[41] Despite his unctuous words, Vergennes continued to deceive his Minister about what he was actually doing at the Porte.

At the same time Vergennes established his relations with his new superior at Versailles, he also grappled with the problems of French relations at Constantinople. In September of 1757, he reported that Osman III was suffering from a stomach ailment, and that he would not take care of himself.[42] For weeks afterward, the health of the Sultan occupied most of his attention. On the 29th of October, however, the vigil ended: *"Il est mort cette nuit."*[43] Sultan Mustapha III, his cousin, succeeded him.

Vergennes found it difficult to understand the new Sultan: he was in poor health, something of a puritan,[44] a hard worker, and seemingly determined to reorganize the financial and military administrations of his state. He had a reputation for being inclined to war, but beyond this well-known reputation Vergennes could find out little about him.[45] He soon learned, to his discomfort, however, that Mustapha III wanted to go to war immediately against Russia, and was restrained only by his advisers.[46] Mustapha also accepted the idea of concluding a treaty of friendship and commerce with Prussia, but Vergennes did not yet know this. In the months ahead Mustapha's intentions and the French desire to keep the Ottoman Empire neutral, constituted the two major concerns of the French ambassador.[47]

In the meantime, the traditional respects and gifts had to go to the new Sultan. When the Sultan hinted that the French ought to free some of the Turkish slaves in the French galleys, Versailles was notified, and thirty Turkish slaves were soon enroute to Constantinople in a French frigate. They arrived in such a pitiful state that Vergennes was ashamed, and felt obliged to distribute new shoes and ten *écus* a head to them before turning them over to the Turks. Nevertheless, he was happy to report that the Sultan was deeply moved by the French gesture. When Mustapha offered to mediate a settlement of the differences between France and England, Vergennes was nonplussed but, after reflection, he suggested that France might accept the mediation, since he knew full well that England would refuse it. "If the refusal of the mediation is going to anger the Turks," he allowed, "it would be better to let the English do it."[48]

At Versailles, Bernis, now deep in the responsibilities of his new post, and overwhelmed by the losses and bloodshed the war was costing France, could give his ambassador very little advice. In fact, the responses of the Minister of Foreign Affairs soon became only cries of desperation. France must keep Turkey out of the war, he urged. Or if they must go to war, Vergennes was to get them to attack Persia, and not Russia or Austria. An attack on Russia or

Austria, Bernis feared, would have the same effect as an attack on France.[49] "If the Ottoman Empire changes its system," Bernis wailed, "the enemies of His Majesy will profit from it to increase their party."[50] "Our situation . . .," he concluded, "is critical."[51] But all of this was but the terrified yapping of a boudoir poodle; Bernis' dispatches were of absolutely no assistance to his ambassador at Constantinople.

Eighteen months after he took office, the chastened Bernis discovered that *his* health, too, was responding poorly to the strain of affairs, so he resigned, leaving France to the aid of heaven.[52] Soon, with a cardinal's hat[53] to comfort him, he retired to his estates. Later, after his health had recovered a bit, he was awarded the ambassadorship to the Vatican and the "Little Saint" rode off to Rome, where, until the end of his days, his cherubic traits and elegant dinners were more than enough to assure his lasting success.[54] At the Ministry of Foreign Affairs he was replaced by the Duc de Choiseul.

Vergennes' reaction to Choiseul's appointment deserves special attention because it was the beginning of a long and sometimes bitter relation between the two men, and one which has been misunderstood by historians. Choiseul, a short, ugly man with a red complexion, had both ability and foresight, despite Horace Walpole's condemnation of his policies as those of a man whose sole ambition it was to "undo his monarch's neighbors."[55] But he was reckless to the extreme.

When he supplanted Bernis as Minister of Foreign Affairs, he had just completed a successful mission as French Ambassador to Vienna where he had been sent to cement the new alliance between Maria Theresa and Louis XV. Earlier he had given a good account of himself as Ambassador to Rome where he had handled the delicate negotiations necessitated by the Papal Bull *Unigenitus*.* After his arrival at Versailles in 1759, he controlled French policy until 1770, although his cousin, Cesar, (Duc de Choiseul-Praslin), actually held the seal of the foreign affairs ministry between 1761 and 1766.

Somehow Vergennes must have learned before Bernis' resignation that Choiseul was a likely contender for the post of Minister of Foreign Affairs. In November, 1758, the Frenchman wrote a long letter to Choiseul at Vienna in which he hinted that he knew that Choiseul was going to become Minister, and went on to court the Ambassador to Vienna with the fawning praise which Vergennes reserved for those who were above him in the hierarchy.[56] After the official announcement of Choiseul's appointment, Vergennes followed up his earlier note with another in which he dared flatter himself that Choiseul would not doubt the lively interest which Vergennes

* Issued by Pope Clement XI in which 101 propositions contained in the writings of the Jansenist Pasquier Quesnel were condemned as scandalous, impious and heretical.

took in the distinction given to Choiseul as a "testimony of the King's confidence and of the justice which the King renders to your superior talents."[57] Choiseul's answer, a rather stiff and formal one compared with Vergennes' letters to him, praised the "wisdom" of Vergennes' reflections, but promised nothing concrete except that he would find occasions with the King to render Vergennes the justice due him.[58] While Vergennes courted Choiseul, Frederick continued to court the Sultan through his emissary in Constantinople, Rexin.

The Prussian King astonished the world, and later historians, with dazzling military campaigns during 1758-59, but the sheer numbers fighting against him took their toll. He hoped to counteract the advantages his enemies had in number by bringing the Turks into the war against Russia and Austria, and relieving the pressure on his own troops. As each year of the war passed, he stepped up his activity at the Porte. His military position demanded that he conclude a treaty of alliance with the Turks.[59]

Vergennes, of course, continued to press the Porte to remain neutral and in April of 1759, he felt he was having some success.[60] But the task became more difficult every day, partly because the French armies seemed incapable of matching the brilliant record of the Prussians and the Turks were almost child-like in their admiration of a military hero.[61] Whenever the French won a battle, Vergennes took special care to report it in great detail to the Porte. The French ambassador also watched to see if the Turkish military forces were becoming more prominent in affairs.[62] At the celebration of the birth of a baby to one of the Sultan's wives, he carefully watched a long parade of Turkish soldiers, and was impressed by the numerous contingent of young men who could form *une très belle armée.*[63]

The worst difficulty in estimating the attitude of the Porte toward Frederick came from the secrecy of the Seraglio; it was extraordinarily difficult to find out what was going on there. The language barrier required that the exchanges with the Porte be handled through a *drogman,* and these interpreters had long ago learned to exploit their positions as intermediaries. Often they went so far as to agree among themselves about the responses to be given a foreign ambassador and refused even to present the problem to the *Re'îs Efendi*. Or if they feared the power of the *Re'îs Efendi*, the *drogmen* might even refuse to bring up unpleasant things which foreign ministers had asked them to raise.[64] As the rumors of a growing Prussian influence with the Sultan accumulated, Vergennes found the *drogmen* more and more difficult to deal with. They were beginning to shut him out. He would not bribe them, because he thought it useless; they simply took the money and then returned with a vague promise to produce concrete information later on, which they never did. The memoranda Vergennes delivered to the Turkish ministers by *drogmen* usually reached their destination, but he always ran the risk that the contents of the memo might soon be for sale to the highest bidder. For a time, Vergennes was reduced to measuring the extent of the Prussian influence by assuming that it was in direct proportion to the number of denials by the Porte that there was any.[65]

Choiseul, however, was not satisfied with his ambassador's efforts. "If the Grand Seigneur has entered into negotiations with our enemies out of some interested motive, and it was English money which determined such an extraordinary maneuver, I do not know of any other means of reducing the inconveniences of any engagement he might make with the King of Prussia than by also offering him some money, in order to extinguish his inclinations toward the Prussians." He ordered Vergennes to make a present of 2,000 *écus* to the *Re'îs Efendi*.

But Vergennes had no faith that money used in such a naked, cynical way could have any effect. "According to my feeble lights," he replied to Versailles, in a dispatch revealing unusual independence, "nothing would be more dangerous than trying to counter-balance the English profusions and opposing negotiation with the force of money." The bad faith and cupidity of the Turks, he told Choiseul, was such that, even if France had temporary success in nullifying the designs of her enemies, the Turks themselves would deliberately revive the designs in order to squeeze new bribes out of the French. Vergennes finally reported to Versailles that, because the *Re'îs Efendi* had been deposed before Choiseul had ordered that he be given 2,000 *écus*, Vergennes had not given the present to anyone.[67]

Instead, he presented the new *Re'îs Efendi* (an "honest, moderate, polished, well-educated" man and "I can say also one of my friends") a long memorandum informing the Turks that he had heard a rumor about an understanding between the Porte and Prussia, and he warned them that such a *rapprochement* put the long-standing Franco-Turkish friendship in jeopardy.[68] But the Porte had the upper hand and knew it. Their response, consequently, was written in a tone of haughtiness and disdain which stung Vergennes to the quick. The *Re'îs Efendi* assured Vergennes that the Ottoman Empire had no need for outside help from anyone to protect its interests. Furthermore, if France needed any proof of the Sultan's friendship, she could find it in the fact that the Porte was not always questioning France about her alliances with Vienna and St. Petersburg.[69] Later, somewhat more moderately, the Turkish minister assured Vergennes that the Sultan had no intention of entering into an alliance which would alter the Porte's "perfect friendship" with France.[70] Nevertheless, he did not deny that there was a treaty in the making.

Vergennes' efforts to fathom the Sultan's intentions finally received some reward when he befriended the Neapolitan doctor of Mustapha III, a certain

Nicolas de Caro. Through this man Vergennes received reports on the Sultan's most intimate conversations. He learned, concerning Frederick, that the Sultan did not quite trust the Prussian monarch, but he did respect him and was flattered by his advances. Vergennes also learned, much to his great surprise, that the Sultan believed he was a relative of Louis XV and, for this reason, he withheld any expression of resentment over the French friendship with Austria and Russia. The doctor also reported an observation by the Sultan about Austria which strikes the modern reader, schooled in the history of the nineteenth century, when the Ottoman Empire was the "sick man" of Europe, as a most precious statement. In his supreme egotism, the Sultan had referred to the Hapsburg Empire as a "vegetating cadaver" kept alive with the assistance of France![71]

Choiseul was pleased with Vergennes' *coup* in winning the Sultan's doctor to his side, and he thought the idea of a familial relation between the Bourbon and the Ottoman rulers a useful discovery. It had "neither truth nor prbability," he judged, but Vergennes could use the "chimera" to France's profit when discussing with the Turks their Empire's relations with France.[72] Yet, in spite of everything he could do, Vergennes had to report to Choiseul, on April 3, 1761, that a treaty between Prussia and Turkey had been signed.[73] Rexin had won, and Vergennes could do nothing but admit it.

At first he was unable to get any details of the treaty, and so could not judge the diplomatic implications for France. But no matter what was in the treaty it must serve to spur on a peace settlement, Vergennes warned, for, after taking this first step, the Turks might let themselves be dragged into the war. And Frederick, not one to hide his victory, publicized it by ordering his agents to maintain a mysterious silence about the nature of the treaty. Now all Europe asked: was the alliance the prelude to the Turks' entry into the war?[74] For a while Frederick managed to keep the answer an "impenetrable mystery."[75] But finally, with the aid of the Russian resident at Constantinople and a liberal distribution of money, Vergennes secured a copy of the secret treaty. He learned for himself that the treaty was only a treaty of friendship and commerce. He was pleased that the Turks had not agreed to enter the war on Frederick's side. Still, the treaty with Prussia, as with the treaty with Denmark, or even the one under negotiation with the Spanish, was not harmless. It would increase the competition for trade in the Ottoman Empire. "It is in the Turks' interest to increase competition," he admitted. But he also knew that it "is in our interest to limit it."[76]

The innocence, militarily, of the treaty did not erase, however, the fact that Frederick's influence at Constantinople was on the rise, and that Vergennes had reached the low point of his influence there. In the long run Frederick's victory was illusory because it led him to nourish false hopes. But, at the moment, this fact provided Vergennes with no consolation.

During the rest of the war, as his armies slowly dissolved, Frederick nourished the desperate hope that the Prussian-Turkish treaty of commerce would be the source of a miraculous salvation. His one star during these black years was the belief that the Turks would soon spring an attack on his enemies, and thereby save him from destruction.[77] His illusory hope was Vergennes' nightmare.

CHAPTER 9

Matters of Prestige

Just after sunrise one morning, Vergennes was roused out of his sleep to receive a *drogman* from the Porte who arrived unannounced with an important memo from the *Grand Vizir* to the "very honorable ambassador of France." The memo informed Vergennes of a recent episode on the island of Stanko* which threatened to precipitate the dreaded break between the Porte and Versailles. Some captured pirates and Christian slaves on the *Ottoman Crown,* the flagship of the Turkish fleet, the memo related, had risen in revolt while the admiral and the captain were ashore at prayer. They had slaughtered or put in chains their guards, stolen the vessel, and escaped to Malta where they sought and received the protection of the Grand Master of the Order of Malta. "His very magnificent, very gracious, very formidable, and very powerful Imperial Majesty, the protector of the World, King of Kings," Mustapha III, was sorely piqued by the arrogance of the prisoners and Christian slaves, and demanded that "His very magnificent and very honored Majesty, the Emperor of France," forthwith arrange the return of the "slaves, ship, and cannon," or else the Sublime Porte would take matters into its own hands and, among other things, dismiss from the Ottoman Empire the French ambassador and French consuls.[1]

The story behind the revolt of the Christian slaves has all the makings of a juvenile Hollywood movie. But its very sensationalism was precisely the thing which irritated the Sultan the most, for he considered his admiralty vessel his "seaborne throne." The Christian slaves had made off with it before the eyes of the entire world, leaving the Turkish admiral standing redfaced on the shore. Not just a ship, but the Sultan's dignity and prestige were involved.

The story of this affair began in June of 1760 when a pirate, Calamata by name, operating out of the mountains of the island of Cerigo (between the island of Crete and Greece), attacked and captured a French merchant Vessel in Turkish waters. At the time of the attack, the pirate's ship was

* Also called Cos. The second largest of the Dodecanese group just off the southwest corner of Asia Minor.

flying the English flag. The French ship was taken into Cerigo harbor and its cargo was shared with a captain of an English ship anchored there.[2] It seemed impossible to deny collusion between the English and the pirates; it was impossible to deny, also, that the act was a glaring violation of the neutrality of Turkish waters.

Vergennes immediately called on the Porte for assistance. The Turks responded by ordering escorts for other French ships sailing into the Gulf of Smyrna, and dispatched two caravelles to find the pirates. They speedily found them, with the French ship still in tow, and, after a brisk exchange of gunfire, captured them. "All of this," Vergennes confessed, "was not accomplished without some expense to me; for there is no free service in this country; but I presume it will cost the English even more. Some Turks were wounded in the combat; and nothing is more costly here than the shedding of Turkish blood."[3] The crew members of the pirate ship were placed in the hold of the Turkish admiral's ship along with eighty or so Christian galley slaves. The admiral received public honors for the deeds of his sailors (one of the commanders of the caravelles was his own son), and Vergennes wrote to him as well as to the Porte, expressing his appreciation for the prompt action.[4]

If the captured pirates had been willing to accept their fate, the story would have ended there; but no sooner were they thrown in with the slaves than they began to plot their escape. When the Admiral and the Captain left the ship at Stanko, accompanied by the ship's soldiers to go to worship, the pirates and slaves saw their chance and took it. After overwhelming the guards left aboard, they cut the anchor cables and headed out into the Mediterranean, where they eventually landed at the Isle of Malta.[5] Hollywood could not have arranged a more bold or dashing escape.

The Sultan, furious, immediately sent an officer to bring back the head of his unfortunate admiral. The unhappy man tried to flee, but in the end his head, along with that of the captain of the admiral's ship, was displayed in the inner court of the Seraglio as a warning to those who blunder.[6] Next Mustapha threatened to break off relations with France unless Louis XV ordered the Order of Malta to arrange a quick restitution of the ship.[7]

The Sultan's threats and anger at France were completely misdirected, because Louis XV had no control over the Order of Malta, an independent, self-governing religious order established in the sixteenth century by the Knights of St. John. There were, to be sure, Frenchmen among the members of the Order, but other nationalities were also represented. At the time of the pirates' escape, the Grand Master was Portuguese.[8] Vergennes tried to explain all this to the Turks, but to no avail. Finally, he realized that he stood in real danger of antagonizing the Sultan if he continued to try to educate him on the subject of the Order of Malta. Some of the Turkish officials, including the *Grand Vizir* sympathized with him, but they all agreed that the Sultan was thoroughly enraged and in no mood to back down.[9] Vergennes also feared that Prussian and English agents had completely won over the Sultan, and that Mustapha was seeking a pretext to sever relations with France. In any event, the critical state of Franco-Turkish relations made it risky to test whether or not the Sultan was actually prepared to go so far as to break off relations. If he did, French diplomatic, religious, and commercial interests in the Levant would suffer a severe blow.

Vergennes could see as many difficulties if his King intervened in the affair as he could see if he did not. If Louis XV succeeded in getting the Order of Malta to return the ship, he would be setting a precedent containing seeds of all kinds of future diplomatic tangles. Perplexed, Vergennes could only write for instructions.[10]

Time did nothing to cool the Sultan's wrath. As Vergennes waited for instructions from Versailles, he kept in touch with the drift of Mustapha's opinions through the doctor, De Caro; what he learned was not promising. Once in a moment of fury the Sultan even threatened to raise a navy and wipe out Malta altogether if his ship was not soon returned. When the doctor suggested that such an undertaking would be indeed expensive, Mustapha explained to him that the Sultan of the Ottoman Empire was not perpetually hobbled by a shortage of funds, as the Christian kings were. He had, he told the doctor, his own personal treasures. He could open one and, if that proved not enough, he would open another. If he lost one fleet sent to destroy Malta, he could build another that would do the job.[11]

The information provided by the doctor De Caro gave Vergennes an idea which could be used, he thought, to convince the Order of Malta that it should return the ship to the Turks, a solution which Vergennes was daily more inclined to favor. Even if the Sultan was only bluffing in his talk of sending a fleet to Malta, a probability about which the Order of Malta could not be certain, the Order would, in any case, be forced to prepare for a possible attack. These preparations, Vergennes predicted, would be extremely costly. He suggested, therefore, that self-interest and economy recommended that the Order return the vessel.[12]

By the first week of the new year, 1761, Choiseul's answer to Vergennes' urgent plea for instructions arrived at Pera. It demonstrated that Louis XV, as well as Mustapha III, had royal pride and concern for prestige. In addition, it also revealed that the war considerably reduced Louis XV's freedom to play the game of diplomatic one-upmanship with Mustapha. The memo began on a tone of haughtiness and cold indignation appropriate to the occasion. "The memo which was given to you from the *Grand Vizir*, Monsieur," Choiseul wrote, "seemed to have merited the King's greatest attention. The consequences [to Louis XV] in it are unjust, indecent, and contrary to [existing] treaties."[13] Vergennes was told to express Louis XV's astonishment on reading in the memo threats unmerited by France's actions, and "unsuitable to the dignity of His Majesty's crown." Choiseul then stiffly repeated Vergennes' old argument that Louis XV had no control over the Order of Malta, and although Choiseul admitted that, several times in the past, France had gotten the Order to make some concession to the Porte, the Sultan was mistaken in believing that France had absolute authority over that religious order.[14]

But Choiseul knew as well as Vergennes that France, already strained to her limit in a world war, could not afford a break with the Sultan and, as his dispatch continued, the tone softened. Louis XV had decided, he told Vergennes, to send a representative to Malta with a commission to buy the Turkish vessel (no mention was made of the slaves); and then, once Louis XV had possession of it, he would present it as a personal gift to the Sultan. That is, if the Sultan indicated that he would accept the gift as a "result of the friendship", and not as a consequence of the threats contained in the Sultan's memo. Choiseul also suggested, no doubt by way of forcing some concession to Louis' pride, that if the King of France succeeded in purchasing the ship, the Sultan should send an ambassador extraordinary to France to thank the French monarch.[15]

If his plan did not work, Choiseul was prepared for the worst, and he ordered Vergennes to draw up a memo containing suggestions about what precautions should be taken to best protect the diplomatic missions and French commerce in the Levant, in case of rupture with the Porte. If things came to that point, Choiseul informed his ambassador, France would back Malta and send its cruisers to assist the Maltese ships in the eastern Mediterranean.[16] Along with these instructions, Choiseul sent an official response to the *Grand Vizir's* memo. Before turning it over to the Turks, however, Vergennes was ordered to read it, and modify it to fit the "style of the court at Constantinople." The official response repeated (somewhat less haughtily, however) the points raised in Choiseul's dispatch, but also raised the question of whether or not the Sultan was looking for an excuse to break with France.[17]

But when Vergennes asked for an audience to present France's official response to the Turk's memo, he was refused. After repeating the request several times and continuing to be unsuccessful, the French ambassador began to despair of ever formally giving his master's answer to the *Grand Vizir*. He was puzzled by the behaviour of the Turkish minister, but he was inclined to believe that it was inspired by the *Grand Vizir's* concern with his own prestige and position. The Turk feared that the Sultan's memo has pushed France too far, and an audience would advertise that fact to the public, and at the same time give France a chance to express publicly its "bitter reproaches."[18] Any reaction that followed might possibly place the blame for the critical state of Franco-Turkish affairs on the shoulders of the Turkish ministers, and not on those of the Sultan. To ease the fears of the *Grand Vizir,* Vergennes arranged a meeting with a *drogman* of the Porte and, in a session that lasted eight hours, he went over the whole affair and tried to get to the bottom of the difficulty. He even read Louis XV's official response to the *drogman,* and the Turk, rather pleased by its unexpected moderation, raised on his own initiative the question of an audience. "What exactly was the reason," the *drogman* asked, why Vergennes demanded a public audience? But Vergennes demurred; he had more to say, he told the *drogman,* but he would say it only at an audience. He assured the *drogman,* however, that the *Grand Vizir* would find no reason for embarrassment in what he would say.[19]

Still the Porte refused to grant the audience, and Vergennes began to think seriously of the consequences if France and the Ottoman Empire broke off relations. France would not be completely helpless in such a crisis, for, as he pointed out to Versailles, a few cruisers could blockade Constantinople and prevent grains and other products essential to the existence of the city from arriving from Egypt and the Black Sea. Within weeks, he predicted, the famine and unrest caused by the blockade would produce "mutinies, alarm, and confusion" in the capital. The Turks, he allowed, would then have reason to repent of their treatment of France.[20]

In the meantime, Vergennes turned once again to the Neapolitan doctor to find out what the Sultan was thinking. The doctor described to Vergennes a scene that occured in the Seraglio, which indicated that Mustapha had not in the least forgotten the capture of his ship, and still held France responsible for its return. Unexpectedly, the Sultan raised the question with the doctor, and immediately all the Turkish officials present prostrated themselves on the floor before the Sultan and begged him not to worry himself with the problem. But the Sultan, becoming angry, refused to calm down. "All right," Mustapha shouted, "if I don't get it back, I'll chase all the foreign ministers from my court." At this outburst all the officials quickly prostrated themselves once more.[21]

Back at Versailles, Choiseul grew daily more impatient that his ambassador at Constantinople moved so slowly. By the end of May, Louis XV had received the ship from the Order of Malta, but he had no intention of giving it up until he received the Turkish response to his memo. Moreover, Choiseul was anxious about the consequences in the Mediterranean if the Turks did build up their fleet and attack Malta. The Italians, especially the Venetians, were thrown into a panic by the prospect, and the Pope had gone so far as to beg the protection of France. At Malta, the Grand Master was calling in all members of the Order to defend the island.[22] "You have seen in my preceding dispatches with what impatience we await your report on the effect in Constantinople of our response concerning the admiral's ship," Choiseul told his representative. "I will not hide from you the fact that the King seems dissatisfied over the uncertainty in which we find ourselves in this affair."[23] Anxious to settle the issue, Choiseul authorized Vergennes to give up the idea of an audience, and get the memo to the Porte in any way he could. Consequently, Vergennes decided to have the memo transmitted to the Porte by a *drogman*.

When the *drogman* appeared to receive the memo, he brought with him another complication. The Sultan, it seems, still believed that he was the proper person to mediate a settlement of the Seven Years War, and he wanted Louis XV to make a formal request that he do so. When Vergennes reported these aspirations, Choiseul grew suspicious of the Sultan's motivations. London and Berlin, he suspected, had suggested the Turkish mediation, in the hopes that France would refuse and thereby complete the Franco-Turkish rift. "It's a new trap," Choiseul warned Vergennes, and he authorized his ambassador to tell the Turks that, if the talks already going on between the belligerents did not achieve any results, France would be agreeable to the mediation of the Sultan.[24] Choiseul was obviously seeking an inoffensive way to stall.

But he was really concerned about whether or not the Porte was going to send an ambassador extraordinary to Versailles to receive the present of the ship.[25] The answer, contained in a new memo from the *Grand Vizir,* was *no.* If the Turks sent an envoy to France, the *Grand Vizir* replied, everyone would think he was going there to pay for the ship, and the Sultan's dignity would "suffer from such a mistaken idea." Nevertheless, the Turkish minister reported that Mustapha "was charmed" by the endeavors of the French "Emperor" to "tighten the knots" of friendship between the two rulers.[26]

Choiseul was exasperated; nevertheless, on January 19, 1762, the French frigate *l'Oiseau,* with the Turkish vessel (flying the Turkish ensigns) in tow, entered the Dardanelles. They were received by an escort of Turkish warships with whom they exchanged cannon salutes. When the ships arrived, Vergennes was indisposed, but a few days later, after the Turkish public had had the opportunity to see with its own eyes how the Emperor of France had granted the Sultan's wishes, the *Grand Vizir,* in a pompous ceremony, paraded before all Constantinople up to the residence of the ambassador of France, where Vergennes officially turned over to him the Turkish ship. In return, the *Grand Vizir* expressed the thanks of Mustapha III, and then paraded back to the Seraglio. After sixteen long months the affair of the pirates and the Turkish ship was over.[27]

Vergennes was delighted at its conclusion. So was the *Grand Vizir,* and, to demonstrate his pleasure, he presented to the French ambassador a richly harnessed riding horse,[28] to the officers at the *l'Oiseau,* fifteen bulls and one hundred sheep, and to the crew one thousand *écus*.[29]

The matter did not close, however, without one more irritation: a rebuke from Choiseul. Taking advantage of the genial atmosphere occasioned by the return of the admiral's ship, Vergennes had asked the Sultan to release to his custody four French sailors held by the Turks as slaves since the time of Vergennes' predecessor. The Sultan graciously obliged.[30] Choiseul, however, did not appreciate the humanitarianism of his ambassador. The request, he admitted, was "just and suitable in itself," but it was badly timed. It should have preceded, rather than followed, the return of the ship, he argued, and then it would not have seemed part of a bargain. As a result of Louis XV's efforts, Choiseul argued, the Turks owed France a large measure of gratitude. Now they could consider the release of the slaves as payment for the return of the ship, and the two things, Choiseul believed, were not at all equal.[31] Vergennes, who had been moved primarily by the fact that the four slaves were the last miserable survivors of seven sailors originally captured, the others having died of ill-treatment, was rather startled by Choiseul's hair-splitting criticism. Nevertheless, he received the rebuke with good grace, and assured his superior that he "reproached himself bitterly" for deserving the minister's disapproval.[32] It is hard to believe that Vergennes felt no resentment of Choiseul's objections.

As Vergennes contemplated the gravity of a possible Russo-Turkish war, another war, one less fraught with European-wide consequences, but one which, nevertheless, required his immediate attention, broke out in the Ottoman Empire. This was a religious war between Greek Orthodox and Roman Catholic Christians, who seemed to believe that they best served the Prince of Peace by killing one another. Upon mounting the Sultan's throne, Osman III had confirmed the various decrees promulgated by his predecessor whereby Europeans, not subject to the tax paid by the Christian and Jewish subjects of the Empire, could freely enjoy their goods and possessions. As part of this confirmation, Osman had ordered that no one molest the Christian religious orders or their places of worship, so long as these did not publicly perform any functions which were contrary to Moslem law and introduced no innovations in their practices or customs.

But in 1757, some Greek Orthodox Christians who were subjects of the Empire, demanded that the Roman Catholics turn over to them some of the principal holy places in Jerusalem. When the Roman Catholics demurred, the Greeks armed themselves and prepared to break the sixth commandment if necessary, in order to dislodge the Roman Catholics from holy ground. One night the Greeks attacked the Church of the Holy Sepulchre, and the Roman Catholics who had been in prayer there retreated to the bell tower, where they defended themselves against the Greeks. The Greeks, frustrated in their attempts to get at the Roman Catholics, retaliated by breaking up or carrying off whatever precious objects they found in the sanctuary.

Vergennes, as representative of the "Protector of the Christian Faith" in the Ottoman Empire, immediately asked the Porte to inquire into the disturbance, but the report that followed (prepared by the Moslem Cadi of Jerusalem) was completely favorable to the Greeks. The Greeks, now apparently convinced that Allah as well as Jehovah was with them, decided to carry the case all the way up to the Sultan's Divan. To ward off a complete defeat for the Roman Catholics, Vergennes requested more time, in order to gather information on the controversy. The time was granted, but the prospects were hardly favorable, because even the Sultan seemed to favor the Greeks.[33]

Osman died and was succeeded by Mustapha III. Vergennes took advantage of the changeover to try to get the Turks to take another look at the controversy before they gave the victory to the Greeks. But, by this time, even the *Grand Vizir* had been won over (Vergennes would have said "bought over"), and Vergennes despaired for the interests of the Roman Catholics.

In the meantime, the Roman Catholics, apparently dissatisfied with the efforts of the French ambassador, decided to take their case to a higher authority and dispatched an urgent letter to the Pope, to whom they described their sufferings and the dangers to Christianity, or at least to the Roman variety, latent in the controversy. The Pope delegated a Franciscan priest, Father Thomas Moraviski, as his representative, and sent him to France to implore Louis XV to do his duty as protector of the Christian faith. "Prostrate at the foot of your throne," Father Moraviski told Louis XV, "I come to implore the powerful protection of Your Majesty and to beseech you, by the blood of Jesus Christ, to order your minister at Constantinople to once again earnestly request the restitution of the Holy Sepulchre and other Holy Places which heretofore have been protected by the monks of Saint Francis . . ." To give greater force to whatever efforts the French monarch undertook, the Pope recommended that the ministers of other Catholic monarchs resident at Constantinople join with Vergennes in approaching the Sultan.[34] Louis XV, sympathetic, transmitted the papal request to Vergennes.

In early 1760, however, Father Moraviski suddenly appeared at Constantinople "with a train and baggage more suited for a minister than a religious mendicant"[35], and began soliciting the assistance of the representatives of the Catholic powers, as well as the ambassador from England. One does not have to read very far in Vergennes' description of Father Moraviski's activity at Constantinople to realize that, from the beginning, the diplomat and the cleric disliked each other. Vergennes resented the interference of the papal envoy, who seemed convinced that he could accomplish more at the Porte than the French ambassador. Vergennes' fury reached its height when the priest tried to involve the English ambassador.

Nevertheless, there was little Vergennes could do about Father Moraviski without becoming enmeshed in a public feud. He had no alternative but to appear to assist him as much as possible. The foreign ministers at the Porte took Father Moraviski's plea under consideration and unanimously decided that, because the Sultan and the *Grand Vizir* were then hostile to the Roman Christians, there was little to be done about the injustices for the moment.[36] Furthermore, they feared that, if Father Moraviski continued to insist, the Sultan might, in anger, expel all foreign religious bodies from the Ottoman Empire. There was nothing further for Father Moraviski to do but return home.

By the time the Franciscan reached France, he had developed some rather harsh judgments about the French ambassador at Constantinople who, he claimed, had done nothing to restore the holy places to the Roman Christians. He even went so far as to accuse Vergennes of being in the pay of the Greeks, and of having connived with them. In a long letter to the Abbé de la Ville, a director in the Ministry of Foreign Affairs and a personal friend of Chavigny, Vergennes indignantly replied to the priest's charges. Vergennes admitted that he had "weakness," but he denied that graft was one of them. In closing the letter, Vergennes expressed the fear that Father Moraviski might have some influence with Choiseul and convince the Minister of Foreign Affairs that the French ambassador at Constantinople was unworthy of his post.[37]

Five weeks later Choiseul himself responded. He had read Vergennes' letter to De la Ville, and he assured the ambassador that his decisions concerning the holy places were very wise. Moreover, Choiseul was not surprised that the other ministers resident at Constantinople had unanimously decided that nothing could be done for the moment. As for Father Moraviski, Choiseul assured Vergennes that he was only a "vain and intriguing monk" and the French ambassador had done well not to listen to him.[38] Vergennes, obviously relieved by Choiseul's dispatch, thanked Choiseul and expressed his consolation at being able to count on the trust of his superior.[39]

Barely had the Greek Orthodox-Roman Catholic controversy died down than the Roman Catholics clashed with the Armenian Apostolic Church. This time, although the conflict started much more violently, Vergennes was able to arrange a more satisfactory settlement.

One Sunday morning in November of 1761, the religious observances at the French ambassador's residence were interrupted by the arrival of a winded and excited servant sent from the church of the Jesuit Society. Turkish soldiers, he reported, had entered the Jesuit Church and convent to arrest all former members of the Armenian Church found worshipping there. The Jesuits, apparently recalling the martial as well as the spiritual exercises of their founder, herded the Armenians into an inner court of the convent, barricaded all the doors and prepared to fight to the last man. At the same time they dispatched the servant to report their troubles to the French ambassador.[40]

The arrests, it turned out, were based on a decree issued by the Sultan to discourage the conversion of Armenians to Roman Catholicism. It provided for the arrest and punishment of all Aremenians found frequenting the Catholic churches. Such a decree was not unusual, but the Turks usually arrested the Armenians outside the churches, and were extremely careful not to enter. This time, however, they were bolder. They began at the Church of the Capuchins, and, led by an Armenian priest, they entered the church and arrested the Armenians who had been in prayer there. Next, still led by the Armenian priest, they marched to the Dominican Church, entered and arrested all the Armenians they could find within. By this time, the Jesuits had been warned, and hastily prepared make-shift defenses. Fortunately so, for their establishment, it seems, held over four hundred Armenians.[41]

Vergennes' first move was to send his French *drogman*, escorted by a janissary, to the Jesuit convent. By the time the two men arrived, the Turks had pierced the outer Jesuit defenses and were closing in for the final attack; but the sight of the *drogman* and the janissary restrained them long enough to permit the hasty negotiation of a truce. They agreed to halt their attack, on condition that none of the Armenians be allowed to escape. By that time, messengers from the Capuchins and the Dominicans had arrived, terrified and incoherent, at the ambassador's residence. They were able to make Vergennes understand that the affair at the Jesuit convent was not an isolated event, and that the situation would have to be taken up formally with high officials at the Porte.[42]

The French ambassador's obvious next step was the presentation to the Porte of a formal protest. But he discovered, as he prepared his protest, that he stood on much less solid ground than he would have preferred. The presence of the Dominican fathers in the affair considerably weakened his case. Although Louis XV considered himself the protector of the Dominicans, as well as other Catholics in the Levant, the Dominican Order had never been specifically named, as other religious orders had been, in the various capitulations agreed upon by France and the Ottoman Empire. The only official recognition of their right to be in the Empire was a decree dating back to the beginning of the reign of Mahmud I (1730), which allowed the

Dominicans to rebuild some Christian churches destroyed by a fire.[43] Vergennes decided, therefore, that the less said about the Dominicans, the better. In order not to draw attention to them, he composed a protest which dealt with the incident of the arrests in much more general terms than he would have liked, lumping together in his text the Capuchin, Jesuit, and Dominican orders. To his *drogman* he assigned the task of steering the protest through the hierarchy at the Seraglio.[44]

The immediate reaction to the protest was surprisingly favorable and unusually quick. The Khaya Bey conferred with the *Re'îs Efendi;* the *Re'îs Efendi* took the protest to the *Grand Vizir,* who called in his provost who had ordered the arrests. Apparently the *Grand Vizir* gave the provost a sharp reprimand, because the French *drogman* saw him leave the meeting in great embarrassment.[45] Meeting the French *drogman,* the provost even apologized, weakly claiming he did not know that the churches were French. But most important of all, he ordered the immediate withdrawal of the Turkish soldiers at the Jesuit convent; although, before the soldiers actually dispersed, the provost tried to extort money from the Jesuits for his raising the siege.[46]

The progress towards a happy conclusion was momentarily blocked when the *Re'îs Efendi* called to Vergennes' attention the imperial order which forbade the Armenians to frequent foreign churches in the Empire. But when Vergennes protested against this restriction, the *Re'îs Efendi* did not insist. Finally, on December 14, 1761, Vergennes received at the ambassadorial palace a procession of Turks led by the provost of the *Grand Vizir* who, formally and publicly, apologized for the violation of the rights of the Christian churches. Vergennes, exploiting the occasion, accepted the apologies but asked, as proof of their sincerity, for the release of all the Armenians arrested during the affair. In keeping with the magnanimous character of the occasion, the provost agreed to this.[47]

Thus, Louis XV and the Chevalier de Vergennes enjoyed the extremely rare satisfaction of a formal and public apology from an official of the Ottoman Empire. Vergennes was justly proud as he reported the occasion to his new superior at Versailles, to Comte de Choiseul, cousin of the Duc de Choiseul who had turned over the Foreign Affairs portfolio to his relative in order to concentrate on the Ministries of War and Marine. "I have seen many disagreeable things happen here since I have been living among them (i.e., the Turks)," he boasted, "and this apology is the first that has ever been given."[48]

The formal apology did not end the discussions of the affair, although it closed it as far as talks with the Turks were concerned. But Vergennes was anxious to prevent its recurrence, and there were still elements in the situation which could blaze up into another incident. Vergennes was especially concerned that Louis XV approach Rome to explain to the Pope the difficulties and limits of the French King's role as protector of Christianity. Although the various Franco-Turkish capitulations protected French Catholics and Roman Catholic dependents of the French crown in the Levant, they did not cover Armenians who were converted. These people, he pointed out, were subjects of the Sultan, and could not expect to be protected by the King of France.[49]

The Comte de Choiseul read Vergennes' recommendations with approval. He praised Vergennes' "dignity and moderation," and agreed that prudence ruled that the French ambassador be content with the apology already accorded him. Like Vergennes, Louis XV's minister did not wish to demand too much of the Turks. Vergennes had actually gotten more out of the Turks than the facts warranted since, in the last three capitulations, the Sultan had agreed that only *French* bishops and priests would be free from Turkish authority as they performed their functions. The release of the arrested Armenians was, therefore, a concession not required by any written agreements.[50]

CHAPTER 10

1764—The Election of the King of Poland

By 1761 the war between France and England had reached a stalemate. The British had defeated the French in the colonies and on the sea, but the French and their allies seemed within sight of a victory in Europe. England's ally, Frederick the Great, had waged a heroic series of campaigns against a multitude of enemies, but his resources were exhausted, and time was against him if the war continued. Prussia was strained to the limit; only a miracle could save her.[1] Frederick hoped the miracle would occur at Constantinople, with a Turkish declaration of war against his enemies. Instead, it occured at St. Petersburg.

On January 5, 1762, the Czarina Elizabeth of Russia died, and was succeeded by her nephew, Peter III.[2] Unlike his aunt, Peter did not detest the Prussian king; in fact, he admired Frederick to the point of adulation.[3] One of the first things he did after his accession, therefore, was to sign a peace treaty with his Prussian hero, restoring all the Prussian territory conquered by Russia.[4]Next, he joined with Frederick to plan a war against Denmark over the claims of Peter's family to Schleswig-Holstein.[5] Almost immediately, Sweden followed Russia's example and reached a settlement with Prussia.[6] With his armies now free of the Swedish and Russian threats in the East, Frederick could concentrate (with a corps of 20,000 Russians furnished by Peter)[7] on the Austrians. The stalemate might now be broken. "[Peter] has only to draw up the treaties as he wishes," Frederick joyfully wrote his envoy at St. Petersburg, "I'll sign them."[8] Luck had delivered him from defeat.

Received as a stroke of fortune at Berlin,[9] the news of Peter's personal diplomatic revolution meant confusion, perhaps catastrophe, at the palace of the French ambassador to the Porte.[10] If Peter and Frederick went to war against Denmark, France would be required to defend Denmark because of treaty obligations. Then, no doubt, Vergennes would receive orders to stop urging the Turks to be neutral and, once again, to encourage them to war against Russia.[11]

But a more pressing worry was that Frederick's *coup* might eventually hurt France at the Porte if Frederick boldly exploited his newly gained prestige. Versailles, clearly alarmed, was concerned about the ominous possibility that Frederick might take advantage of his new position, and his newly formed friendships at the Porte, to incite the Turks to war against Austria, France's ally.[12] Vergennes, anxious to prevent so disastrous a complication, decided he had to direct Turkish attention away from Austria. Now that Russia had deserted France, his target was readymade.[13] He marshalled all his old arguments about a Russian threat, modified them here and there to bring them up-to-date, and presented them to the *Grand Vizir* in the form of a formal memo.

The major theme of the memo devolved around the question: What were the Czar's ambitions? Dictator in Germany? Despot of the North? Master of Poland? Vergennes, to be sure, provided the answer. Russia, he warned, was rapidly becoming the predominant power in the East. "Soon Europe will have no dike strong enough to contain this torrent which threatens to ravage and overturn all who try to block it."[14] The point was intended to touch two chords: the Sultan's interest in maintaining the balance of power in the East, and his jealousy of the achievements of an old enemy. Unfortunately, the Sultan seemed disinterested; his concern for his favorite daughter who was seriously ill, extinguished all other concerns.[15]

When the Sultan's daughter died and he turned once again to the problems of government,[16] he did nothing to indicate that the French ambassador's memo had made the least impression, if, indeed, he even knew about it. Reports arriving at Constantinople indicated that Russian troops were moving into Pomerania in anticipation of joint action with Frederick;[17] and an abundance of rumors and observations led Vergennes to think that Russian and Prussian diplomats at the Porte were trying to persuade Mustapha to launch an attack on Austria's Hungarian possessions. "This is a new development," Vergennes reported, "for which Vienna cannot be prepared, and which betrays the cowardice and depravity of the Russian monarch's heart."[18] Actually, although Vergennes never knew this, Frederick did not need the Turks' help now that he could count on Russia's assistance.[19] Nevertheless, all the evidence seemed to point to a Turkish decision for war. Vergennes learned that Turkish troops were on the move, and that the Sultan had ordered an arms buildup. The military Pasha of Anatolia had been transferred to Bosnia near the Hungarian border; orders went out calling for more artillery; the Turks began construction of a bridge over the Danube; salt-peter reserves were increased; and army supply officers stood ready to act at a moment's notice.[20] A Turkish war against Austria, Vergennes was painfully aware, could shatter the foundation of the

French influence in eastern Europe, most probably bringing his own career at Constantinople to a disastrous close.

But, as Flaubert observed, hostilities are like oysters; they have to be opened, and before Mustapha could reach the decision to open hostilities, his plans were set awry by another unexpected revolution at St. Petersburg. Catherine of Anhalt, the strong-willed consort of Peter III, staged a *coup d'état,* had her husband arrested (and perhaps later assassinated), and became, by the Grace of God, a handful of conspirators, and a few Russian Guards, the Empress and Autocrat of all Russia.[21] "Your conspiracy," Frederick the Great patronizingly wrote her, "was madness and badly planned." He was right, but she had won, and that was the only test she had to meet.

The first act of the new Empress was to confirm the peace established between Peter and Frederick.[22] But she made it clear that she had no intention of going as far as Peter did in giving Frederick military assistance. Her treasury was empty; her soldiers were unpaid. Russia, she believed, needed peace.[23] She ordered all Russian soldiers still in the war zone to return home immediately.[24]

"Before my dispatch arrives," the Comte de Choiseul wrote from Versailles on July 31, 1762, "you will have already learned of the singular event which just occured at Petersburg." This revolution, he predicted, was going to create a new situation in Russia which no one could as yet evaluate. He told Vergennes to wait until France had a chance to see what policies they were going to adopt at the court of St. Petersburg before he said or did anything about Russia.[25]

At the Sublime Porte the reaction to the *coup d'état* was one of surprise and frustration. A gloomy silence settled over the Seraglio, Vergennes noted, for Catherine's revolution had sapped the foundation of the Turks' negotiations with Prussia, and it wrecked their project for conquests in Hungary.[26]

Vergennes' standing at the Porte was improved by the turn of events. He was convinced that the Turks had been preparing an attack on Hungary on the assumption that Russia and Prussia would be sympathetic. But Catherine's behavior, plus the uncertainty about what Frederick now planned to do, inspired the French ambassador to increase his efforts to break the links between Russia, Prussia, and the Porte. "If I were asked to offer counsel to the Porte," he told a Turkish *drogman* in a three-hour-long conference, "it would be that they be in no hurry to take sides." More than one example could be found in the diplomatic archives, he warned, to prove that whenever the Turks decided to move, the Christian powers united. Furthermore, he added, Frederick's word could be trusted only so long as it was to his advantage to keep it.[27] In short, neutrality was the most sound policy consistent with Turkish interests. The *drogman* seemed to agree.[28]

In the meantime, the peace talks between France and London developed into serious negotiations. Louis XV had had enough of a war that was bleeding France white; Pitt, whose hatred of France approached a religious faith, fell from office; France and England exchanged ambassadors. "The existence of our negotiations [with England] is no longer a secret," the Comte de Choiseul informed his ambassador in a dispatch dated September 19, 1762. A reconciliation of the two crowns and a "return to general peace" now appeared within the realm of possibilities.[29]

This news furnished Vergennes with one more weapon and when he used it, it proved extremely effective. The Turks were completely disoriented by the rapidly changing events and decided that, until the diplomatic situation stabilized, they had best temporize. Prudence counseled also that they let their relations with Prussia cool a bit. The King of Prussia, Vergennes proudly reported, can no longer count on "dragging the Ottoman Empire along with his plans."[30] Finally, on November 6, 1762, the Minister of Foreign Affairs notified Vergennes that peace preliminaries had been signed. "In these circumstances," he conjectured, "it is probable that the Porte will abandon the idea of beginning a new war." He could not be absolutely certain, however, for intelligence had come to him through Venice that the *Grand Vizir* had expressed the opinion that the Ottoman Empire "needed a bloodletting."[31]

At the same time, Choiseul proudly notified his ambassador that the name Comte de Choiseul would no longer suffice; for "on the occasion of the preliminary articles of peace which I have negotiated and signed in the name of the King, His Majesty ordered that I be created duke and peer of France under the name of Duc de Praslin."[32] Vergennes, always sensitive to the ego-needs of his superiors as well as to his own need to cultivate favor, quickly responded to the news of the honor with a dispatch devoted entirely to felicitations and congratulations. And having given nourishment to Choiseul-Praslin's ego, he then reminded his superior of the needs of others: "I also dare to ask for the continuation of your favors which you have sometimes permitted me to count on. To merit them is all my ambition, and I can also say the object of all my application, since I can flatter myself to obtain them only by rendering myself worthy of your esteem."[33]

While the Sultan temporized, Catherine flirted. In response to a hint from Frederick that the two of them form an alliance, Catherine coyly sent His Prussian Majesty a basket of fresh grapes and some watermelons.[34] The grapes and watermelons were followed in April of 1764 by a treaty with Frederick which expressed their common understanding regarding the future of Poland.[35] The connection between watermelons and Polish politics seemed farfetched, but Frederick frankly admitted that Catherine united everything "within her sphere of activity."[36]

Catherine had no love for Frederick; but she loved the Polish aristocrat Stanislas Poniatowski, and she wished to place him on the Polish throne[37] after the reigning king, Augustus III "like a fool, let himself die," as Frederick so bluntly phrased it.[38] The bestowal of crowns was to prove, however, less rewarding than the bestowal of watermelons and grapes. In her egotism, Catherine assumed that Stanislas the king would remain as responsive to her wishes as had been Stanislas the lover. In that illusion lay the seeds of her future disappointments, for almost as soon as he became King of Poland, Stanislas introduced reforms which showed an independence not at all in keeping with what Catherine expected.

Estranged from England and not on the best of terms with France, Frederick had entered the agreement with Catherine because he needed an ally against his enemies at Vienna. The two had agreed to act together to further the election of a native-born Pole, thus opening the way for the election of Poniatowski. They agreed, also, to defend the "peace" of the Polish Republic, and to protect the religious rights of the Greek Orthodox Catholics and Protestants. In return for these guarantees in Poland, Frederick received Catherine's guarantee of Silesia, and a promise to come to his aid if he were attacked within his own frontiers.[39] Neither of the two rulers relished the idea of an alliance with each other, but each preferred being diplomatic bedfellows to the alternative of isolation. In addition, the treaty was, for Catherine, the perfect instrument for drastic intervention in Polish affairs.

In France, the response to the election in Poland of a successor to Augustus III was hesitant, confused, and ultimately ineffective. The terrible costs of the Seven Years War, as well as France's alliance with Russia, convinced some French statesmen they must avoid intervention. But Elizabeth's death, Peter's alliance with Frederick, and Catherine's not-very-well-concealed designs on Poland forced a reappraisal. The question returned again and again to the French Councils of State: what could France do to prevent Russian domination of Poland?[40]

In truth, Louis XV never found the answer to the question, and, in lieu of an answer, every faction within the decision-making circles of French high politics went its own way, each trying to convince the King and others that its minority position was or should be French policy. The Dauphine, Marie Josephe, a daughter of the ruling family of Saxony, organized her own party to back the House of Saxony for the Polish throne; French secret diplomacy, pursued by the Comte de Broglie, sought to place the Prince de Conti, a Bourbon prince, on the Polish throne. Louis XV's family ties with the House of Saxony, however, made it difficult for him to favor a prince of the House of Bourbon;[41] furthermore, at the critical moment of the election, Louis XV and Conti were estranged because of a personal quarrel and could not be reconciled.[42] At the last hour, therefore, the secret diplomacy shifted its favor to the Polish General Branicki,[43] then discovered to their dismay that Branicki could muster no effective support among the Poles. French policy then settled into neutrality.

Official policy orginating at Versailles conflicted with both the secret diplomacy and that advocated by the supporters of the House of Saxony,[44] because Choiseul-Praslin inclined to what was probably the most realistic conclusion, that France was neither financially nor militarily strong enough to do anything dramatic in Polish affairs and had best reconcile herself to trying to persuade others to do what she could not do.

The critical weakness of French policy in Poland, however, lay in Louis XV's irresolute personality. For a while he seemed favorable to the House of Saxony[45] but, finding himself caught in the tug and pull of the various conflicting parties, congenitally unable to make difficult decisions, and failing to arouse among other powers any interest in intervening in the Polish crisis,[46] he, in effect, abandoned the Saxons and declared that it was up to the Poles to determine who would be their King.[47] Yet, almost perversely, he continued backstage to pay lip service to Conti's candidacy, although, at the same time, he vowed he would not sacrifice one *sou* or one soldier to have him elected.[48]

In the Council of State, Choiseul-Praslin, in an attempt to clarify French official policy, recommended that France not intervene in the Polish election;[49] yet, in his dispatches to Vergennes, he repeatedly implied another, stronger policy, by urging his ambassador to persuade the Turks they should be prepared to intervene against Russia.[50] Choiseul-Praslin's policy did not go far enough, however, to please the agents of the king's secret diplomacy. They wanted France committed to more aggressive intervention in Poland, against Russia and Prussia, and Choiseul-Praslin's conclusions and Louis XV's vacillation infuriated them.[51] At Warsaw, Hennin, the French resident agent of the secret diplomacy, and friend of Vergennes, bitterly complained to the latter that French policy left him helpless. He felt, he said, that he had no authorization to do anything. Even in Poland, he noticed, confidence in France was waning. "No one listens or will listen to Monsieur le Marquis de Paulmy [French minister to Poland]".[52] As the intentions of the Prussians and Russians became clearer, Hennin became more discouraged: "Neither we nor our allies", he wrote Vergennes, "put into Polish affairs the energy which the opposing party shows; a few words and a little money will not counteract the sums of money the Russians spend, the indirect threats of the Prussians, or the fear of the soldiers who already surround Poland from the North and East." "I predict," he concluded sorrowfully, "that we are not going to play a very brilliant role in this election."[53]

Unfortunately, Hennin was right; French policy never stabilized. When the Russian and Prussian candidate, Poniatowski, approached the French King about the coming election, Louis and Choiseul-Praslin informed him, that for family reasons Louis XV supported the Saxon candidate, but France did not anticipate any great inconvenience if Poniatowski were elected.[54] Yet, as the election approached, Broglie tried to reverse the trend of politics with an eleventh-hour attempt to raise the pro-French Polish general, Branicki, to the Polish throne.[55]

Such a disarray of contradictions and confusion inevitably meant the collapse of all French influence in Poland. Louis XV's public willingness to let the Poles settle their own affairs, although presented to the world as a noble gesture, sprang essentially from his inability to do anything else.[56]

The French ambassador at Constantinople had to make sense, somehow, out of his sovereign's policy. At first Louis seemed determined to reach some kind of concert with the Sultan, because he rightly suspected that the recent Russo-Prussian treaty was only the beginning of further aggression against Poland, and he wanted to lay the groundwork at Constantinople for opposition to such action.[57] On this point, at least, both official and secret diplomacy agreed. Both official Versailles and secret Warsaw ordered Vergennes to arouse the Turks out of their indifference to what was happening in Poland, to get them to stand ready to prevent a Russian move to make a satellite of Poland.[58] The Sultan was interested in the designs fomented at Berlin and St. Petersburg but his response, according to Vergennes, lacked the precision that the critical situation demanded.[59] When a new *Grand Vizir* rose to power, Vergennes became more confident of being able to prod the Turks to action. He was a man of long experience and strong character who would not allow, Vergennes believed, the Russians to dispose of the crown of Poland. But he was aging, and had been out of office in exile, and Vergennes was not certain whether his courage and principles had remained intact.[60] In the meantime, Choiseul-Praslin continued to urge Vergennes to persuade the Sultan to communicate to all the powers of Europe who had ministers at Constantinople his intention to maintain the liberty and the possessions of Poland.

Another factor conditioning Vergennes' response to the Polish election was that, for a time after the death of Augustus III, French diplomats in Eastern Europe did not know who was Catherine's choice for Polish King. When the secret did leak out, they were stunned, not only by her choice of Poniatowski, but by her willingness to back him with a large supply of money and troops.[61] The news of her daring moves threw the agents of secret diplomacy off balance; they simply could not believe that Prussia would back a candidate so obviously Catherine's agent.[62] But as they watched

Frederick's moves and heard his pronouncement their disbelief dissolved. Frederick was collaborating with Russia! Nothing, Hennin wrote to Vergennes, could be more dangerous to Poland.[63]

Poniatowski's candidacy also shook policymakers at Versailles. Choiseul-Praslin informed his ambassador that there was no doubt now that Catherine was determined to exclude all foreign candidates from the throne of Poland and would insist on a Piast; that is, a native-born Pole. And she reserved to herself, continued Choiseul, to name the candidate. "Thus it is very important," he insisted, "that the Porte make some demonstration which could strike fear into the court at St. Petersburg." The Sultan must make it clear, Choiseul-Praslin urged, that he will not stand tranquilly by and watch the oppression of the Poles.[64]

Soon after the death of the Polish King, Vergennes was instructed to muster support at Constantinople for the official French candidate, the Elector of Saxony,[65] but the Elector died, quite unexpectedly, late in 1763, leaving official policy with no candidate. Choiseul-Praslin tried to assure his ambassador that the death brought no change in Louis' policy; Louis would now give his support to one of the princes of the House of Saxony.[66] At the same time, Vergennes was to know that His Majesty the King of France really wanted only the complete liberty of Poland, and he did not want any resolution in the Polish Diet that would exclude a foreign candidate.

Obediently Vergennes labored to get the Turks to declare to all the ministers resident at Constantinople that the Ottoman Empire would not permit anyone to violate Polish liberties, and that the election should remain open to all candidates. And he worked through every contact he had at the Porte, through the *Grand Vizir*, the lesser ministers and even the Neapolitan doctor of the Sultan.[67]

Untiringly he worked to advance French aims as he saw them, but the makers of policy did not always share their rapidly changing plans with him. He was not kept up-to-date about the plans of the secret diplomacy,[68] and official policy was never very clear. Furthermore, conditions at Constantinople sometimes severely inhibited his ability to keep open his lines of communication with Europe and the Porte. In the summer of 1764, for instance, an epidemic of the plague became so dangerous that he was forced to leave Pera and go into the country to avoid contagion. Thus, for a while he was almost completely out of touch with affairs at Constantinople.[69]

Surprisingly, Versailles was nevertheless generous with expressions of its admiration for his efforts, and praised him for his numerous suggestions, which were conceived, Choiseul-Praslin wrote, "with a great deal of intelligence and wisdom."[70] Whatever intelligence and wisdom there might have been in the French ambassador's suggestions, there was not enough strength left in France to make it possible to avoid a diplomatic disaster in Poland.

And to expect the Turks to save the Poles was to add misconception to weakness. France and the Porte had only recently skirted the edge of an open break, and Louis XV's confused policy gave Constantinople no confidence whatsoever that a common policy could overcome the mutual suspicions.

Furthermore, as Vergennes labored, so did his enemies. The Russians and Prussians resorted to every argument possible to convince the Turks that their policies constituted no threat to Polish "liberties".[71] Indeed, according to the positions of St. Petersburg and Berlin, the French and Austrian policies posed the immediate threat of intervention in Poland. In a memo communicated to the Porte, the man who by now had become Vergennes' most active enemy, Frederick's agent Rexin, skillfully argued the point. France and Austria, he claimed, were determined to make a member of the House of Saxony King of Poland. Since the Elector of Saxony also had some distant hereditary rights to the Austrian throne, Rexin hoped to demonstrate to his Turkish hosts that Vienna and Versailles were trying to impose their influence on Eastern Europe. Russia and Prussia had no designs on Poland, he argued, and all the suspicions that they did were created by France and Austria. After all, Rexin observed, it was not Russia and Prussia who wished a foreigner elected to the throne of Poland, and he made it clear that he considered the House of Saxony a "foreign" house. Russia and Prussia, the Prussian envoy insisted, only wanted the Poles to elect one of their own, a "Piast". Rexin concluded his memo with expressions of hope that the Porte approved of his master's policy and that of the Empress of Russia. "In general," Rexin reasoned, "it would be advantageous to the Porte, as well as to the other neighboring powers, if the choice [for a King of Poland] fell on a Piast, who could be easily contained within just limits by the principal Polish aristocrats, rather than have a foreigner elected who would become too powerful."[72]

Caught between the crossfire of argument and counterargument, the Turks procrastinated. But, at last, in a note distributed to the diplomatic community at Pera, the Sultan declared himself. He did indeed wish to see the ancient liberties of Poland remain intact, the Sultan announced. But he went on to say that the King of Poland ought to be freely elected, and he should be a Pole. Rumors arriving at Constantinople, the declaration continued, held that some powers were considering "marching a certain quantity of troops" into Poland to establish as King of Poland "a person sustained by certain Powers." The Porte denied being persuaded by unsubstantiated rumors, but it nevertheless wanted to make its position clear.[73]

What did the declaration mean? Each diplomat read into it his own position. The ministers of Russia, Prussia, and France each claimed that it constituted a victory for his side. "The minister of Russia and that of

Prussia,"Vergennes observed confidently, "in order to mask their embarrassment, are quietly spreading the word that the declaration was their work, and that they had requested it to cut the tangle of intrigues that have developed here in favor of the Elector of Saxony." The French Ambassador quickly dismissed such rubbish. "Unfortunately for them, everyone knows that the Porte had the news of the Elector of Saxony's death twenty-four hours before they delivered the declaration." Modestly Vergennes disclaimed any credit for being "alone" responsible for the declaration. But he did admit to having contributed to the declaration by his advice and reflections to the Porte.[74]

The statement of the Porte did, at first, seem to indicate that the Turks were following France's lead. Like Louis, the Sultan strongly opposed any violation of Polish liberties. But the point was misleading, for the declaration continued to the effect that only a Pole should be elected King of Poland. Since all of the candidates of the confused French policy at that time were foreigners, and only the Russian candidate was Polish, the Porte's statement revealed that Russian and Prussian influences were indeed strong at Constantinople.[75] Perhaps the Porte did suspect Louis XV of planning to impose a King on Poland. The Turkish note could, in fact, be interpreted as a veiled warning to France—a foreign power desiring the election of a non-Pole.[76] Yet, Vergennes certainly did not read the declaration as a threat to France. The powers rumored to be planning to use force, he identified without hesitation as Prussia and Russia. And that "person" they were planning to make king was Poniatowski. "Once you know that," he observed, "everything else explains itself."[77]The statement, as Vergennes saw it, was a public declaration excluding Poniatowski.

Vergennes either did not see the double significance of the Porte's declaration, or else he saw it and preferred to avoid calling attention to what could be considered a major failure on his part. In his dispatch to Versailles, he lauded the Turks for their announcement which left no doubt whatsoever, he believed, that they were opposed to any violation of Polish liberties. He did notice, nevertheless, that the Ottoman government had not taken any formal steps to implement the declaration. While he admitted that the declaration did not say "all that one might desire," he was convinced, or least he wished to convince Choiseul-Praslin, that the Prussians and the Russians would find the statement embarrassing.[78] Even in his response to the Porte, Vergennes maintained the illusion that the Turks' position followed along the lines of his own.[79]

The Turks, apparently surprised by the French ambassador's recently acquired obtuseness, tried once again to explain themselves in another memo, a "Supreme Memoir to Our Very Honored Friend the Ambassador of France."[80] This time they reduced their position to simple ABC's in order to make sure that their "very honored friend" saw the point. Since time immemorial, the note began, the Republic of Poland has been free, and, up to the present, the Sublime Porte has never failed to honor the imperial capitulations which protected this freedom. And as long as the Republic of Poland did nothing to violate these capitulations, "Mustapha," the "ornament of the throne of felicity, . . . [and] the cause of the peace of the human race . . .," would see to it that nothing happened contrary to the capitulation or the rights of peace and friendship between the Porte and the Republic of Poland. Then once again the *Grand Vizir* repeated the Porte's desire that no foreigner be elected to the throne of Poland, but this time he added the observation that, apparently, France's views on the subject "conformed to those of the Sublime Porte."

Then the *Grand Vizir* discussed the danger of foreign troops entering Poland. At all times, foreign troops had entered Poland and sometimes the Poles even received them with hospitality, the Porte noted. The point was a deliberate slap at France who in the last war had persuaded the Poles to consent to the entry of Russian troops on their way to fight Prussia. Such an entry of foreign troops, the Turks stated, violated no treaties or capitulations and, if the troops did not violate the Polish constitution, the Turks would do nothing if it occurred again.[81] The fatal consequences of France's alliance with Russia lay behind these words.

The Porte's position was now clear: (1) it would accept a Pole as King of Poland; (2) it would do nothing to stop entry of Russian troops into Poland as long as they were not used to impose a king; and (3) any attempt by France or any other power to influence any other outcome of the Polish question would be looked upon as "foreign" interference and a violation of Polish liberties. Furthermore, the Porte did not care, the *Réîs Efendi* told Vergennes, who was elected King of Poland. "It is of little importance to us," he explained, "who will be King of Poland. The name means nothing to us. But what interests us is to know how and under what conditions the king will be elected."[82]

Although by now Vergennes must have seen the character of the Porte's position, the Duc de Choiseul-Praslin seems to have first articulated its anti-French implications. "One must admit," he told his ambassador, "that if their [the Turks'] response had been copied from the declarations made by the ministers of the courts of Russia and Berlin it would not have been any different from what it is."[83] Everywhere in Europe, Prussian and Russian agents were exultant about their success at Constantinople. By July of 1764, Louis XV had abandoned all hope that the Turks would act vigorously against the Russians.[84] At Paris, the Comte de Broglie despaired, "We must do the impossible," he wrote to Louis XV, "to at least slow down the execution [of the Russian-Prussian plans]." Nothing must be neglected, he urged, to put "Turkey and the Tartars in movement."[85] But the cry was in the wilderness.

Events proved, however, that neither Praslin nor Broglie, nor even the Russians and Prussians, had fully defined or appreciated the Turks' position. When the Russians began to move troops into Poland, the consequences of their declaration became apparent. Once in military control of Warsaw, the Russians and the Prussians announced that Stanislas Poniatowski was the candidate most worthy of the throne of Poland. The announcement threw the Porte into a fury, for it had had a previous understanding with Berlin and St. Petersburg that, while they all agreed that foreigners should be specifically excluded from the throne, no individual candidate would be indicated.[86] Immediately, the Turks began to have second thoughts.[87]

As Russian troops moved onto Polish soil to insure the election of Poniatowski, Count Branicki, a Polish aristocrat opposed to Russian domination of his country and now supported by French secret diplomacy, dispatched a representative to Constantinople to describe the desperate plight of the Poles.[88] But the awakening came too late at Constantinople. Poniatowski proved to be (at first) not only the choice but the tool of Russia. The Turks suddenly saw a more complete domination of Poland by Russia than they had anticipated. The victories of Russian troops over Branicki's rebel forces, Branicki's entreaties for aid, and the rumor that Catherine planned to marry Poniatowski and unite Russia and Poland completed the dismal picture. The Prussian ministers at Constantinople tried to reduce the Turks' fears of such a marriage by communicating to the Porte Poniatowski's sworn promise to marry only a Pole, but the Porte was not calmed.[89] Now they openly opposed the Russian and Prussian policies.[90]

But their opposition came too late. Louis XV had already abandoned Saxony and agreed to let the Poles have a "free" choice, and Branicki's hopes were destroyed as his military defeat became certain. Moreover, the confusion of French policy made it difficult for anyone to support it. Louis XV's decision to do nothing in Poland constituted the bankruptcy of his secret diplomacy, and the Turks saw it as the diplomatic defeat it really was. Poniatowski was elected King of Poland on September 7, 1764. Versailles, frustrated and unable and unwilling to organize any real opposition to the Russian candidate, affected indifference, but behind the mask of indifference was the blush of humiliation.

The election of Poniatowski dealt a blow to Turkish pride also, because he was the only candidate they had specifically not wanted, and the extent to which the election of Poniatowski was a Russian controlled affair was publicly indicated by the fact that the Turks received official notice of the victory of Poniatowski from the ministers of Russia and Prussia.[91] Vergennes learned of the magnitude of Turkish discontent about Poland only when he met the *Re'îs Efendi* in a specially-arranged, secret audience. This audience, held at the *Re'îs Efendi's* residence, violated all the rules of etiquette and ceremony, and Vergennes appeared at it posing as a doctor. Their dialogue was reported by Vergennes. He probably rendered it a little more dramatic than it actually was, but it is worth sampling. It reveals the Turks' rather strange interpretation of their own late policy and it contains the first statement of the new direction French policy was going to take.[92]

The Re'îs Efendi: The Porte did not care whether the King of Poland was a foreigner or a native Pole, provided that he was freely elected by the will of the nation, because we did not want the Russians to pick the King! Later we were given assurances; we always held to these principles, we have not varied. (*With indignation*) And nevertheless Poniatowski is King. It's a choice that we cannot suffer. Can't we destroy him? This is what I wanted to talk with you about, and I pray you to explain your position.

The Ambassador: (a little surprised by this abrupt question) Nothing is impossible to the Ottoman Empire; such an enterprise has its dangers, however, and is not exempt from the greatest of difficulties. The Porte has, it is true, the resources to eliminate and overcome them, it can extirpate the evil . . .

The Re'îs Efendi: First of all let us see how we can overthrow Poniatowski.

The Ambassador: I see only war; but I can not nor ought not propose it nor counsel you to undertake it; nevertheless, if you are determined to try it, it could be that your efforts would succeed and cause the revolution you propose . . .

Vergennes then pointed out that the Polish election was made by a rump session of the Diet, but the Poles were unable to do anything, because the Russians had 60,000 troops on hand to keep them down. The dialogue continued:

The Re'îs Efendi: Do the Russians have such great numbers; how does one dislodge them?

The Ambassador: Perhaps their numbers are even greater . . . the only hope is a diversion which would cause them enough anxiety to oblige them to look to the defense of their frontiers.

The Re'îs Efendi: Who will make this diversion?

The Ambassador: Only the Porte. It alone is in a position to divert this power [Russia] with the efficacy, but all this depends on their will to do so, and it is only with deference that I discuss this sort of thing.

The *Re'îs Efendi* then suggested that France take the lead. Vergennes demurred. With Prussia and Russia practically surrounding Poland, France had no access. The only rescue route still open was the Ottoman frontier. Where was the Grand General, Branicki? the *Re'îs Efendi* asked. Could he not do something? He was in Lubownia, was the reply, but he was unable to do anything. What about Vienna? She cannot help, Vergennes opined. Her access to Poland was cut by mountains, and if Vienna attacked, Prussia would enter the war against her.

The Re'îs Efendi (agitated): Will Russia then govern Poland?

The Ambassador: No, she will let the King keep the appearance of authority; she will even furnish him with the means to hold his people in subjection; but at the same time, she will have him in such great dependence that he will be to Russia what a khan is to the Ottoman Empire.

The conversation continued along these lines until the *Re'îs Efendi* asked: "If the Porte refused to recognize Poniatowski as king of Poland, what would your court do?" Vergennes had to admit he did not know. But he pointed out to the Turk, no doubt to chide him for his past behavior, that formerly France had been willing to concert with the Porte. As the conversation drew to a close the *Re'îs Efendi,* jumping from "branch to branch," lit on a comic topic.

The Re'îs Efendi (laughing): Well, what could be the cause for the great affection the Czarina has for M. Poniatowski?

The Ambassador (also laughing): I don't doubt but that the Porte is better informed on that subject than I am.

What was the Turks' aim in arranging the secret audience? Did they really wish to plan, at this late date, some joint action with France? Vergennes believed so; he even found the idea of dethroning Poniatowski a "decent" one. Choiseul-Praslin, on the other hand, found it of very little value. At first, he, too, seemed not to have taken the Russian threat to Poland very seriously, but, now that it had materialized, he sought a scapegoat upon which he could lay the blame for the debâcle. The Turks seemed a likely candidate. They were, he told Vergennes, "a little late in their serious concern about the affairs of Poland." And he praised Vergennes for making the Turks understand that they alone were the only ones who could now get themselves out of their difficulties.[93] If the Turks had supported France earlier, he opined, perhaps something could have been done. Now the only dignified response to Poniatowski was to recognize him.[94] After more than a year of bickering and bargaining, the Sultan and Louis XV reluctantly agreed to that sad alternative.[95]

The election of Poniatowski represented the end of the *raison d'être* of

Louis XV's secret diplomacy. It continued to live for another ten years, but its original purpose - to elect a French candidate to the throne of Poland - no longer existed. Millions of *livres* had been spent, an "invisible" and secret foreign service created, and the effectiveness of official policy undermined, to pursue a goal which, when the critical moment arrived, was abandoned in confusion, utter weakness, and humiliation. At Warsaw, the French representative Paulmy became the victim of insults and threats,[96] and Vergennes' contact there, Hennin, wanted only to leave Poland before he too began to feel the personal penalties of defeat. "It is inconceivable," he lamented, "that we could watch with indifference while a Republic which we have always supported perished, and there is founded a monarchy which will, in a short time, change the face of Northern Europe and frustrate our allies in Germany."[97] From Constantinople, Vergennes could offer nothing to dispel Hennin's despair. Unsure as to which candidate his monarch supported or, at least, uncertain as to which one should be given the most vigorous support, he could offer neither Hennin nor the Porte an alternative to frustrating inaction. He knew France did not have the resources to commit itself to a policy of intervention,[98] and he knew full well that the Porte was relying on France and her ally, Austria, to take the lead in containing Russia in Poland.[99] Thus to the rage in Constantinople, over being duped by the Russians into accepting Poniatowski, was added the mutual disillusionment of Vergennes and the Turkish ministers when each discovered that the other would not act alone. Louis XV and the Sultan had separately hoped that the other would do something to prevent Russian domination of Poland. With such a hope as his point of departure, the French Ambassador at the Porte had confined himself to trying to persuade the Turks to do what France was unable to do.[100] Too late, the Turks realized the true intentions of the Russians and, too late, they offered to help France play a role in opposition to the Russian candidate. As Vergennes reflected on the discouraging collapse of French influence in Poland, and on his own inability to produce any reaction at Constantinople to prevent it, he could find no satisfaction whatsoever in the many attempts he had made to persuade the Turks to act. All of them had failed. In the face of such complete impotence, he consoled himself with the illusion that, after all, he was not responsible, for "in the end, Providence disposes of everything."[101]

CHAPTER 11

War

In April of 1776 the French ministers were reshuffled by the Duc de Choiseul. Choiseul-Praslin dropped the Ministry of Foreign Affairs and took up the direction of the Marine. The Duc de Choiseul, who had never really lost control of French policy during the end-of-war and immediate post-war years, gave up the Marine and once again officially took the helm of Foreign Affairs. His return to the office immediately injected more vigor into French foreign policy, but sometimes, (at least as far as France's relation to the Porte was concerned) the vigor overwhelmed sound judgment. Vergennes' attempts to represent the voice of moderation and judgment were interpreted by Choiseul as showing lack of initiative. The differences between the two men resulted in Vergennes' disgrace and the close of his career at Constantinople.

Soon after his return to the Ministry of Foreign Affairs, Choiseul sent Vergennes a resumé of his views on the European situation.[1] He was not at all pleased with the state of affairs. Northern Europe, he found, was almost entirely under Russian domination; the Swedes acted only under the orders of the "Moscovites;" Denmark, out of fear of Russia, was subservient to her; and the King of Prussia followed and backed up all of St. Petersburg's operations. England, Choiseul believed, was behind it all.[2] She supported Russian action with subsidies and worked to prepare a northern league against France. "The only certain way to break up these projects and perhaps tumble the Empress Catherine from her usurped throne," Choiseul concluded, "would be to stir up a war against her. Only the Turks are in a position to render us this service." Whether the Turks won or lost the war did not interest Choiseul; the important thing was that they begin it. While the conflict raged, France might find the opportunity to destroy Catherine's system. If the Turks decided to strike Russia through Poland, Choiseul advised his ambassador that France would answer for Vienna's neutrality, and that Vienna could even assure the Porte of the "tranquillity" of Prussia.

Choiseul then turned his attention to his ambassador and prodded him to action. His comments, in fact, came close to an official chastisement. "It is no longer a question of occupying yourself with the little day-to-day affairs of the embassy," Choiseul scolded, "war by the Turks ought to be the aim of your work and your meditations, if you hope to succeed, if you see it as a possibility. The King wants your ideas [on the subject], and His Majesty will see to it that you are furnished with all the necessary aid in money that you ask for..." Only Vergennes, the King, and Choiseul himself knew of this plan, Choiseul informed his representative, and if it did not succeed (an eventuality which would "pain" the King), it would have to be entirely forgotten. "Don't leave a stone unturned," Choiseul lectured, to acquire in the Divan the same amount of influence that the Russians and Prussians had acquired at French expense. In one stroke Choiseul destroyed all the past arguments in favour of Turkish neutrality. What France now wanted from the Sultan was war; the sooner the war the better.[3]

Vergennes's response to Choiseul's new policy revealed a heretofore hidden facet of the ambassador's personality. He had occasionally suggested to his superiors better means of furthering their policies, but, beyond these occasional suggestions, he had shown very little independence of mind. Perhaps, until now, he had never considered himself experienced enough to question or give advice to Versailles, and his attitude towards those in authority, at times almost servile, most certainly extinguished whatever personal reactions he may have had. But Choiseul's new policy, as well as the indirect reproaches implied by the tone of the dispatch describing it, stung the French ambassador at Constantinople into a new stance. His answer to his chief was a polite, but resolute, lesson in diplomacy.

"The personal letter with which it pleased you to honor me the twenty-first of the past month," Vergennes began, "contained a striking and most impressive picture of the present state of affairs in northern Europe and of the alarming consequences to which the situation seems to point."[4] He then commented on Choiseul's description of Russia's domination of the northern powers and agreed that the Turks were the only power in the position to make war on Russia. "But are they disposed to do so?" Vergennes asked. "And is there any hope that they can be disposed to do so? You have ordered me to express my opinion on this question, and I am going to do so with the utmost clarity possible."

Knowledge of the personal character of those charged with administration, he observed, was not the worst way to judge the direction which an administration will take. And so he proceeded to sketch the "principal traits" of those who formed the Ottoman government. The Sultan, he believed, was vacillating and weak; the *Mufti* was a man whose "venerable exterior, grave composure, and sententious speech" failed to hide his "incompetence and ignorance." The *Grand Vizir,* Vergennes judged, was "sincere," but "without any knowledge whatsoever of the direct or relative interests of the state he governed." The Khaya was a hard worker, but a very sick man. The *Re'îs Efendi* was an "honest," "discreet" and "disinterested" man with sound judgment, but he was overwhelmed with work, and unable to profit from the reflections which his experience furnished him.[5] Vergennes realized that his picture of the Turks was not compatible with the bold plans Choiseul had drawn up for them, "but, prepared to sacrifice everything for the service of His Majesty, I would be committing a criminal act if I withheld the truth which His Majesty did me the honor to ask for." In substance, the Turks were "soft, debased," and "loathed war."[6] Russia might eventually provoke them to war, Vergennes admitted, but he could see no hope for such a war at present and very little hope for one in the future. He admitted, however, that what seemed true about the Turks one day might be false the next.

Having drawn a picture of Turkish inclinations so unfavorable to Choiseul's schemes, Vergennes then proceeded to give his Minister of Foreign Affairs a word of advice on how to carry on negotiations: "The most sure method for succeeding in a negotiation is to understand, as much as possible, the nature and inclinations of those with whom one negotiates . . ." France would make a mistake, he believed, if she abruptly, and without preparation, presented the idea of war to the Turks as an immediate and unavoidable goal; "we would annoy them, and discredit ourselves." Rather, France should try to enlighten the Turks about their own true interests, Vergennes counseled, for they would never go to war unless they were convinced that, in doing so, these were being furthered. He admitted that such an indirect approach would be slower in producing results, but he felt that it was the only effective one, for the Turks could not be pressed or "seduced" into following a policy which contradicted their own convictions.[7] Any high-handed attempts to steer them into such a policy, he implied, would be unsound and reckless.

Vergennes also had something to say about Choiseul's offer to send him all the money necessary to further his plans. Money was not his most pressing need, he informed his superior; it was sufficient that he had been authorized to make "suitable presents" when they might be effective. What he needed most of all, however, was information; facts which would help him reinforce and defend the arguments he planned to present to the Turks.[8]

As he approached the end of his dispatch, Vergennes alluded to Choiseul's comment that he should no longer simply occupy himself with the "little day-to-day affairs" of the embassy. He told the Duke that the day-to-day business would not distract him from the principal objects of his mission. Furthermore, he continued, he hoped that none of the interests for which he was responsible would ever suffer, but if he ever arrived at the point where he could not do everything, the major policies of Louis XV would not be the ones to languish.[9] Having written to his superior as though he were an equal, Vergennes then stepped back into his customary role and closed his dispatch with the fawning formulae so characteristic of letters from bureaucratic inferiors to those above them.[10]

Vergennes' advice to Choiseul had no discernible effect. Choiseul's dispatches continued to press for an immediate Turkish declaration of war, and his arguments in favour of such a declaration ranged from one end of the spectrum of possibilities to the other. The internal affairs of the Ottoman Empire, Choiseul wrote, were in a deplorable state; a "foreign war could alone quiet these internal troubles."[11] On the international stage, Choiseul observed, the prestige of the Sultan had sunk to a new low. A king in Poland had been elected in spite of his opposition; the frontiers between Russia and Poland had been "adjusted" to facilitate an attack on the Turks; and Catherine II was on her way to making her throne superior to that of the Sultan's. War, Choiseul concluded, was the only way the Sultan could win back his old "authority."[12] Use every opportunity, Choiseul ordered his ambassador, to converse with the Turks and "beat their heads with enthusiasm" for war. Spare no expense, and fear no disapproval if you fail but hurry. It was already late in the season to begin a campaign, but the Russians were pushing their operations, and there was only a small margin of time left to remedy affairs.[13]

Vergennes' reluctance to press a policy which he considered unwise was seconded by Nature, which seemed bent on keeping the Sultan's attention away from a foolhardy war. The region of the Bosporus was devastated by a series of earthquakes that left in their wake an epidemic of the plague.[14] Even Vergennes came down with a fever which left him so weak he could hardly stand.[15] Confronted with these catastrophes, the Ottoman government understandably found the suggestion to go to war somewhat remote. Furthermore, Vergennes found it extremely difficult to approach Turks of influence with the arguments suggested by Choiseul. The Turks were simply too vain to respond the way Choiseul assumed they would. If any Turkish official tried to tell the Sultan that his prestige had fallen, Vergennes told Versailles, the result would not be a war on Russia, but the news that the official's head had fallen. Moreover, the Turks would never forgive a foreigner who dared to suggest that their internal administration suffered from weaknesses. Nevertheless, Vergennes assured Choiseul he would do his best, but he reminded him that "it is no more in my power to change and reform the constitution of this country than it is to give to those who administer it the qualities which they lack."[16] Obviously, the ambassador and the Minister of Foreign Affairs were not getting any closer to agreement about the policy to be followed at Constantinople.

By 1767, the tension between Choiseul and Vergennes reached the breaking point. Unable to make his superior in the ministry understand why he could not accomplish at Constantinople everything demanded of him, Vergennes turned to the king. Vergennes had sent Louis XV all of his correspondence with Choiseul, and through the channel of the secret diplomacy he tried to justify his actions. In February of 1767 he wrote: "The approval which you deigned to give me for my efforts to convince the Ottoman ministers to embark on a policy which the glory and security of the administration of their Empire dictates is a glorious testimony to your clemency." It was difficult to convince the Porte of the validity of the French argument, he explained, when the Turks so obviously did not wish to interrupt the tranquillity they enjoyed and which the Empire needed. "Your Majesty will have seen in my correspondence with the Duc de Choiseul," Vergennes continued, "that I have never lost from view the goals which you have assigned to my zeal."

He always tried to lead the Porte's attention back to the ambitious enterprises of the Russians, and he had changed his tactics over and over again to fit the circumstances. He felt he had made some progress in getting the Porte to protest when the Russians forced the Poles to accept an unfavorable boundary agreement. But beyond this meager victory, he confessed, he was unable to go. In fact, he suspected that the Turks did not really care if Poland were reduced to chaos. The religious dissentions in Poland, the destruction by the Russians of the Polish administration, only reduced the Turks' fears that, if the Poles ever became strong, they would war against the Ottoman Empire. Vergennes pled with Louis not to attribute to negligence the slow progress of events. "I never lose any occasion to enlighten the ministers of the Divan, and to encourage them, but I cannot make them do any more than they are inclined to do."[17]

In another letter to his sovereign, Vergennes was pathetic in his attempt at self justification. "I surely cannot reproach myself for neglecting anything in trying to inspire the Turks to a sentiment that would be the most notable, the most elevated, and the most adapted to the circumstances, but the conversion of wills is a supernatural task." He was not exaggerating. Time and again, either personally or through his *drogman* Duval, he tried to persuade the Turks that it was in their interests to go to war against Russia.[18]

When the Comte de Broglie took over the direction of the secret correspondance early in 1767, after the death of Tercier, Vergennes also turned to him and asked for advice. He wanted Broglie's respect and affection, he claimed, and he wanted his help.[19] But the only thing Vergennes received through the network of the secret diplomacy was further exhortations to work harder. The King assured him that he was satisfied with his endeavors. "I exhort you, however, in no way to relax your usual activities in order to move the Ottoman ministry. It is evident that Russia fears its awakening, and that Europe can only gain some advantage from their anxieties in this regard."[20]

But Vergennes could offer no hope. The Turks' "softness," their "indifference" and their obvious weakness and need to continue the *status quo,* frustrated his every effort. Choiseul, he told the King, simply could not understand why the ministers of a great power such as the Porte could not share his own zeal, dignity, and fervor. Choiseul, Vergennes claimed, therefore blamed his ambassador. He admitted his own insufficiencies, but he pointed out that there were other obstacles to his success and some of them were the work of the Turks, and not the result of his own incapacity.[21]

Although affairs of high politics grew daily more pressing, the "little day-to-day" matters continued to demand their measure of attention. A *drogman* of the French consulate at Alexandria was arrested, and put in irons to be transported to Constantinople, on the charge of having deliberately created a rice famine by means of a monopolistic control over the market.[22] Vergennes, ever alert to protect the French business interests in the Levant, protested the *drogman's* innocence to the Porte. The Porte's reaction was immediate and sharp: "The Grand Seigneur is a prince who seeks on his own to get to the bottom of everything and His Highness is convinced of the guilt of the *drogman.*"[23] Vergennes, indignant, asked for and received advice from Versailles and then took the routine steps,[24] to obtain the *drogman's* release. But his efforts were fruitless. The Turks allowed the prisoner to move into more spacious quarters and permitted the Ambassador to send him food. But the concessions were empty ones, for the *drogman,* severely weakened by the prison experience, died. The Ambassador reclaimed the body and arranged a Christian burial.[25] The suffering and death of the unfortunate *drogman* pierced the diplomat's official armour and touched his heart. "My sole consolation," he reflected in one of those rare moments when his human feelings are revealed in an official document, "is that, in sickness and in health, he lacked none of the help that humanity and compassion required that he be given."[26]

In spite of his own reservations, Vergennes followed orders and dutifully worked to lead the Turks into a war. He succeeded in getting them to accept the idea of a protest to the Poles on projected cessions of territory to Russia, but nothing significant came of it even though Louis XV was pleased by this "essential step."[27] Relentlessly, Choiseul continued to drive home his idea that the Turks must attack and, as the Turks refused do so, he grew more and more impatient. Once, after reading a dispatch in which Vergennes repeated the now familiar theme that the Turks were deaf to the idea of war, Choiseul broke into a rage and sat down and wrote his ambassador: "All of this dispatch, which contains nothing but hackneyed and loose reasoning, deserves no other response than the instruction to continue to try to make the Porte understand that, in the interest of foresight, they ought to show some movement."[28] Vergennes, frantic, could only answer, "The Ottoman ministers are very pleased with the information I communicate to them; but they pay no attention whatsoever to the reflections which accompany it." "It seems," he concluded, "that the Porte has decided to abandon Poland to herself."[29]

But Choiseul would not accept Vergennes' estimate of the situation. He grew daily more irritated with the unacceptable advice coming from his representative at Constantinople, whose dispatches, he later complained, "were only amplifications of rhetoric." He had had enough, also, of Vergennes' hesitations and negative attitude. What France needed near the Sultan was someone more aggressive and with more initiative; someone, apparently, who could take the Sultan by the scruff of the neck and pitch him bodily into a war with Russia. Vergennes was not that person. On April 25, 1768, Choiseul gave notice to his ambassador of his decision to recall him.[30] "The King," he wrote, "considering that the duration of your mission has already greatly exceeded the ordinary term, and that your health has for sometime suffered from frequent illnesses which ought to make you desire a rest; His Majesty has decided to make it possible for you to enjoy one by granting you your recall." Vergennes' successor, Choiseul continued, would be the Chevalier de Saint-Priest.[31] Fourteen years of difficult service to the King of France at a post which most diplomats would have considered equivalent to exile was thus abruptly and without forewarning brought to a close.[32]

In the meantime, the Russians consolidated their grip on Poland. The first effective opposition to them developed not at Constantinople but in Poland. In 1768, a small band of Polish nobles and gentry gathered at the little fortress of Bar in Podolia.[33] Their purpose was to form a confederation to defend the independence of Poland against the domination of Russia.[34] At the same time, the Polish Diet began to indicate that it, too, found the Russian yoke too oppressive. They voted a strong resolution asking for the evacuation of Russian troops. In addition, the Polish Senate made no attempt to hide its resentment of Catherine's attempt to impose religious tolerance in Poland. Stanislas, also irked by Catherine's constant interference, was inclined at first to try to mediate between the Confederation of Bar and Russia. But he was in no position to play middle man and, finally, reluctantly, he ordered his armies to Bar to put down the rebellion.

Stanislas' soldiers easily captured the fortress of Bar, but they failed to subdue the rebellion. Instead, the Polish King was soon confronted with an even larger insurrection of nobles combined with peasants. A more indigenous and, therefore, more difficult to control, internal war quickly spread throughout eastern Poland and Lithuania. The ruthlessness of eighteenth-century diplomacy, the high stakes involved, plus the fact that the least important internal rebellion against a government had, or could have, international repercussions, made the next moves in the chain reaction almost inevitable. The Confederation of Bar appealed for outside help. France sent agents to assist the Confederates and, if possible, to reconcile King Stanislas and the rebels.[35] A French secret agent at Vienna reported that every day more and more rumors were circulating that the Porte was considering breaking relations with Russia.[36] A small stream of war *matériel* began to trickle over the Turkish-Polish frontier. Russian troops, under the orders of the relentless Repnin, poured into the Polish provinces to demonstrate brutally what it was like to become a Russian satellite.[37] As he watched the Russians crush the Poles, Frederick of Prussia decided he had either to stop Catherine before she conquered the entire Polish Republic, or else to get something out of the situation for himself: he preferred to get something for himself. Poland, long the cockpit of diplomatic maneuvering by the Great Powers, was on her way to becoming a victim of balance-of-power politics. Gradually, irrevocably, the Polish crisis (to use a modern term to describe an old phenomenon) became "internationalized."

At Constantinople, Vergennes, now recalled but awaiting his replacement, continued to press for war. A contingent of Russian soldiers in pursuit of a band of Polish rebels crossed the Turkish frontier, burned the Turkish town of Balta, and provided a Russian provocation the Sultan could not ignore.[38] On October 6, 1768, well over a month before Vergennes' replacement, Saint-Priest, arrived at Constantinople, the *Grand Vizir* called the Russian minister to the Seraglio and brusqely informed him that the Sultan, angered by the presence of Russian troops on Turkish soil in violation of the Russo-Turkish treaty of 1764, had decided to declare war.[39] Then, in return for the Russian insult to the Sultan's dignity, the *Grand Vizir* ordered the Russian minister and all his staff arrested and made prisoners of state, a provoction which Catherine could not ignore.[40] Choiseul now had the war he so much wanted.

"So war is declared!" the delighted Choiseul wrote to Vergennes and Saint-Priest, "It was the primary objective of all our wishes. The second [objective] is to fight it."[41] Choiseul never saw the fulfillment of the second objective.

When the Sultan declared war on Russia, his armies were totally unprepared to undertake military operations; they had neither the money, the *matériel,* nor the generals needed to fight Russians and protect the Poles. The Baron de Tott, who accompanied Vergennes to Constantinople, worked long and hard training the Turks to use and manufacture modern arms, especially artillery, but the Turks' war machine fell far short of battle readiness.[42] War could only bring a military collapse and a political disaster for the Ottoman Empire, followed by further expansion of Russia, the eventuality Choiseul presumably was trying to prevent. On the river Dniester, at Choczim, in Moldavia and Wallachia, when the Russians struck, the Turks' armies folded.[43] In February, 1769, Austrian troops gave a preview of things to come by occupying the Polish county of Zips. A few weeks later, Joseph II of Austria and Frederick met at Neisse in Silesia to talk and ponder the mutual advantages both parties could gain if they settled their differences.[44] The stage was set for the first partition of Poland.

The Turks were saved from a catastrophic defeat by the sacrifice of Poland.[45] The Russians knew that if they followed up their victories, crossed the Danube and penetrated deep into the Balkans, the Austrians would most probably enter the war against them, not because the Austrians wished to protect the Ottoman Empire, but because they, too, had designs on the Sultan's territories, and could not permit Russia to take more than her share. Frederick, too far away to benefit from a division of Turkish lands, nevertheless feared an upset in the balance of power in eastern Europe.[46] To prevent an Austro-Russian war over the failing Ottoman Empire, and to protect his own position in the balance of power, Frederick urged that the Turkish sick man be left unmolested while the three powers, Russia, Prussia and Austria, partitioned Poland. The two other powers accepted Frederick's invitation and, by 1773, the first partition of Poland was complete. After two further partitions, Poland was carved into nothing; by 1795, she had disappeared from the map of Europe.

The sacrifice of Poland, however, did not permit the Turkish Empire to escape completely unscathed. In the peace Treaty of Küchük Kainarji of 1774, the Russians forced the Turks to allow Russian ships freely to navigate the Black Sea, the Bosphorus, and the Dardanelles Straits; they obliged the Sultan to renounce his sovereignty over the Black Sea Tartars, and they gained acceptance at the Seraglio of the idea of Russia as a protector of Christianity at Constantinople.[47] The Treaty of Küchük Kainarji opened the door of Russian commercial and political expansion southward, and made possible Russian interference in Turkish affairs under the guise of protecting Christians. Russian expansion in any of these areas represented a severe setback for French interests.[48] The Russo-Turkish war changed the political structure of Europe.[49]

Choiseul dug the grave under Poland. He was not, to be sure, the only grave digger at work, but he deserves some measure of responsibility for the partition of Poland, because his thoughtless insistance on a Turkish war against Russia helped to produce the conditions which made the partition feasible.[50] There was very little he could do about Russian domination of Poland, but he could have avoided opening the door to the total disappearance of that Republic. Furthermore, the Ottoman Empire would have suffered a greater defeat than it did if the carving up of Poland had not distracted the eastern powers. Why had Choiseul so recklessly insisted that the Turks gamble with disaster?

It is difficult to suppose that he believed the Turks could effectively wage war against Russia. His ambassador at Constantinople had certainly seen the flabbiness of Turkish power, and Vergennes repeated over and over again in his dispatches that the Turks needed peace. Saint-Priest, his successor at the Porte, recalled that Vergennes' persistent hesitations about suddenly pushing the Turks into a war sprang solely from his recognition that the weakness and ineptitude of the Ottoman government would result in the crushing of Turkey,[51] and consequently, in an increase in Russian power. The prediction proved painfully true. To be sure, the classical "Turkish diversion" to check Russian expansion had been an old and proven instrument of French diplomacy, but by 1768, it had lost its efficacy. Even Louis XV, whose knowledge of affairs was certainly not impressive, saw that the Turks could do very little to save the Poles.[52] Yet Choiseul showed an amazing unconcern about the probable costs and consequences of his policy. He even told Vergennes, it will be remembered, that whether or not the Turks enjoyed a final victory in the war "did not interest" France. In the last analysis, Choiseul's plan for a Turkish war against Russia was but an irresponsible adventure.[53] In allowing his minister to pursue such a policy, Louis XV must have mistaken the man's cynicism and energy for political realism.

There is a sound argument, of course, that it was the Sultan, and not Choiseul, who really committed the blunder of going to war; and, indeed, in the last analysis, the decision was his. But Choiseul, as well as Vergennes, knew that political decisions at Constantinople were often the result of personal whim or ill-considered impulse, and Choiseul should have been working to reduce the number of such decisions rather than increase them.[54]

Vergennes' role in the Turkish disaster was ambivalent. Certainly he was Choiseul's reluctant accomplice. His dispatches to Choiseul-Praslin during 1764 indicate that, at that time, he favoured a Turkish war as a way of stopping Russian expansion. But within two years (by the time of Choiseul's return to the Ministry of Foreign Affairs), he had arrived at the conclusion that the Turks were not prepared, and that a war would be disastrous. From then on, his position did not change. While his correspondence with his superior was usually courteous and respectful, he did not varnish the facts to please Versailles. Occasionally his tone even trespassed the limits of courtesy to drive home the point that he could not provide the Turks with qualities and means which they did not possess. Yet, despite his reservations, he remained until his recall, the obedient servant, and worked to fulfill his instructions. Thus he, too, however unwillingly, contributed to the war which Ottoman Empire was in no position to fight. Moreover, when he returned to Versailles, after his recall, he was not above accepting praise for having helped bring on the war which he had opposed.[55]

Vergennes never clarified his and France's role in urging the Turks to war. Years later, he even denied that he had done anything at all to influence the Porte to go to war. While asking for aid from France, a Turkish prince later reminded Louis XVI that Vergennes had been instrumental in determining his father to declare the disastrous war on Russia.[56] Apparently puzzled by the Turk's insistence on France's responsibility, Louis XVI consulted Vergennes, now his Secretary of State for Foreign Affairs. The conclusions Louis XVI sent to the prince are astounding: "It appears to us, after a thorough examination, that the dead Emperor [sic] of France did not take it upon himself to determine the Glorious Father of Your Imperial Highness to attack the Russians . . ."[57]

Part III

IN AND OUT OF RETIREMENT

CHAPTER 12

Recall

His recall marked the end of an important phase of Vergennes' diplomatic career. It also meant an upheaval in his personal affairs. Little is known about his private thoughts or life up to this point, but it is a certainty that to bring to a sudden close the work of fourteen years in a foreign capital could not fail to create considerable confusion in his private arrangements. In addition, Vergennes had special problems, over and above the ordinary ones associated with a diplomatic transfer. Once again, the contents of the diplomatic pouch give us a rare glimpse of the man's personal life.

In a dispatch dated May 31, 1768, Vergennes wrote that Choiseul had told him, in his letter of recall, to come back to France on the return voyage of the ship bringing his replacement, but "I dare to expose to you an embarrassment in which I find myself, and which afflicts me deeply."[1]

"It is my luck," he revealed to Choiseul, "that my wife is pregnant, and if appearances are correct, the time of her delivery will be around the end of December or the first of January." According to Vergennes' calculations, Saint-Priest could not possibly arrive before September; and it would take at least forty days to introduce the new ambassador to the local situation and to see him through his accreditation. Considering all this, Vergennes could not expect to be ready to return to France before mid-November, and that was the stormiest season of the year. He did not wish to expose his wife, possibly at the risk of her life, to a difficult voyage in the eighth month of her pregnancy. He could, of course, leave her at Constantinople to follow him after the birth of the child, if the King found his immediate return necessary, but he preferred to stay with her if he could get permission to do so.[2] He hoped to charter a merchant ship and return to France in the spring. Although he admitted he would have to have some financial "assistance" to carry out his plan, he agreed that he could not expect to receive the regular earnings of an ambassador. But he was willing to sacrifice earnings in order to be with his wife.

In Ancien-Régime diplomacy, as in Ancien-Régime aristocracy, there was a right and a wrong way to get married. The marriage of an ambassador required the permission of the King. The diplomatic documents contain no evidence of the steps necessary for such an important ceremony; Vergennes was married *without* Louis XV's permission. Furthermore, his wife Anne Viviers was a commoner, a widow and a woman with a rather spicy reputation in Constantinople circles.

Although Choiseul condemned the marriage as "precipitous," it was, in fact, overdue. The marriage contract, dated March 9, 1767, reveals that the man and wife already had two sons out of wedlock, one aged six and the other nearly two.[3] The contract states that the two parties, Charles Gravier de Vergennes and Anne Viviers, desired to execute the reciprocal promises they had made to each other to unite in the sacrament of marriage, which they "had not been able to do until the present for reasons which they did not wish to explain." They wished to recognize their two sons: one born October 31, 1761, "Baptized at the Church of Sainte Marie of the Vines at Pera," named Constantin; and the other named Louis Charles Joseph, born March 17, 1765, and baptized on the 18th at the home of Anne Viviers by the curé of the parish. The contract expressed their intention to legitimatize the sons by a marriage celebrated in church.[4]

Vergennes agreed that he was "content and satisfied" with the token dowry of 10,000 Levantine *piastres* in promissary notes. Both also expressly agreed that there should be no community of property between them. To his future wife, Vergennes promised to give 2,400 *livres* yearly income, plus his furniture, as his share of the marriage settlement.[5] Furthermore, Madame Viviers would live during her lifetime in a furnished apartment at Vergennes' chateau at Toulongeon, or in a furnished house of her choice belonging to him. And, if she wished to establish herself in the country, she should have the use of the gardens and lower courts without having to pay the upkeep. She would also be furnished wood for her heat and that of her domestic help. The contract was signed in the presence of Antoine Viviers, Secretary of the husband and French ambassador, and Alexander Philibert Duval, Secretary-Interpreter and First *Drogman* of France.[6]

Vergennnes' relations with Anne Viviers present a side of his character we have not heretofore met. As an ambassador, he gave the appearance of having renounced the friendship of ordinary human beings in exchange for their deference. His secretary, M. de Lancey, found Vergennes quite accomplished as a man of the world "with the *politesse* and ease of a gallant," and he felt that, if Vergennes had undertaken to seduce the Lucretias of his day with as much dexterity and skill as he put into negotiations, they would not dare boast of having more virtue than the Romans. "He sees them, voluntarily," Lancey tattled, "but only when he is obliged to receive them. They are still captivated by the magnificent ball he gave this carnival." [In] broad daylight, with M le brigadier de Tott and several other equally respectable people, he went to a dinner where the most amiable Levantine-Frankish ladies were assembled." "It seems to me," Lancey judged with the confidence of a *connoisseur,* "that he prefers the company of the prettiest and most amusing in conversation," yet Lancey concluded, "he enjoys this pleasure too rarely to captivate them."[7]

But Vergennes' relations with Anne Viviers were different. In a note dated January, 1760, he revealed how deeply he felt about her: "Wishing to give to Madame the widow Testa the most certain proof of the tender esteem and affection which I have for her, I promise her under the most holy oaths and most sacred engagements of my honor to take her for my wife, to marry her in the church, and to declare her my legitimate wife as soon as I can return to France, or sooner if it can be done, in faith of which I give her the present promise which I pray her to keep absolutely secret, and which I have signed with my hand and sealed with my coat of arms."[8]

The secrecy and mystery surrounding the relationship between Anne Viviers and Vergennes can easily be explained by the fact that the woman's rank in society did not match her charms. Vergennes' nineteenth-century biographers always referred to her as Madame *de* Viviers, and called her brother, later a French diplomat, Claude Antoine *de* Viviers. But their baptismal acts, her marriage registration, and the marriage contract to which her brother was a witness, all list them both as simply Anne Vivier, or Anne Viviers widow of Testa, and Claude Antoine Viviers, the nobiliary particles being absent from documents which most certainly would have recorded them, had the Viviers had the right to use them.[9] Furthermore, one Jean Antoine Monet, who claimed to have known Anne's father, refers to him in a sworn statement as "D'Vivier bourgeois." Dame Anne Viviers was not, therefore, the daughter of a "petit gentilhomme," but the daughter of a commoner. It is not surprising, therefore, that Vergennes had not asked the King for permission to marry; he had known he would be refused.

Anne Viviers was born at Pera, was baptized in the parish of St. Antoine of Pera, and before her marriage to Vergennes she was the widow of a doctor Testa. Her baptismal act gives her date of birth as January 28, 1730.[10] But in 1779, her brother, (perhaps to oblige his sister) claimed that she was not born until February of 1738.[11] Certainly she was a mature woman when she married Vergennes. Her portrait, painted by Antoine Favray, shows her to have been a small, round, almost voluptuous woman, with serene eyes, a wistful feminine face, and soft, exquisite hands. A widow, and the mother of two sons, she was no longer a young girl, but she was not without beauty.

Her maturity, however, did not protect her from the sharp and spiteful tongues of the gossips in the social circles of Pera. Her reputation, no doubt, is a further explanation of why Vergennes could not risk asking the King for permission to marry her. Certainly it explains why he never introduced her into diplomatic society as the ambassadress after the marriage. His liaison with her was as discreet and private as it is possible for such affairs to be.

Madame de Vergennes' reputation and her low origin were to plague them both for the rest of their days. And as his career advanced from diplomat to minister, the question of his wife's position in society and at the court came up again and again. Even before their marriage, they had had a taste of the cruel treatment they could expect from society, in an incident involving Madame Chenier, the mother of the famous French poet, André Chenier. The Cheniers had long been part of the French community at Pera, and one day Madame Chenier received an invitation from the French ambassador to enjoy a boat promenade on the Bosphorus. She accepted the invitation, but was surprised, on entering the boat, that two velvet cushions had been prepared side by side. One was for Madame Chenier and the other was for Vergennes' friend, Anne Viviers. Madame Chenier was thoroughly insulted. That she should be expected to sit next to Anne Viviers was more than she could bear. She drew herself up in disdain, threw her velvet cushion to the other end of the boat, and marched back and sat on it, alone, during the entire trip.[12] From that day on, the future Comtesse de Vergennes had little love for the Cheniers.

Why did Vergennes, always so alert to avoid any blunder that might impede advancement in his career, consent to marry Anne Viviers? The answer is simple, although it is not one that would have met with general approval in eighteenth-century noble society: he loved her, he loved the children she bore him, and both his religion and his conscience demanded that he recognize his responsibilities. In a letter to his friend M. de Tott, he discussed his motives with a sincerity that rings true: "If I have not spoken to you before, Monsieur, of the change in my status, it is not because I distrusted the interest you would take in it. Your friendship for me and your integrity assure me that you are not one of those who would censor me for an act which my religion and my affections have necessitated. I have acknowledged two handsome children of whom the older, who is in his sixth year, has a promising disposition. I could not acknowledge the children without making known the mother; my precipitation has brought me well-merited reproaches . . .; but certainly, if I had hesitated any longer it would have been at the cost of my existence. My health is still recovering from the conflicts I imposed on myself by resisting the natural bent of my heart." The diplomat and aristocrat was caught in the age-old conflict between rank and duty and the need for love and affection. To escape the agony of choosing, he submerged his personal life in secrecy. The result was personal agony and guilt.

"I am very happy in my new state," he told Tott, "My spouse, who has the honor of being known by you, is more dear to me than she has ever been, and

I dote on my children. Secluded in my home, I enjoy an intense peace of soul and the sweet consolation of loving and being loved."[13]

The only trace of the Vergennes' marriage in the diplomatic correspondence is a reference of Choiseul to a letter written by Vergennes April 10, 1767 (the letter itself has disappeared), in which Vergennes announced that the marriage had already taken place.[14] In the dispatch sent less than a week after his marriage, Vergennes mentions nothing but official business.[15] Choiseul chastised Vergennes for his failure to ask the King's permission to marry. "In doing what regulations prescribe," Choiseul wrote, "and what you owe, perhaps as much out of recognition to the King as to your position, your heart would have been able to enjoy an unmixed contentment." Choiseul told his ambassador, nevertheless, that Louis had granted him permission to make public "the marriage you have contracted with a person of a free and honest condition."[16]

Now Choiseul obliged his recalled ambassador and allowed him to remain at Constantinople, but, by the time the letter arrived, the special arrangements were unnecessary. "It has pleased God," Vergennes wrote Choiseul, "to settle things another way." "The motive which had determined me to pass the winter here no longer exists," Vergennes explained to his friend Tott in July of 1768, "my wife having had last month a painful miscarriage for which I must, however, give thanks to God, for there was reason to fear that, if her pregnancy had lasted any longer, it would have cost her life."[17]

But Choiseul did not permit Vergennes' failure to ask the King's permission to be married to go unchallenged. To the Minister of Foreign Affairs, the irregularity of the Ambassador's marriage was just one more example of Vergennes' negligence, and it irritated him.

Vergennes' marriage to Anne Viviers has often been cited as the explanation for his sudden recall from Constantinople in the spring of 1768. And there is no doubt that such an unfortunate marriage was sufficient grounds for recalling a diplomat. If one of his diplomatic representatives became the laughing-stock of diplomatic circles or the object of derision among Europe's aristocrats, the King's prestige suffered and the diplomat's effectiveness was reduced. And, despite his own weakness for women of questionable reputation, Louis XV insisted on a rather puritanical standard for others. He later condemned Madame de Vergennes as that "*vilaine femme.*"[18] Furthermore, there was time between Vergennes' public celebration of his marriage on March 9, 1767, and his recall, dated April 25,1768, for the news of his act to have filtered back to Versailles to influence the King's decision. But, if the marriage was the sole cause for the recall, there was a surprising lapse of time between the cause and the effect.

Moreover, a letter written by Louis XV to Vergennes after his recall indicates that the King was never dissatisfied with his ambassador at Constantinople. In this letter, the King assured Vergennes of "the satisfaction I have had with your conduct during your stay at the Porte, and of the loyalty and discretion with which you have kept the secret [the *secret du roi*] which I confided in you . . ."[19] He then asked Vergennes to compose a memorandum on the state of affairs in Turkey, to be given to the director of his secret diplomacy, the Comte de Broglie, for future use by Saint-Priest, who had now been initiated into the secret.[20] The most interesting part of the letter, however, is Louis' explanation for Vergennes' recall. Not only did he reveal that Choiseul was responsible for it, but, by implication, he indicated to what extent Choiseul had succeeded in gathering the reins of government into his own hands. Louis told his Ambassador that he had consented to the action "only on the representations which M. le duc de Choiseul made to me of the desire you had several times expressed to obtain it . . ."[21] In fact, Vergennes had never asked for recall; the idea was Choiseul's from conception to final decision.

Vergennes' marriage may have influenced Choiseul's decision, but one need only follow the written exchanges between the two men from 1766, when Choiseul returned to the Ministry of Foreign Affairs, to the time of Vergennes' dismissal, to be convinced that there were other, more fundamental, differences between them. Vergennes obeyed the orders forwarded to him by Choiseul, but he did so reluctantly, and he made his reluctance known at Versailles. Basically, the two men differed on matters of policy, and the frictions caused by these policy differences generated a personal hostility between them, a hostility which broke into open expression in their correspondence. Vergennes' subsequent recall was the final act in this personal and political conflict. It was, therefore, not simply a routine recall; it was a personal and political disgrace.[22]

Vergennes' sympathizers have denied the conclusion that Vergennes returned in disfavor, by maintaining that, since he succeeded in driving the Turks to war, Choiseul had no good reason to condemn his actions. But, in the spring of 1768, when he was recalled, it was not apparent that the Turks would go to war that fall, and it was very apparent that the ambassador at Constantinople did not agree with the Minister of Foreign Affairs. Choiseul's condemnation of Vergennes to Saint-Priest is sufficient proof that the minister was dissatisfied with his representative. Furthermore, Vergennes himself knew that he had been recalled in disfavor, and his own awareness of his status overrides the opinion of his well-wishers. In a letter to Broglie, he referred to his recall as *un rappel brusque* "which I attest to you, Monsieur, I neither asked for nor provoked."[23] He never forgot the manner of his recall and, years later, he remembered it with the following words written to his King. Speaking of the childish behaviour of a French ambassador *he* had just brought home for committing a serious blunder,

Vergennes said: "I, too, Sire, have had the misfortune of being recalled, *et très brusquement.*"[24] When Vergennes returned to France, he returned in disfavor, as far as official Versailles was concerned.

In fact, the ambassador had to be punished because his superiors at Versailles could not understand that the Ottoman Empire could no longer serve French diplomacy as it had in the past. The Turks had become, as Vergennes described them, "soft"; they could not stop the Russian advance. French policy at Constantinople had been reduced to a frantic gamble, and France had lost. Thereafter, until the end of the eighteenth century, French diplomacy in the Ottoman Empire was a makeshift delaying action, until Europe found another solution to the "Eastern Question."

The fumblings of French diplomacy at Constantinople, however, were not simply the consequences of Russian power and Turkish weakness. The results of the Diplomatic Revolution, the absurdity of Louis XV's "secret" diplomacy, the contradictions it created in the Polish election and in French relations with the Ottoman Empire, and Choiseul's ill-considered demands for a Russo-Turkish war at all costs, must also be weighed as factors contributing to the confusion in French-Ottoman Empire relations between 1754 and 1768.

CHAPTER 13

To Stockholm

Vergennes left Constantinople with mixed feelings. "I am content to see dawning the hope of a personal tranquillity which is necessary to the preservation of my individual well-being," he wrote his friend Tott. "I will not leave here, however, without regrets." During his many years at Constantinople, he had formed deep friendships among the other diplomats, his staff, including Tott, and even among the Turks, some of whom he had known for years. He was not exaggerating when he told Tott that many of the Turkish ministers, *"les grands"* as well as *"les petits,"* had been sincerely pained by his recall. Also, the French "nation," that is, the businessmen and merchants at Constantinople, had great respect for his competence and judgment. Before he departed, they demonstrated their esteem by presenting him with a golden sword with an exquisitely sculptured golden handle.[1]

Still, the post at the Porte had cost him much, both physically and financially. The unhealthy living conditions, the pressures of his assignment, and repeated illnesses had sapped his energies, and his long separation from France had prevented any efficient management of his estates. "Monsieur le duc de Choiseul has had the kindness to assure me," he explained to Tott, "that His Majesty would demonstrate to me his bountifulness and the satisfaction he has with my services. I have great need of them; not only am I not rich, but I am not comfortably well off. The work here at Constantinople has ruined my health. That is about the only real thing I have earned here."[2] Even after he had spent a hard winter in Stockholm, he still did not regret leaving Turkey.[3]

Vergennes departed for France in January of 1769, aboard the French frigate, *La Sultane*.[4] Upon arrival, he made his final reports to the Ministry of Foreign Affairs, and retired to his estates at Toulongeon near Autun in Burgundy with a pension of 12,000 *livres* plus an extraordinary gratuity of 30,000 *livres*.[5] There, according to one of his biographers, he dedicated himself "entirely to the education of his children, and to the surveillance of his lands."[6] "Happy to be forgotton," wrote another, "he looked neither to the capital nor the court."[7]

These generalizations contain a certain amount of truth. His letters to his son reveal a father who is sincerely concerned about the education of his children. "Profit, my dear Constantin," he said in one letter to his oldest son, "from the kindnesses of M. the Abbé [the boy's tutor, the Abbé Baudet], be docile to his instructions. I willingly flatter myself that I will see the fruits of your applications upon my return, which is not far away."[8] "You are entering the age where you can apply yourself and make progress," he counseled in another letter, "don't waste this precious time which will influence the rest of your life."[9] He was not always so gentle, however. "You must work," he chided his son, "to extirpate the germ of indolence, about which I am sometimes obliged to reproach you"[10] or: "You write to me of your plans to apply yourself with ardor, but why don't you ever tell me that you have begun to do so, or is it that you are so modest that you do not wish to brag . . . We are beginning, my dear friend, a new year; let's get rid of all the infantilisms of the closing one, and arm ourselves with courage for the next."[11] Sometimes, he was almost pleased. "If the letter you have written me is really your own work," he told Constantin, "I am optimistic about the order and clearness that dominates it."[12] And: "You have begun to justify the hopes I have in you . . . ."[13] In all of this advice, Vergennes reveals himself as the true descendant of working magistrates of the courts at Dijon; or indeed, even as a bourgeois "Papa" preparing his son for a career as a substantial member of the governing classes. Later, he did everything possible to facilitate his son's entrance into the military aristocracy and the irresponsible Court life at Versailles, but his present intent was to educate him for a life of service and hard work, to play the role of "*homme raisonnable.*"[14]

In his relations with his wife, Vergennes does not fit the stereotype of the courtly noblemen who idled away their time in dalliance with each others' wives and mistresses. There is a simple tenderness in his urging Constantin, when Madame de Vergennes was ill, to "exhort her, I pray you, to take care of her health as she takes care of yours."[15] Apparently, Madame de Vergennes' health was delicate, for her husband's letters frequently showed a concern about her cold or her melancholia, or reveal pleasure in the fact that her health has been restored, or that she was sleeping and eating well.[16] Vergennes' sincere concern for his wife became the occasion for jokes and mockery among the cynical courtiers at Versailles, but, throughout his life, he treated her with a steady and gentle affection and respect. At Toulongeon, they had the opportunity to know each other more intimately than they had ever had when he was ambassador of France and she was his mistress or secret wife.

But it is difficult to imagine the ex-ambassador resigning himself completely to vegetating in domestic or bucolic peace, and his letters of the period prove that he did not do so. He often visited Paris and the Court. He was a member of a secret organization that gave him access to the King, and he was too ambitious to allow such relations to wither.

After his recall from Constantinople, he made it clear to Louis XV that he wished to continue in his career of public service. In a letter to Louis XV, he wrote: "If I should ever be so happy that Your Majesty would once again want my services, I dare to protest to you in all truth that there is nothing that would keep me from flying immediately to the execution of your orders. My strongest, I can say my unique, passion is to have the honor of serving you. Loyal to your orders, Your Majesty can be assured that I will not keep with less fidelity, on my return to France, the Secret into which it has pleased you to admit me, and that I have kept during my stay in Turkey."[17]

Later, early in 1770, Vergennes once again expressed his desire to return to the diplomatic service, in a request to Choiseul to find him a post, a request which Choiseul received with cold indifference. But Vergennes persevered. "If I expressed to you a desire to continue in a diplomatic career," he answered Choiseul, "it was only in the hope that you would acknowledge and second it. [But] you have answered, Monsieur le duc, in such a way as to render the hope either very feeble, or very uncertain, in telling me that you would gladly find the occasion to put my request before the King's eyes. This cold response on your part, given to someone with thirty years of service, who has just spent fourteen years in a painful assignment amidst the most difficult and the most critical circumstances, and, finally, someone who can claim some good services; this response leaves me in a state of uncertainty. If I must consider your response more a refusal than an encouragement . . .I dare, Monsieur le duc, to demand of you an explanation . . . .I am approaching the age when a wise man ought to be thinking of planning for the future."[18]

But Choiseul showed neither official encouragement nor human sympathy. From behind the protection of his high position, he continued to wound with the weapon of official correctness. "I received, Monsieur," he replied, "the letter with which you honored me the eighth of this month. My answer was the only one my ministry permits me to make, and such as you should have expected. You are not ignorant of the fact, Monsieur, that it is the King who assigns places in the Department of Foreign Affairs, and that the supreme will of His Majesty is my law. And you understand that I cannot make any formal appointments of aspirants to posts, no matter what opinion I may have of the talents of some of them in particular."[19]

Hurt by Choiseul's studied cruelty, Vergennes, nevertheless, refused to give up. A few months later, he sent to Choiseul and the duc de Praslin copies of France's capitulations with the Porte, and again expressed the wish that, even in his retreat, he hoped to "merit the continuation" of Choiseul's "kindnesses."[20] But Vergennes' efforts changed not in the least Choiseul's dislike of his former colleague. Still the diplomat refused to retire into oblivion. He continued, whenever he could, to use his dwindling influence to gain favors for French businessmen, officers, and agents in the Levant,[21] and he kept abreast of the wind changes at Versailles. Furthermore, many of his letters to his son were written from Paris, where Chavigny was living in retirement. It is unbelievable that the conversations between uncle and nephew excluded politics and diplomacy, and talk about what was going on at Versailles.

From Paris, Vergennes could also easily maintain close contact with the Comte de Broglie and the King's secret diplomacy, and there is ample evidence that Broglie consulted him frequently, on questions pertaining to French policy in Eastern Europe and the Ottoman Empire.[22] His differences with Choiseul had by no means destroyed his connections. Vergennes enjoyed the tranquillity of country life when he was at Toulongeon, and he certainly welcomed the companionship of his family, but he never lost interest in affairs of state.

The seigneurie of Toulongeon which Vergennes acquired in 1764,[23] had several times been raised to the status of a *comté* by the kings of France, and in 1757 Louis XV, in a letter of patent issued in favor of the uncle Chavigny, once again gave the owner the right to the title of Comte de Toulongeon. In the same letter of patent, Chavigny, who was unmarried and childless, declared his brother, and after him, his nephew and his nephew's sons to be the legitimate heirs to the property.[24] In 1765, the land was once again raised to a *comté* and so registered at the Parlement of Dijon. This time the registration was in the names of Vergennes and his brother, Jean Gravier, President of the Chambre des Comptes at Dijon.[25] In 1771, just after Chavigny's death, Louis confirmed the transfer of the property and the title with another letter patent.[26] A few years later, in 1779, Louis XVI changed the name of the *comté* from Toulongeon to Vergennes,[27] and thus, this son of a minor *noblesse de robe* and his commoner-wife became Monsieur le Comte and Madame la Comtesse de Vergennes. The lands and the title were never enough to erase the taint of a misalliance, but, the family was steadily rising socially, and the people whom they had left behind could no longer hurt them.

Something of the quality of Vergennes' new social position may be assessed from a description of the property to which he had retreated. The château at Toulongeon was not enormous, but it was magnificently situated.[28] Around the buildings spread beautifully kept gardens, extending outward amid canals, fountains, and clipped trees, toward a terraced hill on the summit of which was a park. "The lands of Toulongeon," recorded a councillor of the Parlement, "are among the most beautiful of Autun."

Located in the parish of La Chapelle-sous-Uchon, the grounds of the château were entered through a long avenue bordered by trees and crossed here and there by a stream. Two other avenues, one leading to a nearby ice cave, and the other to the park on the hill, formed a fan-like pattern. The château itself was composed of two large buildings, four round slate-roofed towers, and four smaller lodgings roofed with lead tile. It was surrounded by a water-filled moat, over which a stone bridge had replaced an earlier drawbridge. The lower court of the château contained stables, granaries, a guard house, and a carriage house on its eastern side; in the southern wing there was a small chapel with a bell tower "to call the people to mass." A description written in 1757 mentions defensive cannonière and embrasures, but these are missing from later accounts.

The drawing room of the château had ceilings of rare woods, and parquet floors. The delicate cabinets, marble-topped tables, and handsome mirrors provided an atmosphere of quiet dignity. Three windows overlooked the grand avenue; three others opened into the inner court. A wide stone stairway swept upward to fourteen different apartments, seven on each of the second and third floors. The apartments were well furnished, and each one had its own water closet and wardrobe. As late as 1757, the upper part of the château had also housed an armory to be used for defense, but by 1765 this area had been converted into living quarters.

The estate extended over three thousand acres. As a seigneur, Vergennes held the power of high, medium, and low justice over the inhabitants, and received a revenue of at least 7,000 *livres* a year from seigneurial dues and obligations.

This, then, was the setting in which Vergennes managed his property, lived a quiet domestic life with his wife and children, and enjoyed the beauties of his gardens and of the Burgundian countryside. This was the home he left on his frequent visits to Paris and Versailles, and from which, one day in 1771, he was to leave and to rarely return for the rest of his life.

The task which was to return Vergennes to public life was the French ambassadorship to Sweden. France's influence in that nation to the north had become increasingly enfeebled, and Louis XV was searching for a veteran diplomat to represent him and, if possible, to reverse the trend.

The quality of Vergennes' assignment and the character of Gustavus III, the Swedish monarch with whom he was to be associated, can be appreciated only with a recapitulation of the history of Sweden during the fifty years following the Constitution of 1720.

The intent of the framers of this Constitution was quite clear: the king was to have no voice in the government. All power, according to the document, was vested in the Diet, consisting of the four Estates — the Nobles, the Clergy, the Bourgeoisie, and the Peasants. The Estates voted separately on every issue, and at least three of them had to give their assent before a law could be enacted. Such an unwieldy system could not but create problems. When the Diet was not in session, executive power was exercised by the Senate, a body of 24 members which jealously guarded its prerogatives and took every available opportunity to extend further its power. The members of the Senate were appointed by the king from among candidates chosen by the Nobles, Clergy, and Bourgeoisie. It is not surprising that they made certain that the monarch was unable to place any of his own men in the Senate.[29] Everywhere he turned, Sweden's king was hedged in by restrictions and laws which limited his role. He could appoint Nobles at his coronation; he presided over the Senate, and he could vote in it; but these functions were absolutely empty of power when it came to manipulating the reins of government, or exercising effective action in times of crisis.[30] The most sinister aspect of the Constitution of 1720, however, was that it could not be changed without the risk of war, for, in the Peace of Nystadt (1721), Russia had stamped her "guarantee" on its terms.[31] She was determined that never again would Sweden be united and made strong under an absolute monarch.

As if to compound the difficulties of an already overly complicated political system, the Swedes were also hopelessly divided into two distinct and hostile parties, the Caps and the Hats. The Caps were pro-Russian, received subsidies from St. Petersburg, and were generally cautious in foreign affairs, particularly when dealing with issues that might harm the interests of Russia. On the other hand, the Hats were aggressive, pro-French, and too willing to sacrifice peace in flamboyant bids for aggrandizement and glory. During the 1740's and 1750's, the Hats received millions of *livres* in subsidies from Versailles to finance their policies and assure loyalty to France. But in 1741, the Hats, who had gained political control in 1738, led Sweden into an ill-advised war with Russia.[32] The only thing that prevented an immediate and wholesale collapse of the unprepared Swedish armies was the fact that neither side dared confront the other for the first six months after the declaration of war. When the two armies did meet, the Russians routed the Swedes. Military activities then ceased while a tacit truce was being arranged by the French ambassador at St. Petersburg. Finally, with their soldiers demoralized and their navy riddled with disease, the Hats began to talk peace. Their skill at negotiation, and the fact that the Russians had domestic problems of their own, saved the Swedes from a crushing defeat.

Nevertheless, the Peace of Abo (1743) left Sweden now committed by treaty to her own destruction. The Russian Empress Elizabeth consented to restore to Sweden most of Finland, but she did so in exchange for the election of her cousin, Adolphus-Frederick, as the Swedish Crown Prince.[33] The reason behind Elizabeth's apparent leniency became clear when

Adolphus-Frederick succeeded King Frederick I in 1751. He revealed himself to be a non-entity who neither desired nor attempted to exercise any authority. He was eventually so far degraded that the Senate tried to remove from his control even the use of the royal signature.[34]

Only his ambitious wife, Louisa Ulrica, sister of Frederick the Great, seemed determined to assert some regal authority, and it was she who attempted to carry out a revolution, in 1756, which ended in disaster and the beheading of many of her followers.

The punishment of Adolphus-Frederick for the attempted *coup d'état*, which he had had neither the courage nor the conviction to lead, was further humiliation by the Estates. In an "instruction" to the tutor of the Crown Prince Gustavus, the Estates informed Adolphus-Frederick and the royal family that kings were the "natural enemies of their subjects" and that, in free States, they exist only "on suffrance."[35] Not only was Adolphus-Frederick told these things, but he was told them publicly. In a solemn ceremony, the instructions were handed to him by the Marshal of the Diet and the Speakers of the three lower orders, and the King was officially requested to pass them on to his son's tutor. Thus, young Gustavus received his education in an atmosphere of public rebuke.

The knowledge that his father had been little more than an impotent figurehead, subject to directives and humiliations from the Senate and the Diet, was to have a predominant influence on Gustavus' life. He was, neither by temperament nor conviction, suited to play such an insignificant role in affairs. Even as a boy, he had intrigued with his mother to get the reins of government back into the hands of his father; and, although the one real attempt in this direction had failed miserably, he was never convinced that the idea was an impracticable one. Defeat had taught him that, if he were ever to succeed, he must have better plans and, above all, he must develop his abilities at deception.

Certainly, Gustavus had the intelligence required to defeat his enemies and to govern well, although, like many a boy, he was reported to have skillfully evaded taxing his intellect during his childhood. One of his discouraged tutors said of him: "the prince is incompetent in penmanship, in spelling, and in grammar; he knows almost nothing of geography. His horror of work is invincible. A stranger to all serious thought, or all religious sentiment, he has an empty heart as well as an empty head."[36] This criticism can be largely discounted, because it came from a new tutor obviously trying to belittle the achievements of his predecessor. Furthermore, since all of Gustavus' tutors were agents of the Senate, placed over him to teach subservience and respect for the anti-monarchical constitution of 1720,[37] it is unlikely that he ever felt free to discuss with them any ideas he might have had. Rather than challenge his political overseers openly, he soon learned to dissemble, and to bide his time until the moment for action arrived. Vergennes' judgment of him was to be that, while his amiable qualities easily won him friends, his facile speech did not make much of an impression on one's mind. He had, nevertheless, "a great fund of acquired information, a just and impartial discernment when he was not led astray by false beliefs."[38]

In time, Gustavus became an expert at concealing his true motives, and his "art of dissimulation" became one of his most striking talents. Referring to the fact that, from birth, the left side of Gustavus' head was flat, giving him two different appearances depending on which side he turned to the observer, one of his earlier biographers concluded that Gustavus' politics were as "double-faced as he was."[39] The generalization is not unfair for, when he came to carry out his *coup d'état* of 1772, he was so adept at deception that he convinced the Senate, the Diet, and even his cunning uncle, Frederick the Great of Prussia, that he had no such plans.[40]

Yet Gustavus was more than a dissembler. Physically he was not handsome; he was of average build, and his body was badly proportioned. The soldier, the Marquis de Bouillé, who described Gustavus as an older man, said he was thin, with a long and narrow face, bad teeth, jutting nose and chin, a large mouth, high forehead, arched eyebrows, and magnificent blue eyes. At court he was completely at home and elegant; he had a superb memory, a persuasive eloquence.[41] At times, he revealed an almost naïve sincerity which won him the affection of those near him. Although, as a child, he had had a strong inclination for girls' clothing (he often went to bed wearing bow ribbons and trinkets),[42] as a man he compensated for this inclination towards transvestism with a strong, indeed an "insatiable, love of glory."[43] This latter characteristic made it painful for him to accept the insignificant role assigned to the monarchy by the Constitution of 1720. His driving personality, so complex and so self-contradictory, demanded a larger stage than that allowed by law, and it was to be one of Vergennes' accomplishments to help him satisfy his ambition.

Before Vergennes' arrival Gustavus could anticipate small promise of assistance from abroad. The Hats' reliance on French aid and advice had brought disastrous consequences to Sweden, but the Caps' subservience to Russia was equally shortsighted. When they came to power they led the ship of state into even more dangerous waters. Although France sent money and willingly gave advice, she was too far away to impose herself militarily. Russia, on the other hand, was Sweden's neighbor and was anxious to expand both her boundaries and her influence in North European politics.

Russia's grand design for the North gave Sweden a role similar to that assigned to Poland before the plan for partition had been hatched: while she was not to be weakened to the point of collapse, she was not to be allowed to grow strong enough to interfere with Russia's ambitions. Furthermore,

Russia was determined to preserve the Swedish Constitution of 1720, because it gave the King no authority, and because the conflicts between the Hats and the Caps made it almost impossible for the Estates to provide strong government. Consequently, with the Caps as her paid fishermen, Russia could fish at leisure in troubled waters. To prevent Sweden's reform of the vicious constitution, Catherine II, not long after she came to power in Russia, arranged (in 1764-65 and 1769) secret treaties with Prussia[44] and Denmark,[45] in which they all agreed to preserve the Swedish Constitution of 1720, even at the cost of war. Then, in 1766, to complete the enchainment of Sweden, the Caps, now wholly puppets of St. Petersburg, also agreed to accept Russia's guarantee of the Constitution.[46] Now, more than ever, any attempt to reform Sweden's domestic politics could easily escalate into an international crisis.

The extent to which Swedish problems had become international ones was clearly seen in 1769 when, after a dangerous crisis brought about by one of Adolphus-Frederick's rare attempts to assert some authority, the Estates were convoked, and a new Diet called for. On the eve of the elections, the Hats party held its general meeting in the French embassy, and the Caps issued a warning that all those who voted against them would suffer the vengeance of Russia. The French and Russian ambassadors attempted to surpass each other in their use of money to assure a favorable majority. As a last desperate move to prevent a Hat victory, the Caps decreed that the Diet would meet at Norrkoping rather than Stockholm, in order to make it easier for the Russian fleet to exert its influence. In spite of all these attempts, Russian *rubles* and Russian naval guns failed, and the Russian ambassador was left with the responsibility of explaining why the French could buy what the Russians could not.[47]

Not long after the victory of the Hats, however, the French ambassador, Modène, discovered that his money had no real power either. During the stress of the election campaign, the Hats had promised him that, in exchange for his assistance, they would, if elected, reform the Constitution so as to give the King more power. When the French ambassador reminded them of this promise, the Hats were reluctant to keep it. The temper of the new Diet opposed strengthening the hand of the monarch, and the Hats themselves regretted having entered into such a bargain. Although defeat was a foregone conclusion, the Hats unenthusiastically presented the matter to the Diet. After a ten months' session, characterized for the most part by paralysis, the Diet dissolved itself. This time, the French ambassador was faced with the necessity of forwarding an explanation to his superiors.

At Versailles, Choiseul, a man of short patience at best, had reached the conclusion that the money spent on the Hats had been wasted. France wanted not only a Sweden ruled by a pro-French party, but also a Sweden sufficiently strong to resist Russian expansion in the North. True, a pro-French party was in power, but the chaos and confusion caused by the internecine strife had left the country too weak to be a shield against Russian aggression. In fact, by supporting the Hats, Louis XV reinforced the very weaknesses Russia and Prussia had been striving to preserve. Disillusioned by the situation, Choiseul decided to reappraise French policy towards Sweden. In the meantime, he cut off all aid, using as an excuse the fact that the Swedes had signed a treaty with England, in violation of the Swedish-French treaty of 1738 in which the former had agreed not to ally with any other power without first consulting France.

Choiseul was not long in finding another way to deal with the Swedish question. He decided to suport a *coup d'état* in Sweden in order to obtain more authority for the King. His new policy, which involved creating a "patriots" party committed to support of the monarch,[48] showed a great flexibility of mind; but, unfortunately, his characteristic impetuosity led him to demand action before circumstances allowed it. The patriots began to form in Sweden, but Choiseul set an impossible timetable for them. As early as December of 1768, he was arguing that "The favorable moment for the revolution has arrived." And he continued to press for an immediate demonstration, although it was quite obvious that the patriots were still too unorganized to achieve success. The French ambassador at Stockholm found himself in the same position as that of Vergennes at Constantinople; attempting to force French policy on an unready group of actors.

Nevertheless, Choiseul and the patriots did make some progress towards their goal. Modène held secret meetings in the apartments of the Queen's reader, a Monsieur Beylon, with various leaders of the revolutionary party, including the Queen and Gustavus. They decided to send Beylon to Versailles to discuss with Choiseul, in person, the situation confronting them. While there, Beylon was to make arrangements for Gustavus to visit France in order that further details of the project, especially the critical problem of French aid, could be worked out.[49] Gustavus was only too willing to participate.

By the time of his departure, Gustavus favored a *coup d'état*. He was aware that the Swedish Diet suspected that there were politcal reasons behind his desire to go to France, for they had voted him the necessary authorization to leave the country with the greatest of reluctance.[50] Consequently, he was extremely careful to hide his real intentions. To avoid giving any official character to his trip, he traveled incognito as the Comte de Gothland, while his brother, Frederick, went as the Comte d'Oland. Furthermore, he kept his party very small. Only his former tutor, the Comte Scheffer, the Barons Ehrensward and Taube, and five others were included in the entourage.[51] To all outward appearances the Crown Prince of Sweden was simply visiting France, the cultural center of Europe, hoping to enrich and complete his education.

Gustavus soon discovered that his trip might prove as non-political, in truth, as he had hoped to make others believe that it was. Upon arrival in Paris on February 4, 1771, he went immediately to the Swedish legation. There he learned that Louis XV had dismissed Choiseul while Gustavus was en route.[52] The very man he had counted upon for advice and assistance was out of favor, and far away from Versailles at his estates at Chanteloup.[53] Moreover, the country was in an uproar as a result of the recent exiling of the Parlement by the reforming Chancellor René Nicolas Charles de Maupeou. For the time being, Gustavus' plans had to be deferred, so he immediately threw himself into the witty and sophisticated life of the Court and the salons, where the affairs of state were pleasantly combined with affairs with beautiful women. "You would be charmed by him," the old Duchesse du Deffand wrote to the Duchesse de Choiseul.[54] He met Madame du Barry and won her favor with a bejewelled collar for her dog. Guided by the historian and writer, Rulhière, he frequented the salons of the Comtesse de Boufflers, Madame de Brionne, and the Comtesse de la Marck, and tested his wits and intelligence against some of the most brilliant men and women of his time. His most pleasant evenings, however, were spent with his "*ardente amie,*" the Comtesse d'Egmont, the charming daughter of the Maréchal de Richelieu. In her he found not only a lively and intelligent companion, but also a friend who would remain dear to him for years to come.[55] He visited the Royal Laboratory of Physics and Optics, and heard a complimentary speech given by deaf mutes trained by the King's interpreter.[56]

Gustavus did not forget the object of his mission, however, even amidst the balls, the theater, and the delightful women. Louis XV still seemed willing to continue along the lines laid out by Choiseul, and Gustavus would not let the matter drop. From someone, he learned that the Duc d'Aiguillon was a strong contender for the post of Secretary of State for Foreign Affairs left vacant by Choiseul and filled, in the interim, by Vrillière. Gustavus' former tutor, the Comte Scheffer, had once served as the Swedish ambassador to France, and during his service he had become a very good friend of D'Aiguillon's mother. Without hesitation, Gustavus used Scheffer to establish contact with the Duchesse d'Aiguillon and the candidate for Secretary of State, in order to prepare the way for discussion of his plans.

No sooner had Gustavus made contact with D'Aiguillon, than news came from Sweden which suddenly changed his status and, consequently, added to the importance of whatever agreements he would reach at Versailles. A messenger brought him word of his father's death. Unless he blundered and antagonized the Swedish Diet, he would be the next King of Sweden. In fact, when Louis XV heard the news, he suggested that Gustavus be immediately and officially received as a monarch. But the young man preferred to remain incognito. Nonetheless, the next day the Swedish legation was hastily transformed into a royal residence, and Gustavus went into official mourning.

Gustavus decided not to leave France immediately; soon he was once again back in society. His critics find his lingering in France and his early return to the salons proof of a frivolous, unfeeling side to his character. But he had come to France to discover what assistance might be available to help him restore the monarchy of Sweden to a position of authority. Now that the office was his, the question of French assistance became critical. He wanted to know something definite before he returned to Stockholm.

In the meantime, he had written a declaration to the Swedish Senate assuring them that he would observe all the laws of Sweden and, especially, the Constitution of 1720. He even went so far as to declare that he considered anyone who attempted to reestablish the sovereignty of the King as an enemy of his person and a traitor to the State.[57] Without this public submission to the Estates, his right to succeed to the throne of his father would have been challenged; and, until he was certain of French assistance, he could not meet his political enemies in open combat.

Before long, however, he *was* sure that France would support his efforts to re-establish his authority. Louis XV was even ready to support his promises with money. France still owed Sweden 10,500,000 *livres* in subsidies from the Convention of 1764, but Choiseul had refused to pay that balance because he felt the money was being wasted in the useless antagonisms between the Hat and Cap factions. Louis now agreed to make this sum available, through payments of 1,500,000 a month, beginning January 1, 1772. Out of this sum, Gustavus was given an advance of 750,000 *livres* to carry him until the remainder arrived. In addition, France promised to provide him with 3,000,000 *livres* to be used to influence the Swedish Diet, which was scheduled to open soon after his return to Stockholm. Backed by these strong commitments from one of the great powers of Europe, Gustavus left Paris on March 18, 1771, confident of the future. Vergennes followed in less than two months.

CHAPTER 14

Coup d'état

Vergennes was not entirely pleased about his appointment as ambassador to Sweden, and neither was Louis XV, whose first choice for the position had been the Comte d'Usson.[1] But the French King was not sure that Usson had the necessary experience for a task that was obviously going to increase in difficulty as time went on. When he expressed his reservations to the Comte de Broglie, the chief of "secret diplomacy" recommended Vergennes: "His reputation in the diplomatic corps and his experience would naturally give him a great influence over a young king, who must have need of counsel; and, besides, this choice would prove to his Swedish Majesty the interest that France takes in his affairs and those of his Kingdom."[2] Louis XV did not immediately concur with Broglie. Although he recognized Vergennes' unquestionable diplomatic qualifications to meet the responsibilities in Stockholm, the King still resented the diplomat's marriage with Anne Viviers and, moreover, feared that the Protestant court in Sweden would take exception to the story of Vergennes' relations with her prior to their marriage. Louis XV ultimately agreed to the appointment of Vergennes, but he refused to allow the Comtesse de Vergennes to accompany her husband to Stockholm.[3]

Prior to his departure from Versailles, the Ministry of Foreign Affairs provided Vergennes with extensive briefing on the situation in Sweden. His formal instructions, consequently, were restricted to expressions of Louis XV's intentions concerning the path he should pursue.[4] Vergennes learned that his first responsibility was to restrain Gustavus from premature action which might be prompted by his youth and bad counsel. The French ambassador was not told to oppose any attempt by Gustavus to gather the reins of government into his own hands; he was merely advised to encourage "prudence and moderation." His next instruction referred to finances — a problem which was to plague Vergennes during his entire stay in Sweden. He was informed that France was prepared to contribute to the election of the right men to the Swedish Diet which was to meet in June, soon after Vergennes' arrival, and the money for this purpose was to be independent of the subsidies Louis had already agreed to with Gustavus. In fact, Vergennes was told that France had already begun to make contributions to the election and the French ambassador should continue this practice by means of a letter of credit provided by Louis XV. Vergennes' orders cautioned him, however, to be sure that he saw the necessity for, and utility of, any expenditures he was to make before he parted with any money. For the last forty years, the King complained, France had been subsidizing Sweden and her politicians without receiving much of value in return. "So onerous an experience ought to serve as a lesson for the future."[5]

Louis told Vergennes that, although the Hat party had always shown a marked loyalty to France, the venality of its members had so corrupted them that they were now held in dishonor. While the Cap party was equally dishonored, there remained among its members some who were honest and disinterested. Both parties, Vergennes was informed, had been responsible for the ruin of Sweden, and neither of them should be shown special favor. Actually, if Sweden wished to rise again, the two parties that divided the country had to be abolished. "This is an important goal that the Comte de Vergennes must never lose from view."[6] He should work to reconcile the two factions, restore the country, and make it possible for Sweden to regain her self-respect and live up to her responsibilities in European affairs.

The problems implicit in the initial instructions, and those he would receive subsequently, became evident to Vergennes soon after his departure from Versailles. He was told to visit Copenhagen on his way to Stockholm to ascertain the Danish attitudes towards the situation in Sweden.[7] The French were apparently not aware that Denmark had signed a secret agreement with Prussia and Russia against Sweden; consequently, Vergennes was ordered to remind the Danish court that reciprocal interests made a Danish-Swedish diplomatic union desirable. The suggestion was made of pure fantasy: Denmark was committed by treaty to an anti-Swedish policy, and Gustavus, as Vergennes was soon to learn, was violently hostile to Denmark. Through rights of his father, Gustavus claimed the duchies of Schleswig and Holstein against Danish counter-claims. The dispute, coupled with Gustavus' personal animosity towards the Danish ruling family, made illusory any thought of conciliation. In fact, once at Stockholm, Vergennes soon found himself directing all his efforts to preventing an open break between the two courts. He became convinced that Gustavus would open hostilities against Denmark the moment he had the power and the means to do so.[8]

When Vergennes arrived in Sweden, the elections for the Diet had already taken place, and the critical moment had come when the deputies reached Stockholm and offered themselves for sale to the various parties. The French ambassador immediately plunged into party politics and, with ready money, tried to insure the election of a favorable Marshal of the Diet. He soon realized, however, that the job required much more money than he had originally estimated. It was not that he was unprepared for the venality of politics in Sweden; on the contrary, he had delayed his departure from Versailles in order to convince Vrillière and the King that he would need two million *livres* to influence politics at his new post. He detested, he said, the venality of the Swedish people, but, nevertheless, he was prepared to exploit their vices. It was not the time, he believed, to reform Swedish morals. If the King refused him adequate funds, he warned, "You can expect me to be absolutely useless in Sweden."[10] Gone now from the ambassador's dispatches was the obsequious Vergennes of former days. Age and experience had toughened him and he had no hesitation whatever about making his needs clear to his superiors. Reluctantly, Louis XV granted the two million *livres;* it proved to be far from sufficient, for, as Vergennes learned after his arrival, Louis XV's Stockholm banker had already advanced "several millions" of *livres* to Swedish political leaders, and he demanded payment as soon as possible.

The difficulties of the new ambassador were multiplied by the fact that, for a time after his arrival in Stockholm, he could get no firm direction from Versailles. The choice of a new Secretary of State for Foreign Affairs was pending and already had been delayed too long.[11] Louis XV's characteristic indecision gave rise to intrigues and rumors which befogged the issue and occupied the time of everyone, including Madame Du Barry, whose lack of knowledge of affairs in no way diminished her determination to influence them. Broglie seems to have wanted the Duc d'Aiguillon to be the new Minister and Aiguillon wanted Broglie, but Du Barry and the Prince de Condé were plotting against them both.[12] At long last, Louis XV selected the Duc d'Aiguillon. Both Vergennes and Gustavus III approved of the appointment. Anticipating that Aiguillon might be the choice, they both had opened their minds to him about Swedish affairs before they left France. What they talked about is not recorded, but it is known that they had agreed on French policy toward Sweden. One of the first things Aiguillon did, upon assuming office, was to assure Vergennes that he "had not changed his way of thinking."[13] France now had a chief of its Department of Foreign Affairs; happily, he and Vergennes were in accord.

Before long, the conflict that everyone expected between Gustavus and the Estates became overt. Aware that he was watching what might prove to be a turning point in Swedish history, Vergennes readied himself to provide the inexperienced Gustavus with "prudence" and "moderation." He soon learned, however, that the Swedish monarch had a mind and some gifts of his own. When Gustavus made a speech on the opening of the Diet, his eloquence deeply moved his audience. Watching the members of the Diet as they listened to their new King's promise not to touch their liberties, Vergennes realized that here, indeed, was a man of talent.[14] Gustavus had a marvelous instinct for winning people to his side. He established public audiences to which anyone, even the lowest peasant, could bring forward his complaints. And when a shortage of flour reduced the supply of bread at Stockholm to a dangerous low, Gustavus personally intervened to help the people and to prevent their being cheated by the bakers who tried to profit from the crisis.[15]

As Gustavus gained popularity, his opponents lost it. The Caps party responded to Gustavus' opening speech with a chorus of inappropriate pedantry, and arrogant reminders that the people were sovereign and that the King of Sweden was elected. Their biggest blunder was committed immediately after the funeral ceremony of Gustavus' father, Adolph-Frederick. Gustavus was so moved at the funeral service that he could not give the oration he had prepared. While he was still grieving, the Diet peremptorily resolved that the King return to their former posts two ex-Senators who had been dismissed by his father. Resenting the tone, as well as the substance, of their ultimatum, Gustavus refused, until the Estates changed their resolution, which he felt was contrary to the spirit of *rapprochement* between themselves and the King. Such a demand, he indignantly responded, was an insult to his honor and to the memory of his late father.[16]

Fearful that Gustavus had challenged the Diet prematurely over an insignificant issue, Vergennes counseled moderation: "I held to the *juste milieu,*" he reported, "by directing my reflections in such a manner as to put him on guard against any precipitous measures."[17] He knew that the Caps, under Russian influence, had superiority in the Diet, and he considered it dangerous to taunt them. Gustavus was equally aware of the situation, but he also had the advantage of a knowledge of his countrymen. He had chosen well the terrain on which to challenge the Diet.

Quick to realize that they were no longer dealing with the docile Adolph-Frederick, and admitting the arrogant tone of their original resolution, the Estates retreated and apologized: "The Estates declare that they had no intention of insulting the memory of the dead King or offending Your Majesty." But they still insisted on the recall of the two Senators, although this time in a more humble petition. Graciously Gustavus complied, expressing the hope that the recall of the two men would help reestablish public calm and tranquillity. He could not resist, however, drawing a bit of profit from his moral advantage. "I owe my blood and my life to my country and to my subjects," he told them, "but, while I must not require of my subjects that they sacrifice their honor for me or the State, they cannot ask me to sacrifice mine for them."[18] Gustavus won the first minor skirmish, and it gave him confidence. Vergennes, armed only with his King's instructions to offer "prudence and moderation," was obviously impressed.

No one, least of all Gustavus and Vergennes, expected the recall of the two Senators to end the struggle between the Estates and the monarch. The next encounter came when the four Orders debated the text of an act of allegiance, called the Act of Assurance, to which Gustavus was to swear. No agreement could be reached on its wording, and the extended haggling resulted in delaying Gustavus' coronation and prolonging the session of the Diet beyond its expected duration.

The extension of the Diet hurt Vergennes, because he was paying subsidies to those members who could be counted on to support Gustavus, and the costs were increasing daily. The government at Versailles, weary of this expensive bickering, determined to stop the drain on an already overburdened treasury. "All that you have done up to the present, with so much wisdom and skill, to strengthen the patriot party and enfeeble the opposition," Aiguillon complained to Vergennes, "has had no success. We find ourselves, after spending 2,500,000 *livres*, no further along than we were six months ago . . ." The poverty of the French treasury demanded caution, explained Aiguillon. He therefore ordered an immediate end to all payments to the Swedes. Aiguillon advised his ambassador, however, that if the Diet could be terminated, Louis XV might be able to make one last effort. He also reminded Vergennes that Louis had understood that Gustavus had plans to repress by force such irresponsible resistance to the throne.[19] Between the lines, Vergennes read the implied question: Was Gustavus ready to break the power of the Estates and establish his own authority?

Vergennes thought that Gustavus was determined to try, first, to reform the government by less violent means. "I do not want to intervene in the deliberations of the Estates," the Swedish monarch told the Senators in an extraordinary meeting, "but at the same time I believe it your duty, as well as mine, to stop in time this continuous agitation of heated minds, before the consequences are fatal to liberty and the State." He announced that he planned to call the Speakers of the four Estates together and discuss with them the dangers confronting the country. "Nothing should be of more concern to all of us. The country wants a prompt remedy." The Swedish Senators were deeply impressed by Gustavus' concern, and especially by his moderation in not wanting to intervene in the affairs of the Estates.[20]

Encouraged by the Senators' reception of his views, Gustavus quickly called the meeting of the Speakers of the four Estates, including, as well, the Marshal of the Diet. In order to insure the continued support of the Senators, he also invited four of their senior members to be present. To the assembled politicians he spoke frankly, telling them that he had for a long time waited in silence for the celebration of his coronation to take place; yet nothing had been done. Instead, he had witnessed nothing but party hatreds degenerating into dangerous altercations. The nation, he warned, was at the edge of an abyss. He stressed that he did not wish to profit from the confusion to increase his own powers at the expense of liberty, but he did want to re-establish some confidence between the Crown and his subjects. He wanted "to become a medium of *rapprochement* and of accord among the Estates."[21]

Gustavus' speech evoked sympathy and approval throughout the country. But in the Diet, the reaction was sullen hostility. Not only did the deputies find the hearsay accounts of the speech disagreeable, but they also refused to allow its official communication to the Diet, on the grounds that it was unconstitutional for the orators or the Marshal of the Diet to transmit any message from the King. When the time came for the orators to speak, they remained silent. In the assembly of Nobles, the speech was recounted by a deputy, but only in a way which gave it no status. A long and bitter debate ensued between the Hats and Caps in the assembly of Nobles, as to whether or not the King should be thanked for his "praiseworthy and patriotic sentiments." The Caps, who opposed any expression of appreciation, carried the vote, and Gustavus' friends were soundly defeated. Encouraged by their victory, the Caps proceeded to bring to trial an editor who had printed Gustavus' earlier speech to the Senators in an effort to bring it to public attention. In this act, the foes of the King turned from inter-party fighting to direct criticism of Gustavus. Vergennes, who saw him soon after this series of defeats, found him *"souverainement piqué."*

Gustavus' position worsened when the French decided to withhold subsidies.[23] Earlier, when he had been given the arrears of the subsidies promised to his country, he had paid the money directly to his political supporters, although he knew that it should have gone directly to the Estates for national defense and other public expenses. He had planned to use subsequent subsidies to make up the deficit, before the Estates became aware of his action. Now, however, with no further subsidies anticipated, he risked discovery and exposure before the Diet, with inevitable loss of the public sympathy he had worked so hard to win. Vergennes was equally concerned, because he foresaw that Gustavus might deny that he had ever received the money. In that case, the French ambassador would be faced with the distasteful alternatives of confirming Gustavus' lie and paying to the Estates the money due them, or of contradicting Gustavus and risking severance of the close ties between the French and the Swedish Kings.[24] The immediate response of both men was to send couriers post-haste to Versailles bearing dispatches begging Louis XV to reconsider his decision. "Do everything in your power," the Swedish minister wrote to his ambassador at Versailles, "to prevent so fatal a blow. I can't believe that it is possible that

His Very Christian Majesty could abandon our young master to so cruel a fate."[25]

Aiguillon had never intended to abandon Gustavus; he had but applied the spur to force the Swedish King into a stronger stance. The moderation, which Vergennes had been instructed to encourage, had only led to a political impasse. Furthermore, the policy was costing France too much money. The threat to stop all subsidies was designed to hasten consummation of more vigorous plans. So that there would be no misunderstanding about what he wanted, the French Secretary sent Gustavus a personal and confidential letter delineating what France expected of him. "You can no longer be in doubt, Sire," Aiguillon wrote, "that your enemies want to establish anarchy in Sweden under the protection of Russia. The Sovereign of that empire is as jealous of your talents as she is alarmed about the use you may make of them. The time has come for you to show her that, even if you do not intend to employ your talents to recover the provinces which have been taken away from the Swedish monarchy, you can suppress the insolence of your subjects whom she has seduced or corrupted, and can make their pernicious projects fail, and you can defend your people and your authority."[26] Going directly to the point, the French Minister then told Gustavus bluntly that he could no longer hope to succeed by using "persuasion and temporization." Success could be achieved only by a *"coup de force,* which has become indispensably necessary." To engage Gustavus' pride, Aiguillon warned him that if he did not act soon he would get the reputation, "not only in Sweden but, even, all over Europe," of being weak. Then, anticipating the question that he knew would be asked, Aiguillon promised that Louis XV would do everything in his power to help Gustavus in whatever action he undertook. While he disavowed any desire to tell the Swedish King how he should manage his affairs, he, nevertheless, suggested that Gustavus employ his loyal troops to force all parties to submit to the "ancient laws and institutions."[27] At the same time, Aiguillon informed the King through normal diplomatic channels that the cabinet at Versailles had decided to renew some of the subsidies.[28]

The characteristic inadequacies of Louis XV's diplomacy are revealed in the 1771-1772 diplomatic exchanges between Stockholm and Versailles. Vergennes was thoroughly pleased with the decision to resume the payment of subsidies, for it eliminated the possibility of a public scandal which, inevitably, would have involved him. Yet he was completely unaware that behind his government's reversal was the determination to have an immediate *coup d'état* in Sweden. In a letter to the French minister to St. Petersburg, he admitted that Sweden was passing through a crisis, but dismissed the rumors of an imminent revolution at Stockholm as the offspring of a "romanesque imagination."[29] Ignorant of the new tack in French foreign policy, Vergennes continued to pursue the old. "I have neglected nothing," he wrote to Versailles, "to combat the taste this Prince Gustavus has, and which he has not hidden from me, for dangerous projects."[30] Gustavus once even confided to Vergennes that there were certain Swedes who favored giving their King absolute sovereignty, but he had refused to accept the suggestion because it would expose him to the blows of fanatics. Vergennes agreed. There would be a general protest against such a move, he thought, and it would offer neighboring powers the opportunity to intervene in Swedish politics. A civil war would follow, bringing with it all the horrors that had desolated Poland. Vergennes left this meeting with Gustavus under the impression that the Swedish King agreed with him.[31] Meanwhile, both Broglie, chief of the secret diplomacy, and Aiguillon continued to instruct the Ambassador to keep the Swedish monarch on the path of moderation.

As Vergennes watched the young monarch during the early months of 1772, he became suspicious that Gustavus planned some bold action. He spoke to the King to warn him of the dangers involved in listening to "flatterers and traitors" who would encourage impractical adventures. Gustavus offered reassurances that he did not contemplate "for the present" a revolution in the government; but he added that, if he ever had a legitimate motive for such an action, he would not answer for what he might do. Vergennes left the interview only partially satisfied, for he was aware of the ease with which Gustavus could find a reason for using force if he so desired. "I fear," he wrote Aiguillon, "that he has only too much taste for the romanesque."[33] From a later meeting, Vergennes concluded that Gustavus would not do anything excessive, but, when he examined the King's plans to manipulate the Estates by means of rewards to the deputies, he decided that they were too complicated and, consequently, too impractical to succeed.[34] Without fully realizing it, Vergennes, too, seemed to be arriving at the conclusion that the way of moderation was doomed.

By now, Gustavus had already decided. Blocked by his enemies in every attempt to exercise authority, he welcomed Aiguillon's suggestion that he use his army to defeat his foes. In direct communications with Gustavus, to which Vergennes was not privy, the French Minister continued to urge action. The Swedes must be made happy "in spite of themselves."[35]

Aiguillon's policy of deception could not continue indefinitely, and Aiguillon must have known that, if his Ambassador learned of the connivance behind his back, he would ask for recall, and France needed him in Sweden. Vergennes was not at all happy at Stockholm without his wife and children, and had even asked to be allowed to return to France.[36] Furthermore, it would have been deleterious to French policy to permit the ambassador and Versailles to continue to work at cross-purposes. Yet Aiguillon was surprisingly slow in revealing his overt plans. "I think . . ., everything considered," he wrote cryptically to his representative, "that you have said enough to this Prince to make him realize the inconveniences to which he will expose himself if he prematurely undertakes anything vigorous; but things have come to such a critical point that perhaps only violent means can remedy them." If Gustavus did carry out a successful revolution, Aiguillon speculated, French money might become more effective in Sweden. "You ought to continue giving the King . . . counsels of moderation," the Secretary of State instructed, "but without opposing any measures . . . which he proposes to follow in order to arrive at his goal."[37]

Vergennes' suspicion that Gustavus had revolutionary plans in mind continued to grow. When the Diet presented the Act of Assurance for his signature, the young man signed it without even reading it, although he had the right to suggest modifications, and although it severely restricted his freedom of action.[38] Suddenly, almost whimsically, he suggested that he make a trip to Russia to see Catherine II to try to convince her to cease her support to the Caps. Vergennes, Aiguillon, and Louis XV were all dumbfounded. Should they encourage the idea or oppose it?[39] Gustavus saved them from their indecision by dropping the scheme almost as suddenly as he had raised it.[40] When the four Orders in the Diet began to fight among themselves over the question of the privileges of the nobles, Gustavus tried to balance the Orders against one another, but the Orders found common ground in restricting the King's right to choose the Senators from a list submitted to him by the Diet.

Frustrated, angry and humiliated, Gustavus reached the end of his patience. "The King of Sweden requested a secret interview with me yesterday," Vergennes began a dispatch to Aiguillon on May 21, 1772. "I found him singularly upset and animated. He no longer accepts the numberless outrages the Estates ceaselessly impose on him." Gustavus, Vergennes reported, now believed he had no choice consistent with his honor but to act to save the independence of his crown. His enemies, he told Vergennes, wanted to force him to wear the yoke of Russia. Gustavus then opened his mind to Vergennes. He revealed a "project, truly bold, but which could be very dangerous, and even fatal, if it failed . . ." "Although I religiously promised the Prince secrecy, Monsieur le Duc, and this Prince even asked me to keep the secret from you for a while, my duty requires that I tell you," Vergennes confided. At the fortress of Sveaborg, near Helsingford in Finland, Vergennes continued, there was a garrison of 1500 soldiers, all of them foreigners, whose ranks and positions were being threatened by the Diet's attempts at military reform. These soldiers had been placed at Sveaborg to guard the maritime establishment there. If they rebelled, and took the ships at their disposal to come to Stockholm, Gustavus would have at his disposal the arms to subdue his enemies. He could then force the Estates to accept a new constitution giving the King more powers and could send them home for a four-year vacation before calling for a new Diet. If, on the other hand, the approaching rebels were discovered Gustavus planned to use the pretext of arresting the rebellious soldiers to march with his own regiment and join them; together, they would return to the capital and carry out his plans. To succeed in his plans, Gustavus estimated, he had an immediate need of 30,000 Swedish *écus* and 5,000 *livres*, and he wanted Vergennes to find them for him.[41]

The astonishment Vergennes felt, as Gustavus revealed the details of his plans, is not difficult to imagine. The career diplomat, whose training and personality had always been characterized by caution, was being asked to plunge into an affair that could easily end in violence and death, perhaps even his own death, if Gustavus failed and his enemies uncovered Vergennes' role in the plot. "I excused myself," Vergennes reported weakly, "from giving any advice, on the grounds of my incompetence in the art of war, and my lack of knowledge about the local situation." Before he agreed to advance any money, he wanted to know how far Gustavus had gone with his project. "And I asked him," he continued, "if he realized that this was a question of all or nothing, without any certainty, and perhaps little probability, of success." Gustaves assured him that he had thought it all through and was fully aware of the danger. He then repeated to the French ambassador all the reasons Aiguillon had used to encourage him to attempt the *coup d'état*: the failure of moderation, the reputation he was getting for weakness of character, and the demand of his own *gloire* that he do something. Furthermore, Gustavus confided, Louis XV was in favor of the plan. Vergennes sent back to his superiors in Versailles all of these revelations with the air of a horrified spinster telling of her first encounter with Don Juan.[42] He had said nothing to dissuade Gustavus; yet, at the same time, he promised nothing. The French ambassador was obviously beyond his depth. He was trained to be a negotiator; Gustavus was asking him to be an adventurer. He was not certain that he could carry on. He confessed that what Gustavus proposed frightened him and he knew it would demand resolution and firmness, which he hoped he could muster.

But Gustavus was committed, and Vergennes' hesitancy could not deter him. Almost immediately after his secret interview with Vergennes, he wrote the French ambassador a personal letter requesting some of the money needed to carry out his plans.[43] And then he left Stockholm for a few days to prepare for his long-delayed coronation. Vergennes, thoroughly shaken by Gustavus' bold decision, dutifully braced himself to play his official role in the coronation ceremonies. But the anxieties caused by Gustavus' revelations overwhelmed him; he bravely began the round of dinners, receptions, and ceremonies, but soon he had to excuse himself from several of them because a severe chill overcame him and sent him to bed. Every crisis in his diplomatic career had ended with an illness; this time, it was a ten-day fever that developed into severe chest congestion.[44]

All during the coronation celebrations, Gustavus said not another word to Vergennes about his scheme. The King gave a warm speech to the Estates, in which he saluted their freedom and independence.[45] Vergennes, although ill, carried on, dancing with the Queen at a costume ball. The four Estates solemnly swore allegiance to the new monarch. After two busy weeks of such whirlwind activity in an atmosphere of renewed popularity of the King, Vergennes began to wonder about the progress of Gustavus' plans for a *coup d'état*.[46] Gustavus had not forgotten. In June, he wrote a personal leter to Louis XV telling him that he was still determined to go ahead. Vergennes received instructions from Aiguillon that the King of France approved of Gustavus' ideas, and authorized Vergennes to advance him the money he needed.[48] Never, however, did Aiguillon reveal to his ambassador the part that he had personally played in encouraging Gustavus to take up arms against the Diet.

As the summer came into full bloom, Gustavus found his role as beloved, but impotent, monarch more and more difficult to play.[49] The Senate and the Diet continued to harass him and to encroach on his prerogatives. Even the secretary to the British envoy to Stockholm, certainly not a man to favor restoring the King to his former power, found himself in sympathy with Gustavus. "The power of the King," he observed, "was almost reduced to nothing."[50] Gustavus, meanwhile, secretly recruited a small band of army officers whom he knew to be loyal, and placed them under the Baron Sprengtporten, colonel of his regiment of guards. He placed under the command of his two brothers several squadrons of soldiers, and ordered them to drill twice a week to improve their discipline and effectiveness. But he had barely begun to shape this instrument of power when the Senate, reacting to rumors that the soldiers at Sveaborg in Finland were discontented and at the point of rebellion, and being somewhat suspicious of Gustavus' intentions, decided to send the Baron Sprengtporten to Finland to improve conditions there and, incidentally, to remove him from the capital. Unintentionally, the Senators were playing directly into Gustavus' hands, for, with Sprengtporten at Sveaborg, Gustavus could have entire confidence in the reliability of the garrison there.[51]

But Gustavus' luck did not continue. When he attempted to transfer ships to Sveaborg to transport the rebellious troops back to Stockholm, the Caps vigorously intervened to prevent the sending of any ships to that station. Although unaware of Gustavus' plans, the Hats, nevertheless, countered this opposition by accusing their opponents of being unpatriotic because of their unwillingness to give the Sveaborg outpost the ships necessary for supply and defense. The Hats triumphed, and Gustavus' plans moved forward, temporarily; but now, nature intervened. The seasonal east winds, which the plotters had trusted to transport the troops from Sveaborg, failed to rise, and Gustavus, fully committed to action, found himself, at the critical moment, separated from his instrument of force by nearly 400 nautical miles.

At this point Gustavus' ingenuity rose to the occasion. In anticipation that something might prevent the use of the Sveaborg troops, he had quietly developed an alternative plan. With his brother, Prince Charles, and a captain of infantry, Hellichius, at the fortress of Christianstad in Scanie, he devised a plan whereby Hellichius would lead a revolt at Christianstad[52] and march his troops to join Charles and his provincial recruits. Together they would go to Stockholm to assist Gustavus. The chances of success of such a move were increasing daily, since the Senate and Diet had stupidly antagonized the Swedish army by ill-advised affronts to the officer corps. Rumors of plans to unseat the Diet and the Senate had now become so public[53] that the opponents of Gustavus took the precaution of placing their King under surveillance. Vergennes found it increasingly difficult to meet with him for private discussions.

Despite his continuing ill health,[54] Vergennes nervously followed the preparations for the *coup*. From time to time, he offered advice to the Swedish monarch, although not all of it was pertinent. The comment, for example, that "more vigor is necessary to sustain a revolution than to make one,"[55] was a platitude, but the French Ambassador's attention to the progress of affairs assured Gustavus of continuing support. And Vergennes' copious reports to Versailles reveal the risks Gustavus willingly faced when he undertook the *coup d'état*. The King, according to Vergennes, was constantly terrified by the thought of assassination. Moreover, he feared that, if he succeeded in carrying out his plans, Russia would intervene and force him to re-establish the constitution which he was working so hard to destroy.[56]

As the day of the *coup* approached, Vergennes became increasingly more anxious. "We are approaching the moment, Monsieur le Duc, of the dénouement of the great project," he wrote Aiguillon. "Soon it will explode into something good, or it will fail; perhaps the first blow has already occurred in Finland." Each detail of the plan, which had earlier seemed so logical, now seemed the plaything of chance. So much depended on favorable winds to bring the pro-monarchist soldiers from Sveaborg. Would Prince Charles arrive at Christianstad at the right moment? Vergennes found assurance only in Gustavus: "The King of Sweden," he reported, "has a firm and tranquil countenance which the uncertainty of events does not shake."[57]

At Versailles the atmosphere was equally tense. Aiguillon had understood that the attempt would take place on the 24th of July. But July ended, August began, and no news. On the 9th of August, Aiguillon could wait no longer. "The special courier, that you would no doubt have dispatched, should have arrived already," he wrote in haste, "and the delay causes us some uneasiness, and makes us fear that the plans have met some obstacle in the execution."[58] Four days later, he still had heard nothing.

Perhaps Gustavus needed money? "Your plan to advance Gustavus all the money at your disposal conforms perfectly with the desires of the King," Aiguillon assured his ambassador. At Stockholm, Vergennes could provide no information. He, too, waited, but his anxiety was increased by the news that unfavorable winds were holding up all movement from Finland. "I don't have to tell you," he wrote on the 13th of August, "with what impatience we must await news of the development of the great event which already should have taken place."[59] Although neither man knew it, the *coup d'état* was already under way.[60]

On August 12, 1772, the soldiers at Christianstad rebelled against the Estates, and the conspirators were fully committed. "Brave Swedes!" the rebellious soldiers exhorted in a manifesto explaining their action to the people of Christianstad and Sweden, "the work is finally begun! Remember your obligations to your King and your country, and show your zeal, each of you in the different Estates! Join with us! It is the only way to save the kingdom from a shameful decline, and perhaps a foreign yoke . . ."[61] The troops arrested the burgomaster and the judges of the city, closed off the fortress, and refused entrance to all except farmers bringing in supplies. By chance, the Baron Rudbeck, a member of the secret committee of the Diet, happened into Christianstad the day of the revolt and became the first outsider to learn of it. Upon being refused permission to see the commander of the fortress, he hastened to Stockholm to spread the news.[62]

Gustavus' ability at dissembling was to prove his greatest asset. General Rudbeck arrived at Stockholm, excited and dusty, bubbling with the news of the revolt at Christianstad, and openly suspicious of Gustavus. According to one report, he had been told by the officer of the guard at Christianstad that the revolt was on orders from their monarch. But Gustavus received him with an embrace, listened to him, thanked him, called him his best friend, and left him convinced of the King's innocence.[63] A few days later, at a party with some officers and Senators, some of whom were allied with the Caps, Gustavus again heard the story of what the officer of the guard had told Rudbeck, Without hesitation, he responded, "Pardon me, you are mistaken. I was present in the Senate when Rudbeck told the story. It was the sentinel, and not the officer, who said it. For, undoubtedly, the officer would have been better informed."[64] The next day, in a long conversation with

Rudbeck, Gustavus diverted himself with work on a piece of embriodery for a lady friend. Not only Rudbeck, but many others, found in the King's indifferent behavior convincing proof that he was not involved in the affair at Christianstad.[65]

Nevertheless, the King's enemies mustered their forces for a showdown. The Senate and the Secret Committee of the Diet declared itself in permanent session; a member of the Caps party was sent to Scanie to put down the rebels, and Gustavus was told to order both his brothers to return to Stockholm immediately. To insure their own security, the Senate and Secret Commitee summoned to Stockholm some of the soldiers in the outlying provinces whom they knew to be loyal to them. At the same time the militia cavalry of the Bourgeois was ordered to patrol the streets and maintain order.[66]

Gustavus, who had already made plans to escape to Hamburg if his *coup* failed, continued to play the role of the innocent.[67] On the evening of the 18th of August, he attended the opera, afterwards inviting to his château a small party for supper and cards. The gambling went on until late at night, and he must have delighted in the fact that the wife of one of the most active of Caps party lost a considerable amount of money to him.[68] But, no sooner had his guests departed, than Gustavus went to his study, hastily wrote notes to various members of his family and to his followers thanking them for their support or explaining his motives. He then made the rounds of various guard posts in the city and retired.[69] At eleven o'clock the next day, he would meet two hundred officers with whatever soldiers they could muster, a force which, he hoped, would be strong enough to overthrow the constitution of Sweden.[70]

During these chaotic days before the *coup d'état*, Vergennes found himself increasingly uninformed. The Caps were successful in their attempt to isolate the Swedish King. On the 16th of August, Vergennes wrote: "This Prince must now take counsel from his courage, rather than from his prudence. I can no longer inspire him. I find it impossible to have any communications with him: he is too much the object of suspicion and is being watched too closely." "May God guide the King of Sweden and protect him."[71] From time to time, Gustavus sent the French Ambassador a note, describing some detail of his plans or to thank Louis XV "for the constant friendship he has shown me and to indicate to him that I hope, tomorrow, to show myself worthy of such a loyal friend."[72] Vergennes found the unfolding events of August, 1772, increasingly incomprehensible.

On the 19th of August, Gustavus arose at the customary hour, had his horse saddled, and left his apartments to meet the group of officers he had, the night before, secretly ordered to assemble at eleven o'clock. As he left his apartments, he turned to a group of officers and officials who acompanied him and said, "If I have the misfortune to be killed, let no one tell my brothers that it was by the hand of a Swede."[73] After reviewing a detachment of the guards, he went on foot to the planned meeting. He arrived as the guard was changing, and he ordered all guards to remain in the courtyard. He demanded that the gates be closed. Surrounded by the officers and the guards, he spoke, describing how the chaos in Sweden was destroying the country, how the political factions kept the nation divided, and how he had been humiliated by the outrages he had endured. He told the soldiers that he had decided to bring the situation to a halt, but he assured his listeners that he had no intention of doing so at the cost of the liberties of the citizens of Sweden. He solemnly asked the soldiers to help him. He was prepared, he told them, to sacrifice his own life to save Sweden.[74]

Not all of the officers had been prepared for Gustavus' message, and some of them were surprised at the request that they violate the constitution to which they had sworn allegiance.[75] Their hesitation was dispelled by the timely intervention of an officer of the guards, who boldly stepped forward and promised his support. Soon all but three of the assembled soldiers were enthusiastically swearing their allegiance to their King: of the three , two were put under arrest and the third fled.[76] While the officers were promising to assist Gustavus, the governor of Stockholm, the Baron Kalling, was outside demanding entrance into the court. He had the right, he shouted, to be present when any orders were being given to the troops. Now, confident of support, Gustavus ordered him to go to the Senate, where he would soon learn the will of the King.[77]

Despite the momentary dismay among some of the soldiers, the number of King's supporters quickly grew. By the time he reached the Senate, the cries "Long live The King!" had become a thunderous acclamation. Certain that whatever was the cause of the enthusiasm for Gustavus was a threat to their interests, several Senators tried to separate Gustavus from the soldiers surrounding him as he entered the Senate, so that he could be placed in Senatorial custody. The soldiers intervened and, instead, the Senators soon found themselves to be prisoners. Courteously, but with authority, Gustavus ordered the Senators into the hall where they customarily met, and placed guards around the exits. He promised them that their needs would be provided for, but he made doubly sure that the doors and gates were locked and chained to prevent their escape.[78]

These preliminary victories not only gave Gustavus more confidence, but also won him more followers. Mounted officers placed themselves under his orders, a detachment of grenadiers joined him, and, as he made his way to the artillery park, crowds of civilians swelled the ranks. General Rudbeck, with a handful of soldiers, tried to block Gustavus' entry into the park but they were easily brushed aside. Once inside, Gustavus gave the troops their orders of the day. He frankly told them that he was determined to put down the aristocrats, and to restore to Sweden its ancient liberties. He did not wish to gain absolute power, he assured the soldiers, he only wanted to be the "first citizen of a free people." Persuaded by their monarch's eloquence, the regiment of artillery vowed allegiance. With the Stockholm arsenal in his hands, Gustavus now held the strategic balance of power in the city. He sent out detachments to secure further key points, to see that all other artillery was in the hands of friends, and to block his enemies' exist from the city, to prevent their raising an army against him outside the gates.[79] The white handkerchief Gustavus had tied around his left arm at the beginning of the *coup* immediately became the symbol of the king's partisans and soon appeared all over the city.[80]

Vergennes followed events as well as he could, but, as he admitted later, he was on the verge of "succumbing under the weight of the contradictions which seemed to become more formidable and more terrifying."[81] He even sent his plate and other precious possessions to the Spanish embassy for safe-keeping until the crisis passed.[82] He saw the crowds in the streets and, later, he secured a copy of the proclamation Gustavus had issued to the Swedish people.[83] Not until the 21st of August, however, after Gustavus had won over the Navy and the civilian administration, and had proclaimed a new constitution for his country, did Vergennes feel confident enough of Gustavus' success to report that he had triumphed.[84]

The journal in which he described the *coup d'état* reveals the ambassador's sense of relief that the crisis seemed to be over and the King was victorious. "It is worthy of notice," he wrote from the security of the ambassador's château, "that a so-little-planned revolution is being accomplished with the least confusion, and without the least bit of violence. One would have said that the concourse of troops and people indicated only the celebration of a festival. Everywhere one sees only serene and content faces; you hear only reiterated acclamations and cries of 'Long live the King!'" After describing how Gustavus dealt with some people of an "agitated and factious spirit," he praised the "presence of mind, the unshakeable firmness, the marvelous way in which the King foresaw everything and provided for everything."[85] Later he admitted that his praises of the King of Sweden might seem exaggerated at Versailles, but, as far as he was concerned, they were "still short of the truth. This Prince has surpassed, during this so-critical occasion, the expectations of his most zealous admirers; he has surpassed even himself; in truth, he has exhibited the character of a hero and the soul of the most humane and most beneficent person."[86]

There were, however, flaws in this near-perfect tapestry. The most serious was that British intelligence had penetrated the secret of the *coup d'état.*

Somehow the British ambassador in France had acquired a copy of a top-secret letter of the King of Sweden to the King of France, had deciphered it, and sent it to London. London, in turn, passed the letter on to its minister at Stockholm, who passed it on to Gustavus' enemies. The letter, fortunately, was couched in such general terms that no specific details of the plans for the *coup d'état* were revealed. Nevertheless, there was obviously a break in security. Vergennes did not think it came from his office since, if it had, Gustavus' enemies would have known more than they did, for his letters were filled with details of the *coup d'état*. Still, the English now had the key to Vergennes' top-secret cipher, and the danger of their learning more was real. Promptly, Vergennes ceased using the cipher and wrote to Versailles for another.[87]

Another problem was that the ambassador was short of funds. The shortage had been chronic since his arrival, but the new circumstances created new demands. Gustavus had drawn heavily on Vergennes' treasury during the crisis of the *coup d'état*[88] and his success had done nothing to lessen the drain. Loyal supporters had to be paid; espionage, Vergennes complained, was "a considerable expense." None of these things came "at bargain prices."[89] Now more than ever before, he predicted, the Swedish people would be in need of assistance from France: "Now more than ever I am unable to close the door on them." While he was on the subject of money, the ambassador also took the opportunity to complain of his own financial straits. His family in France cost considerable to maintain, he revealed, and "this country is excessively dear and costly." And he concluded with the plea: "I invoke your bountifulness, deign to assure me of it; it is by far the most precious thing you could do for me . . ."[90]

The ease with which Gustavus rallied support to his cause in Stockholm explains why so little bloodshed stained the memory of those three days. The opposition simply dissolved in the face of the enthusiasm for the King. In fact, the young man's charismatic appeal was, in the last analysis, almost alone responsible for his victory. Nearly all of his supporters' plans had gone awry. The Caps had learned of the plans for the *coup d'état* before it began;[91] the pro-monarchical garrison at Christianstad never left the fortress in which they had ensconced themselves; the soldiers under Sprengtporten at Sveaborg were so plagued by unfavorable winds that they did not arrive at Stockholm until fifteen days after the *coup* was over.[92] The Comtesse d'Egmont's cry that "Stockholm is free; and Gustavus is victor!"[93] was at least a half-truth: Gustavus was indeed the victor, and his personal victory became one of his strongest assets as he set about re-organizing the government and constitution of Sweden.

Although his role in the success of Gustavus was largely that of paymaster, Vergennes, nevertheless, received his share of the glory. Aiguillon praised him — "No one knows better than I do," he wrote, "the importance and extent of the service you have just rendered your King."[94] Louis XV rewarded his Ambassador by naming him Councilor of State of the Sword,[95] and Gustavus presented him a huge diamond as a token of his appreciation, and a portrait of himself wearing the white handkerchief on his left arm.[96] In the salons of France, where the exploits of the heroic Swedish monarch became a favorite topic, it was generally assumed that the French ambassador had played a heroic role.[97] Although Vergennes was honest enough to admit that he had "so little part in the *coup d'état* that I can not claim much credit for it," he did draw to the attention of his superiors that he was responsible for the Russo-Turkish war, which made it possible for Gustavus safely to flaunt Catherine II and reform his government despite her hostility. "It is worthy of notice," he said, "that, after having participated, in 1768, in bringing about the circumstances which favored the return of Sweden to good days, I have come here precisely at the time when the almost desperate effect came about."[98] He did not remind Aiguillon, however, that, while he had worked to bring about the Russo-Turkish war, he had felt it to be an unwise policy.

The French government admitted to nothing as to its role in the *coup d'état*. It had printed and distributed an official report of the event, but neither France's secret role nor Vergennes' part in the undertaking was mentioned. Nor did the official *Gazette de France* reveal the smallest detail of French involvement.[99] Gustavus knew, however, where his support came from. The night before the *coup d'état*, he wrote Vergennes: "I pray you to testify to your master, the King, my appreciation of the constant friendship he has shown me, and tell him I hope tomorrow to prove myself worthy of a friend so loyal."[100]

Aiguillon, too, received his share of the praise for Gustavus' triumph. The Duc de Broglie, head of the King's secret diplomacy, showered the minister with compliments: "The event that has just occurred in Sweden, Monsieur le duc, is too beneficial to French influence and gives too much honor to its minister who prepared it, for me as a Frenchman, as his servant, and his friend, not to take a part in giving my compliments."[101]

CHAPTER 15

From Stockholm to Versailles

Gustavus' determination to complete the *coup d'état*, rewrite the constitution, and re-organize the administration required constant attention to the reactions of the European powers. He knew that Russia, Prussia, and Denmark did not wish to see a strong and independent Sweden, and he had reason to believe that they might go to war to prevent it. Russia was currently involved in the Turkish war which Vergennes had helped foment; and, along with Prussia and Austria, was deeply engaged in the Partition of Poland. Common sense suggested that she would not plunge into another conflict.[1] Yet Catherine felt deeply the blow to her prestige; in addition, she had signed with Prussia an agreement, to which Denmark was also a party, to protect the Swedish Constitution of 1720.[2] Gustavus could not afford to forget these hostile neighbors whose armies could attack his possessions from three different directions.

Vergennes was painfully aware of the international implications of any posture Gustavus assumed, and he did everything possible to assist him. Through a lively and extensive correspondence with the French ambassadors in St. Petersburg, Constantinople, and Vienna, he kept his fingers on the pulse of events in the courts most likely to challenge Gustavus' moves to consolidate his power. And, with the intelligence he received from these spots, he advised Gustavus.[3] His letters encouraged Louis XV to put confidence in the Swedish monarch and to give him full support. Realizing that, if Prussia were to attack Sweden, Pomerania would be the target, Vergennes repeatedly reminded Versailles that, in 1757, Maria Theresa had guaranteed Swedish Pomerania and the other Swedish territories in Germany.[4] Versailles had acted even before Vergennes had expressed his opinions. Almost immediately after the *coup d'état*, Louis XV persuaded Spain to instruct the Spanish ministers at Copenhagen and St. Petersburg to support the position of the French ministers in these capitals.

English statesmen found it extremely difficult to determine what stance they should assume regarding Gustavus. They had, until now, seconded Russia's efforts to prevent a strong, pro-French monarchy in Sweden, but they were much less inclined to resort to force to get rid of him, now that he had successfully taken over the reins of government. Furthermore, if Catherine crushed Gustavus, Russia would dominate the Baltic.

At the same time, England could not allow Louis XV to send strong military forces to Gustavus' aid. British public opinion and tradition both militated against the admission of a French fleet to the Baltic, and no cabinet member dared openly suggest that perhaps France's and England's interests, for the moment, coincided, since neither of them wished to see Russian influence expand in the north.[5]

The policy finally hammered together was intricate and dangerous. Russia was to be restrained (by refusal of aid) from attacking Sweden; France was to be deterred (partly by menaces, partly by assurances that England would control Russia) from sending a squadron to defend her.[6] Nevertheless, when a Russian invasion of Sweden seemed imminent in the late winter of 1773, Rochfort, the English Secretary of State for the south, risked his political neck and confidentially assured Aiguillon's secret agent in London, the Chevalier de Montagne, that England would do nothing if France intervened to protect Gustavus, provided she did so quickly and her fleet returned to France before the British navy was put on a war footing.[7]

From the very beginning, Aiguillon seems to have detected, behind the smoke screen of England's official policy, the truth that England would not interfere in Sweden.[8] He confidently assured Vergennes that "our worthy ally will not be tormented from the outside."[9] Louis XV was confident that there was "nothing to fear for the present."[10]

In Stockholm, however, the view of the international situation was less sanguine. Frederick's letters threatened the worst. He suspected that French money had played a role in the uprising at Christianstad.[11] "You know, Sire," he told Gustavus, "that I have engagements with Russia; I contracted them long before you undertook the enterprise you have just completed. Both honor and good faith prevent me from breaking them .... You put a knife on my heart," he continued, "by putting me in such a cruel embarrassment from which I see no way to escape."[12] To his sister, Gustavus' mother, Frederick wrote: "I am extremely disturbed that this resort to force obliges me, according to my treaties, to commit myself against my own family."[13] "I am vexed," he warned in another letter, "that you distinguish so poorly between your friends and your enemies."[14] Anxiously, almost pleadingly, Gustavus tried to appease his uncle. In a letter to Prince Henry, Frederick's brother, he wrote: "But tell me then, in the name of God, my dear uncle, what have I done to bring down on my head the storm which you tell me so inevitably threatens?"[15]

But Catherine had already paid too heavily for the war in eastern Europe to leap immediately into another in the north,[16] and Frederick, although apparently willing to use force against Gustavus if necessary, was inclined to do nothing without Catherine's cooperation.[17]

On the other hand, Denmark, the third partner in the alliance, was in an excellent position to block Gustavus, and soon the hostility between the two powers grew so severe that, indeed, a war seemed imminent.[18] Both sides marched troops to the frontiers; suspicions, rumors, and accusations rumbled between the two capitals, and Vergennes' position at Stockholm became almost unbearable.[19]

As the tension heightened, so did the difficulties of the French ambassador's assignment. With great urgency, he tried to convince Aiguillon of Gustavus' deep hatred for Denmark. But he scarcely penetrated the belief of the French Secretary of State that Sweden could be reconciled with Denmark and united in an alliance.[20] In March, 1773, when the strain of the Danish-Swedish crisis reached a peak, and a renewed threat of a Russian invasion loomed on the horizon, Vergennes even toyed with the idea that Gustavus begin a preventive war against Russia. "One could, perhaps," Vergennes wrote Aiguillon, "give Russia a mortal blow by bombarding Reval and Kronstadt before she could deliver hers."[21] Nothing could have been more disastrous for Sweden, where the government was unstable, and where famine claimed the countryside.[22] Had the French ambassador forgotton so quickly the lesson of the Russo-Turkish war? In truth, he was weary, depressed, and in need of rest. "I would abstain, Monsieur le Duc, from communicating to you my fears and my terrors," he confessed to Aiguillon, "if it were not my duty to render you an account of them. I see Sweden in the most deplorable situation."[23]

Vergennes was also ill — the climate of Sweden, he claimed, was incompatible with his temperament. Rheumatism plagued him;[24] he had reached the end of his endurance. The war scare with Denmark dragged on interminably, and the pressure never let up. As his official life passed from one crisis to the next, Vergennes' personal life made the sacrifices. His departure for Stockholm without his wife and family had been for him a soul-tearing experience. "This letter will probably be the last before I leave for Stockholm," he had written to his oldest son, "My heart is torn, I tremble when I measure the distance that is going to separate me from your dear mother and my good friends [his two sons]." But he did it, he told his son, because "some day the sacrifice may be of use to you and your little brother."[25] Yet he wished to remain their father and to share their lives. "Write to me once a month," he had asked. "Tell me about what you are reading, of your studies, and your progress. Tell me the true state of your mother's health and what kind of life she leads. Don't abandon her to her melancholy and sadness. . . . Get her to take walks to dissipate them, and spare nothing to keep her from her own thoughts."[26] His most serious personal concern at Stockholm was the education of his sons, especially Constantin. He demanded periodic reports on the boy's progress from his wife, the tutors, and the boy himself. "The most precious good in the world," he had earlier told his son, "is a good and virtuous education."[27] Constantin was old enough now, he believed, "to realize the shame attached to ignorance."[28] Thus, from Stockholm, the boy was continually exhorted to work at his studies, to hasten his entrance into manhood, to become an *"honnête homme,"* and an *"homme raisonable."* "Cultivate and make fruitful the germs of talent and virtue which providence has put in your mind and in your heart," he charged the boy. "That is the object of my wishes as well as all my ambition."[29]

As the strain of personal and official anxieties took their toll, Vergennes became more and more crotchety. On an occasion when the Swedish Senators preceded him at an audience, he claimed an insult to his rank and created a major diplomatic hassle. At the same time, he became extremely critical, with some justice, of Gustavus' concern with the formal aspects of his new role, and his arrogant imitations of the pomp and ceremony of the court at Versailles. He had even instituted the formal *lever*. Vergennes complained that Gustavus' taste for the pomp and the most vain aping of Versailles were the cause of public derision, and undermined his efforts to gain public support.[30] The relationship between the ambassador of France and the King of Sweden had now deteriorated into a marriage of mutual inconvenience. Vergennes' originally extravagantly high opinion of Gustavus melted away. Later when he was Secretary of State under Louis XVI, Vergennes' disenchantment with Gustavus would have a negative impact on Franco-Swedish relations.

The more Vergennes found himself at odds with the trend of events in Sweden, the more restless he became. By the end of May, 1773, when the war crisis began to abate, his period of usefulness in Stockholm had passed, and he was sensible enough to realize it. Now nearly fifty-four years old, sick and worn out by the almost continuous crisis in Stockholm,[31] he had already begun to think of following in the footsteps of his uncle Chavigny and going into semi-retirement at a post in Switzerland. There he would not be far from his own estates in France, and perhaps, if Louis XV were generous, he would even have his wife and children at his side. "I pray you," he appealed to Aiguillon, "not to forget me when the embassy at Switzerland is vacant."[32]

A year passed, however, before Vergennes was given any hope of leaving Stockholm, and, when he did return home, it was under circumstances which he could hardly have anticipated in 1773. Smallpox brought Louis XV's death in 1774, and the youthful heir to the throne, Louis XVI, needed knowledgeable and experienced advisers. The Comte Charles Gravier de Vergennes was one who could meet the needs of the young King. So he returned to France, not to go into semi-retirement in Switzerland, but to become the Secretary of State for Foreign Affairs for Louis XVI.[33] The career he contemplated bringing to a close in 1773 had barely begun by June of 1774.

The appointment of Vergennes to the post of Secretary of State for Foreign Affairs in 1774 surprised everyone, including Vergennes himself.[34] Marie Antoinette had hoped Choiseul would be recalled and given the appointment;[35] Vergennes' name was not included on the British Foreign Office's list of possible candidates;[36] and Vergennes was too busy trying to arrange his recall from Sweden to speculate on his own prospects. After the astonishment subsided, the question of who was responsible for the appointment began to intrigue the court and the *salons*. Some said that the Chancellor, Maupeou, had suggested Vergennes' name to Louis XVI.[37] Others named the old Jean Frédéric Phélypeox Comte de Maurepas, Minister of Marine under Louis XV, and now once again minister of State under Louis XVI, as the man behind the King's choice. Maurepas, according to one gossip, was looking for someone who would be a docile tool in his hands, and Vergennes was the perfect candidate.[38] According to Mayer, the contemporary biographer of Vergennes, Choiseul deserved the credit for the choice. "I see only the Comte de Vergennes for Foreign Affairs," he is reported to have said when questioned on the subject.[39] But this version of the story is contradicted by the long-standing ill feeling between the two men.[40] It is unlikely that Choiseul would have recommended to Louis XVI a man whom he had so bitterly criticized to Louis XV.

The most credible explanation of Louis XVI's choice of Vergennes is that given in a memoir written by Rayneval, Vergennes' friend and longtime associate in the Ministry of Foreign Affairs. According to Rayneval, Vergennes had been singled out by the Dauphin, the son of Louis XV, as a man worthy of responsibility.[41] Vergennes, the Dauphin wrote, was a person with a "sense of order, sagacious and capable." When the prince died in 1765, and his son, the future Louis XVI became heir to the throne, the latter was much impressed by the soundness of the recommendations his predecessor left behind in his private papers.[42] Later, Madame Adelaide, daughter of Louis XV and much respected by her nephew, Louis XVI, seconded her brother's judgement of Vergennes and warmly supported him before the young monarch. Thus not Maupeou, Maurepas, nor Choiseul was responsible for the choice of Vergennes as Secretary of State for Foreign Affairs. His real patrons were the King's aunt and a man nearly ten years in his grave. Vergennes' reputation as the man behind Gustavus' successful *coup d'état* was the final and perhaps deciding recommendation. In Sweden, Vergennes had engineered, it appeared, a much-needed victory for French diplomacy.

As the word spread of his appointment as Secretary of State for Foreign Affairs, Vergennes' well-wishers multiplied; congratulations came from everywhere, from the great and the small, from former enemies, from relatives, and from those whose names simply implied a relation. A cousin at Dijon congratulated him on being a part of a cabinet of *"des plus honnête gens."*[43] A Monsieur de Langeron assured the new minister that on hearing of the appointment he had congratulated his country.[44] The Duc de Noailles, the Marquis de Noailles, his colleagues in the diplomatic service, Sabatier de Cabre, the Comte de Chatelet, and many others sent their best wishes. Even his old enemy Choiseul wished him success under the double title of "compatriot and former colleague."[45]

Not all well-wishers were disinterested. Both the Duc and the Marquis de Noailles wanted another embassy for the Marquis.[46] Zuchmantel at Venice wanted a better post.[47] The Comte de Chatelet recommended a young man seeking a diplomatic career.[48] A Gravier de Lagellière from Beaune cited his name and a kindness Vergennes once showed his brother, an abbé, as recommendation for a request that Vergennes take his two sons under his protection. Their mother was dead, and he was old, the father told the minister, and "I would die content if you would deign to give me hope that you would not forget them."[49] Even Queen Marie Antoinette had a former valet de chambre who, she believed, deserved to be placed on the rolls of the Department of Foreign Affairs.[50]

Such was Vergennes' first taste of greater power.

"You have studied diplomacy and the interests of princes?" Rousseau had asked in the novel *Emile*. "Good, but what will you do with this knowledge, unless you know how to conciliate the ministers, the ladies of the courts, the heads of the bureaus; unless you possess the secret of pleasing them; unless all find in you the rascal that suits their purposes?" A fundamental question —and, even if the new Secretary of State and Minister of Foreign Affairs did not read Rousseau, similar questions surely flashed in his mind as he left Stockholm to return to the corridors, bureaus and Court of Versailles.

Part IV

THE WAR THAT CHANGED EVERYTHING

CHAPTER 16

The Past, Present, and Future in 1774

Charles Gravier de Vergennes became Secretary of State for Foreign Affairs in 1774, nearly thirty-five years after he first entered the diplomatic service as a young protégé under the tutelage of his uncle Chavigny. And, except for a short time at home at Toulongeon after his recall from Constantinople in 1768, he had spent most of those thirty-five years in service abroad. He knew international politics and the diplomatic world as few other men in France knew them.

But he was a foreigner in his own country, so unaware was he of the many domestic affairs issues that divided Frenchmen. Inevitably, much had changed in France while he labored in foreign courts, and, as he admitted in a letter of 1769, he had become a stranger to France, with "no notions about anything."[1] His ignorance of France embarrassed him, and his enemies enjoyed reminding him of it whenever they got the chance. "Rather than a Minister of Foreign Affairs," mocked the sarcastic Linguet, M. Vergennes is a "foreigner become Minister."[2] His ignorance of domestic affairs and his knowledgeability about world affairs are the keys to both the glory and the failure of Vergennes' career as Secretary of State.

From his various posts as a career diplomat, Vergennes had studied the conflicting forces at work in European international politics in 1774. He had lived on the firing line of Russian expansion; he had felt the jarring effects of Prussia's amazing ability to survive every crisis and grow a little after each one; he had watched with growing concern the merciless and exhausting competition between France and England. But, most of all, he was deeply aware of the risks involved if France engaged in both a continental and a sea war. The Seven Years War, with its humiliations, was to Vergennes a personal as well as a national defeat.

The Seven Years War exhausted France. The state's finances were in a shambles. New debts accumulated on top of unpaid debts from previous wars. The French Navy was in ruins. Vergennes' predecessor, Choiseul, had been forced to give up his plans for an invasion of England because the French Navy was too weak to meet the task. The destruction of the Navy entailed the destruction of French commerce, and France's trade with her colonies fell off to less than a seventh of what it had been before the war. In her weakened state, Choiseul-Praslin realized, France could "fall from first to second rank" among the powers of Europe.[3] At the time of the Peace of 1763, the Duc de Choiseul, his cousin, Choiseul-Praslin, and many others at Versailles decided to try to restore France's power by rebuilding her world commerce and sea power.

In contrast to France, the power of England, France's worst enemy, had increased during that war. England's commerce was flourishing when peace came and, though her war debts were huge, her finances were in good health because her trade and banking institutions supported credit.

The Peace of 1763 left England in control of the keys to world supremacy. In the Americas she monopolized a huge share of the commerce. Her ships dominated the Indian Ocean and she was among the first of the European powers in trade with China. Her traditional ties with Denmark gave her influence at the entry to the Baltic Sea. From Hanover, she profited from the commerce of Northern Europe. Her agents at the French port of Dunkirk jealously watched over her interests in the English Channel. In all the important commercial cities and ports of Northern Europe, from Russia, where she dominated trade, to Amsterdam, the international finance capital of the world, Englishmen traded, borrowed, negotiated, bought, and sold. England's control of Gibralter made her guardian of the entrance to the Mediterranean. At home her commercial development, and the position of London as a financial center second only to Amsterdam, gave her the wealth and the credit necessary to influence international politics.

Still, the exalted position of England in world politics after 1763 was a precarious one. After the peace, England could no longer count on the other powers of Europe to war on France on the continent while England attacked her on the seas and in the colonies. The German states were too exhausted by previous wars to seek willingly a new one. In the Polish partition and the Swedish revolution of 1772, England had refused to take an active part, thereby manifesting to Europe her withdrawl from continental affairs.

It soon became apparent, also, that her overseas possessions could be the source of difficulties as well as strengths. Choiseul-Praslin noted, soon after the Peace of 1763: "The peace," he wrote, "[represents] a remarkable epoch for the English monarchy; but its power is neither stable nor certain; the monarchy must rise or fall .... Its own grandeur is perhaps the seed of its decadence; the vast domains that she has just acquired could lead to losses in two ways: the population of her colonies could grow at the expense of Great Britain; or one day the colonies could become powerful enough to found a state independent of the British crown."[4]

England's inactivity and the budding problems with her American colonists made the time seem ripe for France to play, once more, a role in European affairs which several generations of French monarchs had felt was France's special role in Europe. The conception of the role found its most straightforward expression in the instructions Bernis gave, in 1759, to Choiseul, on his way to be Louis XV's ambassador in Vienna: "The object of the politics of this crown," Bernis wrote, "has been and always will be to play in Europe the superior role which suits its seniority, its dignity, and its grandeur; to reduce every power which attempts to force itself above her, whether by trying to take away her possessions, or by arrogating to itself an unjust pre-emminence, or, finally, by seeking to take away from her [France] her influence and credit in the general affairs [of Europe]"[5] The conception expressed by Bernis had the unquestioned support of Vergennes. He had learned and absorbed it from countless instructions and dispatches he had received as a diplomat. Yet Vergennes knew, from long experience, that no idea from the past readily fitted the present.

Once installed in the Department of Foreign Affairs, Vergennes composed for Louis XVI one of the many memoranda he would write during his ministry to explain and justify his policy. His first one, on the political situation of Europe in 1774, was intended to initiate the young Louis XVI into the mysteries of the international political system.[6]

As Vergennes viewed the system of politics from Versailles in 1774, the event that still dominated the scene was the First Polish Partition of 1772. To Vergennes, the partition, in which Russia, Austria, and Prussia divided among themselves over 80,000 square miles of Polish territory, represented a critical breakdown of the traditional balance-of-power system in Europe, a balance of power in which France had usually exercised considerable influence in Eastern Europe. The partition of Poland, Vergennes told his King, with a moral indignation unusual for him, was political brigandage. Like the defeat suffered by France in the Peace of 1763, the partition of Poland was a terrible blow to the prestige of the French monarchy, for Poland had been a long-time protégé of France.

At the same time, however, the terrible costs of the Russo-Turkish War which had set the state for the Polish partition, as well as domestic unrest at home, convinced the Empress of Russia, Catherine II, that a breathing period of peace was essential. Before he left Sweden to become Secretary of State at Versailles, Vergennes had been assured from several sources that Russia was, for the moment, exhausted, in a "condition in which she could frighten no one."[7] Momentarily, at least, Versailles and St. Petersburg had a common interest in continuing the peace in Eastern Europe.

The other two parties to the Polish partition, Prussia and Austria, caused

Vergennes some concern, although he felt that there was no immediate reason to fear for French interests. The territories newly acquired by Austria and Prussia were either north or east of their own frontiers, and therefore far from French frontiers. And Vergennes recognized that, since the acquisitions were about equal, France could always count on balancing one of them against the other. Yet, such a limited response to the expansion of Prussia or Austria was essentially passive, Vergennes felt, and left little room for France to play the active role she was accustomed to playing in Eastern Europe.

Vergennes especially worried about the ambitious character of Joseph II of Austria. In his opinion, Joseph's mother, Maria Theresa, was the sole person able to control Joseph's limitless ambitions. But Maria Theresa was ill. When she died, who would be the voice of moderation for Joseph? There were ancient claims in Italy that he could exploit, and there were, unfortunately, his father's old claims to French Lorraine. Despite the existing alliance between Austria and France, if Joseph were not somehow bridled, he might seriously threaten French interests.

Despite his distrust of Joseph, Vergennes insisted that France needed her alliance with Austria. The day that Vienna broke her ties with France, he predicted, she could accept England as an ally. After that unhappy day, any war that France became involved in would be a land war as well as a naval war. It did not seem reasonable to Vergennes that Austria, continuously consumed by her conflict with Prussia, would sever her alliance with France, but he knew that errors of judgment and calculation were not unknown in diplomacy. Louis XVI, therefore, had to include the possibility of unreasonable and erroneous decisions in his considerations about Austria. Furthermore, Vergennes warned, if Louis XVI really wanted to keep his allies, he had to keep them constantly aware of the utility of having France as an ally. Louis XVI's allies should fear his resentment if they failed him. "Fear and hope," he told his young King, "are the two great springs of the political, as well as the moral, order."

In order to keep fear alive and nourish it in Vienna, Vergennes wanted Louis XVI to establish better lines of communication with Prussia. Fear of the king of Prussia, he believed, would force Austria to retain close ties with France. "Destroy the power of Prussia," he warned, and there would be no more "dike against Austrian ambition."[8]

In his 1774 memorandum to Louis XVI, Vergennes predicted with startling foresight the difficulties which Louis XVI would face in the future. The death of Maria Theresa, Vergennes believed, would set Joseph free of the restraints imposed by her moderation. When the successions of Berg, Julich, and Bavaria opened, Vergennes predicted, there would be trouble which could easily lead to war. With the example already set by the Polish partition, the smaller powers of Europe were now more than ever at the mercy of powerful predatory states. Could France stand aside, and not become involved, if one or several of the great powers began to devour the small ones?

When Vergennes turned away from the continent and looked to the sea, he saw nothing to reassure his King. England, he said, was a "restless and greedy nation", more envious of her neighbor's prosperity than of her own well-being. She was powerfully armed and ever-ready to strike. Louis XVI could count on the pacific intentions displayed by the English ministers, Vergennes warned, only so long as the domestic difficulties England was having with her American colonies continued. But even the domestic difficulties might tempt England to try to rally the parties that divided her with an external war against France. Moreover, Vergennes added, France might be drawn into a naval war with England against her own wishes and even against those of England. The alliance with Spain obligated France to render aid to Spain, if she went to war, whether the war was offensive or defensive. And there were many opportunities for war, Vergennes saw, in the vast overseas possessions of Spain.

Despite its obvious disadvantages, Vergennes argued, the Family Compact with Spain was, perhaps, more advantageous to France than it was to Spain. England, he explained, carried on a vast trade with Spain and was, therefore, less likely to strike that country which contributed so much to English wealth. On the other hand, England, having nothing to gain from France, was only envious of the prodigious development of French plantations in America, and of French industry at home. What kept England from attacking France, Vergennes believed, was the certainty that the first shot of a cannon directed at either France or Spain would be answered by both Bourbon powers. The Family Compact was, therefore, a cornerstone of French policy, and Louis XVI had to see to it that France had the means and the power to fulfill the obligations of the compact. Otherwise, it would become useless. "May it please God that this never be the fate of the Family Compact!"

Vergennes was insistent, however, that the alliance between France and Spain be on terms of equality. He warned that neither of the allies should abuse the alliance by acting without consulting the interests of the other.

Because the further expansion of any of the great powers would hurt French interests, Vergennes believed that France ought to assume, in Europe, the role of protector of the *status quo* and defender of the properties of all other powers. The second- and third-rate powers, he thought, would welcome France as their protector, now that they had the example of Poland before their eyes. Happily, as the guarantor of the Treaty of Westphalia, France already had the authority to assume such a role in Germany. Indeed,

Vergennes believed that, if France did not assume the role of protector, and arbitrate the troubles of Europe, her indifference to the fate of the small powers would alienate the very powers who traditionally looked to her as their protector. She would then find herself isolated, unrespected, and condemned for not living up to her treaty obligations. To avoid isolation, and to re-establish a *proper* equilibrium of power, that is, one favorable to France, France had to take an active part in Europe's troubles. She would take that part as defender of the *status quo*, protector of the smaller powers, and arbiter of disagreements that threatened to destroy the peace.

Vergennes recognized that, if France became active as the protector of the *status quo* and the small powers of Europe, she would have to be willing to "protect" to the point of military intervention if the issues came to that. In addition, he knew that such a role entailed a self-denying restriction. He believed that, if France stood forth as the champion of the *status quo* in Europe, she could not, without undermining the integrity of her own position, follow a policy of conquest and aggrandizement. France, Vergennes argued, had a fertile soil, and valuable products, which the other nations could not surpass. "[She has] ... zealous and healthy subjects [who are] deeply interested in every kind of business. Her King, like a judge, can look upon his throne as a tribunal instituted by Providence to make others respect the rights and holdings of sovereigns." As Vergennes saw France's future, the increase in French population, the exploitation of France's resources, and the proper development of French diplomatic influence abroad were preferable alternatives to a policy of aggrandizement.

Vergennes' refusal to accept a policy of aggrandizement did not mean, however, that France was resigned to a position as a second-rate power. France, he felt, could best serve her own interests by abandoning all ambitions which tended to create suspicions, fears, and, inevitably, coalitions against her. France could then step forth as the disinterested arbiter and insist that her voice be heard. As the honest broker of Europe, France would earn the influence, respect, and prestige that she deserved, and influence, prestige, and respect were essential ingredients in Vergennes' diplomatic recipe.

The international system, as Vergennes described it in 1774, was anything but orderly, stable, or moral. It was, in fact, a world of dizzy instability, a world of distrust and suspicion, of friends as well as enemies, and it was a world of incessant competition of predatory states which expanded, decayed, and, sometimes, even disappeared. In the midst of the instability, Louis XVI had to defend himself, avoid isolation, and build the prestige and influence which tradition and personal character prescribed. To succeed in these goals, Vergennes seemed to be saying, Louis XVI had to anticipate events by rational calculation of his interests, by reasonable deductions from facts, and by estimates of personal character. As Vergennes analyzed the political picture of Europe, he seemed to be demonstrating to the young Louis XVI an axiom which he had once urged on his son, Constantin: aside from the "impenetrable mysteries" of religion, he had written in a letter from Stockholm, everything should be submitted to the "tribunal of your reason."[9]

Yet it would be a monumental error to conclude that Vergennes' conception of the place of the French monarchy in the international political system was derived purely from rational analysis. In a note to Louis XVI, written in 1782, explaining France's hostility towards England, Vergennes revealed that emotion, vicarious ambition, aristocratic honor, and even his own personal ego were also ingredients in his foreign policy. "Please remember, Sire," Vergennes recalled for his monarch, "the position of France relative to the other powers of Europe when your Majesty took the reins of government and charged me with the Department of Foreign Affairs. The deplorable peace of 1763, the partition of Poland, and many other equally unhappy causes had profoundly undermined the consideration due the crown of France, which in earlier days, had been the object of terror and jealousy; instead there was only the opposite sentiment. Once reputed the first power of Europe, France barely had a place among the second-rate powers. Subjugated, after a fashion, by England, did we not see the ambassador of that power demand an account of our slightest moves, threaten us with war if we did not discontinue re-arming begun in the Mediterranean and which we had to stop? Did I not, myself, watch this same ambassador, in my office, dispute Your Majesty's incontestable right to make civil repairs at Dunkirk, and demand an explanation of the arming of your frigates for the purpose of training your Navy? I confess, Sire, all the arrogance and insults against which my heart revolted made me desire and search for the means to change a situation so little compatible with the elevation of your soul and the grandeur of your power."[10]

Vergennes' policy paper of 1774 also reveals his personal fatalism about the inevitability of war. War, or possibility of war, was an element in every problem, every calculation he studied. Vergennes believed, with an almost mathematical certainty, that the longer peace lasted, the less likely it was to continue to last. A lengthy period of peace was, to him, hard evidence that it would soon end. His view of the certainty of war meant that the priorities and resources of the state had always to be geared to the needs of war. Since Vergennes believed that the future brought only war, the only future he ever prepared for was that of war. His predictions, therefore, were self-fulfilling.

Certainly, war was a constantly recurring theme of Ancien Régime high politics, and diplomatic practice, combined with personal attitudes and the class ambitions of the aristocracy, made it a common occurrence. If one monarch feared another, it was acceptable, in practice, for him to attack his opponent before the latter had a chance to do the same. Or, if a state became an obstacle in the way of a ruler's self-prescribed role in the system, it was by no means indecent to clear away the obstacle with a surprise attack. On the seas, England had the reputation of attacking without a previous declaration of war. On land, Frederick of Prussia held the same dubious honor. But these two powers were hardly alone in their willingness to be convinced by the logic of preventive war.

Preventive war did not necessarily begin with a surprise attack on the enemy. The skillful monarch or statesman could provoke the enemy to attack, and then call into effect the defensive provisions of his alliances. "It is easy to make a war without being, materially, the aggressor," Vergennes told Louis XVI in the spring of 1777.[11] Although he was speaking of Joseph II's relations with Prussia, his statement summarizes beautifully, as we shall see, France's policy of intervention in the American Revolutionary War.

Vergennes' conception of Louis XVI as the arbiter of Europe increased the possibilities for war. The idea was based on a definition of balance of power that gave France a special role in the system. Vergennes did not see France as one power among several who kept the system "balanced" because they were all relatively equal in power and influence. Louis XVI's role, as Vergennes outlined it, was that of the arbiter, who stood, so to speak, somewhat apart from the system, and maintained the balance of power by seeing to it that the other powers maintained an even distribution of power.[12] This definition of balance of power was, of course, the one Englishmen had held for generations. In 1774, when England faced the necessity of withdrawing further from continental affairs, France became her competitor for the job of "holding the balance of power," of being the arbiter. Theoretically, the role required great self-restraint and a sense of duty toward others, especially the smaller, weaker powers. Vergennes recognized that obligation. Furthermore, he felt that, in the Polish partition, England had failed to meet her obligations. He recognized, too, that, to play the role of arbiter, France needed a margin of strength and some diplomatic advantages which she did not have after 1763.

Thus, in 1774, Vergennes was a revisionist, dissatisfied with Louis XVI's position, and determined to change it for one more compatible with his vision of Louis XVI's special role in the international system. England, he knew, would not welcome France's bid to gain that needed margin of strength and the necessary diplomatic advantages. England would not willingly allow France to replace her. England, therefore, was the obstacle standing in the way of Louis XVI's becoming that which Vergennes felt was compatible with the "elevation of . . . Louis XVI's soul and the grandeur of . . . his power."

As Vergennes pondered the map of Europe in 1774, he developed a grand conception of France at the center of the international system. Paradoxically, Louis XVI was to be the arbiter of international politics and the protector, as well as reviser, of the *status quo*. The policy, as he reformulated it, was not just a response to political realities; nor was it simply a plan ready-made from the past. It was, to be sure, a response to what Vergennes considered to be the "givens" of international politics. It was also the result of Vergennes' interpretations of what constituted the history and traditions of the past. And these ingredients were bound together by passionately held values about power, rank, prestige, and honor, which Vergennes inherited from his family and class, as well as from his profession as a diplomat. In addition, his policy grew out of his own perceptions of what the future would bring. War with England was inevitable; the idea of peace with that nation had no immediate future.

Finally, to these ingredients must be added Vergennes' almost complete personal identification with the French monarch's destiny. He found personal gratification when Louis XVI won a victory or saw his prestige rise. He felt shame and indignation when Louis suffered humiliation. Advancing the King's interests was, for him, a way of satisfying, both directly and vicariously, some of his own ambitions. Moreover, it never occurred to him that his monarch's destiny could be worked out in any other arena but that of war and international politics.

Yet, when Vergennes became Secretary of State, the French Navy was totally unprepared for a war with England. During those first months of Louis XVI's reign, Vergennes later recalled, the Navy was in such a sorry state that everything had to be re-done from scratch: "Not a ship in readiness, not a magazine supplied."[13] "At his accession," Vergennes remembered on another occasion, "His Majesty found no Navy and very little provision for its restoration."[14] In such a situation, Vergennes must have felt like a blacksmith without a hammer. France had to become a sea power. The new Secretary of State for the Navy, Sartine, agreed. No sooner was he given authority, than he pressed for the immediate construction of naval ships, and he did so with an energy equal to that of Choiseul.[15]

Vergennes encouraged, helped plan, and closely followed the revival of the French Navy from the moment he took office. And, by mid-year, 1775, the French Navy had been restored to the point where France could defend herself on the sea. Normal operational demands were now met and training cruises, which had been discontinued, were resumed.[16] But, no sooner was the Navy prepared to defend France than Sartine, with the encouragement of Vergennes and Maurepas, began to press for going beyond the needs of defense. When the British responded to the French naval build-up with additions to her navy, Sartine ordered more ships put into service to match the British reaction: what followed was the classical pattern of escalation. When the French government began its secret military aid to the Americans, the French Navy had to expand further, in case the British navy interfered. Each increase in naval armaments increased the fears of attack and, therefore, became further justification for more shipbuilding and stockpiling of supplies. In late 1776, Vergennes wrote: "For two years, France has been occupied with the re-establishment of her Navy and colonies. The progress she has made is considerable, but still not finished . . ."[17] Six months later: "The King now has forty-two ships of the line in readiness, including everything necessary to send them to sea . . ." But Vergennes was still not satisfied: "We have created a sea-going fleet, but we have not yet given . . . [that fleet] the reserve strength that a good use of time will assure."[18] Vergennes, Sartine, and Maurepas were determined that Louis XVI would have a Navy to challenge England's control of the seas.

For the administration of foreign affairs, Vergennes inherited an organization that was, for its time, one of the best organized and most efficient in the world. When Louis XVI, in 1774, dismantled the apparatus of the "*secret du roi,*" Louis XV's parallel and secret system of diplomacy, the Ministry of Foreign Affairs approached the model of an ideal bureaucracy, in that it had a well-defined chain of command; it contained the beginnings of a system of procedure for dealing with routine work activities; and there was a division of labor based on specialization. On the other hand, the Ministry's system of promotion and selection was not based only on technical competence. Family ties obviously played a significant role in the choice of "experts" who worked in the lower levels of the organization; and studies of the backgrounds of ambassadors, and even Vergennes' record of nepotism, demonstrate that class and family, as well as technical competence, played a large role in the selection and promotion of career officers, as well as ambassadors. Thus, in the Ministry of Foreign Affairs, the identity of the state's interest with the particular private interests of family and class was well established. To this institution Vergennes added his own refinements and improvements, as well as his own personal talent for organization and clarity. Thus, when Vergennes came to power in 1774, he took charge of a Ministry of Foreign Affairs which was a model for its time. Neither the Army nor the Navy was equal to all the tasks which the foreign policy he envisaged would create. But the Minister of War, Saint-Germain, and, above all, Sartine, chief of the Navy, helped provide him with the military instruments required to launch his policies.[19]

In the area of public finance, however, Vergennes inherited a clumsy and inadequate public policy. The failure of the structure of French finances to pay the costs of France's role as a great power was a chronic infirmity already recognized by Vergennes' predecessors. To this crucial problem Vergennes brought no solution. Indeed, his failure to give it the priority it deserved was the Achilles heel of his statesmanship.

CHAPTER 17

The Spanish Temptation

Vergennes' Spanish policy began before his administration, in the period immediately following the Seven Years War. He developed it from the lessons learned from the Falkland Islands* dispute. Spain had long claimed these islands because of their proximity to the continent of South America, and because of the Spanish settlements on them. Between 1764 and 1770, however, the English also founded settlements there. The dispute over rival claims began to take on the appearance of war after June, 1770, when the Spanish commander, Bucareli, took it upon himself to remove the English by force. The two countries might very well have gone to war over the islands that year if Louis XV, when approached by Spain, had not refused to lend the aid that Charles III felt was due him according to the Family Compact. In the international dispute which France created when she occupied Corsica, Charles had faithfully stood behind his Bourbon ally. He felt, therefore, that he had a legitimate claim on France's aid. Abandoned, so he felt, by France, Charles had to back down and accept the blame for the crisis, as well as permit the English to return to their settlements.[1] Four years later, the English decided to abandon their settlements of their own accord; nevertheless Charles III had received a blow to his pride and to Spanish prestige. The humiliation was not quickly erased, and Louis XV's part in it remained a sore point in Franco-Spanish relations.

Vergennes believed the Family Compact was useful to France, but he saw in it the potential danger that Spain might use the alliance to advance purely Spanish interests. Vergennes argued, in fact, that Spain had done so in the Falkland Islands affair.[2] Vergennes was aware, also, that any inequality in favor of Spain placed the major policy decisions of the two allies in the lap of the Spanish Minister, Grimaldi, rather than the French Minister. Personally, Vergennes objected to any loss of control over France's decisions. For personal as well as political reasons, therefore, he was determined that French policy would not sail in the wake of Spain.

*Located just off the eastern coast of the southern tip of South America.

In July of 1774, the French ambassador to Spain, Ossun, informed Versailles of a possible outbreak of war between Portugal and Spain. A dispute had arisen over two different, but related, quarrels in South America. According to the French ambassador, Portugal had established military posts on Spanish territory, in the Rio de la Plata region of Brazil. Despite vigorous protests from Spain, she refused to withdraw her troops, even though officials in Lisbon had promised to do so. Unable to get redress through Lisbon and diplomatic channels, Spain decided to take matters into her own hands; she ordered her commander at Buenos Aires to drive out the Portuguese, which he did forthwith.

The second cause of dispute was a Portuguese claim to a colonial establishment on the North Bank of the Rio de la Plata, an establishment enclosed in Spanish territory, menacing the Spanish, both as a military threat and as a center of contraband. The colony had been taken by Spain during the Seven Years War, but returned, at least on paper, by the treaty of peace.

The Portuguese protested that the Spanish had not returned all they had promised to return, and they acted to force the Spanish to accept their point of view by reinforcing their land forces and building up their naval strength in the area. Charles III, angered by this Portuguese impudence, was determined to stand his ground: "if . . . the Portuguese attacked his possessions they would have to answer for it." *"Une petite guerre,"* to use the French ambassador's phrase, seemed to be in the offing. Spain carefully disengaged herself from a costly war with the Moroccans and a disastrous expedition against the Algerians,[3] while Portugal's ally, England, became fully occupied with a nest of difficulties in North America.[4] Spain's opportunity took center stage.

As Vergennes assumed the responsibilities of Secretary of State from his predecessor, Bertin, he saw that the "little war" could very easily grow into a big one. As long as it remained isolated, there was no serious danger to French interests, but the complex and delicate balance of world politics made it extremely difficult to isolate a local war. Furthermore, he knew that Spain had never given up her old idea of uniting Portugal with Spain, and the "little war" in South America offered the perfect excuse to invade Portugal and attempt to bring her under Charles III's authority.

Yet, England considered Portuguese independence essential to her own interests; she had implemented this consideration with an alliance, and would assist her ally in case of a war with Spain if it extended beyond the limits of the small areas under dispute.[5] Louis XVI, bound to Spain by the Family Compact, would then be called upon to stand behind his ally. Other powers of Europe, inspired by the idea that a Spanish conquest of Portugal could upset the balance of power, might also decide to enter the fray. Thus, bullets fired in far-away Brazil could easily ricochet back to Europe. Portugal pushed preparations with an "extreme ardor and vivacity." Spain, after toying with the idea of a non-aggression agreement with England, began a military buildup, and urged her French ally to do the same.[6] Alert French diplomats reported an increase in the activities of English ships and soldiers.[7]

Vergennes felt obligated to assure the Spanish King that Louis XVI stood firmly behind him. Nevertheless, he was embarrassed by the Spanish King's warlike stance, at a time when France's resources were so limited.[8] Although Vergennes admitted that his understanding of state finances was inadequate,[9] he knew that Louis XVI had inherited a crippled financial administration. He recognized also that, if such a "vast machine" were shaken, it could not quickly be restored to normalcy. What France needed most of all was time, time to recover financially, time to put her administration in order, and time to rebuild her navy. For all of these things, peace was a prerequisite,[10] and peace depended on decisions in Spain.

Vergennes also knew that Spain could, if she wished, help France regain her economic strength. One of the obvious ways to rebuild the nation's economy was to encourage industry. To do this, Vergennes believed, France had to increase her exports. In 1768, Spain and France had signed at Madrid a convention defining Article Twenty-four of the Family Compact, which dealt with the commerce and navigation between the two Bourbon realms.[11] A natural market for French goods was Spain, but the Spanish market was not as open to French products as Vergennes would have liked. In fact, the French minister complained to the Spanish, French trade in Spain was not nearly equal to that of England,[12] the archenemy of both Bourbon powers.

Vergennes wanted French goods to be accepted in Spain on equal terms with British goods. It was ridiculous, he argued, that English leather entering Spanish ports should pay only ten per cent duty, while a twenty per cent duty was placed on the same French product. The interests of France and Spain, he claimed required that the two powers hinder, as much as possible, the growth of English wealth. England could be gradually weakened by withdrawing her economic privileges, and reducing opportunities for new gains. This would be even a better way to bring her to terms than war, the Frenchman was convinced, because the outcome of war was "always doubtful and uncertain."[13] Obviously, Vergennes was not ignorant of the weapons of economic warfare.

Vergennes was pleased to find that Spain's initial response to the war crisis was moderate; she insisted on a return of the territory taken by Portugal, but she seemed, at least at first, content to settle the matter on that point. Still, Portugal's sword rattling, exaggerated, he thought, to impress England, frightened the French minister. To assist their allies and protect their own holdings in South America, the English might order a naval squadron to those waters. "A naval force stationed in this area could result in some unfortunate accident," he warned, for "we know the taste the English navy has for rapine. . . ."[14] When he talked over the situation with Lord Stormont, the English ambassador at Versailles, he found the Englishman seriously concerned but, happily, not belligerent. The English hoped, Stormont told him, that the issue could be settled peacefully, or, if not, that the dispute could at least be confined to the interior of Brazil.[15]

Nevertheless, the show of arms continued. Where, diplomats anxiously asked, were the arms going to be used? Reports from across the English Channel indicated that the English build-up was probably a response to the rapidly deteriorating situation in the North American colonies, but, if that crisis died down, the English forces could easily be transferred somewhere else.[16] At the same time, Spanish naval preparations disturbed the English, who sent naval ships to patrol the Bay of Biscay and watch the Spanish fleet.[17] Were the Spaniards going to reinforce their forces in Brazil? Did the British have information that the Portuguese were going to undertake a major campaign in Brazil, and were, therefore, observing Spanish fleet movements for their ally? Suspicions, rumors, and hints were collected, recorded, examined, and re-examined; the tensions that fatigue statesmen in time of crisis gripped the councils of state.

Vergennes wanted to avoid a declaration of war, but, if it could not be avoided, he wanted the war confined to Brazil. His greatest fear was that the Spaniards might launch an invasion of Portugal and drag all of Europe into a general war. He kept insisting, therefore, that, if the Spaniards wanted to protect their holdings in South America, they should send their newly raised reinforcements there, before the English could intercept them.[18] Spain would then have an advantage over the Portuguese in Brazil. Also, such a move (but he did not tell the Spanish this) would reduce the possibility of a Spanish invasion of Portugal by reducing the Spanish means to carry it out. But by now, Spain had taken the bit in its mouth. On October 18, 1775, Grimaldi composed a letter to his ambassador at Versailles which demonstrated that Spain would willingly use the Family Compact to further purely Spanish aims.

Over a month ago, Grimaldi explained, the Portuguese ambassador had opened conversations with Spain which promised an amicable settlement of the dispute in Brazil; also, the ambassador had suggested that both powers order their commanders in Brazil to avoid hostilities. Spain had agreed to this proposal, Grimaldi wrote, and had even asked France and England to withhold mediation proposals made earlier, until Lisbon's true intentions were discovered.

Spain was still awaiting a follow-up response from Lisbon. Portugal's delay raised the suspicion that Portugal and England were hatching some sinister plot against Spain. Spain complained to the Portuguese, Grimaldi reported, and told them the delay could only be interpreted as an artifice. Still there was no answer. It is "shameful", Grimaldi indignantly concluded, "for a monarchy as respectable as the Spanish monarchy to suffer such disdain and insults from the Portuguese ministry."

Grimaldi went on to remind France that England was in trouble with her colonies, but that there was a "moral certainty" that, as soon as she settled this trouble, she would attack the Bourbon powers in order to make good her losses and expenses.

The members of the Spanish council conferred several times together and reached the following conclusions: First, France and Spain "naturally desired peace," and, if Portugal and England would proceed in good faith, the two Bourbon powers would have "little more to do at the moment." But, Grimaldi went on, Portugal had sent "formidable forces" to Brazil, and had invaded Spanish territory. In addition, the Spanish believed that England encouraged, indeed sustained, all this. England had already warned Spain that she was under obligation to back her ally if Portugal was attacked, although Lord Rochfort had explained that the obligation arose only if Spain attacked Portugal in Europe. From these facts the Spanish, somewhat illogically, drew the conclusion that England really had designs on Spain. Finally, the letter said, the Spanish Secretaries of State wished to discuss their conclusions with France.

The Spaniards wanted to know whether the two Bourbon powers should rest on the defensive and wait until it pleased their enemy to attack? Should we not, Grimaldi wanted to know, "profit from the circumstances while their forces are divided?" In order to soothe away any restrictions of conscience that might cloud the desired answer to such a question, Grimaldi pointed out that Portugal was already the aggressor, and, therefore, France and Spain could not be blamed for the war.

The letter also informed Vergennes that Spain had decided not to send more forces to Brazil. Reinforcements would be too expensive and the voyage would be too long. Such an undertaking would cost as much as a "formal conquest," and would deprive Spain of some 8,000 to 10,000 troops which could be used in more important places. The Spanish then reported their opinion that the most economical way to settle the issue was to order troops to the Portuguese frontier, and to send warships into Portuguese waters, letting the Portuguese know that Spain was prepared to fight either in Europe or America, whichever place suited the Spaniards best.

The Spanish note anticipated that such a move might provoke England, and thus set off an explosion. But England was now stripped of her forces at home and had no reserves, as a result of her difficulties in America. In any event, the favorable moment to act was now, before the enemies of the Bourbon family were better prepared.

The Spanish letter closed on a single note: War was inevitable. What was to be done? The Spanish council had been divided. They could send a force to take the Portuguese possessions at San Caetano, and at Rio de Janeiro. This alternative would create a diversion, and relieve the pressure on the Spanish governor of Buenos Aires. But the plan would require more forces than Spain could supply at the moment, and troops sailing such a great distance would not be in condition to go immediately into action. They would need a rest, and a rest would give the Portuguese time to prepare their defenses. Such reflections gave birth to another project: *Spain reinforced by 20,000 or 30,000 French troops, should undertake the conquest of Portugal.* As France's reward, Spain promised Louis XVI the colony of Brazil — after France had conquered it. Brazil, Spain assured France, eventually could be a source of great wealth. Finally, after these two conquests, English pride could be reduced permanently, and the future wars that this "ambitious power" might start out of "ill will and caprice" would be avoided forever. Europe would enjoy a "tranquility unheard of until then." The King of Spain did not want to make such an important decision without hearing the advice of his young nephew, Louis XVI.[19]

With an uninhibited simplicity, Grimaldi thus advanced the classical argument for preventive war. War was inevitable; a preventive war was therefore necessary. The enemy could be humbled, and Europe would live in tranquility forever. Could France, for the second time in less than five years, afford to refuse a Spanish call for assistance? If she did, would the Family Compact survive the refusal?

Vergennes, aware that Grimaldi's propositions deserved immediate attention, submitted them to the King's Council as soon as they arrived. On the twenty-ninth of November, after consideration in Council, the response was formulated.

The mediation efforts of France, Vergennes admitted, had been without fruit. Nevertheless, he was not convinced that Lisbon and London were set on provoking a war. England, he pointed out, had her own colonies to worry about, and Portugal, unaided by England, could have no illusions about the disproportion of her power to that of Spain. Moreover, Vergennes was convinced that "at the present moment England could not, and ought not want to, make war on the two crowns." The American rebellion, he now thought, was going to be a "long-winded affair." Afterwards, England, fatigued by that war and in debt as a result of its expenses, was not likely to provoke still another conflict.[20]

Concerning the moral question of whether fears of an English attack provided justification for an attack on Portugal and England, Vergennes expressed himself clearly: While fears of England *do* exist, he admitted, they could not be used as the motive, or the pretext, for a preventive war against England, even though England had already given the world an example of such an act in 1755. That grief, he continued, was extinguished by the peace treaty. To revive it would be to "soil oneself with a notorious injustice, which would be invincibly repugnant to the feelings and principles of the two monarchs." The two monarchs, he implied, should not violate their "principles."

With the moral objections to a preventive war, Vergennes had other, less idealistic, ones. A preventive war, he pointed out, would cause anxiety throughout Europe. The feeling that an injustice had been committed would take a long time to erase. Furthermore, he continued, European powers were still disposed to fear France more than England. Holland was prejudiced in England's favor. The Russians and English had recently been engaged in negotiations. England, attacked, could very likely secure Russian help. Russia would bring in Denmark, and who would then remain as an ally against this "maritime league?" Only Sweden, and she would be hemmed in by her neighbors, and more of a burden than a help.[21]

The major object of the Bourbon powers, he reminded Spain, was to weaken England, and England seemed bent on that goal, herself. "She unwisely engaged in a war with her colonies, of which the outcome and the end are not easy to foresee." As England's strength declined, the relative strength of the Bourbon powers would rise, and the goal of the Bourbon crowns would be automatically achieved.

Vergennes was careful to point out that France did not excuse Portugal's actions. Nevertheless, he noted, Portugal had disavowed hostilities on the Rio Grande in South America. He confessed that she was slow in negotiating, but in this, she was guilty of bad manners, rather than deliberate injury. If Portugal started a new invasion of Spanish territory in America, he assured the Spanish ambassador, Aranda, there would be time to take action. And, on this point, he could not deny himself the satisfaction of pointing out to the Spanish government that, if they had sent reinforcements to Buenos Aires, as he had earlier suggested, the Portuguese would have been faced with a superior enemy in that theater. Consequently, they would have been less likely to attack, and more eager to settle. In addition, if they tried to defy Spanish arms in South America, the English would not give any effective assistance, for the Court of St. James had made it quite clear that they would assist Portugal only if she were attacked in Europe, or if Spain tried to conquer all of Brazil.

"After all has been said during the course of this letter," Vergennes concluded, "you surely do not expect us to recommend actual land and sea demonstrations against Portugal." The wisest course, he felt, was to let

English weaken herself by dividing her forces. Then there would be time to take "proper measures." Although the idea was "seductive and it was difficult to imagine a more beautiful or richer acquisition" than Brazil, Vergennes stated with finality that territory "does not tempt the King, my master, at all." His Majesty of France, Vergennes declared, was content with his own domain; he wanted to conserve it, and he did not think of extending it. Nevertheless, Vergennes took care to assure Charles III that Louis XVI appreciated his uncle's generous offer.[22]

To reinforce his answer to Aranda, Vergennes also sent a copy of it to his own ambassador to Spain, Ossun, and accompanied it with a letter which contained the further consideration that war was "useless" unless the two crowns were themselves attacked in their "own domains."[23] Later, after the Spanish Minister, Grimaldi, apparently suggested that France was pacifist out of weakness, Vergennes further explained his position to his ambassador: "We do not blush to confess," he wrote, "that we regard war as a very great evil, and we will avoid it as long as we are not forced into it out of duty to our engagements or the bad faith of our rivals." "Let's not dissimulate," he argued, as soon as England saw the two powers take measures to invade Portugal, she would fight, and spare no efforts to bring all of Europe into the war. "Let's not forget," he told Ossun, "that this is the principal resort which has only too often succeeded." France, placed in the center of Europe, could not isolate herself the way Spain could. France, therefore, did not want to furnish the motive for a general European war against the Bourbon powers.[24]

Vergennes had an additional reason why he did not wish to see Portugal conquered by Spain. He suspected that Portugal was weary of its role as protegé of England, and he anticipated that, if Portugal learned not to fear Bourbon domination, she might become an element in his plans for French commercial expansion.

In 1775, he picked up, once again, the threads of commercial negotiations with Lisbon, which he and his uncle Chavigny had left there in 1741. In September, 1775, Louis XVI appointed the Marquis de Blosset his ambassador to Lisbon. In his instructions, Blosset read of the importance of the commercial advantages to be expected from better relations with Portugal.

Once upon a time, the instructions explained, when Spain was part of the Hapsburg holdings, France and Portugal maintained the best relations. But when a prince from the House of Bourbon became King of Spain, Portugal looked elsewhere for protection and friends. She turned to Great Britain and the United Provinces, and she cemented the new alliances by granting commercial advantages to both powers. These advantages had first been enjoyed by France, but had been taken over and extended by the English and the Dutch. In the past France had argued, on the basis of the Treaty of

Utrecht, that the privileges granted to England and the Dutch were automatically those of France. Portugal repeatedly refused to accept such an interpretation.

Louis XVI continued to argue that the old treaties with Portugal still held, but he was willing to concede that France would never persuade Portugal to allow France the privileges granted the Dutch and the English. Until a new treaty could be concluded, French cloth would have to enter the Portuguese market disguised as cloth coming from Holland.

Vergennes had no illusions about the immediate possibility of a *rapprochement* with Portugal. The rivalry between Spain and Portugal, both in Europe and in Latin America, destroyed all chances for better relations. Spain was "indissolubly" united with France, and Portugal was equally united with England. But Vergennes was planting seeds for the future. "Circumstances change," he told Blosset, and, when they did, the French ambassador was to take advantage of every opportunity to open negotiations.

Blosset also read in his instructions that he was to employ his good offices at Lisbon to explore a settlement of the Spanish-Portuguese dispute. Spain had requested such a move, and Louis XVI agreed. He had even agreed to approach England to see if, together, they could contain the "effervescene" of Portugal. On his way to Portugal, Blosset was to stop off at Saint-Iledephonse, where the Spanish court was in residence, to discuss with the Spanish minister what steps should be taken regarding Portugal. Above all, he was to find out what the Spanish King was planning to do in the present quarrel. The Marquis de Blosset was "to listen to everything, without seeming to have any other commission." But, as soon as he learned something, he was to render a complete account to Vergennes. Or, if something very important came up, Blosset was told to write directly to Louis XVI.[25] In the dangerous crisis at hand, reliable information was priceless.

The conflict between Spain and Portugal revealed several components of Vergennes' policies immediately after his assumption of office. From the first, he demonstrated his interest in French commerce. In Spain, and in Portugal, he saw possibilities for the expansion of French trade, and he acted on these possibilities to try to get more markets for France. In both cases, however, the expansion of French trade was to be at the expense of England, France's archenemy. Vergennes' concern with trade was not simply to expand France's commerce. He recognized the value of economic warfare, and wanted to weaken England by striking at her economic advantages. His interest in commerce was always subordinated to high politics.

Vergennes' refusal of Spain's offer of Brazil reinforces the conclusion that Louis XVI did not wish to acquire additional territory, especially colonies, because further acquisitions would arouse Europe against France. Vergennes' concept of balance of power, indeed, had a self-restraining influence on Louis XVI's actions. Vergennes' experience as ambassador at Constantinople had taught him, also, that, with proper treaties and agreements, France could enjoy extensive trade in the world without the administrative expense of colonies. Colonies, he thought, were useless if the commercial advantages they brought could be acquired in another way at less expense.

From the moment he stepped into office, Vergennes opposed war that would involve France on the continent. His refusal to assist Spain in an invasion of Portugal followed from that principle. As long as England remained France's enemy, France had to avoid war in Europe.

How serious was Vergennes' judgment that preventive war was a "notorious injustice?" Did he really have strong convictions about the immorality of preventive war? Personally, yes. Yet, as recently as his ambassadorship to Stockholm, he had suggested that Sweden launch a preventive war against Russia. He used the moral argument as an additional card in his play to restrain Spain's ambition, and to prevent Spain's using the Family Compact to further her own special interests. Its usefulness was a function of the fact that Charles III, a Christian nobleman could not deny traditional morality if someone was so indiscreet as to introduce it into high politics.

CHAPTER 18

The Revolution in America

As Vergennes watched the world diplomatic chessboard in 1775, the revolution in America slowly grew to dominate his attention. He saw both dangers and opportunities for France in the American rebellion, and both were closely tied to the ability of the Americans to field and maintain a viable military force. In July, the French ambassador wrote from England that it appeared to him that the entire British army would be unable to reduce the Americans to submission. This optimistic estimate of the crisis was reinforced by the news of the capture of Fort Ticonderoga by the American forces.[1] With the American resistance growing, Vergennes felt that he could safely test the British embarrassment.

The French and British had long wrangled over the terms of the Treaties of Utrecht and of Paris concerning Dunkirk. Vergennes decided to tell the English that, henceforth, the French would do justice for themselves with regard to repairs at the port of Dunkirk. Furthermore, France would allow no restrictions or prohibitions beyond the strict terms of the Treaty of 1763. Also, he ordered the French representative, Guines, to reopen the explosive question of French rights in the Newfoundland fishery.[2]

But the British were not yet so entangled in the American affair as Vergennes had thought. The almost violent British response to the new French demands startled him and raised, once again, the possibility of a war for which France was not yet prepared. Cautiously Vergennes backtracked. He assured the British that France's intentions were peaceful.[3] His actions demonstrated, however, that, given the right conditions, French diplomacy would not long remain passive.

The critical factor in the Anglo-American problem was whether the rebellious colonies had sufficient force to carry through the revolution that seemed to be developing. Guines, in London, first recognized the lack of any essential information concerning American military strength. To Vergennes, he suggested that Louis XVI send to America someone "capable of taking a good look at them politically and militarily . . . ."[4] He recommended sending Achard de Bonvouloir, a French Army officer who had previously visited America.[5] Vergennes agreed,[6] and soon Bonvouloir was bound for Philadelphia.[7] The curious relationship between the Ancien Régime of France and the new Republic of the United States was thus established.[8]

Before Bonvouloir left for Philadelphia, the King of England, on the twenty-third of August, 1775, proclaimed the American colonies in a state of rebellion. The revolt was now "open and avowed," and the participants were declared traitors.[9] Until this date, Vergennes had assumed possible an eventual reconciliation between England and the colonies.[10] Now, the controversy entered a new phase. Could the American "army of peasants," considered by some to be absolutely ignorant of the maneuvers of war, stand against British regulars?[11]

Vergennes was optimistic. In a dispatch to Guines, he indicated that he did not believe that England could subjugate the Americans.[12] He was, no doubt, influenced by the reports he read from the French dramatist, Beaumarchais. From England, Beaumarchais wrote that the British were sending 40 or 50,000 troops to America. But the number was insignificant compared with the huge American army which the enthusiastic playwright created out of rumors and fact. The Americans, Beaumarchais reported, had 38,000 effective armed men under the walls of Boston. The English army in the town was "reduced to death by starvation, or to seeking winter quarters elsewhere." Along with this formidable force besieging Boston, the Insurgents had 40,000 other troops, "well-armed, and equally resolute," to defend the rest of the country. This was an "army of infuriates whose vengeance and rage animate every effort." "I affirm, Sire," Beaumarchais finished, "that such a nation must be invincible." Vergennes, impressed but skeptical, advised the King, when he passed the letter on to him, that he had no way to verify the estimates.[13] Fortunately for the American cause, it was impossible to verify such reports, for it is doubtful that the Americans around Boston numbered more than 20,000 troops counting officers, noncommissioned officers, and those sick or on furlough.[14] Beaumarchais would have been hard put to find even 10,000 men defending the rest of the country.[15]

Nevertheless, Vergennes was convinced that the American colonists had a force big enough to defend their interests. Also, everything happening in America convinced him that England did not, or at least ought not, want a war with the Bourbon states. His confidence in American strength led him to conclude that the war in the colonies would not end very soon. Afterwards, England, exhausted by civil war, was not likely to seek a war with the Bourbons.[16] Two months later, he was convinced that England was at the point of despair.[17]

Other reports of American strength reinforced Vergennes' cautious optimism.[18] The new year, 1776, was not quite two months old before

Vergennes had before him the first reports of Bonvouloir. Bonvouloir's voyage was not made simply to get military information about the Americans, and historians have rightly stressed the political role which the French agent played in assuring the Insurgents that France had no ambition to regain Canada, and that there were possibilities for getting both trained officers and supplies in France. But the French officer went to America to look at the Americans "militarily," as well as "politically." As Bonvouloir viewed them, the Americans were worthy of respect. "Everyone here is a soldier," he said. "The troops are well clothed, well paid, and well commanded. They have about 50,000 volunteers who do not want pay. You can judge whether people of this stamp will fight." Everywhere in America the situation was the same. There was "inconceivable agitation;" and immense preparation for the next spring. They had besieged Montreal and it had capitulated, and he predicted that Québec would soon be next. Furthermore, the Americans were perfectly entrenched under Boston. According to Bonvouloir, the military situation in America was very much in the Americans' favor. The Americans needed army engineers and supplies; otherwise their prospects were very good.[19]

Bonvouloir's report confirmed information coming from other sources. Beaumarchais had been bombarding Vergennes with letters describing and praising the American efforts, and had been pleading with the French minister to get a project started to aid the Americans. Vergennes was still cautious: as late as May 2, 1776, he told Beaumarchais that it was as "easy to talk well as it was difficult to do well." Nevertheless, Vergennes was now, more than ever, convinced that the Americans could fight, and had an army to do so. Garnier, once again in charge of affairs in London, agreed: "the Americans will be neither discouraged nor subjugated . . . ."[20] Three days later, he noted that "the moment is decisive, ...America has learned to know its strength."[21] Vergennes had all these estimates available when he made his recommendations in the 'Considerations on the Affairs of the English Colonies in America," dated March, 1776.

Vergennes saw the situation as presenting a dilemma. Should France and Spain desire the subjugation or the independence of the English colonies? If the war ended suddenly, either by conquest or by reconciliation, the English would be in an excellent position, in America, to make good their losses at the expense of French and Spanish possessions there. On the other hand, if the Americans succeeded in establishing their independence, they might become expansionists, and equally threaten French and Spanish possessions. Real advantage to the two crowns would follow only if the civil war continued, leaving both victor and vanquished exhausted at the end of the war. A long, drawn-out war would also give France and Spain the time needed to augment their military power.

Vergennes still believed that a war between England and the Bourbon powers was likely. The temptation of exposed French and Spanish holdings in America, the national unity a war would arouse, as well as the desire of individual English ministers to save their own necks with a brilliant conquest, all argued in favor of a British surprise attack. Nor would the English be restrained by moral scruples, Vergennes warned. "Experience has, only too often, proven that they believe to be just and honorable anything they regard as advantageous to the nation and destructive of their rivals." What should be done? Once again, the vision of a quick, preventive war, that would humble England and exalt France, appeared before the cautious statesman. *If* the Kings of Spain and France were warlike; *if* they were not committed by preference to peace; he noted almost wistfully, "*if* they were disposed to give in to their interests, or perhaps the justice of their cause, which is equally that of humanity;" or, more significantly, "*if* their military and pecuniary means were at a more suitable and energetic point of development," it would be necessary to recognize "that Providence had marked out this moment for the humiliation of England." But, there were too many "ifs", his common sense warned him. Returning to his world of scruples and possibilities, the statesman recommended that the two Bourbon Kings continue to assure England of their pacific intentions. At the same time, he advised, they should begin to aid the Insurgents secretly, with munitions and money, to assure a lively resistance. Meanwhile, the two crowns could go on building up their own armed forces.[22] Only Turgot, the economy-minded Finance Minister, was not persuaded of the soundness of Vergennes' recommendations.

The significance of the document, "Considerations," is two-fold. A strong American army insured the "long-winded affair" needed to exhaust both parties in the conflict, and reduce the aggressive potential of England. Secret aid was Vergennes' technique for continuing such a situation. In that sense, secret aid was a defensive device. At the same time, his policy of secret aid contained within itself the possibility, and he clearly saw it, of eventual aggressive action against England. For, while secret aid was a technique for preventing an early British victory in America and, hence, of reducing the threat of a British attack on French and Spanish possessions, it was also a way of giving France and Spain time to build up their armed forces. Secret aid to the colonies could create, for France, the chance to fight a war with England under the most favorable conditions.

Vergennes' "Considerations" reveal another important characteristic of his developing policy. Clearly, he saw his recommendation for secret aid to the rebellious colonists as an alternative to the recently rejected Spanish scheme for invading Portugal. Vergennes never changed his conviction that a Spanish attack on Portugal, in Europe, would lead to a general European war. His belief in an American resistance capable of sustaining a war against England made possible his alternative plan to reduce England's position in world politics, while, at the same time, avoiding the terrifying dangers of a two-front war on land and sea.

Meanwhile, intelligence on the American Army accumulated. A Monsieur O'Reilly, who returned from England and Ireland after talks with Benjamin Franklin and several members of Parliament, wrote to Vergennes that the Americans had, besides a considerable militia, at least 60,000 well-disciplined men under the orders of four officers whose military talents were well known.[23] Mr. Dumas, the American representative at The Hague, turned over to the Abbé Desnoyer, the French Minister to The Hague, information which included the declaration that the entire continent of America was firmly united, and the Americans had had on foot, during the campaign of the preceding summer of 1775, 25,000 men with whom they were not only able "to block up the King's army in Boston, but to spare considerable detachments for the invasion of Canada."[24] The French Minister reported his interview with Dumas on the sixteenth of April, 1776.

When Vergennes composed his next memo on the changing situation in the English colonies, he may not have had Desnoyer's reports on hand. The memo, entitled "Reflections," was dated "April, 1776", but the exact day is difficult to fix.[25] Certain it is, however, that Vergennes had reports from Bonvouloir, which were brought to Paris on the fourth of March by Guines. Also, he very likely had the note from O'Reilly. He seems to have used both in the preparation of the new memo, which constituted a practical plan for carrying out the secret aid recommendations made in the "Considerations."

Vergennes began with the estimate that the colonists had 50,000 regular troops, "well-dressed, well-disciplined, and well-commanded." Furthermore, he noted, repeating Bonvouloir's words, the colonies had nearly as many volunteers "who ask only to fight." From this inflated estimate of American military strength, the Secretary of State for Foreign Affairs drew the conclusion that the Insurgents were, at the moment, capable of resisting the forces which England had in America. They had arms and munitions, consequently there was nothing, at present, to furnish them. Vergennes feared, however, that the colonists would soon exhaust their means. They might then lose courage and submit. Before the American resistance collapsed, Vergennes wanted France to help them. In the meantime, France should make the Americans understand that future assistance depended on their military success, and they could expect help, at the latest, by the end of the next campaign. The plan involved serious risks, for England could only regard such assistance to the rebels as hostile interference in her internal affairs. Secrecy was, therefore, an essential part of the policy. On March first, Vergennes had written to the Foreign Minister of Spain, Grimaldi, and asked for his reaction to the idea of aiding the colonists.

Early in 1776, the belief that the Portuguese-Spanish quarrel had reached a dangerous impasse further quickened Versailles' interest in American military efforts. Portugal, above all, seemed dead set on causing a collision, and Vergennes now saw the American war as a way to divert and tie up the British military in America, if a war came. In February, Vergennes learned that the Portuguese Army had launched an offensive against the Spanish in Brazil, and they followed up their land attack with a naval bombardment of Spanish fortifications at the mouth of the San Pedro River. Soon the Portuguese had deeply penetrated Spanish defenses in Brazil, and were menacing the entire Spanish position there. In April, Spain, once again, was at the brink of war.[26] Grimaldi now believed that the English were secretly in accord with the Portuguese on their new policy of aggression. Charles III was willing to wait a "reasonable time" to see if mediation attempts, undertaken by London and Versailles, would have any effect, but after that, Charles III would "take measures to get satisfaction by force. . . ."[27]

Naturally, Spain expected France to back her, once hostilities began. In fact, Grimaldi wanted France to anticipate the war and send immediately 10 or 12,000 troops to Santo Domingo to defend the island, shared by both Spain and France, against a possible English attack.[28] Vergennes agreed, at once, that Spain should obtain justice for herself if Portugal persisted in refusing to settle by negotiation, but he still wanted to confine the war to Brazil. To implement his hope, he repeated his earlier recommendation that Spain send more reinforcements to her colonies.[29] In addition, he once again made it clear that Louis XVI did not favor, at the moment, a preventive war, especially one that would involve England. "Nothing at the moment," he told his ambassador to Spain, "could justify any war that the two powers [France and Spain] could undertake against England. We have neither motive, nor pretext, I would even add, no real interest, to declare war on her." Experience had taught him, he went on, that war was never an efficacious way of ending quarrels of this sort. The enormous expenses, even when everything went well, soon led to weariness and exhaustion. The war ends because one cannot continue these immense efforts and, most often, the heart of the difficulty was not even touched.[30]

The news of the Portuguese offensive might have triggered the war immediately, had not the Courts of Versailles and Saint James taken steps to calm tempers and mediate a solution. Neither England nor France trusted each other, but, equally, neither power could afford at that time a war between their respective allies. And it was apparent to all that the situation in South America was getting worse. Spain became more and more convinced that Britain's gestures at mediation were a ruse, to give Portugal time to consolidate her victories. Irresistably, Spain and Portugal seemed to be plunging towards open conflict.

As the crisis worsened, and nerves grew taut, Vergennes began to see that his efforts to avoid war were creating a distrust which could break up the Family Compact. The concurrent Anglo-French steps to restrain both Spain and Portugal, and Vergennes' hedging on the Spanish proposals for an attack on Portugal, had a corrosive effect at Madrid. Grimaldi began to have doubts (and he expressed them to his King) about whether France really would assist Spain in the defense of her possessions if England attacked.[31] Worse still, an incident in the Mediterranean publicly demonstrated Spain's resentments, and bred further annoyance between the two Crowns. Two frigates of the Spanish Mediterranean fleet pounced on a French vessel en route to Algeria, took it to Carthage, and declared the goods it was carrying contraband of war going to Algeria. A lively exchange of letters followed, and did not help to smooth ruffled feathers.[32]

Vergennes, obviously provoked by Spanish testiness, but, at the same time, appreciating the cause of Spanish behavior, refused to give an inch. "That nation, so puffed up with its antique grandeur and the show of its forces which are only display," he said of Spain, "believes itself to have the right to give the law to the universe." The King of France, he instructed his ambassador to Spain, would fulfill his treaty obligations and "all his engagements" to the Spanish house. He "would even go beyond them," to give Spain "proof of his tender affection." But if such sentiments were not returned, if Spain's arbitrary decisions and acts were to be the only rewards of French compliance and "vigilant attention to all the interests of a cherished ally," then he could not see how they could continue their alliance. "Let there be no misunderstanding," he continued, "France, although burdened with a considerable debt, is still capable of standing up to any power that dares to challenge her; if the King cherishes moderation, if he makes moderation the basis of his conduct and his counsels, it is because he believes moderation to be preferable to empty bragging, which never was and never will be any good for anything." Furthermore, Vergennes wrote on, his temper obviously warming as he wrote, France would not be dominated by Spain, "We have, for too long, accepted the role of supplicant and Spain, that of the dominant power; it is shameful that we have permitted this difference; it is time to return to equality."

Fortunately, the Secretary of State for Foreign Affairs did not lose complete control of his temper: "You understand, Monsieur," he told his ambassador, Ossun, "that this instruction is not of the sort that can be delivered to the Spanish Minister." He left it up to his ambassador's "zeal, prudence," and "dexterity" to set things straight at Madrid.[33] In a personal letter to Ossun, written the same day, but no doubt much later, for his temper seems to have cooled, he confessed that "I cannot express to you, Monsieur, all the anguish of my soul." Remember, he concluded, "the English want the Family Compact enfeebled even more than they want the subjugation of America."[34]

To the Spanish, the stiff American resistance only added one further reason for the conquest of Portugal: England, now deeply involved in the American scrap, could render her ally little assistance. In July, Spain proclaimed an embargo at Cadiz, and, a month later, an embargo at Galicia and Biscay. Convinced that France was going to be dragged into the headlong dash to war, Vergennes laid the critical situation before the King and Council at Marly on the seventh of July, 1776. "If war between Portugal and Spain becomes unavoidable," he explained, "... it is inevitable that a war with England would follow, and France could not avoid taking a direct part in it." The English, he now thought, were encouraging Portugal, as a way of getting themselves out of the humiliating embarrassment in America. If war came, he declared, France had to concentrate her efforts on the sea, for a land war would lead only to France's losing her principal aim, that of weakening the only enemy France had reason to fear. As for the European powers, he believed Vienna would remain a French ally. Russia was quiet, but might attack Sweden, or even aid England. In Holland, the Republic party, "which has been neglected for too long," had to be encouraged in order to further Dutch neutrality. In addition, the American Insurgents should be told about "the present state of things," and, without committing herself, France should make them see their advantages in the new circumstances. Time was "precious, each instant merits henceforth to be counted and put to profit if we do not wish to be surprised and crushed ...." "We could still have six or eight months of respite; let's not lose them ...."[35]

It was in the early phase of this trying emergency that Vergennes had written to the Spanish Foreign Minister suggesting joint secret measures to aid the colonists. The Spanish answered his suggestion with 1,000,000 *livres*, which was added to the 1,000,000 *livres*, already advanced by Louis XVI to the Roderique Hortelez and Company, organized by the indefatigable Beaumarchais to expedite the shipment of secret aid to the Insurgents. The Spanish were, indeed, interested in Vergennes' plan, but they probably did not see it, as he obviously did, as an alternative to the plan for an attack on Portugal. In any event, for the Americans, the secret aid opened an alternative to the humiliating prospect of surrender.

In the meantime, reports of the American military potential poured into Versailles. Beaumarchais told Vergennes that the time approached when the Americans would be masters of their country. General Lee, he reported, had left 7,000 men in fortified New York and, with the 15,000 which remained, he went straight to Québec. The validity of Beaumarchais' figures can be judged when one remembers that General Lee took, in fact, only his small staff to Québec. Beaumarchais promised that news from Québec was such that there would be nothing to regret. Furthermore, the dramatist believed, the American problem of supply was being eased by the Virginians, who had produced an abundant manufacture of saltpeter. Everywhere, gunpowder was being manufactured. The colony of Virginia alone had 7,000 regular troops under arms, and a militia amounting to 70,000 soldiers.[36] Beaumarchais was not the only purveyor of good news. From another source, Vergennes learned of the evacuation of Boston, and passed this information on to the dramatist. "You are being difficult," he wrote, "if you do not regard the evacuation of Boston as important news." Although Vergennes admitted that he did not know, as yet, how or why the evacuation had occurred, he could not believe "that General Howe abandoned this place of arms for pleasure rather than from necessity."[37]

Vergennes outlined his next move in his rapidly evolving policy in his memo "Considerations on the Position France should take *vis-à-vis* England in the present Circumstances,' dated August 31, 1776. The document reveals a radical conversion of the French Secretary of State to the doctrine of preventive war, the very doctrine he had earlier so energetically rejected. He advanced the bold proposal that France and Spain immediately shift to the offensive, and engage in a joint war on England. Gone now were the high-sounding "principles" of the two Bourbon crowns which he had earlier invoked to resist the Spanish temptation of a preventive war. He still believed that war was the greatest evil that could afflict a society, but the sweet prospect of smashing Britain to her knees dissolved all reservations. This was the moment *le plus beau,* he now argued, for France to erase the shame of the "odious" English surprise attack of 1755.

Why did Vergennes now advocate war? His reasons were several. He was now convinced that England was behind Portugal's warlike agitations; French arms were now in a more respectable state of readiness; the American colonists, having boldly declared their independence, were demonstrating, by force of arms, that they could defend this independence. England, thoroughly entangled in the web of civil war, was vexed, distracted, and completely exposed. The temptation was simply too great. The Council, more and more subject to the influence of the hawkish trio of Maurepas, Sartine, and Vergennes, accepted the recommendation without a dissent. The next problem was to get the Spanish court to agree to such a policy.[38]

The Spanish ministers, not surprisingly, were less than enthusiastic, for the plan had made no mention of their own favorite designs. While all the "appearances," Grimaldi told his ambassador to Versailles, "indicate the war of the colonies ought to endure, Spain wants more than just a prolonged war to exhaust England." In short, the Portuguese bauble still held Charles III in its spell. Grimaldi wanted French support for an invasion and conquest of Portugal and, in addition, he even suggested that Minorca be added to Spain's "advantages," apparently as a tasty *hors d'oeuvre* to the main Portuguese dish.[39]

Grimaldi's response was not at all what Vergennes had hoped for. It still involved the risk of a general European war, which he desperately wanted to avoid. Yet Spain would not discard her scheme for that of Vergennes. The tug of war between the Spanish and the French for the leadership of the Family Compact continued.

CHAPTER 19

Gates and Washington: Saratoga and Germantown

The Spanish answer to Vergennes' "Considerations" was preceded by news that Washington's army had been routed at the Battle of Long Island.[1] Many people now spoke with contempt of the American defenses. Their entrenchments were badly made, the rebels had permitted a redoubt to be surprised, and their retreat was confused and bloodied by heavy losses. Some even said there was nothing for the Americans to do but submit.[2] The military situation in America had suddenly changed to the Americans' disadvantage.

The policy of a joint Franco-Spanish preventive war against England was built on the assumption that the Americans could sustain their military potential. That assumption was now in question. Aware of the effects of such doubts, Silas Deane, the American agent at Versailles, attempted to reconstruct the good opinion Vergennes had earlier held of American strength.[3] But Vergennes again became very cautious. Since the English had a place in New York to winter their troops, he concluded, they would not be an immediate threat to French or Spanish possessions. He decided to continue the aid to the Americans, in hopes they would hold out, but to insist to England on the goodwill of France and go on building up the French arms.[4]

The Spaniards' stubborn refusal to give up the idea of a conquest of Portugal also dampened Vergennes' enthusiasm for war. As long as Spain insisted on making a war with England a war of conquest in Europe, Vergennes was determined to oppose such a war. Fortunately, the Spanish, unable to convince Vergennes of the value of an invasion of Portugal, dispatched a huge armada under Don Pedro Cevallos to undertake operations against the Portuguese in Latin American waters. The new year had barely begun before the Portuguese forces in South America began to reel from the punishment delivered by Spanish guns.[5]

Simultaneously Vergennes continued working, through his representative in London, to mediate the quarrel between Spain and Portugal. As a result of the conversations about mediation, the French Chargé d'affaires in London, Garnier, began to believe that England, more and more involved in America, would very much like to avoid a conflict that would oblige her to aid her ally in Europe. The English government, Garnier noticed, "trembled at the idea of a foreign war."[6] But while England's plight reduced the likelihood that the ministry would decide on war, it raised, at the same time, the danger that her naval captains at sea might precipitate it, while trying to block all the routes through which the Americans were obtaining supplies. The governor of the French colony of St.-Pierre-Martinique revealed the explosive quality of this danger, when he reported that an English frigate, *The Lynx,* had anchored at the entrance of the roadstead of St. Pierre and, at an unguarded moment, boldly entered and captured three American ships which had come to trade.[7] Under such circumstances, the choice of war or peace could easily escape the control of the civilians at Versailles or London and pass to the hands of a zealous commander or naval captain. Clearly, the French decision to aid secretly the Americans had not lessened the danger of war.

During the fall and winter of 1776-1777, Deane in France finished the arrangements with the Roderique Hortelez and Company, and eight shiploads of supplies sailed to the rebels. Seven of these ships slipped through British patrols, and helped make possible the American campaign of 1777.[8] At the same time, the Continental Congress appointed representatives to go to France to negotiate a treaty. Among them was Benjamin Franklin, one of the western world's most imaginative scientists, and soon to become one of America's great diplomats. Their instructions spoke only of a treaty of amity and commerce, but Deane was told, in his letter of appointment as one of the commissioners, that the treaties included with his letter were of commerce and an alliance.[9] Before 1776 ended, Arthur Lee, Benjamin Franklin, and Deane had an audience with Vergennes, who assured them that they had the protection of the French Court and that their interests would receive serious consideration.[10] But the Americans still had to convince Vergennes that the Revolutionary Army was a dependable military force. The task before Vergennes was to go on building France's strength, while bleeding England of hers. At the same time, he had to avoid the war in Europe, which his Spanish ally seemed bound to have.

As 1776 drew to a close, Vergennes, on the basis of new information, began to minimize the Long Island disaster. Reports forwarded to him, through Spanish officials, indicated that although the Americans had suffered a considerable defeat there, they had refused all propositions for a surrender. They seemed still capable of further resistance to the British.[11] Moreover, the energetic Benjamin Franklin contributed to Vergennes' reviving confidence in the American army with a "Memo Concerning the Present State of Late British Colonies in North America." Franklin reported that Congress had resolved to raise eighty-eight battalions for the coming campaign. Their resolution would create an army totalling 68,640 men on paper, and Franklin made no distinction between paper strength and effective strength.[12] Franklin admitted that certain necessities were lacking in order to utilize this force, but he implied that, given supplies, the Americans would soon have an army operating at a number near 68,640 men.

Other reports reinforced the optimistic statements of Franklin. In a "News From London" memorandum passed on to Vergennes, by Deane, in February, the Insurgents were reported to have had actually in service 40,000 men in "spite of the rigors of the season."[13] A memo based on the observations of a French naval officer sent to America by the Comte d'Argent, governor of Martinique, discounted the advantages gained by the Royal Army at Long Island, praised the vigor of Washington's defense, and judged unassailable the encampment where the American General had established himself.[14] In late March, Deane told Vergennes that, although the American army was in great need of artillery, the Insurgents had succeeded in nearly destroying and taking two regiments of English forces, Lord Cornwallis was "retreating" to Amboy, and Kingsbridge, Fort Washington, and "those posts before abandoned by the United States, were retaken by the army under General Washington, Sr."[15] In May of 1777, Deane reported that the quotas of men to be furnished by the several states "were, in some states already completed, and near being so in the rest and the men were engaging for three years or until the end of the war . . . ." "The General," Deane said [with tongue in cheek?], "would now have a permanent army."[16]

With the coming of Spring, Deane reported that, although no big engagement had occurred between the British and American forces, the daily skirmishes usually ended to the advantage of the Americans. The situation, Deane suggested, offered an excellent opportunity for a move against England by some European power. Such a diversion, Deane predicted, would mean the United States would "instantly obtain a superiority by land . . . ." A diversion would also relieve the American commerce by sea, and make it possible for the Insurgents to pay back the money they owed and establish their credit.[17]

American privateers' use of French ports, as place of refuge and for the sale of prizes, made some kind of decision imperative. By the summer of 1777 such activity had become so embarrassing to Vergennes that an ultimatum from the British seemed imminent. Thus pressed, Vergennes once again urged in a memo to Louis XVI that France enter the war. The moment had come, he stated, for the Bourbon powers to prepare for a close defensive and offensive alliance with the Americans. It was necessary, "either to abandon America to herself, or to help her courageously and effectively." Secret aid, he felt, was no longer enough. If the Bourbon powers were not willing to help, then "humanity and honesty" required that the Americans be told so. On the twenty-sixth of July, a copy of this memo, which had been approved by Louis XVI, was sent on to Madrid for submission to Jose-Moñins Conde de Floridablanca, who had replaced Grimaldi as the Spanish Chief Minister in 1776.[18]

Soon after the writing of this memo, there was a blackout of information concerning the American military situation. Repeatedly, during the late summer and fall of 1777, Vergennes asked his Ambassador to England, the Duc de Noailles, to send him information on the movements of Generals Howe and Burgoyne, and the activities of Washington. What Vergennes and Noailles saw developing in America were the conditions for major engagements between the Revolutionists and the British forces. The outcome of such engagements would verify or destroy the reports concerning the intentions, as well as the capabilities, of the American Army.[19]

Meanwhile, Sartine, in close collaboration with Vergennes and Maurepas, continued to strengthen the French Navy. The naval budget skyrocketed. At the death of Louis XV, the cost of the Navy was between 20,000,000–25,000,000 *livres* a year. But, in 1776, Sartine spent 34,000,000.[20] By 1778, the annual naval budget was pushing beyond 100,000,000 *livres*.[21]

October, 1777, was a critical month to the French diplomats and ministers observing the American Revolutionary War. The British were engaged in a large-scale, two-pronged operation to cut the heart out of the American resistance. Howe was moving to engage Washington near Philadelphia, and Burgoyne was marching south from Canada to meet Clinton's column moving northeastward. The Revolution approached a point of crisis. "I will neglect nothing, Monsieur le Comte," French Ambassador to London, assured Vergennes, "in order to be in a condition here, next Friday, to render you a more detailed account of these different objects. . . ."[22]

The following Friday, Noailles kept his promise in a letter about the military situation in America. In England, he said, everyone was in a state of uncertainty about what had become of General Howe. On the other hand, it was generally believed that Burgoyne had passed Albany in his advance. Noailles added that he had "spared no pains or cares" to find out for certain what appeared to him to be doubtful; he could not believe that Burgoyne had arrived at Albany so quickly. The British general had been reported at Skenesboro, New York, on July 11, and even if he had met with no resistance, physical difficulties made such a fast descent difficult, if not impossible. Nevertheless, British opinion held that, on August 28, Burgoyne had not only reached Albany, but had passed it. Moreover, it was believed that Clinton was departing by the North (Hudson) River, on his secret expedition to join Burgoyne. Noailles thought that, if Burgoyne had actually reached Albany, he would surely winter there.[23]

The retreat of the Americans before the British advance was disappointing; it had the appearance of a flight. The Insurgents seemed to have been "struck by terror" at the advance of the Royal troops. Worse still, the militia, the military institution on which many Europeans placed their hopes for American success, was said to have refused to join the Army. For this reason, the Americans were too weak to dispute Burgoyne's advance. Refusing to doubt the patriotism of these citizen-soldiers, Noailles observed that: "It appears that this defection of the militia is more the effect of indiscipline than of a discouragement which would be fatal to the American cause." Nevertheless, the Insurgents were failing in their attempts to stop Burgoyne.[24]

In his reply to Noailles' dispatch, Vergennes could paint no brighter picture of what was happening farther south in America. He reported that Howe had taken a position between Baltimore and Newcastle, and threatened to divide the colonies in two. It was impossible to tell whether the British were going to force a battle. Such a move seemed to depend, Vergennes continued, on whether General Washington intended to fight to protect his supplies.[25]

For a time thereafter, only rumors and contradictory reports reached the French Foreign Affairs office. Lord Stormont, the British Ambassador to France, reported to Vergennes that Burgoyne was master of Albany, and had been joined by Clinton. The American General Philip Schuyler had suffered a crushing defeat, and had surrendered with 1,500 men. The British General Barry St. Leger was master of the Mohawk River up to the Hudson. Farther south the Americans were also in serious trouble, for Howe had advanced up the Susquehanna River and debarked in Lancaster County, Pennsylvania. Vergennes, in his report of this news to Noailles, called it "pure babbling" by the British. But the "pure babbling" caused some anxieties.[26]

While waiting for more reliable news, Noailles and Vergennes speculated on the seriousness of the events developing across the Atlantic. The distress of Washington, Noailles pointed out, would be extreme if Burgoyne managed to surmount the many obstacles in his path. Washington's communications with the south were already presumably cut by Howe, and his communications with the northern forces would be severed if Burgoyne met Clinton.[27]

November brought no clarification of the confusing reports. Indeed, rumors became even more contradictory. Noailles reported to his chief that the English were celebrating the defeat of Washington, the taking of Philadelphia, and continued successes of Burgoyne. But official sources,Noailles added, gave no cause for such exhibitions of joy. Even Howe had admitted, Noailles wrote, that the taking of Philadelphia would decide nothing in favor of England, if the army of Washington remained intact. Burgoyne was rumored to have had minor successes against the Americans, and was reported to have been at Saratoga on August 20.[28] A letter from Lisbon, Portugal, dated November 4, reported that Howe had been beaten by Washington.[29] Later, Vergennes wrote to Noailles that he had heard that Washington had been defeated and Philadelphia taken.[30] When Noailles tried to obtain more certain information from Lord Weymouth, the British Secretary of State for Foreign Affairs, Weymouth repeated rumors favoring the British, rumors which he said "merited some belief because they had come from New York."[31] By November 21, Vergennes was speculating on the consequences that would follow if Howe actually had defeated Washington.[32] Finding himself in this confusion, Vergennes ordered his commercial agent, John Holker, then going to America, to find out just "what was the situation and position of the English armies," their strength and resources, as well as the number of regulars and militia troops fighting for the Insurgents, and their attitude toward their leaders.[33] The news of the battles of Germantown and Saratoga arrived in France at this critical psychological moment.

The reports of the successes of the American Army were brought to the American agents in France by Jonathan Loring Austin, the secretary of the Board of War of Massachusetts. The correspondence the Massachusetts Council sent to Benjamin Franklin, Silas Deane, and Arthur Lee, translated copies of which were turned over to Vergennes,[34] contained not only the news of Burgoyne's surrender at Saratoga, but also information, some of it in a letter from General Washington, concerning the position and condition of Washington's forces after Germantown.

In the Northern Department, the dispatch said, Major General Gates had surrounded the enemy, had taken their provision boats, and cut them off from their line of retreat. Burgoyne had the choice of escaping by forcing his way through the American troops, or surrendering. "It seems he chose the latter." The victory helped "inspirit" the American troops throughout the continent, and intimidated and dispirited the British. The Northern Department would soon be secured for the American cause, predicted the Americans, because General Gates was forwarding troops to retake Ticonderoga, and Forts Montgomery and Independence. The Massachusetts Council had little doubt that these positions would soon be in American hands.[35]

The report of the Saratoga victory, however, did not constitute all the good news. Information concerning Washington's movements indicated that there was no occasion for British rejoicing over Washington's defeat at Germantown. The battle, reported the Massachusetts Council, was a near victory for Washington. He would have soundly beaten the British if the smoke and fog had not created disorder among the American troops. The council's interpretation of the battle was somewhat oversimplified. Washington's retreat was also the result of lack of ammunition among the forces of General John Sullivan, the disobedience of orders on the part of Major General Adam Stephen, and the lack of coordination so characteristic of this citizen army, even when there was no smoke or fog.[36] But the Americans were in "high spirits" even though victory had, barely, escaped them. The Massachusetts Council was in hopes that they would soon hear that Howe's army was cut off from retreat and would find itself in the same predicament as Burgoyne's before his surrender.[37] The Northern Department, then, was securely under the control of the American forces; in the central theater of war, Washington's army, far from being destroyed or beaten as has been rumored, was intact, in high spirits, and had succeeded in placing Howe in danger of having his own line of retreat and supply cut off.

The letter in which Franklin, Deane, and Lee forwarded the news to Vergennes repeated this optimistic forecast of the military situation.[38] Beaumarchais, who hastened to report the news to Vergennes, especially emphasized the favorable position which Washington had achieved as a result of the engagement at Germantown. The American general, he assured Vergennes, had permitted Howe to enter Philadelphia without any opposition, and then had set about to encircle him there. In order to avoid such an encirclement Howe had to leave the city, and on October 6 — the battle actually took place on October 4 — there had been a general engagement between the two armies at Germantown. The English, according to Beaumarchais, lost about nine hundred men, including three generals, while the American losses were only half that number. A storm, Beaumarchais continued, had forced the two armies to separate before either side gained a decisive advantage. Howe then re-entered Philadelphia, and Washington cut him off from exterior communications.[39]

The campaign in Pennsylvania was further developed in a letter sent to Ferdinand Grand, a broker in Paris who acted as one of the intermediaries between the American commissioners and Vergennes. The letter, dated from London on December 5, was passed on to Vergennes. The English Ministry and public were of the opinion, according to this correspondent, "that, while the Americans maintained such a powerful army in the field as that under General Washington, it was idle to suppose they would listen to any terms which the British Commissioners might offer them." Furthermore, the attack upon British troops at Germantown was "allowed by all

Howe's officers to have been secretly and ably conducted, and that, if General Gray had not seasonably arrived, and with a large reinforcement supported Howe, he would have been defeated." It was also agreed, the letter continued, "that the Americans had made an excellent retreat from Germantown . . . ."[40]

The French ambassador at London saw the significance of the Battle of Germantown.[41] According to the news Vergennes received from Noailles, the English stationed on the Elk River had abandoned this point of communication with their Navy in order to make themselves masters of Philadelphia. The American Army had disputed the terrain every step of the way. There had been a general action at Brandywine, and the American Army, reported at a strength of 15,000 troops, had retired in good order. There was no indication in the dispatch that Noailles knew how close Washington came to utter defeat at Brandywine. Nor did Noailles question the number of American troops reported engaged. Actually, the British had the 15,000 troops; the American forces did not exceed 11,000.

After reporting the action at Brandywine, Noailles discussed the "second general engagement," at Germantown, which had begun entirely to the advantage of the Insurgents and had been more bloody than the first. The victory had been disputed for a long time, with the advantage going first to one side, then to the other. Finally, without losing a single cannon, Washington returned to camp. Noailles concluded: "the American Army intact, experienced, no longer fearing to attack, or defend itself, is camped sixteen miles from the English Army, and able to receive all sorts of aid in provisions and men, while General Howe has not yet been able to establish communications with his Navy which is, nevertheless, his only resource for subsisting in a position where he will soon be encircled on all sides." To add final proof that the British recognized the gravity of the situation in America, Noailles noted that there had been a sharp drop on the British Stock market.[42] Five days later, Noailles redrew his sketch of the situation in America, and suggested that the time had come for the King of France to make hard decisions concerning the American war.[43]

Vergennes was again enthusiastic.[44] In November, it had appeared that a two-pronged British attack was threatening the very existence of the American armies in the north and middle colonies. Now, in December, it appeared that one of the prongs of the British offensive had been completely smashed at Saratoga, and the other — that led by General Howe — was in danger of being bottled up in Philadelphia by Washington's forces, which, contrary to earlier rumors, were very much intact and capable of meeting the British in general engagements. The Battle of Germantown had demonstrated this to the French. Vergennes was so encouraged by this state of affairs that he saw hope of Howe's being forced to submit to the same conditions as Burgoyne.

"This event seems very possible," he wrote. He confessed, however, that he would not see it happen without anxiety. Should Howe surrender, France would earn little favor from the Americans, since she had so far contributed so feebly to the establishment of their independence.[45] "All this," Vergennes concluded, "seems to bring us closer to the moment of crisis which I have always foreseen."[46] The day these words were written, Louis XVI approved Vergennes' recommendation that the American commissioners be received publicly by the French government, to arrange "a closer understanding between the Crown and the United Provinces of North America."[47] Moreover, the French merchant and fishing fleet was home safely, and out of reach of the British navy.

Meanwhile, Washington's army settled down at Valley Forge for the winter. Half of his troops were without proper clothing, most of them without blankets, and a quarter of them wholly unfit for duty because of lack of supplies. The fact that, during this winter at Valley Forge, Washington's army dwindled to but 3,760 men fit for active service would indeed have caused some hesitations in the French Ministry, if it had been known. The American Army, contrary to the French estimates of it, was disorganized and demoralized. Even the Battle of Germantown itself was partly responsible for this state of affairs. The army of George Washington had actually suffered twice as many losses in casualties and prisoners as the British, and, although the British later decided to evacuate Philadelphia, it was not from excessive fear of encirclement by the feeble American forces. At any moment during the winter of 1777-1778, General Howe could have descended upon the meager, unsheltered forces at Valley Forge and destroyed what was called Washington's "army".

Fortunately, French officials were not aware of these disturbing realities. Although the hoped-for possibility that Washington would bottle up Howe in Philadelphia did not materialize,[48] when the American Army finished its campaign for the year, its position at Valley Forge appeared to the French to be formidable. A close study of the documents brings one to the same conclusion John Adams reached when writing to a member of the Continental Congress about the importance of the battles of Saratoga and Germantown: "General Gates was the ablest negotiator you had in Europe; and, next to him, General Washington's attack on the enemy at Germantown. I do not know, indeed, whether this last affair had not more influence upon the European mind than that of Saratoga. Although the attempt was unsuccessful, the military gentlemen in Europe considered it as the most decisive proof that America would finally succeed."[49] A letter of Louis XVI's to Charles III confirms Adams' judgement: "The destruction of the army of Burgoyne, and the very confined state in which Howe finds himself," he wrote, "have totally changed the face of things. America is triumphant and England beatan."[50]

The Battle of Germantown, as well as the victory at Saratoga thus played an important role in the making of the Franco-American alliance of 1778. The battles demonstrated to the French that the British attempt to crush American resistance during the campaign of 1777 had failed in both the northern and central theatres of the war. Also, the Battle of Germantown, as it was reported in France, reinforced French confidence in Washington's military capabilities, and seemed to add proof to the estimates of American strength. Finally, according to Noailles' interpretation of the battle, the Americans had shown that their army was very much intact, was experienced, and not afraid to attack the British in force. For the first time in Vergennes' lifetime, England was now caught in the trap she had so often sprung on France. She was tied down on the American continent in a difficult land war with a tenacious enemy, while France was free to strike her on the sea. The only flaw in this near-perfect opportunity was still the uncertainty of whether Spain would play the game on Vergennes's terms.

CHAPTER 20

The Decision to Intervene

The costs of French participation in the American Revolutionary War, historians generally agree, were an important factor precipitating the French Revolution. The question of who was responsible for the decision to intervene is, therefore, of considerable significance. "The supreme decision was made by the King," Vergennes wrote in a private letter to the French ambassador to Spain. "The influence of his ministers was not decisive; the evidence of the facts, the moral certainty of danger, and his conviction alone determined [the decision]"[1] Later, in a memo to the King himself, Vergennes repeated the statement: "It was as a consequence of (His Majesty's) orders that I opened the negotiations with the Americans."[2] At the time, Louis XVI did not deny his Minister's statement.

As an older man, however, Louis felt differently. Just after the French Revolution began, the Sultan Tippoo of Mysore, India, approached Louis XVI to petition for French assistance in ridding his realm of British control. Louis' response indicated that he came to believe that the decision to intervene in the American war was not altogether his own. "This occasion [the unrest in India]," he told the Sultan, "greatly resembles the American affair, of which I never think without regret. On that occasion, they took advantage of my youth, and today we are paying the price for it."[3] The "they" Louis refers to could only have been the persons who advised him during the months he was pondering intervention: Maurepas, Sartine, and Vergennes.

Young Louis XVI had been determined to be the ruler of France. At court and in diplomatic circles, many expected the strong-willed Marie Antoinette to direct affairs and so they, at first, ignored Louis and tried to gain the Queen's favor. But Louis surprised them all by excluding the Queen from what he called his "business." He was, in fact, so overly jealous of his authority that he revealed himself for what he actually was: an uneasy, inexperienced lad who feared guidance, but desperately needed it. For the first few weeks of his reign he turned to the only person he really trusted, his Aunt Adelaide. But soon the minister, Maurepas, replaced the aunt.

Maurepas promised to teach Louis XVI "how not to need a prime minister." The boy-king readily accepted Maurepas' guidance. "I am only twenty years old," he confessed to him, "and I do not possess all the knowledge which I need."[4]

Maurepas always remained a power behind the throne, but Louis XVI also found still another guide in Vergennes. Louis was a serious student of statecraft. He studied and worked, sometimes ten to twelve hours a day, reading official papers, financial figures, and notes from his ministers. During the first months after he became Secretary of State, Vergennes wrote to the King dozens of letters explaining and suggesting policies, but always scrupulously deferring the final decision to his "Master." Louis XVI was flattered and, no doubt, relieved to find a man of experience who was self-effacing and respected the King's prerogatives. Gradually the two men came to trust each other. Soon Vergennes, working with Maurepas and Sartine, was part of a powerful triumvirate that made policy for Louis XVI.[5] Vergennes never challenged Maurepas' court role as mentor to the King. And, as long as Maurepas lived, Vergennes carefully checked with him before recommending anything to the King. Also, he readily accepted Maurepas' suggestions.[6] But, even before Maurepas died, Vergennes was one of the dominant members of the King's Council. To Louis XVI, Vergennes forever remained the servant; he made no bids to assume the official role of First Minister. He always discussed each step of the American policy with Maurepas, Sartine, and Louis XVI, but he insisted that only the King made decisions.[7]

Vergennes, nevertheless, carried a great deal of the responsibility for the decision to intervene in the American Revolutionary War. The "evidence of the facts," which he claimed determined the King's decision, was ultimately under his control. He helped sift the military estimates, and he made evaluations. With Maurepas and Sartine, he set the aims and strategy of the war. His memos helped establish options.[8]

Among the rejected alternative options open to Louis XVI was one suggested by Turgot, Louis' Comptrolleur-Général of Finance from 1774-1776. Turgot perceived, better than many others in the government, that Louis XVI inherited a structure of state finances that could not provide the money required, if France went to war. The social and legal system exempted from taxation many who could best afford to pay. At the same time, the tax system was especially onerous for the unprivileged, who paid the largest share of the taxes. The fiscal system failed completely to provide enough money to cover the price France paid to be a great power. Moreover, the accounting system of the French treasury was a mystery even to those who were responsible for it,[9] and the costs of war confused the State's finances beyond all comprehension. Turgot's suggested option was based on the judgment that France's problems at home were more urgent than any problem abroad. He tried, during his short term in office, to persuade Louis XVI that major reforms had to be undertaken in France, to create a prosperous state and provide social justice. In order to do these things, he insisted, the government had to economize. Economy, he saw, required peace.

But to Vergennes, the rebellion in America was a once-in-a-lifetime opportunity to strike at England, and raise France to her rightful "superiority of consideration and influence." To Turgot, war was a deceiving temptation. "You know the state of your finances," he explained to Louis XVI in one of his often-quoted memos. "[You know] that, despite economies and improvements already made since the beginning of the reign, there is a 20,000,000 *livres* difference between receipts and expenses.... The path of economy is possible; to follow it requires only a firm will."[10] To go to war, he insisted, would be the "greatest of misfortunes, since it would make reforms impossible for a long time, if not forever."[11]

No new taxes, no new loans, strict economy and, above all, peace. From the perspective of history, Turgot's option seems clearly the wisest. He was concerned with survival, through reform, of French traditional society and monarchy.[12] Turgot appreciated the seriousness of the financial situation, and saw that war imposed a killing burden. Vergennes knew as well as Turgot that French finances were in a bad state; yet he did not have the same sense of urgency about the problem that Turgot had. Furthermore, Turgot did not fear the social consequences of the reforms he advocated. Vergennes feared them and resisted them. Turgot, moreover, did not completely identify with the code of values which gave top priority to rank and influence in the international system, while the vision of Louis XVI as arbiter of Europe was the very marrow of existence to Vergennes, a career diplomat.

Unfortunately, the differences between Vergennes and Turgot may not have been presented to the King in as clear a contrast as they should have been. Louis XVI was too young and inexperienced to see that Turgot's critique of Vergennes' foreign policy was usually oblique, never direct, and it probably sometimes left the monarch wondering what the real issues were. Turgot's critics charge him with being too brusque and uncompromising.[13] But, in the debates and memos on the American war, he was not brusque enough; he compromised too much. He came to accept secret aid to the Americans; he reluctantly agreed to the build-up of the French Navy; and he even conceded that, if necessary, France could support a short war.[14] Since Vergennes was already arguing that the war was, indeed, necessary, Turgot, in effect, provided his opponents with the weapon they needed to discount his opposition.

From the viewpoint of traditional diplomacy, the advice Vergennes gave to Louis XVI, during the crisis of the American war, was persuasive. It demonstrated the Secretary of State's thorough understanding of the international situation, as well as his superb mastery of the techniques of diplomacy. Nevertheless, it was based on a shocking misunderstanding of how serious the fiscal and economic difficulties of the French government were, and [15] it ignored completely the growing cry for social justice in France. Vergennes' advice was limited by a professional and class bias which subordinated even the most serious domestic problems to foreign affairs. He apparently even allowed himself the illusion that war would somehow help solve the problems of the state debt because the King could impose extraordinary taxes during wartime, and his subjects would not complain. When the Comptrolleur-Général of Finance, after 1776, Jacques Necker, embarked on the controversial policy of meeting France's wartime financial needs by administrative reforms and the expedient of further loans, Vergennes supported him. "If he [Necker] can end the war without straying from this system," Vergennes applauded in 1779, "he will be a great man in the field."[16] And Necker's apparent success was, indeed, extraordinary. Without Necker, Louis XVI's foreign policy would have been ham-strung.[17] But the long-run consequences of these loans were still to unfold. Furthermore, after 1781, Necker's administrative reforms were undone by his successors, Joly de Flemy and Lefevre d'Ormesson. Both direct and indirect taxes were raised and further loans were floated.

Another factor in Vergennes' decision to recommend war was a product of his long professional training. Like a veteran boxer, the career diplomat had learned by experience to exploit the enemy's mistakes and embarrassments. For decades, French diplomats, especially those such as Vergennes, who were privy to the *Secret du Roi,* had lived with the galling belief that England was responsible for France's humiliations; England was the obstacle in the way of France's return to a position of authority in Europe. Now England, for a fleeting moment, was off-balance, exposed, and vulnerable. To the veteran diplomat, this was a unique opportunity. It was, as Vergennes said, the moment *le plus beau.*[18] To erase the shame of earlier defeats, his deepest reflexes told him he must strike; so he struck. The opportunity to inflict damage became, therefore, a motive for doing so.

Preventive war was justified by diplomatic practice, but Christian morality and aristocratic honor certainly condemned an unprovoked attack on the enemy without warning. Vergennes personally appreciated this moral position; he had used it to argue against the Spanish King's plans for a preventive war.[19] His argument to Charles III may have been only tactical, but it came from deep within a part of his character. His distaste for the Polish Partition, Frederick's attack on Silesia, and England's unprovoked attacks at sea was sincere and reflected a personal repugnance for deceit and naked force as means in the affairs of men and states.

How, then, did he justify, to himself and others, an aggressive intervention in the American Revolutionary War? Clearly, he saw the decision as one of necessity, not choice. Since war with England was "inevitable," there was no moral choice to be made. Peace, to him, was not an option. Herein lies the essential difference in the perceptions of Vergennes and Turgot. If Turgot could have persuaded Louis XVI and Vergennes that peace, not war, was a necessity, the history of Louis XVI's reign might have been different. Vergennes never saw peace with England in this light. The area of his professional concern became, therefore, strategic: when and under what conditions could France best fight the war?

Convinced that war with England was coming, Vergennes could not provoke the war before the French Navy was prepared. The longer the Americans held out, the longer France had, to rebuild her Navy. Vergennes' advocacy of secret aid to the Americans bought the time needed to build up naval strength. Despite Vergennes' rhetoric about military strength's being the best guarantee of peace, France did not build up the French Navy to preserve the peace, but to win a war.[20] That war did not occur before 1778, partly because the French Navy was not ready for it. Nevertheless, veteran observers in Europe saw that, when France was ready, war would become "more or less probable."[21]

Vergennes signed a commercial treaty with the Americans, because commerce was a major consideration in his general policy. He saw that French commerce might benefit from American independence, and he was anxious to develop new markets for French goods. An expanding market meant increased tax revenues for the government, and Louis XVI's treasury needed any revenues it could get.[22]

More importantly, Vergennes saw commerce as a weapon in diplomacy. England's international position, he believed, could be weakened by striking at her economic and commercial privileges abroad.[23] Moreover, he felt that French power could be restored by increased trade. He had already argued both points with regard to Spanish domestic and imperial commerce.[24] Unquestionably, he saw the commercial treaty with the Americans in the same light: a way of weakening England's international position by striking at her commerce.[25] But the commercial aspects of the Franco-American alliance were always instrumental in Vergennes' overall policies. In fact, all of the commercial treaties he negotiated during his administration were fundamentally political: to advance the power and influence of Louis XVI. The American treaty was no exception.

Nor was the desire for new colonies a significant aim of Vergennes' American policy. His decisions and writings, again and again, manifest the fact that he saw little value in acquiring colonies. Furthermore, his long experience in the Ottoman Empire taught him that, by treaty and wise diplomacy, France could enjoy the economic advantages of commerce without the burdensome costs of colonial defense and administration. He refused Spain's offer of the colony of Brazil, with the response that additional territory "did not tempt the King, my Master."[26] There is nothing in the diplomacy of the American Revolution that indicates he had changed his mind by 1778.

Vergennes deliberately provoked a war with England, and he provoked it to recover for Louis XVI a role in European affairs which the French King had presumably lost in 1763. While self-defense was a concern of every statesman in the unstable and harshly competitive conditions of eighteenth-century high politics, self-defense was not the principal reason why Vergennes wanted war with England. More important to him was the fact that he saw England as a formidable obstacle to Louis XVI's becoming the arbiter of Europe. And England was vulnerable.

Nevertheless, there were compelling personal, as well as diplomatic, reasons why Vergennes did not want Louis XVI to appear to be the aggressor in the war. Personally, his own deeply held Christian moral scruples opposed an open attack on England. Furthermore, the alliance with the Americans was a defensive one, which came into effect only in the event that Great Britain "should break the peace with France, either by direct hostilities or by hindering her commerce and navigation."[27] It is not likely that either the French or the Americans would have quibbled much over whether a French war with England was defensive or offensive, since both governments wanted French intervention. Still, by provoking England to attack first, Vergennes left no room for dispute over whether or not the alliance bound France and the United States together.

Moreover, diplomatically and militarily, Vergennes had nothing to gain from a French surprise attack on England. French aid to the Americans, and the Treaty of Franco-American commerce, placed George III in an untenable position, since it denied his legal authority over the Americans and provided the means to resist that authority. The longer the British allowed that situation to continue, the stronger the Americans and French became, and the more George III's authority suffered. Yet, until the French publicly announced their treaty with the rebels, England preferred to overlook the intervention of France, because she preferred to ignore it rather than precipitate open warfare with the French Navy."[28]

Vergennes did not want France to strike first. An attack on England would bring into play England's defensive alliances, and might bring European powers, especially the Netherlands, into the fray. The war would then no longer be confined to the American continent and the seas, and France would lose the strategic advantage Vergennes hoped to exploit. Moreover,

Vergennes was convinced that Britain's allies would stay out of the war if at all possible; they hoped to profit from the trade the belligerents would have to abandon.[29] French interests, therefore, required that England have no claim on her allies.

Perhaps Great Britain might have avoided even longer an open break with Louis XVI, if the latter, on Vergennes' suggestion, had not presented George III with a diplomatic note, delivered by the French ambassador, which publicly recognized the independence of the United States, and announced the signing of the treaties of February 6, 1778. The note was a deliberate challenge to the British monarch before the eyes of Europe, and it came because Vergennes felt France was ready to fight. Vergennes, of course, insisted that the note was not intended to provoke England to war, but other Europeans saw the matter in another light. The Danish Foreign Minister, Bernstorff, remarked that the French ambassador's note "was the signal for war."[30] A diplomat said the note made war "inevitable"[31] The French chargé d'affaires at Copenhagen predicted that the note would be promptly followed by a British declaration of war.[32]

The fiction that England was the aggressor became very important to Vergennes when the Bavarian succession crisis developed. It gave him an advantage in dealing with Austria. Joseph II ordered his troops into Bavaria and then asked Louis XVI to support him, in accordance with the Franco-Austrian alliance of 1756. France refused, on the grounds that the alliance was only defensive and Joseph's act was an offensive one. Earlier, the French ambassador to Vienna had broached to Joseph the subject of Austrian aid to France if France were attacked. Joseph was reluctant to commit himself.[33] After the British attacked the French frigate *La Belle Poule,* Vergennes went to great lengths to convince the Austrians that the British were, indeed, the aggressors.[34] But Austria would never admit that the English were the aggressors.[35] Vergennes continued to insist, however, and repeatedly reminded Joseph that the English aggression against France gave Louis XVI equal right to demand Austrian assistance. Finally, Vergennes offered Joseph a deal. The two allies, he suggested, ought to recognize each other's positions, and stop embarrassing each other by claiming aid.[36] Throughout the Bavarian crisis Joseph continued to demand help; Vergennes continued to respond that France's right to Austrian aid was equal to Austria's right to French aid. The response never convinced Joseph, but it blunted the effect of his demands on France. By maintaining the fiction that England was the aggressor, Vergennes persistently fended off Joseph's attempts to divert France's military efforts away from the American war.

Experienced diplomats were hardly taken in by Louis XVI's claim that England had aggressed against France. As early as 1776, European diplomats knew of Beaumarchais' comings and goings, they knew American ships were loading munitions at Le Havre, and that Vergennes and the British ambassador had clashed over the French interference in the British Empire.[37] The Danish ambassador to Madrid remarked in January, 1777, that there would probably be no war that year, because England was too busy with her colonies, and France and Spain were not yet ready for it. But he correctly predicted that developments in the coming year would make war likely.[38] The Danish ambassador at Versailles saw that the French were determined not to appear the aggressors in the coming war, but he also saw that the decisions being made to put the French Navy in operational readiness were a "decisive" sign of war with England.[39] His superior at Copenhagen agreed. After the British attack on *La Belle Poule,* Bernstorff openly questioned France's attempts to demonstrate England's guilt for starting the war. France, he noted, wished to date the beginning of the war with the *La Belle Poule* affair; but England dated the beginning of the hostilities much earlier.[40] In Austria, Joseph II, told the French ambassador the same thing. To Joseph, the Franco-American treaty began the war, because it made it "inevitable" that England attack France.[41] To Joseph, the attack on *La Belle Poule* seemed only a skirmish in a war already begun by French action.

Vergennes' plans for war also entailed unsuccessful attempts to deceive. While he prepared for war, he tried to convince the British that Louis XVI did not seek to profit from the embarrassment England found herself in, in America.[42] Later developments made it clear that Vergennes' statements to the British were blatant lies, but Vergennes continued the official stance: France would not use the American revolt to embarrass England.[43] Again, the diplomats were not deceived. From the beginning of Franco-American contacts, British spies kept London informed of what was happening at Versailles.[44] And, even if the British spy system had been incompetent, alert English diplomats could have learned of the French deception from other European diplomats. The Danish minister, Bernstorff, followed, in Copenhagen, the course of French intervention, step by step.[45] From Madrid the reports of his representative, St. Saphorin, were amazingly accurate.[46] If the Danish diplomatic corps was so well-informed, the diplomats of other powers must have been aware, also, of the deceptions of the French government. Louis XVI knew this. When he tried to explain to Charles III why he had signed treaties with the United States without full consultation with Madrid, he mentioned, as one reason for his haste, that French involvement was no longer a secret, and the British were threatening vengeance.[47] If Louis believed that the breakdown of secrecy brought England closer to an attack on France, did he not see, as Vergennes surely did, that a public announcement in London of a Franco-American alliance treaty would likely provoke England to open war? The Treaty of February 6, 1778, and the public announcement of it, was Vergennes' way of beginning the war "without being, materially, the aggressor . . . ."[48]

In short, the Anglo-French war was a preventive war in which France played the role of provocateur, while trying to maintain the fiction that England was the aggressor. Vergennes evaded the moral responsibility for his acts, on the grounds that they were determined by necessity. Turgot, on the other hand, argued that peace, not war, was the real necessity. The intervention demonstrates Vergennes' mastery of the techniques of international diplomacy. It also demonstrates his blindness: he could not take seriously the warnings about the inability of the King's treasury to pay for his foreign policy.

The French intervention required considerable deception on the part of a man who personally cultivated the reputation of being honest. Vergennes did not deceive the veteran diplomats of Europe. Did he deceive himself into believing that his actions were consistent with his personal Christian morals? It is impossible to say. Certainly the argument of "necessity" is frequently used by statesmen as a shield to hide, from themselves as well as from others, the inconsistencies between their actions and their professed private morals. Vergennes' justification of his actions on the grounds of necessity smacks of this sort of self-deception. Whatever the case, he continued to cultivate at court the image of the honest, hard-working, Christian family man,[49] while he privately admitted to his colleagues in the field that the limits for what is permissible in ". . .politics are not quite as strict as [they are] for morality . . . ."[50]

France's plans to exploit the war in America depended, of course, on the continued existence of an American military force. A professional diplomat, trained to calculate and measure power, Vergennes had taken each step of the road to intervention with the confidence that the Americans could field a reliable army. Once the alliance was sealed, however, that confidence began to erode. Reports from America began to draw a picture of an Army in desperate straits, and very much in need of help. The soldiers needed everything, "clothes, arms, money, or even still more, effective support."[51] As early as the latter part of 1777, the French government had contingency plans for an expeditionary force to America, if necessary. After the joint French-Spanish attempt to end the war with an invasion of England was aborted, repeated reports from America described an American army on the verge of collapse. Louis XVI's council decided to send to America an expeditionary force.[52] France was now totally and tragically committed.

CHAPTER 21

Spain Enters the War

The Franco-American alliance of 1778 presented to Charles III of Spain an unwanted war. While Spanish policy had been indeed warlike against Portugal, Charles III had no desire to fight in a war that encouraged independence movements in the American hemisphere. The idea of political independence was contagious and could spread too easily to the Spanish colonies.[1] Furthermore, Spanish soldiers and sailors returning home from their minor war in Brazil, against Portugal, would be easy targets for the English Navy. In any case, before they could plunge into a new war, they had to have time to rest and recuperate. Moreover, the Spanish treasury was drained.[2].

Additional considerations also led Spanish ministers to want peace. The Spanish Navy appeared formidable against the Portuguese in Brazil. But could it maintain that reputation against the British Navy? The question arose not only because of Spanish pride, but from Spanish needs: a successful British blockade of Spain, or repeated interceptions of Spanish shipping, could disrupt Spanish commerce and create chaos in the Spanish economy.[3]

There were other reasons why Spain suddenly became pacific. The Spanish ministry, especially Floridablanca, and Charles III personally, resented that a major decision had been made by their ally at Versailles with very little consideration for opinions at Madrid.[4] Louis XVI had presented Charles III with a *fait accompli*. The Spanish King was "not content."[5]

Surely Vergennes had known how Spain would react to Louis XVI's decision. Vergennes was too experienced a diplomat to have made a blunder inadvertently. Did he count on the fact that the Spanish would be so compromised by their ally's intervention in the war that they would have no choice but to follow the French lead?[6] Either he intended to compromise Spain, or he was indifferent to the reactions of the Spanish government because he firmly believed Spain would follow Louis XVI into the war. The latter belief seemed almost certain to him because it periodically received confirmation from Montmorin, French ambassador to Madrid.[7] Moreover, the Spanish ambassador to Versailles, Aranda, was almost as favorable to the idea of immediate Spanish entry into the war as was Vergennes. Unfortunately, however, Aranda did not enjoy the complete confidence of Floridablanca,[8] although the Spanish knew, of course, that, if they did not assist France, they risked seeing the Family Compact come apart. Vergennes counted heavily on the strength of the family ties of the Bourbon dynasty and the Family Compact to hold together the Franco-Spanish alliance.[9]

Louis XVI tried to nurse Charles' wounded pride by explaining to his uncle that time and circumstances simply did not permit him to inform the Spanish and wait for their opinions. Louis allowed, however, that Charles' advice would have been "most precious" to him. The separation of America from Great Britain, Louis said, deprived England of an important source of her power. It was in the Bourbons' interests, therefore, to prevent a reunion.[10]

Charles' answer was coolly polite, but non-committal. He was appreciative, he said, of Louis' gesture of friendship in informing him of the treaty with the Americans, but he noted that Louis had announced the alliance against England before Charles had received notification of it. He would, therefore, decline giving an opinion on it. Then, in a deliberately sarcastic statement, Charles told Louis that he had no doubt but that the "foresightedness" of his nephew had led him to take all the "necessary measures" the circumstances required to avoid possible dangerous consequences of his decision. Since one of the "necessary measures"[11] Louis had not taken was to get Spanish consent beforehand to guarantee Spanish assistance, Charles' statement was a warning bell at Versailles.

Louis XVI, Floridablanca later complained, treated Charles III as though he were a viceroy, or governor of a province.[12] Floridablanca felt that, while the alliance might benefit France, it promised very little for Spain.[13] He had expressed his objections to Vergennes at least two weeks before the latter signed the treaty with the Americans. And Vergennes had tried to answer Floridablanca's objections barely a week before he signed the alliance.[14] Floridablanca had also pointed out to Vergennes that the Spanish treasure fleet from Mexico and Rio de la Plata would not arrive in Spain until the end of June. An alliance with the Americans made hostilities with the English Navy inevitable, just at the moment when these Spanish fleets would be on the high seas. The British Navy certainly would hunt down such prime targets, if Spain joined the Franco-American Alliance. When Vergennes offered to send French ships to help protect the Spanish fleets, Floridablanca scrupulously declined.[15]

Thus, in the spring of 1778 Charles III stood, balancing the risks of war and Spanish interests against the dangers involved in breaking the Family Compact. Vergennes revived their argument that war was a way of protecting the Spanish from a possible British surprise attack, or even an Anglo-

American attack, if the Americans re-united with the mother country. But the reasoning now seemed farfetched to Floridablanca. The Spanish minister argued , with good reason, that the moment chosen by France to intervene on the American side actually increased, rather than diminished, the threats to Spain.[16] Moreover, Floridablanca did not believe that the Americans were on the verge of accepting peace terms that the British government and Parliament could accept.[17] The French treaty with the Americans, Spain insisted, was premature.[18] Thus Charles III was polite, but he firmly refused to rush headlong into hostilities. To insure that England understood that France had concluded the American treaty without Spanish concurrence, Floridablanca officially informed the British of that fact.[19]

Whatever the Spanish thought about Louis XVI's alliance with the Americans, the war created a situation which Spain could exploit to her own advantage, and Floridablanca was intelligent enough to perceive the opportunities. Spain had the choice to remain neutral, to mediate a settlement of the war, or to enter the war. Her decision as to which of these choices she would take would depend ultimately on which offered the most benefits. Charles III did not intend to deny himself any reward the war might present to him. The old Spanish minister, Grimaldi, had written in 1776: "...the goal of all wars is to conserve one's own possessions and to take those of someone else, so that the losses one suffers will be inferior to the advantages. Otherwise war would be ruinous and ought, consequently, to be avoided."[20] In 1778, Charles III and Floridablanca found Grimaldi's principle a good rule of thumb for formulating Spanish reactions to the American Revolutionary War.

Because of the slight to Spanish opinion shown by France when Louis XVI concluded the Franco-American Alliance, Vergennes never dared to ask Spain to enter the war with England as an obligation formally required by the Family Compact.[21] And Floridablanca was quick to indicate to Versailles that Spain would limit her operations to only auxiliary ones, if Louis XVI did insist that she enter the war to fulfill the obligations of the Family Compact.[22] Nevertheless, Vergennes' insistence that Britain was the aggressor made it theoretically possible to call for Spanish help, according to the obligations of mutual defense stipulated in the treaty: "Whoever attacks one [Bourbon] crown attacks the other."[23]

France badly needed the Spanish Navy in the maritime war made inevitable by the alliance with the Insurgents. Vergennes was confident that the French Navy had, in the spring of 1778, at least effective parity with the British Navy,[24] because the British could not immediately man all the ships which they had ready or under construction. For a few months, therefore, France could count on meeting the English at sea on fairly equal terms, but only for a few months. Once the British manned their warships, the French Navy would be outnumbered. To Vergennes, consequently, the help of the Spanish Navy, even if it served only to divert and tie up the British Navy, was absolutely indispensable to a French victory. Furthermore, the Spanish help had to be available before the French Navy lost its effective parity with the British. After that, France would become the underdog in a naval war that could be disastrous.[25]

Louis XVI needed the Spanish Navy. That irreducible fact was the axis of Vergennes' Spanish diplomacy immediately after the signing of the Franco-American treaty. But Louis XVI would have to pay for it and, no doubt, pay dearly. During the months after the announcement of the American treaty, Vergennes spent his time trying to determine exactly what the Spanish price would be.

In numerous dispatches to Montmorin, Vergennes outlined, one after the other, Louis XVI's offers to Spain, each one designed to bring Spain into the war. Vergennes suggested Minorca, a share of the Newfoundland fisheries, Jamaica and Florida, and Gibraltar.[26] Vergennes expected Gibraltar to be a particularly effective bait, because Floridablanca had indicated Spanish concern for that fortress soon after he learned of the Franco-American treaty.[27]

The Spanish demand for Gibraltar was a useful one to Spain because it could be used to bargain with England, as well as France.[28] England, presumably, would be willing to pay to keep Spain neutral. Was she willing to offer so dear a prize as Gibraltar? If so, Spain could gain from the war simply by staying out of it.[29] Knowing Charles III's interest in Gibraltar, the British government was willing to talk, listen attentively, and stall, with the knowledge that every moment that Spain remained out of the war increased the burden on France and bought the time needed to bring the British Navy up to full strength.

As Floridablanca discussed neutrality with England in exchange for Gibraltar, he simultaneously, in April, 1778, advanced his project for Spanish mediation of a peace settlement. The Spanish attempted to make it appear that it was the British government that asked Spain to be mediator. But Vergennes refused to believe the story. The Spanish, he correctly concluded, were the authors of the plan for mediation; they were maneuvering for more time. They did, in fact, need more time, for in May, the British turned down the Spanish offer to trade neutrality for Gibraltar, and temporarily suspended any discussion of the matter.[30] By now, Vergennes was beginning to have doubts about the readiness of Charles III to aid his nephew. Nevertheless, he unenthusiastically informed Madrid of Louis XVI's acceptance of Charles III as mediator. To have refused would have created still another resentment at Madrid. Vergennes insisted, however, that France would not agree to any settlement that did not include American independence.[31]

The perplexing behavior of Spain did convince Vergennes that Spanish assistance could not be taken for granted. Thenceforth, he began actively to cultivate Spanish ministers to win their support. He paid assiduous attention to every Spanish opinion. Time and again he made it clear to Madrid that Louis XVI put a very high value on Spanish co-operation.[32] But the appointment, by Madrid, of the Conde d'Almodovar to be the new ambassador to London to replace the chargé d'affaires, Escasano, only increased his uncertainty about Spanish reliability. The presence of the experienced Almodovar at London, Vergennes observed, indicated that the Spanish placed a high value on their negotiations with England.[33]

In August, 1778, Spain pressed, once again, her twin notions of neutrality—for a price—and mediation. Almodovar subtly fished for an offer from Great Britain to pay for Spanish neutrality, and reminded the British government that Spain could not wait forever.[34] The Spanish treasure fleet and the expeditionary force from Brazil were now safe at home, so Floridablanca spoke in a more energetic tone. When Almodovar's subtleties did not work, the Spanish declared outright that they wanted Gibraltar and Minorca, but more especially Gibraltar, in exchange for neutrality.[35] The British Minister of War, Barrington, hinted that England might yet be persuaded to turn over Gibraltar and Minorca to Spain.[36] Spain asked both parties to draw up their demands, so that Spain could compose a formula for a mediated peace settlement. Vergennes' official demands were accompanied by a secret list to Spain of Louis XVI's minimum demands. No sooner were the discussions under way than it became clear that the two sides were too far apart to expect a settlement. France refused to compromise on her demand for a British withdrawal from all occupied territory, on her wish to have the British commissioners removed from Dunkirk, and on her determination that Britain recognize the independence of the United States. Britain set as a pre-condition for any negotiations with France that Louis XVI withdraw all aid, military or otherwise, to the Americans.[37]

Floridablanca had once written Almodovar to tell the British that what Spain did not get "by negotiation, we know how to get with a club."[38] Floridablanca now reached for the club. In an inquiry to Versailles, he asked: in case mediation failed, what might be the "benefits" Spain could anticipate, if she entered the war? Floridablanca also requested information on plans for possible combined Franco-Spanish military operations, should Spain enter the War.[39] Both Montmorin and Vergennes already knew that the benefit Spain most wanted was Gibraltar. Vergennes dispatched to Madrid France's plan for combined operations.[40] It was constructed on the premise that, together, Spain and France could put to sea a fleet of ships of the line that outnumbered the English, by 107 to 92.[41]

During the winter of 1778 and the early months of 1779, Spain became more and more irritated by the vague British notes that said nothing and settled nothing. Charles III was disappointed in the progress of mediation and Floridablanca warned England that she had to show some concrete desire for peace.[42] Moreover, on the seas, British corsairs were steadily increasing their harassment of Spanish shipping. When Madrid demanded reparations for what she considered illegal seizures, the British resorted once again to vague and evasive replies.[43] The distrust between Spain and England became so great that the idea of mediation could not advance beyond diplomatic form. By the spring of 1779, a majority of the British Parliament had come to favor a war with Spain.[44]

Nevertheless, Charles III was not satisfied with his Bourbon relative, and Louis XVI and Vergennes did not trust Floridablanca. Floridablanca suspected that France did not want Spain to get Gibraltar, and some of the other rewards that Vergennes had dangled before Spanish eyes—Jamaica and most of Florida—Spain simply did not want.[45]

Yet early in August, Floridablanca informed Vergennes that Spain was building up her naval squadrons, and reinforcing her troops in Havana.[46] He also suggested, but only as his own personal thought, that, if France and Spain combined their naval resources, they would have the strength to invade England and impose a peace settlement at London.[47]

Floridablanca's personal thoughts only exasperated Vergennes. By the end of December, 1778, the first naval campaign season of the war was closed, and there were no combined operations with Spain in sight.[48] To remind Floridablanca that England was the eternal enemy of the Bourbons, Vergennes drew up a detailed list of grievances the two Bourbon monarchs had against England, and sent them off to Madrid.[49] As long as he hoped that England might make Spain an offer, Floridablanca would not give his endorsement to the statement of grievances. He also asked that Vergennes postpone its publication, because he realized that, if such a statement were made public, it might be taken as a declaration of war on England.[50] Vergennes deferred to Floridablanca's request, but continued to discuss the details of the statement with the Spanish minister. The list of grievances Almodovar presented to the British government on June 15, 1779, when he demanded his passport,[51] was an offspring of this early attempt by Vergennes to involve Spain in the war.

Thus, by the close of 1778, Spain had taken several large strides in the direction of collaboration with France, despite the fact that she still explored the way of mediation to achieve her aims. With Floridablanca's encouragement, Vergennes had drawn up a war plan based on the premise that the Spanish Navy would be available for combined naval operations. If Spain could not find a market in London for her neutrality, she obviously had one for her Navy at Versailles. The next step, if mediation failed, was an agreement on the price France would pay if Spain entered the war. The agreement was the Convention of Aranjuez.

From the perspective of historical hindsight, the step-by-step involvement of Spain in the American Revolution appears, as it indeed was, a logical conclusion to Vergennes' Spanish diplomacy. Yet such a view is misleading if it ignores the uncertain context, for, at no time during 1778 or up until the last moment in early 1779, was Vergennes completely confident that Charles III would enter the war. The Spanish monarch's attitude perplexed Vergennes and confounded his hopes that Spain would quickly come into the war.

The alternatives for France, if Spain did not enter the war, were bleak. As the campaign of 1778 closed, Vergennes planned for the next campaign on the assumption that the Spanish Navy would be an active ally of France by the spring of 1779. He did so, in part, because Floridablanca's call for a plan of war encouraged him to do so. Yet, as spring approached, Charles III made no concrete commitment. Anxiously Vergennes pointed out to the Spanish that, after the opening of the campaign season, the British Navy would equal, then surpass, the French Navy if the latter had to operate alone. To operate alone required that the French Navy implement a strategy very different from that which it could undertake if combined with the Spanish fleet. Yet, as late as mid-March, 1779, Vergennes was still uncertain, and increasingly anxious, about which way Spain would go.

Moreover, if Spain joined France, the fleets of the two Bourbon monarchs needed time to learn to maneuver together before they met the British. If Spain joined France, but joined too late, Vergennes warned, the military consequences would be almost as disastrous as they would be if she did not join at all.[52] Time, then, became a crucial element in Vergennes' calculations. France needed Spain's assistance, and she needed it soon. Vergennes' letters to Montmorin, and his private notes to the King, show a growing impatience with Spain and a desperate willingness to agree to almost anything suggested by the Spanish that would bring Charles III into the war. "I will not dissimulate, Sire," . . . .he wrote in a private note to Louis XVI, in December, 1778, " . . . .the views and pretensions of Spain are gigantic, but remember that time spent countering them will be time lost that should be spent establishing combined operations . . . ."[53]

In Spain the French ambassador shared the same anxieties. When, at the beginning of 1779, Montmorin suggested to Floridablanca that the Spanish minister draft a convention detailing the benefits Spain might gain from a war, Floridablanca refused. Such a draft, Floridablanca explained, should come only from France and be a closely guarded secret, for he did not wish Spain to do anything that would be out of keeping with her role as a neutral.[54]

In answer to Floridablanca's suggestion, and as a result of several conversations with him, Montmorin took the initiative to draw up a list of points that could form the basis of a Franco-Spanish convention. Montmorin then proposed that Vergennes use the French ambassador's items to draw up a formal Franco-Spanish convention and send it to him along with the appropriate power to sign. Somewhat more confident, Montmorin confessed that he believed Floridablanca was acting in good faith.[55]

Vergennes was ecstatic. "I read your dispatch with the zeal of patriotism and the emotion of friendship," he wrote to Montmorin. "I immediately passed it on the King, who will surely be satisfied with it."[56] Later reports from Madrid kept up the spirits of the Secretary of State. England's response to Spain's latest offers for mediation continued to be vague. Floridablanca, Montmorin gleefully reported, expected nothing more from them and was turning, increasingly, to the details of a formal convention and combined military operations. Floridablanca, Montmorin reported, "awaited with impatience" Vergennes' draft of a Franco-Spanish convention.[57]

Together Louis XVI, Maurepas, and Vergennes quickly drew up a draft of the convention, based on Montmorin's recommendations, and dispatched it to Spain. The first Article of the draft, the "keystone of the edifice," as Vergennes called it, would set the time when Spain would declare herself a participant in the war. In the draft Vergennes left a blank space for the date for Floridablanca to fill in.[58]

Article II outlined a plan for combined Spanish-French military operations.[59] The essential element of this plan was a combined invasion of Ireland using 30,000 French and Spanish soldiers. Vergennes also counted on an Irish uprising that would add to the numbers of the invaders.[60] But Floridablanca refused to provide troops for the Irish operation.[61] Vergennes, therefore, proposed an alternative plan. The Bourbons' combined fleets would gain naval superiority in the channel, and then exploit their superiority by pursuing the British fleet into Britain's own forts and destroying them, or by trapping the enemy fleet in the road of Spithead between Portsmouth and the Isle of Wight. While the Bourbon warships swept the Channel of British ships, a 20,000-man expeditionary force would land, first on the Isle of Wight, and then at Portsmouth.[62] The plan was not as dramatic as the earlier one, but it did satisfy the Spaniard's determination to "attack Carthage at Carthage . . ."[63] rather than in the Americas.

The idea of a direct attack on England was not new.[64] The Comte de Broglie, one of Vergennes' old chiefs and collaborators in Louis XV's *secret du roi,* had introduced Vergennes to the idea in 1774 when he outlined a plan to invade England. When Louis XVI had ordered that Broglie's papers be destroyed, Vergennes had personally intervened to save Broglie's invasion plans.[65]

Vergennes hoped that the idea of a descent on England would appeal to Floridablanca; it would bring the Spanish into the war with a dramatic *éclat*, an entry especially pleasing to Charles III, and it promised, as all such grandiose military plans inevitably promise, to end the war quickly. The Bourbons could then dictate a peace from London. Before promising full Spanish participation in the war, Floridablanca wanted a French commitment for a total war against England; a war like the one the Romans had fought against the Carthaginians, a war, in short, that shifted the central theatre of operations away from America and back to Europe.[66]

A war to crush Britain, as the Romans had crushed the Carthaginians, was foreign to Vergennes' conceptions of war and politics. The French Secretary of State wished only to reduce English power and influence, relative to that of France, and he wanted to force a modification of British foreign policy, but he had no desire whatsoever to destroy England's presence in the balance-of-power system. Moreover, he was sure that the other states in Europe would not stand by and allow such an operation to succeed. If France abandoned her politics of moderation, much of Europe might coalesce against her.[67]

The plan to gain naval superiority in the English Channel and then land troops on British beaches was also very costly.[68] Such a combined operation would require from 30 to 50 French ships of the line and 20,000 troops.[69] Finally, such an armada would be exposed to thousands of unforeseen risks and dangers. Storms, unfavorable winds, disease, and bad fortune could turn the "grand design," as Vergennes called it, into a terrible catastrophe such as the one which had befallen an earlier Spanish armada.[70] Heretofore, Vergennes had opposed such an operation because it shifted the center of military operations away from America to Europe. But, now, to bring Spain into the war, he was willing to agree to almost anything. Vergennes made it clear, however, that, while Spain was free to choose the time when the operation would be carried out, it had to be done before England was strong enough to oppose it successfully.[71]

The article in the draft of the convention concerning the United States created the most difficulty in Spain. It stated that United States independence was the principle base of the relations between the United States and France, and provided that the two Bourbon powers agree not to put down their arms until United States' independence was recognized by England.[72] Vergennes had predicted the article would cause difficulties; his predictions were confirmed.

Five separate articles of Vergennes' draft convention detailed the advantages both France and Spain expected to draw from the war.[73] Article XI reconfirmed the Family Pact.[74] Article XII, returned to the thorny issue of

United States independence, and provided that, on the day when Spain entered the war, she would recognize the independence of the United States either by acceding "purely and simply" to the Franco-American alliance or by any other "public act" that Charles III found appropriate.[75]

In one of the several letters that accompanied Vergennes' draft to Madrid, the French Secretary of State repeated Louis XVI's desire to accept Charles III's plans to mediate a peace. But he predicted that England—"drunk from past successes"—would reject them. And, if the British did not make a formal reply soon, Spain ought to interpret "their silence, and their evasive tactics", Vergennes told Montmorin, as a sign of their bad intentions. By now, Vergennes believed that the Bourbon monarchs could, together, command one hundred and sixteen ships. "The English, for sure, do not have the equivalent."[76]

Vergennes rejoiced over the reports of the step-by-step transformation of Spain into a fighting ally. But, in reality, Charles III was still not in the French camp. Floridablanca set the middle of May as the date when Charles III would make an open declaration against England, if the British ministry continued to be dilatory. Too late, Vergennes answered. Spanish sailors had very little experience sailing in large squadrons; they did not have the experience in maneuvering that a combined operation required. They needed additional time to gain the necessary experience. "Press the signing of the convention . . .," he urged Montmorin.[77]

The most difficult obstacles to the signing of the convention came from Floridablanca. He complained that Vergennes' plans for the combined naval operations were inadequate,[78] and he insisted on waiting for a response from London that would tell him something more concrete about what the British were going to do.[79] Most of all, he had a multitude of objections and reservations about the convention draft sent him by Vergennes. Floridablanca had assured Montmorin, after his first reading of the draft, that the two parties would reach an accord quickly. Several days later, however, he changed his mind. He went through the draft with Montmorin, article by article, and developed his objections. The First Article set the time when Charles III would enter the war against England. To Vergennes, it was the "keystone of the edifice"; to Floridablanca, it was "absolutely useless."[80] The article concerning American independence he found "out of place" as well as "useless." Since the independence of the Americans was the "first and, indeed, the only cause" of the war, it was superfluous to promise not to put down one's arms until that goal was obtained.[81]

Montmorin agreed that the independence of the United States was truly the first cause of the war: for that reason it ought to be in the convention. Floridablanca refused. As they discussed the issue, Floridablanca grew angry. The article guaranteeing the independence of the United States, he noted with irritation, was much more precise than those promising benefits to Spain, or even to France. According to Vergennes' draft, the Bourbons would "not put down their arms" until Great Britain recognized the independence of the United States. But the draft provided only that they "make every effort to procure" the benefits desired by the Bourbon monarchs.

Montmorin tried to satisfy Floridablanca's objections by suggesting that they use the same expressions for both sets of articles. Abruptly, Floridablanca changed the subject to the military plan of operations. Once the two parties reached total agreement on their military plans, the other issues would "arrange themselves." Floridablanca ended the discussion with the comment that he would draw up his own draft of a convention.

Montmorin was now thoroughly confused. Had Floridablanca changed his mind after further reflection on Vergennes' draft? Was he reflecting Charles III's reluctance to commit himself until he had a definite answer from England? Whatever the case, Montmorin once more saw Floridablanca escape him. The Spanish minister was a difficult person to manage, confessed the French ambassador.[82]

"Monsieur le Comte de Floridablanca," Vergennes responded when he read Montmorin's latest report, "is creating pretexts for new delays." Spain, Vergennes demanded, must tell France what her intentions were. Bitterly Vergennes pointed out that, by her repeated delays, Spain was leaving France militarily exposed. If Charles III had told Louis XVI that the French could not count on Spanish help, the French government would have adopted a military strategy more suited to a Navy whose numbers did not equal those of the enemy. Furthermore, it was too late to change plans. ". . . I very much fear," Vergennes concluded, "that the only service our ally will end up rendering to us will be that of having made it impossible for us to take the only measures which could assure our defense."[83]

Floridablanca, Vergennes believed, was taking advantage of France's need for Spain. The Spaniard, Vergennes told Montmorin, wanted Spain to profit from the war without risking any of the dangers. He wanted to reap without having sown. Growing sarcastic, Vergennes attributed Floridablanca's tactics to the man's "fiscal spirit which was the essence of his original profession." Floridablanca had begun his career in government finances, in the Council of Castile. Vergennes' contempt for men who busied themselves with the concerns of the State's finances was almost unqualified.[84]

But sarcasm did nothing to bring Spain into the war, so Vergennes turned once again to meet Floridablanca's objections. In two documents, one addressed to Montmorin, and the other to Floridablanca, he tried once more to outline plans for a joint military operation that would satisfy the Spanish. Vergennes again promised that the joint military operation would open with a strike at the British fleet in the Channel, followed by attacks on the British ports, and an expeditionary force against the Isle of Wight and Portsmouth. If the Spanish King agreed, Vergennes advised, the "junction of the two Bourbon fleets should take place between the first and the fifteenth of May." Vergennes recommended that the French Lieutenant General, the Comte d'Orvilliers, be the commander of the operation, but Louis XVI, Vergennes assured Floridablanca, was willing to allow Charles III to name a Spanish commander, if the Spanish forces involved equaled, or were superior to, those provided by France.[85]

By the beginning of March, the perplexed Montmorin, on whom Vergennes depended for advice on how to deal with Charles III and Floridablanca, had given up trying to fathom Spanish motivations. He turned his attention simply to ways of getting the Spanish into the war. France, he proposed, should go ahead with the plans for combined military operations; she should announce to Spain the departure date of the French fleet from Brest, and indicate to Madrid that the French expected to join whatever number of Spanish ships Vergennes judged necessary to the success of the operation. Once the Spanish were in the war, Montmorin counseled, necessity would make them more easy to deal with.[86] This tactic involved a risk that could possibly end in disaster; but the Spanish treasure fleets were safely home, and the Spanish naval squadron assigned to cooperate with the French fleet was ready and waiting for orders. France, Montmorin suggested, must decide for Spain. "Once the decision is made by you, there will remain here no pretext to retreat."[87]

But it was British muddleheadedness, rather than French craftiness, that finally drove Spain into the war. When they eventually answered the latest Spanish offer to mediate, their answer contained unacceptable conditions. They agreed to accept a truce between France, the Americans, and England that would allow Spain time to mediate a settlement between France and England. During the truce, Louis XVI would be free, the British conditions provided, to treat with Great Britain concerning any interest he might have in Europe or in the Americas, but he would not be allowed to mix his interests with the "alleged interests of those that France affects to call *her allies* (i.e. the United States)." The "Colonies" would be free to draw up their complaints, the British reply went on, but, at the same time, the "legitimate government" would be reestablished during the truce. Then one would see if a "direct and immediate conciliation" were possible.[88]

The British conditions would have destroyed the intent and letter of the Franco-American alliance. If Charles III had accepted the British conditions, the acceptance would have been a personal and diplomatic affront to his nephew at Versailles. It is difficult to say whether the British appreciated what their response meant at Madrid. Vergennes saw that it provided the additional push necessary to drive the Spanish into war. Charles III and

Floridablanca interpreted the British response in the same way. Even the English ambassador to Madrid, Lord Grantham, apparently realized that his government had passed the point of no return; for several days he deliberately avoided any contacts with the Spanish government.[89]

Floridablanca and Charles III prepared the document that would be the instrument of Spain's entry into the war. At the same time, Floridablanca worked out with Montmorin the final plan of the combined military operation. The diplomatic pouch carrying the Spanish ultimatum was to be delivered to the English ambassador at Madrid and would reach London at the latest the thirteenth or fourteenth of April. Lord Weymouth would then have eight days, that is until the twenty-second, to consider it. Almodovar would then request an answer. If Weymouth asked for more time, Almodovar would give him two or three more days. On the twenty-fifth the Spanish ambassador would send a courier to Madrid by way of Paris with the British response, if there was a response, or with the notification of no answer whatsoever. The courier would arrive in Madrid around the sixth of May. If the response was silence, or unsatisfactory, the Spanish fleet would be ordered immediately to sail from Cadiz to meet the French on the twentieth of May. The French fleet would sail from Brest between the tenth and fifteenth of May, in order to make the *rendezvous.* If something happened to delay the *rendezvous,* Floridablanca suggested prolonging the conversations at London to give the squadron time to unite. Floridablanca also recommended that Louis XVI prohibit all travel between France and England so that British spies, if they penetrated the secret plans, would not be able to communicate with their government.[90]

The ultimatum prepared by Charles III was officially submitted to Paris and London. It provided for an indefinite suspension of arms between France and Great Britain, which would not be broken without a warning one year in advance. Following the suspension of hostilities, the two crowns would undertake a general disarmament in European seas within a month; within four months in American seas; and from eight months to a year in the seas of Africa and Asia. The plenipotentiaries of the two courts would then assemble to negotiate a definite treaty of peace, and to "regulate the respective restitutions and compensations." Charles III would act as mediator to this assembly and he invited the plenipotentiaries to make Madrid the place of their meeting.

At the same time, the ultimatum continued, by the mediation of Charles III, George III would grant to the "American Colonies" a separate suspension of hostilities which would be continued unless Great Britain notified Spain, one year in advance, of her intention to break it. Meanwhile Spain, as mediator, could facilitate disarmament and the drawing of limits on places and territories occupied at the moment of ratification of the ultimatum. The colonies would send one or more commissioners to Madrid to meet with Great Britain under the watchful eye of the mediator. During this time the Colonies would be treated as "independent in fact." Finally, if any or all of the participating powers so demanded, Great Britain and France or Spain would guarantee the treaty settlement.[91] In its public declaration, Spain professed that it was unbelievable that Great Britain could refuse to accept the ultimatum.[92] But in the corridors of the Prado and Versailles, neither Floridablanca nor Vergennes believed Great Britain would accept.[93] The provision most likely to cause difficulty in the British ministry was that which granted the United States *de facto* independence.

His common sense told Vergennes that England would not accept the ultimatum; yet fears plagued him that she might, for he had deep reservations about its provisions. In the first place, Charles III and Floridablanca had composed and sent it off to England without consulting France. The truce it established would have left British soldiers in control of a large portion of territory the Americans considered part of their new country; and it would have placed the future of the young United States under the protection of Spain, rather than France. Charles III had no obligations to secure independence to the United States; whereas Louis XVI was bound by treaty to secure it. "I do not know . . ., how we would reconcile this engagement [the Franco-American treaty]," Vergennes wrote to Montmorin after he received a copy of the ultimatum, "with a truce which would leave in the hands of their [the Americans'] enemies the islands and other territories which they have had taken away from them during the war." He confessed that he was sorely embarrassed by what he called "this sort of defection."[94] "The more we examine and weigh them [the stipulations of the ultimatum]," Vergennes complained to Montmorin in another dispatch, "the less we see how to reconcile them with what the King [Louis XVI] owes to himself and to his new allies; if we stipulate for them a truce in which each party remains in possession of the territory it now occupies, America will be able to believe, with good reason, that she is abandoned by us, and, at that moment, believing herself released from all obligations toward us, she will, it is to be feared, place herself once more in the leading strings of England." Vergennes reminded Montmorin that Charles III had repeatedly promised that he would look out for the "dignity" of Louis XVI in his negotiations with Great Britain. It would be useless to object to the fact, Vergennes went on, that Charles III had sent the ultimatum to England without consulting France, but Louis XVI did want to "scrupulously fill his engagements."[95] Even if the British rejected the ultimatum, and he was morally certain they would, it could be used by them to create suspicion among the Americans about French trustworthiness. After the British had refused the Spanish ultimatum, Vergennes still pondered what might have happened had the

British accepted it. "It is fortunate, Monsieur," he wrote to Montmorin, "that the English ministry did not sense the benefit it could have drawn from it."[96] Vergennes fully appreciated that the British ministry had had, momentarily, the means to create serious tensions within both the Franco-American alliance and the Family Compact.

An additional effect of the ultimatum was that it applied the pressure of time to the negotiations over the Franco-Spanish Convention of Aranjuez. Floridablanca had promised to re-edit Vergennes' draft of the Convention, but days turned into weeks and he produced nothing. Every day Montmorin asked about it, and Floridablanca assured him it was forthcoming. Finally, just a few days before the ultimatum was due to reach London, Floridablanca produced his version of the Convention. Hastily, Montmorin read it and re-read it, and hurried off to find Floridablanca, who was ready to sign.

Montmorin had a minor objection to Article One which Floridablanca accepted with little difficulty.[97] The two negotiators then reached the articles concerning the Americans, and the real differences between Spanish policy and French policy once again came to the surface. In his draft, Vergennes had wanted to commit Charles III to a formal guarantee of American independence: "... The two contracting powers," Vergennes' draft of Article Four read, "mutually engage themselves not to lay down their arms until the independence of the United States is recognized by the English crown."[98] Floridablanca refused to agree to this article. Charles III, he told Montmorin, would not recognize the independence of the United States until the English were forced to do so by the peace settlement. The Spanish King did not want to encourage such "an example" so near his own possessions. Floridablanca would only agree to insert in Article Four a statement to the effect that Louis XVI had "proposed and demanded" that Charles III recognize the independence of the United States on the day war was declared. But, since Charles III had not concluded a treaty with the Americans, in which their reciprocal interests could be outlined, he promised nothing, other than not to arrange any treaty with the United States without concerting with Louis XVI.[99] In Article Twelve of his draft, Vergennes had included the phrase: "The Catholic King [of Spain]declares that, the day he enters into war with England, he will recognize the sovereign independence of the Unites States of America, either by acceding purely and simply to the [Franco-American] treaty of friendship and commerce ... or by some other public act that His Catholic Majesty finds appropriate."[100] The discussion between Floridablanca and Montmorin on this reference to American independence once again was heated and when it ended, Vergennes' entire Article Twelve was erased from the Convention.

Montmorin noted two significant changes in the articles which listed the benefits Spain wanted to achieve from the war. Vergennes had placed Gibraltar at the end of a list of five items; Floridablanca placed it at the top of the list. Also Floridablanca had added Minorca as item number six. When Montmorin protested this addition, Floridablanca replied that he did so to achieve symmetry in the Convention. France had asked for six things; equaity demanded that Spain do likewise. Montmorin protested that France's demand for its rights in Dunkirk were not exactly the equivalent of Spain's demand for Gibraltar, but Floridablanca refused to back down. And he knew that Montmorin could not refuse. The French ambassador noted that, formerly, Spain wanted possession of only Mobile River and the fort, and Pensacola, but there now appeared with these places the phrase, "with all the vast of Florida which extends along the Canal of Bahama." That territory, Floridablanca retorted, was absolutely essential to Spanish navigation of the Gulf of Mexico. Once again, Montmorin returned to the point that six did not equal six in the lists of demands by the two Bourbons. So Floridablanca agreed to add to Article Nine that, if France did not achieve the abolition of English rights over Dunkirk, Louis XVI could choose some "other object". Both parties agreed not to lay down their arms, or make any treaty of peace, truce, or suspension of hostilities, until Spain achieved Gibraltar and France recovered her rights at Dunkirk or the vague "other object."

Floridablanca and Montmorin signed the Convention of Aranjuez the twelfth of April, and Louis XVI ratified it six days later. By the fourteenth of May, Vergennes knew that the British ministry had refused the Spanish ultimatum. "Fortunately," Montmorin noted with relief, "England . . . has cut through all the difficulties."[101] The combined naval operations could now get underway; the Franco-American treaty and Family Compact were still intact. Vergennes had successfully walked the tightrope.

If Britain had accepted *de facto* independence for the Americans while a peace was negotiated under the mediation of Spain, Vergennes would have been confronted with an agonizing dilemma, for the terms of the Spanish ultimatum were nearly as unacceptable to France as they were to England. A suspension of arms which left British troops occupying large portions of American territory certainly would have denied one of the main purposes of the war.[102] Nor would he have found palatable a peace settlement which made Charles III the arbiter of American, French, and European interests. That role Vergennes reserved for Louis XVI. Spanish mediation would have shifted the center of gravity of the Family Compact from Versailles to Madrid and, for personal as well as policy reasons, Vergennes did not wish to see Louis XVI forced into an auxiliary role in his alliances with either Spain or Austria.

The Convention of Aranjuez complicated French relations with the United States and had a significant impact on the military strategy of the war. During the first year of the war, Vergennes had used French military forces in Europe only to divert British attention, while the major thrust of French military action took place elsewhere, against the outposts of the British empire, especially in America.[103] The Franco-Spanish plans for a joint naval operation against England shifted the center of military strategy back to Europe. The new strategy did not please Vergennes, but he had to accept it to insure full Spanish participation in the war. Otherwise, Spain would have given only the minimum aid required by the letter of the Family Compact.[104]

Nevertheless, the new plan did offer the promise of some advantages. If successful, the plan might, indeed, bring the war to a swift conclusion. Furthermore, Vergennes was aware from intelligence sources that rumors, alone, of such an attack on England created panic in London. Panic, Vergennes felt, would certainly constitute a concrete advantage for Louis XVI, if it interrupted English commerce and created chaos in English financial circles. Certainly, the latter advantage could have been achieved as easily with a threat of an invasion as with a real attack, but such a gesture had no appeal in Spain.[105]

But the risks entailed by the combined Franco-Spanish plans became greater as each day passed. To succeed, the operation had to be undertaken early in the campaign season, so as to be completed before the bad weather in the fall. And yet, Vergennes had been unable to impress upon Floridablanca the importance of time. Furthermore, Floridablanca had continued, up until the last minute, to insist that Vergennes, Maurepas, and Louis XVI keep all the plans secret, even from the French military commander, until Spain learned how England planned to respond to Spanish offers to mediate. Thus Vergennes, of necessity, had to assume the task of improvising a plan of military operation with the help of Maurepas, Sartine and Louis XVI, without being able to consult with all the key military officers involved. Even the Spanish ambassador at Versailles, Aranda, was not privy to the military plans germinating at Versailles and Madrid. The situation made Vergennes uneasy, for he knew for certain that when Aranda learned he had been kept in the dark about such essential matters, there would be a "vigorous explosion."[106]

Vergennes had set May first as the critical date for combined Franco-Spanish operations. Once the two fleets had joined, the Bourbons would have at least forty-five ships of the line to oppose the thirty-five British ships which, French intelligence estimated, were in the Channel.[107] But May first came and passed, and nothing was ready. Vergennes had not been able to bring the appropriate military commanders into the discussions of the plans until April, and the French commander of the combined fleets, the Comte d'Orvilliers, did not leave for Brest until the end of May. His instructions communicated the anxiety which now dominated Versailles: the operation had to be undertaken immediately, before it was too late.[108]

Now delays plagued the fleets. The Spanish commander was so slow in putting his part of the operation into motion that he was dismissed.[109] The French fleets waited for the Spaniards at the *rendezvous* point, while their reserves of water and supplies began to run out. Worst of all, an outbreak of malaria and smallpox appeared on board the French ships.[110] The sickness became an epidemic. Every day a frigate made the rounds of the port, taking off the sick and dead.[111] Meanwhile, the British, who now knew of the Bourbon intentions, exploited the time available by concentrating troops on their southern coasts. George III was to take personal command.[112]

Finally, the combined fleets were ready to sail, forty-nine days after the French departure from Brest. Immediately, they ran into bad winds. The exhaustion of supplies, the sickness, and the irreparable loss of time had reduced the operation to a disaster. Already there were 140 dead from disease. On the fifteenth of August, the decimated armada appeared off Falmouth, England, and for three days created the panic Vergennes had hoped for. As he predicted, the stock market fell.[113] But England did not fall. The French army that was to land at Portsmouth and the Isle of Wight embarked on troop ships from French channel ports, but storms and bad winds made the soldiers seasick. "I do not know what the weather at sea is," Vergennes thought, " but it is frightful here at Versailles .... If the same weather reigns at sea ... our fleets must be suffering terribly."[114] On the seventh of August, already dreadfully late in the season, Vergennes gave up the idea of landing on the Isle of Wight, and substituted a plan, this one the brainchild of the Spanish ambassador, for an invasion and occupation along the coasts of Cornwall.[115]

But the substitute plan had no more chance of success than the original one. The shortages of supplies grew worse; the steady progress of the epidemic left some ships without sufficient sailors to keep the vessels at sea.[116] On the twenty-fifth of August, following a seven-day storm which had badly mauled the combined fleet, the Comte d'Orvilliers decided to seek out and pursue the fleet of British Admiral Charles Hardy and, if possible, to destroy it. If they did not find the enemy fleet, however, he decided that they would return to Brest.[117] Failing to find the British, the ships of the armada turned and sailed into Brest. Many who witnessed the return lauded the magnificence and imposing nature of the assemblage of naval power. But, inside the French ships, more than 8,000 men were on the sick list or dead.[118] The enterprise had failed, just short of a catastrophe.

Nevertheless, Spain was in the war, the Family Compact and the Franco-American alliance were still intact and, for a few short weeks, Europe had watched the British fleet and public intimidated by the combined navies of

Louis XVI and Charles III. The costs were terrible. The abortive attack on England added an additional 100,000,000 *livres* to the war expense and, from a military point of view, very little had been accomplished.[119] A recent study of that Channel campaign rightly concludes that the "Isle of Wight expedition was potentially the worst French strategic mistake of the war."[120]

CHAPTER 22

Dutch Neutrality: 1776-1782

The Dutch Patriots' Party's bid for power in the United Provinces in the late 1770's created an atmosphere favorable to France. It is impossible to say whether the Patriots were shock troops of a major re-orientation in Dutch politics away from the traditional English alliance, or whether they were simply the forlorn hope of an old opposition to the semi-royal Stadholder.[1] Vergennes did not trust the Stadholder, William V, who was pro-English, but he was slow to break the official stance of courtesy towards him, and even slower to place any confidence in the reliability of Patriots. But more importantly, he did not want to commit Louis XVI to any political alliances with the Dutch while France's resources were tied up in the American Revolutionary War.

On the other side, however, the Patriots saw great value in an alliance with France. Louis XVI's navy could defend Dutch colonies overseas and help convoy Dutch merchant ships in the event of war with England. To this idea, Vergennes strongly objected. The French navy, even after the Spanish added their ships to those of Louis XVI, did not have the strength to take on such a task. Furthermore, as the Dutch trade steadily grew with the Americans, France, and Spain, in armaments and supplies during the American war, it became apparent to Vergennes that the United Provinces could perhaps contribute more to the war as neutrals than as belligerents. He hoped, therefore, to keep the Dutch neutral, and trading. He also saw, of course, the obvious diplomatic and military disadvantages of England if the Dutch insisted on their rights as neutrals.

Catherine's 1780 Declaration of Neutral Rights[2] which strongly defended the principle of "free ships, free goods" dovetailed with Vergennes' evolving policy regarding neutrality. As early as September of 1778, he had urged the northern powers to get together and find a way to defend their rights as neutrals against Great Britain.[3] The Franco-American Treaty of Commerce of 1778 contained principles similar to those advanced by Catherine,[4] and

France's increasing need for war supplies spoke for more vigorous protection of neutral rights. On April 25, 1780, Vergennes officially notified Catherine of Louis XVI's satisfaction with her Declaration.[5]

Frightened that the new League of Armed Neutrals being formed by Catherine might become an anti-Spanish instrument, the Spanish government also notified Catherine in April, 1780, that it recognized and respected the rights of neutrals as she had outlined them, although Spain refused to lift its blockade of Gibraltar.

Diplomatic eyes now turned to the United Provinces. If only the northern neutrals, Sweden and Denmark, joined Catherine, her League would remain only an *entente* of Baltic powers. But if the Dutch joined her, it became a European league.[6] The King of Prussia saw this, and pressed the Republic to adhere to the League;[7] Vergennes also encouraged the Dutch to join.[8] But from London the British signaled warnings to the Dutch not to adhere to the League.[9] And the British could not be ignored. The ability of the British navy to interrupt Dutch shipping was already a demonstrated reality. While Catherine loudly proclaimed the rights of the neutrals, she was far away from the United Provinces and her navy was too weak to give the Dutch much assistance against the British Navy. The Estates General of the United Provinces thus deliberated a long time over Catherine's Declaration of Neutrality. As a neutral power the Dutch favored the plan to protect neutral trade.[10] But they were, at the same time, afraid that the English would attack them if they joined it. Most of all, the Dutch feared for their colonial possessions if they went to war with England.[11] They were certain they wanted neutrality, but were unclear as to how to defend neutrality without losing it.[12]

In April of 1780, an order in Council by the British government increased English harassment of Dutch shipping.[13] Seemingly, the Dutch were being punished for a decision they had not yet made. Simultaneously, England suspended all treaties of alliance between England and the United Provinces. Fears among the businessmen of Amsterdam and Rotterdam became so intense that they began demanding an embargo on all Dutch shipping until some way could be found to protect it.[14]

The Dutch reaction to the growing harassment from England was twofold. They began preparations to put to sea armed convoys, to protect their merchant shipping.[15] And they launched a diplomatic campaign to escape the isolation in which their differences with England had left them. Vergennes approved of the Dutch decision to establish armed convoys,[16] and he encouraged the United Provinces to turn to Catherine of Russia and her League of Armed Neutrality as a way to escape isolation. Louis XVI had too many commitments to offer the United Provinces a hand, and Vergennes considered Catherine's League an available shield against English attacks on the Dutch.[17] He wanted the Dutch to accept Catherine's Declaration without reservation.

But he was disappointed that the Dutch ministers departing for St. Petersburg carried with them a demand that Catherine guarantee Dutch overseas possessions as a condition to Dutch adherence.[18] The French ambassador at The Hague, LaVauguyon, recommended that Louis XVI support the idea and persuade Catherine to agree to it.[19] Such a guarantee, he argued, was in complete conformity with French notions that in case of an Anglo-Dutch war, any Dutch possessions taken by the English be restored at the end of the war.[20] But LaVauguyon's personal stance became embarrassing to Vergennes because it encouraged a growing desire, on the part of Dutch officials, that Louis XVI back all Dutch demands through his minister at St. Petersburg.[21] Vergennes responded that the idea was unacceptable. Not Catherine, Sweden, nor Denmark, he saw, wanted to give a guarantee that would surely embroil them in a direct confrontation with England.[22]

Vergennes finally agreed to authorize Vérac, his minister to St. Petersburg, to ask the Russian Minister, Panin, to listen "favorably" to the Dutch demand for a guarantee, but beyond that he would not go.[23] Perhaps, he suggested, such a guarantee could develop as a consequence of Dutch adherence to the League of Neutrals, but it should never be a condition for joining it.[24] The unique concern of Catherine's Declaration, Vergennes pointed out to LaVauguyon, and, by way of the ambassador, to the Dutch, was freedom of commerce and navigation for neutrals. The Dutch insistence on anything beyond that annoyed him considerably,[25] for, he had earlier noted, it confused two separate issues which might embarrass the negotiations on Armed Neutrality and cause them to fail.[26] With France in no position to help the United Provinces defend themselves, Vergennes saw Catherine's League as the only alternative open.

As Vergennes made it clear that Louis XVI did not favor Dutch insistence on a guarantee at St. Petersburg, the Patriot Party came up with another proposal. Perhaps Catherine would be more willing to grant a guarantee if Louis XVI himself did so first.[27] Vergennes' patience began to wear thin. The Dutch were taking a great risk, he felt, if they continued, by such demands, to delay their adherence to the League of Neutrals.[28] "We need all of our means to protect our own territories," he told LaVauguyon.[29] Moreover, if the slightest political ties were established between France and the Dutch Republic, the latter would cease to be a neutral. She would become suspect among the neutrals, and would offend England even more. It was France's interest to strengthen the Armed Neutrality League; hence, let the Dutch seek help there.[30]

Nevertheless, LaVauguyon continued to press for the idea of Louis XVI's using his influence at St. Petersburg to get the guarantee the Dutch wanted.

He was convinced that the demand for a guarantee from Catherine had universal support in the United Provinces.[31] Vergennes kept his promise and ordered Vérac to ask Panin to listen favorably to the Dutch demands. But, at the same time, he also asked Vérac to suggest to Panin that he get from the Dutch plenipotentiaries, when they arrived, a categorical response as to whether or not they wished to associate with the League of Neutrals.[32] Time, he felt, was running out. British hostility toward the United Provinces was growing.[33] The Swedes and Danes had joined Russia; why did the United Provinces continue to hold out? Vergennes knew that, if England declared war on the United Provinces before their joining the League, the Dutch would be abandoned to themselves.[34]

In the meantime, at St. Petersburg the Dutch plenipotentiaries presented their demands for a guarantee of Dutch colonial possessions. They received a flat rejection. Either the Dutch entered the neutrality convention as neutrals, without strings attached, Catherine responded, or there would be no agreement. She was not prepared to defend Dutch possessions overseas.[35] Confronted with Louis XVI's refusal to back them, and with Catherine's blunt demand that they give her a "prompt and categorical" response, the Dutch plenipotentiaries stopped insisting on guarantee, but refused to act until they were instructed from home.[36] Dutch opinion, worried by Britain's open menaces, had come to accept the idea of adherence to the League without guarantees, but the Stadholder, the French ambassador thought, still had reservations; LaVauguyon busily tried to persuade him to change his mind.[37]

As the Dutch moved closer to joining the League, the British government became more exasperated. From London, it seemed far better to declare war on the United Provinces than to see them come under the protection of Catherine's Armed Neutrality League. If the Dutch were members of the League it would be more difficult, and more dangerous, to stop their trade with the belligerents. The British Ministry decided, consequently, that a way had to be found to declare war on the United Provinces, but the war must appear unrelated to the issue of neutrality. England wanted to avoid antagonizing Catherine and the League.[38]

Meanwhile, Vergennes moved heaven and earth to facilitate Dutch trade. When he revoked, on March 1, 1779, the neutral privileges granted by his liberal decree of July 26, 1778, he exempted the ships of many of the Dutch cities from the provisions of the revocation.[39] In 1780, he announced that certain duties placed on Dutch commerce were suppressed.[40] But the power of the British navy in the channel made him seek other ways to transport naval provisions and munitions from Amsterdam to France. From Holland came the idea of a system to move goods from the United Provinces over interior routes, by canals, rivers, and land, rather than by sea.[41] The new system, put into operation by the Rimberg firm of Bruges,[42] worked so well that by June of 1780, Vergennes expressed to LaVauguyon his "enormous satisfaction" with it.[43]

But there were obstacles to the smooth working of the interior system because the goods had to pass through the Austrian Netherlands. Sartine suggested that Vergennes try to get an agreement from the government of the Austrian Netherlands to allow naval stores to pass freely through her territory.[44] If Vergennes could not obtain an entire exemption of Austrian duties for naval stores coming from the United Provinces, Sartine wanted him to get, at least, a sharp reduction.[45] Vergennes raised the question with the government of the Austrian Netherlands and got what he wanted: the government exempted all naval munitions moving from Holland by interior routes to France. They agreed that duties would continue to be levied by the cities which the naval stores passed through, but the merchants would later be reimbursed.[46] This arrangement was an attempt to avoid public recognition of the nature of the commerce, for Vergennes was determined to keep it a secret.

Later LaVauguyon negotiated with the Dutch themselves to exempt from certain customs duties those French merchants who were shipping Dutch goods to France by interior canals. The specification of the goods was left vague, for reasons of security, but the exemption automatically included naval stores.[47] After the Dutch entered the war, they prohibited the export of naval supplies to foreign countries, but they specifically exempted France from the prohibition.[48] At The Hague, the British ambassador's intelligence system learned of the new transport system.[49] There was little the British could do to close up the interior supply lines, but they instituted naval visits of all the ships entering Dutch ports, in order to intercept the supplies, if possible, before they were reloaded onto carriers plying the interior routes.[50]

In October, 1779, the Continental Congress gave Henry Laurens instructions to negotiate with the Dutch Republic a loan of 10,000,000 *livres* at the lowest possible rate of interest. When he was commissioned to proceed to The Hague, however, his final instructions also included an order to explore the possibility of a "treaty of friendship and commerce" with the United Provinces.[51] But Laurens delayed leaving to take up his mission. Months passed, and the Continental Congress voted to ask John Adams to raise the loan, while Laurens repeatedly announced, and then withdrew the announcements, that he was leaving. Almost a year later, on August 13, 1780, he boarded the *Mercury* scheduled to leave from Philadelphia.[52] The first week of September, when the *Mercury* was within sight of Newfoundland, an English frigate, the H.M.S. *Vestol,* spotted her,[53] gave chase, and captured her. Laurens was captured and taken to London. Most importantly of all, however, his papers, including the draft of a treaty of friendship and commerce with the Dutch Republic, fell into the hands of his captors.

The British had long suspected that the Dutch were in communication with the American rebels, and the Laurens papers confirmed their suspicion. The papers contained a batch of correspondence between Dutch individuals and American agents, along with the project for a Dutch-American treaty. To the British, the project for a treaty was proof that the Dutch were playing a double game. While insisting, on the one hand, on the rights and privileges of neutrals; on the other hand, they had secretly intrigued to ally with the Americans. The fact that the treaty was only a draft, and that none of the correspondence was with officials of the Dutch government was, to the British, irrelevant. How else would a government begin to establish relations with a rebel government? Had not the French government aid to the insurgents first been arranged through private individuals and companies ostensibly independent of the official apparatus?

The idea of a Dutch-American treaty especially infuriated the British Ministry, for it contained the basis for wide-ranging economic relations between the Dutch and the Americans. It also defined contraband according to the rule of "free ships, free goods," a principle which England could not accept. Strictly speaking, the treaty project contained nothing in violation of Dutch neutrality; furthermore, it was only a proposal for a treaty.[54] What was particularly abrasive to the British, in their moment of distress, however, was the willingness of the Dutch to consider the Americans as masters of their own sovereignty. They were insurgents, resisting the legitimate authority of George III, and the Dutch had the indecency to discuss with them the rights of neutrals, and consular exchanges, as though they constituted a sovereign, independent power. As the Dutch daily moved closer to joining the League of Neutrals, the British searched high and low for a way to stop them. The charge of complicity with the belligerent Americans was as good a justification as any to go to war against the Dutch.

Lord Stormont passed the Laurens papers and the treaty draft to his ambassador at The Hague, Sir Joseph Yorke, who, in turn, communicated them to the government of the United Provinces. Yorke let it be known that he wanted an immediate public disavowal, and punishment of those persons involved in the communications with the Americans.[55] The secret Committee of the Dutch Estates General and the Estates of Holland studied the papers, but they failed to see evidence that justified punishment. The draft of a treaty hardly had any legal value; in any case, it dated from 1778, clear evidence that the Dutch had been in no hurry to make such a treaty. What was the cause of such English indignation?

The real causes of British indignation were in St. Petersburg, where the Dutch plenipotentiaries would soon receive instructions, if Dutch opinion continued on its present trend, to accede to the Neutral League with no guarantees attached.[56] Even the Stadholder, as he saw how Yorke's attitude provoked Dutch resentment, was embarrassed by British haughtiness.[57] Nevertheless, Yorke kept pushing. Finally, blinded by the arrogance of the power he represented, he publicized his conclusion that the Dutch would be persuaded only by force.[58] To the courts of Vienna, Berlin, Copenhagen, and Stockholm, Yorke distributed memos charging the Dutch with "high treason" against the Anglo-Dutch treaty of 1674.[59] Whatever else Yorke communicated, one thing was certain: England was prepared to declare war rather than see the Dutch drift out of the English orbit.

The Dutch faced a nasty dilemma. Either they punished their citizens for "crimes" the English ambassador charged them with, or they exposed themselves to the destructiveness of the British navy. On November 27,1780, the Estates General of the United Provinces voted a resolution disavowing those who had been in communication with the Americans. And they adopted the motion, passed by the Estate General of Holland, that only the city of Amsterdam was responsible for the contacts with the American insurgents. But they said nothing of punishment.[60] It was not what Yorke demanded, but it was the most the Dutch could do and keep their self-respect.[61]

Time was pressing now. The English ambassador to Russia, Sir James Harris, was trying to persuade the Russians that the Dutch were double-dealing and not to be trusted.[62] At The Hague Sir Joseph Yorke brandished the Laurens papers and threatened terrible consequences if the Dutch did not meet his impossible demands.[63] And all the while, the British Navy preyed on Dutch neutral shipping with furious violence. Stripped of its diplomatic niceties, Yorke's behavior at The Hague was nothing less than political bullying, and the Dutch recognized it as such.[64] On November 20, 1780, the Estates General of the Dutch Republic voted to authorize its representatives at St. Petersburg to sign the Convention of Neutrality without further insistence on guarantees.[65]

At London, Count Welderen, the Dutch ambassador, courageously defended the Dutch cause, but Lord Stormont would have none of it and, finally, even refused to see him.[66] The London representatives of the three members of the Neutral League, Denmark, Sweden and Russia, attempted to mediate the Anglo-Dutch dispute. Above all, they tried to explain to Stormont that Dutch neutrality did not constitute an act of aggression against Great Britain. At The Hague, Galitsin, strove to restrain Yorke and to persuade him to accept the Dutch disavowal. But Yorke refused, partly from the belief that Galitsin was an agent of Prussian and French diplomacy and did not represent the Empress Catherine.[67]

By now, London knew that the Dutch plenipotentiaries had been instructed to sign the convention with Russia; they were determined to open hostilities with the United Provinces before the signing took place. Thus, when the Dutch plenipotentiaries signed the convention on January 4, 1781, the British government already had recalled Yorke, and George III had already issued his manifesto explaining why Great Britain was compelled to go to war against the United Provinces. The manifesto listed every reason but the real one: that Great Britain did not wish to see Dutch shipping protected by the Armed Neutrality League. The manifesto made belligerents of the Dutch a few weeks before they became members of the League of Neutrals.[68]

From the outbreak of the American Revolutionary War up to the outbreak of hostilities between the United Provinces and Great Britain, Vergennes felt that Dutch adherence to the Armed Neutrality League was in the best interests of Louis XVI, and the French ambassador at The Hague worked to advance that cause. Vergennes resisted both the Patriots and the Stadholder, however, when they demanded guarantees. He even found it necessary to resist Louis XVI's own ambassador, when LaVauguyon became a spokesman in favor of guarantees.

Vergennes did not wish to make allies of the United Provinces. The supplies the Bourbons and their allies needed could be better assured if the Dutch remained neutral and, more especially, if they became members of Catherine's Armed League. Moreover, Vergennes feared that, as allies, the Dutch would be more of a burden to Louis XVI than a help, since they would claim aid as belligerents which Louis XVI could ill afford to give.

Louis XVI's stance meant that Catherine emerged as the hope of the United Provinces and as the defender of the principles of Neutral Rights. Her shadow loomed ever larger over the map of Europe during the war, and began to eclipse Louis XVI in his role of arbiter. But, given the circumstances of the American War, Louis could hardly do anything but encourage her.

The war between the United Provinces and England was a painful diplomatic reversal for the Dutch.[69] For fifty years before the American War, neutrality had served their interests about as well as they could be served in the dangerous and unstable world of the eighteenth century.[70] Catherine's League of Neutrals, therefore, appeared as the only way out of an impossible position. But the British government could not allow Dutch ships to sail behind the shield of the Armed League. In retrospect, the ability of the Dutch to remain neutral during the period from the outbreak of British-French hostilities in June of 1778 until the British manifesto of December, 1780 was, in itself, a diplomatic accomplishment of considerable significance.[71] There is no evidence, as has been suggested, that Vergennes manipulated the European situation and Dutch diplomacy to bring war to the United Provinces.[72] Dutch adherence to the Armed League produced an Anglo-Dutch war, but that was not the aim of Vergennes.

The Anglo-Dutch War was the result, primarily, of the actions of the British government, their continued misreading of Catherine's policy,[73] and their simple-minded belief that any opposition to their military or diplomatic policies at The Hague, at St. Petersburg, or anywhere else in Europe, was the result of French (or Prussian) intrigue and plots.[74] In a letter to the Princess of Orange, Frederick of Prussia put it this way: the war came because of British vanity, ignorance, pride, lack of diplomatic skill, and the determination to establish a royal despotism, and because brainless political leaders wanted it:

"Tu l'as voulu, tu l'as voulu, Georges Dandin."[75]

Part V

A MASTER JUGGLER PERFORMS

CHAPTER 23

The Bavarian Crisis: I

At a dinner party in Vienna in March of 1778 the French ambassador, the Baron de Breteuil, was engaged by Joseph II, the Emperor of the Holy Roman Empire, in conversation. The year 1778 would be a notable one, Joseph observed, for three absolutely unrelated wars threatened the tranquility of Europe. How would such a year end, Joseph asked the French ambassador? Breteuil replied that he personally hoped there would be no war. And he observed that if Joseph hoped the same thing, at least one war would probably not take place. Joseph protested. Of course, he wanted peace, but . . .(princes rarely spoke of peace without a counterpoint of "buts"). But, Joseph went on, he could not accept peace if people interpreted his desire for peace as a sign of weakness, or as a sign that he feared the King of Prussia. Above all, Joseph insisted, he wanted no one to think he feared the King of Prussia. Breteuil politely applauded Joseph's "noble resolution." Joseph then launched on a discourse on the skill of his soldiers, on the talents of his generals, and, of course, on the sincerity of his own "good will."

An experienced diplomat, Breteuil knew what Joseph's "but" really meant: The Emperor itched for a chance to test himself against Frederick of Prussia.[1] Intelligent, restless, and imbued with the aristocratic notion that warfare was the trade of kings, young Joseph placed peace much lower on his hierarchy of values than did his aging mother, Maria Theresa.

The three possible wars that momentarily absorbed the Emperor and the diplomat were the American Revolutionary War, a possible Russo-Turkish war arising from the dispute over the Crimea, and a war crisis caused by the death, in December of 1777, of Maximilian Joseph, the Elector of Bavaria. Joseph spoke of these crises as separate events; Vergennes, however, saw them as intricately related, because French interests were at stake in each.

The death of Maximilian Joseph extinguished the male line of his branch of the Wittelsbach family. By a series of family agreements Maximilian Joseph had guaranteed that the succession would pass to another branch of the family, that of the Elector Palatinate, Charles Theodore. The solution was simple enough, and, according to the opinion of the French envoy to Bavaria, consistent with public law and custom.[2] But in the wild maze of German imperial politics a simple solution had little chance of survival. The dowager Electress of Saxony had indirect claims to the succession, Maria Theresa of Austria had vague claims as Queen of Bohemia, and Joseph II had claims, even more vague, based on his pretensions as Emperor.[3]

Early after he became Secretary of State, Vergennes recognized that the Bavarian Succession, when it came, might produce a war.[4] But coming as it did, at the very moment, when events in America provided the opportunity for France to settle accounts with England, the Bavarian Succession dispute was a trap which Vergennes now wanted to avoid at all costs.

The crisis over Bavaria strained the French-Austrian alliance almost to the breaking point. Vergennes and Louis XVI saw the relationship as a way of assuring peace on the Continent, while France concentrated on a maritime war with England. Joseph, on the other hand, saw the alliance as a useful tool in his plans to expand and to challenge Frederick the Great. Vergennes did not want France to become Joseph's military auxiliary, nor did he wish to see the power of Frederick destroyed. The vision of an Austria-dominated Germany haunted French monarchs. If Joseph acquired Bavaria he would nearly double his German possessions: his German holdings would be linked with his Italian ones; Austrian revenues would grow with the addition of 15 to 18,000,000 *livres* in taxes; and the Bavarians would add 20,000 men to the Austrian army.[5]

Joseph's expansionist ambitions were common knowledge in Europe.[6] Frederick II had predicted that Europe would go up in flames the moment Joseph became master of the politics of Austria, because he felt, that Joseph was "devoured by ambition."[7] In 1774, when Vergennes sent Breteuil to Vienna, his primary concern was to communicate to Joseph the idea that, while Louis XVI viewed the Austrian alliance as central to his political calculations, the French monarch was not inclined to agree to everything Joseph did simply because the latter was his brother-in-law and ally.[8]

The warning had little noticeable effect. In 1775, Joseph took advantage of the situation created by the Russo-Turkish War to invade the Turkish territories of Bukovina and Moldavia. When peace came, most of Moldavia was restored to Turkey, but Joseph kept Bukovina because it formed a strategic link between his provinces of Transylvania and Galicia. Vergennes responded to Joseph's plundering with a warning that Louis XVI would not stand by and see the Ottoman Empire dismembered. At the same time, he also told the Emperor that France would not agree to any further territorial acquisitions by Joseph.[9] A move by Joseph against Bavaria would challenge this policy.

To follow up his concern over the Bavarian Succession, in 1776 Vergennes sent the Chevalier de la Luzerne to Bavaria to represent Louis XVI. While Vergennes and Louis XVI seemed prepared to accept an alliance between Austria and Bavaria, because Bavaria was, in itself, only a "light-weight in the balance," they would not accept an Austrian assimilation of that territory. Already, Vergennes felt, the European balance of power had begun to tip in favor of the three powers which had combined to despoil Poland. If Bavaria fell to Austria, France would be confronted with a new system totally hostile to her own role in Europe as Vergennes and Louis XVI conceived it. At Munich La Luzerne was to watch the Austrian diplomats and keep his ears open.

In the spring of 1777, Joseph II wrote to Louis XVI announcing his plans for a journey to France. The friends of the Queen took heart. Vergennes knew that Joseph's presence at Versailles would strengthen the hand of the Austrian Ambassador, Mercy, and of Marie Antoinette. Both had already begun to suspect that Vergennes disapproved of Joseph's extravagant ambitions.[11] He wished to annex Bavaria as soon as the Elector Maximilian died, and the collapsing Ottoman Empire continued to arouse his cupidity. Did Louis XVI find these ambitions agreeable? If he did, Joseph suggested a cession to Louis XVI of a part of the Austrian Netherlands.

Vergennes reminded Louis that France's only interest in the alliance with Austria was to maintain the general tranquility of Europe, and it was useful to Louis XVI only so long as it contributed to that goal.[12] Peace in Europe gave France the freedom to come to terms with England. If Joseph came seeking an increase in the assistance Louis XVI would give him in case of war, it could only be because he wished to use the alliance to crush Frederick of Prussia. Vergennes, again and again, insisted that he carried no brief for Frederick as an individual, but, from the point of view of the political system of Europe, France had to see that the integrity and power of Prussia was preserved. If the King of Prussia were destroyed, he predicted, ". . . there would be no longer a dike against the ambitions of Austria." Even the security of the Bourbon possessions in Italy, Vergennes believed, depended on the existence of a powerful Prussia. Vergennes was even willing to see Prussia expand a bit, as long as she did so on the Oder or the Elbe and not on the Rhine, to guarantee that she remain a counterweight to Austrian power.[13]

Vergennes apparently did not expect Joseph to come to France with a plan to absorb Bavaria. Yet he had anticipated the nature of the bribe Joseph would offer to get Louis XVI's consent. Even if Joseph offered all of the Austrian Low Countries, Vergennes reasoned, Louis XVI could not accept the offer without arousing the hostility of the Dutch Republic and throwing them into the arms of England.

France, Vergennes believed, derived positive advantages from the fact that the Low Countries belonged to Austria. In the Netherlands, France had an Austrian hostage, and it would be unreasonable to change a situation which was so useful for containing Austria.[14] Vergennes, therefore, repeated to Louis XVI his principle that France should not seek new territories. Louis XVI's role in Europe was to be that of supreme judge, his throne should be the tribunal instituted by Providence to see to it that the rights and properties of sovereigns were respected.[15]

But, in defending his policy to restrain Joseph II, Vergennes ran the risk of a public bout with a powerful segment of the court. Joseph expected to use his sister, the Queen, as his channel of influence, just as Hapsburg women in the Kingdom of the Two Sicilies and in Parma were the agents of Hapsburg influence in Italy. "Everyone believes," the British Ambassador observed, "that the Queen will gain influence over the mind of the King, and, in this case, the court of Vienna will run France even more than she has heretofore done."[16]

Vergennes had hardly assumed the responsibilities of his office, before he realized that his greatest enemy at Court would be the Queen and her faction which included not only courtiers, domestics, and spies, but also the Emperor's ambassador to Louis XVI, the Comte de Mercy d'Argenteau.

There was, fortunately, another faction equally powerful, one bitterly opposed to the Austrian alliance. It included veterans of Louis XV's secret diplomacy, key members of the Ministry of Foreign Affairs, such as Rayneval, as well as several *grands* of the court. Vergennes sympathized with this group, but he never gained their total support because his own solution to the problem of the Austrian alliance was too moderate for them. He would not break with Austria, as they wanted to do. He hoped only to change the conditions of the alliance so that it would be of use, and not a burden, to France.[17] When Vergennes brought Joseph's offer into the King's Council, he openly challenged the Queen and her coterie.

To find leverage for his policy, Vergennes returned to the idea of using Frederick to restrain Joseph. Despite the collaboration between Prussia and Austria during the partition of Poland, Vergennes all along had felt that the rivalry between the two powers was "indestructible". Now that Frederick was stronger and richer as a result of his banditry in Poland, Joseph had even greater cause to fear him, especially since Austria's newest acquisitions were exposed to an attack by Prussia.[18] Frederick was now an old man. Pale, skinny, and suffering from gout, he seemed nearer dead than alive to the French minister, the Marquis de Pons, when he returned to Potsdam in 1775.[19] But nothing restored Frederick's zest for life more quickly than a diplomatic scrap. "These people think I'm dead," he shouted, when he learned that Joseph had designs on Bavaria, "but I'll prove just the contrary to them."[20]

Vergennes followed the graph of Frederick's wrath with sympathetic interest. He did not trust the Prussian King. He knew as well as anyone Frederick's record of deception and betrayal. Yet the Bavarian issue, as well as concern for the balance of power in Germany, provided the occasion for France and Prussia to establish a working understanding.[21] Now that Frederick no longer needed Joseph to divide up Poland, he had no reason to continue to wear the mask of friendship.

The opinion in France favoring a Franco-Prussian *rapprochement* already existed.[22] Frederick's claque at Paris and Versailles was probably as articulate as Joseph's. There were many who openly advocated a Franco-Prussian alliance that would join together Sweden, Prussia, and France to protect the Turks and Poles from Catherine and Joseph. Also, Maurepas was a personal friend of Frederick's ambassador, Goltz.

Vergennes was not prepared to execute a reversal of alliances, because he believed that would be tantamount to falling into a trap set by Frederick, whom he suspected of wanting to see France and Austria go at each other.[23] Also, an abandonment of Joseph would inevitably lead, he felt, to a new Anglo-Austrian treaty against France. Yet an informal relationship with Prussia, that would restrain Joseph but not rupture the alliance, would be a useful way to free France from subjection to Austria without making an open enemy of her.

The news of the Elector of Bavaria's death had barely reached the capitals of Europe, before Austrian troops marched to the Bavarian frontier and ominously "awaited orders." In the background, the diplomats arranged a convention. According to reports received by the French ambassador at Vienna, Joseph had warned the Palatinate Elector that either he agree to the Emperor's claims, or Austria would take all of Bavaria. When the Palatinate Elector's envoy described the negotiations to Breteuil, he tearfully confessed that he accepted Joseph's demands only under duress. A convention was signed (January 3, 1778) and Austrian troops marched into Bavaria. Bavarian troops, who had been ordered not to resist, obediently retreated before them. The entire operation was done quickly and without violence.[24]

Joseph was jubilant. To show his appreciation to his minister Kaunitz, who arranged the triumph, he turned up unannounced at Kaunitz' birthday party, sat down at the table *en famille,* and spent the evening praising the father of the household before his family. The cynical French ambassador found it characteristic that Joseph only recognized Kaunitz' talents when they were devoted to the seizing of other people's territory.[25]

Maria Theresa was depressed. She had hoped to die before the Bavarian succession issue unsettled Europe. Apparently she, too, doubted the legitimacy of her son's claims. Nevertheless, she stoically set about doing her duty to sustain them.[26] Whether she would be willing, in her old age, to plunge

Europe into a bloody war to defend those claims still remained, however, a moot point.

When Joseph calculated the risks of the Bavarian invasion, he expected Frederick to oppose it, but he apparently operated on the assumption that Frederick would not find anyone in Europe who would share his animosity toward Austria. Faced with an Austria backed up by her alliance with France, Frederick could rage and threaten, but, if he decided to go to war, he would be alone. His only two possible allies, Russia and England, were busy in the Crimea and in America. If this, indeed, describes Joseph's reasoning, therein lay his most serious error.

As expected, Frederick II was the first power to react against the Bavarian invasion. When the Palatinate Elector notified Frederick of his succession, he did not use his new titles because he had signed them away in the January Third Convention. Frederick responded to the Elector's note by deliberately using the Palatinate Elector's new titles, thereby indicating that he did not recognize the changes wrought by the Convention.[27] A grand fief of the Empire could not be dismembered, or ceded, or rendered allodial, he responded, without the consent of the Diet of the German Confederation. Frederick's refusal to recognize the Convention of January Third was the first step in bringing the German Diet into the Bavarian dispute.[28]

That Joseph had miscalculated became manifest when the *chargé d'affaires* of the Duke of Deux-Ponts arrived at Munich. The Duke of Deux-Ponts was next in line of succession, and Imperial custom required that he ratify the January Third Convention. Since the Duke of Deux-Ponts had a son, he did not contemplate the January Third arrangement with the same eye as did the Palatinate Elector.[29] Along with Deux-Ponts, Saxony[30] and the Duke of Mecklenburg[31] also had pretentions to Bavaria. With these small German powers, Frederick began a vigorous anti-Austrian campaign in the Empire. By March of 1778, the Duke of Deux-Ponts, with Frederick behind him, had thrown the question into the lap of the German Diet at Ratisbon.[32]

Frederick opened the verbal war at Ratisbon with a public declaration that the Convention of January Third was incompatible with the constitution of the German Empire, with the Treaty of Westphalia, and with various other treaties.[33] He demanded that the succession of Bavaria be reestablished as it was before the Austrian occupation, and that negotiations be undertaken in conformity with the Imperial constitution. Frederick then invited all states to join him. He backed up his diplomatic rhetoric with conspicuous preparations for war.

Frederick's charge that the January Third Convention was contrary to the Treaty of Westphalia was a master's thrust at French sensibilities. Vergennes had always insisted that, while Louis XVI would neglect nothing to protect the alliance between France and Austria, the French monarch could never forget that he had even older responsibilities towards Germany as a result of the Treaties of Westphalia. Frederick's minister at Verailles, M. Goltz, wasted no time in turning Frederick's general request for support into an explicit demand for a French guarantee of the Treaties of Westphalia. Vergennes confessed that the request sorely embarrassed France. He resented Joseph's having forced him into a corner.[34]

As Vergennes waited for Vienna to explain the basis of her claims to Bavaria, the Prussian King bombarded him with urgent questions. What would Louis XVI do, he asked, if a war broke out between Vienna and Berlin? Frederick's envoy, Goltz, made it clear to Vergennes that Frederick only wanted France to remain neutral. Goltz cornered his friend, the Comte de Maurepas, and suggested the same thing. Both Vergennes and Maurepas answered that, as yet, Louis XVI had not had time to deliberate the question. Goltz' insistence convinced Vergennes, however, that the Prussian King had resolved to settle the dispute by war. He told the Prussian Minister, therefore, that whatever Louis XVI decided, if Frederick was determined to go to war, any concert between Louis XVI and Prussia became impossible. If, however, Frederick was looking for possible avenues of conciliation, Louis XVI would willingly act to facilitate a peaceful settlement.[35]

Vergennes was wary of Frederick in his new role as defender of justice, especially when he coupled his high-sounding principles with under-the-table offers to France of the Austrian Low Countries, and a suggestion that, when war broke out with England, France in alliance with Prussia could easily create a diversion for England by attacking Hanover. What Frederick really wanted, Vergennes feared, was to lure France into a step that would compromise her vis-à-vis Austria. As Goltz returned again and again to offer advise, temptations, and even veiled threats, Vergennes repeated the theme that Louis XVI was not disposed to break his alliance with Austria; nor did he wish the Bavarian Succession to be the cause for war.[36] Nevertheless, he continued to insist to Frederick that Louis XVI was willing to play the role of conciliator, if Prussia were not dead set on war.[37]

As the Bavarian Succession passed from war crisis to serious negotiations, Frederick very carefully kept Vergennes informed of his exchanges with Austria. Because Joseph and his minister, Kaunitz, very often kept Louis XVI in the dark about what was going on, Frederick's steady supply of information was more than welcome at Versailles.

Joseph's invasion of Bavaria had presented Louis XVI with a *fait accompli* at the very moment when France's involvement in the American War made her wish to avoid, at all costs, any military commitments on the Continent. And Joseph was not even considerate enough to inform his ally of the legal basis for his claims. Furthermore, his ambassadors in Germany encouraged the opinion that the entire Bavarian operation had been carried out with Louis XVI's approval. When Vergennes discussed that false opinion with the Austrian ambassador, he was astonished that Mercy, himself, believed it was true.[38] Immediately, Vergennes sent to all Louis XVI's ministers in Europe a memo denying, categorically, that there had been any concert between Joseph and Louis XVI in the Bavarian Succession.[39] Vergennes followed up his memos with a personal letter to Breteuil, in which he expressed Louis XVI's resentment that such rumors had been circulated, and he demanded that Joseph provide Louis XVI with the justification for his claims to Bavaria.

Breteuil's request for the justification surprised Kaunitz. At first he smoldered, then he flew into a rage. Who was the power, he asked, that would question the rights of Maria Theresa? The armed forces of the House of Austria, he continued, feared no one. The bewildered Breteuil asked him if he was referring to Prussia — or France? Avoiding the question, Kaunitz went on to declare that, of course, Austria's claims were valid. But Breteuil waited in vain for the evidence.[40] When Kaunitz heard of the memo Vergennes had circulated to the French embassies in Europe, he boiled over once more, this time insisting that the Empress and Emperor needed no one's consent in order to negotiate a convention with the Elector Palatinate.[41]

Kaunitz' fury at being asked to justify his sovereign's action convinced Breteuil that the Austrian Minister did not feel confident about the legality of Austria's claims.[42] When Vergennes questioned the Austrian ambassador, he was amazed when Mercy tried to urge upon France what Vergennes saw as an "ingenuous parody of the memos which had been published to justify the partition of Poland." Never, Vergennes wrote to Breteuil, had anyone assembled "in such a small space, so many false principles and so many blatantly-invented facts."[43] Later, Maurepas told Mercy that Louis XVI had little confidence in the legitimacy of Joseph's right to be in Bavaria. He assured him, however, that Louis XVI would avoid setting himself up as a judge of Vienna's claims.[44]

The recognition that Austria's claims were at best inadequate, if not illegal, and Kaunitz' repeated temper tantrums whenever France asked to examine Austria's claims, posed a dilemma for Vergennes. It became more and more obvious every day that Joseph's demands on Bavaria had no convincing legal basis: they were nothing less than an act of aggression. Yet to advance Louis XVI as a guarantor of the Treaties of Westphalia would lead France to an unwanted rupture with Austria. Nevertheless, Louis XVI could not remain silent while his ally pulled him into a Continental war. Step by step, Vergennes threaded his way through the diplomatic minefield. He first accepted the Austrian agreement with the Elector Palatinate, but made it clear that France in no way had given her approval. Next he cultivated the confidence of Frederick in order to stop, if possible, the formation, on Frederick's part, of a coalition in Germany that might tempt the Prussian King to gamble on a war against Joseph. The true interest of Louis XVI, Vergennes believed, was to maintain an equilibrium between Frederick and Joseph and, above all, to preserve the peace.[45]

This preliminary position was difficult to maintain. Frederick continued to challenge the legality of Joseph's invasion of Bavaria. He insisted that the Treaties of Westphalia had been violated, and his agents were everywhere in Germany trying to arouse the smaller powers against Austria. At Ratisbon, the Duke of Deux-Ponts was in his camp with a protest to the German Diet. Soon Deux-Ponts was joined by Saxony.[46] Frederick encouraged rumors that he would fight Austria to the death rather than suffer the subversion of the constitution of the Empire or the aggrandizement of his rival.[47]

Soon preparations for military operations occupied the soldiers. War seemed every day more likely, and Joseph again and again repeated that he counted on French aid when the war came.

To Vergennes, French participation in a war over Bavaria could end only in catastrophe. By now, Louis XVI expected to hear of hostilities with England with each messenger who came to Versailles. Furthermore, Vergennes was convinced that French participation in a war to defend Joseph's invasion of Bavaria would totally undermine France's age-old commitments as guarantor of the Treaties of Westphalia. By March of 1778, he had reached the conclusion that the treaty with Austria guaranteed only the territories Austria had had at the time of the treaty. France was not obligated to defend any territory, such as Bavaria, that Austria later acquired. Furthermore, he argued, Louis XVI did not see the Franco-Austrian treaty as a means for expansion. Vergennes insisted on Louis XVI's allegiance to the treaty with Austria, but he scrupulously refused to approve of Joseph's actions in Bavaria. Nor would he promise to help him in case of war.[48]

When Vergennes sent the dispatch to Breteuil, outlining France's decision to exclude the Bavarian Succession from the terms of the alliance, he suggested that Breteuil read the document to Kaunitz, so there would be no mistake about what Louis XVI meant to say. Breteuil dutifully followed instructions. What he probably expected to happen, happened. When Breteuil read that Louis XVI would not go to war over Bavaria, Kaunitz had him repeat the phrase. Breteuil did so, word for word. Then he recommenced his reading. When he got to the phrase which stated that Louis XVI did not recognize the present crisis as *casus foederis,* Kaunitz took his pen and scraped across what he had written. "I can't listen any longer to this," he shouted. "Nor can I tell the Empress .... I will not use it unless you put it in writing." Breteuil answered that his orders were to read the declaration. "In that case," Kaunitz continued, now in a fury, "the Empress will never know about it." Breteuil began reading again. Kaunitz listened in silence. When Breteuil finished, Kaunitz wearily observed that it was useless to make treaties if commitments could be so arbitrarily interpreted.

Kaunitz surely told Maria Theresa of the dispatch. For three days she refused to speak to the French ambassador. Oddly enough, Joseph tried to make up for his mother's behavior. Breteuil was pleased to find him less determined to take on the King of Prussia.[49] Did Joseph misunderstand? Breteuil several times repeated to Kaunitz that Louis XVI did not believe that the Franco-Austrian alliance required that France provide aid in a war over the Bavarian Succession. Louis XVI would remain neutral, he once again carefully explained. Finally, Joseph, too, understood and he became less cordial. As he perceived his situation, his major ally was deserting him just as he prepared to leave Vienna to take command of his armies in the field. At the court of Vienna, experienced observers were betting that the Franco-Austrian alliance would not outlast the year.[50]

Kaunitz, in an attempt to salvage something, asked Louis XVI to consent, at least, to guarding the Austrian Netherlands for Austria. Also, would France speak to Frederick in a language the Prussian could understand; that is, threaten him with force? Breteuil gave no satisfaction. Louis XVI refused to budge. Moreover, he saw no value in shouting at Frederick.

To Vergennes, Louis XVI's neutrality established a proper relationship between Austria and France. He did not want French policy determined at Vienna any more than at Madrid. Yet neither Louis XVI nor Vergennes wanted to break up the alliance with Joseph II. As they built their case for neutrality on the one hand, they simultaneously attended to Austria's dignity on the other. Louis XVI would remain neutral in a Bavarian war, Vergennes insisted, but he would not make a public declaration to that effect, because he did not want to embarrass Joseph or encourage Frederick. Also, Vergennes later agreed that Louis XVI would not allow Frederick to attack the Austrian Low Countries.[51]

Louis XVI's solicitude for his ally's sensibilities was also noticeable in his decision not to act as guarantor of the Treaties of Westphalia. When Catherine of Russia entered the Bavarian Succession as a defender of the liberties of Germany, Vergennes argued that Louis XVI had a better title to that role as guarantor of the Treaties of Westphalia. But, he told his ambassador at Vienna, the "intention of His Majesty is to abstain from all steps that could be interpreted as condemning his ally's procedures." Later, when Frederick and the government at Vienna began negotiations, Vergennes acted as a conciliator by encouraging both sides to abandon the dispute over legal rights. It was a dispute, Vergennes knew, which made Kaunitz and Joseph uneasy, and embarrassed them before the public opinion of

Germany. Vergennes recommended, instead, that they talk of compromises and equivalents.[52] Joseph continued to find Louis XVI's pacificism exasperating. Kaunitz complained to Breteuil that France had caused Joseph nothing but dissatisfaction.[53]

Yet despite Louis XVI's unwillingness to support his ally, there was much bluster and talk in the Austrian army about the coming contest between Austrian and Prussian soldiers. At court, the aristocratic officers openly expressed their desire to test themselves against Frederick. According to the French ambassador at Vienna, war had become as necessary to the Austrian officers' pride as it was to impose Joseph's claims on Bavaria.[54]

As the campaign season approached, Austrian troops were readied in their billets in Bohemia and Moravia while Frederick massed his troops at the frontiers. All the while, Joseph and Frederick incited each other to combat with a slanging match of challenges, declarations, accusations, and expressions of mutual admiration. Vergennes tried to establish lines of communication between Berlin and Vienna by way of Versailles, but his hopes and his efforts bore no fruit. Kaunitz did not always inform his ally of the contents of the letters he sent to Frederick and Vergennes held back on his suggestions to Vienna because if he suggested that Joseph give up too much, Joseph could accuse his brother-in-law of despoiling him. If he suggested that Austria give up very little, his ally would expect Louis XVI to back up the suggestion with force.[55] In an exchange of letters early in 1778, Frederick and Maria Theresa, the latter acting on her own initiative, accomplised the only positive step toward eventual negotiation: both parties expressed a sincere desire to avoid another exhausting war, and Frederick ceased to require that, before negotiations could take place, the situation in Bavaria had to be re-established as it was before the death of Maximilian Joseph.[56]

The war that everyone expected began in a way that no one expected. Frederick suddenly stabbed deep into Bohemia. The ease with which Frederick accomplished his move startled everyone. Later, Kaunitz explained to Breteuil that Joseph had allowed Frederick to enter Bohemia so that there would be no uncertainty about who was the aggressor. Only Maria Theresa seemed to regret the opening of hostilities. The idea of a war in her old age haunted her. She cried continuously, Breteuil reported. But the French ambassador predicted sarcastically that she would "familiarize herself" very quickly with the idea. The Prussian minister at Vienna asked for his passport and left. "Henceforth the cannon will decide," Kaunitz declared in a pompous attempt to be grandiloquent. "And then diplomacy," Breteuil soberly observed.[57]

Frederick's invasion of Bohemia provided Joseph II with leverage he did not have following his own invasion of Bavaria. Now he was the victim of attack and, according to the Austrian view of the matter, deserving of French aid according to the Treaty of 1756, as well as the Treaties of Westphalia. Again Louis XVI refused with the argument that the Maritime war France was now engaged in with England required all of France's resources. Furthermore, Vergennes reminded the Austrian ambassador at Versailles, once more, that Louis XVI could legitimately demand aid from Austria, since France had been attacked by England. Joseph recognized the maneuver; he was using it himself.[58] Each time Kaunitz raised the question, Vergennes countered with the excuse that the war against England was already a heavy drain on French resources, and his reply always contained the implication that France was showing great restraint in not asking Austria to provide to France the aid required by the Treaty of 1756.

By the summer of 1778, the outlines of Louis XVI's policy in the Bavarian war were clear. France would remain neutral in a war between Prussia and Austria. But, for the sake of Austrian sensibilities, and in order not to provide Frederick with the dangerous hope that the Franco-Austrian alliance was dead, Vergennes never gave Frederick clear assurances of French neutrality. When Joseph II's demands were extravagant, Vergennes encouraged Frederick's opposition. When Frederick became abrupt and rigid, Vergennes admonished him, but never with the threats and harsh language Kaunitz and Joseph desired. Vergennes wished only to strengthen French ties with Frederick; he did not wish to join him in an alliance system. In performing these complicated diplomatic exercises, Vergennes always tried to avoid antagonizing Austria to the point where she would abandon the alliance with France. The performance called into play every skill he had learned in his long career as a diplomat.

CHAPTER 24

The Bavarian Crisis: II

Louis XVI's desire for peace in Bavaria was shared by Maria Theresa. In July, soon after the outbreak of hostilities between Joseph II and Frederick, Maria Theresa, without consulting her son, sent her own envoy, François Thugut, to Frederick with propositions which she hoped would become the basis for a suspension of arms. She wanted Frederick to know just how much she desired to have peace in Europe. Her letter proposed that Austria return to the Elector Palatinate all of Bavaria, except for a portion of territory that would yield a revenue of 1,000,000 *florins* a year. She suggested that Austria negotiate an exchange of her possessions with the Elector Palatinate for another part of Bavaria where the revenues did not exceed 1,000,000 *florins*, where the territory did not border on the Imperial city of Ratisbon, and where the exchange did not cut Bavaria into two parts. In her third proposal, Maria Theresa offered to unite her good offices with those of Frederick to find a "just and equitable" arrangement between the Elector Palatinate and the Elector of Saxony in order to settle claims on Bavaria.[1]

Frederick answered immediately. He wanted the Empress to give up some of her rights over the fiefs of Saxony, rights which she claimed as Queen of Bohemia. In addition, could not the Empress, Frederick asked, accommodate the Duke of Mecklenburg with some little fief of the Empire? Could they not reach another agreement to settle the succession of Bayreuth and Ansbach in Frederick's favor? And, finally, Frederick asked, could not Joseph raise the blockade of Ratisbon where the Diet of the Empire was assembled?[2] The latter question, especially, was tailor-made to provoke Joseph. It did.

When Joseph learned of his mother's initiative, he was outraged. As Maria Theresa's subject, he admitted, he had to accept whatever she ordered him to accept. But as her son and Emperor, he would never enter into a negotiation such as that outlined in the letters carried by her messenger Thugut.[3] The exchange of letters between Frederick and Maria Theresa continued, but Joseph fumed, anxious to break off all negotiations. Finally, Joseph himself came up with a counter-proposal to Frederick's response that achieved his aim.[4] The Empress, his counter-proposal suggested to Frederick, would sacrifice all of her claims and possessions in Bavaria; she would annul the Convention of January Third and re-establish the Elector Palatinate in full possession of Bavaria, if Frederick would renounce all of his claims to the Margraviates of Franconia. Frederick, of course, found this proposal "inadmissible." Once again, the next move passed from the diplomats to the generals.[5]

According to the French ambassador, Joseph's joy at this turn of events was without bounds. He had nothing but contempt for his mother's foolish gestures for peace. The distance between mother and son became so great, according to the French ambassador, that the Grand Chamberlain, the Count de Rosenberg, and Kaunitz had to forget momentarily the dispute with Frederick, in order to negotiate a reconciliation between mother and son.[6]

Convinced now that Louis XVI would not help Austria, Kaunitz was painfully aware that some new alternative had to be found if Austria was to escape a long war with Frederick; a war in which the latter played the role of defender of justice, and of the small powers against Austria.[7] Joseph's clumsy attempts to justify his actions confirmed the opinion that the Duke of Deux-Pont's cry for justice was justified. Furthermore, Frederick's agents in Germany circulated declaration after declaration expressing the Prussian King's pain at having to resort to arms to protect the laws of the Empire.[8]

By mid-summer of 1778, the government at Vienna had become quite alarmed at the unanimity of opinion hostile to Austria. Kaunitz was truly anxious about what he called Frederick's "crusade" in the Empire. The Austrian point of view seemed rejected everywhere and public confidence in the Emperor suffered.[9]

Joseph's counter-proposal to Frederick was directed at public opinion. Kaunitz hoped that Frederick's refusal would bring opinion around to Austria. Furthermore, Kaunitz added, somewhat illogically, if Frederick refused, there would no longer be any illusions about who started the war. France would have to come to the aid of Austria.[10]

Despite France's repeated rejections of the worn-out request for aid, Kaunitz continued to dangle lures before Louis XVI's eyes. If Prussia refused to accept Austria's "counter-proposal", he said, France could do much to help Austria in her moment of embarrassment. And Austria, perhaps, could, in turn, assist France. "We could concert on several things relative to the Electorate of Hanover," Kaunitz suggested. Hanover, Kaunitz said, had sided with Frederick against Joseph in the issue of the Bavarian succession. Austria was prepared, therefore, to act with regard to that power in any way that suited France. Breteuil once again explained that France had enough to do in her maritime war. She did not wish to attack

Hanover.[11]

As the diplomats debated and the soldiers strutted, the pawns in the game of high politics became restless. The confusion caused by changes of sovereignty in Bavaria, the added taxes, and the violence imposed by military occupation created pockets of misery and discontent that flared up fitfully, becoming miniature previews of the insurrections and revolutions of the next decade. The new Elector of Bavaria (the Elector Palatinate), trying to reorganize what little was left of his recent inheritance, introduced his own Protestant soldiers into a Catholic Bavarian regiment of guards. The result was an outbreak of quarrels, riots, and violence. As Austrian Walloon troops passed through Bavaria on their way to the front, they added plunder and rape to the disorder. The members of the old Estates of Bavaria, obviously seeking a way to resist the Austrian domination, approached La Luzerne, the French envoy in Munich, and asked him what the Bavarians should do under the present circumstances. Even the Duchess of Bavaria, a relative of the Elector, secretly at first, then openly, formed with Frederick projects of resistance to the settlement imposed on Charles Theodore. Desertion in the Austrian armies went on as it usually did in wartime , but, this time, with the widespread assistance of the peasants of Bavaria. Soldiers allegedly trying to keep order and force payment of taxes only increased the violence.[12]

The failure of Maria Theresa's gesture to Frederick raised, once more, the question of Louis XVI's role in the Bavarian dispute, for plainly the two adversaries had reached an impasse. Louis XVI remained firm in his neutrality. But what did it mean to be neutral when one of the belligerents in a dispute was an ally? Joseph and Kaunitz felt that the least Louis XVI could do was to speak up to Frederick, and let him know that in the last analysis Louis stood behind Joseph.[13] When Louis XVI refused to change the tone of his voice with Frederick, Kaunitz accused Vergennes of being pro-Prussian.[14]

But the French ambassador to Vienna believed that Vergennes was too pro-Austrian. Breteuil felt that Louis XVI should take a hard line against Joseph. If Louis adopted a more "clearcut tone," Breteuil advised, Joseph would be more inclined to make peace, for he was fully aware of the value of France's friendship.[15]

Only after it became clear that nothing was likely to bring Louis XVI into the war, did Joseph show some interest in Louis XVI's offers of his good offices.[16] When he did so, Vergennes immediately sent a conciliatory note to Frederick, to establish a line of contact and prevent, if possible, further blood letting. The note contained no hint of belligerency towards Frederick. He did not want to force Frederick to seek closer ties with Russia or England, or to try to form a league of the Protestant powers of the North.

At the same time, Vergennes recognized that the request from Vienna for Louis XVI's good offices was humiliating for the Austrians. He was extremely careful, therefore, to show great concern for their interests, as he gradually re-established the lines between Prussia and Austria. This was despite the fact that he was becoming more and more irritated by Kaunitz' refusal to give France the information needed to keep Louis XVI up to date on what was going on.[17]

Moreover, Louis XVI did not hesitate to admonish Frederick when he thought the Prussian King was insincere or in error. Both Vergennes and Maurepas, for example, personally informed the Prussian minister at Versailles that Louis XVI was displeased with abrupt manner in which Frederick had broken off negotiations with Vienna. As the role of providing "good offices" developed into the role of official mediator, Louis XVI and his Secretary of State for Foreign Affairs scrupulously maintained the stance of honest broker, although they were increasingly more exposed to the criticisms of both parties.[18]

But the peaceful settlement of the Bavarian War was finally assured by the intervention of Catherine of Russia. As the crisis over Bavaria deteriorated, both Frederick and Maria Theresa kept an eye on Catherine II, whose intervention in the affair might mean the difference between victory and defeat. Frederick transmitted to Catherine, as he did to Louis XVI, all the documents relative to his negotiations with Vienna, and Maria Theresa did likewise. Frederick denied that Austria had any right whatsoever to Bavaria and the Empress of Austria tried to demonstrate to Catherine that Joseph's claims were well-founded.[19] But Frederick had an advantage in this campaign to win Catherine, for his treaty of alliance with Catherine (1777) stipulated that she should aid him with a corps of Russian auxiliary troops in case of a war with Austria.

Nevertheless, while Catherine recognized her obligations to Frederick, she also knew that her ambitions in the Ottoman Empire made it dangerous to make an enemy of Joseph. She apparently thought seriously of forming a triple alliance of Russia, Austria, and Prussia, which could dominate Eastern Europe and control any settlement made in that part of the Continent. Both Frederick and Joseph had seemed ready to negotiate seriously for an alliance, when the Bavarian crisis interrupted their relationship.[20]

When she entered the scene as mediator, Catherine was not completely free of her entanglement with the Turks.[21] But she was freer than Louis XVI, who was thoroughly occupied with the American war. And when she spoke, she spoke with authority. She wanted to end the Bavarian dispute, and she knew that to do so would enhance her prestige and influence in Germany.[22] Louis XVI's role as arbiter of European politics was dramatically upstaged by the Empress of Russia.

Joseph and Kaunitz had counted on a Russian dispute with the Turks to keep Catherine out of German affairs. Frederick, they had erroneously supposed, would then be powerless because he would have no support or active assistance from his Russian ally.[23] Kaunitz was convinced, or, as Breteuil put it, he was trying to convince himself, that Catherine was determined to fight the Turks and she would therefore remain neutral in the event of an Austrian-Prussian war. But by the fall of 1778, the threat of a Russo-Turkish war faded and Catherine was free to deal with the Bavarian problem.[24]

Vergennes was not anxious to have Catherine enter the arena of German politics. ". . . Let's avoid assigning her a role in the present crisis, if we do not want to add to our embarrassment and to that of our ally . . .," he had written to Breteuil.[25] Vergennes did not think that Catherine wanted to go to war over the Bavarian issue. He felt, however, that Catherine, although intelligent, was not always exempt from miscalculation. Furthermore, he feared that her desire to play a principal role in Germany, and her passion for prestige, might lead her much further along the road to war than Louis XVI wished to go.[26]

But as Vergennes and his ambassador to Vienna reflected further, they both came to admit that Catherine's presence might have a good effect, especially since she had influence with her ally, Prussia. Her freedom of action could also play a role in persuading Maria Theresa and Joseph to settle. Vergennes had concluded that Austria was more swayed by fear than by any other motive, and Catherine's threats could produce the necessary fear.[27] In October, 1778, Vergennes wrote to Louis XVI's representative at St. Petersburg, Corberon, that the talks resulting from the Thugut mission had failed and negotiations had once again ceased. Louis XVI, Vergennes said, had directly intervened with his good offices to try to persuade Frederick to reach a settlement. Louis XVI had tried also to influence his ally to reach a joint settlement. If Catherine would do the same toward her ally, perhaps both parties would be more flexible and agree to some kind of conciliation. "It would be a role worthy of the magnanimity and humanity of the Empress of Russia," he declared, if she would use her good offices to stop the calamities that were about to flood Germany and Europe. Vergennes did not propose that Louis XVI and Catherine concert their diplomatic activities, but he indicated that one of the reasons why Louis XVI was communicating with Catherine was that he wanted to convince St. Petersburg of his sincere interest in effecting an understanding with her. Later, Vergennes suggested that St. Petersburg authorize its minister at Vienna to concert with the French ambassador there, on steps to bring Frederick and Joseph to the peace table. To facilitate the concert, Vergennes ordered Breteuil to co-ordinate with the French envoy at Berlin.[28]

Catherine's entrance onto the scene startled everyone. She made no attempt to conceal her hostility to Joseph and her sympathy for Frederick. Joseph's claims to Bavaria, she informed Europe, were outright violations of the Treaties of Westphalia, which formed the basis of the public law of Germany, and his invasion of Bavaria was a violation of "Sacred peace." His actions, in short, were a disturbance to the order and equilibrium of all of Europe and, therefore, a threat to the Empire of Russia. She then invited Frederick and Joseph "and other interested parties" to find a legal and amicable settlement of the Bavarian succession. If there were no peaceful settlement, she threatened to do what she felt was "suitable" to protect the interests of her Empire and her friends and, "above all, to her obligations towards her ally."[29] Her manner and what she said were, in fact, what Joseph and Kaunitz had ardently wanted from Louis XVI when he spoke to Frederick.

Catherine's intervention was not what Vergennes had had in mind when he suggested that Catherine concert with Louis XVI. Momentarily, it seemed that peace was further away than ever before. And if Russia entered the war, which she seemed determined to do if the Bavarian issue were not settled by the next spring of 1779,[30] could Louis XVI continue to withhold assistance to his ally? Maurepas, Vergennes, and Louis XVI met to determine what to do next. They decided that, while the Russian declaration was definitely partial to Prussia, Louis XVI was not going to make any suggestions to Vienna as to how to respond. In his orders to his diplomats Vergennes did note, however, that, in spite of the curtness of Catherine's words, she clearly expressed a desire for peace. Louis XVI hoped, therefore, that Austria would seize the occasion to reopen negotiations.[31]

At the same time, Vergennes dispatched a communication to his envoy at St. Petersburg, in which he allowed that Louis XVI was "infinitely touched" by the fervor of Catherine's desire for peace. But Vergennes then went on to note that, if the two sovereigns were agreed on the need to stop the war, there seemed to be a noticeable difference in their way of going about it. Catherine's stance showed too much deference to her ally; it was cutting and even menacing toward Austria. Louis XVI, on the other hand, had tried, Vergennes explained, to be friendly and conciliatory toward Frederick. The role of mediator, Vergennes observed, requires more use of persuasion than threat of force. Persuade the Russians, Vergennes advised Corberon, to use the French methods. Nevertheless, Louis XVI was ready to concert with Catherine to find a way to peace.[32]

Kaunitz watched Louis XVI welcome Catherine as mediator, with fury and despair. Could France not now see the necessity of supporting Austria against the terrifying combination of Prussian and Russian might? But Louis XVI plainly did not see such a necessity.[33] He was now convinced that

Frederick and Catherine really wanted a peaceful settlement and, furthermore, he was exceedingly annoyed that Joseph was, once again, demanding a large portion of Bavaria; this time, a territory equivalent to what Frederick would receive when he inherited the Margraviates of Franconia.[34]

With France unwilling to assume the role that Catherine played in support of her ally, Austria had the choice of backing down or fighting alone. By November, 1778, the Ministry in Vienna was split over the question of war and peace, with Maria Theresa urging peace, Joseph determined to remain firm, and Kaunitz, in great misery, caught in the middle. Toward the end of the month, however, Breteuil learned that Joseph had admitted to his mother that he was coming around to agreeing with her.[35] Before the year closed, Russia and Prussia had reached a definition of Russia's military obligations to Frederick. Frederick was never satisfied with the assistance Catherine agreed to provide, but any aid at all was more than Joseph could expect from his ally.[36] The moment was obviously not favorable to Joseph's plans.

In March, 1779, after agreeing to a truce, the two warring parties came together in the town of Teschen, in Austrian Silesia. Breteuil, representing France, and Prince Repnin, representing Russia, acted as mediators. There, less than three months later, the Bavarian War came to a close. It did not end at all the way Joseph had wanted it to end. His enemy's ally had made it clear that she would stand behind Prussia if peace failed. Louis XVI had refused to make a similar commitment. Joseph felt abandoned. He backed down ". . . in order to make a better jump [the next time]."[37]

The settlement at Teschen ended the war. Each side agreed to cease all hostilities and to evacuate any territory that belonged to the other.[38] In the war zones where the ordinary peasant competed with the armies for food, this aspect of the peace was the essential one. In the settlement, Joseph renounced the territorial pretensions contained in the Convention of January 3, 1778. He received, in return, that part of Bavaria situated between the Danube, Inn, and Salza Rivers. The Palatinate Elector recovered, therefore, most of Bavaria which he had given up in the Convention of January Third.[39] At the same time, the Elector reluctantly agreed to the suggestions, on the part of the great powers mediating the settlement, that he pay a 6,000,000 *florins* indemnity to the Saxon Elector in return for Saxony's renunciation of her claims to Bavaria.[40] The Duke of Mecklenburg received the good offices of the contracting powers to advance his desire that the Emperor grant him the privilege of *non appelando,* a privilege that would free him from the jurisdiction of Imperial Courts.[41] The Duke of Deux-Ponts acceded to the agreements because they protected his rights of inheritance to Bavaria. Thus an inheritance all but lost to him in 1778, once again seemed secure.[42]

The most welcome benefit for Frederick was Joseph's agreement not to stand in the way of the eventual union of the Franconian Margraviates, Ansbach and Bayreuth, with Brandenburg. Frederick received indisputable recognition of his succession upon the extinction of the family line which then held them.[43]

Although, in Germany, Catherine shared the role Vergennes wished Louis XVI to play in Europe, the outcome of the crisis represented an important victory for Louis XVI. It was the supreme test of Vergenne's skill and talent, and beautifully illustrated his ability to accomplish large aims by little steps. He wanted, above all, to avoid a Continental war. He wished to change the nature of the Franco-Austrian alliance so that Versailles, not Vienna, would have freedom of decision. He wanted to encourage Frederick as a counterweight to Austria, but he did not want to be taken in by him. He wanted to prevent, as much as possible, the aggrandizement of Austria. And he did not want Joseph to exchange the Austrian Low Countries for Bavaria. In all of these aims he succeeded.

At the same time, at home, he skillfully threaded his way between the Queen's powerful and hostile coterie which wanted France to render aid to Joseph, and the increasing fury of the anti-Austrian faction, which wanted stiffer resistance to Joseph's demands. In the Bavarian crisis, Vergennes' estimate of personalities, his knowledge of European politics, and his influence with the King were all used with consummate skill to achieve his ends.

The most dramatic outcome of the Bavarian Succession crisis was Catherine II's greater visibility and prestige in Europe. As a co-mediator she shared the authority and applause that Vergennes sought for Louis XVI. Catherine now appeared alongside Louis XVI and Frederick as a "protector" of the smaller powers of Germany. She, too, spoke as the defender of the Treaties of Westphalia. Furthermore, her ally, Frederick, claimed the victory in the Bavarian War.[44]

The collaboration of France and Russia created a temporary *rapprochement* between Louis XVI and Catherine II. Catherine and Frederick both made separate overtures to Versailles, which hinted at another revolutionary reversal of alliances if Louis XVI agreed. "If we were as disposed to a revolution in the political system as some too readily suppose," Vergennes wrote, "it could be accomplished, perhaps, in three months."[45] But Louis XVI did not wish "to change the face of Europe." Vergennes saw no advantages to be gained from breaking the Austrian alliance.

Nevertheless, the collaboration with Catherine provided the basis for reducing the tensions between France and Russia. Vergennes hoped that the understanding achieved between Louis XVI and Catherine II during the Bavarian crisis might set the stage for "commercial arrangements."[46] He knew, of course, that the major issue between Russia and France — the fate of the Ottoman Empire — had not been settled by the collaboration at Teschen. France had provided the Turks with secret military aid during the recent Russo-Turkish war, and was still very much committed to protecting the Ottoman Empire against Russian and Austrian aggression.[47] But, at least, a minimum of mutual understanding had been achieved. Furthermore, Catherine was aware that she owed to Vergennes "more than one 'thank you'" for his part in the satisfaction she had felt as a participant in a major European settlement.[48]

CHAPTER 25

Mogilev

In the spring of 1780 in the Russian village of Mogilev, a "miserable village, of wooden buildings and streets of mud," the young Joseph II, Emperor of the Holy Roman Empire, sat reading a letter from Catherine II, Empress of Russia. The Empress, the letter said, would soon arrive at Mogilev where she would make a grand ceremonial entry into the village and then proceed to the village church. Her letter, as well as her couriers, made it clear that she wanted to see Joseph very much, but something in her sense of proprieties rebelled at the idea of first seeing him among the milling crowds of onlookers observing her entrance. Could she see him for the first time, alone, at a place she had had especially built for the meeting?

Such an apparently whimsical request flattered the ego of the young Emperor, but Catherine had probably anticipated Joseph's reaction, and it was not whimsy at all which motivated the request; it was a calculated part of a complex diplomatic maneuver. Joseph and Catherine were on the verge of an affair, not a romantic affair of the heart, but an affair of high politics. Of course, Joseph had agreed to grant Catherine the favor she asked. When they met in Catherine's chosen spot, Joseph, who had been waiting patiently for her, moved gallantly to kiss her hand, but he was pleasantly stopped in mid-motion by Catherine's full embrace. They sat down and began to talk, and it quickly became obvious that Catherine was in a "particularly good humor." From "their first words, they seemed to agree with each other."[1]

The Russo-Austrian affair really began much earlier in the winter of 1779 with a conversation between the Russian ambassador to Vienna, Prince Galitsin, and Joseph II. During the conversation Joseph, who made a hobby of visiting the sovereigns of Europe, expressed a desire to meet the Czarina Catherine. The Russian ambassador immediately saw a host of interesting possibilities swimming in such an idea, and he quickly notified his sovereign of Joseph's wish. Although she pretended to be unwilling, Catherine was delighted.[2] Austrian support, or at least its consent, was essential to the successful fulfillment of some of her more grandiose ambitions and she found Joseph's wish in "perfect conformity" with her own sentiments.[3]

Catherine was already planning a trip to Mogilev, and she wrote Galitsin that her voyage offered the perfect opportunity to grant Joseph his wish. She wanted so much, she told her representative (who was, of course, expected to tell Joseph) to "render justice to the eminent qualities which assigned him so distinguished a rank among the sovereigns of this century."[4]

The meeting with Catherine was a part of Joseph's own personal diplomacy; he arranged everything before consulting his Chancellor Kaunitz or telling his mother. And he told them about his plans only after he had received Catherine's reply and agreement to meet him. His motivations are a cause for a lively historical dispute. According to the historian, Arneth, he had become thoroughly disillusioned with his French alliance during the American War for Independence. There is no doubt that he harbored deep resentments against Louis XVI for his refusal to allow him a free hand in the Bavarian succession crisis.[5]

But Joseph's desire to meet Catherine was not simply a reaction to France's stubborn refusal to assist him in his conquests; he also acted with one eye on his bitter enemy, Prussia.[6] Russia was one of Prussia's key allies, and any policy that might pry Catherine away from her Prussian attachment was worth the attempt. Furthermore, Joseph was an extremely ambitious young man. He burned to redraw the map of Europe to Austria's advantage. Vergennes had effectively blocked his ambitions in the West, in Germany; so he turned to the East. Before he could move in that direction, however, he had to reach some kind of an understanding with Catherine (unless he was prepared to fight with her), because he rightly suspected that she, too, was already determined to violate the *status quo* in the area now under Joseph's covetous eye. Could they not, together, reach some mutually advantageous agreement?

Having completed his own arrangements for the meeting with Catherine, Joseph then turned to Kaunitz for recommendations as to what he should tell the Russian Empress. The Austrian Chancellor was rather surprised at Joseph's independence, but not so much so as to be unable to offer advice: Joseph should try to arrange an alliance between the two Empires which would give reciprocal guarantees of the territories of both parties. In addition, and more importantly, Kaunitz also told Joseph to make it clear to Catherine that he was ready to reach an understanding with her on the delicate question of the Ottoman Empire.[7]

Once the two were together at Mogilev, a lively conversation began immediately in an atmosphere of amiability. But under the masks of sociability lurked the beasts of ambition. The question worrying both sovereigns was whether or not their ambitions would lead the two of them down the same path of policy. If the answer were to be yes, the social graces could give way to a more profitable relationship. But if the answer were to be no, if their ambitions were mutually exclusive, it was definitely best that each not reveal too much to the other. Thus carefully, cautiously, each weighed the other's words and selected his own with care. When the time came for Catherine's departure from Mogilev, it was decided that Joseph would go with her to St. Petersburg. Along the way they could continue their conversation in the privacy of Catherine's carriage.

After days of delicate prodding, probing, and exchanging amiabilities with Catherine, Joseph concluded that she had at least two ideas she wanted to communicate. First, she was obviously suspicious of Prussia. Was she hinting that she was ready to quit her alliance with that kingdom? Secondly, Joseph noted that every time he mentioned the Ottoman Turks, Catherine mentioned Italy, and "when she speaks to me of Rome, I always speak to her of Constantinople."[8] Each sovereign made certain quickly to assure the other that neither of them really had ambitions in the direction of these two cities, but the steady and mechanical repetition of such assurances only reduced the likelihood of their sincerity. When Joseph broached to Catherine the subject of a defensive treaty of alliance between the two powers, a treaty that would guarantee the territories of both, he noticed it was "well-received."[9] Catherine's favorite, Prince Potemkin, asked, however, if such a guarantee would include future conquests that Catherine might make. Joseph demurred. The benefits of such an agreement would not be reciprocal. Potemkin easily found the way out of that difficulty with an offer to guarantee all the conquests Austria might make. Joseph was impressed, but not yet prepared to go that far. But when Potemkin asked him not to make an alliance with the Turks against Russia, Joseph hesitated. Such an agreement, he told Potemkin, ought to be taken up at the ministerial level. As Joseph prepared to leave, he knew that nothing definite had yet been decided between himself and Catherine, but he felt confident that, if he let things continue along the path they had taken, he could "tranquilly await the outcome."[10]

The *adieux* of the two rulers were as touching as their meeting. He kissed her hand; she seized his hands and kissed them, and began to cry. The parting was so tender (and so public) that it set French diplomats to worrying. Breteuil reported the details of it to his superiors at Versailles.[11] Such an exhibition of sentimentality, he recognized, was not likely a spontaneous outpouring of the affection of one sovereign for another. It was staged to be noticed and, to him, that meant trouble.

A veteran of fourteen years as ambassador at Constantinople, Vergennes did not need to be told how important the continued existence of the Ottoman Empire was to France. This weak, unpredictable, obviously decaying power certainly was not the ideal ally, but she was the only thing available, at the moment, to block Russia's drive to the Dardenelles. Vergennes' earlier opposition to Choiseul's reckless policy, of pushing the Turks prematurely into a disastrous war, was grounded on this irreducible fact. In addition, France's commercial interests in the Levant were certainly safer under the protection of the Sultans, even with their erratic personalities and policies, than they would be if subject to the authority of the brilliant and aggressive Czarina of Russia.

Vergennes also saw that Joseph's affair with Catherine did not augur well for the Franco-Austrian alliance. The Treaty of Teschen left Joseph thoroughly dissatisfied with Louis XVI and his Foreign Affairs Minister, and Vergennes was very much aware that the death of the aging Maria Theresa, which everyone daily expected, would place the alliance in further jeopardy.[12] Yet Vergennes knew that Joseph could not afford an abrupt break with France, especially if Catherine loosened her ties with Prussia, for a firm alliance between the two abandoned powers would threaten Joseph's flank and rear, and make it a risky business to undertake any military action against the Ottoman Empire. This possibility, so clearly dangerous from Joseph's point of view, was Vergennes' trump card, but it had to be played with extreme care because Vergennes did not want to make an enemy of Joseph, especially while France was straining every nerve and sinew to gain a victory in the American War.

Vergennes could not easily understand why Joseph wanted to expand to the East, nor why Joseph was willing to let Russia expand in that area. If Joseph and Catherine became close neighbors, even with buffer zones between them, friction would inevitably develop.[13] To Vergennes it was illogical and, in the long run, against Joseph's interests, to want to create such a potentially explosive situation in the Balkans. The history of that region in the nineteenth and twentieth centuries would prove the logic of Vergennes' reasoning. Nevertheless, Vergennes' long experience in diplomacy had taught him that the logic of long-range, enlightened self-interest was only one of many elements of traditional diplomacy. Joseph's personality, his passionate longing for prestige, his consuming ambition to expand were at least as strong factors in the make-up of his policies as long-range self-interest.[14] In short, Vergennes perceived in Joseph a fault he bore himself: he sometimes failed to see that the requirements of prestige and those of long-range self-interest do not always coincide.

The thing that most worried Vergennes, and made him fear for the future of the Ottoman Empire, was the example of the earlier combination of Russia, Prussia, and Austria which had ruthlessly carved up Poland. Such a combination had seemed improbable to many experienced diplomats, who had for years watched the three powers shuffle and reshuffle their alliances in order to fight each other more efficiently. But the Polish feast had been too rewarding to the diners to expect them to forget it quickly. When

Vergennes saw Austria and Russia once again in secret huddles, he quickly jumped to the conclusion that a new feast was being planned, and he strongly suspected the main dish might be the Ottoman Empire. He was absolutely correct, but he also knew that Catherine's need for an understanding with Joseph, and the dilapidated state of her finances, which were still suffering from the last war with the Turks, held her momentarily in check.[15]

At first, the strongest opposition to Joseph's plans came from his mother. For political and moral reasons, his mother was not at all pleased with his sudden diplomatic infatuation with the Czarina of Russia, for she rightly feared that any political child born of such a union could only be, in her eyes, illegitimate. The partition of the Ottoman Empire, she felt, "would constitute an event more critical than the partition of Poland." Not only would the Austrian House lose its reputation for good faith if it undertook such an enterprise, but, if the enterprise succeeded, it would bring Austria only a few miserable and worthless provinces that would more than likely exhaust, rather than augment, the power of the Hapsburg monarchy.[16]

But Maria Theresa was getting old and Joseph was still young; he could therefore safely afford to wait until the death of his mother removed her old-womanish scruples. In the meantime, he had to make certain that nothing smothered his and Catherine's political child before it had a chance to mature. Joseph carefully instructed his ambassador to Russia, Cobenzl, in the ways to nourish the project while, at the same time, warning him to keep the negotiations secret. His Chancellor, Kaunitz, willingly offered his assistance in advancing the project, although he could not resist tinkering with it. To Kaunitz's mind, gains made in Italy for Austria would not be the equivalent of Russian gains in the Ottoman Empire; he was clearly of the opinion that true reciprocity would also involve Austrian acquisition of Turkish territory.[17]

The death of Maria Theresa in the fall of 1780 cleared the way for the implementation of Joseph's projects. Now free of the restraining hand of his mother, Joseph was not likely to continue her pacific policy. Vergennes recognized the dangers inherent in the new situation: dangers for the Ottoman Empire and, most of all, the dangers for the Continental peace so essential to his American policy. Fortunately, Joseph, too, saw the dangers likely to be spawned by his policy, and was therefore inclined to proceed with caution. He expected Louis XVI to oppose his eastern policy, because France had traditionally protected the Ottoman Empire. And Joseph was also aware that Prussia, still an ally of Catherine, could too easily wreck his plans if Frederick chose to do so.

Nevertheless, the young Emperor was not inclined to abandon his ambitions. On January 9, 1781, barely two months after the death of his mother, he re-opened negotiations with Catherine. By the latter half of May, they had hammered out the basics for a defensive alliance. The precise details for common action in the Ottoman Empire were not yet settled, but a long stride toward the goal had been taken. This accomplished, Joseph decided to make a journey to Versailles — his second — to take the temperature of opinion there before proceeding on the more drastic action.[18] A charming guest, because he knew how to be charmed by his hosts, Joseph dazzled the ladies, sampled court opinion, and measured the force of Vergennes' opposition to Austrian plans. He also reminded the French Queen, his sister, that, underneath her French robes, she was still an Austrian and must keep her Austrian heart. He meant by that, that she should be the principal agent in Versailles for his foreign policy. After a six-day visit he departed in a puff of powder and pomp.[19]

Once back in Vienna, Joseph pressed his negotiations with Catherine, and by September he got from her a set of formal propositions containing a detailed formula for partitioning the Ottoman Empire. As her share of the spoils, Catherine wanted the Crimea, a strip of territory on the eastern shore of the Sea of Azov, the northern littoral of the Black Sea which had been declared independent in the Treaty of Küchük-Kaynarji (1774), and she hoped to create an independent domain of the province of Dacia.* If successful, such an extensive acquisition would bring under Catherine's ownership the entire northern shore of the Black Sea, and the boundaries of Turkish influence in the Balkans would be pushed back to within three hundred miles of the very heart of the Ottoman Empire, Constantinople.

But Catherine was generous, especially with the lands of the Turkish Sultan. Joseph wanted, and she consented to his acquisition of, Bosnia, Serbia, and even certain territories belonging to Venice in Dalmatia. For compensation to Venice, they planned to give either the strategically-placed Turkish island of Cyprus (which had once belonged to Venice), or the territory of Moria (old Peloponnesus) which the Turks had taken from the Venetians in 1718.

Catherine's ambitions did not stop at a mere division of Turkish lands. Behind her extravagant claims to Turkish territory was the even more extravagant desire to destroy completely the Ottoman Empire. If the Sultan could be chased out of Constantinople, she suggested, why not restore the old Byzantine Empire and place her second grandson, whose name, prophetically, was Constantine, on the throne as Emperor?[20] Catherine's

* The Ancient province of Dacia lay along the left bank of the Danube between the Temes River on the west and the Pruth River on the east, comprising the plateau of Transylvania, the plain of Wallachia, and a portion of modern Hungary and Moldavia. But Catherine seems not to have had the same boundaries in mind. In her plan, the limits of the province of Dacia would be the Dniester and the Black Sea on the east and the Aluta and Danube on the west and south.

designs, seconded by Joseph, constituted not a simple theft of territory from a weak and vulnerable neighbor, but a veritable revolution in the structure of European politics. Not even Peter the Great had dared reach so far.

As the rumors of the Russo-Austrian plans for partitioning the Ottoman Empire began to leak out, they aroused concern in other European courts, as well as at Versailles. The Republic of Venice was especially sensitive to any modifications of the Turkish boundaries, especially any changes along the littoral of the Adriatic Sea and the Eastern Mediterranean. Venice would have preferred to see the territorial integrity of the Ottoman Empire remain intact, but, at the same time, she was prepared, if matters came to the point of division, to advance her own claims to a share of the spoils.[21]

For the King of Prussia, the implications of Joseph's radical new system were most unsettling. At first, Frederick seemed astonishingly unworried about Joseph's plans. His complacent attitude was partially based on the belief that Russia, already tied up with a multitude of difficulties in the diplomacy of Armed Neutrality, was not likely to go seeking new problems. In addition, Frederick trusted Catherine enough to believe that his own treaty with her would hold her to her obligations to him until 1788. His ties with Catherine were also reinforced by his adherence to the Armed Neutrality in May of 1781.[22] But as information on the Russo-Austrian plans began to accumulate, it became more and more obvious to Frederick that there was indeed something to worry about.[23] If Russia abandoned him in favor of Austria, he would be left isolated on the Continent, with both France and Russia bound to his archenemy to the south. The prospect of such an ugly turn of affairs was discomfiting, and now Frederick, who, in his own youth, had recklessly lighted the fires of general war, assumed the role of chief of the fire brigade, sounding the alarm for all of Europe to hear. First he tried to knock together a quadruple alliance between Prussia, the Ottoman Empire, France, and Russia, but his efforts led to nothing substantial. Then he turned to England for a way out of his isolation, at the same time ordering his ministers at the Porte to goad the Turks into shoring up their rickety defenses, even promising to aid them if they became objects of aggression.[24] His real hope, however, lay in the possibility that Austria's designs on Turkey would antagonize France, and open the way for a Franco-Prussian *rapprochement*.[25]

Joseph, too, saw the danger of a Prussian *rapprochement* with France. He knew that he could not plunge into a diplomatic escapade in the East without the consent of his neighbor to the West. To gain this consent, he decided to invite France to the division of the spoils. In August of 1782, he carried his plan to the Marquis de Breteuil, the French ambassador at Vienna, and made his offer: it was no less than the entire province of Egypt, one of richest territories of the Ottoman Empire.[26]

Joseph's offer of Egypt was a clever one, for, since the time of Saint Louis, that "salubrious country" had fascinated Frenchmen. Three times during his reign, Louis XIV had tried to open up the territory to French influence by negotiating for access of French ships to the Port of Suez and the Red Sea. Throughout the seventeenth and eighteenth centuries French philosophers, travelers, and diplomats extolled the riches of Egypt. The philosopher Leibnitz had gone so far as to urge its conquest by France. Between 1750 and 1760, the Marquis d'Argenson had toyed with the amazingly prophetic idea of creating a canal between the Red Sea and the Mediterranean. Yet Choiseul seems to have been the first statesman who seriously considered taking advantage of the disintegration of the Ottoman Empire and taking Egypt. In 1769, according to Talleyrand, at least, Choiseul had contemplated the idea as a way of replacing the losses in production and commerce suffered when the American colonies were torn from French control at the end of the Seven Years War.[27] Vergennes had met the notion of acquisition of Egypt in a memo submitted to the Ministry of Foreign Affairs in 1776 by his old acquaintance of the Constantinople embassy, the Baron de Tott. Tott recommended the acquisition of Egypt on the grounds that the destruction of the Ottoman Empire was inevitable, and, unless France established for herself a strong position there, her commercial interests in the Levant would suffer.[28]

Joseph learned of France's interest in Egypt during his visit to France in 1777. At that time, Vergennes' successor at Constantinople, Saint-Priest, was on leave in France and, during a two-hour conversation between Joseph and Saint-Priest on the terrace at Versailles, it is fairly certain that Saint-Priest revealed to Joseph his own idea that France should either make a determined effort to assist the Ottoman Empire, which he believed was "incapable of defending itself," or else "let it fall and appropriate to herself whatever pieces of the debris it would be to France's advantage to have."[29] To Saint-Priest's mind, the most tempting piece of "debris" was Egypt.[30]

When Joseph had earlier tried to bribe France into accepting his annexation of Bavaria, by offering Louis XVI the Austrian Low Countries, Vergennes had refused to rise to the lure. But this new temptation was a tribute to Joseph's resourcefulness. To refuse it, Vergennes would have to go against the current of generations of thinking about Egypt, as well as against the opinion of several experts that France needed Egypt in order to protect and extend French commercial interests in the Levant. And along with these pressures urging the acquisition of Egypt was the fear that, if France did not snatch the ripened fruit, Austria or Great Britain might.[31]

Vergennes was not surprised by Joseph's offer to Breteuil, but it sorely embarrassed him, for it forced into his lap a cluster of spiny alternatives. Not only was an important segment of Court and Ministry opinion in favor of taking Egypt, but his own Ambassador to Constantinople, Saint-Priest, had originally raised the issue with Joseph. Within the Ministry, Sartine, the Minister of Marine, seemed to be, though hesitantly, encouraging such a policy. In fact, Sartine had sent the Baron de Tott on a secret mission to Egypt in 1777, to reconnoitre the situation there and report back to him whatever "symptoms of decadence" there were which tended to loosen the ties of Egypt with Constantinople.[32]

But Joseph's offer violated the very basis of Louis XVI's foreign policy, and Vergennes knew it. France, he felt, should not seek further acquisitions. History, as he interpreted it, demonstrated that, whenever France expanded, Europe coalesced against her. France's role in Europe, as he conceived it, should be that of the stabilizer, the protector of the small powers and the *status quo*. And, even though his support of the Americans contradicted his pronouncements in favor of the *status quo*, he could easily argue that, if France was to play the role of defender of the *status quo* in Europe, she had to reduce the relative power of England in order to prevent English interference. Only then could France keep the initiative, and freely play her self-assigned role. Considering the problem from this point of view, Vergennes rejected Joseph's offer and he convinced Louis XVI to do so. But the way to this difficult policy decision was not an easy one, and Vergennes' ideas emerged triumphant only after a bitter, exhausting struggle within the Council, a struggle which partially contributed to the defeated Sartine's loss of his post and left behind dangerous land mines of resentment against the Minister of Foreign Affairs.

CHAPTER 26

Peace Appears Trailing Clouds of Ambitions

"History teaches us," Harold Nicolson has wisely observed, "...that coalitions begin to disintegrate from the moment the common danger is removed." The Battle of Yorktown did not immediately remove England, the danger common to France and her allies, but the year 1782 opened with expectations that such a thing could soon happen, for with the surrender of Cornwallis, hopes for a British victory in America all but collapsed. Peace, like a maturing pupa, began stirring in the minds of statesmen. And, to quote further Harold Nicolson, at the "basis of any alliance or coalition, is an agreement between two or more sovereign states to subordinate their separate interests to a single purpose . . . So soon . . . as ultimate victory seems assured, the consciousness of separate interests tends to overshadow the sense of common purpose."[1]

This period of Vergennes' career was to be the most difficult of his life. The alliance system which he had hammered together was a jerry-built structure, strained by internal contradictions and conflicts, unjoined at critical spots, and cemented together only by a fear of the common enemy. But when that common enemy showed signs of weakening, the conflicting aims of France and her allies began to dissolve the effects of fear. Furthermore, as the vision of peace approached, Vergennes began to see that the fever of ambition in Spain, the United States, and France, and the inevitable disputes over the division of the spoils opened the way to the Englishmen to divide the allies and win, at the peace table, the war they had lost at Yorktown.

The constant fear during the war, that one or another of his allies would make a separate peace and leave France to hobble along alone or with fewer allies, haunted the French Minister. And the dangers of a separate peace did not diminish as peace approached, for a break in the ranks now could undermine his position at the bargaining table and result in a diplomatic defeat. Moreover, it should always be kept in mind that, while Vergennes worked to shepherd home safely a peace in the West, the French position in eastern Europe was daily becoming more precarious. A satisfactory peace in the West was necessary to any effective action in the East. In addition, the disquieting financial malaise of the French government confronted Vergennes with a situation so complex, changeable, and, indeed, so desperate that one false move could bring the collapse of the entire system he had struggled so hard to erect.

Although Vergennes opposed any of his allies' making a separate peace, he had no objections to their engaging in separate negotiations. "We are and shall always be," he wrote to his minister at Philadelphia, "disposed to consent that the American plenipotentiaries in Europe should treat according to their instructions directly, and without our intervention, with those of the Court of London, while we, on our side, shall treat in the same way." The only condition which he set was that the two negotiations proceed at the same rate, and that the two treaties be signed the same day.[2] Again and again he repeated this idea to LaLuzerne, to the British, and to Franklin,[3] and there is no reason to believe that, when the American commissioners opened separate negotiations with the English during the summer of 1782, they were doing so against the wishes of the French Minister of Foreign Affairs.

The separate peace which Vergennes feared was, of course, England's greatest weapon. Like a doctor probing the patient's body in search of internal weaknesses, British diplomats and agents again and again probed the minds of Spanish, French, and American representatives, in search of signs of a break in their enemies' concert, but without success.[4]

Unperturbed, the British kept up the pressure. In March of 1782, just before his ministry fell, Lord North tested once more the solidarity of the alliance with separate offers to each. To the Dutch, he offered a separate peace on the basis of *uti possidetis*; that is, the belligerent parties would keep those possessions they had acquired by arms during the war, with the exception of territory captured from the British by the French. To the French, a British agent promised *uti possidetis* along with a British agreement to give up her rights in Dunkirk and concessions in India. Franklin, at Paris, and Adams, at The Hague, were likewise approached to discover their intentions, but no one went for the bait. Through Vergennes' undersecretary, Rayneval, Franklin kept Vergennes informed of everything that went on, and Vergennes reciprocated. At The Hague, the French ambassador used his personal influence with the Patriots to indicate to the Dutch the grave consequences that would follow if the Dutch were tempted by English propositions to make a separate peace.[5] The alliance held fast, and the North ministry fell, having failed at making peace as well as war.[6]

Charles Fox then became Secretary of State for Foreign Affairs, and Lord

Shelburne Secretary of State for the Colonies, under the new Rockingham ministry. Together they continued the search for cracks in the enemy's wall. Shelburne shrewdly divined that the Americans' allegiance to their allies was the weakest point in the alliance system, for the French, the Dutch, and the Spanish all had European and world-wide interests for which the Americans had no concern. At the same time, he knew that American interests on the continent of America conflicted with those of Spain, and the jealousies created by these conflicts could easily be fanned into an open dispute. Shelburne carefully nourished the jealousies. He dispatched General Carleton and Admiral Digby to America to offer the Americans independence "in the first instance." "The advantages which we expect from such concessions," Shelburne told the two officers, "are that America, once apprised of the King's dispositions to acknowledge the independence of the Thirteen States, and of the disinclination in the French court to terminate the war, must see that it is from this moment to be carried on with a view of negotiating points, in which she can have no concern. . . ." "These facts being made notorious," Shelburne concluded near the end of his letter, "it is scarce conceivable that America . . . will continue to make efforts under French direction . . . ."[7]

But, in his choice of means, Shelburne failed to consider the man with whom he hoped to deal. Once in America, Carleton addressed himself to General Washington, the most unlikely person to be tempted. Washington not only refused to discuss Carleton's proposals, he even refused to convey to the Continental Congress the reports on the proceedings of Parliament which enabled George III to treat with the Americans. When the Continental Congress heard of Carleton's mission, it backed Washington, and denied a passport to the messenger who wished to deliver to the Congress the report on Parliament's dispositions. Congress firmly closed the incident with a ringing resolution condemning England's "insidious steps."[8]

As the spring advanced into summer, the English multiplied their attempts to find or create a break in their enemies' line. Once, the English thought Franklin had looked "in the direction of separate peace," and they jumped to the conclusion that Franklin was really ready to approve of such a peace. They were soon undeceived.[9]

When Rockingham died in July, and Lord Shelburne became Prime Minister, Vergennes' alliance system was still intact. But he knew that he could not relax. The new English cabinet, he warned, "will lend itself only with the greatest repugnance to a general peace, and will not negotiate seriously and in good faith until it has lost all hope of dividing the allies by treating with each separately."[10]

But the stepped-up contacts meant that the British Cabinet was anxious to talk peace. And this knowledge compelled Vergennes to hasten his preparations for the coming negotiations. His position, on entering the peace talks of 1782-1783, was not a very happy one. It was similar, in important respects, to the position of William III of England during the negotiations preceding the Treaty of Ryswick. Like William III, Vergennes headed an alliance system which contained dissonant members with conflicting interests. Vergennes was to find (as did William III) that it was next to impossible to satisfy each of his allies in the final treaty, for they all, monarchical Spain, the Dutch Republic, and the United States, approached the end of the war with expansionist ambitions, and these ambitions conflicted. Compared with the claims being staked out by her allies, France's claims were extremely modest, considering how much of the war burden she had carried. She demanded American independence, the freeing of Dunkirk, restoration of French fishing rights in Newfoundland, and some minor territorial exchanges in the colonies.

Vergennes had no objection to his allies' gaining from the war. But he had to make them realize, and he had to do so without antagonizing them, that France's resources were not inexhaustible, and that France was neither inclined nor able to prolong the war to insure the satisfaction of all of their demands. With careful husbanding of means, he might hope to meet the obligations required by his treaties with the United States and Spain, but beyond that he could not go. Such a position did not mean, it should be clearly understood, that France would veto any gains her allies could make, but it did mean that the Spanish and American diplomats could not count on having the French Army, the French Navy, and the French treasury at their backs to second their every wish.

Caught between the growing, and what he considered extravagant, claims of his allies, Vergennes was also harassed within his own government. In 1780, the Director General of Finances, Necker, discouraged with the financial disarray of the French treasury tried, secretly, to open negotiations himself to make peace with the English. Through the Abbé Veri, Necker contacted the English banker Thomas Walpole, who was visiting Paris in the summer of 1780. Together Veri and Walpole discussed "peace" overtures between Maurepas and Lord North, which would have neatly excluded Vergennes.[11] Maurepas was politically wise enough to suspect that Necker might be behind the intrigue, so he was never enthusiastic about it.[12] Furthermore, he was too sick with the gout to embark on private negotiations. In any case, George III did not trust Walpole enough to allow him to become his negotiator. Nor was the British King yet ready at that time to make any settlement that recognized America's independence.[13]

But Necker also tried other ways to end the war. In the summer and fall of 1780 he also used the Swiss historian, Paul Henri Mallet, to make contacts with Mountstuart, the new British envoy to the court of Savoy. To obtain the desperately needed peace, Necker was apparently willing to settle for a good deal less than Vergennes was demanding. He seemed responsive even to the idea that only one province of America, for example, New England, become independent, while Britain recovered her sovereignty over the others.[14] But George III refused to give Mountstuart the necessary authority to follow up his preliminary talks with a trip to Paris.

In December of 1780, Necker tried once more to begin his own peace negotiations.[15] This time, he secretly contacted Lord North by letter. Again George III stubbornly refused to go for the bait. And Necker's attempts to usurp Vergennes' position came to a halt. Vergennes somehow learned, perhaps through the *cabinet noir,* which secretly opened letters, that Necker was in contact with the British. And at court he cleverly undermined Necker by casting doubts on his competence. "I will not express my opinion of Necker's financial operations," Vergennes told the Austrian Ambassador, Mercy d'Argenteau, "but in all other parts of the administration he is shortsighted and ignorant."[16]

While Necker intrigued for peace, the French "War Party," led by the Maréchal de Castries, Minister of the Navy, demanded escalation of the war. He insisted that France, too, make the American War for Independence a war of expansion, and urged the deployment of French soldiers and sailors with that idea in mind. Such a war was in clear contradiction to Vergennes' concept of Louis XVI's role in Europe and the world, but the fact that France's two allies were demanding additional territories gave Castries leverage in the Court and Royal Council. In 1781, when Spain decided it might include Jamaica along with its other demands, Castries went into a fury. In the Royal Council of September twenty-fifth, he railed "against the indecency of letting Spain have her way and alone gather all the profit from the alliance."[17] As the negotiations began, the expansionist faction led by Castries incessantly bombarded Vergennes with memos and plans for extending French colonialism in India.[18]

In the King's Council, Vergennes countered plans for aggrandizement with the realities of financial facts; facts, ironically, provided by Necker. France simply did not have the resources to carry on the kind of war Castries and others wished to undertake. Consequently, the Minister of Foreign Affairs argued, both the war and the claims against England had to be limited. Happily, Louis XVI agreed and Vergennes' policy carried the day. But Castries never gave up. While Vergennes fought off attempts to usurp his authority, while he talked to moderate his allies' war aims, the French Minister of the Navy continued pressing for breaking off all discussions of peace and going on the offensive.[19]

Necker's and Castries' attempts to undermine Vergennes' policies were not due to personal ambition alone. Historical hindsight clearly demonstrates the wisdom of Necker's understanding that peace was absolutely necessary. While Castries' attempts to expand French war aims were ill-advised, they are understandable in the context of the expanding aims of Louis XVI's allies. On the other hand, both men had very high opinions of their own talents and both, without doubt, knew that if they challenged Vergennes successfully they would replace him in the King's confidence.[20]

Vergennes also had to deal with the personal ambitions of the representatives of the various powers, who were arriving in Paris to negotiate peace. Each man carried with him instructions reflecting the policies of the various states, but each also had his own private ambitions, personal peculiarities, and quirks that complicated the peace negotiations. Long experience in diplomacy had taught Vergennes not to ignore the influence of personal character in negotiations.

The United Provinces was represented at Paris by Ambassador Lestevnon de Berkenrode, and Gérard Brantzen who arrived in Paris as an "adjunct." Vergennes objected to the dilatory tactics of both men, but he was especially distrustful of Brantzen. He had even ordered LaVauguyon to intervene at The Hague, to try to prevent the choice of Brantzen as an adjunct. Against Brantzen, Vergennes had argued, for Dutch consumption, that the greater the number of persons involved in the negotiations, the greater the number of complications and indiscretions. But, if the Estates General insisted on an adjunct, Vergennes wanted LaVauguyon to take "confidential steps" to have them select some one more favorable to France. LaVauguyon had found it impossible to satisfy his superior; Brantzen was sent to Paris.[21]

At Paris, he confirmed Vergennes' suspicions of him by repeatedly blaming Vergennes for the way negotiations proceeded. The French, he told the American, John Adams, were "devilishly cunning" and were playing each power off against the other, in order to satisfy their own state's interests.[22]

To Vergennes it seemed that Brantzen arrived at Paris with an extraordinarily pretentious set of demands, considering the Dutch contribution to the war.[23] The Dutch refused to enter into any negotiations for peace until Great Britain recognized all neutral rights, and freedom of the seas, embodied in the principles of the Armed Neutrality. All of Holland's possessions conquered by Britain during the American war were to be returned. Since some of these possessions had been retaken by France, the negotiations here were really with France. Finally the Dutch demanded, with the "greatest of force," that Great Britain pay for the losses and damages caused to Dutch citizens by Great Britain during the war.[24]

Vergennes was willing to agree not to make peace with England without the Dutch,[25] but he insisted that the Dutch had to show moderation in formulating their claims.[26]

The French Ambassador at The Hague and Vergennes were never free of the nagging anxiety that, if the Dutch were unsatisfied, the United Provinces, or even one of the Dutch provinces — most likely the province of Zeeland — might seek a separate peace on its own.[27] When Vergennes tried to communicate to the Dutch Ambassador, Berkenrode, that it was Louis XVI's desire to have all the negotiations proceed at the same pace, and that no one power should agree to a final settlement without the others, Berkenrode objected. He felt that, if Holland could make a favorable separate peace, she should be under no obligation to continue the war. Vergennes warned him that, if France and Spain adopted the same attitude, the Dutch might find themselves completely alone and still fighting England.[28] After considerable wrangling and threatening, Vergennes finally got Berkenrode and the Dutch to consent to the formula that no peace, armistice, or truce would be signed by the United Provinces unless all the other allies were ready to sign similar agreements.[29]

The United States sent three men to make the peace. Benjamin Franklin was a cosmopolitan who appreciated the foreign culture of France without denying his own. A famous scientist, he never lost the curiosity which made him want to listen to others. He also saw the value of preserving confidence in diplomacy without becoming the dupe of it. He had no illusions about the essential goodness of mankind; still he avoided the equally dangerous oversimplification that all men, especially foreigners, were evil. Franklin, unlike his two colleagues, Jay and Adams, accepted conflicts of interest as natural and it was, therefore, possible to disagree with Franklin without running the risk of being suspected of treachery or evil intent. He was always alert to include his two American colleagues in the peace negotiations, yet he did not raise a public outcry (which would have hurt the cause he represented) when they refused to share with him their diplomatic secrets. For months he worked to lay the foundation for a peace with England, yet he watched his colleagues, who obviously distrusted him, take the initiative out of his hands and begin a settlement on their own terms. Even here, however, the man's greatness was not diminished. Secure in his own reputation, he let the younger men make theirs. Indeed, perhaps, this was his finest moment, the moment when "self elimination was the price of peace," not only with Great Britain, but within the American delegation.[30] What might have happened to the American cause at Versailles, if Franklin had been as rigid or vindictive a person as John Adams?

Until the Continental Congress established a commission for negotiating peace in June of 1781, the only American authorized to negotiate for peace was John Adams. He was a human generator of unintegrated passions and contradictions. He believed that "the honest man is seldom forsaken,"[31] yet he suspected nearly everyone of plotting against him. He criticized Franklin's French, which was fluent but ungrammatical. Yet, when Adams was presented to Louis XVI, he was unable to utter a word of French.[32] The French people, he claimed, were "light and lazy," lacking in virtue, in fact, degenerate; yet he was embarrassingly hungry for their flattery. Although he spent a great amount of his time abroad trying to borrow money to keep his struggling country from bankruptcy, he insisted again and again (and again) that the United States was dependent on no powers. He was thoroughly conscious of the expansionist interests of the young Republic he represented, yet proclaimed these interests in the name of Providence, thereby making opposition tantamount to opposing the Almighty. He recognized that the search for time, fame, beauty, or praise was not an admirable "Christian endeavor," but there is evidence enough that a fierce personal ambition burned in the inmost core of his soul.[33] But his private ambitions were always couched in the language of patriotism. Perhaps, because he was personally an obnoxious man, historians have strained to be fair to John Adams. And he was not without virtues. He tried to be scrupulously honest, and when his jealousies or prejudices did not blind him to the truth, he *was* honest. He accepted responsibilities, worked diligently, and noted it all, detail for detail, in his "Diary", to convince himself (for he was his own most pitiless critic) that he bore his share of the world's work. When he arrived in France, for the first time in 1778, he failed to announce his arrival to Vergennes, as polite diplomatic conduct required, but he did note that the public business of the American commissioners at Passy had "never been methodically conducted. There never was, before I came, a minute book, a letter book, or an account book . . . ."[34] Franklin, busy with other affairs (not all of them strictly diplomatic), paid scant attention to such things. Adams put his feet under the table and straightened out the records, brought some order into the commission's financial affairs, and gave greater regularity to the correspondence. As a diplomat, John Adams had much to learn, but he revealed very early an unusual talent as an embassy clerk.

When Adams returned to France for the second time in 1780, this time to negotiate peace, he remembered to report his presence to Vergennes, but he obviously had not yet learned much about the elementary courtesies of diplomacy. He opened the discussions with Vergennes in such a way as to suggest that he was trying to go over the head of Benjamin Franklin, whom he considered duped by the French, and even senile. At the same time, by his self-righteous rudeness, he tactlessly destroyed any possibility of replacing Franklin at the French court.

The third American Commissioner, John Jay, was a son of a wealthy colonial merchant, grew up with the advantages provided by wealth: private tutors, books, and self-confidence. He was, according to one source, a "serious," "grave," and "sedate young man," although as he grew older his self-confidence "begat a not disagreeable vanity."[35] His admission to the bar, at the age of twenty-three, launched him on a career as a successful lawyer in New York City. Intelligent, well-established, and at home in the proper social circles, John Jay seems never to have been tortured by the conflicts and passions that consumed John Adams. Nor, in his philosophical speculations, did he ever range so far or so daringly as did Benjamin Franklin. Nevertheless, he was capable of deep commitments and, once he became committed, he was completely committed, as his work in the Continental Congress testified.

Jay's debut into diplomacy, however, broke the habit of success and was, for personal as well as public reasons, unfortunate. Leaving a world where he was respected as an established and responsible leader, he was sent to Madrid to win recognition and assistance for the United States. The task was an impossible one from the start, and could only lead to frustration for him. In Madrid, neither he nor his country were respectable, and irritated contempt, rather than respect, became his lot. Floridablanca said of him: "His two chief points were: Spain, recognize our independence; Spain, give us more money."[36] From his humiliating purgatory in Spain he was called, in 1782, to go to Paris and become a commissioner to negotiate peace. He journeyed to Paris in spite of "bad roads, fleas, and bugs," carrying in his heart deep suspicions of European diplomats, and a determination to succeed. He arrived in Paris on June 23, 1782.[37]

When Fox resigned from the Foreign Office in July of 1782, his representative at Versailles, Thomas Grenville, "sent without any authority" in May, immediately demanded his own recall. "It being my fixed purpose," Grenville admitted, "to decline any further prosecution of this business."[38] Allyne Fitzherbert replaced him. The negotiations for the Peace of 1783 became the stairway to promotion for a handful of young British diplomats, and among them was Fitzherbert. He was not quite thirty when he arrived in Paris in July of 1783. A graduate of St. John's, Cambridge, he began his diplomatic career in 1777 as Minister to Brussels, where he remained until Lord Shelburne sent him to Paris. Although he did not see the peace negotiations to their final signatures, Fitzherbert it was who helped frame the necessary preliminaries. He was a popular conversationlist, a raconteur, and of above average intelligence, according to his friends, but indifferent about business, "and not attentive enough to his post,"[39] as one of his critics later complained. At Paris, however, he demonstrated an unusual competence.

The chief Spanish negotiator at Paris continued to be the Count d'Aranda. He received from Charles III his full powers to negotiate, in August, 1782.[40] The significant fact about his role in Paris was the growing rift between Aranda and his superior, Floridablanca. While Floridablanca was willing to move heaven and earth to obtain Gibraltar, Aranda always felt that the value of Gibraltar to Spain was secondary to the value of the Spanish Empire in America. This difference between them, Aranda's independence of character, and his personal resentments against Floridablanca, who often treated him with contempt, were to have important consequences as the peace negotiations drew to a close.

Spanish plans for peace early in the war were based on the idea of a long truce, with the belligerents on the American continent remaining in possession of whatever territory they controlled militarily. At Philadelphia and Versailles, that idea was never considered as anything other than a bad settlement. But, in Spain, the notion of a truce based on *uti possidetis* was never completely abandoned; it remained a virile arrow in Floridablanca's diplomatic quiver for the remainder of the war. In the secret Hussey-Cumberland negotiations, the same formula was once again taken out of its wraps and given serious consideration.[41]

Franco-Spanish discussions of a truce, during these early exchanges, have raised questions in some minds as to whether Vergennes honestly wanted to secure the independence of the United States. The answer is an unequivocal "Yes." While a long-term truce was not the most desirable outcome of the war, it did not deny the guarantee of independence. Article Eight of the Treaty of Alliance had, in fact, provided for a possible truce, and history demonstrated to Vergennes that such a route to independence, while not the ideal one, was not impossible. The Dutch Republic had, in fact, achieved its independence this way. Furthermore, to assure the United States that France would stand behind American independence, Vergennes even suggested a further treaty to assist the Americans if, at the end of a truce, the English tried to subjugate them.

Yet, there is no question that a truce based on *uti possidetis* was a difficult pill for Americans to swallow. Vergennes also found this solution distasteful. For that reason, he never considered it as anything but a solution *in extremis.* But there were bleak months during the long and exhausting war when even the most dedicated and loyal Americans had to consider the terrifying prospect of defeat. Vergennes also looked defeat in the face. He did so, especially, as his confidence in American military potential was shattered, and as Necker ceaselessly hounded him with the undeniable fact that France could not continue to bleed herself financially to support the war.

In September, 1780, several members of Louis XVI's Council concluded that France had to make an immediate peace, and that she should inform Spain. Vergennes fought the move because he was not yet ready to give up: "Yesterday Your Majesty heard," he wrote in a note to Louis XVI, "what M. le Comte de Maurepas said about the situation of His Majesty's finances. It is truly alarming, and seems to leave no other alternative but peace, and the most prompt peace."[42] Spain's need for peace, Vergennes was certain, was just as pressing as that of France. Nevertheless, he stressed that he did not wish to confess to Spain that France had exhausted her resources and needed Spain to procure the peace. He did not wish, of course, to confess the bankruptcy of his own policy. Furthermore, if Spain made the peace, the initiative would pass from Versailles to Madrid, and Vergennes' own pride rebelled against such an alternative. In addition, he knew that Spain had no reason at all to respect France's commitments to her American allies. Thus, if Spain made the peace, Louis XVI's influence as protector of the small powers might be jeapordized; Vergennes wanted to preserve that influence if he could.

Vergennes' alternative to a Spanish-initiated settlement of the war was to accept a formal offer of Catherine II, made in December of 1780, to be mediator. Now riding the crest of prestige as a result of having welded together an Armed Neutrality block, Catherine sought further avenues of influence in European politics. Vergennes, who never abandoned the idea of a *rapprochement* with Catherine, accepted her offer to mediate. The British, who knew that their declaration of war on Holland had displeased Catherine, did not wish to displease her further, so they, too, accepted, requesting, however, that Austria be asked to serve as co-mediator. Spain preferred not to abandon her own secret negotiations, carried on with the two English agents, Thomas Hussey and Richard Cumberland, but when England recalled Cumberland, Floridablanca accepted the Austro-Russian mediation as second best; Spain, too, was nearly exhausted.

Vergennes had qualms about the British request that Austria be a co-mediator. If Joseph succeeded in getting the diplomats to come to Vienna, he would surely find an opportunity to avenge Vergennes' earlier opposition to his ambitions. Furthermore, Joseph's intimacy with the English, plus the fact that the Russian ambassador at Vienna was a weak man who could be led around by the Austrians, displeased Vergennes. In this discouraging situation, Vergennes again considered the possibility of a settlement providing for a long-term truce based on *uti possidetis* except for New York, which, he insisted, the British must evacuate. But he clearly recognized that Louis XVI would be "somewhat violating his engagements," and "that he would be giving the Americans just cause for complaint or, at least, distrust, if he should propose to Congress to sign a truce leaving the English what they possessed on the American continent. Therefore, only the mediators, who were bound by no ties, could make a proposition so painful to the United States." These were, indeed, "the blackest days of the war."[43]

Vergennes' position does not mean, however, that he prepared to make a settlement behind the backs of the Americans. He called in John Adams and laid the unpleasant facts before him. Understandably, Adams refused categorically to treat with the British unless the mediating powers "would acknowledge and lay down as a preliminary the sovereignty of the United States, and admit their minister to a Congress."[44] Neither the mediators nor King George could accept these conditions, and Vergennes was faced with the choice of either abandoning his allies or fighting another costly campaign. He chose the latter course, but, in doing so, he led his King another step closer to bankruptcy. The war continued, the deficit grew, and John Adams assured himself (and others) that *he* had saved American independence.[45]

CHAPTER 27

The Crisis of 1783

In June of 1782, a revolt broke out in the Crimea against the Khan of the Crimea, Shahin Girai, a Russian puppet.[1] Suddenly he found himself face to face with an insurrection of Tartars led by his own brother. Alienated from his subjects by a record of almost-animal brutality and cruelty, the Khan was unable to muster any assistance. He gave up and fled. His brother, momentarily the popular hero, was elected Khan.

According to the Treaty of Kuchuk Kaynarji (1774), the Crimea was "entirely independent of every foreign power, governed by their own Sovereign, of the race of Ghengis Khan, elected and raised to the throne by all the Tartar peoples."[2] The Tartars, therefore, had a perfect right to exercise their sovereignty by electing whomever they pleased as Khan. But almost immediately the Porte and St.Petersburg began circling the crisis, looking for an opportunity to exploit it. The Porte declared that if Russia agreed to stay out of the Crimea, so would she. But the Porte's benevolence was conditioned by the gratifying knowledge that the deposed Khan had been Catherine's tool. Catherine, on the other hand, found neutrality the least acceptable of all the possible responses. The revolt furnished the perfect occasion to fish in troubled waters, and advance her own and Joseph II's plans of expansion. Furthermore, the overthrow of the Khan Girai was a blow to her prestige. The rumor that the new Khan was in favor at the Porte, and would, perhaps, even receive help from them, did nothing to restore her composure. By August, 1782, the affair had grown into an ugly crisis. Catherine loudly accused the Turks of having instigated the rebellion. It was obvious to everyone that she was broadcasting her justification for intervention.

If Russia moved into the Crimea, the Porte would find it difficult to stand aside. Joseph would be tempted to follow his heroine into the fray, and Frederick could not allow Joseph to expand unless he did too. As the dominoes in Eastern Europe began to tumble, Vergennes had to make the difficult choice between backing Austria's aggressions or bailing out the sinking Turkish Empire. In either case, France, as well as all of Europe, might slide into the jaws of war.

Vergennes' experience at Constantinople had made him very skeptical of the Turks' ability to undertake a major war, and he did not wish to make the mistake that he felt Choiseul had made, of urging the Turks into a foreordained military catastrophe. His first reaction to the crisis, therefore, was to warn the Turks of the dangers of a premature intervention in the Crimean crisis; and the Turks, at least at first, seemed content to accept his warning, although they made it clear to the Russians that they felt the Tartars were well within their rights to get rid of one Khan and elect another.

Catherine could not accept such a view. She regarded the new Khan as not representing the "Tartar nation." Certainly, he did not represent *her* interests in the Crimea, and she did not intend to recognize him. After a brief warning to the Tartars, she blockaded the ports of the Crimea and ordered her cumbersome war machine into motion.[3] Her aim was not simply to restore the deposed Khan, but to incorporate the entire Crimea into her own Empire. Furthermore, as the French ambassador to St. Petersburg clearly saw, the ambitions of Catherine were not limited to the Crimea: "Many are persuaded," he wrote to Versailles, "that Russia seeks less to establish the Khan than to force the Turks into a war which would provide the occasion for the execution of the Czarina's grand projects."[4] The time to harvest the fruits of the rendezvous at Mogilev had arrived. By November of 1782, the conclusion that Catherine was determined to open a war was confirmed by her stubborn refusal to consider any offers of the Porte (offers originally suggested by the French Ambassador) to establish a commission of inquiry to look into the Crimea problem. Rebuffed by Catherine, the *Re'îs Efendi* was left to face the specter of war. Within a week, it appeared in a Russian *ultimatum*.

The *ultimatum*, dated November 15, 1782, and drawn up with the consent and cooperation of Austria, contained a list of specious Russian grievances against the Ottoman Empire, followed by a series of extravagant demands. The *ultimatum*, like a scorpion, had its stinger in its tail: "The acceptance of these propositions which the Court of Russia offers to the Ottoman Porte," the *ultimatum* ended, "constitutes the only way to prevent disagreeable events . . . ." A note attached to the *ultimatum* made it unmistakeably clear that Austria stood firmly behind Russia and would not view a refusal "with indifference." To emphasize this point, Joseph backed up words with a flurry of troop movements along the frontier of the Ottoman Empire. In the Crimea, the former Khan, Girai, escorted by fifteen thousand Russian soldiers, marched back into his former realm and overwhelmed his opponents.[5]

As soldiers marched to the east, Joseph kept an eye on his neighbor in the west. He wrote to his ambassador at Versailles, Mercy d'Argenteau, and explained the details of his maturing project, and pointed out to him how vital France's assistance or, at least, her neutrality was to the success of his plans. Louis XVI and Vergennes had already made their decisions regarding the partition of the Ottoman Empire and they did not leave room for Joseph's plans. The coming peace between England and France, Vergennes warned the Austrian ambassador, would make the Empress Catherine "think twice" before she took up arms, "for she cannot be unaware that there is not a single Power in Europe which will not risk its last man, and its last penny, to prevent the ruin of the Ottoman Empire."[6] Mercy d'Argenteau left his interview with Vergennes with no doubts as to the French position on his master's policies. But Joseph refused to be deflected from his course.

Simultaneously Vergennes labored to make peace with England. He knew (and he knew that Catherine knew) that, when France freed herself from the American war, she would be in a much better position to make her influence felt in the East. But Catherine was also aware of the importance of time. She had launched her adventure when she did in order to complete it before the English and French settled their quarrel.[7] The maneuvering of Catherine and Vergennes over the Ottoman Empire took on the character of a match of two able champions, and destroys the neat conception of eighteenth-century diplomacy as operating like a mechanical and balancing device. In the winter of 1782, the Anglo-French War was not yet settled and, until it was, Catherine held the trump cards. Unable to turn his full attention to the East, Vergennes resigned himself to a limited victory for the Czarina, but he wanted to avoid the total destruction of the Ottoman Empire. To do this, he decided to encourage the Turks to give Catherine some satisfaction. Such a game was extremely dangerous, and Vergennes played it with no illusions. He hoped to gain time, until France was in a better military and diplomatic position. At Constantinople, the French ambassador, Saint-Priest, even collaborated with the Austrian ambassador to persuade the Turks to meet the Czarina's demands.[8]

At the same time, Joseph would not enjoy Catherine's sense of achievement. Vergennes advised the Porte to cede to Russia and to resist Austria, who was much more exposed to a French attack. Vergennes knew that Joseph was not likely to continue his association with the Russians if he did not share in the rewards. Thus he worked to blunt the Austro-Russian aggressive alliance, and save whatever he could of the Ottoman Empire. He also tightened up the Franco-Prussian *rapprochement* already cautiously begun. His tactics became more effective with time. As the spring of 1783 approached, the Anglo-French peace was all but settled. France daily gained more freedom of action. Joseph's freedom, inversely, became more restricted.

But Joseph was too committed to bow out gracefully. He continued his arms build-up on the frontier of the Ottoman Empire and continued to press Egypt into Louis XVI's hands. Louis XVI remained uninterested, but the problem, unfortunately, did not grow any less serious. Encouraged by success, Catherine now sought a pretext for another thrust at the Turks. A Russo-Turkish commercial treaty in the process of negotiation offered a variety of causes for provocation.[9] Vergennes grew concerned about whether or not the Ottoman Empire really could be saved. The Turks frantically offered France a treaty of defense, but France was in no position, either financially or geographically, to fight Russia. But if France refused, would the Turks write off French friendship as useless? Cornered, Vergennes tried to get out of his predicament with flattery: The Sultan surely had no cause to borrow the forces of outside powers. He could defend himself with his own resources.[10] But, Vergennes surely asked himself, could he really?

The critical situation, however, was not hopeless. Vergennes learned that Frederick of Prussia was maneuvering at Constantinople to form some sort of agreement that might give Catherine pause. In Frederick's moves, Vergennes saw France's opportunity. He advised the Turks to consider seriously Prussia's offers of an alliance,[11] and he thereby planted one more seed of cooperation between Frederick and Louis XVI.

At the same time, Vergennes tried to woo Joseph away from Catherine with the idea of a concert between France and Austria designed to "prevent and contain the disorders which menace Europe because of Catherine's ambition."[12] Joseph, still not convinced that France really would block his ambitions in the East, gave a vague, non-committal answer. This only increased Vergennes' concern, as the Russians negotiating with the Turks on the commercial treaty were now openly belligerent. Once again Vergennes decided that the best of the bad alternatives was to appease Russia and stand firm against Austria. Again Saint-Priest was told to recommend such a policy to the Turks.

But the Turks were reluctant to back down on every issue, especially on issues which involved important economic interests. By April, 1783, Catherine's military was again poised, ready to move, and Joseph once more gave her his support. There was nothing in the way, now, of an all-out strike against the Turks. Catherine needed only a pretext, and it came when an agent of Catherine's puppet, the Tartar Khan, was assassinated under mysterious circumstances. It was not difficult to hold the Turks responsible for the killing; Catherine now had her justification for war.

Catherine's actions forced Joseph to step up his contacts with Versailles for he could not safely play his part in the coming war without French acquiescence. Once more he dangled Egypt before Vergennes' eyes. "Egypt!" Vergennes exploded, exasperated. "We would not accept those

Muslims if you gave them to us."[13] France neither wanted nor needed new conquests, he once again explained. Furthermore, he could not see what Joseph expected to acquire in this adventure.

As the implications of his position closed in on him, Joseph became more and more uncomfortable. "What a difference," he wrote to Catherine in a lament, "between your Majesty's position and mine . . ."[14] Catherine would not wait for Joseph to secure his rear.

Aware that the human costs of war require some kind of justification, Catherine declared her "love of humanity," and her firm desire for a solid and permanent peace,[15] and ordered Potemkin to the Crimea to take charge of the army. The Khan of the Crimea, her own puppet, resigned and she took possession of the entire province. Her action was only the beginning of a plan to unite the Crimea, Kuban, and the Isle of Tamon with her Empire. If the Turks opposed her (her action was a brutal violation of the Treaty of Kuchuk Kaynarji), she self-righteously vowed to "oppose force with force."[16] To her ally *le plus intime*, Joseph, she advised that now was the time to "round out and augment his possessions at the expense of the common enemy."[17] Joseph's upright and virtuous mother had never provided him with the experience to deal with such a woman. He needed time to prepare for his own security, and he feared a Franco-Prussian agreement against him. He temporized. He urged the Turks to give in. If only France would come around. He could do nothing without France, and France, it seemed, could neither be bought nor bribed. Nevertheless, he decided to try once more.

On a pleasant Monday in June of 1783, the Austrian ambassador the Comte d'Argenteau, stepped down from his carriage and entered the garden of the home of the Comte de Vergennes.[18] It was the day before their customary weekly meeting at the Ministry of Foreign Affairs. They exchanged pleasant good days and, after a turn in the garden, Vergennes invited Mercy into his study. There he offered the Ambassador a chair at his desk and took another directly across from him. When both men were seated Mercy opened a copy of a document written by the Empress of Russia and addressed to Prince Galitsin, her ambassador to Vienna. Solemnly, Mercy began reading it aloud, but Vergennes, realizing at once the significance of the document, asked to read it himself. Willingly Mercy handed the manuscript over to Vergennes who, slowly and with great attention, began to read. When the Frenchman finished reading the communication from Catherine, Mercy then showed him several dispatches from Joseph. For nearly an hour Vergennes read on, stopping occasionally to take notes, while Mercy, seated opposite him, carefully watched the Minister's face for signs of a reacton. Vergennes revealed nothing. The only thing his face did not conceal was his obvious appreciation that the affairs treated in the papers before him were grave.

And indeed they were! For Joseph had revealed to Vergennes all of Catherine's projects and told him that a decision could no longer be postponed. He considered it extremely dangerous to be a "spectator" while Russia expanded southward, yet he was in no position to stop such expansion unless France was willing to assist him, with "all her forces," against Prussia, whom he suspected of being ready to pounce on Austria if Joseph should oppose Russia. Furthermore, Joseph wanted from Versailles some kind of clearly drawn plan that could assure the preservation of the Ottoman Empire. He confessed, however, that he really did not believe that such a plan could be devised, for, already, Russia had established an unshakable position in the Crimea. Joseph admitted that he could remain neutral and let Catherine have her way, but this alternative, he feared would probably end in Russian preponderance in Eastern Europe. The only acceptable alternative, as far as Joseph could see, was for Austria to assist Russia in the partition of the Ottoman Empire, and "appropriate to herself a part of Turkey." Joseph was already prepared to go to war to carry out this alternative, but he needed the approval of France and reassurance that, if Prussia attacked him in the rear, France would carry out the obligations of the Hapsburg-Bourbon alliance.

Catherine's letter and Joseph's dispatches left Vergennes numb and depressed. "That day," Mercy later recorded, "Monsieur de Vergennes was almost completely disheartened. He complained of a fate that plagued him. No matter where he was, there were always difficulties to unravel." Vergennes tried to tell Mercy, who disiked him immensely, what embarrassment the communications caused him. He needed time to reflect, he told the Austrian. But Mercy could not wait; he wanted an answer by early the next day. Vergennes protested. Such serious problems had to be taken up with the King and the Council. It was impossible to make a decision so soon. Still, Vergennes sadly closed the conversation with a weak promise that he "was going to preach moderation to Petersburg and patience to the Porte."

The next day, Mercy found Vergennes recovered from his depression and (to Mercy's discomfort) now, more than ever, determined to protect the Ottoman Empire as much as it was in his power to do so. Furthermore, he was in no mood to accept Joseph's thin rationalizations for dividing up that tottering Empire. If Joseph took Turkish territory to maintain the equilibrium with Russia, Vergennes pointed out, then Prussia would have to take something to maintain the equilibrium with Austria, and so on *ad infinitum.* The stability of Europe would be completely undermined by such a chain reaction.[19]

Yet Mercy was still under orders to make as strong a case as possible for his master's position, so he repeated his formula about the need to guard the balance of power, and reminded Vergennes that, after all, the reward (Egypt) that Louis XVI would get if he went along with Joseph would be *fort belle*.[20] Still not tempted, Vergennes countered with the argument that, if Austria took Moldavia and Wallachia, the frontiers of Russia and Austria would be moved together. How could Austria avoid trouble with such an aggressive neighbor? Mercy dodged the issue by saying that he did not know what Joseph would want as his share of the territory.

But Vergennes was not yet prepared to join a conspiracy to precipitate the death of the Ottoman Empire. He knew as well as everyone else that the Sultan was ruling on borrowed time, and that, eventually, there would have to be a settlement of the "Eastern Question," and probably partition, but he wanted the settlement to be a gradual one that would not suddenly knock the very foundations out from under the European system. Until a less radical solution was found, he preferred "to remedy the present evils."[21]

While the two diplomats talked at Versailles, Catherine's soldiers completed the conquest of the Crimea and rolled on into the Kuban. Knowing that his own monarch desperately needed peace, and that the Ottoman Empire could not plunge into war without risking its very existence, Vergennes continued to follow the only route he saw open: further appeasement of Russia. We must "ward off the storm by giving satisfaction to the Empress. . . ." At the same time, however, he was determined to hold Joseph in check. His decision was not a happy one. He knew it could lead to further and further demands by Catherine, and it would put a dangerous strain on the Franco-Austrian alliance. His choice might even lead to war at the end of the labyrinth, and another war would push France over the edge of financial chaos. He wrote to his friend and ambassador to Spain, Montmorin: "By showing ourselves indifferent we would have committed a crime in the eyes of the Turks, and they would have presented our behavior to all Europe as indicative of at least a tacit agreement [with the aggressor], and our weakness would have attracted to us the contempt of all Europe. We have no other choice but to disapprove and to excite the Court of Vienna to opposition." "If we succeed," he concluded, "it is most probable that we will prevent the fall of the Ottoman Empire. If we fail, the King will at least have performed his duty, and his Majesty will then have the right to act according to his own interests and as circumstances permit. . . ."[22]

Throughout the month of June the crisis deepened, and the strains on Vergennes' physical and mental resources accumulated. Before long his health deteriorated, until he was so feeble that he was unable to get out of bed. Still his work did not stop. He confessed to Mercy, who came to visit him in his bedchamber, that he was "hardly able to think." He managed to compose a reply to Mercy's demand for French assistance or neutrality, a reply which stimulated the disappointed Mercy to complain that Vergennes' answer was more "the writing of a lawyer than the language of a Minister of Foreign Affairs of a great Power." The acts suggested by Catherine and Joseph, Vergennes had written, represented a new and dangerous "system of political jurisprudence" which could easily "prepare the way for successive revolutions and the most extraordinary confusion." Joseph, Vergennes went on to advise, should intervene *vis-à-vis* Catherine to try to bring her to the "principles of moderation and equity." At the same time, he promised, France would "raise her voice" to try to "deflect or calm so frightening a storm."[23] The issue, as Vergennes clearly saw it, was whether or not a "grand Empire which held a place in the general balance" would continue to exist.[24]

Louis XVI was particularly disposed, Vergennes told Mercy in the sick-room interview, to work with Joseph, and "all other well-intentioned Powers, in favor of public tranquility." When France took such a position, Vergennes predicted, "Europe would join her." He then proposed a mediation between Russia and the Turks. Vergennes knew that such a mediation would lead to further Russian acquisition of Turkish territory, but at least some of the Empire would be saved. In any event, the affair would be localized, and Joseph would get nothing. To add a sprig of fear to his already unsavory offering, Vergennes suggested that Austria and France bring Prussia into the affair. Both Mercy and Joseph knew that they could never work with Frederick on this problem, but they were intelligent enough to see that, perhaps, France and Prussia might manage a *rapprochement.* Both were wise enough, also, to see that Vergennes' suggestion was, in effect, a veiled threat that France might seek just such a *rapprochement.* With France and Prussia collaborating, Joseph would not dare to undertake a military adventure in the East. When Mercy received the sick Vergennes' answer, he, too, was sorely discomfited. How could Louis XVI, he protested indignantly, not attend to the needs of the Emperor, his master, when he had seen all of the confidential documents?[25]

But Vergennes, affecting a gaiety he could hardly have felt, chided Mercy on the suddenness of Joseph's requests, and then coldly reminded him that, if Austria and Russia had an alliance, France had never been officially informed of it. Mercy, in turn, hotly reminded Vergennes that, if France looked upon the aggrandizement of Austria as less acceptable than the aggrandizement of Russia, then the Austro-French alliance had indeed reached a critical state.[26]

Little by little, both men ran out of anything to say to each other. Vergennes sick and weary, dropped his face into his hands and muttered that he had nothing more to add to his King's response. He had another appointment with the Ambassador of England, and the Comptrolleur Général was already waiting outside the door of the sick-room to see him. Discouraged with his failure to change Vergennes' mind, Mercy left the sick man, mumbling that he had come "only for the good of the two Courts." He had hoped to hear from Vergennes "something more pleasant."[27]

Joseph had one more arrow in his quiver: his sister, Queen Marie Antoinette. Mercy immediately went to her and, playing upon the theme that the alliance between her husband and her brother was breaking up, he advised her to approach the King behind Vergennes' back. The Queen's first impulse was to call Vergennes to her chambers and demand an account of his actions, but Mercy counseled the less dramatic, but (he thought) more effective, route of wifely pressure on the King. Obediently, the Queen followed Mercy's advice. But Louis XVI, showing an independence of character that often failed him, would not ditch his Minister of Foreign Affairs in the crisis.

While Joseph and his ministers angrily fumbled with France's refusal to give them permission to despoil the Ottoman Empire, Vergennes, still working from his sick-bed, began the task of sounding the alarm bell and informing Europe of his King's stand, in order to gain whatever support he could for his policy. Spain readily approved, even though the American war left her too weak to do anything.[28]

Vergennes wrote to Catherine and the Porte offering Louis XVI's good offices to help settle the Russo-Turkish conflict. And he could not help reminding Catherine that the legal status of the Crimea had already been fixed by the Treaty of Kuchuk Kainarji.[29] But Catherine made it clear that she was in no mood to debate points of legality. She had made her move, her armies were in possession of the Crimea, and she was well aware that France could do nothing effective to move them out. Her answer made Vergennes realize, more than ever, that his major efforts had to be aimed at containing a further advance towards Constantinople, rather than rolling back the new frontiers.

To develop this alternative he needed the help of Frederick the Great. Consequently, in a memo to Louis XVI, he advanced the proposal that his King and Frederick collaborate to hold Catherine in check.[30] Vergennes knew, when he advanced the idea, that he was personally challenging the Queen of France. Her concern for Joseph's interests at Versailles, and her own personal hatred of Frederick, meant that she would fight with every weapon at her disposal to prevent the King's approval of such a policy. Furthermore, Mercy lost no opportunities to warn her that this crisis could prove to be the very "touchstone" of her reputation and influence. If she failed here to influence policy, if she failed to undermine Vergennes' hold over the King, no one would ever again take her political influence seriously.[31]

Yet, in spite of everything Marie Antoinette could do, Louis held firm. He backed his Minister's recommendation, and Vergennes ordered Louis' representative at Berlin to open discussions of the question with Frederick.[32] Vergennes was resigned to the Turkish loss of the Crimea, but he hoped Catherine would be satisfied with that territory and Kuban. An understanding with Frederick was the instrument to convince her to be satisfied.

The progress of Vergennes' policy was hindered by the English Ambassador at St. Petersburg, Harris, who seemed indifferent to what Catherine did to the Turks. England was apparently content to let Russia destroy the Ottoman Empire. In fact, when Harris was asked by the Russian Chancellor what would be England's reaction to a war between Russia and the Turks, with France possibly supporting the Turks, Harris assured the Russians that England would back the Russians with "real assistance" if France intervened. England learned to regret that policy in the nineteenth century.

Once Joseph accepted the fact that France would not support him, he tried another tack. He asked France to mediate a settlement between Austria and the Turks, hoping to get what he wanted by these means.[33] But Vergennes simply would not participate, in any fashion whatsoever, in an Austrian division of the Ottoman Empire. He accepted the Russian aggression only because he could do nothing about it, but his means of restraint were not so limited in the case of Austria. Even Mercy seems to have been amazingly slow in recognizing the true shape of Vergennes' policy, and as he did, his personal anger with Vergennes increased in proportion as the truth dawned. Mercy was not alone in his fury. When the Austrian Chancellor Kaunitz learned of Louis XVI's course of action, he stormed and shouted at the French Chargé d'affaires, Barthélemy, as if the poor man had himself been the originator of the policy.[34]

Satisfied, for the moment, with her enormous gains, Catherine agreed to accept the good offices, proffered by Vergennes, to settle the Russo-Turkish dispute, although she refused in advance to give up the Crimea or Kuban. Her finances were in utter disorder, and her army was disintegrating from the bacteria of the plague; she welcomed a settlement. Vergennes accepted Catherine's conditions, but also advised the Porte to cultivate further a *rapprochement* with Frederick, in case Catherine and Joseph did not show moderation.

The French acceptance and encouragement of a Prussian role at Constantinople delighted Frederick.[35] He considered his friendship with Russia dissolved, as a result of the collaboration and alliance of Joseph and Catherine, and Catherine had confirmed his opinion by refusing to renew the alliance with Frederick.[36] Frederick also saw the opportunity as a chance to cut the ties that bound France to Austria. Vergennes, however, was not prepared to go that far. He did not want Austria to use the alliance with France to further Austrian expansionist ambitions, but he by no means wanted to destroy it. Furthermore, Frederick, now an old man, was not really anxious to risk a war to gain France's friendship.

Nevertheless, Vergennes' ostentatious preparations for treating with Frederick had the desired effect. Joseph was forced to recognize how far Vergennes might go to save the Turks. Diplomatically, Joseph was boxed in, and, militarily, he was outnumbered. Without France's good will he could do nothing in the East, and, if he deliberately cut himself loose from his French alliance, he created the conditions for a Franco-Prussian alliance. These realities were Vergennes' trump cards and he played them with supreme skill. Led astray by a bold woman, and outpointed by a master diplomat, Joseph had to admit defeat. "Like a gallant knight," he wrote to Mercy, "I have renounced all temptation, for it is the only way I can, at the same time, keep my relations with Russia, my alliance with France, and save the Porte."[37]

Mauled and wounded as they were, the Turks were saved — at least momentarily. In the treaty signed with the Turks in 1784, Catherine kept the Crimea and Kuban, and the Isle of Tamon. Vergennes, now more conciliatory, assured Joseph that France had made no alliance with Prussia. He was telling the truth: there was no alliance with Frederick, for an alliance had not been necessary. The simple threat of one had been enough to force Joseph to abandon his reckless schemes. The terrible vision of losing his friends in the West had made Joseph more sensitive than ever about protecting his alliance with his brother-in-law. Recognizing this, Vergennes let the Prussian negotiations drop, and busied himself with repairing the alliance with Austria. He replaced his ambassador to Vienna, Breteuil (who had borne the brunt of Austrian wrath), with the Marquis de Noailles, and gave his new appointee orders to do everything possible to soothe Austrian tempers and restore Franco-Austrian relations to their former strength.[38]

France emerged from the crisis of 1783 a shaky arbiter and spokesman for European peace and Louis XVI, momentarily, enjoyed the respect and honor of the role. Nevertheless, the Turks had lost Kuban, the Crimea, and the Isle of Tamon, and the Treaty of Küchük Kainarji had been shamelessly violated. Even so, Catherine had not achieved all her aims. Her dream of a new Byzantium with her grandson on the throne remained only a dream; her plans and Joseph's to carve up the Ottoman Empire had to be discarded.

Skillfully Vergennes had halted Austrian expansion and, at the same time, preserved the French alliance with Joseph. This accomplishment was no mean feat, for it had been necessary to bring a good deal of unpleasant pressure to bear on Joseph. Yet, while doing so, Vergennes could never forget that his monarch could not afford to break with Austria, for, the "day that the Court of Vienna separates from France," he had earlier written, "she will have England for an ally."[39]

In the process of executing his delicate task, Vergennes had found further grounds for common action with Frederick of Prussia. To be sure, no alliance was made, but the possibility of one was now real, and the possibility alone could be useful as leverage against any future adventures by Joseph. Vergennes was fully aware of the value of this new relation with Prussia, and did not hesitate to point it out to his King.

When the storm passed, even Catherine found reason to be pleased with France. By treaty she was now in a position to dominate the Black Sea and enjoy considerable commercial advantages in the area. Since France was the leading trading nation in the Levant, the next logical step in the Franco-Russian *rapprochement,* so tentatively begun in 1774, was to link up the commercial interests of the two powers.[40] Furthermore, if Catherine would accept commercial expansion in the East as a substitute for political destruction of the Ottoman Empire, a serious point of friction betwen France and Russia could be eliminated.[41]

When the year 1783 closed, Vergennes saw the end of the most trying year of his diplomatic career. The peace with England, the agony of the Ottoman Empire, Catherine's uncontrollable ambitions, and Joseph's reckless irresponsibility had taxed his intelligence, strength, and health to the utmost. Throughout his life every unusually demanding responsibility always left him exhausted and ill. But the young Vergennes always sprang back; whereas the older Vergennes (in December of 1783 he celebrated his sixty-fourth birthday) found his capacity for renewal seriously diminished. Fortunately, after 1783 the diplomatic situation in Europe became less critical and the strain was less trying. But the calm in international affairs only meant that the problems of the exhausted treasury and the cries for domestic reforms in France would now come forward. "The burdens of affairs pile up around me," Vergennes had earlier complained, "and no matter how much energy I spend trying to expedite things, I fear that they are going to crush me under their weight."[42]

Perhaps the most dramatic result of 1783, however, was that, as a result of Vergennes' guidance, the great powers of Europe had become aware of the Turkish problem. Turkey soon became the "sick man" of Europe and under the guardianship of Europe. Vergennes himself summed up the achievements of his policy in the East: "No matter how great the sacrifice of the Turks appears, it is a great deal less serious and less fatal than it would have been if there had been a war. . . .[If] there had been a war, the Ottoman Porte, fighting against the two Imperial Courts, would most certainly have succumbed."[43] Thus France helped guarantee that the "sick man" of Europe would linger on into the nineteenth century.

CHAPTER 28

The Vergennes Family

Vergennes moved in the society of the court at Versailles with several social and personal disadvantages. Those who counted in society knew that his wife, the Comtesse de Vergennes, did not have respectable family credentials. They undoubtedly knew that the marriage had occurred without the King's permission, and that Louis XV had refused to allow Madame la Comtesse to accompany her husband to Stockholm because he feared that her reputation might cause a scandal at that Protestant court. When she arrived at Versailles, therefore, she was snubbed and rejected, just as she had been, earlier, at Constantinople.

Vergennes, at least, brought with him the titles of the nobility of the robe. But as Secretary of State he no longer enjoyed the protective coloration of the diplomatic bureaucracy. His faults and social inadequacies became public targets. Furthermore, his inadequacies were readily apparent. He did not enjoy what he called "the dissipations and frivolous amusements" of court life.[1] He was incapable of the light conversation that society found so charming. "I converse with M. de Maurepas," the Spanish ambassador noted, "I negotiate with M. de Vergennes."[2] His attempts at gaiety were sad and "ridiculously bourgeois." His jokes were in bad taste; his stories never ended.[3]

Furthermore, no matter which way he turned, he found enemies who opposed him. Also, when he failed to find posts for his friends, he only added to the number of his enemies.[4] Moreover, the deceptions required for the French intervention in the American War eroded his reputation for honesty, and gave credence to vicious rumors that he used his office for his own personal profit.[5] Even his friends found it difficult to respond to the rumors.

The stresses created by his position and the competitive atmosphere at court frequently left Vergennes or his wife ill. He always contended that the only thing he had earned in his career as diplomat was the ruination of his health. His personal letters often spoke of his rheumatism, his black depressions, and the pains of advancing old age. At Versailles, the pressures accumulated. No matter how much time and effort he devoted to work, the burdens grew heavier. He feared they would crush him.[6]

The Comtesse de Vergennes came to Versailles with delicate health. She frequently suffered from insomnia and melancholy. The few glimpses we get of her are those of an insecure, neurotic woman who had great affection and concern for her husband and sons, but whose life at Versailles was a constant struggle for acceptance and rank. Vergennes himself realized that her frequent fatigue and poor health were the result of the anxieties caused by the never ending visits, ceremonies, and engagements required by their official and social position.[7] Nevertheless, they both continued to make the sacrifices, to suffer the discomforts and pains of life at Versailles, for their family. "It is no longer for ourselves that we live," he once reminded his wife. "It is for our children. A sense of duty has a part, no doubt, in my going on, but do you think I would be so persevering, and that a sense of duty . . . would give me the strength to resist the inconveniences of the climate, and the many other moral and physical mortifications, if I did not hope that my sacrifice will benefit them, and if I could not see my work as breaking ground from which they will harvest the fruits."[8] Vergennes thus devoted his life to his family interests as well as to those of his monarch. Inevitably the question arises: what if he had been forced to choose between the two? According to a contemporary, when Vergennes was asked that question, he refused to answer: "I don't know," he is said to have replied. "Don't press me on that point."[9]

Whether Vergennes harbored a greater loyalty to his family than to his King, we will never know. One thing is certain, however; he expected the King not to forget the interests of the Vergennes family,[10] and certainly Vergennes did not forget them.[11] While Vergennes served as Secretary of State and Minister of Foreign Affairs, he saw to it that position after position went to members of his family. His brother became an ambassador. His brother-in-law, Viviers, and a cousin each received a post as Minister Plenipotentiary. To a nephew went a diplomatic post at Munich. For his two sons he found prestigious assignments in the army, as well as the diplomatic corps.[12] Vergennes' nepotism was not exceptional, of course; he lived in an age when political and social power readily converted into family rank and prestige. In this respect, his actions were representative of his class and his time.

Success carried with it many rewards. Vergennes was born into a noble family of only modest means, and his marriage had brought him no additional wealth or property. One of his contemporaries noted that, in fact, he received nothing from his marriage to his "pretty Greek" but children.[13] Nevertheless, during his lifetime, he systematically accumulated estates and titles that enhanced the family's assets and reputation. He was Secretary, and then Grand Treasurer, of the prestigious Order of Saint Louis. At his death he possessed the comté de Vergennes, which he had inherited from Chavigny as the comté de Toulongeon.[14] He held the baronie d'Uchon,[15] and a seigneurie de Bordeaux. As minister, he not only had an apartment in the palace of Versailles, he also acquired a town house on the Avenue de Paris at Versailles.[16] During his ministry, he requested and received from Louis XVI additional lands of persons who died without successors.[17] He also purchased the seigneuries of Fravenberg and Welferdins in Lorraine.[18] These acquisitions represented substantial additions to the family holdings.[19] The property he accumulated between 1774 and 1787 was valuable and produced a sizeable income.[20] According to his will of 1784, Vergennes' lands, buildings, official posts, and the numerous gifts of furniture and jewels given him by the sovereigns of Europe were worth over 2 ½ million *livres*. The income from his lands totaled 72,000 *livres*.[21] The charge made by his enemies that his office brought him riches, therefore, has some basis in fact.

Vergennes always spoke of his wealth as meager, but his notions of his wealth are deceptive. If a commoner had possessed his wealth, he no doubt would have felt himself rich and with the means to "live nobly." The argument of poverty was sometimes a form of pressure put on the King to grant more favors, and was not unusual during the Ancien Régime.[22]

Yet it is true that Vergennes' income never equalled his expenses. While he was still Ambassador to Stockholm he complained of his inability to meet the costs of his position. "I am not rich," he wrote. Yet the role of diplomat entailed huge expenses if he carried out his assignments in a "noble and decent" manner.[23] The role of Secretary of State, with its added social and official burdens, was even more expensive. The property acquired during his years as Minister hardly met the needs of a family whose social and political responsibilities, now more than ever, had to be carried out in a "noble and decent" manner. Like the French monarchy, the Vergennes family found it increasingly difficult to meet the costs of the role it played and the rank to which it aspired.

When he died, Vergennes' widow and children were so desperately short of resources that they went begging to the King for help. A family friend and official, Gojard, intervened in the widow's behalf and reminded Louis XVI that he had promised the family his benevolence and protection. The "calumnious rumors" of Vergennes "pretended wealth" were "atrocious lies," Gojard told the King. The family urgently needed help. Louis agreed to accord the widow a pension of 20,000 *livres* and 8,000 *livres* each for her sons.[24] The pension was considerably less than widows of earlier ministers received, but the almost-bankrupt treasury could provide no more. Nevertheless, Madame de Vergennes was not satisfied. Furthermore, she was not certain, nor was the government, whether the 20,000 *livres* included, or was in addition to, two earlier pensions totaling 16,000 *livres* which Louis had promised her upon Vergennes' death and the death of her brother. After months of wrangling and negotiation, the two earlier pensions were cancelled and the Comtesse received a pension of 24,000 *livres*.[25] Even this was short of the 30,000 *livres* ordinarily granted to the widows of ministers.

Vergennes knew that his enemies accused him of using his office for personal gain, and the accusation hurt him deeply. In defending himself before the King against his accusors, he denied that the desire for riches motivated him. "I have always preferred esteem to riches," he insisted. And he suggested that, if Louis XVI were not convinced of his rectitude, he would gladly resign his office.[26] Louis XVI was persuaded that he was not abusing his office, for Vergennes' tenure outlasted that of twenty other ministers who served the King.

The humiliations suffered by the Comtesse de Vergennes because of her origins were surely compounded by her husband's desire to promote the family. His conception of her role at Versailles was an impossible mixture of incompatibles. On the one hand, he saw his family as separate from the Court, his home as an escape, a sanctuary, where he could retire from the pressures of affairs of state and find harmony, solitude, and the affections of the family circle. He spent nearly every afternoon and, usually, all day Friday *en famille* playing games with his children or nephews. No one was invited to his house to dine on Friday except the family.[27] In this scene the Comtesse de Vergennes played the role she had played at Constantinople, when she was his secret mistress. She provided an atmosphere of warmth, affections and tranquility, an atmosphere in sharp contrast to the high pressure and aggressive competition of the Versailles bureau and court.

On the other hand, Vergennes also encouraged his wife to be a figure in court society, despite her origins, and despite the painful rebuffs she had received at Constantinople when he tried to introduce her into French society there. The opportunities provided by international politics assisted him in this ambition, as they did in other cases when he wanted to advance members of his family.

Not long after Vergennes became Secretary of State for Foreign Affairs it occurred to the Empress Maria Theresa of Austria and her ambassador to Versailles, Mercy d'Argenteau, that Vergennes might accept the "beneficence and protection" of Marie Antoinette and thereby be under obligation to the Queen's pro-Austrian coterie at Versailles. The most obvious assistance which Marie Antoinette could offer to Vergennes was to become the patron of his wife and introduce her into court society in such a way that it was apparent to everyone that she had the Queen's blessings. The presentation of the Comtesse de Vergennes was a delicate matter, and involved some serious difficulties, but Mercy's circumspect diplomacy and the Queen's willingness to go along with her mother's wishes soon overcame them. The Queen broached the subject to the King, and he agreed to give his support. Marie Antoinette then called in Vergennes and announced to him that the Comtesse would, indeed, be presented at Court.[28] Before the Queen and, later, before Mercy, Vergennes overflowed with gratitude. To the Queen and the Empress, he said, he owed the good fortune of his existence. And he promised that for the rest of his life, he would remember their kindness.[29] Mercy was greatly pleased. The Queen, he thought, already had the loyalty of the Comptrolleur Général of Finances and the Minister of Marine. Now she had certainly won the attachment of the Minister of Foreign Affairs.[30] With such a circle of "protégés," in positions of power, Austrian interests surely would not suffer. On November 20, 1774, therefore, the Comtesse de Vergennes, the Comtesse de Dama, and the Comtesse de Bassompierre were formally presented to their Majesties Louis XVI and Marie Antoinette and to the royal family. The Comtesse de Vergennes was presented by the Marquise de Juigné, whose social and noble respectability no one could challenge.[31] From then on the Comtesse de Vergennes became two persons. She was the affectionate and considerate mother and wife, who shielded her husband and family from the inevitable attrition and cruelties of public life. She was, at the same time, a competitor in that fierce social and court arena.

The Comtesse de Vergennes' life at court became unbearably trying, for Vergennes did not prove to be the Queen's "man". In the King's Council he stoutly resisted the efforts of the pro-Austrian party, and personally led the opposition to Joseph's ambitions. The Queen was enraged and the Comtesse de Vergennes suffered, for the Queen could take away as well as give. Yet neither Vergennes nor the Queen ever gave up using her for their own purposes. Vergennes continued to arrange places for his wife in court society, and the Queen never gave up trying to get political leverage out of the Comtesse's social inadequacies. In 1782, when the future czar of Russia, Paul I, and his wife visited France as the Comte and Comtesse du Nord, Vergennes went to the Queen and suggested that his wife do the honors of conducting the Comtesse de Nord. The Queen agreed, no doubt to put Vergennes under an obligation to her. Vergennes rushed to inform his wife that to perform her social duties she had to be ready that day at noon, or "even a little before," to arrive on time at the apartment of the Comtesse du Nord to accompany her to see the Queen. Vergennes was sensitive enough to realize that such a task, performed on such short notice, would cause his wife "a little embarrassment," but he insisted, nevertheless. "Make use of your good sense," he glibly advised.[32]

Later, when Marie Antoinette wished to have a member of her coterie, the Comte de Guines, re-appointed ambassador to England (Vergennes had earlier dismissed him), she tried, once again, to use the Comtesse de Vergennes. She invited her to dinner in the King's apartment. The Queen was especially considerate to this woman whom Louis XV had contemptously referred to as that "vilaine femme," insisting that the Comtesse sit next to her.[33] But to no avail; Vergennes refused to re-appoint Guines, and the King backed his minister. It is difficult to believe that the Queen allowed the affront to go unpunished, for Madame de Vergennes was much too vulnerable.

Despite the Queen's hostility, the fortunes of the Vergennes family steadily climbed. Their name became one to be reckoned with at the Court, and even among the political and social élite of Europe. But Vergennes recognized that, however much the King rewarded him and his relatives for services rendered, the future of the family fortunes depended as much on the next generation as it did on his own. Therefore, as he worked to promote his family's immediate interests, he also prepared his eldest son, Constantin, to take up, eventually, the family burdens. While the younger son Louis Charles Joseph, was not ignored, the father placed on Constantin's shoulders the family's future.

The education he planned for his sons reflected many of the values of that segment of the French nobility that remained dedicated to the authority of the monarch and service to the King. The father tried to instill in them an appreciation for hard work, loyalty, and, above all, the esteem of those in power. At the same time, the father was determined to find a place for the sons among the nobility of the sword, because the nobility enjoyed greater social prestige than did the nobility of the robe.

From the time when Vergennes returned to France from Constantinople until his death in 1787, his special interest in Constantin's education and social advancement never flagged. At Paris, at Stockholm, and at Versailles he directed and arranged his son's studies. To do this he carried on a continuous exchange of letters with his wife, Constantin, and his tutors.

The Vicomte Constantin de Vergennes received his formal instruction from tutors. Schools and colleges in Ancien-Régime France received sons of the nobility, but, among the nobility and those who aspired to live nobly, the instruction of the young was usually the responsibility of a tutor. It was the thing to do, and it avoided the harsh competition of the college classroom, a competition which sometimes resulted in the implicit ranking of students according to criteria other than social class. Such ranking was apt to be humiliating to a child of noble birth. Once, when Constantin, at the age of 13, was being especially lackadaisical about his studies, the angry father threatened to dismiss the tutors and send the boy to a college if he did not improve. At a college, the father wrote sarcastically, "he will have the glorious advantage of being associated with boys of seven or eight years old.[34]

We know the names of three of Constantin's tutors, and something of the character of two of them. They were the Abbé Baudet, the Abbé Balmain and the Abbé Sabatier de Castres. The Abbé Baudet is mentioned in a letter as Constantin's tutor a year after the family's return to France from Constantinople. The boy was then seven. The father described the Abbé as a "second father", who loved the boy "no less than the father." From this description, we can infer that he had already been in the household for some time. We know very little else about Baudet, however, except that the father considered him an "excellent mentor."[35]

In February of 1771, the father's letters indicate that the Abbé Balmain had become Constantin's tutor. This was, no doubt, François Balmain, a Jesuit, who returned in 1770 to Autun, where he had earlier been a professsor, after the suppression of the Jesuit Society in Lorraine in 1768.[36] The Abbé Balmain seems to have been Constantin's tutor until early 1774, when a sharp conflict of personalities between the two ended in another change of mentors. In a letter to his wife, Vergennes speaks of this *changement de main,* but without much sympathy for the son whose "nonchalance", lack of "application", and refusal to be docile tried the father's patience.[37] Soon after, we find Balmain in Paris, where he remained until the Revolution. He was executed there, in 1792, for refusal to take the oath to the Civil Constitution required of the clergy. The Abbé Baudet returned to the family in 1774 to replace Balmain. Constantin was now thirteen and entering a difficult period of adolescence.

The most famous of Constantin's teachers, however, was the Abbé Sabatier de Castres. He was appointed *instituteur* of the Vergennes children in January, 1776. According to an author of the *Mémoires Secrets* of Louis Petit, Bachaumont, the Abbé Sabatier was the sworn enemy of the "party" of the *philosophes*. And he owed his appointment, still according to the author of Bachaumont's *Mémoires Secrets*, to his reputation as a conservative and *anti-philosophe*. The father, Bachaumont thought, was one of the "old types, a religious man and [an] enemy of the dogmas of modern philosophy."[38] Vergennes, the author implied, had selected a tutor who would speak for the values and interests the father wished to see protected and perpetuated. To attract Sabatier to Versailles, Vergennes, now Secretary of State, paid him 12,000 *francs* annually, and gave him lodging at the Palace of Versailles. When the Revolution exploded in 1789, Sabatier was among the first *émigrés* to leave France.

The writings Sabatier left behind contain contradictory evidence of his opinions and values, and leave the strong impression that he was a literary opportunist. In his early twenties, he had been known for his caustic tongue, his *libertinage*, his "licentious" stories and poems, and as a protégé of the *philosophe* Helvétius. But he soon discarded this role and began publishing works attacking Helvétius, as well as Voltaire, and other *philosophes*. Before long he had gained renown and acclaim as a defender of traditional religion and morals, although his enemies maintained that he had neither.[39] His detractors also claimed that he was a "literary pigmy." A sampling of his writings makes it difficult to contradict the judgment.[40]

Vergennes wanted Sabatier to instruct his children because he spoke for the conservative and traditional interests which the father wished to see protected. What were these interests? Essentially they were three: the Church, the throne, and landed property. The enemy of all three, Sabatier felt, was the new wave of critical thought. If the new thinking continued, Sabatier predicted in 1768 in a letter to Helvétius, before the end of the century France would see the "fall of the clergy, which in turn will bring down the throne, which in turn will bring down the great landed property owners."[41]

Vergennes' attempts to educate his sons reveal something of the character of the father. When fatherly counsel had no immediate effect on Constantin's adolescent tendency to stray from his studies, the father resorted to other means. The year 1774 was Constantin's year of adolescent crisis. Between thirteen and fourteen years old, he exasperated his parents and tutors with his nonchalance and unwillingness to apply himself. The "material" was there, Vergennes said of his son, but the "will" was lacking. A change in tutors did not seem to help. In a letter to his wife, Vergennes expressed his angry disappointment in Constantin's progress. He confessed that he did not have the *sang-froid* to write to the boy directly. But he told his wife to make it clear to Constantin that he had to work, to merit his father's esteem. If that threat did not arouse him, the father suggested, she should try to frighten him with the threat of withdrawal of parental love. Or strike at his *amour propre,* even humiliate him, the father suggested: "It is the only way, perhaps, to direct him towards the most salutary goals."[42]

With his formal instruction, the young aristocrat also needed a place among those who exercised power and influence, if he were to establish his reputation and esteem. In eighteenth-century France, proper placement meant a rank in the army where one would enjoy the social distinction of the nobility of the sword; it meant being at Versailles where one could mingle with Court society, and it meant being so placed that one would have frequent personal contacts with the King, from whom all distinction and power ultimately flowed. When Constantin was barely a teenager, his father began to make the arrangements to fulfill these requirements.

In 1775, a year after the father became Minister of State, and after months of working together had created a certain bond of trust between King and Minister, the Comte made his first request for his son. In Alsace, certain fiefs had been left without heirs when the holder died. "Sire," Vergennes began his note to Louis XVI, "I have two sons; I am raising them to have sentiments of patriotism and *vertu;* but I have little fortune to leave them, and we are not of that class of those who can aspire to outstanding favor." He then asked the King to grant to him and his sons the reversion of ownership of a fief in Alsace. The request was granted.[43]

Encouraged by his success, a year later Vergennes made a further request. "My oldest son [Constantin]," he wrote, "has attained the age required by regulations to enter the military service; his education, which has been reasonably successful, has nourished in his heart those seeds of *vertu,* that I would fear for if he went somewhere away from my surveillance ..... " To avoid the danger of the son's escaping his surveillance, Vergennes asked the King to grant the lad a commission in the *Gardes Françaises de la Porte du Roi,* who were stationed in Versailles. Vergennes explained to Louis XVI that he had already discussed the commission with the Maréchal de Biron, the commander of the regiment. Biron was willing to admit Constantin in the guards, but there were "others," whose names Vergennes did not mention, who prevented it. Vergennes requested that Louis XVI let Biron know that it was agreeable to the King that Constantin enter the guards as soon as there was an opening.[44] Apparently Louis XVI did let Biron know it was agreeable to him. In January, 1777, Constantin entered the *Gardes Françaises* as an *Ensigne.* Three years later, when he was nineteen, he was promoted to *sous Lieutenant,* and, in December of 1783, he was appointed *Capitaine-Colonel des Gardes de la Porte du Roi.* The father's role in these appointments is well-documented. Whatever else Constantin learned from his father, he also learned from him how power and influence was exercised.

The courtier, Bachaumont, claimed that Vergennes' bid for the *Capitaine-Colonel's* position for his son was, in fact, a brutal exercise of power. The Court was shocked by Vergennes' ruthlessness and many reproached him for the way he had "supplanted" the previous *Capitaine-Colonel* in order to secure the position for Constantin.[45] Undoubtedly there was a good deal of petty jealousy in the reproaches; at the same time, there is no question but that the post of *Capitaine-Colonel* experienced an abrupt change of personnel, and that the young Vergennes came out on top. With this appointment, Constantin soon received a commission of colonel of infantry and, in 1786, he was promoted to the rank of *Maître de Camp, lieutenant en deuxiéme,* in the Dauphin regiment of the dragoons.

All of these military appointments and promotions carried with them social distinction, but that of *Capitaine-Colonel des Gardes de la Porte du Roi* was the choicest plum. It was, above all, a position of social and military prestige, and to an ambitious young man it was most useful. At the same time, the position was lucrative.[46] The regiment of the *Gardes de la Porte* was reputed to be one of the oldest of the *Maison du roi;* its origins were said to date back before the time of Saint Louis. The military duties of the *Gardes de la Porte* were light. They had the responsibility, at six every morning, of receiving from the *Gardes du Corps* the keys of the doors to the court of the King's lodging, and they stood guard at the principal entries of the palace until six at night, when they returned the keys and responsibilities to the *Gardes du Corps.* They saw to it that no one entered the palace with any arms other than a sword; they were present at the first and last audiences of ambassadors, they stood guard while the King exercised his own troops at the palace, they saw to it that no carriage or *chaise à porteur* was allowed in the palace court except those of the dignitaries who had rights of entry. These duties brought considerable prestige, because they were associated with the protection of the King himself.

But there were additional privileges. The *Gardes de la Porte* were exempt from taxes, and they had special privileges of justice before the courts. The King himself furnished them with a pint of wine a day and bread for their table. After twenty years of service, a *Garde* could sell his position at a high price and still retain his social, fiscal, and legal privileges. The *Capitaine-Colonel* had additional privileges. When he entered service, he received his ebony and ivory baton of command from the hands of the King himself. But, most importantly of all, he accompanied the King wherever he went.[47]

Vergennes was not content to rest here. In 1781, when Constantin prepared for his marriage, the father asked Louis XVI to grant his son the honor of entering the carriage of the King and following him at the hunt. If granted, Vergennes told the King, the honor would contribute immensely to the successful establishment of the household of the young man, who was on the verge of marriage to *demoiselle* de Lentillhac de Sedières. With the privileges of entering the King's carriage, of accompanying Louis XVI on the hunt, and those belonging to the post of *Capitaine-Colonel des Gardes* Constantin soon moved among the most select, in an aristocratic court that was itself a social and political élite.

Constantin's entry into the military increased his father's surveillance of his development, the steady flow of advice from father to son. Despite the fact that the father's governmental duties consumed most of his time, he still wrote to Constantin. He warned him, as Constantin began his training in the army, not to wear heels during his marching exercises. "It is an excellent way," he said, "to make yourself lame." When Constantin mentioned that his military apprenticeships would undoubtedly take a long time, Vergennes urged him to work hard and shorten it, revealing once again the father's mania to accelerate the young man's education. "You must do so well," he insisted, "that no one will be able to consider you an apprentice for very long." And he reminded Constantin that, when he finished his army apprenticeship, there were some interesting things at Versailles in which he could be instructed, an allusion, no doubt, to Vergennes' determination that Constantin would follow his father in diplomacy.[48]

The father reminded the son to be sure to pay social visits to all the officers of his company, after he had heard a complaint that Constantin was not prompt in fulfilling his social obligations. This was a "duty" that had to be taken seriously, the father declared. When Madame la Comtesse de Vergennes found the social life of the Court painful, "contrary to her taste," and "fatiguing," her sacrifices were described to the boy as her contribution to the son's future career. "The sensitivity of your heart assures me," the father wrote, "that you feel the price of your obligation."[49]

When Constantin finished his military apprenticeship, the father was sincerely pleased and congratulated him. But he did not relax the pressure. Now that Constantin was free of his military duties, the father wanted him to return home. There were still "so many things to learn and I am afraid that, if you get away from your instructors, you will lose the elementary learning that you have [already] received."[50]

As Constantin approached twenty-five years of age, his place in court society was assured. He was an officer of a regiment of the *Maison du roi,* his post guaranteed the opportunity for personal contact with the King, and he was living under the continued surveillance and protection of his father. He was not always as careful of small social obligations as others felt he should be, but he could be excused on the grounds of youth. He did not work as hard as his father wanted him to work, but he had perceived, no doubt, that, while hard work played a role in his father's rise up the social and political ranks, his own position in society was the result of his father's connections and influence. He was certain enough of this fact to allow himself from time to time to indulge his "taste for dissipation," a taste which caused his father great concern.

In 1786 the father judged him ready for the next stage of his education, a tour of Europe that would take him to Sedan, Liège, Brussels, the principal cities of Holland and the Hague; then, on to Dresden, through Bohemia, and finally to Vienna. From Austria, he was to return to France by way of Munich and Strasburg. The itinerary was planned by the father, and, since the United Provinces were torn apart by political dissension, the tour gave birth to rumors that the young man was carrying out a special commission for the father. The father denied that he was using Constantin for such a purpose.[51] If Constantin had a diplomatic commission to carry out in 1786, it was secondary to the main aim, which was to complete the young man's education, to familiarize him with the geography and courts of Europe, and to introduce him to the people who would be of use in his career.[52]

When Constantin arrived at The Hague, the French Ambassador there, the Marquis de Vérac, briefed him on the political situation in the United Provinces.[53] As he travelled north, the father arranged for him to meet the Comte de Maillebois, because, he said, a young army officer ought to pay homage to a general of his experience.[54] When Constantin reached Vienna he had been told to try to win the esteem of the Prince Kaunitz. "It is very important," the father lectured, "that he think well of you and, even, that he let it be known that he does."[55] At Vienna, Constantin was advised to "cultivate everyone who had rank [place], and all those who are responsive to respect."[56] The French Ambassador at Vienna, the Marquis de Noailles, was ordered to present Constantin tő the Emperor. It was arranged for him to meet the Prince de Colloredo and the Comte de Coblenzl. As he returned to France he stopped at Strasburg where his father had arranged for him to meet and talk with the military commander there, the Marquis de Salle.[57]

Constantin was advised, also, to keep his eyes open to the geography, to military affairs, as well as to men and politics. When Constantin had to wait in Bohemia for the Emperor to return to Vienna, the father told him to spend his leisure seeing nearby battlefields where many of the critical battles of European wars had been fought. The city of Vienna, Constantin read, offered a more vast "field of instruction." There one could study "men and affairs."[58]

Since the father intended the tour as an exercise in gaining esteem, he read the reports of each stage of the way with special interest. When Constantin was attentive to the requirements of *politesse* and the principles of *honnêteté*, the father was proud.[59] When he heard praises of the young man's modesty, the father was pleased, although he warned Constantin to be careful and not allow modesty to degenerate into timidity.[60] "Occupy yourself exclusively to merit a good opinion," the father urged, as the young man approached Vienna. The reports arriving at Versailles satisfied the father, but the thought of his son at Vienna made him anxious. "Use, [at Vienna], he wrote to Constantin, "more than anywhere else, your wisdom and prudence . . . ." "Try to win the esteem of Prince Kaunitz."[61]

While Constantin was away from Versailles, his father protected his interests. He watched over the health of his son's young wife and, like a doting grandfather, sent news of the two grandchildren.[62] When details of Constantin's regiment had to be taken care of, Vergennes arranged for them to be handled by the influential Maréchal de Ségur. When Constantin had a candidate to recommend to Louis XVI, to replace an officer who had just resigned, the father saw to it that the recommendation was placed before the eyes of the King. Louis XVI agreed to follow Constantin's recommendation.[63] In more ways than one, Constantin's tour of 1786 taught him the secrets of how power was exercised in Ancien Régime Europe.

In 1787, when bankruptcy threatened the French government, the regiment of the *Gardes de la Porte* was discontinued. By now, however, Constantin, at the age of twenty-six, was ready to follow the footsteps of his father into diplomacy. In September, 1787, he was appointed Minister of Louis XVI to Coblentz. He had travelled through the United Provinces, into Germany and the Holy Roman Empire. He had made contacts there among the men of power. It was quite logical, therefore, that, like his father, he begin his diplomatic career in Germany.

Vergennes, the head of an aristocratic family, was seen by many of his contemporaries as decidedly "bourgeois". The term, no doubt, was intended to be an insult arising from his reputation as a faithful husband. Vergennes enjoyed the domesticity created by his marriage to Anne Viviers. The *comte* and *comtesse* lived together, loved each other, and "did not blush about it."[64] Nevertheless, the Vergennes family record adds more evidence to the view that the nobility of France enjoyed great political influence in the eighteenth century.[65] The family shared with so many other French noble families the rewards and prestige of making the pilgrimage from the provinces to Versailles.[66] The social status gained as a result of his public functions, the accumulated new lands, the military posts gained for his sons, as well as his personal contacts with the King, all contributed to the steady rise of the family. Yet, we must not forget that the rise probably would not have occurred so dramatically if Vergennes and his wife had not been willing to accept the personal sacrifices, the hard work, and even the occasional abuse, from their enemies at Court. The rewards at Versailles were great, but the personal costs were equally so.

CHAPTER 29

Gibraltar

During the spring and summer of 1782, when Grenville was still at Versailles, Vergennes explored with the Englishman several points which needed to be clarified before serious peace talks could begin.[1] Grenville and Vergennes reached an understanding that the negotiations would take place in Paris, not Vienna, and without the mediation of the Imperial powers. The French Secretary of State continued to insist that a preliminary condition for peace was the recognition of the independence of the United States. Also, Louis XVI wanted King George to understand that "justice and generosity" required that France not abandon the United Provinces, since Great Britain was responsible for Dutch participation in the war.[2] Louis admitted, however, that he was not bound by any treaty to stand by the United Provinces, and his willingness to do so cooled perceptibly as he became more acquainted with Dutch demands.

In May of 1782, George III agreed to recognize the independence of the United States, and Grenville notified Vergennes of this on June fifteenth.[3] But the concession was made by the British with the hope that, with her principal demand met, the United States would not be inclined to continue the war to satisfy Bourbon demands.[4]

Grenville also suggested, in another conference with Vergennes, that the Treaty of Paris of 1763 be the basis of the coming peace. At first, Vergennes objected to this suggestion. He could not hear the Treaty of Paris mentioned "without trembling," he told Grenville. He wanted to forget the Treaty of Paris and all preceding treaties, and settle their affairs according to "principles of justice and reciprocal convenience."[5] But, despite his righteous indignation, Vergennes knew that he could not abrogate the Treaty of Paris, which contained settlements involving most of the major powers of Europe. To discard it would have been an irresponsible act.

The North ministry fell, and the Shelburne ministry came to power. With preliminary steps towards peace already taken, the real work of peacemaking remained to be done. The settlement was of worldwide dimensions and despite Vergennes' willingness, indeed insistence, that the negotiations between the various powers be carried on separately, the participants, in fact, could not so easily separate the negotiations. If something were granted by England to one power, it obviously could not be granted to another power. Furthermore, since the diplomats saw the world map in terms of balances, they were continuously bickering over whether one piece of territory, or one concession, really equalled another item offered in exchange. Were Orán or Santo Domingo equal to Gibraltar? Were eighty villages in India the equivalent of the island of Tobago?

On his first mission to London in September of 1782, Rayneval took with him a list of items which Vergennes considered the "means of achieving the preliminaries of peace." The first aim of the war, American independence, was now apparently settled.[6] But Rayneval was to get assurances. Shelburne reassured him on that point; American independence would be "without restriction." Their conversations about other issues, however, led to less definite conclusions. Sénégal, formerly a French possession, Louis XVI now wanted back, with its dependencies. In his instructions to Fitzherbert, Shelburne stated his belief that what France really wanted, when she asked for Sénégal, was a base which provided for "easier purchase of slaves than ... they now have," and not the entire area that was then called Sénégambia. Although Shelburne felt that perhaps some other area might as easily serve the purpose, he did not openly oppose the cession as long as England was left with a share of the gum trade just north of the Sénégal River.[7] George III confessed that he did not know enough about the subject to reach an opinion, but he admitted he would be happy to get rid of a place where the climate "sweeps off a terrible number of my subjects."[8]

France wished to be "re-established" in India, as she had been before the Seven Years War. Vergennes made it clear that Louis XVI did not want to reacquire large territories there. What he wanted were small districts that could serve as security, and provide income for the French commercial houses in India. France wanted a "safe and free commerce in India."

Shelburne advised Fitzherbert that France could not expect to be allowed any fortifications whatsoever in Bengal, but he readily allowed that commercial houses (*comptoirs*), without the surrounding districts, might be allowed in Chandenagore and Musulipatam in Bengal. At Pondichéry and Calicar, England was even ready to allow the French "a sufficient amount of land to protect their town and pay their expenses."[9]

France also wanted the restitution of Santa Lucia, and the retrocession of Dominica.[10] Shelburne was favorable, recognizing that these demands were, in effect, to pay for the French restitution of all the English islands captured during the war.[11]

Finally, Vergennes insisted that England abrogate the articles in the 1763 peace treaty which gave George III the right to maintain a British Commissioner at Dunkirk to prevent the rebuilding of the naval and military installations dismantled and razed after 1763. This aspect of the peace of 1763 was a constant public humiliation for France, according to Vergennes, and he wanted it eliminated. Shelburne recognized that France held this issue "much at heart." Nevertheless, he did not immediately concede to the demand because he hoped to use it for bargaining on other issues.[12] George III agreed: "Dunkirk is certainly of much less consequence than many other points, and therefore, if it can render other terms better, ought not to be in the least an object with us."[13]

In the Franco-English treaty signed at Versailles on September 3, 1783, these minor issues were ironed out. George III ceded to Louis XVI the territory of the Sénégal River with its dependencies, including the forts. In addition, George III restored to France the island of Gorée, which his navy had captured. In return for this cession, Louis XVI guaranteed Great Britain's possession of the territory of the Gambia River with its fortifications. The two parties to the peace also agreed to charge a commission with the responsibility for working out conflicting boundary limits in Africa, and further agreed that, as far as the rest of the African coasts were concerned, Englishmen and Frenchmen could continue their rights of visit according to their custom.[14]

Great Britain returned to France the island of St. Lucia, and ceded to France the island of Tobago. Louis XVI, in turn, promised to respect the rights and religion of British inhabitants in both places and agreed to allow them to emigrate if they so chose.[15]

In India, according to the treaty, Great Britain would return to France any French establishment conquered from France on the coast of Orixa or in Bengal, as well as Mahé and the commercial houses at Suratte. Furthermore, George III promised the subjects of Louis XVI a "free and independent" commerce at Mahé and Suratte and along the coasts of Orixa, Coromandel, and Malabar.[16] Pondichéry was to be returned to France and its possession guaranteed by Great Britain. In return, France was not to exercise her newly-granted rights in such a way as to threaten British subjects in India.[17]

The British concession on Dunkirk pleased Vergennes immensely. As a "sincere proof" of his desire for "reconciliation and friendship," George III consented to the abrogation and suppression of all the articles relative to Dunkirk in any Anglo-French treaties from the peace of Utrecht in 1713 to 1783.[18]

Finally, the two powers agreed to restore to each other all territorial conquests made during the war which were not covered by specific articles in the treaty. They promised to restore them "without difficulty" or "without requiring any compensation."[19] On the question of prizes and seizures, they agreed that all decisions about prizes and seizures made before hostilities began would be submitted to prize courts of the nation which made the capture or seizure and settled according to public law and treaties.[20]

The direct negotiations between England and Spain in 1782 were a final effort in a series of unsuccessful Spanish attempts to make an advantageous peace, with or without France. The Hussey-Cumberland talks of 1780 had explored the possibility of an Anglo-Spanish separate peace and the cession of Gibraltar to Spain, in exchange for some territorial or monetary equivalent.[21] But at the time, Floridablanca was not nearly so ready to make peace as he appeared to be, partly because the combined Bourbon fleets had won an important victory off Cape St. Vincent. Also, Vergennes, now cognizant of the purpose of Cumberland's mission, was doing everything he could to prevent its success.[22] Finally, the British ministry could not bring itself to give Spain a clear-cut answer regarding Gibraltar.[23] In February of 1781, Cumberland received his recall from Madrid, and this episode in Anglo-Spanish relations ended.[24]

The failure of the Hussey-Cumberland mission to produce a peace advantageous to Spain stirred Floridablanca to look with some favor on the attempts, first of Russia, and later of Austria and Russia together, to mediate a peace.[25] Spain dispatched an agent, the Marqués de Torre, to St. Petersburg with the Spanish terms for settlement. Once again, Gibraltar appeared as the principal demand.[26] The Russian and Austrian mediators submitted their proposals for a settlement in May of 1781.[27] As we have seen,[28] John Adams objected strenuously to the mediators' plan, and indicated that he was not willing to treat at all with Great Britain unless the two Imperial courts recognized the United States to be a "free, sovereign, and independent State."[29]

George III also objected. The proposal appeared to him as outside intervention in Britain's internal affairs. At the same time, the Spanish monarch found the terms were not acceptable because Gibraltar was not admitted as a subject for negotiation.[30] Thus, the attempt to make peace in Vienna failed.

Spanish final negotiations with England began on October 7, 1782, when Aranda presented Charles III's peace terms to Fitzherbert in Paris. In a conversation with Fitzherbert, Aranda emphasized that the demands for Gibraltar, Minorca, West Florida, and the withdrawal of English logwood rights in Yucatan, Campeche, and Honduras constituted an *ultimatum*. In return for Gibraltar, Spain indicated she was willing to cede to Great Britain either Orán, or some other equivalent.[31] To facilitate the negotiations, Charles III later sent Don Ignacio Heredia to London to deal directly with Shelburne.[32]

When he arrived in Paris, Fitzherbert had concluded that France and

Spain were in no hurry to negotiate. The reason, he learned, was that the Bourbons awaited the outcome of the blockade of Gibraltar. But Vergennes was not as keen on delaying the negotiations as Floridablanca, and when the French Admiral de Grasse returned from London with information that convinced Vergennes that London was sincerely inclined to negotiate, Vergennes quickly dispatched Rayneval to London to verify the Admiral's report.[33] Admiral de Grasse had proposed on behalf of Spain that England cede or agree to regulation of her conquests in the Gulf of Mexico; that England grant to Spain Minorca or Gibraltar, whichever Spain chose; and that, in return, Spain grant England a port in the Mediterranean for her commerce to the Levant.

At London, Rayneval learned that Shelburne was not prepared to cede either Gibraltar or Minorca. Rayneval had no authority to discuss Spanish demands,[34] but he indicated to Shelburne, nevertheless, that, personally, he thought that the cession of Gibraltar was a *sine qua non* of the peace.[35] Shelburne continued to insist strongly that it seemed to him impossible that England would ever cede Gibraltar. When Shelburne discussed his talks with George III, the latter told his minister, ". . . . if [Gibraltar is] not taken, I hope Puerto Rico may be got for it."[36] Later Shelburne raised with Rayneval the possibility of an exchange of Gibraltar for Puerto Rico, but Rayneval replied that, since Spain wished to gain control of the Gulf of Mexico, the cession of Puerto Rico was hardly possible. When Rayneval reported his conversations to Vergennes, he stressed the point that the Spanish demand for Gibraltar would surely cause "great difficulties," for England clearly wanted West Florida or Puerto Rico in exchange.[37] In Paris, Fitzherbert was told that, if ever the Spanish ambassador mentioned Gibraltar to him, Fitzherbert was to refer the topic immediately to London, along with a detailed report on everything Aranda said about the proposal.[38]

The diplomatic perspective on Gibraltar changed, however, when news began to filter back to London, Madrid, and Versailles that the combined Bourbon forces had totally failed in their attempt to take the Rock by assault.[39] Spain stubbornly continued the siege for almost a half a year longer, but Louis XVI withdrew the French troops besieging Gibraltar.[40] Thus, without French military assistance, Spain's only chance to get Gibraltar lay in the negotiations.[41]

Predictably, the British ministers found the Spanish demands "exorbitant and inadmissible." Even if the Spanish had captured Gibraltar, Grantham later wrote to Fitzherbert, Great Britain would not have given up Gibraltar for the territories Spain was offering.[42] But Fitzherbert was instructed to offer Aranda West Florida and the abandonment of the Central American logwood settlements, if Spain would guarantee England their right to cut logwood along the coast. In return, England asked that Spain return

Minorca, with its fortifications restored, and that Spain drop its demands for Gibraltar.

Fitzherbert's instructions suggested that cession of Gibraltar was not negotiable. Yet, in fact, the door was not closed. Grantham told Fitzherbert that if Spain did not drop her demand for Gibraltar, England would consider cession if Spain restored to England all the territories she had conquered during the war, and if Spain came up with an offer of exchange which England considered equivalent. The British felt that Orán, which the Spanish had several times mentioned as their offer for Gibraltar, was not an equivalent.[43] In fact, Floridablanca himself considered Orán a positive liability.

British insistence that the Spanish drop the question of Gibraltar, unless they were willing to come up with some equivalent more attractive than Oran, forced Floridablanca to modify his instructions to Aranda. Now he instructed Aranda to offer Spanish Santo Domingo for Gibraltar, if the British agreed to meet Spain's other demands.[44]

Since France shared control of Santo Domingo with Spain, Floridablanca's offer to exchange Spanish Santo Domingo for Gibraltar was of special interest to Louis XVI. To overcome a possible French objection to sharing Santo Domingo with England, Floridablanca simultaneously offered to cede to France Spain's half of Santo Domingo. For compensation, he asked Louis XVI to agree to cede Corsica or the French West Indies to Britain, as equivalents for giving up Gibraltar to Spain. As part of this triangular bargain, Vergennes was to promise to persuade England to accept all of the other Spanish demands.[45] At Versailles the Spanish "deal" did not appear nearly so attractive as it did at Madrid.[46] Vergennes refused to allow Corsica to be brought into the negotiations. Floridablanca's proposal, however, gave Vergennes the opening to intervene in the negotiations over Gibraltar.[47]

Vergennes first suggested that Charles III raise the ante. Orán was not equal to the price England wanted for Gibraltar.[48] He suggested the two Floridas, or even New Orleans and the American territory between the Mississippi and the western boundaries of the United States. Vergennes had, all along, argued that the Mississippi territory not occupied by the United States and Spain already belonged to England, but Rayneval's talks with Shelburne had led Vergennes to believe such an offer might be acceptable. The idea was still-born; Floridablanca rejected it outright.[49]

Vergennes continued to look for some exchange that would appeal to the English. He was convinced that Charles III would not end the war until Gibraltar was in Spanish hands, and the treaty of Aranjuez had bound Louis XVI to that goal. Nevertheless, France's ability to carry the war into another campaign season was in serious doubt. The inability of the French people to pay the war taxes was apparent now, even to outsiders. According to the British diplomat, Fitzherbert, Vergennes exhibited "an unequivocal desire to put an end to this war."[50] The Spanish government was hardly better off, according to an American observer there.[51]

Furthermore, by the first week of December, 1782, there were no other important unsettled issues obstructing a Franco-British or Anglo-American settlement. The Americans had agreed to their preliminary peace settlement with Great Britain, and, in fact, had let it be known that, if France delayed the peace much longer to satisfy Spain, they would sign separately.[52] In England, the ministry wanted to settle the question of whether there would be another year of war before Parliament opened. As the pressures to end the war mounted, Vergennes busily explored two avenues to peace: he labored to persuade the Spanish to modify their demands; at the same time, he sent Rayneval back to England to determine if there was any real possibility that the English government would relinquish Gibraltar and, if so, at what price.

Meanwhile, Vergennes conferred with Aranda again and again on the proposals, counterproposals, and ultimatums passing to and fro across the Channel with increasing frequency. The result was a development that history sometimes creates to mock human affairs: when George III and the English Cabinet finally agreed to give up Gibraltar [53] for an equivalent, Vergennes persuaded Aranda to give up the Spanish demand for Gibraltar.

On November twenty-eighth Rayneval left for London, carrying instructions from Vergennes and a Spanish *ultimatum* which contained the latest results of Franco-Spanish discussions. The *ultimatum* provided that England abandon the logwood settlements on the Bay of Honduras, and give up all authority over the logwood establishments on the coast of Campeche. In return, Spain would agree to furnish England an agreed upon amount of wood every year at a stipulated price. The logwood trade would be carried in English ships. Spain would keep West Florida, and extend its boundary into East Florida to Cape Canaveral.

On the issue of Gibraltar, the *ultimatum* proposed another three-way trade: England would cede Gibraltar to Spain (but keep possession of the arms and munitions they had there); Spain would restore Minorca to England (and likewise keep possession of the arms and munitions they had there); and France, to indemnify England for her cession of Gibraltar, would grant the islands of Guadeloupe and Dominica to England.[54]

When Rayneval reached London on December first, the expectations for peace were high. The opening of Parliament had been delayed so that George III might begin the new Parliament with a dramatic announcement about the coming peace. The fact that Rayneval brought Vergennes' son, Constantin, with him greatly increased confidence in the sincerity of the

French government. King George himself was now prepared to accept Guadeloupe and Dominica for Gibraltar, if necessary, in order to make the peace which, he now believed, was "so desirable," and "so essential."[55]

The British answer to the Spanish *ultimatum* came almost immediately. In a long cabinet meeting on the third of December, they voted approval of the cession of Gibraltar for Puerto Rico; or Guadeloupe, St. Lucia, and Dominica; or Guadeloupe, Dominica, and Trinidad, although two members objected, and one of these even threatened to resign if Gibraltar were exchanged for Guadeloupe.[56]

Meanwhile, at Versailles, Vergennes had been chipping away at Spanish determination to hold out for Gibraltar. It was apparent now, as Floridablanca recognized, that the "only obstacle to the conclusion of peace" was Gibraltar.[57] "If the King of Spain could be persuaded to give Gibraltar," Vergennes wrote Rayneval, "how much easier it would be for the English ministry and for ourselves . . . . "[58]

In a letter to Aranda, Floridablanca had stressed that Charles III would insist on having Gibraltar "with all his might," but, at the same time, he asked to know what Charles III might expect for compensation if he did give up his demand for Gibraltar.[59] This passage may have been the signal Vergennes was looking for: it meant that Charles III might accept the "sacrifice" of Gibraltar for a price, although it was by no means an indication that he was ready to do so. In conversations with Aranda, Vergennes noted also that the Spanish Ambassador was not very keen on the exchange of any West Indian territory for Gibraltar. He felt that English possession in the West Indies would contribute a positive threat to Spanish interests there, and would place Spain in an "unfortunate position in that part of the world.[60]

In any event, Vergennes immediately instructed Rayneval to discuss openly the possibility of a settlement which did not include Gibraltar.[61] The French Secretary of State hoped that he could influence Charles III to give up the demand and offered to try to persuade Charles to do so. He suggested that the English tell Rayneval, frankly, the peace terms they wanted with Spain. If such a proposal did not appeal to the British ministry, Vergennes suggested that the parties return to the offer of Guadeloupe and Dominica for Gibraltar. Vergennes also offered a proposal to settle one of the last problems separating France and England. If England's demand for St. Lucia were granted, he noted, the French island of Martinique would be indefensible. He suggested, therefore, that it, too, be ceded in return for some English equivalent in the West or East Indies.[62]

Vergennes' newest proposals surprised George III. By now he was reconciled to the loss of Gibraltar, and was holding out for a valuable offer in return for it.[63] Nevertheless, the British Cabinet agreed on a response containing an option which did not include Gibraltar. England offered to grant the two Floridas and Minorca to Spain, if the latter restored the Bahamas and permitted, with restrictions, the continued cutting of logwood in Honduras. France, the British proposal continued, should cede Dominica back to England.[64]

By this time, Shelburne had concluded without the "least doubt" that Vergennes was anxious to settle whether or not Spain received Gibraltar,[65] and he was dead right. When the British counterproposals arrived at Versailles, Vergennes was ecstatic. He notified Aranda of their arrival, and spoke of them as terms "with which I hope you will be satisfied," for the terms were not the ones he had been instructed to seek. Nevertheless, he took upon himself the responsibility for accepting them. Vergennes was astonished, according to his letter to Rayneval,[67] as indeed, he must have been, for a great deal of the responsibility for dropping Gibraltar from the Spanish list of demands lay with Vergennes and *not* the Conde d' Aranda. Fortunately for the peace, Floridablanca, in Madrid, did not overrule his Ambassador at Versailles. Whether he was persuaded by Aranda's argument that the territorial equivalents that would have gone to England in exchange for Gibraltar would have placed English sea power in a position to threaten Spanish possessions in America, is a moot point.[68] In London, George III still harbored the notion that he could have made a better deal if he had given up Gibraltar and received Minorca, the two Floridas and Guadeloupe. But he accepted the settlement with Spain, on the grounds that it made peace certain.[69] There was a last-minute flare-up of tempers and distrust, when France refused to give up Dominica as the British believed she had offered to do, but that potentially explosive issue was settled by compromise. England granted to France Tobago and some minor territories in India, in exchange for Dominica.[70]

Despite the unauthorized "sacrifice" of Gibraltar, Floridablanca accepted the peace agreed upon by Vergennes, Aranda, and the British Cabinet. It was a profitable peace.[71] The treaty granted to Spain Florida and Minorca, both of considerable value for her military and trade.[72] George III, in fact, felt that the potential trade of Port Mahon, in Minorca, made that island even more valuable than the *"proud fortress."*[74] And Floridablanca, too, put more value on these two territories, than on Gibraltar.[74]

Furthermore, since France and the United States had already come to terms with England, Floridablanca had no other option. Spain lacked the resources to fight England alone, and the Dutch, who still had not reached a settlement with England, had proven to be more of a liability than an asset.

The Anglo-Spanish treaty also settled the long-smoldering dispute over the English rights to cut logwood in Honduras, but almost as an afterthought. The preliminary treaty of January, 1782, assured British subjects in Honduras that they would not be molested in their cutting and transporting of logwood.[75] When Fox became Secretary of State, however, he decided that the boundaries within which British subjects could cut wood should be extended. He even questioned the Spanish assumption of domination in the area.[76] The results of the discussions thus reopened did not satisfy Fox, but they ended in a much more precise phrasing and definition of British rights in the Spanish American settlement. In the definitive treaty, the Spanish recognized the British right to "cut, load, and transport wood" in specified areas between the Wallis and Rio Hondo Rivers. The English outside of the newly-defined area were to be ordered to move to the specified area within eighteen months. Finally, George III promised to demolish all fortifications built by his subjects in the designated area. Within the area, the British subjects enjoyed fishing rights for their subsistence.[77]

In return for these British concessions, Spain restored the Isle of Providence and the Bahamas to England, promised to give back any conquered territory not covered specifically by the treaty, and agreed to name commissioners to make new commercial arrangements with England as soon as the treaty was ratified.[78]

Charles III and Floridablanca emerged from the American war with further cause for resentment against Louis XVI and Vergennes. From the moment Vergennes took office in 1774, the Spanish government had watched Vergennes grasp for more and more control of joint Bourbon foreign policy and they watched him use the Family Compact to advance policies which, they felt, were not always in Spain's interest. Even more difficult to accept was that Vergennes had begun the war, and he ended it, by presenting Charles III with a *fait accompli.*

But Vergennes had had to submit to the force of circumstances. It has been argued that Vergennes never wanted Spain to have Gibraltar, because the British presence there bound Spain to the French alliance.[79] The hypothesis is correct in explaining the general motives of France during the negotiations for the peace of 1783. But to this political aim must be added the stark facts about French capabilities in 1782. Vergennes now believed that France did not have the resources to risk another year of war.[80] Despite his strong belief that foreign policy should always take precedence over domestic issues, the reality of an empty treasury dominated the agenda of the Secretary of State for Foreign Affairs.

CHAPTER 30

The Right to Catch Fish

Historians usually consider Gibraltar the major stumbling block in the peace negotiations preceding the treaty of 1783, and, indeed, the bickering and trading that went on over that fortress justify its reputation as a rock in the negotiations, as well as in the sea. But, in 1782, the French Secretary of State for Foreign Affairs would have placed additional problems alongside Gibraltar as likely hindrances to a quick conclusion of the war. One of these was the explosive tangle of various claims to the Newfoundland fisheries, claims which, he feared, might very well prolong the war, and even split the alliance system he had built.

France had long had an interest in the Newfoundland fisheries, not only because of their economic value, but also because she felt that a flourishing fishery was directly related to the strength and training of her naval fleet. The fisheries question was always one of the most hotly disputed issues in the peace negotiations ending every war between France and England during the late seventeenth and eighteenth centuries. By the Treaty of Paris of 1763, England had regained the position in the fisheries which she had earlier lost to Louis XIV and, from then on, she rapidly extended her efforts to eliminate French fishermen from the Newfoundland fisheries in order to undermine French naval and economic strength. The 1763 treaty had given the French the "liberty" to engage in shore fishing at Newfoundland between Bonavista and Pointe Riche, but prohibited the French from fishing within three leagues of the Gulf of St. Lawrence, and within fifteen leagues of the Cape Breton coast. In return, Great Britain granted France the islands of St. Pierre and Miquelon to serve as places of shelter for French fishermen, provided the islands were never fortified.[1]

Even these moderate concessions to France caused a great deal of public criticism of the British cabinet. William Pitt, the American colonies, and the London merchants all wanted the French totally excluded from the fisheries, and they were disappointed that the Treaty of Paris had not so provided. In truth, the restrictions imposed by the Treaty of Paris, and especially the English interpretation of the word "liberty," left the French fisheries to die a slow death rather than a sudden one, for, after 1770, French fishing enterprises at Newfoundland sharply declined. When the French signed their treaties with the Americans in 1778 and went to war with England, they saw their fisheries collapse and their establishments on the islands of St. Pierre and Miquelon totally destroyed.[2]

Yet Vergennes, as other ministers before him, never forgot the fishery question, and his belief that a prosperous fishing industry was essential to French naval and economic strength helped make the question a "constant sore" with the British. But every time Vergennes raised the problem with the British Secretary of State for the Southern Department, he aroused such a testy reaction that he withdrew it. The American Revolution gave him the opportunity to further his country's interest in the fisheries, however, and one of his objectives in signing the alliance with the Americans in 1778 was to regain France's ancient position in the Newfoundland fisheries. It is "very probable," he wrote in a memorandum in 1776, "that, as a result of events, we could recover a part of the possessions which England took away from us in America, such as the shore fishery, that of the Gulf of St. Lawrence, Cape Breton Island, etc., etc. We are not speaking of Canada."[3]

In the negotiations with the Americans concerning the treaties of 1778, Vergennes was careful to provide for the future of French fishing interests. In the Treaty of Alliance with the United States, he made sure that no article barred eventual conquests of the Newfoundland and island fisheries, and Gérard, Vergennes' spokesman, made it clear to the Americans that, while France wanted nothing on the American continent, Newfoundland and the islands of the Gulf of St. Lawrence were open to conquest of either or both parties to the alliance. To this possibility the Americans agreed, and during the war Admiral d'Estaing persistently tried to get the Americans to participate in a joint expedition against the fisheries.[4]

In the Treaty of Amity and Commerce between France and the Thirteen United States, French interests in the fisheries were specifically safeguarded. In Article Nine the "Subjects, Inhabitants, Merchants, Commanders of Ships, Masters and Mariners of the States, Provinces and Dominions of each Party respectively, shall abstain and forbear to fish in all Places possessed or *which shall be possessed* by the other party." And if any vessel "shall be found fishing contrary to the Tenor of this Treaty," it would be confiscated. The article made it abundantly clear that Vergennes thought of acquiring more fishing territory in American waters. There is evidence, too, that, as early as 1775, he had even considered making an exchange of fishing territories with the British, thereby acquiring fishing rights in a zone different from the one assigned to France in the previous treaties.[5]

Article Nine illustrates, also, that the Americans did not deny themselves the possibility of acquiring fishing rights. They agreed only that whatever the

French acquired would be reserved exclusively to the French, with the exception, however, "that the Exclusion stipulated in the present Article shall take place only so long, and so far as the Most Christian King or the United States shall not in this respect have granted an Exemption to some other Nation."[6]

In the light of later disputes among historians as to whether or not Vergennes' demands on the English in 1782, for "exclusive" privileges in the Newfoundland fisheries, constitute a plot against American interests, Article Nine, as well as Article Ten, is of the utmost importance. The articles did not exclude Americans from all the fisheries; they only indicated that Vergennes hoped that the fishermen from the various nations fishing off Newfoundland would be restricted to separate zones, and would not be permitted to trespass on each others' territory. The long history of squabbles between French and British fishermen and diplomats over fishing rights and privileges made such a precaution necessary.

Article Ten clarifies the point. The Americans agreed that, even if France did not better her position in the fisheries as a result of the expected American war, the United States would continue to recognize France's rights to the fisheries left to France by the Treaties of Utrecht and Paris. "The United States their Citizens and Inhabitants," the article provided "shall never disturb the Subjects, of the Most Christian King in the Enjoyment and Exercise of the Right of Fishing on the Banks of Newfoundland; *nor in the indefinite and exclusive right* which belongs to them on the Part of the Coast of that Island which is designed by the Treaty of Utrecht; nor in the Rights relative to all and each of the Isles which belong to his Most Christian Majesty; the whole conformable to the true Sense of the Treaties of Utrecht and Paris."[7]

In 1778, John Adams obtained from Ralph Izard, another American agent, copies of British papers containing the argument that the Treaties of Utrecht and Paris said nothing at all about "exclusive" rights. Adams, congenitally suspicious, immediately jumped to the erroneous conclusion that the Americans had probably fallen for some French trick. He vowed that he would look into the question, for a representative of a young nation, struggling for survival amongst the wicked powers of Europe, could not be too careful.[8]

But Vergennes' motives contained no intent to deceive. The history of the squabbles and disputes over rights in the Newfoundland fisheries clearly demonstrated to him that some sort of an agreement was necessary, to prevent trouble. Articles Nine and Ten of the Treaty of Amity and Commerce were motivated by the desire to establish some such preventive measures.

More importantly, these articles reflect a principle which France had consistently and vigorously defended for generations. In 1686, for example, France and Great Britain signed the Treaty of Whitehal, which contained a provision (Article Five) that the "Subjects, inhabitants, merchants, ship-captains, skippers, and sailors of the Kingdoms, provinces, and lands of both Kings respectively, shall abstain and keep away from trade and fishing in all places which are occupied or shall be occupied by one or the other party in America . . . ." Any ships caught violating the tenor of this article would be confiscated.[9] Article Five, in effect, recognized that France and England shared the Newfoundland fisheries and that there was to be no intermingling of the fishermen of the two powers. In Newfoundland, France had exclusive rights on the south and west and part of the north-east, while England enjoyed them on the east.

Later, in the Treaty of Utrecht (1713), the French were forced (in Article Thirteen) to cede to the English the island of Newfoundland, but they were allowed to keep their fishing rights from Cape Bonavista to the extreme northern tip of Newfoundland, and from there down the western coast to Pointe Riche.[10] This treaty narrowed the area along the coast from which Frenchmen could take fish, but said nothing about changing the nature of their rights retained within the new limits. These rights, the ones defined in the Treaty of Whitehall, remained intact, and, as Louis XIV said, the Newfoundland coast was still partly "specified" for English fisheries. From 1713 to 1755, English practice in Newfoundland fully recognized the French position and their "exclusive" rights.[11]

During the negotiations to settle the Seven Years' War, however, English diplomats, in order to satisfy the demands of their own fishing interests, began to argue the doctrine of "concurrence," a doctrine which meant that the restricted area left to the French had to be shared with English fishermen. France quickly and vigorously objected to this innovation which would effectively ruin her own fisheries. When the Treaty of 1763 was finally signed, France felt she had secured her fisheries rights, and she based her belief on the fact that the Treaty of Paris generally reconfirmed the Treaty of Utrecht, and the fisheries clauses in the treaty specifically renewed those of the Treaty of Utrecht.[12]

Nevertheless, the wording of the Paris treaty considerably weakened the French case. Instead of providing for French *rights*, it spoke of *liberties* to fish, and the distinction was of no small significance. Rights were generally considered to be permanent; liberties, on the other hand, were privileges granted by a sovereign power, in this case Great Britain. Exploiting the advantages derived from this wording, British diplomats again revived their argument of "concurrence," and stated that exclusive rights were no longer retained by France; instead, French fishermen had been granted the privilege to fish in certain areas under British control, along with British subjects. The French refused to accept the British position, and the dispute became a bitter one between the two powers; it grew more heated as the American Revolution approached. Choiseul, in fact, marched to the brink of war over the issue.[13]

Immediately after assuming office, Vergennes seems to have momentarily admitted the British right to share the fisheries with the French, but Sartine, the Minister of Marine, convinced him of the dangers implicit in the British notion of "concurrence," so Vergennes abandoned his view, and returned to Choiseul's position.[14]

Essentially the French position was founded on the principle that the wars between Great Britain and France, which followed the treaty of 1686, did not abrogate the fisheries rights defined in that treaty. Interestingly enough, the English themselves sometimes seemed to accept the principle. In 1753, for example, both the Attorney General and the Solicitor General of the British Crown gave an opinion that the fishery clauses of the treaty of 1686 were still in force. And, as late as 1765, that is, two years after the Treaty of Paris, the Advocate General of the Crown, Sir James Marriott, went against the views of his fellow officers, the Attorney General and the Solicitor General, to give the opinion that the Treaty of 1686 was still "subsisting," because it was never abrogated.[15] The use of the term "exclusive" in the Franco-American treaty of 1778 was not, therefore, inserted to trick the Americans, but grew quite logically out of the position taken by the French since 1686 and pressed forward in every negotiation with the English since that date.

One further point is pertinent to an understanding of Adams' belief that French claims to exclusive rights in the fisheries were an attempt to deceive. Article Nine of the Franco-American treaty of commerce of 1778 is very similar in word and meaning to Article Five of the Treaty of Whitehall of 1686, suggesting that the earlier treaty was the mode for the later one. John Adams studied the Treaty of Whitehall for his own "model" for a commercial treaty with France.[16] Yet, somehow, he managed to complete his study in total ignorance of the perfectly respectable and, for years, publicly proclaimed French position in the bitter controversy over the exclusive rights which that treaty formalized. If Adams had known the history of the controversy, he surely would have recognized that the words "Exclusion" and "exclusive" in Articles Nine and Ten of the Franco-American commercial treaty did not indicate a plan to dupe anyone, but were simply a means of making explicit the century-old French position in the Anglo-French conflict. In signing the treaty, the Americans had, in effect, consented to side with the French against the British on this disputed issue.

Curiously enough, when Adams did finally look into the background of the word "exclusive," he accepted the British position in the controversy which, as we might expect, held that the French had no exclusive rights. Vergennes, he believed, had indeed hood-winked the "Thirteen United States." Thus, while the treaty of 1778 formally obliged the United States to side with the French on the old issue of fisheries rights, John Adams seems personally to have sided with the British.[17] It is ironic, therefore, that the basis of the French argument in the dispute — that a treaty is not abrogated by subsequent wars — was the very one advanced by Adams' son, John Quincy Adams, to defend *American* fishing rights in Newfoundland after the War of 1812.

As subjects of George III, the New Englanders had long enjoyed the right to fish off Canada and Newfoundland, until Lord North's bill to restrain trade barred them from the North Atlantic fisheries as of July 1, 1775. When the Americans denied the sovereignty of King George, the British monarch naturally argued that, as a result of their action, they had lost for all time any rights they may have enjoyed as his subjects. Only a grant from the King could restore such rights.

Still, like the French, the Americans never forgot the value of the fisheries and, hence, were unwilling to lose them when they rejected the sovereignty of the mother country. From the beginning, they claimed rights to the fisheries, and based their claims on the principle that they still retained the "common rights" to the fisheries of Newfoundland and Canada which they had earlier enjoyed. The argument from "common rights" was traditionally based on the theory that the sea cannot be owned by anyone, and, hence, no restrictions can be put on its use. Such an argument was not without precedent, since it was based on ancient classical theory and had even earned the fervent support of the great jurist Grotius. The basic difficulty with such a position, however, was that, although it was based on a very respectable and consistent legalist tradition of natural law, it ran head-on into the facts of history, for, time and again, restrictions had been put on the use of seas, and the practice had been accepted by the great powers in formal treaties. In both the Treaty of Utrecht and the Treaty of Paris, to mention two relevant examples, England had forced France and Spain to accept limitations and restrictions on their use of the fisheries off Newfoundland and Canada, and the most sincere appeal to the classical jurists and their touchstone, Natural Law, could not exorcise the power of the British naval guns, which effectively continued to enforce these restrictions.

Furthermore, since the Renaissance, a counter-doctrine had developed which proclaimed that the sea was, indeed, susceptible of dominion, and that the history of laws and customs of men of all ages demonstrated the practical acceptance of such a doctrine. If a sea had passed under the dominion of a prince, the theory held, it follows that the prince can grant, withhold, or limit its use.[18] Thus, by the eighteenth century, the common rights to fish on the seas, in practice, meant the common right to fish only on the "high seas", as distinguished from "territorial waters" which were subject to the jurisdiction of the prince. Now, of course, the field of dispute shifted to the question of what constituted territorial waters.

Perhaps to acommodate themselves to the facts of British practice, the Americans developed a third and rather imaginative interpretation of the doctrine of "common rights." They did not argue only that everyone had "common rights" to the fisheries, but that *they* specifically had rights, arising from the fact that they had long enjoyed them in common with English subjects before independence, and that these "common rights" remained with them even after their break with the mother country. Robert Livingston, the American Secretary of State, explained the American point of view in a letter to Franklin dated January 7, 1782: "The argument on which the people of America found their claim to fish on the banks of Newfoundland arises, first, from their having once formed a part of the British Empire, in which state they always enjoyed, as fully as the people of Britain themselves, the right of fishing on those banks." Livingston went on to argue that American rights were not invalidated by the separation, which was forced on them by British oppression, "and it can not certainly be contended that those oppressions abridged our rights or gave new ones to Britain."[19] In the same letter to Franklin, Livingston buttressed his first principle with the prestige of another, namely the classical one that "the sea cannot in its nature be appropriated," and, therefore, by the "laws of nations" Americans, as well as anyone else, had the common right to fish on the high seas outside the territorial limits of a nation. The advantage of advancing both principles was considerable: the appeal to traditional "common rights" to fish on the high seas reinforced American claims to fish there; the principle of "common rights" based on rights earlier shared in common with British subjects, implied the right to fish inside the territorial waters of Newfoundland and Canada, or wherever the Americans had earlier enjoyed the right to fish, a claim which could not have been sustained with the older principle of common rights.

By claiming their rights as possessions held before the war, the Americans could insist that Article Nine of the treaty of alliance with France — a mutual guarantee of "possessions" — obligated Louis XVI to guarantee these American fishing claims.[20] The American demand was, basically, one for a partitioning of the British Empire between the two sovereignties, King George III and the new Thirteen United States, with the two separate sovereignties carrying with them all their possessions and rights enjoyed prior to the partition.[21]

The American position was indeed a novel and bold one. With imagination and skill, they had threaded their way, on the one hand, between idealistic adherence to a purely abstract principle, cut off from practice, and, on the other hand, submission to the English ministers and sailors who had excluded Americans from the fisheries since 1775. Vergennes, however, was in no position to applaud the American argument simply because it was novel. In his eyes, its very novelty was its greatest disadvantage. He very early concluded that it was highly unlikely that such a principle would convince anyone — and the subsequent long history of Anglo-American fishing negotiations proved he was right — and, therefore, the only way the British could be obliged to grant American fishing rights would be by force of arms. Was France, then, going to be asked to prolong the war to force acceptance of an ingenious, but altogether novel, principle of fishing rights?

From his first contacts with the Americans, Vergennes sought to discover the nature and extent of American interest in the fisheries. In July of 1776, he discussed at length with Silas Deane the future of the rebellious colonies, and he carefully questioned the American as to whether or not the colonies could subsist without the fisheries. Deane assured Vergennes "that the fisheries were never carried on but by a part of the colonies, and by them not so much as a means of subsistence as of commerce; that, the fisheries failing, those employed in them turned part to agriculture and part to the army and navy."[22] It is impossible, of course, to say how much Deane's assurances influenced Vergennes, but there is no doubt that he came to hold that the fisheries were not absolutely essential to the existence of the fledgling nation, and, therefore, should never become *sine qua non* of the peace negotiations. In 1778, John Adams was of the same opinion.[23]

Nevertheless, Vergennes had no objections to the Americans' gaining rights to the fisheries, as long as their demands did not destroy French claims, and as long as France was not asked to continue the war to secure them. And in his discussions with Deane previous to the treaties of 1778, he gave no indication that he felt that French and American interests in the fisheries were irreconcilable. In March, Silas Deane even offered France the possibility of the conquest of Newfoundland, with a division of the fisheries between France and the United States, in return for entry into the war against England.[24] Later that same year, Vergennes confidently assured his ambassador at Madrid that, if the Americans succeeded in driving the British off the continent, he was certain they were disposed "to satisfy" France and Spain with respect to the fisheries.[25] But the Spanish desire for a share of the fisheries was never satisified. Among the many demands put forward by Spain, in October of 1782, was that of a share in the Newfoundland fisheries. This was a revival of a similar claim made at the peace negotiations ending the Seven Years War. The demand never got beyond the October proposals, for the British flatly refused to consider it. "The absolute claim of the fishery," Shelburne told Fitzherbert, "is out of the question."[26]

The British early saw that suspicions between the United States and France over the fisheries were very likely and could easily be exploited for Britain's benefit. Consequently, British intelligence agents carefully noted any signs of such suspicions. In May of 1777, the American representatives in Paris were alarmed by rumor that the English and French were making some "accommodation, injurious to the colonies" respecting the fisheries. The accommodation, presumably, would be in return for French neutrality in the American war. The British spy in the American ranks, Dr. Edward Bancroft, carefully noted the American reactions in his report to his superiors.[27] In August of 1780, a British agent in New York reported to William Eden, the head of the British intelligence service, that Ralph Izard had just arrived in America, and was propagating the idea that Franklin and Deane, in France, had "given the Fishery to France and the Floridas to Spain." Izard's language, another report on the same incident claimed, "filled the country with Jealousies." The American agents, Izard was reported to have stated, "were duped by the Cabinet of Versailles. . . ." "Dr. Franklin was superannuated," and all the American agents were "unfaithful and deceived except for the Lees."[28] Suspicions such as these were tailormade for British use when the peace talks opened, if only they could find an American representative who could be led astray by them.

Whether or not distrust between France and the United States concerning the fisheries grew or diminished depended, ultimately, on the form which the American claims took. If they grew to a point where they directly harmed French interests, Vergennes was duty bound to moderate them. Such an intervention would place him in an unenviable position, for many New Englanders considered their claims to the fisheries to be God-given and self-evident, and woe unto the wretch who dared interfere with God's will. There were three points, essentially, where American claims might impinge on French interests: (1) if the American demands were impossibly high, and they refused to accept a peace until they gained them, the war might be prolonged for purely American gains; (2) if the Americans insisted that France guarantee their fishing rights, they would have to be refused, because Louis XVI simply could not take on any additional obligations; and (3) finally, if the Americans insisted on rights in *all* the territory where they had earlier fished, France's claims to "exclusive" rights on the shores of Newfoundland would, of necessity, be narrowly restricted to the limits assigned by the treaty of 1763, since the Americans, as British subjects, had fished everywhere else. As the Franco-American treaties of 1778 demonstrate, Vergennes had hoped to gain a larger fishing area for France, and had written such a hope into the treaty with the United States.

The debate in the Continental Congress, as to the direction American policy on the fisheries should take, cropped up over and over again and with a surprising degree of passion, indicating that the Americans themselves had not completely settled in their own minds how far they should go with their claims. Vergennes, of course, followed the debates with great interest, and tried to make his influence felt whenever the debate took a turn which threatened to put France and the United States at odds with each other. He was especially interested, for example, in the discussion and resolutions of the Congress during the summer of 1779, when the Americans seemed to be hammering out a formal policy regarding the fisheries. In June, the Congress appeared to be moving toward the position that peace could come only after the American fisheries rights were recognized by Great Britain. It is "essential to the welfare of these United States that the inhabitants thereof at the expiration of the war," a resolution of June 19 read, "should continue to enjoy the free and undisturbed exercise of their common rights to fish on the banks of Newfoundland and the other fishing banks and seas of North America, preserving inviolate the treaties between France and the United States." To add braces to the resolution, they further resolved that an explanatory note be prepared and sent to the American minister at Versailles, "whereby the said common right to the fisheries shall be more explicitly guaranteed to the inhabitants of these United States than it already is by the treaties aforesaid."[29] In short, the peace would come only after the American fisheries rights were recognized, and Louis XVI should stand behind the American claim.

Yet, by the middle of August, when the Congress was drafting its instructions to the Commissioners to be appointed to negotiate a treaty of peace, the Congress had backed away from its earlier extreme stand, or, at least, from its earlier tactics. In its instructions for a treaty of peace with Great Britain, the Americans took the position that, although "it was of the utmost importance to the peace and commerce" of the United States that their common rights to the fisheries (as well as the cession of Canada and Nova Scotia!) be guaranteed to them, "yet a desire of terminating the war hath induced us not to make the acquisition of these objects an ultimatum on the present occasion."[30] On the same day, however, they drafted the instructions for a treaty of commerce with Great Britain, to be made after the peace, and, in the instructions, they provided that "the common right of fishing shall in no case be given up;" they instructed Franklin, in Paris, to that effect and further ordered him to try to get a formal engagement from Louis XVI, that he would make common cause with the Americans in a war against Great Britain if any of their rights to the fisheries were disturbed after the peace.[31]

Vergennes' response to the American claims was honest and frank: Louis XVI simply could not back them. "It should, therefore, be well established," he wrote to LaLuzerne in September of 1779, "that, from the moment when the colonists published their Declaration of Independence, they have ceased to own a share in the fisheries, because they have forfeited, by their own act, the qualification which entitled them to such a share; that, consequently, they can offer to the court of London neither title nor actual possession. From this comes another result; viz., that, the Americans having no right to the fisheries, we can give them no guarantee on that head."[32]

For a while, the demands for making the fisheries claims a *sine qua non* of the peace seemed to abate, but the approach of peace brought them forward once again, this time in force. In October of 1781, the Massachusetts General Court instructed its delegates to urge the Continental Congress to include the American claims for fisheries in any peace negotiations, and the first committee of Congress which took up the Massachusetts proposal agreed that the "common rights" to the fisheries should be secured at the peace negotiations. In addition, it was once more recommended that Louis XVI be urged to back his allies' claims on Great Britain. Another committee then took up the question, and eventually drew up a report equally as strong in favour of the claims to "common rights" in the fisheries.[33]

When this report was debated in Congress, however, it was strongly opposed by a number of congressmen. It is customary to dismiss this repeated opposition to such an extreme position as the manifestation of France's control over members of the Continental Congress. But it is most doubtful that LaLuzerne's influence on Congress was as great as such a simplistic explanation assumes; nor, for that matter, was it as great as LaLuzerne himself liked to assume. In truth, some members of Congress sincerely believed the fishery question to be a strictly sectional interest of New England "radicals", and that a war begun in the name of political liberty should not be prolonged for the right to catch fish.[34] Quite understandably, Vergennes was alarmed by the revival of these extravagant claims, and he would have been doing less than his duty if he had not enlightened the Americans as to the limits of Louis XVI's responsibilities. The resources of France were not inexhaustible, and Vergennes very wisely wished to avoid being maneuvered into assuming more burdens than his treaties required.

But many New Englanders refused to appreciate the French position, and even went so far as to suspect France of hostility toward the United States because Louis XVI refused to assume the additional burden. When LaLuzerne tried to discuss the matter with Lowell, for example, the leader of the New England fishing block in the Continental Congress refused to listen. France could by no means be expected to assist the Americans in such extravagant demands on the English, LaLuzerne told Lowell. In that case, Lowell replied, New England would refuse to accept a peace without the fisheries. LaLuzerne persisted in trying to moderate Lowell's position by showing him that the insistence on "common rights" was, in fact, no claim at all, since it was based on a principle which England did not and never would recognize. Lowell abruptly closed the conversation (and his mind) by repeating that the fisheries were a "common right" of all nations.[35] It did, indeed, appear that the war begun for liberty would be continued for the privilege of catching fish.

Nevertheless, Vergennes refused to give comfort to this American tendency. "As to ourselves," he wrote LaLuzerne in August of 1781, "we will make no sacrifices of our own fisheries, and we will not prolong the calamities of war to force England to sacrifice hers."[36] "France would not dispute the Americans' right of fishing on the open seas," he told LaLuzerne in another letter, "but the rights of coastal fishing belong to the owner of that coast, Great Britain, and he is at liberty to exclude from it whomsoever he thinks fit." The Americans, he concluded, "have absolutely no claims thereto."[37]

In March of 1782, Barbé-Marbois, the secretary of the French legation at Philadelphia, summed up, in the temporary absence of LaLuzerne, the French position on the fisheries in a letter to Vergennes.[38] Unfortunately, he also added a few of his own presumptuous recommendations for action to be taken. Samuel Adams of Massachusetts Bay, Marbois reported was "using all his endeavors to raise, in the State of Massachusetts, a strong opposition to peace if the eastern states are not thereby admitted to the fisheries . . . ." There was not a "fitter engine, than the fisheries," Marbois opined, "for stirring up the passions of the eastern people. By renewing this question, which had lain dormant during his two years' absence from Boston, he has raised the expectations of the people of Massachusetts to an extraordinary pitch . . . ." It was now repeated in the Massachusetts General Court, Marbois continued, that there would be "no peace without the fisheries." Marbois thought it would be dangerous for France to raise a public cry over the issue, but he thought Louis XVI should intimate to Congress and the American ministers his surprise that the Newfoundland fisheries question was to be included in the new instructions. Louis XVI should promise Congress, Marbois believed, that he would give his assistance in procuring, for the Americans, admission to the other fisheries, although he was "not answerable for the success," and "he was bound to nothing as the treaty makes no mention of the article."

Except for some of his own personal suggestions, Marbois' letter contained nothing new on the French position on the fisheries, and that position had already been fully explained to the Continental Congress by Gérard and LaLuzerne. Nevertheless, the eager young secretary's letter proved to be diplomatic dynamite, for it fell into the hands of the British, and they skillfully made use of it and other information to incite the panicky John Jay into opening separate negotiations.[39] For the rest of his life, John Jay was convinced that his hasty action had frustrated a French attempt to betray the Americans in the peace negotiations of the Treaty of Paris, and Jay's later justification of his action has convinced many historians that he was right.[40]

The definitive Anglo-French Treaty awarded France the islands of St. Pierre and Miquelon, near Newfoundland, and defined the respective rights of the parties granted fishing privileges in Newfoundland. Louis XVI agreed to accept for his subjects an area beginning at Cape St. Jean, going northward and then descending southward to Cape Raye. French fishermen were to enjoy the right to fish as they had enjoyed it under the Treaty of Utrecht. To Vergennes, this last stipulation meant that the French had won their "exclusive rights", for that was the interpretation placed on Article Thirteen of the Treaty of Utrecht, by both the English and the French, from 1713 to 1755.[41]

The United States, according to their final agreement with England, gained the right to fish on the "Grand Banks and other banks" of Newfoundland, and in the Gulf of St. Lawrence, and "all other places in the sea where the inhabitants of both countries used at any time heretofore to fish." But, on the coasts of Newfoundland, American fishermen could fish (but not dry or cure) only at those places used by British fishermen. The peace treaty, therefore, reinforced the Frenchmen's "exclusive" rights to their fishing area,[42] as well as increased that area.

The evidence available reveals how unfounded was Jay's view that Vergennes wanted to divide the Newfoundland fisheries between Great Britain and France to the exclusion of the Americans, and that, in order to achieve his goal, Vergennes was prepared to deceive the American delegates at Paris. Although Vergennes thought that the American claims to Newfoundland were extravagant, he had no objection whatsoever to American acquisition, or even Spanish acquisition, of fishing rights, as long as such claims were not at the expense of France's claims or as long as Louis XVI was not held responsible for forcing George III to recognize the claims. His subsequent willing acceptance of the Anglo-American agreement on American fishing liberties is proof enough of this point. Moreover, Vergennes' demands for "exclusive"rights to the fisheries were not, as John Adams suspected, a device for excluding the Americans from Newfoundland waters, but were a restatement of a longheld French policy of trying to avoid the conflicts and disputes which inevitably arose when the fishermen of Great Britain and France fished in the same areas. The policy was based on the reasoned principle that a war did not abrogate a treaty.

Vergennes objected to the Americans' claim that the right to fish was already their possession because they had shared it in common with the

British before the Revolution. The argument, he believed, was spurious, and France could not be expected to make sacrifices or prolong the war to force Great Britain to accept it. In this opinion, Vergennes was not only trying to preserve his monarch's limited resources, he was also upholding a view which had become a part of the public law of Europe: that is, that the rights of coastal fishing belonged to the owner of that coast.

CHAPTER 31

The Mississippi Boundary

The American claims to the Mississippi Valley were a vexation for Vergennes, not only because of the risk that they might antagonize Spain, but because he believed that they might prove costly to France. The treaty with the United States had obliged Louis XVI to guarantee the possessions of the young republic, but the American interest in Nova Scotia, Canada, Florida, and the Mississippi Valley indicated that the new nation's conception of what constituted its possessions was not fixed. Furthermore, the representatives of the United States were thoroughly committed to territorial expansion. Vergennes, like Bismarck later, took the position that France was "satiated"; she had no need to acquire further territory. In this divergence lay a great danger to his policy. If his allies were not restrained, France would find herself fighting and paying for territory that others would enjoy, and French policy would be subverted at a tremendous cost in French resources. Furthermore, Vergennes would not permit his allies, whether they be Austria, Spain, or the new United States to maneuver him into a position where French resources became an instrument of the policy of some other sovereign. For personal as well as political reasons, he did not wish to have French policy determined in Philadelphia, Vienna, or Madrid, rather than Versailles.

The Mississippi issue grew out of clause XI of the Franco-American Treaty of 1778. In that clause Louis XVI guaranteed to the new nation:

> Their liberty, sovereignty, and independence, absolute and unlimited, as well in matters of government as commerce, and also their possessions, and the additions or conquests that their confederation may obtain during the war ... the whole of their possessions shall be fixed and assured to the said states at the moment of the cessation of their present war with Great Britain.[1]

The guarantee of American independence in this article is unequivocal; it is "absolute and unlimited." But the extent of the guarantee to "possessions" is not. Did the Mississippi territory fall under this head? Or was it one of the "additions" or "conquests?" Also did not the stipulation that the limits of possession be "fixed" at the end of the war encourage the Americans to tack onto their confederation as many "additions" as possible before the peace?

Vergennes, of course, had no pre-conceived moral or legal objections to demands for exchanges of territory. Few wars ended in the eighteenth century without some transfer of land and people, and his attitude reflected the customs of Ancien Régime diplomacy. On the other hand, the spokesmen for the American demands to territory presented no arguments that convinced him that France was, by treaty, obliged to guarantee them. He would have found unconvincing the argument that America's destiny made expansion to the west irresistible.[2] And he would not have been impressed with the claim that the future development of the United States required acquisition to prevent Americans being "cooped up" between the Atlantic Ocean and the Appalachian Mountains.[3] The argument of *Lebensraum* did not then enjoy the status it later acquired.

The key to Vergennes' position *vis-á-vis* American policy concerning the Mississippi territory was the fact that the Americans were not demanding that England grant them the territory, they were claiming *that it already belonged to them;* it was a "possession." Herein lay the danger to France. If the Mississippi territory did, indeed, constitute a part of American possessions, Louis XVI was committed by treaty to continue the war until England recognized American ownership. The costs of such a commitment were, of course, unpredictable, but, from the vantage point of Versailles in 1781-82, there was no question but that the cost certainly would be more than France could afford. The debate over whether or not the western lands were, indeed, American possessions was, therefore, not an exercise in theoretical hairsplitting; it ultimately reduced itself to a definition of France's diplomatic obligations.

Americans, of course, could formulate designs on the western territory, they could insist with the English that such territory be granted to them, and Vergennes could not object. But, when the Americans argued that the territory already belonged to them, and that Louis XVI was obliged by treaty to see to it that Great Britain recognized the Americans' title, he objected. Such an argument committed Louis XVI to defend an American claim which Vergennes found untenable.

The Americans advanced several arguments to prove that the Mississippi territory was, indeed, their possession,[4] but Vergennes and his representatives found them all unconvincing. The notion that the original charters of the colonies gave the United States title to the area was the most vulnerable to criticism.[5] In the Proclamation of 1763, George III had effectively set aside those charter boundaries when he strictly forbade, on pain of his displeasure, all his "loving subjects" from making any purchases or settlements in the Mississippi region, without his "leave or license."[6] The Quebec Act of 1774 further nullified the western claims of the colonies.[7] Before 1763, France claimed possession of both Canada and the Mississippi Valley, and had nearly exhausted herself in a long, bloody, and expensive war to defend that claim. Certainly Vergennes could not now be expected to argue, before George III's representatives, that, in fact, the Americans had, all along, been the rightful owners of that land. Furthermore, by Articles Four and Seven of the Treaty of Paris of 1763, Louis XV had ceded the territory to his Britannick Majesty, not to the American colonies,[8] and Vergennes saw no reason to revise the Treaty of 1763 on that point. Finally, claims based on charters granted by a sovereign the Americans no longer recognized were self-contradictory; one could not deny sovereignty and, at the same time, base claims on it.

A claim to the West based on conquest or occupation was open to the Americans, and Article Eleven of the Treaty with France made it explicit.[9] But, in fact, the Americans had conquered or occupied very little of the territory they demanded, and had, later, even evacuated some portions of what they had occupied.[10] Hence, their claim based on conquest and occupation was very weak. But, more significant still, a claim based on the right of conquest or occupation was equally open to Spain,[11] for Spanish troops had also conquered and occupied a small portion of the territory. If Americans based their claims on conquest or occupation, they ran the risk of undermining their claims to other portions of the territory they wanted, but had not won.

The Americans also reasoned that, when the King lost his sovereignty over the American people, he also lost all rights incidental to that sovereignty; that is, rights to the western lands. They argued from the assumption that the rights to the land devolved on the people of the United States, as a result of the break with Great Britain. But this argument was strongly contested, even by Americans. Representatives of the various states rightly saw that such a claim denied the individual states' claims based on ancient charters.[12] Furthermore, the argument had no status whatsoever in the public law of Europe. The notion that the rights of the British crown devolved on the United States was sheer "extravagance," as James Madison quite honestly admitted.[13]

As early as September, 1779, Vergennes stated the French position regarding American possessions. Louis XVI's guarantee, he warned Americans, "bears only on the independence of the United States," and this guarantee "only eventually bears on their possessions, whatever these may be."[14] Within this statement there was infinite possibility for American expansion, but there was nothing there that committed the money and military forces of Louis XVI to securing that expansion. LaLuzerne repeatedly echoed that conclusion. The United States, he argued, could not substantiate any of her claims, because she did not actually hold possession, and she could make no claims based on a sovereignty she had clearly renounced in the Declaration of Independence.[15] The Franco-American alliance, LaLuzerne reminded the Americans, had been formed to secure American independence, not to underwrite territorial conquests.[16]

Nevertheless, the question of who would possess the Mississippi territory would not be argued away. Vergennes recognized the British as rightful owners, but, as the time for peace negotiations approached, he was also confronted with the unpleasant fact that both of his allies wanted the territory. His response, therefore, was an attempt to restrain his allies, and find a compromise. His actions were conditioned by two important considerations. He had to see that his commitments were in line with French power and, secondly, he had to avoid a breakdown of his alliance system. He hoped, above all, to prevent an open conflict between his Spanish ally and his American ally over the division of the western territory. Furthermore, American resentment, over Spain's humiliating and repeated refusals to recognize them and give them more aid, greatly increased the friction between the two countries, making a compromise solution between the two more difficult as it became more necessary.

Moreover, in the Spanish ministry and among the American plenipotentiaries, there were men who were deeply suspicious of France. Vergennes had to be extremely careful that he not compromise himself with either Spain or the United States, by appearing to favor one or the other. For that reason, in 1780, and even though, a year earlier, he had supported Spain's claims to the Mississippi territory, he withdrew that support. "It is not for us to decide this question," he explained to LaLuzerne, "and prudence imposes upon us a strict duty not to articulate an opinion in this regard." "Only silence," he warned later, "will be without disadvantage."[17] He also advised his ambassador to Spain not to take sides on the issue.[18]

By mid-1782, however, his hands-off policy became increasingly difficult to maintain. Vergennes began to see that France had to assume the role of mediator. But the Spaniards' pride and the Americans' suspicious sensitivity made any compromise highly unlikely. No matter what he did, he was not likely to avoid irritating one or the other, or both, of his allies. Perhaps he had vaguely hoped that the fortunes of war would settle the dispute, but, by the summer of 1782, nothing at all had been settled, and the subject had become a potential danger to allied unity. Spain and the United States suspiciously eyed each other, watching for signs of treachery. Vergennes could no longer avoid the task of trying to reconcile two irreconcilable claims. The only possible and honorable way he could achieve this goal was by means of compromise, and it was the route he ultimately chose. But he never seemed sufficiently aware that both Spain and the United States would consider any compromise a sell-out; he was, in reality, trapped in the web of contradictory claims.

During the month of July, 1782, John Jay had been unable to participate in any of the negotiations because he and his family were abed with influenza. By the first week in August, he was, once again, on his feet and, although still suffering from the fatigue of his illness, he was ready to negotiate. On the third of August, he had his first interview with the Spanish ambassador to France, the Conde d'Aranda. From the first, the two men disliked each other. Aranda soured the atmosphere by refusing to receive Jay as an official representative of the United States, because Spain still stubbornly refused to recognize the United States. So Aranda received Jay as a "Spanish nobleman." This only added insult to injury. Jay detested the Spanish, and had no sympathy for noblemen. It was an inauspicious opening to the solution of their differences.

The results of their first meeting are well known. The two diplomats did agree that some clearly-marked line should constitute the western boundary of the United States,[19] but, having agreed that the new nation should have a western boundary, they parted ways. When asked where he would draw the boundary, Jay traced with his finger a line down the Mississippi to New Orleans. Aranda, somewhat surprised, asked him if he was not even going to leave to Spain West Florida. "Not only was that formerly ours," he pointed out to Jay, "but we have reconquered it from the English."[20] Jay was not moved. Since the Colonies took "by subrogation the rights of England, and the latter had these well-known boundaries, these same cannot be gainsaid from the source of the Mississippi to where the real boundary of West Florida begins."[21]

Aranda contested Jay's claim with one equally as farfetched, and soon both men were busily comparing ancient grants and counter-grants made by the Spanish and English crowns. Finally, Aranda came to the truth of the matter by bluntly admitting that ". . .both of our parties have equally good, or, indeed, equally reasonable rights. Let us remember this in marking out for ourselves the major landmarks; then each of us may clothe the naked body as best he can."[22]

The great gap that really separated Jay and Aranda did not become so obvious, however, until Aranda drew his line for the western boundary of the United States. This boundary began at the western end of Lake Superior, then traced the shore line of the Great Lakes to the western edge of Lake Erie. From this point, a line was dropped down to the confluence of the Grand Kanawha and Ohio Rivers. Then another line was drawn from there to the source of the Flint River, and thence to a spot near the headwaters of the St. Mary's River at the northern line of East Florida.[23]

Following a tradition as old as diplomacy itself, the two men were cold-bloodedly partitioning the territory of a power with whom they were at war. On the great Mitchell map used by Aranda and Jay in their boundary conversations, the claims of the two men were inches apart. But on the American continent, the two lines represented thousands of square miles of rich land, and the access to a major waterway.

When it became obvious that neither Jay nor Aranda would retreat from the lines they had drawn as the western boundary of the United States, Vergennes was brought into the discussions. Jay noted, during the first interview which included Vergennes and Franklin, that the French Secretary of State for Foreign Affairs "was very cautious and reserved," but that his secretary, Rayneval, "thought we claimed more than we had a right to."[24]

It was Rayneval's opinion that lighted Jay's suspicions that France was considering a betrayal of the United States on the boundary issue. But, in truth, Rayneval was only repeating what the American already knew: that Louis XVI considered the Americans' claims to the West to be extravagant. Jay's suspicions burned even brighter a few days later, however, when Rayneval attempted to minimize, before Jay, the significance of Aranda's lack of powers to treat with Jay.[25] Surely, he concluded, there was a plot afoot.

Aranda was pleased that Vergennes had been called into the boundary discussions, and, no doubt, he was further satisfied when Vergennes assured him that the arguments Aranda had used to counter Jay's claims were in order. Jay's claims, Vergennes believed, were excessive, but he pointed out to Aranda that there were, west of Aranda's line, several American settlements. Aranda allowed that these settlements would have to be taken into consideration. Aranda then expressed the opinion that, if Vergennes wished to "take the trouble to intervene," Aranda "would be grateful to him for it, but let him begin by explaining things concretely to Jay."[26]

Vergennes' attempts to reconcile the positions of his two allies culminated in a compromise proposal drawn up by Rayneval. The western boundary line suggested by this proposal went from the "eastern angle of the Gulf of Mexico, which makes the section between the two Floridas, to Fort Toulouse, situated in the country of the Alabamas; from thence the River Loneschatihi should be ascended, from the south of which a right line should be drawn to the Fort of Factory Quenasse (Kanassee); from this last place the course of the River Euphasee is to be followed till it joins the Cherokee; the course of this last river is to be pursued to the place where it receives the Pelissippi, this last to be followed to its source, from whence a right line is to be drawn to the Cumberland River, whose course is to be followed until it falls into the Ohio."[27]

One need only to trace this line on a map, to be convinced of the compromise nature of this French proposal.[28] It bisects the area disputed by France's two allies, and it was as favorable (or detrimental) to the Spanish claims as it was to the American ones. The fact that Aranda seemed ready to accept Rayneval's boundary, and Jay was not, indicates only that the veteran Spanish ambassador was more willing to accept a compromise than were the Americans. For not only Jay, but Franklin and Adams, refused to back up one inch on this question. There was nothing immoral about the Americans' refusal to compromise on this point, and the subsequent negotiations proved the effectiveness of such a tactic, but the point at issue here is whether Vergennes was guilty of duplicity when he suggested a compromise. Unless one reads more into the evidence than is actually there, the answer is clearly, "No."

Vergennes' and Rayneval's refusal to second Jay's bid for the western territory has been singled out as proof that Vergennes really favored the Spanish claims, rather than the American ones. But those who make such charges usually fail to point out that Vergennes and Rayneval were equally dubious about the Spanish claims. "The Americans," according to the French position, "had acquired no rights over the territory east of the Mississippi south of the Ohio." But, at the same time, the "proprietary rights of Spain to the east of the same river do not extend beyond her conquests." The land belonged to England, according to the French view, and Louis XVI did not wish to commit his dwindling resources to force England to submit to the demands of either of his allies.[29] Nevertheless, Jay perceived this position as an act of treachery.

When Rayneval presented his compromise proposal to Jay, Jay refused to consider it; furthermore, he told Rayneval that Aranda's lack of power to treat officially was sufficient cause to break off the conversations. Rayneval did not insist, for Vergennes had no more desire to impose the compromise proposal than he had to force the acceptance of the claims of either ally. Nevertheless, as the "honest broker" in these complicated talks, Rayneval felt compelled to advise Jay to see Aranda again, and make him a "proposition of some sort or other . . . ." Moreover, Rayneval still felt that the compromise embodied in his memo "was the most proper to make a reasonable conciliation."[30]

Rayneval closed his letter with the news that he was going to be "absent [from Versailles] for some days." A few days later, Jay learned that Rayneval had gone to London. The news that Rayneval was leaving aroused, once again, Jay's suspicions. The additional information that, on the morning of Rayneval's departure, the Conde d'Aranda, "contrary to his usual practice," had gone to Versailles and spent two or three hours in conference with Vergennes and Rayneval before the latter left for London, confirmed Jay's suspicions. Now he was certain that Vergennes was intriguing behind the backs of the Americans.[31]

By now, Jay was thoroughly convinced of the existence of a plot against American interests. And, once the plot thesis became fixed in his mind, nearly every move the French made was interpreted as proof of duplicity. Fully aware of Jay's attitude, the British helpfully shoveled coals onto the fire. Three days after Rayneval sailed for London, a British agent handed to Jay the famous intercepted Barbé-Marbois letter. This letter repeated the French denials of American rights in the Newfoundland fisheries. Whatever the British paid their agent for passing this letter on to Jay was money well spent. Jay now decided that Vergennes was no longer trustworthy, and the Americans had to strike out on their own, independently of France. Jay even decided that he had to go behind the back of his own colleague, Franklin, and against Congress' instructions. This was to be shirtsleeve diplomacy in the grand style; dramatic enough to raise the blood to the cheeks of future generations of American patriots, but, in truth, little different from the cunning of many a small power caught in the tangle of Ancien Régime diplomacy.

Jay concluded that Rayneval had been sent to London primarily to undercut all of the important American claims. According to Jay, Rayneval would tell the British that the "demands of America, to be treated by Britain as independent previous to a treaty, were not approved or countenanced" by France. He would sound out Shelburne, to discover if the British would agree to divide the fisheries with France "to the exclusion of others." Rayneval, Jay believed, "would impress Lord Shelburne with the determination of Spain to possess the exclusive navigation of the Gulf of Mexico," and Spain's desire to keep the United States from the Mississippi, as well as "to hint the propriety of such a line as, on the one hand, would satisfy Spain and, on the other, leave to Britain all the country north of the Ohio." Also, he would "make such other verbal overtures to Lord Shelburne as it might not be advisable to reduce to writing . . . ." And, if terms agreeable to France did not seem possible, Jay believed, "an immediate stop might be put to the negotiations."[32]

Jay was wrong on every count.

The real object of Rayneval's mission was not to do in the Americans, but to test the sincerity of Shelburne's apparent inclinations for peace.[33] The French Admiral de Grasse, while a prisoner in London, had had several interviews with Lord Shelburne, interviews in which not only terms for peace were discussed, but terms which, at least as the Comte de Grasse understood them, indicated Britain's willingness to cede Gibraltar. When the Admiral was ransomed and returned to France, he presented to Vergennes a report of his interviews which included a series of articles which, the

Admiral felt authorized to say, would be approved by the British minister. Britain seemed willing, according to Grasse, to cede Gibraltar in return for St. Lucia or Dominica in the Caribbean, and to grant the Americans "the most complete and absolute independence, without condition or modification."[34] These articles differed so radically from those carried by Fitzherbert that Vergennes, hopeful, but at the same time perplexed, immediately dispatched Rayneval to clarify Shelburne's intentions.[35]

The first article of Rayneval's instructions insisted upon American independence as a preliminary to peace.[36] Furthermore, when Rayneval reported to Vergennes on September sixteenth, he stated: "independence, this is agreed upon. It shall be without restriction."[37] Shelburne, he said, "found independence a pill . . . difficult to swallow and digest, but one which he had to take."[38] Later, Rayneval reported that "as independence was agreed upon, there is nothing to report on that subject."[39] It was eventually John Jay, and not Vergennes, who relinquished the demand for independence as a preliminary condition to peace.[40]

The "English ministers," Rayneval's instruction read, "may speak to M. de Rayneval about the affairs of America and the United Provinces; he will declare that he has no authority to treat on these topics."[41] When Shelburne questioned Rayneval about the American claims to the fisheries, the French envoy replied that he "was ignorant of the views of Congress concerning the subject in question, but thought that he might venture to say that the King would never support unjust demands; that he was not able to judge whether those of the Americans were just or not, and that, besides, he was without authority in that respect."[42] When Shelburne said he hoped that Louis XVI "would not sustain the Americans in their demands," Rayneval answered that he did not doubt the earnest desire of the King [Louis XVI] to do all in his power to restrain them within the boundaries of justice and reason." And he further added, "that the English minister ought to find in the negotiations of 1754, relative to the Ohio, the limits which England, then the sovereign of America, believe it proper to assign."[43]

Rayneval clearly intimated, therefore, that France would not stand behind all of the American claims. But such a position can hardly be called an act of betrayal. Vergennes had never promised to back the Americans on every demand, and was not prepared to prolong the war by making demands on the British which he felt the British could not possibly accept. His estimate of what Britain would concede to the Americans was wrong, but error does not constitute treachery. Viewed in this light, Rayneval's performance in London showed amazing consideration for American interests, for, even though Vergennes and Rayneval considered the American claims extreme, Rayneval said nothing to indicate that France was opposed to any British concessions to them.[44] But more importantly, Rayneval returned to France convinced that Shelburne could be trusted, and that he sincerely wanted peace.[45]

The secrecy which veiled Rayneval's mission has occasionally been cited as "proof" of French perfidy. But such "proof" rests on an anachronism, and a misreading of Rayneval's words. We must remember that the conditions of eighteenth-century diplomacy favored, indeed required, secrecy, and that the modern notion about open negotiations did not carry the odor of sanctity which it later acquired. In the Ancien Régime, it was not so readily assumed that secrecy was evil or a sure sign of misdealing. But, more importantly, the widespread practice of speculating in public funds and insurance imposed the necessity of secrecy for political and financial reasons. Stock-jobbers and gamblers who got advance notice of an approaching peace could easily make a killing on the market, sometimes in collusion with government or cabinet officials. Earlier in his career, Lord Shelburne had seen his predecessor at the Peace of 1763 burned by a stock-jobber scandal, and the example left him extremely anxious to avoid such scandal in his own administration.[46]

Furthermore, George III had a personal horror of stock-jobbing, and Shelburne was aware of his King's sensitivity on this point.[47] Not surprisingly, therefore, Shelburne wanted secrecy to be "most faithfully guarded . . . ." "My lord [Shelburne] fears gamblers in the public funds," Rayneval explained to Vergennes, "and would be extremely desirous to frustrate their endeavors." Rayneval answered Shelburne that they "could arrange to conclude in the greatest secrecy, so as to throw the curious off the scent."[48] Later, Shelburne wrote to Richard Oswald, his commissioner in Paris. "I have nothing else to add, except the particular satisfaction which it gives me to find that what has passed hitherto in the American and French negotiations has given rise to no speculation in the funds. I need not tell you the numbers which are upon the watch, and of how much importance it is to the reputation of every person concerned to avoid the possibility of it."[49] Shelburne's special desire to keep knowledge of the talks from the Americans and Dutch does not prove a plot; it suggests that the Americans and the Dutch, and the British spies who had infiltrated their ranks, had especially bad reputations for speculation.[50]

Shelburne soon concluded that a rift had developed between the Americans and the French over the American claims, but it is highly unlikely that Rayneval's words convinced Shelburne of this truth.[51] In all probability, Shelburne was enlightened by the British agent, Benjamin Vaughan, who became John Jay's emissary. As soon as Jay learned of Rayneval's departure on a secret mission, he decided to disregard his instructions and strike out on his own and negotiate, independently of Vergennes. He sent Vaughan, post-haste, to London to get Richard Oswald's commission changed, to permit serious negotiations between the Americans and the English. And, from that date until his death, Jay seemed to have been convinced that whatever he did was justified by the existence of a French plot against American interests.

But Jay's actions, at this critical turning point in the diplomacy of the American Revolution, cannot be sufficiently explained by the hypothesis that he was motivated only by a suspicion of French treachery. His refusal to confide in Franklin, when he made his momentous decision, can only be explained by the hypothesis that, either he did not trust his American colleague, or else he was so panic-stricken by Rayneval's departure that he forgot to consult his partner. The fact that he had established contacts with Benjamin Vaughan as early as July twenty-fifth[52] raises the suspicion that his decision to go it alone was not unpremeditated, and that Rayneval's departure was the occasion, and not the cause, of Jay's deliberate disregarding of his instructions from Congress. Jay suspected his allies, and, perhaps, even his colleague, of treachery, but whatever convinced him that he could trust Benjamin Vaughan, an enemy agent and, paradoxically, an agent whom the British government itself did not trust? George III had said of Vaughan "... by what I have seen from the correspondence of Mr. Vaughan I have but little opinion of his talents ...."[53] And, even after Vaughan's breathless mission to London, George III did not change his mind: "As to poor Mr. Vaughan," he wrote, "he seems so willing to be active, and so void of judgment, that it is fortunate he has had no business, and the sooner he returns to his family the better."[54]

John Jay's behavior suggests one other hypothesis. Jay and his other colleague, John Adams, were both extremely ambitious young diplomats, who may very well have let their own personal desires to make a *coup* override their sense of loyalty to the older and more experienced Franklin. Their later attitude toward Franklin, and their exaggerated attempts at self-justification, suggest that their consciences were certainly not completely clear as far as Franklin was concerned. This hypothesis gains credence, also, when we remember that, once Jay had taken the initiative for the negotiations out of Franklin's hands, he was the first to compromise on the issue of independence. Earlier, he had condemned Vergennes, and by implication Franklin, for even contemplating just such a compromise.

In any event, John Jay led the rebellion against full consultation with Vergennes, and began to negotiate a preliminary peace with the British as soon as Oswald returned. When John Adams arrived in Paris from the Hague in late October, he enthusiastically seconded Jay's decision.[55] And, in keeping with his characteristic bad manners, this time he refused to see Franklin until Matthew Ridley persuaded him of the necessity of a meeting.[56] By now, Adams thoroughly distrusted Franklin's "cunning,"[57] he spoke "freely of what he thought of Dr. Franklin,"[58] and, when he finally saw Franklin on the twenty-ninth of October, he told him bluntly that he "was determined to support Mr. Jay to the utmost of my power in . . .the principles, wisdom, and firmness with which [he] conducted the negotiations." Franklin heard Adams "patiently but said nothing."[59] The next morning, however, he had decided to "go on with the gentlemen in this business without consulting the French court."[60] By the fifth of November, they had negotiated with Oswald and a new British envoy, Henry Strachey, a set of articles which became, except for minor changes, the preliminary peace treaty.

All three of the American commissioners clearly saw the advantages to be gained for the United States by breaking away from the restraining hand of Vergennes, and exploiting the situation in which the European powers found themselves. The temptation to do so would probably have been too great to resist, even if Vergennes and Rayneval had given them no grounds for suspicion. Jay and Adams incorrectly assessed the motives of Vergennes, but the two men, along with Franklin, correctly assessed their position *vis-à-vis* France and England. Both powers desperately needed peace; to prolong the war would have demanded sacrifices and involved risks which both governments were reluctant to demand. Thus, by pressing every advantage, by considering some issues not negotiable, by threatening even to prolong the war; in other words, by shrewdly taking advantage of Europe's distresses and rivalries, the Americans returned home with a peace that astounded everyone. The American gains, Vergennes exclaimed in amazement, "exceed all that I could have thought possible." And Rayneval probably put his finger on the truth of the matter when he concluded that the settlement with the Americans was "a dream, and the English ministers in according it [must have] had in view ultimately the defection of the Americans."

But, in fact, a defection never occurred, because the war was not prolonged. Although the American commissioners certainly disobeyed their instructions, they did not violate any principle of the Treaty of 1778. They would have been foolish to do so, for, even though Adams and Jay loved to proclaim about American independence, they knew that the United States was, in fact, not yet independent. Franklin, at least, knew that the United States was still dependent on France for money to help keep the new nation solvent, and it was Franklin who patiently accepted Vergennes' criticism of the commissioners' behavior; it was Franklin who tactfully apologized; and, of course, it was Franklin who got a new loan from Vergennes.

Americans have been fiercely proud of the ability of the American commissioners in Versailles to take advantage of the rivalries of Europe and gain advantages for the infant republic. Certainly, the peace settlement between

England and the United States was a rich harvest for the American republic. Great Britain recognized the independence of the United States, and the young nation extended its boundaries to the Mississippi. Great Britain accorded fishing rights to Americans off Newfoundland and Nova Scotia, and liberty to dry and fish along the unsettled shores of Nova Scotia, Labrador, and the Magdalen Island. The debts due to creditors of each country, by debtors of the other, were validated. In return, Congress pledged to recommend (and no more) to the State legislatures, that they restore the rights and properties of the Loyalists. Finally, the British promised to evacuate all their land and sea forces "with all convenient speed" after the cessation of hostilities. Without a doubt, the Americans gained far more than they would have if they had remained in close collaboration with their ally. One cannot conclude from this fact, however, that their victory was preordained, that their demands were valid under public law, or even that Vergennes was obliged to favor their claims. Jay's and Adams' victory was not a triumph of Good over Evil, and Providence probably had no interest whatsoever in the outcome of the war. In simple truth, Jay discovered that it was possible, under the circumstances, to make demands which Vergennes could not support, and he made them; England, anxious to make a peace, conceded.

Vergennes did not plot against the Americans' interests, but the American diplomats' suspicions of him are understandable. They knew, as well as other diplomats of Europe, that Vergennes was capable of intrigue and plotting. Vergennes' role, as French Ambassador, in the Swedish *coup d'état* of 1772 was public knowledge.[61] And the Americans, themselves, had participated in his deceptive maneuvers against Great Britain, in the months that preceded the Franco-American alliance. Thus, Vergennes' reputation as a man capable of intrigue and deception was public knowledge that Jay, or Adams and Franklin could not ignore. The episode demonstrates the truth of Français de Collière's observation that deceit always leaves a "drop of poison" behind that will plague the diplomat for the rest of his career. The intelligent diplomat, Collière advised, would be very careful to establish a reputation for "plain and fair dealing so that men may know that they can rely upon him."[62]

Part VI

EVE OF DISASTER

CHAPTER 32

The Legacy of the American War

The peace of 1783 was hailed by Frenchmen and Europeans alike as a great victory for Louis XVI. The announcement of it in Paris was made, by order of the Lieutenant of Police, in cafés and theatres and created a great outburst of joy and relief.[1] At his town house in Versailles, Vergennes celebrated with a dinner for Fitzherbert, Aranda, Franklin, and his colleagues. Great Britain had been forced to recognize the independence of the United States. Friends of Vergennes were exultant.[2]

But the debate on Vergennes' policy in the American Revolution began during his lifetime and still continues. Despite Vergennes' pro-American propaganda campaign at Court, Marie Antoinette had little enthusiasm for the support given to the American revolutionaries,[3] and Charles III of Spain saw the intervention in the American War as a policy forced upon him by Vergennes and Louis XVI.[4] In Louis XVI's cabinet, the Secretary of State for the Navy, the Marquis de Castries, never reconciled himself to the fact that, while most of the burdens of the war were on France, most of the benefits were for her allies.[5] Castries' complaints echoed throughout France.[6] American historians, mindful of the fact that Vergennes did not vigorously support every American demand at the peace table, have found Vergennes and his policy a striking example of the deception, cynicism, and trickery that characterized Ancien Régime diplomacy.[7] But, in fact, Vergennes did not deceive or betray the Americans in the peace settlement. If he deceived anyone, it was England during the early stages of French intervention, when Vergennes repeatedly assured England that France wanted only peace while, in fact, France prepared for war. If Vergennes betrayed (the word is perhaps too strong) anyone at the peace table, it was Spain, for Louis XVI had promised to continue the war until Gibraltar was Spanish, but Vergennes skillfully manipulated the negotiations to relieve France of this obligation.

French historians have praised Vergennes' American policy as the high point in Louis XVI's reign. The ministry of Vergennes, claimed a typical French historian, "is one of the most glorious epochs of our history."[8] But a more searching look at the American war reveals an ambiguous legacy. The American war and peace settlement were, perhaps, the "last ray of glory"[9] for the Ancien Régime, but the price of that glory was bankruptcy. In the achievement of his foreign policy goals, Vergennes unintentionally helped to destroy the society and monarchy he wished to conserve.

When the peace treaties were finally signed in 1783, and the war ended, Vergennes felt obliged to summarize for Louis XVI the result of almost five years of war and diplomacy.[10] It is difficult to gauge just how much he believed his justification of past decisions. He was under severe pressure and criticism, from various factions in the French government and court, because he refused to continue the war to gain more territory for France in India.[11] Castries vigorously resisted Vergennes' peace.[12] If Vergennes had any reservations or disappointments about his past diplomacy, he wasn't inclined to articulate them; his enemies could use his words againt him. His perceptions of the results of his diplomacy are, therefore, as much briefs for the defense as they are objective analyses.

Nevertheless, his comments about the war contain several recurring ideas worth noting. It is clear, for example, that he did not regret having brought France into the war, despite the government's near-bankrupt treasury. In March of 1784, he argued that England's pride, ambition, violence, and injustices had provoked Louis XVI to intervene, in order to prevent the American Revolutionary War from developing into something "prejudicial" to France.[13] The intervention was just one among several examples, according to Vergennes, of Louis XVI's desire to preserve public order, and to act as the arbiter. France had no need for aggrandizement or conquests, but, as the arbiter of Europe, she was concerned with maintaining the balance of power.

In addition, Vergennes claimed that, as a result of France's moderation during the war, the small powers no longer feared France's ambitions. Even the Dutch, he pointed out, after more than a century of suspicions of France, had broken with their long-standing ally, England, and fought with France during the war. This about-face, Vergennes believed, was a major victory for France.[14]

Vergennes admitted that the progress of the war had not always developed according to plan, and that there had been mistakes committed, and reverses suffered. But he reminded his monarch that the primary aim of the war — American independence — had been, in fact, achieved.[15]

Vergennes also felt that the war justified the government's earlier decision to give top priority to the expansion of the French Navy. While he admitted that orderly finances and a well-constituted Army were important, he insisted that a well-organized and carefully maintained Navy should always have first priority. "I humbly plead with you," he urged Louis XVI, "to keep the Navy on a respectable footing."[16] Power, he told the King, was still the most certain way to gain respect, especially if the power was used wisely and for justice.[17]

The peace treaty signed with England made provision for negotiating an Anglo-French commercial treaty, which Vergennes hoped could begin a *rapproachement* between England and France, and Vergennes continued to press for the treaty until it was signed in 1786. Yet, despite his official stance, he still saw Great Britain as France's first enemy. This "proud and haughty" nation, he warned Louis, would reopen a war with France again whenever she believed herself able to win it. In fact, Vergennes concluded, England was already busily building the ships to fight that next war.[18] Thus, the war did nothing to change Vergennes' conviction that war was inevitable, and France must forever spend her resources preparing for it. One should not "flatter oneself" with the idea of a long peace, he declared. The newly-won peace was "absolutely precarious"[19]

Nevertheless, the war forced Vergennes to recognize France's growing inability to find resources to fight wars. He knew, of course, that France needed to put her finances in order, and that England had better means to finance war than France. Still, it was England, according to his perceptions, who was really exhausted by the war. And it was England, he informed Louis XVI, just four years before France went bankrupt from the debts of the American War, who emerged from the war "bent under the weight of an enormous debt which was crushing her."[20]

The American War cost at the very best more than a billion *livres*.[21] The costs of these loans, that is, the interests and redemption payments, came out of the ordinary expenditures of the budget. In his *Compte rendu* of 1781, Necker claimed that revenues exceeded ordinary expenses enough to cover the interests on the war loans of 1781.[22] Furthermore, Joly de Fleury, in 1783, claimed that at the end of the war the credit of the government had been maintained "beyond all expectations."[23] But Necker's claims were challenged from the beginning and had been a bone of contention among historians ever since.[24]

Nevertheless, the French debt of 1783 totalled over 3 billion *livres* with annual interest costs of over 165 million *livres*. And while Joly de Fleury and Vergennes may have been sanguine about the health of post-war finances, in fact, France had borrowed its money at rates of interest that were much more burdonsome than the interests on British loans. By 1788 the State debt in France absorbed over 50 per cent of the ordinary budget. The expenses of the military and diplomatic affairs absorbed another 26 per cent.[25] Those who paid taxes in France paid dearly for France's role as arbiter of Europe.

And the burden would prove to be more than the traditional economy and privileged social structure of France could carry. In these financial weaknesses lay some of the explosive origins of the French Revolution.

Vergennes did not approve of the social and political ideas advanced by the Americans Louis XVI had supported. Proof of this lies in his haste to crush other revolutionary reformers, when their actions did not further French foreign policy.[26] In the spring of 1782, the bourgeois and "natives" of Geneva clashed with the ruling "patricians" of that city, and after two days of sharp street fighting, the revolutionaries were masters of the city. Since the "natives" (descendants of immigrants to the city) formed an economically and socially underprivileged class in Geneva, the new revolutionary government, in which the natives shared power with the bourgeois, represented a social and political revolution. The patricians, who formed only a small minority, seemed helpless in the face of this popular movement. Realizing their impotence at home, they appealed to foreign powers, to Berne, Zurich, to Piedmont-Sardinia, and especially to France. Vergennes was more than willing to help. The revolutionaries were dangerous, he thought, because they believed "that sovereignty lies with the people." An alliance was soon formed between France, Sardinia, Berne, and Zurich to intervene militarily in Geneva. France promised to send 6,000 troops. The other allies promised 6,000 more. In July 1782, when the French and Sardinian troops stood before the walls of Geneva, the Genevan revolutionaries vowed to "live and die free," but the overwhelming odds against them took the heart out of their cause. By November, the revolutionaries had surrendered and their leaders were in prison or exile. With the aid of French troops, the Ancien Régime was restored and made more oppressive. Vergennes was completely frank about his reasons for destroying this popular uprising: "The insurgents whom I am driving from Geneva are agents of England, while the American insurgents are our friends for years to come. I have dealt with both of them, not by reason of their political systems, but by reason of their attitudes toward France. Such are my reasons of State."[27] There is no clearer expression of an Ancien Régime statesman's inability to see revolutionary activity in any way other than in the context of international politics.

Nevertheless, historians have traced the transfer from America to France of the revolutionary ideas that played a part in the causal pattern of the French Revolution.[28] This diffusion of revolutionary idealism was the direct consequence of Vergennes' foreign politics; indeed, the carriers themselves were usually diplomatic agents. French unofficial and official agents spread in France a glowing picture of American political ideas, and of the American society. The writings and personal popularity of the American minister to Louis XVI, Benjamin Franklin; the French government-sponsored publication, in the European press, of American state constitutions and the Declaration of Independence; French diplomatic recognition of American agents; as well as the reports of some French soldiers who returned from the French Expeditionary Force in America, all encouraged the spread of ideals and hopes which had a revolutionary effect. Jefferson observed the result when he was the American minister to France: "Though celebrated writers of this and other countries had already sketched good principles on the subject of government, yet the American war seems first to have awakened the thinking part of this nation in general from the sleep of despotism in which they were sunk."[29] The ideals of the American Revolution, circulated in France through the good offices of the Minister of Foreign Affairs, played a crucial part in the moral and ideological preparation for revolutionary activity in France.[30] Yet, Vergennes himself did not believe that the republicanism of the Americans would ever be a serious threat to Louis XVI. He disdainfully dismissed such beliefs in republicanism as the "idols of . . . fanaticism."[31]

The American war forced the government of Louis XVI to recognize that the financial difficulties of the State could no longer be avoided.[32] The needs of war had also revealed the inability of the government's right hand to know what its left hand did. A Secretary of State, such as Sartine, could, on his own, secretly expand his military budget. The Comptrolleur of Finance had neither the status nor the influence to stop such practices.

Attempts to respond to the situation brought a rash of governmental committees in the last decades before the revolution. The Abbé de Veri noted in his journal that committees had become a necessity of the times, because government officials had been forced to see the relationship between one governmental endeavor and another. "Finances, war, or any foreign affairs, and even, sometimes, jurisprudence," he noted, "all have an influence on each other; and the head of one [branch of government] cannot take a sure step without concert with the other parties."[33] One can only marvel at a government in which the obvious appears as a dramatic conceptual breakthrough.

The new *Comité contentieux des finances,* created in 1783, was an example of this type of response, and its fate is representative of how the Ancien Régime failed to meet the crisis. There had been an earlier committee with the same name, but this new one, organized by the Comptrolleur-Général of Finances, Joly de Fleury, had as its ostensible aim the liquidation of the American Revolutionary War.[34] It was to oversee, coordinate, and reduce the expenditures of the different ministers, and even to enter into the deliberations of the various ministers on questions relating to expenditures. The committee was supposed to meet at least once a week and usually included the Keeper of the Seals, the head of the Royal Council on Finances, that is, Vergennes, and the Comptrolleur-Général of Finances. But, in reality, the committee's main purpose was soon blunted and the committee was used as an instrument, in the hands of Vergennes, to control or to try to force the resignations of the Secretary of State for War, Ségur, and the Secretary of the Navy, Castries. Their differences with Vergennes over foreign policy had become unbearable.[35] Moreover, on the occasions when the committee tried to implement its original aims, it threatened too many high persons at Court. Hardly a month after he organized the committee, Joly de Fleury was forced to resign. His successor, Lefevre d'Ormesson, suffered the same fate. Like Fleury, he was no reformer; he only demanded that the heads of the ministries provide him with an accurate accounting of their departments. But their response continued to be hostility and non-cooperation.[36] The committee ceased to meet, and, in 1784, it was suppressed at the request of the new Comptrolleur-Général, Calonne.

The example of the committee of finances symbolizes the futile gropings and internal conflicts of a government faced with a desperate crisis, but virtually paralyzed in its inability to initiate and carry through any policy which threatened the powerful, the entrenched, and the privileged. Instead of bringing radical financial reform, the post-war years until Vergennes' death in 1787 were years of piece-meal remedies, half-measures, or, years of "reaction,"[37] Joly de Fleury, Lefevre d'Ormesson, and Calonne did not try radically to overhaul an outworn system; they simply tried to make it work. Their basic conservatism explains why Vergennes gave them his support. Yet, even so, whenever they proposed plans which smelled the least bit of radical reform, they were harried out of office. Furthermore, whenever anyone tried to appeal, over the heads of the King and his ministers, to the public, as Necker did in 1781, in his misleading, but pioneering, *Compte rendu,* Vergennes was the first to act in the name of authority: "His [Necker's] *Compte rendu* is a pure appeal to the people," Vergennes warned Louis XVI. "For a long time Your Majesty will not close the wound done to the dignity of the throne."[38] With the Keeper of the Seals, Miromesnil, and Maurepas, Vergennes, who earlier had supported Necker, urged Louis XVI to accept Necker's resignation. Vergennes admired Necker's obvious ability to raise money for the war, but he resented Necker's interference in foreign affairs, he resented his appeal to public opinion, and he distrusted him as a reformer.[39]

Another consequence of the peace of 1783 was that Louis XVI appointed Vergennes as President, or chief, of the Royal Council of Finances. Given the government's now-urgent concern about the deteriorating financial situation, the post gave to Vergennes something of the role of first minister, although without the title. The appointment of Vergennes to an office concerned with finances seems absurd, since never had he shown any real understanding for such problems. The most simple explanation for the appointment is that Louis XVI, equally ignorant,[40] was rewarding Vergennes for services rendered in diplomacy, rather than for his abilities in finance. Indeed, the letter patent awarding the post said, outright, that the post was a reward for services in the Department of Foreign Affairs, and, principally, for his work in making the peace.[41] Bachaumont saw the appointment as purely honorific, rewarding Vergennes with the place left vacant by the death of Maurepas.[42] But Bachaumont rightly saw that the new position did place the Comptrolleur-Général of Finances under Vergennes' authority.[43]

By a combination of circumstances, this appointment provided Vergennes with the experience he should have had much earlier in his career. The Royal Council of Finances was composed of nine members, including the Keeper of the Seals.[44] The seat in the Council brought Vergennes face to face with the pressing questions of economics and finance. The Royal Council approved the accounts of the Royal Treasury, prepared replies to petitions, and judged matters of litigation related to financial affairs.[45] As a member of this Council, Vergennes, rather belatedly, began his education in economics and state finance.

Vergenne's enemy, Turgot, had earlier argued that the State's financial difficulties grew out of weaknesses in her economy. A prosperous economy, so went his argument, would provide the revenues required by government. Such a simple theory had an appeal in 1783, because, it suggested a way whereby Louis XVI could escape bankruptcy while, at the sametime, avoiding more radical fiscal, administrative, and social reforms. In 1783, one of Turgot's protégés, DuPont de Nemours, co-head of the Bureau of the Balance of Commerce, became one of Vergennes' trusted economic advisers. As we shall see, DuPont suggested to the Secretary of State for Foreign Affairs ways in which the financial difficulties he pondered in the Royal Council of finances might be relieved by diplomacy,[46]

In 1786, the French Treasury showed an annual deficit of 112,000,000 *livres.* The Comptrolleur-Général of Finances, Calonne, attempted to come to terms with the problem with a plan to reform administration, to increase taxation, and cut expenditures, but all of this depended on increasing the prosperity of the economy, and getting the approval of a significant segment of the privileged classes, for his reforms involved, in some cases, abolition of privileges.[47] At first Vergennes tried to avoid Calonne's reforms,but soon he conceded that something had to be done. Personally, however, he wanted the King to impose his authority on the Parlements and force them to accept the King's fiscal policy. [48] Calonne's reforms probably appeared, to the conservative Vergennes, although we have little evidence of this, as much less dangerous than calling the Estates General, which some radicals were demanding. Vergennes probably agreed with the Cardinal de Bernis who wrote to him: "Everybody has gone off their heads. We are back in the disorders of the Fronde . . . . The assembling of the States General will change or modify the existing constitution . . . . I am pretty old, but I wish I were older. The future makes me afraid."[49].

To implement his reforms, Calonne devised the plan to call together an assembly composed of Notables of the realm, chosen by the King. Calonne hoped that the Notables, flattered by the King's request for their advice, would rally behind reforms. Their approval would go a long way, Calonne hoped, toward marshalling public opinion in favor of reform.[50] But how could one get one hundred forty-four Notables to agree to reform, when the ministers of the King themselves could not agree? The Secretary of State for the Navy, the Duc de Castries, vigorously opposed calling the assembly, and complained to the King that the decision to do so had been made without his being consulted.[51] The Minister of War, the Maréchal de Ségur, saw the assembly as "the seedling of the Estates General."[52] Vergennes reluctantly accepted Calonne's plan, but, along with Miromesnil, he urged Calonne to move slowly, to introduce the reforms in well-spaced stages. When Calonne refused, because the gravity of the crisis required speed, Vergennes and Miromesnil became his enemies.[53] Vergennes took the matter to the King and got a promise that the first meeting of the assembly would be delayed. Vergennes died on the thirteenth of February, before the Assembly of Notables met. It is impossible, therefore, to say for certain how he would have reacted to the Notables' refusal to support Calonne, and their demand for the calling of an Estates General, but his past performance and his innate conservatism point to the conclusion that he would have balked at any suggestion of radical reform, and the monarchy could have been saved only by such radical action.

CHAPTER 33

The Scheldt River Dispute: 1780-1785

In the spring of 1780, as part of its determination to force the Dutch to reconsider their drift toward the Armed Neutrality pact and friendship with France, the British government suspended all treaties with the Dutch government.[1] The immediate meaning of the suspension was clear. The English found unacceptable the Dutch behavior in the American Revolutionary War: Dutch goods had supplied the rebels since early in the war.

But the announcement contained another meaning which soon became apparent. By treaties dating back to 1715 and 1718, England was one of the major supports of the Dutch in their determination to maintain garrisons in the "barrier fortresses" in the Austrian Netherlands, and in their refusal to open the Scheldt River to navigation, a situation which strangled all commercial competition from the city of Antwerp. The Diplomatic Revolution of 1756 and Dutch neutrality during the Seven Years War had frayed the traditional lines between the United Provinces and Great Britain, but at the beginning of the American War, Britain was still obliged by treaty[2] to go to the aid of the Dutch, in case they were attacked, as the Dutch, in turn, were obligated to assist Great Britain, in case she were attacked. When England suspended the treaties with the United Provinces, she left the Dutch isolated in an international crisis that daily became more dangerous. Fear of isolation sent the Dutch scurrying to find new friends. But until she found new friends, the Republic was vulnerable and exposed. Emperor Joseph II saw her weakness, and exploited this critical moment to settle old accounts with the United Provinces.

The growth of the city of Antwerp in the Netherlands, potentially one of the great international seaports of the world, had been thwarted by the Peace of Westphalia (1648), which provided that the Scheldt River and the seaways leading to it be closed to navigation. The effect was the destruction of Antwerp's seagoing commerce. In the Barrier Treaty of 1715, the Austrians, who inherited the Netherlands from the Spanish, had to accept the same conditions. The Scheldt remained closed, and Antwerp languished.

Joseph II, however, was not content to be deprived of the use of a river whose economic value was readily apparent. Furthermore, the establishment of Dutch garrisons in the Austrian Netherlands by the Barrier Treaties had never pleased him. Now that England had withdrawn her support from these treaties, Joseph was free to act. In 1780, he occupied some forts along the canal from Bruges to Shirs, and in 1782, he unilaterally abrogated the Barrier Treaties. He also began to ponder the possibility of opening the Scheldt and restoring to Antwerp her freedom of commerce.[3]

His actions were, without doubt, encouraged by English diplomats.[4] But Joseph needed no outsiders to show him the opportunities created for him by Dutch-English hostilities. Not only would a flourishing Antwerp bring economic advantages, but the opening of the Scheldt would ultimately provide a means to extend his influence along the Rhine. In 1784, at Brussels, Dutch and Netherlander commissioners met in conference to discuss relations between the United Provinces and the Austrian Netherlands. The Scheldt River was one of the principal subjects of discussion. The Dutch seemed confident, however, that they could avoid any changes in the status of the Scheldt by dragging out the talks and consenting to nothing.[5] But Joseph believed otherwise.[6] He demanded the free navigation of the Scheldt.[7]

The Dutch were astonished. Joseph demanded not only territories, villages, and fortresses, which he claimed the Dutch had "usurped"from him, he also wanted the key Dutch fortress of Maastricht, indemnities for "injustices" committed by Dutch agents, payment and interest on the tax and customs losses he had suffered because of the Dutch, and the return of munitions and artillery he had loaned the Dutch garrisons in the barrier fortresses. But, above all, he wanted the Scheldt River opened to navigation.[8]

The Dutch were shaken. They recognized how weak they were, now that England no longer guaranteed the treaties of 1715 and 1718. Joseph was, in effect, unilaterally annulling those treaties. In their panic, the United Provinces asked Louis XVI to include in the Dutch-French alliance, then under negotiation, a commitment to defend the United Provinces with land forces in case they were attacked. There were even rumors that the Dutch Stadholder was considering approaching England to ask her good offices.[9] Both the United Provinces and Joseph wanted Louis' support and both asked him to extend his good offices.[10] Louis agreed to make available his good offices, but reluctantly, for he felt that he did not yet understand the extent of Joseph's demands on the Dutch.[11] Moreover, when Vergennes learned that the King of Prussia was advising the Dutch to hold firm and not give in to Joseph's demands, he was even more cautious. The issue had the ingredients of a European War.

The Dutch rejected Joseph's demands. They answered, point by point, each of the Emperor's claims and reduced them to nothing. The leaders of the Dutch Patriot Party felt they could make no concessions to Joseph, for reasons of internal politics as well as high politics. If they did, they would surely be accused of betraying their country. "The continuation of their influence," the French *chargé d'affaires* at The Hague believed, "requires that they [the Patriots] be the most zealous defenders of its rights."[12]

The dispute took a more ominous turn when the Dutch announced they were going to reinforce their troops along the Netherlands frontier.[13] The authorities in the Austrian Netherlands responded with the threat that, if the Dutch increased their frontier forces, they would do the same.

As the lines between the two disputants began to harden, Vergennes became uncomfortable. Louis XVI was involved in treaty negotiations with the Dutch, and Joseph was already his ally. Furthermore, if Joseph did not significantly lower his demands, Vergennes warned his ambassador at Vienna, Louis XVI would not even attempt to conciliate the dispute.[14] Joseph answered that if the Dutch did not accept his "ultimatum", including the point about opening the Scheldt, he was going to sail one of his ships up the Scheldt from Ostende to Antwerp and back. And if anyone tried to stop or hinder it, he warned, he would take the appropriate measures.

The Dutch were willing to give a little to satisfy Joseph. They agreed to withdraw from some of the barrier fortresses which, Joseph claimed, threatened him. And they were prepared to negotiate the differences over boundaries. But they refused to budge on the question of the opening of the Scheldt.[15] To demonstrate that they meant what they said, the Dutch ordered armed vessels to patrol the mouth of the Scheldt, and reinforcements were sent to the fortress of Maastricht. In April, 1784, an Austrian merchantman sailed up the Scheldt toward Antwerp, past the Dutch batteries, and it was fired on. The Prussian minister to the United Provinces intimated that his monarch did not disapprove of the Dutch action.[16]

To the Dutch concessions, the Austrian Minister of State, Kaunitz, returned a flat rejection, and then announced that a ship flying the Emperor's flag would force the passage of the Scheldt.[17] In the meantime, Austrian soldiers in the Netherlands moved into positions to respond to the reinforcement of Maastricht.[18] The result of the decision was predictable: the ship openly flying the Emperor's pennant sailed within the range of Dutch batteries and the latter opened fire. An armed Dutch frigate then stopped the intruder and refused to allow it to proceed.[19] Immediately, Joseph recalled his minister to the Dutch Estates General[20] and announced that an army of 80,000 men would obtain satisfaction for the outrage against his flag and his dignity. To his sister, Marie Antoinette, he wrote: "I assure you positively that I do not desire the destruction of the Dutch Republic, nor to make any conquests there, but I confess to you at the same time that if they continue their arrogance, and do not give me some satisfaction ... I will employ all the force that I believe proper to make them repent . . . ."[21] "The result is serious," Noailles wrote to Vergennes from Vienna, ". . . A war declared between these two powers and the fighting to take place near our frontier."[22]

At Versailles, the crisis looked as explosive as it did at Vienna, and Vergennes was deeply distressed. Louis XVI and the Dutch were close to agreement on an alliance, and, although Vergennes had insisted that the Scheldt dispute be exempted from the terms of the alliance, he, nevertheless, believed that Louis XVI could not stand by and watch Joseph satisfy his ambitions at the expense of the Dutch. Even without treaty obligations, Louis XVI's role as arbiter of Europe did not permit such a policy. Still, Vergennes was hesitant to take a public stand in favor of the Dutch for fear it would stiffen their resolution not to compromise. "In case of a war," he warned his representative at the Hague, "we foresee that the Republic will lose its exclusive rights over the Scheldt."[23]

But Vergennes also believed that Joseph II was the one most responsible for the crisis. Joseph, he told Louis XVI, had deliberately ordered his ship to sail up the river, and had then labeled the Dutch resistance insulting and a declaration of war, although the Dutch had the legal right to stop the ship. Joseph was undoubtedly counting on a quick victory imposed by his superior land forces.[24] He was also counting on his alliance with France. Louis XVI, Vergennes argued, could easily accept the Scheldt being opened or closed. But France could not stand passively by and allow the Dutch Republic to be reduced to the will of the Emperor. French interest, Vergennes argued, required that she not abandon the Dutch Republic at the very moment when it was seeking to establish ties with France.[25] Louis XVI was in danger of becoming a principal actor in a major European war.[26]

If war broke out in the Austrian Low Countries, Vergennes concluded, Louis XVI would send an army to his Belgium frontier as a warning to Joseph. At the same time, Louis XVI could open a direct personal correspondence with his brother-in-law to encourage him to moderation and peace. If these measures failed to settle the dispute, Vergennes advised, Louis XVI would have to take more "coercive measures" to prevent the ruin of the Dutch Republic, and check his brother-in-law's "torrent of ambition."[27]

In case of war, Vergennes predicted, France would need Prussian help, but he cautioned that Prussia had a reputation that made it difficult to count on her. Furthermore, Prussia would surely make costly military demands. For example, she would probably require that France field an army on the lower Rhine. She would, perhaps, want a subsidy. Prussia would probably insist that the Elector of Saxony be brought into the alliance, with France shouldering whatever costs that entailed.

In the South, the help of the Court of Turin would be indispensible in a war against Austria but this, too, would cost additional money. Spain might enter the war on the side of France, Vergennes believed, but, if she entered (which he felt unlikely because of her financial disorders), she would be interested only in Italy.[28] Nowhere else in Europe did Vergennes see any possibility for help.

In a war with Austria over the Scheldt River, France would field three armies, one in the Low Countries, one on the lower Rhine and the third in Italy. Altogether the three armies would amount to 140,000 troops. The cost of fielding such a military force, plus the additional war subsidies, Vergennes anticipated, would be considerable, especially if the war spread to the sea. Moreover, Vergennes recognized, Louis XVI could not count on England's "indifference" if a war broke out on the Continent. Discreetly, Vergennes had approached the British government asking for a British disapproval of Joseph's treatment of the Dutch, but he had received nothing but hostile indifference.[29]

As Vergennes outlined the possible costs and consequences of a new war, he was led inevitably to the Minister of Finances, Calonne. He was the expert, Vergennes advised, who could judge whether France's resources could meet the expenses of such a war. And Vergennes cautioned that it would be a dangerous error to assume, hypothetically, that a war would last only two or three years. It is very difficult, he warned, recalling, no doubt, the still-recent peace negotiations, to get one's allies to put down their arms before they have satisfied all of their ambitions.

Thus Vergennes drew a sober picture of what a war with Joseph might mean. But unlike the Vergennes of 1778, the one of 1784 was considerably more aware of the relationship between international politics and finances. The financial shambles caused by the American War had, indeed, taught the Secretary of State for Foreign Affairs to be more sensitive about the relations between capacities and commitments.[30] Perhaps, he admitted, he was now more "timid." But he warned Louis XVI that "people often engage in war without calculating the burden of expenses or the possibility of long duration." It would be a dangerous error, he believed, for Louis XVI to undertake a commitment beyond his means.[31]

Vergennes still saw Louis XVI as the arbiter of Europe, but in 1784 the arbiter was faced with difficult options. Because of the paucity of resources, the margin of freedom and power required to exercise the role of arbiter was severely reduced. From this cramped base, Vergennes gambled for his King. He asked Louis XVI to get written responses to the crisis from the other ministers.[32] In the Council of State, Calonne found Vergennes' reasoning about the situation "incontestable." The Maréchal de Ségur, Minister of War, saw the Emperor's acts as violations of formal treaties and public law, and therefore, felt it his duty to ask for orders to move 60,000 troops to the frontier. The Maréchal de Castries, Minister of the Marine, agreed with Ségur: Holland had to be helped before it was too late. The influential diplomat, Breteuil, heartily agreed. If France wished to maintain the present "system," she must not permit the Emperor to overpower the Dutch. If she did, she would lose her support among the small powers. In addition, Breteuil saw Vienna's behavior as a deliberate attempt to obstruct France's treaty with the Dutch.[33] These were the issues, the ministers agreed, on which Louis' prestige and security rested.

Louis XVI decided, therefore, to back the Dutch, but to do so in a way that made the Estates General understand that war would not be in their interest. Vergennes told his *chargé d'affaires* in the Dutch Republic to point out to the Dutch Patriots what a dangerous tactic was the bombardment of Joseph's ship.[34] The Republic would do better to talk with Joseph, before it rushed headlong into war.[35] To facilitate the talking, Louis XVI again offered his good offices. At Vienna, the French ambassador made the same point. War was a dangerous game, and Joseph would do better to talk.

The Austrians were especially piqued that France had not spoken "more firmly" to the Dutch about their actions. Vergennes could only recommend that the French ambassador remain reserved and circumspect in the face of Austrian resentment and the "too flammable" temper of Kaunitz.

In the meantime, Joseph held councils of war, but nothing warlike, according to the French ambassador's sources, was decided. The councils of war concluded that a war with the United Provinces involved unpromising difficulties. The season for campaigning was already well advanced; the Emperor's troops had to march through the territories where he recruited many of his mercenaries, and the council agreed that, once in their homeland, the mercenaries would desert. Furthermore, the Dutch could defend themselves by flooding their lands, and create for the Imperial army almost impossible obstacles.[36] Even more critical difficulties arose at home. The Imperial army found itself in short supply of forage. And, in Transylvania, where Joseph's officers were at work forcibly pressing the peasants into the army, there was rebellion against military conscription.[37] Aroused by the violent propaganda of the Patriots against Austria, the Dutch determination to resist mounted day by day.[38] Whatever Joseph may have once expected, it was now clear that a war with the Dutch would not be a holiday affair.

At the same moment, Louis XVI pointed out to Joseph that his demand of the Dutch to open the Scheldt River was out of order. The Dutch, Louis XVI reminded his brother-in-law, had enjoyed, for nearly a century and a half, the right to keep the Scheldt closed. The right was assured by solemn treaties, and they regarded it as the very foundation of their prosperity, . . . "even their existence."[39] Louis warned Joseph that, if he continued to make such demands on the United Provinces, he would excite a general uneasiness among the powers of Europe and they would take the appropriate "measures". In fact, Louis XVI told Joseph, he had found it necessary, himself, to assemble troops on his frontiers because of the insecurity created by the conflict. France could not be indifferent to the fate of the Dutch Republic, Louis XVI explained, especially at the moment when the diplomats of France and the Dutch Republic were about to conclude a Franco-Dutch treaty. If Joseph would only suspend all of his hostile actions against the Dutch, and listen to the voice of moderation and humanity, Louis XVI promised to help to procure for both sides a just and suitable peace.

Vergennes knew that the advice and veiled threats in the report that Noailles gave to Joseph would cause discomfort at Vienna. It was painful, he wrote to Noailles, to oppose one's ally. But, Vergennes suggested, Louis rendered Joseph a service by pointing out to him some useful truths,even at the risk of displeasing him. Furthermore, in a personal letter to Noailles, Vergennes said he hoped the ambassador would sweeten the bitter pill to be administered to Joseph, without altering the essentials.[40] He promised Noailles that he was doing everything he could to get the Dutch in a proper mood to negotiate.[41] But, if the Emperor holds to his "ultimatum," Vergennes told Noailles, the Dutch appeared to be ready to risk everything.

Once again, Vergennes warned Joseph, through the French ambassador, that Louis XVI would not stand by and watch Joseph subvert the entire system of public law, and endanger the property, as well as the tranquility, of all nations.[42]

Confronted with Louis XVI's refusal to go along with his plans and the increasing obstacles to his military forces (a heavy snow, for example, had all but closed the routes over which Austrian troops had to march),[43] Joseph changed his tactics. He raised with Louis XVI the possibility of exchanging with the Palatinate Elector, most of his lands in the Austrian Netherlands for Bavaria. He was prepared, he said, to grant the Elector sufficient territory to guarantee him a revenue which would exceed that which he drew from Bavaria.[44] Joseph's ambassador pointed out to Vergennes that, if Joseph relinquished his Netherlands, he would have no reasons for maintaining close relations with England. Joseph would forever remain an ally of France. Furthermore, Mercy explained, if Joseph could consolidate his forces, he would be in a better position to stand up to Russia. Was Joseph hinting that Austria might be willing to second France's determination to defend the Ottoman Empire against further encroachment?[45]

While the Palatinate Elector desired the exchange, according to Joseph, care would have to be taken to lead the Duc de Deux Ponts to consent, since, as the eventual successor to the Elector Palatinate, his approval was required by public law. This task, of bringing the Duc de Deux Ponts to consent, Joseph expected Louis XVI to perform.[46]

Louis XVI responded to Joseph's plans by a private letter. He assured Joseph that he wanted to cooperate with him, but the proposal to exchange the Low Countries for Bavaria, he pointed out, would "derange" the balance-of-power system and arouse opposition.[47] Joseph had best concern himself with ways of satisfying that opposition, Louis XVI warned, before he made a move. At least, Louis XVI advised, the Emperor had better consult the King of Prussia.[48] Louis offered to consult the King of Prussia for Joseph, if the latter wished.

Earlier, the King of France had also told Joseph that, if he continued to insist on the opening of the Scheldt, the Dutch would fight, and had a right to.[49] It was clear now that Louis XVI would not back his Austrian ally. Furthermore, at Berlin, Frederick was in negotiations with a Dutch agent seeking Prussian military aid.[50] Joseph could not even count on French neutrality, the French ambassador informed Kaunitz, if the Emperor decided to force his own justice by means of war.[51]

Confronted with an increasingly vigorous opposition, Joseph reluctantly agreed to accept Louis XVI as the mediator between the Dutch and the Austrians. He even ceased to insist on the opening of the Scheldt River.[52] In return, however, he insisted more energetically on some of his other demands, among which was the demand for the strategically important city of Maastricht,[53] and the withdrawal of the Dutch garrisons from the barrier fortresses. The garrisons, Joseph claimed, were a humiliation to him. He could defend his possessions without Dutch help. The Dutch were ready to evacuate most of the barrier fortresses in Austrian territory, but they balked at giving up Maastricht.

As mediator, Louis XVI pressed on each party the seriousness of the situation. The Dutch, Vergennes warned, must consider carefully whatever proposals they made to Joseph, in order to avoid war, and they ought to give him some satisfaction for what he claimed was the insult to his flag.[54] On the other hand, Louis indicated to Joseph that France's role as guarantor of the Treaties of Westphalia and Teschen required that she consider with great circumspection the idea of the exchange of Bavaria. Louis wanted, especially, to sound out the opinions of other interested parties. Prussia's policy was already clear. Frederick sent his brother, Prince Henry, to Versailles, where he was received with such public applause and personal acclaim that Marie Antoinette rightly suspected that he was involved in some anti-Austrian intrigue.[55] By July of 1785, Frederick had organized, with the Electors of Saxony and Hanover, a league of German princes to protect the liberties of Germany against Joseph's ambitions.[56] By a secret article of the agreement, they promised to resist Austria if she invaded or tried to seize Bavaria. Under the mounting pressure, Joseph began to back down.[57]

With extraordinary finesse and tact, Vergennes kept open the lines between Vienna and The Hague, cajoling, warning, and pushing to bring the two parties to the negotiating table. In the spring of 1784, at the Brussels conference, the Dutch had agreed to evacuate the barrier fortresses in Austrian territories. The uncompromising resistance of the Dutch to the opening of the Scheldt, and Louis XVI's support of their rights, argued in favor of Joseph's giving up that demand.[58] The opposition of Louis XVI, Frederick, and the multitude of German princes to the exchange of Bavaria left Joseph little choice (short of a difficult war) but to give up that idea, too.[59] He was left with a handful of secondary demands and his important claim to Maastricht.

The Dutch, Louis XVI told Joseph in a private letter of December, 1784, had shown, in their various responses, a willingness to satisfy most of the other demands. But they were not willing to cede Maastricht.[60] Louis suggested, therefore, the idea of separating the fortress of Maastricht from the city and its surrounding lands and forests. The United Provinces, he offered, might agree to cede the city of Maastricht with its surrounding territories to Joseph, if Joseph agreed to cede back to the Dutch the fortress, and some part of the territory, in return for payment of money. If Joseph found the idea acceptable, he was to let Louis XVI know, confidentially, how much money he thought the deal was worth. Louis assured him that he had not yet told the Dutch of the idea. "If you accept," Louis XVI pled with his brother-in-law, "I cannot beg you enough to halt, if it is still possible, the march of your troops, or, at least, order them to take positions which will not increase anxieties . . . ."[61] In January, 1785, Joseph agreed to accept a suspension of arms until May 1,but he warned that, if the United Provinces had not agreed to some accommodation by that time, he would settle the issue by force of arms.[62]

In the laborious negotiations carried on at Paris under French auspices, the diplomats wrangled well into September before the preliminary articles were ready for signatures, but the guns remained silent. On November 8, 1785, the definitive treaty was signed at Fontainebleau.

The treaty incorporated, in a modified form, Louis XVI's suggestion for a compromise over Maastricht. Joseph renounced all of his rights and claims to Maastricht and, in return, the United Provinces agreed to pay him an indemnity of 9,500,000 *florins*.[63] Each party agreed not to construct fortresses or artillery batteries within cannonshot of each other, and they promised to demolish any such fortresses or batteries then in existence.[64] The Dutch agreed to evacuate, demolish, or turn over to Joseph several fortresses, including Fort Lillo, whose cannons had bombarded the Austrian merchantman in April, 1784.[65] Commissions were established to settle the several boundary differences and the claims for damages made by individuals against the two sovereigns.[66]

Both parties made minor re-adjustments and exchanges of territory.[67] The Dutch agreed to pay 500,000 *florins* for the damages caused to Joseph's subjects by the flooding carried out by the United Provinces as part of their military defense.[68] Finally, Joseph was recognized as sovereign over the Scheldt from Antwerp to Sanftingen.[69] But beyond Sanftingen, the Dutch remained sovereign and the Scheldt remained closed in conformity with the 1648 settlement, which was recognized and confirmed by the Treaty of Fontainebleau.[70] To the final treaty, Vergennes signed his name as the representative of Louis XVI, who, as mediator, guaranteed the treaty.[71]

Louis XVI agreed to pay a share of the Dutch payments stipulated by the treaty. But Louis' agreement quickly divided the French and the Dutch when they sat down to define what Louis XVI's share should be.[72] The French ambassador was too close to what he thought was a total triumph, however, to let the matter of money become an obstacle. He urged Vergennes to pay whatever the Dutch demanded,[73] and came up with a Dutch promise to give France two warships, armed with 100 guns apiece, if Louis paid the share demanded by the Dutch. Under the mounting pressure, Vergennes agreed.[74] Louis XVI paid 4,250,000 *florins*.[75] Thus, the prestige which Louis XVI enjoyed as the mediator of this dispute was dearly paid for.

The treaty of Fontainebleau granted to Joseph some additional territory in Limburg and Borabont, a little more sovereignty over the Scheldt River and 9,500,000 *florins*. But it is doubtful if the sum total of all these concessions equalled the costs of raising, moving, and maintaining an army in the Netherlands, and the more hidden costs arising from the disorder and confusion created by the preparations for war. Furthermore, Maastricht remained in the hands of the Dutch, the Scheldt remained closed, and the idea of exchanging the Austrian Netherlands for Bavaria was stillborn. The Treaty of Fontainebleau was, in fact, a humiliating defeat for Joseph. And, for that, Joseph and the Queen's party held France responsible.

But neither Louis XVI nor Vergennes was totally responsible for the Emperor's defeat in the Scheldt River dispute. Frederick II's determination to protect the *status quo* in the Empire rallied the smaller powers to resist Joseph. Joseph's new ally, Catherine II, offered him very little assistance. She did not oppose his ambitious demands, but did little to help him achieve them, beyond a bland note to the Dutch Estates General, in which she expressed her hope that the Emperor's just demands would be satisfied. Thus, Joseph's containment and frustration sprang from several corners of Europe, not just from Versailles.

Nevertheless, there is no doubt that Louis XVI's support, or, at the least, acquiescence, was essential to the success of Joseph's plans, and Louis XVI, at the critical moment, refused to acquiesce. Joseph felt betrayed; "I believe I have done everything possible as an ally and friend of Louis XVI," he wrote to his sister, the Queen of France. Yet, Joseph complained, Louis XVI interfered with his achieving a "just satisfaction" from the Dutch, and refused to contribute to the exchange of the Austrian Netherlands for Bavaria. The Austrian-French alliance, Joseph concluded, was now subordinated, at Versailles, to friendship and alliance with Holland, to the King of Prussia, to the Ottoman Empire, and a lot of little German princes. Joseph felt that he had been treated shabbily. France had handled him with "duplicity, if not falsely . . . ."[76]

Marie Antoinette agreed with her brother. With the Austrian ambassador, Mercy, she had vigorously pushed Joseph's demands, and she had expected Louis XVI to grant her wishes. She was, after all, his wife and, until March of 1785, pregnant. Moreover, she believed that the Scheldt River affair would have been settled sooner, if Louis XVI's "personal intentions had been better seconded by those who have the responsibility for carrying them out" [77] Her scapegoat was Vergennes. He had deliberately created delays and difficulties, she wrote to her brother, and would have created many more if she had not spoken to him in an "imposing manner."[78] Vergennes, she charged, was dishonest,[79] insincere,[80] and equivocating.[81] When the King's Council, with Vergennes arguing against Joseph's claims, decided to warn Joseph not to expect Louis XVI's assistance, Marie Antoinette intervened in a rage, and actually delayed for seven days the departure of the courier who was to carry what she called the "odious dispatch" to Vienna.[82] When she became disgusted with Louis XVI's vague responses, she turned her wrath on Vergennes. She wrote to him explaining her brother's policy,[83] and she confronted him with her brother's arguments in the presence of the King. [84] But her methods failed to produce the desired effect. Vergennes wanted to explain himself to the Queen, but the King discouraged the idea. Louis knew Marie Antoinette's tempers; perhaps he wanted to spare his Minister. But Vergennes and Marie Antoinette were on a collision course. Each time the Queen confronted Vergennes, she found the Minister respectful, but the resistance to her brother continued. At last, she became so enraged that she forgot her role as Queen. Mercy d'Argenteau, who witnessed the scene, said she shouted at Vergennes and accused him of deceit. The latter, visibly shaken by the Queen's attack, was unable to speak at first; then he offered to resign, since he caused her so much discontent.

The Queen did not want a resignation; she wanted a change in policy. She went over, once again, her brother's cause, point by point. Vergennes listened, but answered only that the matter ought to be deliberated in the King's Council. Louis XVI, who, up to that point, had watched the entire spectacle in awed silence, finally interrupted the discussion and brought it to a close.[85]

The next day, Mercy went to the Queen and told her that such attacks on Vergennes could lead only to unfortunate consequences. Very well, the Queen responded, there was no other alternative but to dismiss the Minister, "... my dignity and my credit require it." But, as the Queen and Mercy considered the matter further, they began to hesitate. In order to dismiss Vergennes, they would have to get rid of many other people. And who would succeed him? The more they speculated, the more complicated the question became.[86] Nevertheless, the Queen continued to see in Vergennes the enemy of her brother. "Always remember, Monsieur," she is reported to have said, one day, to Vergennes, "that the Emperor is my brother." "I remember, Madame," Vergennes is said to have answered, "but I recall, above all else, that Monseigneur le Dauphin is your son."[87] Whether or not such an exchange took place, it neatly symbolizes the relationship between Marie Antoinette and Vergennes.

Not only with the Queen, but also with the Austrian ambassador, Vergennes' day-to-day meetings became more and more disagreeable. As the contacts between the Dutch and the Emperor became more abrasive, Vergennes met with Mercy only when a third party, usually his Undersecretary, Rayneval, was present. During these meetings, the atmosphere was tense, and the work laborious. Mercy doggedly fought to win Joseph's demands, and Vergennes tried to find an avenue of conciliation for the United Provinces and Vienna. Once, even Vergennes lost his temper, in a heated exchange with Mercy. "During the ten years I have handled affairs with him," Mercy later reported, "this is the first time I have seen him forget himself."[88] In November of 1784, just as Louis XVI made his decision not to back Joseph, Vergennes characteristically fell ill. From that date, his illnesses became more frequent, his fatigues more deep-seated. "It is painful to oppose one's ally," he had earlier observed. When the peace settlement was signed in November of 1784, he had personally experienced, again and again, the agonizing truth of his statement. Only a soul of galvanized iron could have escaped untouched from the ceaseless rigors of his position. Like the French nation, he too, needed peace. Peace and rest.

CHAPTER 34

Relations with Italy: 1774-1787

French relations with the Italian states during the administration of Vergennes (1774-1787), reveal in a compact form the motivations, successes, and failings of French foreign policy during the last years of the Ancien Régime. But, in Italy, the stage was beautifully arranged for Louis XVI to play the role of arbiter that he wished to play in Europe. Geographically, France was well placed to hold the balance of power in Italy. She was in a position, similar to that of an insular power, enjoying a certain detachment from the arena of competition. Louis XVI could play the arbiter in preserving the balance between the two major power blocks in Italy, the Spanish Bourbons and the Austrian Hapsburgs. His right to play the role was guaranteed by his alliances with both the Spanish Bourbons and the Austrian Hapsburgs.

French-Italian relations were also conditioned by strategic and military considerations. In northern Italy, Savoy-Sardinia, Parma, Tuscany, Genoa, and Modena were of key importance. Through these states ran all the roads from western Europe to Italy. From Marseille or Barcelona, the route to Parma or Modena ran through Genoa. Since the Sixteenth century, these northern Italian states had been the battlegrounds where France had fought the Hapsburgs, or they provided, in times of European wars, the additional weights which could turn the balance of power for or against France.

In the Mediterranean, Vergennes was confronted with the fact that his two major allies— Austria and Spain — pursued conflicting policies. In a position to benefit from the disintegration of the Ottoman Empire, Austria was a threat to the *status quo* in the eastern Mediterranean after 1774. From her strong position in Italy, she strove to consolidate her power, and gain support for her ambitions in the eastern Mediterranean. The Spanish Bourbons, on the other hand, wanted to maintain the *status quo* in the Mediterranean, after having played the role of revisionist earlier in the century. Between these two contradictory tendencies, Vergennes had to guide French policy in Italy, always alert to any move that would radically change the balance of power.

Austria had large possessions in northern Italy and exercised considerable imperial authority there. By her facility of communication with Tuscany and Modena, especially after the acquisition of Modena through the marriage of the Archduke Ferdinand with Marie d'Este in 1771, she enjoyed tremendous military advantages there.[1]

The expansionist tendencies of Joseph II worried Vergennes, for his imperial ally's ambitions conflicted with Louis XVI's desire to maintain the *status quo* in Europe, including Italy. He knew that Joseph had old claims to Parma and Plaisance, which he could advance if he wished. And a longstanding dispute between Genoa and Austria about the territory of San Remo, over which Austria claimed sovereignty by title of a fief of the Empire, created fears that the Emperor might even invade Genoa if a favorable opportunity arose. France was determined to protect Genoa, and had made her determination known at Vienna. In 1754, Louis XV had openly threatened to march 50,000 troops to the aid of Genoa if Austria tried to settle her dispute with Genoa by force. Fortunately, in 1774, Maria Theresa still acted as the "voice of moderation" with her son.[2]

But what Austria could not do with military force in Italy, she continued to do by marriage contracts. In Modena, Naples, and Parma, marriages of ruling families with Hapsburg children did more to advance Austrian policies in Italy than all the soldiers Joseph II could muster. And the rules of the diplomatic game, as well as common respect for public decency, made politics by marriage more difficult to oppose. Unlike the daughter of the French regent, Charlotte Aglae, who married the Duke of Modena and ran off to France whenever she got the chance, the Hapsburg women stayed at their posts and performed their duties. Their "duties" included looking out for Hapsburg interests.

The island of Corsica, once the territory of Genoa, was the possession of France. A French army had defeated the army of the rebel patriot, Paoli, and had occupied the island in 1769. It remained for Vergennes to clean up the numerous petty difficulties created by the occupation and to establish the definitive recognition of French control over Corsica; this control shifted in favor of France the power relations in the western Mediterranean, with a French naval base on Corsica posing a serious threat to the British navy in the whole region.

When France occupied Corsica it agreed, in a treaty with Genoa, to pay Genoa an annual subsidy of 200,000 *livres* a year for ten years.[3] In 1777, the question of the continuance of the subsidy provided Vergennes with the occasion to spell out his interpretation of the treaty which had led to France's occupation of Corsica. Vergennes argued that it had been the intention of

Louis XV to acquire the island of Corsica when he occupied it. Furthermore, when France overcame the resistance of Paoli, she had established her right of conquest over the island.[4] Vergennes recognized that the French treaty with Genoa provided the possibility of Genoa's recovering the island by paying France for the cost of occupation, but such a possibility "is and will always be an illusion," Vergennes believed, for the Republic of Genoa would never be able to raise the considerable sums of money that the submission of Corsica had cost France. Furthermore, if the Genoese did recover Corsica, Vergennes pointed out, they would lose it again, because they did not have the means to hold it. Vergennes insisted that "the Isle of Corsica ought to be regarded as a domain belonging to France."

The annexation of Corsica by France created a number of difficulties over property rights, which threatened Franco-Genoan relations. Louis XV had agreed to recognize the property rights of the Genoans and Corsicans who had had their property confiscated, occupied, or detained during the brief war with Paoli, and complaints and claims arising out of this agreement were numerous.[5] One of the more complex property problems was a consequence of Louis XV's suppression of the Jesuits. Once France came into possession of Corsica, the French government confiscated Jesuit property there for use for education.[6] But it was not always easy to determine the amount of property held by the Jesuits of Corsica, especially since they had invested money outside of Corsica. These claims and complaints over Corsica caused serious concern at Versailles. Vergennes did not wish to see a situation develop that might lead to conflict with Genoa, especially in time of other wars.

The war with England brought into the open new fears that Paoli, who had escaped to Tuscany after his defeat in Corsica, would organize an invasion of the island with England's support. Rumors and reports about Paoli's agents flew from Versailles to Genoa and back. Louis XVI began to take police action against those whom he suspected, in Corsica, of favoring Paoli, and he gave warning to Florence that he would not tolerate the hostile activities of Paoli and his "bandits," who had escaped to Tuscan territory.[7] At the same time, the French kept a systematic watch on English warships, corsairs, and merchants' ships in the western Mediterranean to discover if England was trying to rekindle the old troubles in Corsica.[8]

Officially, Genoa observed a policy of neutrality in the American Revolutionary War, but she allowed France and Spain to enroll sailors in her port. Sartine, the Secretary of State for the Marine, had the responsibility for arranging the enrollments through the French consul at Genoa. But the French envoy, Monteil, soon became involved in the task. The enrollment of sailors for the Bourbon fleets could easily become a political issue, because there were powerful merchants at Genoa with pro-English leanings.

Nevertheless, the sailors who were to be recruited somehow had to learn the details of the French and Spanish offers.[9] Also, Vergennes assigned to the diplomat and consul at Genoa the equally delicate task of trying to get back into the French navy the thousands of deserters who had fled to Italy during the war to serve on neutral ships in the Mediterranean.[10]

In the great conflict between the Hapsburgs and the Bourbons, Savoy-Sardinia allowed herself no long-term loyalties. As a neutral, she watched each crisis develop and determined her alliances on estimates of what she could gain. In the War of Polish Succession, Savoy-Sardinia had joined the Bourbons; in the War of Austrian Succession she had fought on the side of Austria. At the same time, she became a protégé of England, a fact that increased her importance in the eyes of Frenchmen. After each war, she returned from the peace table a little fatter. Her ability to exploit the conflicts of the great powers seemed unlimited.

But the shape of the Balance-of-Power System in Europe and Italy, when Vergennes came to power, boxed-in Savoy-Sardinia. In 1752, in the Treaty of Aranjuez, Bourbon Spain, Hapsburg Austria, and Savoy-Sardinia agreed to a mutual guarantee of the territories of each. Since this treaty applied especially to the territories of each in Italy, it dampened somewhat the Hapsburg-Bourbon conflict on the peninsula, and made it difficult for Savoy-Sardinia to exploit the old antagonisms. The Diplomatic Revolution completed the process.[11] "This intimate union [between France and Austria] . . .," the French diplomat, Chauvelin, observed, "forms an obstacle, as solid as it is powerful, to the aggrandizement of the House of Savoy."[12] Vergennes, too, noted with satisfaction that the union of France and Austria held Savoy-Sardinia in check.[13]

In reality, Savoy-Sardinia could no longer play the political combinations which had provided her with so many opportunities in the past. Her new and passive role was not one, however, that she would continue to play, if new opportunities arose. When strains between Austria and France developed, she hoped for a break between them. But it never came, so Savoy-Sardinia established a line to Prussia. Victor Amadeus III, King of Savoy-Sardinia, exchanged envoys with Frederick II. The move worried Versailles. It seemed to point to an eventual return of Savoy to active politics by means of a Prussian alliance.

The golden opportunity turned up in the Bavarian crisis. Austria, on the verge of war with Prussia, had to draw many of her troops out of Milan. Sardinia watched and waited for the moment. As an ally of Prussia, she could do great damage to Austria's territories in Italy. But her hopes collapsed at the Peace of Teschen. Savoy-Sardinia retreated, once again, into inactivity.

Another serious crisis of the Franco-Austrian alliance came in 1784, when

France intervened in Joseph II's quarrel with the United Provinces over navigation of the Scheldt River. Vergennes knew that, if a war broke out over Joseph's attempts to open the Scheldt River, France would find herself in opposition to Austria. As he considered this grave possibility, Vergennes' eye fell on Savoy-Sardinia. "... it would be ... indispensable to have the assistance of the Court of Turin," Vergennes recommended to Louis XVI. "It seems that there would not be a great deal of difficulty in associating her with us: the dismemberment of Milan, the conquest, even, of this Duchy, has always been, and is still, an object of ... [Savoy-Sardinia's] wishes and her ambitions." The only problem Vergennes could discover in such an eventuality was that Savoy-Sardinia was in serious financial difficulties. But, for this problem, Vergennes had the customary answer: subsidies from Louis XVI.[14] However, the diplomatic settlement of the crisis once again left Savoy-Sardinia unrewarded.

The Diplomatic Revolution of 1756 had brought the Duchy of Parma back into the French alliance system. The Family Compact of 1761 confirmed the return by guaranteeing the possessions of the Duke of Parma, as it did those of the other Bourbon princes: France, Spain, and the Kingdom of the Two Sicilies. But Parma, like Naples, was not easy to keep as a Bourbon satellite. Her territories were surrounded by those dominated by Austria or Savoy-Sardinia, and the marriage of Ferdinand, the Duke of Parma, to the Archduchess Marie Amelie, daughter of Maria Theresa, created at the Court of Parma a situation similar to the one at Naples. Like her sister, Marie Antoinette, Marie Amelie was strong-willed and pro-Austrian. France's principle support at Parma was the Marchese de Felino, but he soon became the target of Marie Amelie's campaign to bring Parma closer to Austria. France watched this subtle woman destroy the agents of French influence in Parma and replace them with agents of Austrian influence. When he was Secretary of State, Choiseul had tried to keep Parma in line by ordering his representative at Parma to clear out, by brutal purges, all those who seemed disloyal or indifferent. But his high-handed methods brought Parma no closer to France. Vergennes' response to Parma was in sharp contrast: he saw to it that France's relations with Parma were friendly, undramatic, and without serious conflict. Although Parma could no longer be counted on as a Bourbon appendage, he did not wish to create a reaction to unsettle the *status quo*.

Vergennes inherited one problem, however, which he could not allow to remain unsolved. The Duke Ferdinand of Parma tolerated the distribution in his territory of extracts from the papal bull, *in coenae Domini,* which was openly hostile to the French principle of Gallican Liberties. Since the bull had been earlier suppressed in the Bourbon states, including Parma, the Spanish minister at Parma made a vigorous protest. Flavigny, Louis XVI's agent at Parma, seconded the Spanish minister. The Duke claimed that the distribution had not been approved by his government, but had been the work of the printer himself, a young man who was promptly arrested and, though later released, was not given permission to reopen his shop. The whole incident, according to the Duke of Parma, was simply a "misunderstanding." Both the Bourbon ministers at Parma found the Duke's story difficult to believe; they believed that he, along with the Archbishop, had had a part in the printing. Nevertheless, when the Duke forbade the circulation of the tract to confessors, who had been using it for the direction of the faithful, the Bourbon courts did not press the issue any further.[15]

The Republic of Venice remained extremely important to France in the eighteenth century, not because of her power, which had diminished considerably since the sixteenth century, not even because of her commerce, since France traded very little with Venice, but because of her strategic position in the eastern Mediterranean. Also, Venice made an excellent listening post for Versailles. Having decided, after the Peace of Passarowitz in 1718, that neutrality was the stance most consistent with her interests, Venice ceased to play an aggressive role in European politics. In Italy and the eastern Mediterranean, she still vigorously defended her political and economic interests as she saw them, but even a war so close as the Russo-Turkish war of 1768-1774 did not draw her out of her aloofness; she remained a neutral observer.[16]

By 1774, however, Venetian neutrality was being rapidly undermined by both European and domestic politics. At home, the disarray of her government and military steadily weakened Venice and made her a vulnerable target for her expanding neighbors, and the pressures of what historians have agreed to call the "Eastern Question" steadily pulled her into the maelstrom of eastern Mediterranean politics.

At Versailles, Vergennes watched these two independent historical threads draw closer together. A veteran of many years as French Ambassador at Constantinople, he knew that France relied on the continued existence of Venice. Her weakness worried him; if it continued, he prophesied, the Republic of Venice would soon disappear, for, every year, she became more exposed to the greed and ambitions of her neighbors.[17] In the spring of 1750, Austrian armies had suddenly occupied a piece of the territory of Venice. Louis XV believed that the occupation was proof of Austria's designs on Venice.[18]

In 1779, Vergennes appointed his brother, the Marquis de Vergennes, to be Louis XVI's Ambassador to Venice. In his instructions to his brother, Vergennes emphasized that the destruction or possession of Venice by her neighbors would constitute a great misfortune for French politics.[19]

Any Italian sovereign who invaded and conquered Venice, Vergennes informed his brother, would soon control Lombardy and Piedmont.[20] To the north and east of the Republic of Venice lay the Empire of Austria: a "most dangerous enemy" of Venice, Vergennes told his brother. The partition of Poland had already demonstrated Austria's willingness to prey on her weak neighbors. Standing between Austria's possessions in Germany and those in Italy, Venice was, indeed, a temptation.

The expansion of Russia at the expense of the Ottoman Empire also drew attention to the strategic position of Venice. Feeble, and without great credit in European affairs, Venice, nevertheless, remembered a time when her power and influence were enormous. As her power declined, she lost some of her possessions to the growing Ottoman Empire. But, by 1779, the repeated victories of the Russians over the Turks had demonstrated the inability of the Ottoman Empire to resist attack. Perhaps Venice could recoup her ancient losses to the Ottoman Empire by allying herself with Russia. Vergennes knew that the Russians had already tried to win the friendship of the Venetians, and to draw them out of their neutrality by offers of spoils. Louis XVI did not wish to see this happen; it was a "capital point," Vergennes insisted.[21]

The most important role of the French ambassador at Venice, however, was that of lookout for his King. To his brother, Vergennes stressed the great importance of his being, above all, the eyes of the King at Venice. Yet the situation of a foreign ambassador at Venice was rendered difficult by the numerous restrictions that hindered his movements and contacts. Venice was one of the first countries to exploit the possibilities of the permanent embassy as a center of intelligence gathering. The reports of her ambassadors, about the peoples and countries where they were stationed, were models of objective and imaginative reporting. For this reason, perhaps, Venetians regarded all foreign ambassadors to Venice as spies. Consequently, their movements and behavior were hemmed in by a web of regulations. No ambassador could have any personal contact with members of the Venetian nobility, in whose hands the government of the Republic rested. Ambassadors were isolated from society and, almost always, suspect.[22] Aside from the audiences granted upon arrival and departure, there were no other official personal contacts acceptable under law. To obtain information, and to influence affairs, ambassadors used agents, priests, nuns, and courtesans as go-betweens.[23] When Bernis was French Ambassador to Venice, he took advantage of the carnival festivities to make forbidden contacts. Behind carnival masks he conversed, personally, not only with nobles of the Senate, but with the Doge himself.[24] Despite the restrictions, Vergennes wanted his brother to find out what was going on in the Mediterranean. He insisted, again and again, that the Marquis de Vergennes "employ every care" to find out, in particular, what the courts of

Vienna and St. Petersburg were doing at Venice.[25]

In contrast to the dramatic, and sometimes violent, disputes between Versailles and Rome, before 1774 and later, during the French Revolution and the Reign of Napoleon, relations between the papacy and Louis XVI were tranquil.[26] The great issues of Gallicanism, Jansenism, and the strife over the papal bull, *Unigenitus,* were, if not dead, at least exhausted. Although the courts of Europe still accorded papal nuncios special honors of precedence, in the system of European politics the voice of the Pope was little more than a familiar whisper. He could not threaten the secular authority of the French crown, for the power he could exercise was hardly more than a "phantom"—the word is that of the French Minister, Puysieux in 1748.[27] In turn, the crown of France, less fearful of papal authority, was now less prone to interfere in affairs at Rome.[28]

Nevertheless, Louis XVI could never forget Rome. As long as he exercised authority derived from Divine Right, the King of France had too much in common with the Pope to ignore him. And his own devotion to Christian beliefs implied a veneration of, as well as a deep sense of duty toward, church authority and its moral judgments. The title, *Fils ainé de l'Eglise,* given to the French monarchs by the papacy, was taken seriously at Versailles.

Moreover, the French embassy at Rome reflected honor on the French monarch. It was the center of the social life of European diplomacy and aristocracy. In the diplomatic corps, the French Ambassador, the Cardinal de Bernis was the undisputed champion of receptions, dinners, ceremony, and display. The name of his chef enjoyed a greater renown in Rome than did the names of most of the minor diplomats there. As long as prestige remained a goal of European diplomacy, the embassy at Rome remained important. Also, Rome still retained its reputation as a major gossip shop.

Louis XV had banished the Jesuits from his realm in 1764. In July of 1769, the ambassadors of the three Bourbon crowns, France, Spain, and Naples, confirmed their own individual acts against the Jesuits with a memo submitted to Pope Clement XIII, urging the total abolishment of the Society of Jesus. Charles III followed up the memo of 1769 with continued pressures, executed by his energetic *chargé d'affaires* at Rome, Don José Monino, the Conde de Floridablanca. Feeling less strongly about the issue than the King of Spain, Louis XV approved of whatever Charles III did at Rome to destroy the Jesuits. "If Spain is content," his Minister, d'Aiguillon, observed, "so are we . . . ."[29] In February, 1769, Clement XIII died. His successor, who took the name of Clement XIV, promised, before his election, to suppress the Jesuits. In the summer of 1773, he yielded to Bourbon demands and kept his promise.

Vergennes was just becoming familiar with his new responsibilities of

Secretary of State, when he learned that Pope Clement XIV was ill and then, in September, 1774, dead. The diplomatic system awarded considerable prestige to the monarch who could influence a papal election. Vergennes never let slip by a chance to enhance the opinion the world had of his Monarch's influence.[30]

Louis XVI's Ambassador at Rome, the Cardinal de Bernis, was eminently prepared to play a leading part in the conclave, called in 1774, to elect the new Pope. He had participated in the election of Clement XIV; he knew intimately many members of the Sacred College; he was confident of his influence at Rome; and he had wisely taken the precaution to plan every step he took, with the cooperation of Don José Moniño, who represented Spain.[31] Indeed, reading the correspondence between Vergennes and Bernis concerning the Conclave of 1774, the historian gains the impression that Bernis probably had more to do with Louis XVI's Roman policy, in 1774, than Vergennes did.

"Discontent" and "fury for vengeance" were the words Bernis used to describe to Vergennes the pro-Jesuit party, soon after the opening of the conclave to elect a new Pope in October, 1774. Their hatred for Pope Clement XIV had been so uncontrolled that they made no effort to conceal their joy at the news of his death. "No Pope," according to Clement's biographer, "was ever treated in such a savage manner after his death."[32] Acts of vandalism against Clement's corpse became so frequent that Bernis felt obliged to hire guards to watch over the body day and night.[33]

Soon after the conclave opened, Bernis saw Clement's enemies, mostly Italian Cardinals, attempt to precipitate an election of one of their own party before the cardinals coming from outside Italy could arrive. Alarmed, Bernis immediately contacted the *doyen* of the Sacred College, and the two of them quickly composed a memo which declared, without equivocation, that a premature election would be taken as an open insult "to the monarchs of the House of Bourbon."[34] This blunt approach threw the cardinals into an unusual flutter and fume, but it made some of the hotheads pause and reflect. For the benefit of those "fanatics" who continued to intrigue, Bernis repeated the warning a few weeks later. When the tardy cardinals began to arrive, the anti-Clement XIV — pro-Jesuits — group was still venomous and dangerous, but had not yet enjoyed any successes at the conclave. From France the Cardinal Paul d'Albert de Luynes came, to second Bernis and take part in the conclave.[35]

Charles III and Louis XVI had agreed not to give their cardinals specific instructions regarding their candidate for the papacy. They agreed to leave the negotiations to the "discernment" of their Ministers. Vergennes assumed, as did the Spanish Minister, that the Bourbon King of Naples would adopt the policy of his more powerful relatives regarding the papal election.

Vergennes ordered Bernis and Luynes, therefore, to admit the Cardinal from Naples, Orsini, into their concert. The Austrian minister, Kaunitz, announced, soon after Clement's death, that he intended to send no one to the conclave. But he later changed his mind. His views on the election were similar to those of the Bourbons, who were more than happy to have the Austrian cardinals at Rome. As a gesture of friendship, Vergennes sent to the Imperial Court the general plans for the election, which Louis XVI and Charles III had agreed on.[36]

Bernis' *Journal of the Conclave* reads like a description of a national convention to select a candidate for the Presidency of the United States. For 137 days the cardinals proposed, bargained, wheeled and dealed, and cast their votes. In his periodic reports, Bernis included the final tally of every ballot. As the cardinals grew weary, Bernis, the Popemaker, prepared his compromise candidate, the Cardinal Brashi.[37]

Bernis tried, early in the conclave, to advance Brashi's name but without success. Without pressing the matter, Bernis withdrew his support of Brashi, and supported other candidates advanced by others. Each failed to gain enough votes, but, after each failure, Bernis had a few more friends. As the other candidates were checkmated, Bernis talked, explained, listened to other proposals, agreed to support others. He worked especially hard to dissolve the opposition of those who feared Brashi might be a creature of the ultra-montane, pro-Jesuit party. Meanwhile the cardinals grew weary. When they felt that the psychological moment had arrived, the Bourbon cardinals proposed Brashi's candidacy, once again, to a small caucus. He won immediate approval. On February 15, 1775, he was elected, and chose the name Pius VI. Brashi, Berni's compromise candidate, was not among those candidates whom the Bourbons had originally picked as "agreeable candidates," but they were confident at his election that he would maintain with the "Catholic Sovereigns" a close union. That meant, of course, that he would not try to restore the Jesuits.[38]

At Naples, Ferdinand I, King of the Two Sicilies, and Queen Maria Carolina personified the muted conflict that continued to go on between the Spanish Bourbons and the House of Austria in the Mediterranean, despite the Treaty of Aranjuez (1752) and the Diplomatic Revolution (1756). Ferdinand, a Bourbon and son of Charles III of Spain, had become King of Naples and Sicily in 1759. His throne was guaranteed by treaties signed with both the Bourbons and the Hapsburgs.[39] In 1768, Ferdinand had married Maria Carolina, another daughter of Maria Theresa of Austria. Almost immediately, the new Queen became suspect at Versailles. She had gone to Naples with the notion that the Bourbons had usurped the Kingdom of Naples from the House of Hapsburg, and her anti-Spanish, pro-Austrian prejudices marked her influence as a potential threat to Bourbon interests.[40]

Influence was, above all, what she wanted. The marriage contract between Ferdinand and Maria Carolina had stipulated that she had the right to enter the Council of State as soon as she gave Ferdinand an heir. She was no sooner pregnant than she insisted on exercising her right, and entered the Council of State. Ambitious, and skillful at intrigue and administration, she soon began to reach for the reins of government. Ferdinand was unable to resist the force of his wife's personality. He was pushed aside, much to Vergennes' regret.[41]

In 1774, the Bourbons relied on the Prime Minister, the Marchese de Tanucci, to be their spokesman at the Neapolitan court. A former professor of law at the University of Pisa, Tanucci was intelligent and knowledgeable. But his almost total submission to Madrid, his anti-clericalism, and his reputation for chicanery had made him many enemies. To compensate for his subservience to the Bourbons at Madrid, he showed an exaggerated defiance toward the Bourbons at Versailles. Even the pettiest problems became occasions for dispute.[42]

Despite Tanucci's pettiness toward France, Vergennes counted on him as the Bourbons' man at Naples, and French ambassadors were repeatedly told to cultivate his confidence, and to avoid entering any intrigues against him. But, in 1774, he was very old, and his age plus his numerous enemies were reasons enough to arouse fears for the Bourbon cause. In 1776, French and Spanish fears were realized; Tanucci fell from office.[43]

The Baron de Breteuil, French Ambassador to Naples since 1772, was first told to cultivate the confidence of Maria Carolina. But the futility of the tactic was soon apparent to Vergennes. He recognized that, no matter what ties Maria Carolina had with the House of Bourbon, her first loyalty was to the Austrian dynasty. She was hostile to Spain, Vergennes concluded, because she wanted Ferdinand to get out from under his dependence on Charles III.[44] After 1776, the policies of Naples began more and more to diverge from those of Madrid and Versailles.

The agent of Bourbon frustration was John Francis Edward Acton, an Englishman brought to Naples, in 1779, by Queen Maria Carolina, to reorganize and reform the Neapolitan navy. Acton agreed with Maria Carolina that a pro-Bourbon policy was not in the interests of the Kingdom of the Two Sicilies and, first as Commander-in-Chief of the navy, then Minister of Finance, and, finally, Prime Minister, he soon had the power to implement his aims.

Vergennes immediately saw the threat posed by Acton's rapid rise to power, but, for a long time, he remained unaware of all the resources behind the man. Acton was not simply an agent of Queen Maria Carolina, nor even of Austria, but of England. By 1785, however, Vergennes better appreciated Acton's power, but he still did not seem to understand the extent of support for Acton, provided by English money through the British ambassador, Lord Hamilton. England was financing another shift in the balance, in Italy and the Mediterranean.

At Florence, in the Grand Duchy of Tuscany, the marriage, in 1764, of the Hapsburg Archduke, Pierre-Leopold, with the Spanish Bourbon, Marie Louise, created a period of conciliation between the Bourbons and the Hapsburgs at Tuscany. The politics of Duke Leopold were pro-Austrian but his own interests conflicted very little with those of France. During the American Revolutionary War, however, the free port of Leghorn, already an important British trade center, became a repair and supply center for British naval ships in the Mediterranean, especially after the British lost Port Mahon in Minorca to the French and Spanish.[45] Leghorn even served as recruiting centre for British garrisons.[46] The fact that the British recruited many of Paoli's "bandits" into their forces created, among the French ministers in Italy, a fear that the British were using Tuscany to sponsor an invasion of Corsica.

But the most interesting aspect of Tuscan politics was the Grand Duke Leopold himself. Among the most talented of the "enlightened despots" of the eighteenth century, Leopold kept the bureaus at Versailles fascinated with his willingness to make his state, to use Vergennes' phrase, a "country of experiment."[47] When the Comte de Durfort became Louis XVI's minister to Tuscany in 1784, he was specifically charged with the responsibility of providing Vergennes with precise and complete information on reforms.[48] Durfort's diplomatic dispatches are excellent illustrations of the role which the resident ambassadors played in collecting and processing information to be relayed to the home government.

Both Durfort and Vergennes saw the significance of the reform movement in Tuscany. "You will see, Monsieur, in the correspondence of your predecessor," Vergennes wrote to Durfort, "that I have often exhorted him to profit from the leisure that a Minister of the King has at Florence, to examine the results of all the changes that the Grand Duke had made in every part of the administration of his states. It is, so to speak, a fortunate thing that there is a Prince who has tried to do nearly everything, in legislation, in agriculture, and commerce, that has come out of the heads of writers for the last twenty-five years. Do his people find these things good? That is another question."[49]

"Certain it is," Durfort answered, "that here the modern *philosophe* can be judged . . . ."[50]

Durfort put his finger on the point that interested Vergennes the most. By 1784, the American Revolutionary War had brought France to the edge of bankruptcy. In the salons, in the King's Council, even in the streets of Paris, there were those who cried reform, and drew many of their ideas for reform from the *philosophes*. Systematically and without great publicity, Vergennes resisted the reformers. He was, as Bachaumont said of him, of the "old school" of thought. The reforms of the Grand Duke of Tuscany thus seemed to him as both a threat and a boon. If they worked, they were a threat. If they were unsuccessful, they were a boon; he could then argue that the theories of the modern writers and *philosophes* had been tried, and had failed. "The operation [to suppress the monasteries] merits examination in the greatest detail," Vergennes observed, "if only to have objections to oppose to projects of this type." Thus the reforms of Tuscany were scrutinized for arguments against reform, rather than to discover whether the reforms might be useful to Louis XVI.

Again and again, Durfort composed long descriptions of Leopold's reforms. Leopold's suppression of religious establishments, and of tax exemptions for nobles, his reform code, his commercial reforms were examined, one by one. Each fell short of convincing Vergennes that Leopold, or the modern thinkers, had anything to teach Louis XVI or France. While he admitted that Leopold had shown great energy in his reforms, Durfort also remained unconvinced of their value, and contemptuous of their supporters: "... [The] results are very much below those the oratory talents and academic discourses had foretold."[51] Vergennes seconded Durfort: "It appears," he observed, "that they are not all happy."[52] The destruction of the monasteries had led to a rise in agricultural prices.[53] When the new "Code Leopold" appeared, Durfort searched through every volume of it to demonstrate that the results had not been as good as hoped.[54]

When Leopold's reforms produced some successes, Vergennes and Durfort took a different tack. Even if reforms in Tuscany worked, one could not argue their value for France. After all, Tuscany was not France, and Duke Leopold was not King Louis XVI. France had a population twenty times that of Tuscany, and even if free trade in grain[55] worked in Tuscany, it would not necessarily work in France. When the Grand Duke streamlined his administrative apparatus, and cut his budget by getting rid of surplus personnel, Vergennes reacted with the observation that "... the affairs of the Grand Duchy of Tuscany can be administered without the apparatus of various departments necessary to a monarchy." Therefore, there was nothing "astonishing or interesting" in Leopold's administrative reforms.[56] When Leopold's tax reforms appeared to be bringing more money into the treasury, Vergennes suggested that Leopold's concern with his treasury was not quite in keeping with the dignity of a prince. "Perhaps," the French Secretary of State observed, with his characteristic contempt for finances, "... the Prince [of Tuscany] allows the interests of his treasury to enter too much into the calculations of the novelties he adopts every day [!]"[57] Vergennes used the reforms in Tuscany to defend the *status quo* in France.

Thus, as Italy ceased to be less a battleground of Bourbon-Hapsburg conflict, France spent less of her resources and energies intervening in Italian politics. "If it becomes necessary," Vergennes even admitted to Louis XVI, "to opt between the conservation of the branches of the House of Bourbon in Italy and that of Prussian power in Germany, we should not hesitate to abandon the first and maintain the other." The Bourbons in Italy, he explained, were a "political luxury."[58]

Nevertheless, Vergennes understood that Italy could not be isolated from the dynamics of European high politics. Russia's pressure on the Ottoman Empire was felt in Venice and Turin. Austria's desire to revise the *status quo* in the Mediterranean implied a clash with Spain, who desired to protect the *status quo*. Both were Louis XVI's allies; they confronted each other in Italy. Austria's threat to Genoa and Venice, the rebel Paoli's threats to Louis XVI's control of Corsica, the establishment of diplomatic lines with Prussia by Savoy-Sardinia, the religious issues which forever complicated Italian politics, and the tangle and intrigues of dynastic politics, each contained potentially explosive power that could destroy Italian tranquillity. For that reason, Vergennes and his subordinates at Versailles read, with special attention, the continuous stream of political news flowing to Versailles from the permanent embassies in Italy.

Less perceptible to Vergennes, perhaps, but nonetheless of future importance to French policy, was the fact that the English economic and diplomatic presence in Italy was growing, despite the English setbacks in the western Mediterranean during the American Revolutionary War. In Naples, the rise of Acton to power in the Ministry was a clear loss to French commerce, and a boost to British trade. By 1784, the Italian peninsula was one of Britian's largest European customers, and the source of a large share of British imports, especially raw materials.[59] By comparison, French commercial interests in Italy were considerably less important. And the growing economic presence of England in Italy could eventually translate into a diplomatic problem for France, for Vergennes was fully aware of the tendency of close commercial relations to be translated into political relations.

Vergennes' response to the reforms of the Duke of Tuscany is typical of his conservatism, and highlights, once more, his greatest failure as a statesman. Leopold's reforms in Tuscany, according to Vergennes, had no value for France. He dismissed the example as not relevant to France because the differences between the Duchy of Tuscany and France were too great. And Leopold's concern with his treasury, Vergennes found undignified; his taste for "novelty" unbecoming. When speaking of the single-tax system being discussed in Tuscany, Vergennes argued that revenue was so necessary to meet Louis XVI's financial commitments (i.e., Louis' commitments as a great power), that there was really no latitude to permit experiments with a new system. He admitted that this was unfortunate, "... but, on the other hand," he observed, revealing his basic fear of innovation, "... perhaps the spirit of novelty would be even more dangerous, if it could be exercised more easily."[60] Thus, while the Duke of Tuscany took advantage of peace to reform his state, Vergennes used the urgency of war and high politics to argue that France could not experiment with "new systems." The priorities of high politics, which created the financial crisis in France, therefore, also served to resist the reforms which might have warded off the bankruptcy.

CHAPTER 35

Commerce and Diplomacy I: The Anglo-French Commercial Treaty of 1786

In 1785, The French treasury was on the verge of bankruptcy. Its troubles, however, did not spring from a lack of wealth in France. The state, because of age-old privileges and inefficiencies, simply could not tap the wealth available, without a thoroughgoing reform of its fiscal and social structure. But many in France, including Vergennes, were determined that thoroughgoing reforms must not take place. The government, consequently, had to find other ways of raising the much-needed revenue. The idea of increasing foreign trade to raise customs revenues was appealing. Increased trade and customs revenues would provide the French treasury with the means to carry on as a great power, and help silence those who demanded more radical solutions.

An estimated three-fourths of the merchandise imported into France in 1786 was contraband, prohibited by law or by high tariffs,[1] and it was reasonable to assume that if such prohibitions were removed, and replaced by moderate duties, the illegal trade could be converted into a source of revenue.[2] Vergennes certainly saw the advantages of such a trade policy.

On May 21, 1786, Gérard de Rayneval read, before the Council of State, a paper outlining some additional gains which could be expected from a liberal trade agreement with England.[3] It was a mistake, according to Rayneval, for every nation to try to produce all the products it needed. Individual countries could produce some products much more economically than could others. A freer trade system would allow the countries within the system to produce and sell, at home and abroad, those things it could best produce, while it could easily buy those products it could not produce cheaply. Furthermore, as Rayneval saw the situation, and on this point he agreed completely with the Physiocrats, the cultivation of the soil was the most solid basis for the prosperity of France;[4] it was, therefore, an obligation of the state to encourage agricultural production. This could be done in France by opening new markets abroad. If France opened her ports to English manufactured goods, English ports could be opened to French agricultural products.

Rayneval admitted to the Council that such a liberalization of trade policy would cause some immediate hardships to French manufacturers, whose machinery was technologically behind that of the British. Yet he felt that the interests of French agriculture, and even the consumer, should be preferred to those of the French manufacturers. If France sent to England its wines, brandies, vinegars, and salt, all products of the soil which England could not as efficiently produce, England could supply, in return, cotton goods and hardware. Products such as woolens, which were produced by both countries, could be handled by arrangements of reciprocal advantage. In addition, the competition introduced by a trade agreement might provide the stimulus needed to force French manufacturers to quicken their pace of modernization.

Vergennes, moreover, was convinced that a commercial treaty would be a useful instrument for establishing a *rapproachement* with Great Britain. Such a radical departure in foreign policy would certainly raise cries of appeasement in both countries. Yet France needed peace, and Great Britain was her most likely enemy. "His Most Christian Majesty [Louis XVI]," the British commissioner William Eden wrote, "in receiving the King's letter [of credence], was pleased to say several sentences to me respecting his eagerness to promoté a commercial intercourse between the two countries, as the best means of maintaining a pacific system."[5] Whenever Vergennes spoke to Eden, he dwelt a good deal on the effect that a French - English *rapproachement* would have on preserving the peace.[6] To Vergennes, the commercial treaty opened a path to possible co-existence.[7]

English motives were equally complex. In England, the old Mercantile and protectionist notions still seemed to dominate economic thought.[8] Yet Shelburne, who began with France the discussions which led to a commercial treaty, recognized the virtues of a more liberal trade policy, and he later praised the treaty because it was inspired by the "great principles of free trade."[9] But Shelburne fell from office in February of 1783, and Pitt replaced him.

Pitt held no consistent economic theory, yet he appreciated the argument's of the liberal economists, and he wanted England to gain the benefits such theories promised.[10] Nor was Pitt ignorant of the financial reasons for reforming the traditional mercantile system. At the close of the American Revolutionary War, the British treasury deficit was 3,000,000 pounds. Yet the British Exchequer lost 280,000 pounds a year, on customs on French wines smuggled into England.[11] If prohibitions were dropped, and replaced by moderate levies, the Exchequer stood to gain.[12]

The treaty-makers of 1786, therefore, had a multitude of aims. They were advised of the possibilities for increased trade, and customs revenue, through a more liberal trade policy; the French hoped that a more competitive environment would stimulate technological improvement in French manufacturers; both sides, especially Vergennes, saw in a treaty the possibility of a thaw in the Anglo-French cold war; and, surely, they were aware that the new economic theories taught that free trade was consistent with the public good. Such a broad conception of interests is a tribute to their talents.

Article Eighteen of the Peace Treaty of 1783 provided that France and England name commissioners, after the exchange of ratifications, to negotiate new commercial arrangements. The Article stipulated that these arrangements should be concluded within two years after January 1, 1784.[13] The English had hoped, apparently, that Article Eighteen might be buried in the Foreign Office archives, but Vergennes was determined to the contrary.[14] He saw so many advantages in an Anglo-French commercial treaty that he could not let the opportunity pass. On his initiative, therefore, commissioners were named and exchanged, and negotiations opened.[15] And it was his constant pressure that brought the negotiations to a final conclusion.

Despite Vergennes' determination to conclude a treaty as soon as possible, serious negotiations did not begin until the spring of 1786. The uncertainties resulting from the fall of Shelburne and the rise of Pitt made it difficult to embark on a new policy in foreign trade. And, even after he was finally established in power, Pitt did not give first priority to the Franco-English treaty. The British appointed a commissioner, as required by the Eighteenth Article of the Versailles Treaty, but the commisioner, George Craufurd, remained in England for six months, studying the question of how much French contraband entered England. And, when he finally did reach Paris, he arrived without instructions, and spent much of his time trying to avoid the French commissioner, Gérard de Rayneval.[16]

Lord Carmarthen, the British Foreign Secretary, saw no reason to hurry into new arrangements with France. The commercial provisions of the Treaty of Utrecht were still in force and quite consistent, he thought, with British interests.[17] In addition, his distrust of France made him doubt that any real benefits could follow from opening new negotiations.[18]

Progress towards a treaty was not assisted, either, by the hostile attitude of the French Ambassador at London, Adhémar de Grignan, and his *chargé d'affaires,* Barthélemy. While Vergennes and Rayneval worked, at Versailles, towards a *détente,* the two Frenchmen in London remained adamant in their belief that hatred of France was part of the English character.[19] Furthermore, they had no hesitation in expressing their opinions: "It is an evident truth that the English are irreconcilable enemies. Rivalry, competition, jealousy, national hatred, spirit of vengeance, all are opposed to a *reapprochement* with this nation ...."[20] Such inflexibility made it difficult for Vergennes to deal with England through his ambassador there; consequently, most of the negotiations were carried on in France.

Vergennes was determined to make a treaty. At the same time, he was in a hurry to do so, since he feared that delay would give the opposition in France a chance to consolidate against him.[21] His first move, made in September of 1784, was a suggestion, through Rayneval, to the British, that the principle of reciprocity be the basis for the negotiations.[22] But the British refused to rise to the bait. They did not even bother to answer. Irritated, Vergennes decided to administer a stiffer medicine. "If the intention of the English minister is to while away the time allowed by the last treaty of peace," he wrote to the French ambassador in London, "we have neither the means nor a reason to oppose him. But when the two years have passed, we will regard the Treaty of Utrecht as lapsed ... and we will regulate our commerce with Great Britain as it suits our interest to do so ...."[23]

Vergennes' threat to consider the Treaty of Utrecht no longer binding was a move which Carmarthen had not expected, and certainly did not wish to see carried out. "...we intend to hold to the Treaty of Utrecht," he told the French ambassador. "In that case," the latter replied, "you deceive yourself absolutely." Obviously shaken, Carmarthen protested, but Grignan refused to argue the matter. Vergennes had made it perfectly clear to the British, when he was negotiating Article Eighteen of the 1783 treaty, that the treaty they were then discussing could, in no manner, be a confirmation or a renewal of the Treaty of Utrecht.[24] England was not acting in good faith, Grignan told Carmarthen, and he advised the Englishman to read the various explanatory memos that Vergennes had sent to London.[25]

But the British still were not ready to negotiate in earnest, so Vergennes tried another form of pressure. To convince them of France's good will, he had earlier allowed a generous number of British products to enter France.[26] Since the British had not responded to the carrot, he tried the whip. In February of 1785, the French government decreed a sixty per cent *ad valorem* duty on the English carriages that were becoming so popular in fashionable French society.[27] This move was followed, in July, by more government decrees: one forbidding the importation of saddlery, woolens, hosiery, hardware, and most articles of polished steel,[28] and another which forbade the entry of foreign cottons, muslins, gauzes, and linens.[29] Still another excluded all foreigners from sharing the French trade with the Barbary states.[30] Although England was not specifically named, she was obviously the target of these decrees. Carmarthen, piqued, remarked, after the heavy duty was placed on English carriages, that the tendency of Vergennes' actions was "to prevent that spirit of conciliation and friendly liberality so necessary at this time to produce any good effect from those commercial arrangements now in contemplation . . . ."[31]

The hammer blows snapped the British government to attention, but it still refused to accept the principle of reciprocity as the basis for negotiation. "Mutual benefits and reciprocal advantages are indisputably the objects we are inclined to pursue in the adjustment of this business," Carmarthen wrote to Craufurd, "but to say, at once, that the two nations shall be entitled to those privileges which are, alone, allowed to the most favored nations, by the way of a basis to the negotiations, and without weighing the nature and consequences of such privileges, is totally impossible."[32]

Now that he had the attention of the British foreign secretary, however, Vergennes would not let up the pressure. On October 21st, the French government registered a decree further forbidding importations into France.[33] Three days later, Vergennes announced that, at the close of 1785, France would no longer adhere to the provisions of the Treaty of Utrecht.[34] When Carmarthen objected to these decrees, he received the bland reply that, since the new duties were general, they did not show any special hostility to England.[35] France was completely in the right in imposing such duties, Rayneval told Craufurd, as long as no new commercial arrangements were being negotiated.[36]

Fortunately, in the British embassy at Paris, there was an individual, David Hailes, who understood the significance of Vergennes' ostensibly hostile acts, and he took the opportunity provided by the absence of his superior, the Duke of Dorset, to spell it out for London. "The slow progress of the treaty of commerce," wrote Hailes, "has occasioned a great deal of ill-humor towards us."[37] After the decrees of October, Hailes again explained to London that the action of the French government was taken "to stimulate us to a conclusion of the commercial treaty as soon as possible."[38]

Carmarthen found it difficult, however, to believe that French motivations were so innocent. He suspected that Vergennes was plotting a sinister plan to ruin England. Happily, Pitt was not so rigidly convinced of France's hostility, and it was just at this moment that he stepped into the affair. From then on, the negotiations were pursued with more energy, if not more speed. Having been involved in an unsuccessful attempt to conclude a free-trade agreement with Ireland, Pitt had not been able to give much attention to the faltering Anglo-French discussions. But his Irish project had fallen through, and now he was free to turn his attention to Versailles.[39] He was encouraged to do so by a London merchant, one Benjamin Eyre, who assured him that Great Britain would have a decided advantage over France in any trade agreement which opened the ports of each country to the trade of the other.[40] To facilitate matters, therefore, Pitt instructed Craufurd to ask

Vergennes for a six-month extension on the abrogation of the Treaty of Utrecht, a request that Vergennes readily agreed to, and then he replaced Craufurd with William Eden, a sympathetic negotiator who soon became convinced of the sincerity of the French Secretary of State. "Whatever may be their political motive," Eden wrote to Pitt, "it is not to be doubted that they wish to come to a conclusion."[41] Gradually, even Pitt came around to admitting that perhaps in commercial matters the French could be sincere, although he was not yet willing to accept the "protestations of political amity."[42]

In September of 1785, Vergennes had suggested that, if the English did not like the French proposals, they should advance some of their own. France, he wanted to assure London, would certainly consider them in a spirit of conciliation.[43] Consequently, when Eden embarked for Paris, he carried with him the minutes of a treaty he had drawn up. This was the first hard evidence that Vergennes had had that the British were ready to engage in serious negotiations.

Once the British demonstrated a willingness to negotiate, Vergennes turned over to his numerous aides the various tasks auxiliary to the making of a treaty. Gérard de Rayneval, a long-time confidant, became his chief negotiator at Versailles. Behind the scenes, in a role not so public but equally important, worked the Physiocrat, DuPont de Nemours.

Rayneval's contribution will become apparent as the narrative progresses. DuPont's role in the commercial treaty of 1786 deserves a moment's description because it illustrates how Vergennes used expert advisors in his policy making. Vergennes knew very little about economic affairs, but he had the good sense to make use of the specialist, when he felt he needed him.

DuPont began his career as Turgot's protégé,[44] but Turgot's disgrace left him without a patron. Consequently, he offered his services to Vergennes, first as a secret agent to the rebellious Americans.[45] On this occasion and several later ones, Vergennes chose not to use DuPont as an intelligence, or diplomatic, agent. But he respected DuPont's talents and reputation as an expert on economic matters. And it is in this area that DuPont made his contribution to the commercial treaty of 1786. In 1779, he became Inspector-General of Commerce[46] and, thereafter, Vergennes employed him in numerous tasks relating to French commerce and the economy. When the Spanish asked to float a loan in France, DuPont was consulted for an opinion.[47] When the council considered the question of opening Bayonne as a free port, DuPont was called upon to give his recommendation.[48] Continuously, he gathered data on French commerce and the economy, and sifted it for use in the discussions in council. His data lacked the precision of twentieth-century economic data; nevertheless, he brought together an impressive amount of information about French trade and manaufacturing.

The information, plus his international reputation, combined to give his opinions considerable weight in the government. In 1785, DuPont became a member of a consultative committee on agriculture, under the direction of Vergennes' nephew, Gravier de Vergennes. In the same year, he became Co-director, along with Boyetet, of the Bureau of Balance of Commerce.[49] Boyetet and DuPont came to sharp disagreement over the Anglo-French commercial treaty. In fact, Boyetet became one of the most articulate spokesmen for the opposition. He felt that the commercial treaty would harm French manufacturers, and he disapproved of the French government's refusal to consult the local chambers of commerce, and bring them into the discussions about the specifics of the treaty which directly concerned their interests.[50] The Bureau of Balance of Commerce drew up reports on French trade, and suggested ways in which it could be improved and expanded.[51] Working through this bureau, DuPont became an extremely important aid to Vergennes in the making of the Anglo-French commercial treaty.

DuPont never participated in the negotiations as Vergennes' representative. That role was well-filled by Gérard de Rayneval. And, certainly, DuPont did not entirely write the treaty, as one of his biographers believed.[52] Of the fifty-five articles in the treaty and the convention which followed, only seventeen were new; the rest were copied from the Treaties of Utrecht, either verbatim or with alterations. And the alterations were the offspring of many people: Pitt, Eden, the Advocate General of Great Britain, the English Solicitor of Customs; Rayneval, Vergennes, the French Controlleur-Général, as well as DuPont.

DuPont's role was, nevertheless, significant. He gathered together and interpreted statistics. He organized information needed by the negotiators. And he was a very articulate "idea man", who promised to save France from its financial difficulties by means of commercial treaties. Vergennes and other members of the government used DuPont's ideas, his memos, and his arguments, in the Councils of State and in the negotiations with the English. When the opposition organized against the making of a treaty, DuPont provided Vergennes and his aides with answers to the critics. In 1786, DuPont wrote six different memos,[53] in which he argued in favor of a commercial treaty with England. His arguments can be summarized as follows: both sides could gain by opening up their markets to each other. A commercial treaty could be the first step in a *détente* that could eventually unite France and England so that, together, they could have tremendous influence in world affairs. Prussia and Austria, DuPont believed, could only fight when France and England were foolish enough to subsidize them. France and England did not have opposing interests in commerce, DuPont argued. France could not take away England's achievements in the production of tea and woolens, and England would never be able to compete with France in the production of wine, silk, and olive oil. DuPont admitted that there would be some rivalry in certain hardwares, in fashions, and cottons, but he pointed out that competition could be beneficial to both sides.[54]

DuPont's arguments were the most imaginative when he turned to state finance and peace. Both countries, DuPont stressed, needed peace. Wars were exhausting them, necessitating loans, absorbing public resources, and thus forcing increases in taxation. France and England could continue fighting with each other, but neither side could ever win a decisive victory; the results would always be mutual exhaustion. A commercial treaty, DuPont believed, could be an important step toward reconciliation.

Furthermore, a commercial treaty would provide a remedy for the financial ailments England and France suffered from previous wars. If prohibitions and high tariffs were lifted, goods which had been smuggled into both countries, illegally, could enter legally. If moderate duties were placed on goods, the treasuries of both countries would gain. The only losers would be the smugglers, who could no longer compete.

DuPont's most effective weapons were the statistics and quantitative data he gathered to demonstrate that France would gain economically from a treaty with England. Although he admitted that his estimates were not perfect, he organized an impressive body of evidence to prove that, when England opened her ports to French wines, brandies, and vinegars, French agriculture would receive a significant boost. French machines, he believed, could be perfected to equal English models, if the French government and French manufacturers began an enlightened policy of modernization. Competition with England would be a healthy spur to that modernization. In any case, DuPont pointed out, French manufacturers were already competing with English manufacturers, because of the enormous quantities of English manufactured goods smuggled into France every year. In fact, DuPont concluded, the treaty would simply legalize imports in some cases, and put money in the French treasury, rather than in the pockets of smugglers.[55] As Vergennes and Rayneval negotiated the trade treaty, DuPont continued to supply them with necessary information and arguments in favor of the treaty, for the debate over the advisability of the treaty continued right down to the signing and after.[56]

Eden specified, in the minutes that he brought from London, that England was not prepared to establish the two nations on the footing of most-favored nations, because existing treaties with other nations made this impossible. He was referring, especially, to the treaty England had with Portugal, the Methuen Treaty. Also, each power should retain the right to give particular advantages to other nations.[57] Despite these reservations, Vergennes was pleased with the attitude now adopted by England.

Together, Rayneval and Eden set to work and soon worked out a "Project" for a commercial treaty.[58]

The only article in the "Project" that gave Vergennes misgivings was the first, which concluded with the statement that each power reserved for itself the right to make subsequent alterations after a six months' notification to the other.[59] Vergennes, who continued to think in terms of his long-range goal of reducing tensions, did not wish to commit himself to an agreement that could be radically altered after six months. Nonetheless, he agreed to send the "Project" on to Pitt for comments.

Pitt, too, disliked Article One. He rightly saw it as a "most favored nation" clause in disguise, and he correctly concluded that, if France placed a general prohibition or duty on cotton or hardware, England would lose the only real advantages from a treaty.[60] Even if France had no general prohibitions on any goods now, she could impose them in six months without violating the terms of the treaty. Such a clause gave France an advantage over England, because England's treaty obligations with Portugal made it impossible for her to impose general prohibitions on products such as wine. Pitt wanted to liberalize trade with France but protect English trade interests with the rest of the world.[61] He also wanted to be certain that Ireland benefited from any treaty made with France.[62]

Although he embarrassed Eden by doing so, Pitt also refused to admit French silks into England. He feared a sharp reaction from English silk manufacturers; silk "must be kept out of the question."[63] He was somewhat concerned, too, about the repercussions in Portugal, if England agreed to admit French wines. The Methuen Treaty with Portugal gave Portuguese wines special advantages which they would lose if a treaty with France were concluded. On this latter point, however, Pitt was inclined to give way.[64] In spite of his objections, Pitt entertained "sanguine hopes" as to a final agreement on a treaty.[65]

Pitt's insistence on working out the details of specific goods to be exchanged between the two countries irritated Vergennes, because Eden had, earlier, insisted on a statement of general principles, and had argued that details could wait until later.[66] The British change of front only delayed the conclusion of a treaty. When Eden returned to Versailles after a short absence, he found Rayneval "less cordial and conciliatory than in our former conference." In fact, Eden wrote, his manner bordered on peevishness.[67] Still, the English offers were much more liberal than Vergennes had expected;[68] expediency dictated that he push on with the negotiations. When Eden presented to Vergennes a formal "Declaration"[69] incorporating Pitt's objections, he expressed his "earnest desire to reach a proper conclusion to the business in question."[70] Carmarthen was much impressed that the British proposals received such a conciliatory reception.[71]

The English "Declaration," like the earlier "Project," advanced the idea that the navigation and commerce of the two countries be placed on a most-favored-nation basis, but it allowed for exceptions, in cases where special privileges had been granted to other powers. In addition, it suggested that arrangements be made for establishing the amount of duties on specific articles where it was convenient. "In order to give stability" to the commercial relations between the two powers, the "Declaration" contained the proposal that both parties agree not to alter the arrangements for ten years.[72] Within ten days, Rayneval returned to Eden a "contre-Declaration," which contained all the essentials of the British "Declaration."[73] The two parties could turn now to a consideration of the specific duties to be placed on the articles admitted into their ports.

With Vergennes anxious to get an agreement before the opposition in France found a way to prevent the conclusion of a treaty, and Pitt determined to consider and re-consider, in detail, each article in the treaty, the negotiations during this period taxed the patience of all the participants. To Vergennes, the most important item in the treaty was the article setting the duties on French wines. King George had demonstrated a willingness to abolish all prohibitions which would place French subjects at a disadvantage *vis-à-vis* the subjects of other States. But he made one exception, and it was precisely the one that hurt France most: Portuguese wine would continue to enter at a lower duty than French wine.[74] Nevertheless, Pitt did agree that French wines should enjoy a lower duty in English ports; consequently, he suggested that they be lowered more than one-third. Pitt also agreed to admit French vinegars and brandies at considerable reduction.[75] In return for these concessions, France was expected to allow entry of British hardware, woolens, and worsteds at "reasonable rates." The British duties on French linens would be reduced to equal those placed on similar goods from Holland and Flanders. The prohibitions on French cambric and lawns were to be lifted, and these goods admitted at moderate duties of twelve to fifteen per cent. Cotton goods would be admitted into each country on a basis of reciprocity.[76] Vergennes, Rayneval, and Calonne, the Finance Minister, all agreed that France should continue to insist on the opening of British ports to French silks,[77] but Pitt would not have it; the pressure from British silk manufacturers was simply too great.[78] To compensate the French for their disappointment, however, Pitt agreed to allow French fashions to enter at no duties, other than those imposed on the goods of other countries, and he took into consideration a French request to admit French plate glass. In return, however, England asked that her pottery be admitted into France at a low duty.

By the month of August, Rayneval and Eden had made great strides toward the signing of a treaty, and Vergennes, now very ill, began to look forward to the conclusion of the wearisome negotiations. He was not willing to bring the discussions to a close, however, until France obtained a better arrangement on the question of its wines. England's offer to lower duties on French wines by one-third was a step in the right direction, but it did not go far enough. It left the Portuguese with the advantage.[79] France was willing to concede to Britain on the question of the entrance of French silks,[80] but not on the question of French wines. Because he felt so strongly about this question, Vergennes himself intervened, and personally urged Eden to try to get London to agree to admit French wines at rates equal to those on Portuguese wines.[81] Within three days, London agreed that, "if necessary," the duties on French wines could be lowered to be equal to those *then* placed on Portuguese wines.[82] England reserved the right, however, to make further reductions of the duties on Portuguese wines.[83]

Vergennes chafed at the numerous delays, and urged that the negotiations be brought to a prompt conclusion, but Pitt refused to be rushed. He was concerned about the effects the treaty might have on Irish trade, and he wanted to assure himself that Ireland would reap some benefits.[84] Even Eden, who was satisfied with the concessions France had made, and who shared Vergennes' fear of the opposition in France, felt obliged to urge his home office to speed up the negotiations.[85] But Pitt insisted on keeping his political fences in repair, and so we find him, during most of the month of August, questioning Irish leaders, getting their views on the treaty, and suggesting changes in the treaty that would benefit them.

Not until September 21, 1786, therefore, did the diplomats succeed in composing a draft of the treaty to which all could agree. On the twenty-sixth of September,[86] Rayneval and Eden affixed their signatures to the treaty[87] in a small ceremony at Versailles. Two weeks later they exchanged ratifications.[88]

The commercial relations established by the Anglo-French Commercial Treaty of 1786, or the Eden Treaty, as it was called in Great Britain, are remarkable in their liberality. Absolute freedom of commerce and trade between England and France and their European dominions was not established, but the terms of the treaty provided that there be "a reciprocal and entirely perfect liberty of navigation and commerce between the [European] subjects of each party . . . upon the conditions and in such manner and form as is settled and adjusted in the following articles." In Article Six, the two powers listed the specific conditions and duties to be placed on certain goods. Great Britain could charge no more duties on French wines than were then paid on Portuguese wines. There was no restriction, however, on Britain's lowering, at a later date, the duties on Portuguese wine. Duties on French vinegars and olive oils were considerably lowered. Both parties agreed that no duty on gauzes, hardware, cutlery, cabinet ware, or turnery, as well other goods of iron, steel, copper or brass, could exceed ten per cent *ad valorem*. Duties on cottons, woolens, millinery made of muslin, linen, cambric or gauze, as well as porcelain, plate-glass, and pottery were fixed at twelve per cent *ad valorem*. Saddlery was to be taxed at fifteen per cent *ad valorem,* linens at the rate charged by the most-favored nation, Holland, and cambrics and lawns duties were lowered to five shillings, or six *livres Tournois,* per demi piece of seven yards and three quarters, English measure.

The highest duty established was on beer, which received a reciprocal duty of thirty per cent *ad valorem*. The prohibition which the negotiators had been unable to eliminate was that on silk, "all manufacturers of cotton and wool mixed with silk . . . shall remain prohibited on both sides." On all other articles not specifically listed in the treaty, the rates of the most-favored European nation would apply. In addition, both parties agreed that countervailing duties might be placed on certain articles.

Aside from its purely commercial articles, the treaty is unusual in its attempt to further an Anglo-French *rapprochement* by establishing rules and principles to govern the relations between the two states, as well as among the subjects of both sovereigns. Any subject of either king, for example, could travel freely in the dominions of the other "without license or passport." Agreements were reached regarding privateering and smuggling, and contraband was defined narrowly so that only arms, ammunition, belts, helmets, horses, and harnesses could be declared contraband in time of war. England's willingness to abide by such a strict definition, in time of war, remained to be proven, however. Both powers agreed that the terms of the treaty could not be revised or re-examined for twelve years.

The Anglo-French Commercial Treaty was signed on September 26, 1786, but it did not become effective until July of 1787. The two powers did not open their ports to each other until May of 1787. Nevertheless, there developed a widely accepted belief, in France, that the treaty was one of the principal causes of the economic crisis that struck France in 1786-1787. But the crisis reached its climax in the latter part of 1786, and by mid-1787, when the treaty went into effect, it had begun to ameliorate. The treaty coincided with the crisis, but could not have caused it.[89]

Nevertheless, many manufacturers, and Vergennes' enemies, saw a cause and effect relation between the treaty and the failing economy, and they raised an outcry. Picardie, the region hardest hit by the depression, raised a lively protest,[90] but it was the Chamber of Commerce of Normandie that raised the most publicized objections, in the famous *Observations de la Chambre de Commerce de Normandie sur le traité . . . entre la France et l'Angleterre*.[91]

Vergennes' and Louis XVI's policy had to be defended. Once more,

DuPont stepped forward. In a long *Lettre à la Chambre de Commerce de Normandie,*[92] he answered the critics. There had been some difficulties in getting the treaty underway, he admitted. Calonne had departed from the government, Vergennes had died, and there was some confusion involved in the transition to the new system. Furthermore, the collection of duties by the French customs had been lax, and many English goods were entering France at a lower declared value than they were really worth.[93] The result was competition stiffer than had been anticipated. The undervaluation of British goods meant that customs receipts were also considerably lower than anticipated. But DuPont reminded the critics, once more, of the long-range benefits to be gained from the treaty.

As for the economic crisis, DuPont pointed out that the problems of French manufacturers were more complex than the Chamber of Commerce of Normandy realized. Furthermore, their difficulties were not related to the commercial treaty. French tanneries were in decline long before the treaty was signed, he noted.[94] Changes in fashion, and not the treaty, were the cause of the dip in sales of textiles.[95] Some textile industries, he said, simply charged too much.[96] The luxury trade, he explained, had been seriously hurt by government economies in pensions,[97] while the failure of the raw silk crop had severely damaged the silk manufacturers.[98]

Any attempt to connect the treaty with the weaknesses in the French economy was misleading, DuPont argued. Furthermore, he still believed that the long-range benefits, and the implications for peace in the treaty, made it worth support. The competition from England would accelerate the modernization of French manufacturing, he insisted.

Later historians have also questioned the relation between the economic crisis and the treaty. French manufacturers were already losing the European market before 1786, and the Anglo-French Commercial Treaty was in no way related to this problem.[99] Long before the treaty with England, for example, Austria, Prussia, and Spain had severely undermined French gauze manufacturing by closing their frontiers to this French product.[100] Furthermore, English competition was not new to French manufacturers. For years, English goods entered France as contraband; one cannot argue, therefore, that the treaty suddenly introduced competition where there had been none at all. There is no escaping the conclusion that the French economy was in a serious slump, but the causes were deeper and more complex than the treaty of 1786.

A more valid criticism of the treaty is that it was made and thrust upon French merchants and manufacturers without enough preparation. It is not true as one critic claimed, that the French Ministry prepared the treaty, without consulting the interested parties. "This important act," the critic argued, "was concluded clandestinely" and "without the necessary information."[101] Nevertheless, this criticism, coming from an Inspector-General of manufacturers and commerce, Cliquot-Blervache, was a serious one, and it represents the hostility towards the Treaty of a good many men of the business community in France. Vergennes, Castries, Calonne and other government administrators, such as DuPont and Boyetet, spent many hours gathering information to be used in the preparations for the treaty, but, by and large, the final treaty did not please the French Chambers of Commerce, manufacturers, and merchants; they did not agree with the diplomatic or economic rationale behind the various agreements. Already severely shaken by the depression, the business structure of France simply did not want to cope with so many new developments. Boyetet later claimed that he warned the treaty-makers that, at least, the Chambers of Commerce should have played a larger role in the preparations for the treaty,[102] but the fear of arousing a formidable opposition prevented their doing so. As a result, the French business community, already in a state of crisis, found itself overwhelmed by the changes produced when their ports were opened to British goods.

Ideally the introduction of British goods should have been so phased as to give French merchants and manufacturers time to prepare for it. But, even if such a policy had been considered, it probably would have been overruled by Calonne because of the desperate needs of the French treasury. The French government needed a sharp rise in customs revenues from a flood of British goods into France, and this consideration blinded it to the hardships that such a policy would impose on French business. The Englishman, David Hailes, clearly saw that French treasury needs were taking precedence over the needs of French business: "But I think I can take upon me to assure your Lordship," he wrote to Carmarthen, "that there exists another, and no less principal, cause of the eagerness of France to conclude the commercial arrangement. I mean that of the immediate relief of the *Trésor Royal* by the increase of the revenue, an increase which, it may be presumed, will prove immense, from the sudden influx of all sorts of British merchandise paying the legal duties, as soon as the Treaty shall take effect."[103] Thus, wherever one turns at the end of the Ancien Régime, there is evidence of the damaging effects of the inability of the government to reform. The French government, in effect, forced the French manufacturer to sacrifice to meet the needs of diplomacy and the treasury.

The English government carefully considered the opinion of English merchants and manufacturers each step of the way. Pitt and Eden agreed, soon after Eden's appointment, that it was important "to cultivate every channel of information . . . ." "It cannot be too generally understood," Pitt wrote Eden, "that our sole object is to collect, from all parts of the Kingdom, a just representation of the interests of all the various branches of trade and manufacture which can be affected by the French arrangement . . . ."[104] By January of 1786, Eden was spending "*every* morning, and all morning, in examination of merchants and manufacturers upon various branches of commerce."[105] And, even after Eden left for France in late March, the British Council of Trade continued to inquire into the opinions of merchants, manufacturers, and members of the General Chamber of Manufacturers of Great Britain.[106] By the time Eden began serious negotiations with France, he knew fairly well who was in favor of opening trade with France, who was in favor of it but with reservations, who was "divided or doubtful," and who was against it.[107] The English and French preparations for negotiating the commercial treaty provide interesting insights into the decision making processes of Ancien Régime governments.

Vergennes died before the English treaty was tested. But if he had lived, he would have been discouraged with the results. His long time opponent in Louis XVI's cabinet, the Minister of the Navy, the Maréchal de Castries, repeatedly differed with Vergennes and Calonne, the Comptrolleur Général of Finances, over the new commercial relations during the negotiations for the treaty. Castries' objections were partly the result of his own abrasiveness, partly his jealousy of the prerogatives of the Ministry of the Navy which, he thought, did not have its proper role in the negotiations. But Castries also differed fundamentally with Vergennes over the issue of whether British ships should be allowed to carry goods of other countries into French ports, when French ships were not allowed the same right in British ports.[108] Later, Castries raised difficult, but legitimate, questions in the negotiations over the exchange of consuls, and he wanted more clarification of consular jurisdiction. Anxious to conclude a treaty, Vergennes and Eden had agreed that the rights and privileges of consuls had to conform to the "constitutions of the two Kingdoms . . .," but the Maréchal de Castries demanded absolute reciprocity.[109]

After Vergennes' death, Castries continued to insist on his views as the British returned again and again to iron out their differences with the French. Vergennes' replacement, Montmorin, was too inexperienced to settle the conflict himself and too weak to bend the will of the Minister of the Navy. The issue remained in deadlock with the French and the British refusing to cede on essentials. A recent historian of Castries part in the consular negotiations sums up his role this way: "[Castries] insisted upon exact reciprocity or nothing — and *got nothing*"[110] France received no English consuls until after the Napoleonic Wars. Every commercial dispute, every complaint, therefore, had to be handled through the ambassador, who was never on the spot and rarely well informed. The treaty, intended to facilitate better relations between England and France, thus created further occasions for complaint and distrust.[111]

CHAPTER 36

Commerce and Diplomacy II: The Franco-Russian Treaty of 1787 and Other Treaties

The Franco-Russian trade treaty of 1787 was Vergennes' last achievement. He died before the final negotiations were completed, but the diplomatic spadework for the treaty, and the conception of its role in French policy were his. The treaty was a piece in Vergennes' plan to use diplomacy and trade to revive the French economy and to solve the problems of French finances. And, as with every commercial treaty he negotiated, commerce always remained the instrument of high politics.

Throughout the eighteenth century, there were several attempts to establish better trade relations between France and Russia; all of them failed. Deep political differences, and ineptness on the part of both Russian and French diplomats and statesmen, probably would have made any agreements unworkable, even if concluded.[1] There were many obstacles to better trade relations between France and Russia. One of the most important was the reluctance of French merchants to venture into the Baltic in search of trade with Russia.[2] Added to this difficulty, was the scarcity, in Russia, of French merchants to handle French Baltic trade. In 1757, one observer remarked that there were "no French merchants at St. Petersburg . . . only a number of ragged peddlers without credit or reputation . . . ."[3] The situation was no better in 1785.[4] Furthermore, those French merchants who were in Russia did not enjoy the success or confidence enjoyed by their English counterparts. They complained of the mediocrity of profits, and of the many restrictions and inequities they suffered at the hands of the Russian bureaucracy.[5]

Critics of French merchants, however, believed that the cause of the difficulties lay closer to home. French merchants in Russia spent many of their profits on unproductive luxuries and, hence, were never able to accumulate the capital needed to expand their activities.[6] Unlike the English merchants, the French merchants refused to cooperate with each other to protect their common interests and, despite their repeated cries to Versailles and Paris for assistance in setting up new French trading houses in Russia, in reality, they intrigued to prevent any new competition.[7]

French merchants did not, in fact, enjoy in Russia the same privileges enjoyed by English merchants. The latter enjoyed the right to quick and impartial settlements in Russian courts; they could pay custom duties in Russian currency and this meant, for the English, a savings of about one and one-half to two per cent on the payment of duties. Finally, the English enjoyed preferential tariffs.[8] English merchants were trusted, and they knew the country. This situation, according to the French, explained the English "monopoly". Many of the French merchants in Russia resorted to smuggling and illegal activities to survive.[9] The French government accurately summed up the situation in 1763: "[Russia] knows our merchandise, but she has hardly seen our merchants, so there has resulted the presupposition that France can be of no use to Russia in the balance of commerce."[10]

The obstacles in the way of direct French trade did not mean, however, an absence of French goods in Russia, or, for that matter, an absence of Russian goods in France. Statistics regarding commerce in the eighteenth century are notoriously imprecise. Calonne's figures on the trade for 1785 estimated that imports from Russia, directly to France, amounted to nearly 6,500,000 *livres;* while French exports, directly to Russia, amounted to nearly 5,500,000. But these figures did not include the totals of indirect trade or smuggling.[11] The Russians, according to an earlier estimate of 1757, consumed yearly nearly 100,000,000 *livres* worth of French merchandise, and France purchased almost 30,000,000 *livres* annually of Russian products.[12] This estimate included all trade, direct and indirect, between the two countries. Most of it, however, was carried on Dutch, English, Hanse, or Scandinavian ships.[13] By 1786, the overall total of direct and indirect trade must have been considerably greater, for Vergennes and several of his informants were persuaded that Franco-Russian trade was increasing.[14]

One of the vexing difficulties with the trade figures was that they were contradictory at the point where they needed to be the most precise. Who enjoyed the favorable balance of trade, France or Russia? In direct trade, Russia seemed to enjoy a slight favor,[15] but, in overall trade, including smuggling, France seemed to enjoy a considerable balance in her favor. Furthermore, Vergennes argued, if France enjoyed the favorable balance in peace, Russia compensated for the difference in wartime.[16] The reliability of the figures became a matter of some dispute among the diplomats negotiating the Franco-Russian commercial treaty, because neither party wished to make any agreements that would leave them with an unfavorable balance of trade.[17]

Moreover, some influential Russians felt that a large volume of French goods coming into Russia represented an unhealthy influence, since the French products were, by and large, wines and luxury goods. Not only did these luxury products drain Russia of her specie, they would, also, according to the Russian minister, Voroncov, "corrupt our morals."[18] In 1757, Russia had, indeed, raised a formidable obstacle to direct and legal Franco-Russian trade relations, by establishing a near prohibitive tariff on French luxury products. Every attempt to persuade Catherine to remove or lower the tariff failed.

At another level, the almost chronic lack of understanding and coordination between the French embassy at St. Petersburg and the French consuls in Russia did nothing to advance Franco-Russian trade relations. One despairing consul accused the ambassador of making life "a living hell for me." In turn, the French ambassador blamed the consul, personally, for the chaos of Franco-Russian commercial relations.[19]

Despite the numerous difficulties standing in the way of Franco-Russian commerce, there were many French observers who believed that France could increase her trade with Russia, if she ceased trying to block Russian expansion southward. Let the Russians move into the area now slipping from Ottoman control, they argued, and French traders could then link up with them and tap new markets in the Black Sea and the Levant.[20] One of Vergennes' earlier collaborators at Constantinople, Peysonnel, developed, at length, the argument in favor of Russian expansion, by insisting that it would help facilitate a commercial arrangement which would certainly bring the Black Sea trade to France, and unlock markets in Russia hitherto monopolized by England.[21]

Catherine's dissatisfaction with England's role in the American War led her to resent her almost-exclusive dependence on English trade.[22] Catherine's confidant, the Prince Potemkin, favored a closer relation with France based on commerce, and he especially wanted to encourage Black Sea trade, in order to develop the economy of the southern territories recently taken from the Turks.[23] Unfortunately, however, this "most unexplainable man who ever existed," Ségur wrote to Vergennes, "understands everything quickly, but never follows up anything."[24] Still, Catherine believed that she would benefit economically if she established her trade with the world on a more competitive basis.[25] Her new political role as arbiter of Europe required that she become independent of England.[26]

The Russians had long sought navigation rights on the Black Sea,[27] and they gained them in the treaty of *Kuchuk Kainarji* in 1774. After 1774, Russian commercial vessels sailed the Black Sea and, through the newly opened gateway, to the Eastern Mediterranean. The treaty made it possible to convert the Black Sea from an exclusively Ottoman lake into a Russo-

Ottoman lake. Since the French had favored the Turks in the war against Russia, Catherine was under no obligation to stand aside and allow French merchants to move in and reap all the rewards provided by the opportunities. Furthermore, the fear of Russian competition in an area where they had, hitherto, operated almost exclusively made many Frenchmen wary of the appearance of Russian ships in the Mediterranean.[28] Observers outside of France agreed: Russian ships in the Black Sea would constitute a sharp challenge to the French Levant trade.[29]

Moreover, it soon became apparent that the treaty of *Kuchuk Kainarji* would be the pretext for almost-constant agitation along the common frontiers of the Ottoman Empire and Russia. If the Czarina took up arms and exploited her susperiority over the failing Turks, France's traditional role as friend of the Turks would be severely tested. Unless France decided to abandon altogether her policy of protecting the Turks, she had to continue to defend them against Russian encroachment. To encourage Russian economic expansion southward, and, at the same time, try to keep in repair the Ottoman dike designed by France to stop Russian expansion,[30] was to court a diplomatic catastrophe. If Catherine II continued to execute her expansionist ambitions, the veteran diplomat, Broglie, believed, there was no hope for a Franco-Russian *rapproachement.*

Despite all the potential dangers, Vergennes found attractive a commercial treaty with Russia. There was an opinion among French diplomatic observers that England's relations with Russia offered a model for France. During the eighteenth century, England had studiously tried to avoid political alliances with Russia. She believed it was not in her interest to bind herself too closely to a power whose aims were, in many ways, so different from her own.[32] Yet, by means of her flourishing commercial relations with Russia, England seemed consistently able to draw Russia into continental politics on her side, whenever she needed Russian help.[33] Could France increase her influence at St. Petersburg by means of a commercial treaty? The subtle influence of economics might prove more effective in calming Russian aggressive tendencies against the Turks than the promises, expensive presents, and military advisors[34] France sent to Constantinople. By now, Vergennes was convinced that Louis XVI desperately needed a prolonged peace, in order to recover from the debts of previous wars. Any policy that tended to reduce the chances for a European war was worth thoughtful consideration.

In his instructions to his young and recently appointed Ambassador to St. Petersburg, Louis-Philippe Ségur, Vergennes admitted that political considerations were paramount in his reflections on trade with Russia. Perhaps Catherine could be weaned away from English influence, by means of commerce.[35] If Catherine's designs against the Turks could be moderated by such roundabout tactics, Vergennes was prepared to use the tactics. His ambassador agreed. Perhaps, Ségur speculated, peace in Europe could be assured with a Franco-Russian *rapprochement,* "of which a treaty of commerce would be the base and first step."[36]

Unlike most of his predecessors, Louis-Philippe Ségur immediately won the attention and respect of Catherine and many members of the Russian court, when he arrived at St. Petersburg in March, 1785.[37] And, most importantly, Ségur quickly began to enjoy the friendship and eventual confidence of Prince Potemkin.[38] Soon Ségur moved with ease in the St. Petersburg Court and society. The anti-French members of the government and Court began to fear his "flatteries."[39]

Once established, Ségur began the laborious task of dissolving suspicions of France and, at the same time, placing before the Russian ministers Louis XVI's views about a Franco-Russian commercial treaty. In his preliminary talks with the Russians, Ségur tried to persuade them to grant to France equality with other nations. If French merchants enjoyed the same trading privileges enjoyed by the merchants of other countries, and if these privileges were protected by a formal treaty, Ségur believed, French merchants would be more willing to take risks and embark on new projects for Russian trade.[40] Such a condition of equality could be easily guaranteed by a "most-favored-nation" clause.[41]

The Russians were not ready to grant France the equality Ségur demanded. Experience had taught them, they argued, that the most-favored-nation clause led to so many abuses and disputes that it actually interfered with commerce. Furthermore, the Russians wished to reserve the right to grant preferential treatment to some countries, Portugal and Spain, for example, because their distant geographical location from Russian Baltic ports required that they be given special treatment. Russia, indeed, wanted to free herself from dependence on English trade, but she reasoned that this could be best accomplished by attracting to her ports as many foreign ships as possible. To do this, she had to reserve the right to grant special privileges to certain countries.[42]

The Russians felt that they could refuse absolute equality to France, because they were convinced that their products were absolutely essential to the well-being of France. France sold Russia only luxury items, while Russia sold France naval stores. France needed wood more than Russia needed wine. Vergennes informed the Russian minister at Versailles of the fact that the United States, with whom France already had a commercial treaty, also produced naval stores.[43] But the information failed to move the diplomats at St. Petersburg. Furthermore, they contended, if Russia admitted French wines on the basis of equality — that is, with lower customs duties — the Russian government would suffer a significant loss of revenues. Customs duties, according to the Russian minister, Voroncov, represented a major source of revenue for the Russian government. It could not be expected to sacrifice these revenues.[44]

Nevertheless, the two parties were now in tacit agreement that they wanted to encourage direct Franco-Russian trade.[45] Any concessions made, therefore, would apply only to goods carried on Russian or French ships. Russian or French goods carried on the ships of third parties would not benefit from any agreement between the two countries.

Most of the Russian goods imported into France were raw materials, already permitted entry with very little duty. The Minister of Marine and the Chamber of Commerce of Marseille, however, wanted to continue a twenty per cent duty on goods coming from Russia, which were similar to those which French traders ordinarily shipped from the Levant. In the subsequent discussions, Ségur agreed to give up this prohibitive duty, in exchange for a reduction of Russian duties in the Black Sea ports.

One of the frequent complaints of French traders in Russia was the lack of parity between English traders and French traders regarding the currencies used for payments of duties.[46] The English paid in local currencies, while France had to pay half of the total duties with the Dutch *Riksdaler*. Ségur estimated that the savings to the English were probably not as significant as French merchants claimed;[47] but, nevertheless, it was a discrimination against French merchants that he was determined to eliminate.[48] At first, the Russians seemed willing to allow French traders to pay duties in local currency.[49] But later, when the diplomats began talking of specifics, the Russians stiffened their position. Progress toward a settlement came to a halt.[50] But Ségur knew that he had the support of Potemkin on this issue, so he refused to back down.[51]

In the negotiations, two products, French wines and Russian iron, emerged as critical for Franco-Russian trade: French wines represented one of the most important French exports to Russia. Also, a tremendous quantity of French wines were shipped to Russia disguised as Spanish wines, because Spain, along with Portugal, enjoyed special tariff privileges not enjoyed by France. Ségur was confident, too, that Russian consumption of French wines was increasing, in spite of the tariff advantages enjoyed by the Portuguese and Spanish wines. Furthermore, Ségur believed that the demand in Russia for French wines was so great that it would exceed the supply, regardless of the duties paid.[52] Nevertheless, he continued to press for lower duties because he felt France should enjoy, at least in part, equality of treatment with Spain and Portugal.[53]

In the last months of the negotiations, the Russians startled the French with the demand that the French lower by twenty per cent all duties on Russian iron. The demand was embarrassing, even though France imported very little iron from Russia.[54] It was a shrewd attempt to enter the competition with Sweden, whose iron exports to France were considerable. The demand also contradicted French trade agreements recently signed with Hamburg, Sweden, and England. Ségur firmly objected, and urged his superiors at Versailles not to accept it.[55] But, before Vergennes received Ségur's urgent note to refuse the Russian demand, he had conceded that France might agree to a twenty per cent reduction of duties on Russian iron imports, if the reduction was not rigidly tied to duties placed on iron coming from other countries. Vergennes offered even more: for example, that France offer to lower by one fifth its duties on Russian tallow.[56] But, at St. Petersburg, Ségur ignored Vergennes and offered the Russians only a "most-favored-nation class" on iron. To his surprise, the Russians accepted.

In January, 1787, Ségur signed the commercial treaty with the Russians, and sent it to Versailles for ratification. In the articles dealing with Franco-Russian commerce, French merchants gained most of the rights heretofore enjoyed by the English.[57] On the other hand, nearly one-half of the articles in the treaty dealt with rights of maritime powers in times of war and peace. The articles echoed the rights demanded by Catherine, in her Armed Neutrality of 1780, and represented, therefore, substantial Franco-Russian agreement in this area. In this respect, the treaty represented Louis XVI's recognition that Russia was now a permanent part of the European international system.[58]

From a historical perspective, we can see that the treaty represented a significant step in the direction of freer trade. It was negotiated on the premise that a moderate amount of free exchange would profit the economies of both countries. Furthermore, as in the Eden treaty, Vergennes assumed that the lowering of tariffs would increase the volume of trade, while, at the same time, reducing smuggling. The result, he hoped, would be an increase in revenues from duties.[59]

Unfortunately, before the year 1787 ended, Russia and the Ottoman Empire were once again at war, and Franco-Russian commerce in the south was stillborn.[60] Commerce, however, had been neither Catherine's nor Vergennes' only interest in making the treaty. Catherine had sought the treaty as a means of gaining some diplomatic independence from England without suffering great economic and commercial losses. The treaty was a political instrument in her foreign policy.

Vergennes hoped the commercial treaty would give Louis XVI more political leverage in dealing with Catherine. In place of an openly hostile stance toward Russia, Vergennes wanted to find a more subtle instrument for influencing Catherine, and moderating her ambitions against the Ottoman Empire. The commercial treaty was a further extension of his earlier "good offices" in dealing with the explosive Russo-Turkish conflict. French interest in the preservation of the Ottoman Empire remained an unsurmountable obstacle to a true Franco-Russian *rapproachement* and Vergennes was not willing to relinquish that interest.[61] Catherine knew this, and remained suspicious of France. The treaty did, however, open a door wider to French mediation in Russo-Turkish disputes. The treaty reflected, therefore, the deep ambiguities of Franco-Russian relations on the eve of the French Revolution.

The commercial treaties with England and Russia were not the only negotiations Vergennes sponsored to encourage French commerce and increase revenues. Between 1774 and his death in 1787, he had a hand in at least fifteen other treaties, conventions, or diplomatic talks, which, in one way or another, represented an attempt to facilitate French commerce or customs collection. During the period, Louis XVI issued numerous edicts and letters patent, to implement trade agreements or to make uniform, or to clarify, customs and consular procedures.[62]

One of the activities costing the state too much in revenues was smuggling. But, in order to tighten control over smugglers, and protect customs revenues, France and her neighbors had to clarify exactly where their mutual frontiers were. In 1778, Vergennes negotiated an agreement with the Bishop of Liège, settling boundary and territorial differences which, in some cases, were over 200 years old.[63] In 1778, the Secretary of State also put his signature to a convention with the Elector of Trier, bringing to a close boundary disputes predating the time when the young Vergennes represented Louis XV at Trier.[64] In November of 1774, Vergennes signed a *précis verbal* with the Swiss canton of Berne, which clarified the frontiers between the French territory of Gex and the canton of Berne. This settlement was one of several attempts to define more precisely boundaries which, presumably, had been agreed upon in the Treaty of Lausanne in 1564.[64] In 1776, at Nancy, Louis XVI and the Prince of Nassau-Weilbourg settled their boundary differences in a treaty, ratified by the Empire in 1785.[66] In 1777, the "frequent dissentions" between the French and the Spanish regarding possessions, boundaries, and authority of commands on the island of Santo Domingo, were settled by treaty. In this treaty, Vergennes put his signature to a shameful document which placed human slaves and "all beasts" in the same category, for the purposes of regulating their trade, pursuit, and capture.[67]

Vergennes continued to pursue his goal, expressed from the moment of his entry into the government, to substitute France for England in the commercial lives of Spain and Portugal. In 1774, he completed a convention and, in 1785, a treaty with Charles III which aimed at defining their mutual boundaries, and working out ways to stop smuggling, especially in salt and tobacco, over the frontiers and in the ports of France and Spain.[68] In March of 1778, the Spanish-Portuguese Treaty of Prado ended hostilities between the two powers and promised mutual guarantees and better commerce. Both powers agreed that they would reciprocally enjoy all the commercial "privileges, liberties, and exemptions" enjoyed by the most favored nation, in this case, England. And Portugal further conceded that the commercial rights, granted in her 1667 treaty with England, would be granted to Spain, "with no modifications nor explanations." In return, any rights Spain had granted to England were to be granted to Portugal.

Article Seventeen of this treaty provided for the accession of other powers to the treaty. Vergennes immediately set to work to get Spain and Portugal to include France in the commercial arrangements agreed upon by them. On August 8, 1783, Louis XVI acceded to the treaty, and France became a party to the Spanish-Portuguese commercial arrangements.[69]

In 1779, Louis XVI signed a treaty of commerce with the Duke of Mecklenburg. The treaty promised attractive commercial benefits, because of Mecklenburg's location on the Baltic Sea and along the Elbe River. Louis XVI granted, to the subjects of the Duke of Mecklenburg, the same commercial privileges in France as those enjoyed by the merchants of the important city of Hamburg. The Duke, in turn, promised to reduce the import tariffs on French white and red wines, *eaux de vie,* sugar, coffee, and Indigo.[70] In July of 1784, Vergennes completed negotiations with the King of Sweden on a secret treaty, which contained assurances to France of an outlet for her products in the Swedish port of Goteborg.[71]

Vergennes also worked for other kinds of agreements to clear away obstacles to foreign trade. In treaties, or in articles within treaties, he abolished the *droit d'Aubaine.* This ancient custom gave the King of France the legal right to inherit the property of foreigners who died in France without heirs. The *droit d'Aubaine* was a clear nuisance to foreign merchants residing in France. In treaties with the Bishop of Liège,[72] with twenty-three of the cities of the Holy Roman Empire,[73] the Duke of Württemberg,[74] the United States,[75] the Duke of Hesse-Darmstadt,[76] the Duke of Mecklenburg,[77] and Russia[78] Louis XVI agreed to abolish the *droit d'Aubaine* in return for a reciprocal concession in each case, on the part of the other party to the treaty. Vergennes also included in these treaties mutual agreements to maintain roads, open rivers, and build bridges to facilitate commerce.[79]

One of the aims of these treaties was to place French merchants and shippers in a favorable competitive position, not only in world colonial trade, but in internal European trade. The Rhine River, the Meuse River, the Moselle River, the Saar River, and the Elbe River, were seen by Vergennes as vital communication routes to the interior of Europe, as well as to the outside world. Many of his treaties were conscious attempts to open these routes to a freer navigation and trade for France and other European powers.

We also find, in these treaties, Vergennes' attempt to incorporate into the public law of Europe the rights of neutrals, which had been the cause of so much controversy during the American Revolutionary War. One expects to find, and finds, Catherine's principles on neutral rights in wartime spelled out in the Franco-Russian Commercial Treaty. But in Article Twelve of the treaty with the Duke of Mecklenburg, Louis also promises to recognize the neutral rights of the ships of Mecklenburg, in case France goes to war against a third party. Vergennes was careful, however, to exempt from this promise a war between France and the Emperor or the Empire.[80]

In the definition of contraband of war, in the treaty with Mecklenburg Vergennes and the other diplomats who signed it held to a conception of public law which tried to restrain man's inhumanity to man. Contraband, according to the conventional definition, was: arms, munitions, horses, saddles, and "generally all the other things serving for instruments of war." But, specifically exempted from this definition of contraband, were wheat, grains, vegetables, wines, oils, salt and "generally anything that serves as nutrition and sustenance for life."[81] Behind the dull, conventional prose detailing these exemptions were assumptions, about war and humankind, which illuminate the infinite gulf that lies between Vergennes' world and our own.

Vergennes' vision of France as arbiter of Europe, as guardian of the smaller powers, and as guarantor of the Treaty of Westphalia required that France no longer appear as a threat to her neighbors, large or small. The role of arbiter was shared with Russia, of course, after the Peace of Teschen in 1779, but the fears aroused in Germany by the manifest ambitions of Joseph II provided Louis XVI with ample opportunity to appear the disinterested guardian of the *status quo* in Europe. In this role, Louis XVI returned to a policy which made him a conservative force in Europe. Louis XVI was especially conscious of this role, in his relations with the small Rhineland states.[82]

Other political aims are also apparent in the various commercial treaties Vergennes negotiated during his thirteen years in office. The treaties with Spain, Portugal, Russia, and the United States were attempts to undermine English influence in these countries, by establishing economic ties that would bind these powers more closely to France. In this respect, Vergennes' commercial policy was a consequence of his lifelong belief that France's greatest competitor in the international system was England. His attempts to substitute French commerce for English commerce, therefore, were simply high politics in another form.

Vergennes saw expanding commerce and shipping as keys to world power. He had, long ago, given up the notion that commerce depended upon a system of colonies. Shipping and commerce could be developed by means of treaties, and the wealth amassed would pay the bill for membership in the ranks of the "great powers."

The trade treaties with Russia and England had additional motives. Now that the American war had been settled, Vergennes was determined to keep Europe peaceful. The determination was consistent with his policy of maintaining the *status quo* in Europe, but, more importantly, it was dictated by the state of the French Treasury. A *rapprochement* with England, he felt, could lessen tensions between London and Versailles, and could lead to cooperation in restraining the ambitious powers of Europe. England and France, together, could bring telling pressures to bear on Russia or Austria, if either persisted in its expansionist schemes. The treaty with Russia was an attempt to bring Catherine into Vergennes' system, by making it economically painful for Catherine to ignore French wishes. The word "*rapprochement*" is too strong a word to describe the Franco-Russian contacts established by the commercial treaty, but the intent was, surely, to establish a relationship with Russia which made Louis XVI less of an adversary in a system where both powers had mutual interests.

The trade treaties failed to live up to some of Vergennes' hopes. The French accession to the Spanish-Portuguese treaty did not, in fact, greatly improve opportunities for French commerce in Portugal,[83] and the relative positions of French and English commerce in Portugal changed very little. Nevertheless, Portugal had indicated its determination to be more independent of its old ally, England, and that impulse for independence justified the treaty in Vergennes' eyes. Later, Portugal even suggested that she accede to the Franco-Spanish *Pacte de Famille,* but Vergennes, who never advanced in anything except by slow stages, insisted on waiting to see what the new commercial arrangements would bring.[84]

The Franco-American commercial treaty failed, also, to produce significant commercial advantages for France. Admittedly, Vergennes may have counted less on the commercial rewards of this treaty with the Americans than on the political rewards. But once politically independent, the Americans returned to their English tastes and habits, and bought the overwhelming quantity of their imports from England. Britain, in turn, took most of the American exports. The British also facilitated the increase of American commerce by offering her former colonial subjects generous credits.[85] At the end of the war, the United States took advantage of its right to sell raw material to the French islands. But with its profits, it bought English, not French, goods.[86]

During the five years that the Eden treaty regulated Anglo-French trade, it increased trade in certain commodities, especially wine, it helped to control smuggling, and it did stimulate manufacturing. But, as a commercial arrangement, it had limited success.[87] Moreover, as a plan for *rapprochement,* it broke apart when the hostile political parties in the Dutch United Provinces decided to settle their differences by violence, and called to the great powers for help.

The Russian treaty gave to French merchants the equal treatment they demanded, and opened the way for a new Franco-Russian relationship in the future. It also provided a market for the depressed French wine industry. But the outbreak of a Russo-Turkish War, in 1787, strangled direct Franco-Russian trade in the south. The political and domestic unrest in France, in 1787 and 1788, interfered with both Franco-Russian and Anglo-French trade. But, most importantly, both treaties came too late to provide the substantial revenues the State needed to survive its financial crisis. Thus, the time needed to make the treaties work for France was never available. Vergennes died, and Louis XVI lost the benefits of his experience and commitment to the commercial treaties. Bankruptcy opened the gate to revolution. Turgot's warning that France needed, above all, time, and that time could only be provided by peace, was no longer a warning, but an epitaph to lost opportunities.

Nevertheless, in a very important sense, the treaties Vergennes made with the European powers marked a significant era in European trade relations. The dogma that the prosperity of nations always required high tariffs and prohibitions was challenged by a policy which contained the seeds of the later liberal doctrines of free trade. In this sense, it is no exaggeration to see in the trade treaties of Vergennes' administration, and especially in the Anglo-British Treaty, seeds of the twentieth-century European Common Market.[88] Vergennes' trade policy represents his great claim to the title of statesman.

CHAPTER 37

The Dutch Entanglement: 1783-1787

In 1778, the French monarchy supported, in America, a minority political party struggling to gain power in a society torn apart by political strife. The Americans requested and received from France diplomatic support and economic aid, and, with the help of French military intervention, eventually succeeded. In the peace of 1783, France celebrated a prestigious diplomatic triumph. In the mid-1780's, the opportunity for a second such triumph seemed to be developing in the Dutch United Provinces. After some hesitation, France, once again, committed herself to the minority party. This time, however, the outcome was very different, suggesting, perhaps, that the successes of the past are not always reliable guides to policy.

Vergennes had preferred that the United Provinces remain neutral in the American War. Dutch neutrality, he felt, would assure France of the necessary military and naval supplies, and Dutch membership in the Armed League would shift any responsibility for protecting the Dutch to Catherine's shoulders. The British government appreciated, as well as Vergennes did, however, the advantages her enemies gained from Dutch neutrality, and decided that a war with the United Provinces, before they adhered to the Armed League, was the least of several evils. But the question that nagged London and British Ambassador Harris at St. Petersburg was: would Catherine come to the aid of the Dutch?

Vergennes, apparently, had a momentary hope that British hostilities against the United Provinces would, indeed, arouse Catherine to a vigorous reaction against Great Britain.[1] But his common sense warned him that such a hope was hardly realistic. Catherine was personally *"piquée au vif"* by the British war against the Dutch,[2] but she had too much to lose in a war with England and much to gain, diplomatically, by remaining a neutral at the head of a League of Armed Neutrals. And, as it turned out, she had much to gain, by advancing herself as a mediator rather than a belligerent, in the war.[3] Furthermore, Catherine was not anti-British. While the American war brought her closer to France, that "closeness" never meant more to her than neutrality and the opportunity to advance what she considered to be Russian interests. Vergennes appreciated the advantage Catherine gained from such a policy, and did not expect her to give it up voluntarily.[4]

As the actions of the British government made it clear that an Anglo-Dutch war was clearly the aim of the English, Vergennes encouraged the Dutch to prepare to defend themselves.[5] He recognized, of course, that, if Catherine did not come to the assistance of the United Provinces, the Dutch would expect Louis XVI to do so. Such expectations disturbed the French Secretary of State, for the French Treasury was already over extended.

Hostilities with England had barely begun, before the Dutch Grand Pensionary suggested to the French Ambassador a "solid system of union" between Louis XVI and the United Provinces.[6] The suggestion was nothing more than a suggestion, in January of 1781, because the Dutch were still not certain about Catherine's disposition towards the new war.[7] A Dutch courier, with French blessings, was on his way to St. Petersburg to claim help from the neutrals,[8] but Catherine's response, when it came, was ambivalent; she offered to mediate.[9] But Harris, the English Ambassador at St. Petersburg, assured London, on the authority of Catherine's former lover, Potemkin, that Russia would never give the Dutch any effective aid, even if the English refused to accept mediation.[10] Harris was involved in a negotiation with Catherine, to cede to her the Mediterranean island of Minorca, and he was confident that she would do nothing to interfere with the negotiations. Catherine ultimately refused to be "led into temptation"[11] for Minorca. She realized, of course, the risks involved in gaining a naval base in an area of the Mediterranean which had become the cockpit of Anglo-Bourbon disputes. But she also refused to order her admirals to defend the privileges which the Dutch presumably enjoyed, as new members of the League.[12] Furthermore, she informed the British government that she would treat the Dutch as belligerents, as far as their relations with Great Britain were concerned.[13] Her decision was immediately seconded by Denmark. The United Provinces were, in effect, abandoned.[14]

Catherine's move left the Dutch with no choice but to seek a closer association with France. Vergennes anticipated that the Dutch would turn to Louis XVI, if Catherine refused them.[15] Dutch political and mercantile leaders frequently conversed with the French Ambassador about the need to protect Dutch shipping and Dutch East and West Indian colonies.[16] LaVauguyon was instructed to tell the Dutch that Louis XVI had ordered his fleet commanders to protect all Dutch ships that asked for help.[17]

But the Dutch wanted something "more special and more certain." Deputies of the Dutch Company of the Indies arranged a meeting with LaVauguyon to tell him that a fleet from the Indies, carrying more than

50,000,000 *livres'* worth of merchandise was scheduled to sail for Holland in January, and it was too late to change its sailing orders. If the English captured it, not only would the Company of the Indies be ruined, but England would gain an enormous prize. LaVauguyon, of course, saw the need to keep the Dutch ships out of British hands, but he refused to give any encouragement to the deputies of the Company of the Indies. He suggested that they take their request to the Dutch Estates General, which could officially seek French aid. Nevertheless, when he relayed the conversation to Vergennes, he gave his opinion that it was clearly in France's interest to protect the Dutch Indies fleet. LaVauguyon further suggested that Vergennes ask Spain to add some of her fleet to this operation.[18] LaVauguyon wanted to give the Dutch a general assurance that whenever they requested help through formal diplomatic channels, they would receive it.[19] Even the Stadholder, LaVauguyon later reported, wanted French help to protect the Dutch fleet.[20] The mounting Dutch interest in securing aid from Louis XVI appeared at Versailles, therefore, as more than just the desire of the Patriot Party. On this issue, merchants, the Grand Pensionary, the Stadholder, as well as the Patriots, seemed to be united.

Vergennes raised with the Minister of Marine, the Marquis de Castries, the question of protecting the Dutch Indies fleet with a combined French-Spanish squadron, and Castries rejected the idea. It was impossible, he argued, to organize and implement, on such a short notice, so difficult an operation. Castries offered to detail two frigates to join the Dutch squadron at the Azores, to intercept and protect the Dutch Indies fleet.[21] But, when the suggestion was forwarded to the Dutch Admiral Bylandt, he rejected the idea, and was soon joined by other Dutch naval commanders, because it entailed sailing under the orders of French commanders.[22] Nevertheless, however inauspiciously, the wartime association of France and the United Provinces had begun.

The war brought further conventions and concerts between the two powers. In February of 1781, the Dutch and French reached a mutual agreement on procedures to facilitate the return of ships, which had been taken as prizes by the British, but later recaptured by the French or Dutch.[23] In March, 1782, the French government agreed to treat as French, all Dutch ships entering French ports with products from the colonies, thus eliminating most of the customs duties.[24] Near the close of the same month, the Dutch sent Vergennes a plan to organize a combined Franco-Dutch military concert.[25] Louis XVI agreed to the plan and took the initiative to coordinate it with Spanish military operations.[26]

But Franco-Dutch combined military operations never achieved any striking successes, and they left both parties disappointed and exasperated. France sent troops to the Dutch India Company colony at the Cape of Good

Hope, to help protect that important colony, and the operation soon was the cause of an acrimonious dispute. The French Minister of Marine, the Marquis de Castries, complained that the Dutch governor at the Cape of Good Hope, one Plettenberg, failed to meet his commitments to the French soldiers sent there. Long after their debarkment, Castries charged, French soldiers were without the bedding, lodging, and food promised by the Dutch. Castries was irate. French soldiers, he complained, were treated worse than slaves. He accused Plettenberg of harboring "a criminal partiality for the English", or a "very marked indifference to French interests."[27] Castries demanded Plettenberg's recall.[28] He later moderated his opinion of Plettenberg,[29] but, by then, France and the United Provinces were attempting, unsuccessfully, to co-ordinate still another naval operation. This time, a combined fleet was to cruise in the Gulf of Gascony and northward toward the Channel. One of the purposes of this fleet was to provide a diversion for the English ships standing outside of the West Frisian island of Texel, and give the Dutch fleet, blocked up in its ports, opportunity to leave port for operation in the North Sea.[30] But the Spanish-French fleet was delayed, waiting for the necessary winds. The British withdrew part of its fleet before the French or Spanish navy appeared, but the Dutch ships remained in port, partly because many of the Dutch sailors were ill with influenza.[31] When the Franco-Spanish fleet made its appearance, Vergennes urged his ambassador at The Hague to see to it that the Dutch ships put to sea, in order not to lose the opportunity. He was not at all confident, he told LaVauguyon, of the vigor of the Dutch admiral in command.[32] On July Seventh, the Dutch fleet did leave port. Now, at last, LaVauguyon hoped, there was some possibility for a naval concert.[33] The Dutch suggested a concerted attack against England.[34] Vergennes refused, because the Spanish fleet was soon to be withdrawn to participate in the siege of Gibraltar.[35] The Dutch opposed the withdrawal, and asked that the fleet remain. Vergennes refused.[36] For a while, the Dutch patrolled the North Sea, while the Spanish and French fleets patrolled farther south until they were ordered to Gibraltar. Then a violent storm, plus the return of units of the British fleet, sent the Dutch fleet scurrying back to port at Texel, where it remained, for the most part, until the peace.

When the negotiations to settle the American war began in earnest in 1783, Vergennes was irked by the Dutch tendency to demand what he considered to be much more than their military contribution to the war warranted. At the peace table in Paris, the Dutch made three demands. They wanted England to recognize the principles of Catherine's Armed Neutrality, they wanted England to return any colonies captured during the war, and they demanded damages for ships captured by the British in violation of neutral rights. The Dutch held out, especially, for the return of the Indian port of Negappinam, captured by the British, but Vergennes, discontented with Dutch demands and delays, pulled the rug out from under these negotiations, when he notified them that France was going to sign the final peace treaty, with or without the Dutch. If the Dutch wished to make a suitable peace, Vergennes felt, she should have made an effort proportionate to the conditions she proposed. "Ask the Stadholder," he wrote to LaVauguyon, "what conditions of peace he expects to obtain, with a fleet which never leaves port and, when someone urges that it go to sea, [its commanders] dare refuse because of lack of provisions and gear."[37] Another time, when Vergennes saw what he considered to be dilatory tactics of the Dutch peace plenipotentiaries in Paris, he again expressed his dissatisfaction. "They make war so badly," he told LaVauguyon, "that they ought to want, more than anyone else, to get it over with."[38] He charged LaVauguyon to try to convince the Dutch that, since they made very little contribution to the war, they could not expect anything but sacrifices at the peace.[39]

The word "sacrifices" best describes the Dutch capitulation at the peace negotiations. Over the heads of the Dutch, Vergennes worked out with the British an agreement to return Trincomale in Ceylon to the Dutch, but retain Negappinam. In addition, the Dutch had to concede to the British the right to trade and navigate freely in the Eastern Oceans, a concession that proved to be a very valuable asset to British trade. England, however, agreed that freedom of commerce, according to the principles of Armed Neutrality, would be accorded to all nations.

Their isolation at the peace table left the Dutch anxious to convert the wartime association with France into an alliance. The French *chargé d'affaires,* Bérenger, who took over LaVauguyon's responsibilities while the latter was on leave in France, noted that the Patriots, above all, wished an "indissoluble tie" with France.[40] Heretofore, Vergennes had consciously avoided building his Dutch policy on what, he knew, was only a political faction. At the Hague LaVauguyon had treated with the Stadholder, as well as the Grand Pensionary, the Estates General, the deputies of the Company of the Indies, and the Patriots. Vergennes had not encouraged the Patriots' campaign against the Stadholder, because he knew that the King of Prussia would consider such a policy a hostile move by France against Prussia,[41] since the Stadholder's wife, the Princess of Orange, was Frederick's niece. Vergennes wanted to dampen the internal political conflicts in the United Provinces. Yet, as the conflict between the Patriots and the Stadholder's party daily grew more serious, LaVauguyon and his successors, Bérenger, and later, the Marquis de Vérac, found it more and more difficult not to be drawn into it. The offer for a Franco-Dutch alliance issuing from the Patriots Party was, therefore, a development that required circumspection at

Versailles.

In June of 1783, the Dutch plenipotentiaries at Versailles submitted to Vergennes Dutch proposals for a Franco-Dutch treaty of commerce. Vergennes was favorable, but cautious.[42] The Dutch then answered with a much more elaborate proposal for a defensive alliance.[43] By this date, however, a Dutch dispute with Joseph II, over the navigation of the Scheldt River, was in full bloom and taking a grave turn for the worse. Vergennes readily sensed the dangers presented to France by that crisis. Prudence required, therefore, that Louis XVI avoid the role of ally to the Dutch, at the moment when another ally was quarreling with them. Caution was especially appropriate since, as Bérenger so aptly put it, the Dutch had a vexing tendency to interpret the most simple "politesse" as a political commitment.[44] Vergennes saw, too, that a premature commitment to the United Provinces might encourage the Estates General to refuse all compromise with Joseph II.[45]

But, one by one, various provinces of the United Provinces, Utrecht, Frisia, Holland, and Overijssel, took the initiative to request an alliance with France.[46] As Bérenger relayed each of these requests to Versailles, it became more apparent that Louis XVI had to make a decision. Should he commit himself to a formal alliance with the United Provinces? If so, how? By a treaty of commerce, or a defensive alliance? Vergennes' initial response was in favor of a commercial treaty because it would commit Louis XVI the least. Nevertheless, LaVauguyon's reports back to Versailles reveal the two salient points that would eventually force an altogether different French policy: The Patriots did not want a simple commercial alliance; they wanted a defensive alliance with France, which included a maritime and colonial union. Furthermore, by now, LaVauguyon was an enthusiastic supporter of the Patriots.[47] And he recommended that Versailles abandon its attempts to reconcile the various internal factions, and place its full confidence in the Patriots. Vergennes remained reluctant, for he saw that an alliance which formed a maritime and colonial union would appear to be aimed directly at England, and he did not want to give umbrage to any European power.[48] Moreover, he had long ago concluded that the Patriots' primary interests were not those of Louis XVI.[49] Vergennes apparently still thought in terms of a Dutch policy based on a broader foundation than the Patriot Party. But his ambassador was, in fact, dealing every day more exclusively with the Patriots.[50]

Unfortunately, individual members of Louis XVI's cabinet agreed with LaVauguyon. The Baron de Breteuil and the Chief of Finances, Calonne, favored placing more faith in the Patriot Party and, consequently, argued for a more general political alliance.[51] Thus, according to an in-house memo written after the fact, when LaVauguyon returned to The Hague in April of 1784, after a leave at Versailles, he returned as a spokesman for Breteuil and

Calonne, and an advocate of a political alliance.[52] Vergennes yielded to the pressures favoring a political alliance, but it is unlikely that he considered the new course the wisest one.

In reality, the Patriots controlled only the province of Holland. The power of William V, the Stadholder, was not destroyed. And the Army, large segments of the landed nobility and peasantry, and some of the urban population were still loyal to the Stadholder and the Orangist course.[53] But William V's personal failings crippled him as a leader. The Orangist party needed leadership and that was soon provided, not by the Stadholder, but by the British Ambassador.

Why did Vergennes yield to the pressures for a political alliance? The answer lies, no doubt, in his awareness of the growing opposition in France to his policies and to him, personally, as Secretary of State for Foreign Affairs. The American Revolutionary War had spawned a host of critics, who saw Vergennes as the man responsible for Louis XVI's policies and debts.[54] He was stung and humiliated by rumors that he was using his office for personal gain. The Queen looked upon him as the main obstacle to the success of her brother Joseph's foreign policy, and intrigued to get rid of him.[55] Within the King's Council his authority was increasingly disputed. The Minister of Marine, the Marquis de Castries, found him too pacifist, while, earlier, Necker had found him too warlike. Neither man was above intrigue to usurp Vergennes' powers, or even replace him.[56] In addition, his persistent illnesses drained his energies and his confidence. The end result was a defensiveness and uncertainty on Vergennes' part, and a willingness to compromise against his better judgment.[57]

Once the negotiations for the Franco-Dutch alliance were underway, LaVauguyon took leave and returned to France, and to a new post as Ambassador to Madrid. He was replaced at The Hague by the Marquis de Vérac, a man who, by common consent of his friends and enemies, was a non-entity.[58] He proved to be no match for the new British ambassador to The Hague, Sir James Harris, later the first Earl of Malmesbury.

Harris, like Vérac, had previously served his King at St. Petersburg, where he tried, with little success, to develop a pro-British party around the Prince Potemkin.[59] In contrast, at St. Petersburg, Vérac had enjoyed some success because Catherine's and Louis XVI's foreign policy brought Russia and France closer together. At The Hague, however, the roles of the two diplomats were reversed. By skillfully rebuilding a pro-British party around the Stadholder, Harris isolated the Patriots and left them more and more dependent on France. The success of Franco-Dutch relations therefore increasingly depended on the Patriots.

Vergennes was never completely reconciled to this new policy. Vergennes told Vérac, in his instruction, to take no part in the domestic party disputes in the Dutch Republic, and to work to prevent the growth of an excessive party spirit. Moreover, Vérac was to advise the Patriots not to try to subvert the constitution of the United Provinces by their attacks on the Stadholder. Vergennes told Vérac, however, to continue LaVauguyon's policy of cooperation with the Patriots, to prevent the Stadholder from reviving a pro-British policy.[60] Vérac's instructions contained, in short, the contradictions within Louis XVI's Dutch policy. Vergennes still argued for a Dutch policy that remained above factional and domestic disputes. Yet he yielded to the pressures at home and in the United Provinces, to deal only with the Patriots and to tie Louis XVI's Dutch policy to the fortunes of a single political party.

The first moves of the British Ambassador Harris at The Hague were calculated to dissolve the suspicions of the Patriots that he was there to restore the old Anglo-Dutch alliance and to destroy the Patriots. In late 1784 and early 1785, the British government did not want to commit herself to a policy that might require armed intervention in the United Provinces.[61]

Harris, therefore, spent his early months at The Hague establishing his household, quietly renewing acquaintances, and gathering around himself a clutch of agents who would serve him. He even made a passing attempt to woo the Patriots.[62] He knew the Dutch language, he had old friends in the Netherlands, and he made new ones. The pro-British party needed a chief, and he was on his way to insinuating himself into that role. During these early months, his alert mind also played over the possibilities open to him. One of the most pregnant possibilities was one that very nearly predicted the manner in which the Patriots would be brought to heel, and French policy brought to a humiliating defeat. "Were England and Prussia to unite their operations here;were proper advantages taken of the disposition of the people; were the conduct of France clearly stated to them; and were the friends of the Prince [the Stadholder] assured of a support, I have little doubt that either the Patriotic body would soon dissolve itself, or become an easy victim to a short popular insurrection."[63] Thus, the domestic conflicts of the United Provinces offered the great powers of Western Europe the temptation to meddle, to serve their own interests.

Meanwhile, Vérac talked of a Franco-Dutch alliance. Vergennes had earlier assured the Dutch of Louis XVI's willingness to conclude some kind of an alliance,[64] but, before Vérac's arrival, he did very little to encourage the idea.[65] The consequences of such apparent indifference on the part of France were soon manifest. In debates in the Estates of Holland, the pro-English party accused the Patriots of raising false hopes of French support, and the Patriots, in turn, became more insistent that Louis XVI give them some tangible evidence that he was, indeed, willing to commit himself, one way or another, to Dutch protection.[66] Before his departure, LaVauguyon had warned that, if Louis XVI did not respond favorably to the demand for a defensive treaty, the Patriots would be discredited.[67]

While Vergennes tried to persuade the Patriots that they could count on Louis XVI's friendship, his rhetoric was not confirmed by his actions. When the Dutch marched to the brink of war with Joseph II, in the Scheldt River crisis, Vergennes demurred. Heretofore, he had argued that Louis XVI did not wish to make a treaty that seemed to be directed against England. Now, he wished to avoid a treaty that could be interpreted as being directed against Joseph II. But the confrontation with Joseph only made the Dutch more insistent.[68]

Vergennes suggested that, perhaps, a treaty should exclude the Scheldt dispute from its provisions. The Patriots at first objected, then suggested a secret article defining the conditions and limits of the treaty.[69] Vergennes agreed,[70] and, with this major obstacle out of the way, nothing stood in the way of the conclusion of a treaty.

Yet, Vergennes was still unwilling to conclude. He wanted no formal alliance with the Dutch until the Scheldt River issue was settled. While he wanted to contain Joseph II's ambitions, he did not wish to provoke him to an open break with France. Thus, the negotiations for the Franco-Dutch alliances were deliberately drawn out, and the signing was delayed until after the Dutch settled with Joseph II at Fontainebleau in 1785.

Louis XVI's refusal to commit himself unambiguously to the defense of Dutch interests was a ready-made weapon in the hands of the British Ambassador, Harris. He argued that Louis XVI would never be a reliable ally. Nevertheless, the day after the Dutch and the Emperor Joseph concluded their dispute over the Scheldt River, Louis XVI agreed to a defensive alliance with the United Provinces.[71]

The treaty of alliances between Louis XVI and the Estates General of the United Provinces stressed in its title, as well as its articles, that it was "purely defensive," and not directed against any power. The purpose, according to the preamble, was to render stable the recent peace and preserve the general tranquility. The two powers agreed to a reciprocal guarantee of the territories of each, and promised to protect each other against aggression anywhere in the world.[72] In case either party were threatened with an attack, the other party promised to use its good offices to prevent hostilities and arrange a conciliation.[73] But, if good offices failed to bring about a conciliation, the two contracting parties promised to render assistance by sea and land. Louis XVI agreed to furnish the United Provinces with 18,000 infantry, 2,000 cavalry, twelve vessels of the line, and six frigates, in case the latter found herself at war. In case France became involved in a maritime war, the United Provinces promised to assist with 5,000 infantry and 1,000 cavalry, or the equivalent in money.[74] Each 1,000 infantrymen were evaluated at 10,000 Dutch *florins,* and each 1,000 cavalrymen were evaluated at 30,000 *florins*.[75] Both powers agreed that, in case of a maritime war in which they took no part, they would mutually guarantee freedom of the seas and support the principle of free ships, free goods.[76]

Louis XVI and the Estates General promised to negotiate a commercial treaty, to provide that the Dutch merchants be treated, in France, as those of the most-favored nation, and French merchants would receive the same treatment in the United Provinces.

Since the dispute between the Emperor and the Dutch Republic had been settled the day before this treaty was signed, there was no need to exclude that dispute from the final provisions of the treaty. In a separate article, however, Louis XVI did guarantee the settlement between the United Provinces and the Emperor Joseph II.[77]

At The Hague, the British Ambassador, Harris, did his utmost to prevent the signing of the Franco-Dutch alliance.[78] According to rumors gathered by the French Ambassador, Harris offered 100,000 *écus* to anyone who could delay, even for six weeks, the signing of the alliance.[79] The rumor may very well have been planted by the Dutch, to stir Louis XVI to sign the treaty which had been so long held in suspension by the Scheldt River crisis.[80]

When the signatures were completed, the indefatigable Harris then made every possible effort to prevent ratification.[81] Again he failed. The Dutch settlement with Joseph II had been ratified by a slim majority of four of the seven provinces, but the Franco-Dutch alliance was ratified with no significant opposition.[82]

In August of 1786, Frederick the Great of Prussia died. With his passing, Vergennes set about to preserve, at Berlin, the atmosphere favorable to France and France's Dutch policy. Prussia's attitude toward the United Provinces, he saw, was absolutely critical to the success and stability of French policy there. Through the French envoy, D'Esterno, Vergennes arranged to put Prussian officials on Louis XVI's payroll.[83] He encouraged the efforts of Prince Henry of Prussia and the Prussian Minister of State, Finckenstein, to win the new King over to a pro-French stance, and he secretly contributed to the campaign to weaken the influence of the pro-English Minister, Hertzberg.[84] He also sent the Vicomte de Mirabeau on two missions to Berlin, in 1785 and 1786, primarily to gather intelligence on the opinions and possible directions of the new King.[85] At Berlin, Mirabeau realized that the key to Prussian reactions to French policies in the Dutch Republic was the Patriots' behavior. France must see to it, he advised, that the Patriots moderate their attacks on the Stadholder. If they did not, he warned, they could be a positive threat to the peace of Europe.[86]

A month after Frederick's death, Frederick William II sent Count Goertz to The Hague to view the situation there, and to assure the Stadholder and the Princess of Orange that the King of Prussia would continue to support them. But Goertz' instructions also included the astonishing idea that the French minister at The Hague would cooperate with Goertz in restoring the Stadholder to the command of the garrison at The Hague,[87] a post of which the Estates of Holland had deprived him earlier in the year. How Goertz was to persuade Vérac, already deeply committed to the Patriots, to cooperate was not made clear in the instructions. Since Vérac was steadily dragging Vergennes into the orbit of the Patriots, Goertz' instructions seemed totally out of touch with reality, if we assume that he seriously tried to implement them. In fact, at The Hague, he did not conceal the fact that he advocated the cause of the Princess of Orange and the Stadholder, that he detested the Patriots, and that he harbored a strong bias against France.[88] Frederick William's response to Goertz' anti-French reports was a sharp rebuke.[89] And his pro-French minister, Finckenstein, reasonably concluded that Frederick William had decided that the confused politics of the United Provinces could be left to the French to sort out.[90] With Prussian diplomats and ministers holding the opinion that Frederick William had decided not to oppose France in the political storm in the United Provinces, it is not surprising that the British Ambassador to Berlin, Dalrymble, reached the same conclusion.[91]

On the surface, such a response from Berlin seemed ideal for France, but it proved to be her undoing. Frederick William II's seeming tolerance of the growing French influence in the United Provinces did not change his basic commitment to the Stadholder and the Princess of Orange. He assumed that French influence would keep the Patriots in check. But Vérac was daily becoming more and more their agent, rather than their counselor. And the Patriots' vision of their future included no compromise with the Stadholder. Vergennes operated on the faith that the chances of any hostile action on the part of the Prussian King, to protect the Stadholder, were minimal, because of the influence of the pro-French party at Berlin. Thus, as the Patriots organized to overthrow the Stadholder and revolutionize their government, the French and Prussian governments, both misled by illusions, blindly maneuvered onto a collision course.

One of the difficulties of understanding French policy at The Hague was the multiplicity of French agents there. Each of them claimed to be representing a different French minister, and each one contradicted the other. Few of them coordinated their activities with Vérac.[92] The confusion illustrates in sharp outline how much the control of foreign affairs had slipped from Vergennes' grasp. He was sick, soon to die, and yet the work accumulated. "Europe seems to have conspired . . . to crush me with work," he wrote to Rayneval, " . . . [My] health is not getting any better."[93] Three weeks later, his health had further deteriorated. He suffered from gout; he was unable to exercise and, for two months, he had been unable to eat a normal diet. But, worst of all, was the unceasing pressure of work. "I have not a moment to myself . . . ," he wrote to Rayneval in a pathetic call for help.[94] Before the month ended, he was dead.

Vergennes saw, as clearly as anyone, that he was losing control of French policy in the United Provinces, and that France risked being forced down a path chosen by the Patriots, rather than by the French King. "We cannot abandon our system to men who act without consulting us," he warned Vérac, "and who treat us like puppets in their hands."[95] Louis XVI, he reminded Vérac, had negotiated with the Estates General and allied with the Dutch Republic, not with a political faction.[96]

Since Vérac seemed totally under the influence of the Patriots, Vergennes decided to send Rayneval to The Hague, as a fact-finder and as his personal representative. Vergennes had complete confidence in Rayneval, and had used him before on missions that required intelligence and good judgment. Rayneval received no written instructions, but it appears, from other evidence, that Vergennes wanted him to reach some kind of understanding with Prussia on the respective roles of France and Prussia in the United Provinces. In addition, Vergennes obviously wanted Rayneval to return from The Hague with a clearer picture of what was happening there than he had been getting from Vérac and the numerous other agents crawling over the countryside.

At The Hague, Rayneval quickly appreciated the fact that the political ferment in the Dutch Republic was extraordinary, and that the Patriots were uncompromising in their determination to change the government of the United Provinces. Nevertheless, he concluded that Louis XVI must continue to work with them; France had no other base for influence in the United Provinces.[97] Rayneval saw that there was a real danger that the Patriots might lose control of the political explosion they were creating. But this possibility did not modify his opinion that France give them support.[98] Their dependency, presumably, would guarantee their obedience to French authority. Neither Rayneval nor Vergennes saw that the Patriots were not simply the creatures, or pawns, of international politics. They were the harbingers of a vast political and social upheaval in Europe that would eventually destroy even the monarch of France.

The second major conclusion Rayneval brought back from The Hague was that the Stadholder was an imbecile, completely dominated by his wife, and he deserved to be turned out of office by the Patriots. According to Rayneval, he had no real power to resist the Patriots.[99] The latter judgment grew, no doubt, from the fact that Frederick William II appeared to have lost patience with the Princess of Orange, who refused to accept his plan to conciliate the dispute in the United Provinces.[100]

Thus, Rayneval returned to Versailles, as an advocate of the Patriot

Party, and holding their opinion that the only way to deal with the Stadholder was to get rid of him. Furthermore, Frederick William II no longer appeared to be the defender of his sister and her husband, the Stadholder. Even the Princess of Orange, herself, had apparently decided to write off Frederick William as her protector.[101] England alone, and Harris in particular, seemed to be the the only obstacle in the way of a complete victory for the Patriots. And the Patriots, according to French officials, would obey Versailles because they were dependent on France. They had, according to Rayneval, "... no other existence but that which France gave them."[102] Thus, Rayneval accomplished what Vérac had been unable to do. He convinced Vergennes of the soundness of a policy which the Secretary of State for Foreign Affairs had, with good reason rejected when it came from Vérac.

The policy was a recipe for disaster. Despite the personal differences that separated the Princess of Orange and the Stadholder from Frederick William II, the King of Prussia would not stand aside and watch his sister and his brother-in-law destroyed. His prestige and his sense of dynastic honor would not allow it. Furthermore, if the pro-French Patriots Party came to dominate the United Provinces, the other western powers of Europe would certainly interpret such a development as an unwelcome shift in the balance of power in Western Europe. The obvious response to such a turn of events was a coalition of Prussia and England, and a military intervention to protect the Orangists. If Vergennes had learned nothing else from his forty years in the diplomatic service, he certainly had learned this elementary lesson. But he was a man struggling to protect his personal political influence, while sickness drained away his very life. Thus, France, in 1785 and 1786, played a dangerous game in the United Provinces, a game which they had won in America, but one that could be won now only if France committed herself militarily. The Patriots expected support from France, but would not be controlled by her. Since the French treasury was exhausted, and French domestic affairs were rapidly approaching chaos, warnings from Versailles that France would support the Patriots militarily, were interpreted as bluffs, as indeed they were.

The moment of decision came in 1787, after Vergennes' death. The Patriots and the Orangists reached an impasse, where both sides decided to resort to arms. When the conflict became violent, Frederick William of Prussia reconsidered his original decision to stay out of Dutch affairs and made contact with England. The French government, on the verge of bankruptcy, had to reconsider its earlier commitments. The Patriots, operating under the illusion that Louis XVI was still their protector, stiffened their determination to defeat the Orangist party. On September Fourteenth, a Prussian army invaded the United Provinces and the British navy began preparations. France's choice was simple: as the British Minister, Pitt, said, the French had either to "... give up their predominant influence in the Republic or ... *fight for it.*"[103] After a flutter of indignation, the protector of the Patriots and arbiter of all Europe collapsed in a shower of diplomatic rhetoric. There was no other choice: Louis XVI could no longer play the costly game of high politics. Problems which Vergennes had only belatedly faced now crowded onto center stage.

Epilogue

In the latter part of January, 1787, a steadily increasing fatigue and fever became so acute that Vergennes' close friends began to fear for his life. The continuous fever sapped his energies; dark spots appeared on his skin. On the Twenty-fourth of January, he was unable to attend the meeting of the Council of State.[1] For three weeks, he lingered on; but his body was exhausted. During the night of February 13, 1787, he died, in his sixty-eighth year. He was buried in the cemetery of the parish of Notre Dame at Versailles by the curé Jacob.[2] Legend has it that the King appeared in public with tears in his eyes as Vergennes was dying. "I have lost," he is reported to have said, "the only friend on whom I could count, the only minister who never deceived me."[3]

At his death, Vergennes' titles included Comte de Vergennes, Baron d'Uchon and Saint-Eugène, Seigneur de Bordeaux, Saint Simphouen, Marmagne, Pondevaux, Morly, and Barnault, Councilor to the King, Commander of the King's Orders, Chief of the Royal Council of Finances, Councilor of State of the Sword, and Minister and Secretary of State. But during the French Revolution his grave disappeared, and his sepulchral monument, ordered in 1788, was put in place empty, in the parish Church of Notre Dame, during the Restoration in 1818.[4] Thus, neither in his life nor his death, did he find rest.

Vergennes had wanted Louis XVI and France to be arbiter of Europe, with the prestige, influence, and power which the position implied. He did not hesitate to launch a war, when he thought it would advance his King's position. His aristocratic and professional background provided the justification for war: it was an honorable and a necessary mediator of human affairs.

He was a devout Catholic and, at the Court, enjoyed the reputation of a morally upright family man. But, as a professional diplomat, "Reasons of State" took precedence over Christian morality whenever the two loyalties came into conflict. When Reasons of State demanded, he lied and deceived.

Was he a great statesman? Certainly, his American policy temporarily reduced the power of England, relative to that of France. The peace brought Louis XVI enormous prestige. But the hoped-for flourishing of postwar Franco-American trade never materialized. And, when England chose to return to Continental politics, as she did in the Dutch crisis of 1787, the position and prestige which France had won in the American War proved to be hollow. Exhausted by the costs of high politics, and tormented by internal conflict, France was exposed as diplomatically impotent. Prussia, backed by England, invaded the United Provinces and destroyed the pro-French Patriot Party. Vergennes was unable to stem the long-term trend of England's rise to international power.

On the Continent, Vergennes helped keep the peace. He had restrained the ambitions of Spain against Portugal, and of Joseph II against Bavaria and the Ottoman Empire. He kept for France the balance of power between Austria and Prussia, whose growing antagonism was one of the central developments of eighteenth-century high politics. But the intervention of Louis XVI to check the ambitions of Joseph II was the last effective role Louis XVI played in German politics, and the éclat of this role was diminished when Catherine II forced Louis to share with her the role of arbiter. In Eastern Europe, Vergennes could not prevent the advance of Russia against the Ottoman Empire, for French resources were tied up in the American War. Catherine reduced French policy in Eastern Europe to that of a delaying action, while France and Europe began the long search for another solution to the Eastern Question. Nevertheless, Vergennes' performance as a peacekeeper was a magnificent display of skill and intelligence.

Vergennes has a solid claim to greatness for his attempts to reinforce the public laws of Europe by treaties. In the peace negotiations with England, the Newfoundland fisheries issue gave him the opportunity to reinforce the precedents of public law concerning the use of the seas. His several efforts to forge a clearer definition of contraband, and to advance the rights of neutrals in wartime also deserve acclaim. Also, his conceptions of the role of commerce in international affairs and the numerous commercial treaties he negotiated were the work of a man of political vision.

But Vergennes never overcame his greatest failing: his inability to understand that France could not go on skirting the edge of bankruptcy to pay for its costly foreign policy. War brought higher taxes, inflation, and destruction; the victims of these plagues were never rewarded with estates, titles, prestige, and grandeur. Vergennes had little understanding of the social consequences of his diplomatic decisions. His vision was limited by the blinders of class, rank, and professional traditions. Ordinary French men and women, by the millions, had crying needs that could not be satisfied by diplomatic victories and international prestige. Vergennes did not understand these contradictions of his own society, and became, therefore, an unwilling midwife to historical change.

Thus, Louis XVI followed the grand and heroic, but exhausting and self-destructive illusion that he could be the self-appointed arbiter of Europe. Vergennes' experience, his reputation for realism, his extraordinary diplomatic skills, and his killing capacity for hard work gave to that illusion the appearance of reality.

In March of 1795, Citizen Commissioner J.A. LeBrun, of the French Revolutionary Government, stood examining some portrait engravings before him: one of Louis XV, one of Prince Kaunitz of Austria, and one of George Washington, Commander of the Revolutionary Army of the United States of America. All three engravings, Citizen LeBrun allowed, were worth no more than thirty *livres*. He jotted down his estimate, and moved on to a larger engraving, a map of the city of Constantinople. Methodically, he measured the map. Value? Sixty *livres*, he recorded as he automatically moved to the next object.

Next, Citizen LeBrun came to a copper plate of portrait engraved by Vaugetiste. He counted the prints made from the plate, and read the inscription on the portrait: "Charles Gravier, Comte de Vergennes, Councilor of State Ordinary, Minister and Secretary of State and Chief of the Royal Council of Finances."[5] In 1795, Louis XVI or Louis Capet, as the French Revolutionaries called him, was dead, his head severed from his body by Revolutionary Justice. The man enclosed in the rectangular engraving, seated at his desk with a note addressed "To the King" in his right hand, had known nothing of the public execution of his master, whom he had served for thirteen years. Vergennes had died six years before the execution. It would have been inconceivable to Vergennes, at the time of his death, that this Citizen LeBrun, agent of the First French Republic, would ever be making an inventory of the *objets d'art* left by Vergennes to his oldest son, Constantin. But Constantin, deprived of his titles and fortunes by the Revolution, had fled the country to join the army of emigrés who were determined to return to France and crush the Revolution.

And yet, even at the time of Vergennes' death, in February of 1787, the structure of the French monarchy was cracking. The State tottered on the edge of bankruptcy, the aristocrats were rebellious, and ideas of reform circulated in the body politic. Indeed, the history of the monarchical system which Vergennes served and loved seems to demonstrate the thesis that societies produce, within themselves, the seeds of their own destruction. France's unceasing struggle for power, rank, and prestige, pushed to its final limits, led to a self-destroying inversion: a collapse of power, and then chaos. Ironically, by performing his duties as he understood them, by being among the most competent and responsible royal servants which his class and profession produced, Vergennes helped to destroy the social and political world with which he identified. In a curious way, therefore, there was a linkage between the Comte de Vergennes and Citizen Commissioner LeBrun, but it is doubtful that either man, in his wildest fantasies, would have acknowledged the relationship.

Notes

Preface

1. "Critique of Hegel's Philosophy of the State" in Loyd D. Easton and Kurt D. Guddat, *Writings of the Young Marx on Philosophy and Society* (New York, 1967), p. 186.

2. *Ibid.*

3. See, for example, the conclusions of Sigmund Freud, *Civilization and Its Discontents* (New York, 1961); W.H. McNeill, *The Rise of the West* (Chicago, 1963).

4. "Inventaire des objets d'art laissés chez M. de Vergennes, émigré (1793)", *Archievs Nationales* F 17^{A} (1268) 17°, 226.

Chapter 1. War of the Austrian Succession

1. Gaston de Bourge, "Le Comte de Vergennes; ses débuts diplomatiques en Allemagne auprès de l'èlecteur de Trêves et de l'électeur d'Hanovre", *Revue des questions historiques,* XLIV, p. 43. On the cost of the appointment to the diplomatic corps. See "Extrait de minutes de sa Chancellerie de l'ambassade de France à la Porte Ottoman," *Archives de la famille Vergennes.* Hereafter cited as *AFV.* For the opportunity to consult the Vergennes family papers I am extremely grateful to the late Odon de Vergennes of Paris, and to M. et Mme. Pierre de Tugny, now living at Marly le Roi, France.

2. "Mémoire pour servir d'instruction au sieur de Chavigny . . .etc., 12 February, 1740," Vicomte de Caix de Saint-Aymour, editor, *Recueil des instructions donneés aux ambassadeurs et ministres de France depuis les traités de Westphalie jusqu'à la révolution française:* (Paris, 1886), III, "Portugal," 287-301.

3. John J. Meng, *The Comte de Vergennes: European phases of His American Diplomacy* (1774-1780) (Washington, D.C., 1932), 15.

4. "Chavigny to the Cardinal de Tencin, 30 August, 1745," Quoted in Gaston de Bourge, ses débuts diplomatiques en Allemagne auprès de l'électeur de Trèves et de l'électeur d'Hanovre, *Revue des questions historiques,* XLIV, 95; Chavigny repeats the wish in a letter dated 22 November, 1745. Papiers Chavigny: Union de Frankfort. VI bis, *AFV.* See also: "Chavigny to Paris du Verney, 3 June, 1745," *ibid.*

5. "Chavigny to the Prince de Conti, 18 August, 1745." quoted in Bourage, "Le Comte de Vergennes, ses débuts diplomatiques en Allemagne auprès de l'électeur de Trèves et de l'électeur d'Hanovre," *Revue des questions historiques,* 94; Charles de Chambrun, *À l'école d'un diplomate: Vergennes* (Paris, 1944), 36.

6. Jules D'Arbaumont, *Amorial de la Chambre des Comptes de Dijon,* (Dijon, 1881), 75.

7. *Ibid.*, 75-76: Claude Carloman Rulhière, "Le Comte de Vergennes; première

cause des États-Généraux," in *Oeuvres* (Paris, 1819), I, 148; Bonneville de Marsangy, *Le chevalier de Vergennes; son ambassade à Constantinople* (Paris, 1894), I, 1-2; Charles de Chambrun, *À l'école d'un diplomate: Vergennes* (Paris, 1944), 5; Meng, *The Comte de Vergennes,* 11.

8. J.D.'Arbaumont, *Amorial de la Chambre des Comptes de Dijon,* 76.

9. *Nouvel État Général et Alphabétique des Villes, Bourgs et Paroisses* . . . etc., (Dijon, 1783), 326-327; Abbé Expilly, *Dictionnaire Geographique, historique et politique des Gaules et de la France* (Amsterdam, 1768), vol. 5, p. 364.

10. Archives de la Côte d'or, État Général, Serie B 11078, Côte 17.

11. Archives de la Côte d'or, État Général, Serie B, 12142 24vo -28.

12. M. Courtpré, *Description Générale et particulière du duché de Bourgogne* (Dijon, 1848), 166-167.

13. Was he the plaintiff in 1708 against Edmée Menestrier in a dispute over debts? See: Archives de la Côte D'or. Serie E 912, féodalité; titres des familles.

14. "Registres Paroissiaux, État-Civil, Dijon, 1718-1720," *ibid.;* Archives de la Ville de Dijon, Supplément à la Serie B - État Civil. For the family coat-of-arms see: H. Beaune et J.D'Arbaumont, *La Noblesse aux États de Bourgogne* (Dijon, 1864), 84, 91.

15. "Registres de Baptême, mariage et Sépulture de la paroisse de Saint-Jean de Dijon pour l'année mille-sept-cent-dix-neuf," État-Civil: Dijon, 1718-1720, dated 29 December, 1719. An imperfect version of Vergennes' act of Baptism is printed in Marsangy, *Vergennes à Constantinople,* 1, 4fn; Charles Joseph Mayer, in *La vie publique et privée de Charles Gravier de Vergennes* (Paris, 1789), 7fn, incorrectly gives Vergennes' date of birth as the 28th of December, 1719. *The Encyclopedia Britannica* (Chicago, 1962), XXIII, 80, incorrectly gives Vergennes' birth date as December 20, 1717. See also: C.N. Amanton, "Biographie - Le comte de Vergennes," *Annales de la littérature et des arts* (Paris, 1827), XXVIII, 22-25.

16. My information concerning the Vergennes home is based on the research of M. Pierre Gras, Conservateur, Bibliothèque de la ville Dijon, M. Gauchat, former Directeur du Service du Plan de la Ville Dijon, M. Jean-Claude Garreta, of the Bibliothèque de la ville Dijon, and M. Bernard Savouret, of the Archives Municipales de Dijon. These scholars very generously assisted me in my research at Dijon, and they provided me with answers to many questions concerning the location of the Vergennes home. For their assistance I am most grateful. See also: *Rolles de Tailles des Annees 1719, 1720, 1721, 1722,* Archives Municipales de Dijon, Lno 274; *La véritable connoissance des temps ou des saisons pour l'annees,* 1722, 1723, 1730, 1732, 1734, 1735; Victor Lagier, *Manuel de L'Étranger à Dijon* (Dijon, 1824), 543; F. Vernillat, "Promenades dans Dijon," (Unpublished MS), Bibliothèque de la Ville de Dijon, MS. #1733, 1908, p. 129; Jacques Nicolas Vallot, "Promenades dans Dijon faites en 1817," (Unpublished MS.), Bibliothèque de la ville Dijon, Fonds Vallot, #7, MS. 1484, p. 25; *Almanach de Palais pour le duché de Bourgogne,* 1721, 1723, 1724, 1726, 1727-1736. Archives Départementales de la côte d'or, Serie G. II, Clergé Séculier, G. 1258, p. 172. *Mémoires de l'Académie des Sciences, arts et Belles Lettres de Dijon,* (1854), 2eme Serie, Tome II, Annees 1852-1853, xli-xlviii; Eugène Fyot, *Dijon; son passé evoqué par ses Rues* (Dijon, 1927), 99, 339.

17. "Contract du Mariage Entre M. Charles Gravier et Dlle Marie Françoise Chevignard," 15 February, 1718," Serie C, 8615, Notaire Gaudrillet, Archives de la Côte d'or, 51.

18. Maurice Garden, "Niveaux de fortune à Dijon au milieu du XVIIIème siècle," *Cahiers d'histoire publiées par les universités de Clermont, Lyon et Grenoble* (1964) IX, 226. See also: *Annales de Bourgogne,* tome XXXVII, annee 1965, fascicule 2

avril-juin, 138-142.

19. Maurice Garden, "Niveaux de fortune à Dijon au milieu du XVIIIème siècle," *Cahiers d'histoire publieés par les universités de Clermont, Lyon et Grenoble* (1964) IX, 226, 243.

20. *Ibid.*, 230-231.

21. *Ibid.*, 226.

22. "État-Civil: Dijon, 1721-1723," Archives de la Côte d'or.

23. Eugene Fyot, *Dijon; son passé évoqué par ses rues* (Dijon, 1927), 79-80.

24. "Diplômes Universitaires: 1738-1739," Papiers Vergennes. *AFV;* Marsangy, *Vergennes à Constantinople,* I, 4fn.

25. On Chavigny see: A.de Boislisle, editor, *Mémoires de Saint-Simon* (Paris, 1906), XIX, 23, ff. In Appendix III, 452-493, Boislisle has included a long article on Chavigny with sources and bibliography. See also the article on Chavigny in *Dictionnaire de Biographie Française,* edited by M. Prévot and Roman d'Amat (Paris, 1959), VIII, 1094-1095; The Baron de Besenval in his *Mémoires* (Paris, 1805), II, 213-218, obviously drawing on Saint-Simon, also discusses Chavigny's background; "Histoire des deux Chavignys," in Berton du Rocheret *Oeuvres choisies; mémoires et correspondance* (Châlons-sur-Marne, 1865), 23-38; *Mercure Galant,* July, 1708, 1er partie, 80-91; Philippe de Courcillon, Marquis de Dangeau, *Journal du Marquis de Dangeau;* edited by MM. Soulé, Dussieux, de Chennevieres, Montz, de Montaeglon et Feuillet de Conches (Paris, 1854-1960), XII entries of 4 and 13 February, 1710, 96-97, 100-100.

26. "Mémoire pour servir d'Instruction au Sieur de Chavigny allant à Ratisbonne pour le service du Roi en qualite de Ministre de Sa Majesté près la Diète de l'Empire," Bertrand Auerbach, *Recueil des Instructions données aux ambassadeurs et ministres de France* (Paris, 1912), XVIII, 115-174; "Addition à l'Instruction de Sr. de Chavigny, ministre du roi à la Diète de Ratisbonne, 5 September, 1726," *ibid.*, 174-178.

27. Duc de Luynes, *Mémoires du duc de Luynes sur la cour de Louis XV* (Paris, 1860-1865), V, 328-329.

28. Fredericka-Sophia Wilhelmine, *Mémoirs of Wilhelmine Margravine of Bayreuth,* translated by Princess Christine of Schleswig-Holstein (New York, 1887), 448; See also: "Instructions due roi du Sieur Comte de Bavière ... etc.," in André Lebon, editor, *Recueil des instructions données aux ambassadeurs et ministres de France depuis les traités de Westphalie jusqu'à la révolution française: Bavière, Palatinat, Deux-Ponts* (Paris, 1889), VII, 256.

29. Auguste le Page (ed.) *Mémoire de l'élection de l'Empéreur Charles VII* (Paris, 1870), iii.

30. *Gazette de France,* 13 January, 1742, 17-18; 3 February, 1742, 70; 10 February, 1742, 73-77; 17 February, 1742, 88-89; For a detailed description of the election ceremony see: Auguste le Page (ed.) *Mémoire de l'élection de l'Empéreur Charles VII,* 208-259.

31. Fredericka-Sophia Wilhelmine, *Mémoirs,* 445; *Gazette de France,* 26 October, 1743, 517.

32. *Gazette de France,* 2 November, 28 December, 1743, 526-527; 619-620.

33. *Gazette de France,* 9 May, 1744, 226.

34. André Lebon, *Recueil des instructions,* VII, 223.

35. Louis-Augustin Blondel and the Comte de Lautrec also represented France at the court of Charles VII. See Bertrand Auerbach, editor, *Recueil des Instructions* (Paris, 1912), XVIII, 199-201; Andre-Lebon, editor, *Recueil des Instructions,* (Paris, 1889), VII, 199-221.

36. "Memoire pour servir d'instruction au sieur de Chavigny allant de la part du roi près de l'Empéreur, Fontainebleau, 4 Octobre, 1743," Lebon, VII, 224-239.

37. "Instruction pour le sieur de Chavigny retournant à Frankfort sur-le-Mein, Marly, 19 January, 1744," *Ibid.*, 240-246.

38. *Ibid.*, VII, 296; *Gazette de France,* 18 September, 1744, 446-447. According to Argenson, the Treaty of thew union of Frankfort cost France 28,000,000 *livres* in subsidies and grants. See René d'Argenson, *Mémoires* (Paris, 1825), 352 fn.

39. *Gazette de France,* 16 January, 1745, 26

40. Zévort, *LeMarquis d'Argenson,* 116. Charles' return to Munich is described in Broglie's *Marie Thérèse: Impératrice,* I, 23-24, 95-96, 130.

41. Zévort, *Le Marquis d'Argenson,* 116.

42. *Gazette de France,* 5 February, 1745, 63.

43. "Intructions du roi au sieur comte de Bavière . . . etc.," in Lebon, *Recueil des instructions,* VII, 247-268; *Gazette de France,* 7 December, 1743, 592.

44. Sir Richard Lodge, *Private Correspondence of Chesterfield and Newcastle:* 1744-46 (London, 1930), xviii.

45. Duc de Noailles, *Mémoires,* edited by C.B. Petitot (Paris, 1829), III, 395.

46. Lodge, *Private Correspondence of Chesterfield and Newcastle,* xviii.

47. "Chesterfield to Newcastle, March 9, N.S., 1745," Lodge, *Private Correspondence of Chesterfield and Newcastle,* 19.

48. Edgar Zévort, *Le Marquis D'Argenson et le Ministère des Affaires Étrangères du 18 Novembre, 1744 au Janvier, 1747* (Paris, 1880), 112; Duc Albert de Broglie, *Marie Thérèse: Impératrice* (Paris, 1890), I, 304.

49. Zévort, *Le Marquis d'Argenson,* 118-119; Broglie, *Marie-Thérèse: Impératrice,* I, 293-295, 300.

50. *Gazette de France,* 17 April, 1, 22, May 1745, 197-202, 223-224, 259.

51. *Ibid.*, 25 September, 1745.

52. "Mémoires et lettres concernant S. A.M. le Prince Guillaume de Hesse et le traité des 6,000 Hessoise," Dossier: 1742-1745; "Lettres important," *AFV*.

53. "Lettres de M. de Lantingshausen à S.E. Chavigny et à M. de Vergennes pendant l'année 1744." Dossier: 1742-1744; "Lettres important," *AFV*. Also: "Vergennes to Chavigny, 31 October, 1744," in "Trois lettres de M. de Vergennes à S.E. de Francfort le 20 et 31 Octobre, 1744," *ibid.*

54. "Vergennes to Chavigny, 20 October, 1744," *ibid.*

55. Broglie, *Marie Thérèse: Impératrice,* I, 319-320.

56. *Ibid.*, I, 316.

57. *Gazette de France,* 1 January, 1746, 6.

58. Bourge, "Le comte de Vergennes; ses débuts . . .," 94.

59. Zévort, *Le Marquis d'Argenson,* 123.

60. *Ibid.*, 209.

61. *Ibid.*, 210. See also: "Mémoire pour servir de supplément à l'instruction du sieur de Chavigny . . . etc., 2 August, 1746," Saint-Aymour, *Recueil des instructions,* III, 304-305.

62. Marsangy, *Vergennes à Constantinople,* I, 29.

63. Chavigny and Vergennes returned to Lisbon in October of 1749. *ibid.*, I. 39.

64. Zévort, *Le Marquis d'Argenson,* 211-212.

65. *Ibid.*, 212-213: "Mémoire pour servir de supplément a l'instruction du sieur de Chavigny . . . etc., 2 August, 1746," Saint-Aymour, *Recueil des instructions,* III, 302.

66. Zévort, *Le Marquis d'Argenson,* 214.

67. *Ibid.*, 213.

68. *Ibid.*

69. *Ibid.*

70. *Ibid.*, 214; On the general problem of the mistakes of d'Argenson's ministry, see: albert de Broglie, "Fin du Ministère du Marquis d'Argenson:" Part I, "L'expédition d'Écosse et la prise de Bruxelles;" Part II, "Affaires d'Espagne et d'Italie-Project de confédération italienne," in *Revue des Deux-Mondes* (Paris, 1889), XCVI, 313-349; 720-750; Part III, "Suite du project de confédération italienne," *ibid*, 1890, XCVII, 54-85.

71. D.B. Horn, *British Diplomatic Service: 1689-1789* (Oxford, 1961), 95.

72. *Ibid.*, 106.

73. Zévort, *Le Marquis d'Argenson*, 284.

Chapter 2. A King of the Romans

1. Quoted in A. de Boislisle, editor, *Mémoires de Saint-Simon* (Paris, 1906), XIX, 488. In Appendix III, pp. 456-493, of this volume, Boislisle gives an excellent summary of Chavigny's career with bibliographical references.

2. *Gazette de France*, 21 January, 1746, 36.

3. Boislisle, *Mémoires de Saint-Simon*, XIX, 491

4. Gaston de Bourge, "Le Comte de Vergennes; ses débuts diplomatiques en Allemagne auprès de l'électeur de Trèves et de l'électeur d'Hanovre," *Revue des questions historiques*, XLIV, 100.

5. Vicq d'Azyr, *Eloge de M. le Comte de Vergennes* (Paris, 1788), 8. A slightly different version of this statement, but one which says essentially the same thing, is in Charles Joseph Mayer, *Vie publique et privée de Charles Gravier, Comte de Vergennes* (Paris, 1789), 21.

6. "Mémoire pour servir d'instruction au sieur de Chavigny ... allant en qualité d'ambassadeur du roi auprès de la République de Venise, 14 September, 1750," Pierre DuParc, editor, *Recueil des instructions données aux ambassadeurs et ministres de France* (Paris, 1958) XXVI, 209-218.

7. See document dated 6 May, 1750, *Archives des Affaires Étrangères - Documents Personnel*, LXVIII, 5. Hereafter referred to as *AAE-DP*. Vergennes' letter of credence is dated 27 July, 1750. *Archives des Affaires Étrangères - Correspondance Politique - Trèves*, XVII, fol. 24. Hereafter referred to as *AAE-CP-Trèves.*

8. "Pelham to Lord Chancellor Hardwicke, Nov. 7, 1748," and "Hardwicke to Newcastle, November 8, 1748." Philip C. Yorke, *The Life and Correspondence of Philip Yorke, Earl of Hardwicke, Lord High Chancellor of Great Britain* (Cambridge, England, 1913), II, 10-11.

9. V.H.H. Green, *The Hanoverians, 1714-1815* (London, 1956), 68.

10. "Newcastle to Chesterfield, 22 February, 1744/45," Sir Richard Lodge, *Private Correspondence of Chesterfield and Newcastle 1744-1746* (London, 1930), 12-17.

11. On the origins of the project for the Election of the King of the Romans, see D.B. Horn, "The Origins of the Proposed Election of a King of the Romans, 1748-1750," *The English Historical Review* (1927), XLII, 361-370. Also the same author's *Sir Charles Hanbury Williams and European Diplomacy (1747-58)* (London, 1930), 48-50. Johan Christoph Adelung in *Pragmatische Staatsgeschichte European von dem Ableben Kaiser Carls 6 an bis auf gegenwartige Zeiten* (Gotha, 1766), VII, pt. I, 146, states that the election project was the result of a secret agreement made between George II and Maria Theresa after the Peace of Aix-la-Chapelle. He gives no evidence for his statement, however, and the evidence uncovered by Horn contradicts the hypothesis.

12. Sir Richard Lodge, "The Continental Policy of Great Britain, 1740-1760," *History* (1931-32), XVI, 302.

13. D.B. Horn, *Sir Charles Hanbury Williams*, 83.

14. Kaunitz, the Austrian ambassador at Paris, felt that the Newcastle plan was sure to lead to difficulties, but even he admitted that the "idea was a good one, and conformed to a sound policy." See "Kaunitz to Koch, 20 September, 1750," Hanns Schlitter, *Correspondance Secrète entre le Comte A.W. Kaunitz - Reitberg, Ambassadeur impérial à Paris et le baron Ignaz de Koch, Secrétaire de l'Impératrice Maria Thérèse, 1750-1752* (Paris, 1899), 30.

15. Sir Herbert W. Richmond, *Statesmen and Seapower* (Oxford, 1946), 48.

16. See, for example the eighteenth-century pamphlets: Anonymous, *A Second Letter to the People of England on Foreign Subsidies and the Consequences to the Nation* (London, 1756); Anonymous, *A Sixth Letter to the People of England on the Progress of National Ruin* (London, 1757).

17. "Pelham to Hume Campbell, 1 September, (o.s.), 1750," Marchmont Papers, II, 388-389, quoted in D.B. Horn, "The Cabinet Controversy on Subsidies in Time of Peace, 1749-1750," *The English Historical Review* (1930) XLV, 466.

18. "Newcastle to Hardwicke, 25 August (o.s.), 1749.": Quoted in *ibid.*, 463-464.

19. Reinhold Koser, *König Friedrich der Grosse* (Stuttgart and Berlin, 1904). I, 563.

20. "Frederick to Comte de Podwils, 25 August, 1750," *Politische Correspondenz Friedrich's des Grossen* (Berlin, 1882), VIII, 59-60; Also, Letters to Klinggraeffen, Frederick's representative at Hanover, 10 and 12 September, 1750, *ibid.*, 76, 78; "Kaunitz to Koch, 11 December, 1750," Schlitter, *Correspondance Secrète*, 48.

21. "Frederick to the Baron Le Chambrier at Paris and Fontainebleau, 25 September, 13 October, 24 October, and 21 November, 1750," *ibid.*, 84, 107, 120, 160-161.

22. "Mémoire pour servir d'Instruction au Sr. chevalier de Vergennes allant résider près l'électeur de Trèves en qualité de Ministre du Roi," *AAE-CP-Trèves*, XVII, 2-7vo ; Vergennes' letter of credence, signed by Louis XV, was dated 27 July, 1750, *ibid.*, XVII, 24; "Copie de la lettre de créance du Roi au Chevalier de Vergennes, son ministre auprès de l'électeur de Trèves,"*Archives de la Famille Vergennes*. Hereafter cited as *AFV*. Also, Georges Livet, *Recueil des instructions données aux ambassadeurs et ministres de France depuis les traités de Westphalie jusqu'à la révolution française* (Paris, 1966), vol. XXVIII, "Electorat de Trèves," 171-176.

23. "Vergennes to Puysieux, 5 August, 1750," *AAE-CP-Trèves*, XVIII, 25.

24. "Vergennes to Puysieux, 18 August, 1750," *ibid.*, XVII, 27.

25. "Vergennes to Puysieux, 23 August, 1750," *ibid.*, XVII, 28.

26. "Mémoire pour servir d'Instruction au Sr. chevalier de Vergennes allant résider auprès l'électeur de Trèves en qualité de Ministre du Roi, 27 June, 1750," *ibid.*, XVII, 2-2vo.

27. "Vergennes to Puysieux, 23 August, 1750; 14 December, 1750," *ibid.*, XVII, 29, 118-119.

28. "Mémoire pour servir d'instruction . . . ." *ibid.*, XVII, 2vo-4; The possibilities for intrigue and intervention in an election of a co-adjutor presented themselves to Vergennes, but he wisely refused to exploit them. See, for example: the exchange of letters between Vergennes and Sickengen, 10 February, 13 February, 1752; *AFV*.

29. "Mémoire pour servir d'instruction . . . ." *AAE-CP-Trèves*, XVII, 4vo-5; "Vergennes to Puysieux, 28 September, 1750," XVII, 35bis, *ibid.*

30. "Mémoire pour servir d'instruction . . . ." *ibid.*, XVII, 4-5; "Vergennes to Saint-Contest, 6 December, 1751," *ibid.*, 291vo.

31. "Vergennes to Spangenberg, 17 August, 1750," *AFV*.

32. "Vergennes to Puysieux, 14 September, 1750," *AAE-CP-Trèves,* XVII, 36-36vo; "Vergennes to Puysieux, 21 September, 1750," *ibid.*, XVII, 39; Also folios 30bis-31bis.

33. "Vergennes to Saint-Contest, 6 December, 1751," *ibid.*, XVII, 292-292vo.

34. "Vergennes to Puysieux, 18 August, 1750," *ibid.*, XVII, 28-30; See also, on François-Georges de Schönborn; Georges Livet, *Recueil des Instructions données* aux ambassadeurs, etc., Vol. XXVIII, "Trèves," CIX-CXXIV.

35. "Concordat germanique fait entre le pape Nicolas V d'une part et l'empéreur Frederic III et L'Empire d'autre part, sur la manière de pourvoir aux bénéfices d'Allemagne, confirmé par bulle du même Pape le 18 mars, 1448," DeBoug, editor, *Recueil des édits déclarations, lettres patentes, arrêts du conseil d'État et du Conseil souverains d'Alsace* (Colmar, 1775), I, LV.

36. "Vergennes to Saint-Contest, 6 December, 1751," *AAE-CP-Trèves,* XVII, 295vo-297.

37. Attached to Vergennes' dispatch of 21 September, 1750. *AAE-CP-Trèves,* XVII, 295vo-297.

38. *Ibid.*, XVII, 33bis; "Vergennes to Puysieux, 28 September, 1750," *ibid.*, XVII, 35-35vo. Also: "Vergennes to Puysieux, 26 October, 1750," *ibid.*, XVII, 53-54.

39. *Ibid.*, 35vo-36vo.

40. "Puysieux to Vergennes, 18 October, 1750," *ibid.*, XVII, 44-44vo.

41. "Vergennes to Puysieux, 2 November, 1750," *ibid.*, XVII, 62-63.

42. "Vergennes to Puysieux, 2 November, 1750," *ibid.*, XVII, 63-63vo.

43. "Réponse au comte de la Peubla de la part du Roi dans l'affaire de l'élection d'un roi des Romains," 30 October, 1750," *Politische Correspondenz* VIII, 129; Adelung, *Pragmatische Staatsgeschichte* VII, pt. I, 149-150. The "Réponse", dated 30 October, was given to the Austrian minister, Comte de la Peubla, the 1st of November, 1750. The circular letter was dated 7 November, 1750. See also: "Koch to Kaunitz, 28 November, 1750," Schlitter, *Correspondance Secrète,* 36.

44. "Vergennes à Puysieux, 30 November, 1750," *AAE-CP-Trèves,* XVII, 89-92.

45. "Traduction de la lettre de l'Électeur de Trèves à sa Majesté le Roi de Prusse, 21 November, 1750." *ibid.*, XVII, 83. See also; folios 87-88.

46. Alfred von Arneth, *Maria-Thèresa nach dem Erbfolgekrieg, 1748-1756* (Vienna, 1870), IV, 293.

47. *Ibid.*, IV, 294.

48. "Klinggraeffen to Frederick II, 26 September, 1 October, 6 October, 1750;" "Frederick II to Klinggraeffen, 3 October, 6 October, 1750," *Politische Correspondenz,* VIII, 91, 107, 113-14.

49. "Bedford to Albemarle, 22 November, 1750," L.G. Wickam Legg, editor, *British Diplomatic Instructions, 1689-1789* (London, 1934), VII, "France," Pt. IV., 1745-1789, 13; "Koch to Kaunitz, 28 November, 1750," "Kaunitz to Koch, 4 December, 1750," Schlitter, *Correspondance Secrète,* 36, 38.

50. "Frederick II to Podewils, 13 November, 1750," *Politische Correspondenz,* VIII, 152. See also Kaunitz' opinion that the election was going badly: "Kaunitz to Koch, 29 November, 1750," Schlitter, *Correspondance Secrète,* 30-31.

51. Adelung, *Pragmatische Staatsgeschichte,* VII, 147; "Frederick II to Warendorff, 26 September, 1750," *Politische Correspondenz,* VII, 86.

52. "Frederick II to Warendorff, 12 September, 1750,"; *Ibid.*, VIII, 77.

53. For the details of the diplomatic episode see: *Preussiche Staatsschrift aus der Regieungszeit König Friedrich II, 1746-1756* (Berlin, 1885), II, 238-256.

54. "Vergennes to Puysieux, 15 February, 1751," *AAE-CP-Trèves,* XVII, 152.

55. "Puysieux to Vergennes, 31 December, 1750," *ibid.*, XVII, 127-127vo.
56. "Koch to Kaunitz, 17 April, 1751," Schlitter, *Correspondance Secrète,* 96-97.
57. "Vergennes to Puysieux, 15 February, 1751," *AAE-CP-Trèves,* XVII, 153vo.
58. "Vergennes to Puysieux, 17 May, 1751," *ibid.*, XVII, 210.
59. "Vergennes to Puysieux, 12 April, 1751," *ibid.*, XVII, 184-185.
60. "Puysieux to Vergennes, 25 April, 1751," *ibid.*, XVII, 197-197vo.
61. "Vergennes to Puysieux, 12 April, 1751," *ibid.*, XVII, 187-187vo.
62. "Vergennes to Puysieux, 17 May, 1751," *ibid.*, XVII, 210-210vo.
63. "Vergennes to Saint-Contest, 4 October, 1751," *ibid.*, XVII, 277-278; "Vergennes to Saint-Contest, 6 December, 1751," *ibid.*, XVII, 296-297.
64. "Vergennes to Puysieux, 17 May, 1751," *ibid.*, XVII, 210-210vo.
65. "Holderness to Albermarle, 12 December, 1751," *British Diplomatic Instructions,* VII, 20.
66. "Holderness to Yorke, 8 July, 1751," *ibid.*, VII, 16-17.
67. "Vergennes to Saint-Contest, 24 January, 1752," *AAE-CP-Trèves,* XVIII, 26.
68. "Saint-Contest to Vergennes, 18 February, 1752," *ibid.*, XVIII, 45vo.
69. "Vergennes to Saint-Contest, 3 March, 1752," *ibid.*, XVIII, 53vo.
70. *Gazette de France,* 28 September, 1751, 454.

Chapter 3. The Congress at Hanover

1. D'Argenson, *Journal,* edited by Jennet (Paris, 1857), I, 941; II, 45.
2. "Albemarle to Newcastle, 31 August/11 September, 1752," quoted in L.G. Wickam Legg, *British Diplomatic Instructions; 1689-1789* (London, 1934), France, VII, Part IV, xvi.
3. Comte Charles de Chambrun, *À l'école d'un diplomate: Vergennes* (Paris, 1944), 47.
4. *AAE-CP-Brunswick, Hanovre,* LI, 5; *AAE-Dossiers Personnels,* LXVIII, 6.
5. Gaëtan de Raxis de Flassan, *Histoire Générale et raisonnée de la diplomatie Française* (Paris, 1811); V, 186.
6. Louis Bonneville de Marsangy, *Le Chevalier de Vergennes; Son ambassade à Constantinople* (Paris, 1894), I, 62.
7. On the negotiations for the Saxon treaty see: D.B. Horn, *Sir Charles Hanbury Williams and European Diplomacy* (London, (1930), V, 68-100.
8. T.C. Hansard, *The Parliamentary History of England from the Earliest Times to the Year 1803* (London 1813), XIV, 1132-1198.
9. *Ibid.*, 1137-1149.
10. *Ibid.*, 1175-1184.
11. Basil Williams, *Carteret and Newcastle* (Cambridge, England, 1943), 187.
12. Hansard, *The Parliamentary History,* XIV, 1134, 1178.
13. *Ibid.*, 1136.
14. *Ibid.*, 1175; William Coxe, *Memoirs of the Right Honourable Henry Pelham* (London, 1829), II, 208.
15. *AAE-CP-Brunswick-Hanovre,* LI, 156-157.
16. "Holderness to Albemarle, 13 February, 1752," *British Diplomatic Instructions,* VII,20.
17. "Holderness to Albemarle, 26 March, 1752," *ibid.*, VII, 22. See also: "Koch to Kaunitz, 27 May, 10 June, 1752;" "Kaunitz to Koch, 17 June, 1752," Hans Schlitter, *Correspondance Secréte entre le comte A.W. Kaunitz-Reitberg...et le Baron Ignaz de Koch, 1750-1752* (Paris, 1899), 222, 232, 237-238.

18. *Gazette de France,* 29 April, 13 May, 1752, 212, 233.

19. "Newcastle to Albemarle, 27 April/8 May, 1752," *British Diplomatic Instructions,* VII, 24.

20. Coxe, *Pelham,* II, 415.

21. "Mémoire pour servir d'instruction au Sieur de Vergennes allant à Hanovre, 17 April, 1752," *AAE-CP-Brunswick-Hanovre,* LI, 7-10; Also in "Papiers Vergennes: Mission à l'Électeur d'Hanovre, 1752," *Archives de la Famille Vergennes.* Hereafter referred to as *AFV.*

22. *British Diplomatic Instructions,* VII, xxi fn.

23. *Ibid.,* V, 62.

24. *Ibid.,* VII, xxi fn.

25. "Newcastle to Albemarle, 27 April/8 May, 1752," *British diplomatic Instructions,* VII, 25.

26. "Vergennes to Saint-Contest, 12 May, 1752," *AAE-CP-Brunswick-Hanovre,* LI, 30; *The Gazette de France,* 3 June, 1752, 267, reported, apparently erroneously, that Vergennes was not received until the 12th of May.

27. "Vergennes to Saint-Contest, 12 May, 1752," *AAE-CP-Brunswick-Hanovre,* LI, 30vo-32.

28. *Ibid.,* 32-34vo.

29. *Ibid.,* 35-35vo.

30. "Newcastle to Albemarle, 13/24 May, 1752," *British Diplomatic Instructions,* VII, 27.

31. See: *AAE-CP-Brunswick-Hanovre,* LI, 44vo-46vo.

32. See: *British Diplomatic Instructions,* VII, 25-26.

33. Hans Schlitter, *Correspondance Secrète,* 19, 31, 217.

34. "Saint-Contest to Vergennes, 26 May, 1752," "Vergennes to Saint-Contest, 3 June, 1752," *AAE-CP-Brunswick-Hanovre,* LI, 70-73vo, 76-79vo.

35. "Vergennes to Saint-Contest, 3 June, 1752," *ibid.,* LI, 80-80vo.

36. *Ibid.,* 89vo.

37. "Koch to Kaunitz, 4, 11 March, 15 April, 1752," Schlitter, *Correspondance Secrète,* 181-182, 190, 217.

38. "Newcastle to Pelham 3/14 June, 1752," Coxe, *Pelham,* II, 426. See also: "Koch to Kaunitz, 10 June, 1752," Schlitter, *Correspondance Secrète,* 231.

39. "Newcastle to Lord Chancellor Hardwicke, 18/29 June, 1752," Coxe, *Pelham,* II 430-431.

40. "Vergennes to Saint-Contest, 19 June, 1752," *AAE-CP-Brunswick-Hanovre,* LI, 145-146vo.

41. "Newcastle to Pelham, 12/23 June, 1752," Coxe, *Pelham,* II 429; "Koch to Kaunitz, 10 June, 1752," Schlitter, *Correspondance Secrète,* 233.

42. Coxe, *Pelham,* II 228.

43. Coxe, *Pelham,* II, 226, says the Palatinate's pecuniary claims were reduced to 1,200,000 *florins* as a result of Newcastle's efforts. Vergennes believed, however, ("Vergennes to Saint-Contest, 4 July, 1752," *AAE-CP-Brunswick-Hanovre,* LI, 153vo.) that Newcastle suggested to Vienna an offer of only 1,000,000 *florins.*

44. "Vergennes to Saint-Contest, 4 July, 1752," *ibid.,* 239-240vo. Also: 421-423.

45. Stadion presented his credentials at Hanover the 2nd of June, 1752. *Gazette de France,* 17 June, 1752, 292.

46. "Vergennes to Saint-Contest, 28 June, 1752," *AAE-CP-Brunswick-Hanovre,* LI, 192-195.

47. "Papier donné à M. le Baron de Vorster par les ministres de Sa Majesté, le roi de la Grande Bretagne, Électeur de Brunswick-Lüneberg; de S.A.E. de Mayence et

de S.A.E. de Bavière, 27 June, 1752," *ibid.*, LI, 172-173vo.

48. "Project de Protocole de conférences tenus en conséquence du précis de la réponse de Vienne, 1 July, 1752," *ibid.*, LI, 252-254; "Vergennes to Saint-Contest, 7 July, 2 August, 1752," *ibid.*, LI, 241-250; 315-332.

49. "Vergennes to Saint-Contest, 7 July, 1752," *ibid.*, LI, 249.

50. "Vergennes to Saint-Contest, 27 June, 1752," *ibid.*, LI, 192-195.

51. "Newcastle to Pelham, 9/20 May, 1752," Coxe, *Pelham,* II, 418.

52. "Newcastle to Pelham, 24 June/5 July, 1752," *ibid.*, 435.

53. "Vergennes to Saint-Contest, 7 July, 1752," *AAE-CP-Brunswick-Hanovre,* LI, 249-250; See also: "Koch to Kaunitz, 10 June, 24 June, 2 September, 1752," Schlitter, *Correspondance Secrète,* 232, 240, 276-277.

54. "Baron de Wrede to S.A. Electrol Palatinat, 26 June, 1752;" "Vergennes to Saint-Contest, 27 June, 1752," *AAE-CP-Brunswick-Hanovre,* LI, 152-156, 190vo-191vo.

55. "Vergennes to Saint-Contest, 28 June, 7 July, 1752," *ibid.*, LI, 195-195vo, 232-234.

56. *AAE-Mémoires et Documents-Allemagne,* CIV, 170-171.

57. "Vergennes to Saint-Contest, 4 July, 1752," *AAE-CP-Brunswick-Hanovre,* LI, 235-235vo; "Saint-Contest to Tilly, 16 July, 1752," *AAE-CP-Palatinat,* LXXVII, 45vo-46vo.

58. "Vergennes to Saint-Contest, 27 June, 1752," *AAE-CP-Brunswick-Hanovre,* LI, 187; See also: dispatch of Baron von Wrede to S.A. Electoral Palatinat, dated 26 June, 1752, *ibid.*, LI, 152.

59. "Vergennes to Saint-Contest, 4 July, 1752," *ibid.*, LI, 236vo-237.

60. "Vergennes to Saint-Contest, 23 July, 1752," *ibid.*, LI, 299-299vo.

61. "Vergennes to Saint-Contest, 23 August, 1752," *ibid.*, LI, 367vo-368vo.

62. See "Koch to Kaunitz, 24 June, 1752," Schlitter, *Correspondance Secrète,* 240-241.

63. "Pelham to Newcastle, 1/12 July, 1752," Coxe, *Pelham,* LI, 437.

64. "Newcastle to Chancellor Hardwicke, 18/29 June, 1752," *ibid.*, II, 430-432.

65. "Pelham to Newcastle, 1/12 July, 1752," *ibid.*, II, 437.

66. "Vergennes to Saint-Contest, 23 August, 1752," *AAE-CP-Brunswick-Hanovre,* LI, 368vo-372vo.

67. *Ibid.*, 372vo-376vo; Coxe, *Pelham,* II, 229.

68. "Newcastle to Pelham, 5/16 August, 1752;" "Pelham to Newcastle, 28 August, 1752;" "Chancellor Hardwicke to Newcastle, 27 August, 1752," *ibid.*, II, 442, 445-447.

69. "Pelham to Newcastle, 1/12 July, 1752," *ibid.*, II, 437.

70. "Vergennes to Saint-Contest, 23 August, 1752," *AAE-CP-Brunswick-Hanovre,* LI, 378vo-379.

71. *Ibid.*, LI, 376vo.

72. *AAE-CP-Brunswick,* LI, 395-398.

73. "Pelham to Newcastle, 28 August, 1752," Coxe, *Pelham,* II, 445-446.

74. "Newcastle to Pelham, 19 September, 1752," *ibid.*, II, 447.

75. "Newcastle to Keith, 20/31 August, 1752," *ibid.*, II, 443.

76. Rex's communications with Newcastle were well publicized, however. See *Gazette de France,* 8 July, 1752, 330-331.

77. The Comte d'Haslang arrived in Hanover the 20th of June, 1752, *ibid.*

78. Gaston de Bourge, "Le comte de Vergennes; ses débuts diplomatiques en Allemagne auprès de l'électeur de Trêves et de l'électeur de Hanovre . . . 1750-1752," *Revue des questions historiques* (1888), LIV, 137.

79. Grimaldi arrived at Hanover the 1st of July, 1752, *Gazette de France,* 22 July, 1752, 354. See also: *ibid.,* 28 October, 1752, 527; "Vergennes to Saint-Contest, 4 July, 1752," *AAE-CP-Brunswick-Hanovre,* LI, 237-237vo; "Vergennes to Saint-Contest, 11 July, 1752," *ibid.,* LI, 283vo-284. Grimaldi left Hanover late in November, 1752. "Vergennes to Saint-Contest, 3 November, 1752," *AFV.*

80. Bourge, "Le comte de Vergennes; ses débuts . . ., 28;" *Gazette de France,* 13 May, 8 July, 12 August, 28 October, 1752, 233, 330-331, 390, 413, 527.

81. "Saint-Contest to Vergennes 9 September, 1752," *AAE-CP-Brunswick-Hanovre,* LI, 488vo; "Vergennes to Saint-Contest, 30 August, 16 September, 1752," *ibid.,* LI, 393vo-394, 494vo-495.

82. "Vergennes to Saint-Contest, 16 September, 1752," *ibid.,* LI, 494vo-495.

83. "Newcastle to Pelham, 20 September, 1752, 'Postscript to letter of 19 September, 1752,'" Coxe, *Pelham,* II, 447.

84. "Vergennes to Saint-Contest, 27 September, 1752," *AAE-CP-Brunswick-Hanovre,* LI, 499vo.

85. "Newcastle to Pelham, 28 September, 1752," Coxe, *Pelham,* II, 449.

86. Bourge, "Le comte de Vergennes; ses débuts . . .," 158, 161.

87. "Newcastle to Pelham, 28 September, 1752," Coxe, *Pelham,* II, 447.

88. "Newcastle to Pelham, 28 September, 1752," *ibid.,* II, 449.

89. "Newcastle to Pelham, 'Postscript' 29 September, 1752 to letter of 28 September, 1752," *ibid.,* II, 447.

90. "Vergennes to Saint-Contest, 7 October,1752," *AAE-CP-Brunswick-Hanovre,* LI, 515vo-516.

91. Philip C. Yorke, *The Life and Correspondence of Philip Yorke, Earl of Hardwicke, Lord High Chancellor of Great Britain* (Cambridge, England, 1913), II, 536. Coxe, *Pelham,* II, 230, 350, 450, 459.

92. "Newcastle to Chancellor Hardwicke, 12/23 October, 1752." *ibid.,* 459-460.

93. *AAE-CP-Brunswick-Hanovre,* LI, 537, 438vo.

94. *Ibid.,* fol. 539-54.

95. *Ibid.,* fol. 547-548vo. These documents are also in "Papiers Vergennes: Mission à l'Électeur d'Hanovre, 1752," *AFV.*

96. "Declaration de M. le duc de Newcastle, 29 October, 1752," *AAE-CP-Brunswick-Hanovre,* LI, 567-567vo.

97. "Vergennes to Saint-Contest, 29 October, 1752," *ibid.,* LI, 561-562. Also: "Papiers Vergennes: Mission à l'Electeur d'Hanovre," *AFV.*

98. "Vergennes to Saint-Contest, 29 October, 1752." *AAE-CP-Brunswick-Hanovre,* LI, 563-564vo.

99. "Vergennes to Saint-Contest, 3 November, 10 November, 1752," "Papiers Vergennes: Mission à l'Electeur d' Hanovre, 1752," *AFV.* Also: *AAE-CP-Brunswick-Hanovre,* LI, 572.

100. "Saint-Contest to Vergennes, 7 November, 1752," *ibid.,* LI, 571-571vo; also "Papiers Vergennes: Mission ài' Electeur d' Hanovre, 1752," *AFV.*

101. *AAE-CP-Palatinat,* LXXVII, 205, 239; "Saint-Contest to Tilly, 16 January, 1753," *ibid.,* LXXVIII, 35; See also the interesting exchange of letters: "Kaunitz to Koch, 29 May, 1752," Hanns Schlitter, *Correspondance Secrète entre le comte A.W. Kaunitz-Rietberg et le Baron Ignaz de Koch: 1750-1752* (Paris, 1899), 226-229; "Koch to Kaunitz, 17 June, 1752," *ibid.,* 235.

102. "Holderness to Albermarle, 28 December, 1752," L.G. Wickam Legg, *British Diplomatic Instructions, 1689-1789* (London, 1934), France, VII, 33.

103. "Saint-Contest to Wachendonck, 9, 22 November, 1752," *AAE-CP-Palatinat,* LXXVII, 199-204vo, 206-213vo.

104. "Vergennes to Wrede, 17 December, 1752," *ibid.*, LXXVII, 274-276vo; See also: "Saint-Contest to Tilly, 21 December, 1752." *ibid.*, 300vo-301.

105. "Saint-Contest to Tilly, 16 July, 1752," *ibid.*, LXXVII, 45vo-46; "Tilly to Saint-Contest, 26 December, 1752," *ibid., LXXVII, 315vo;* "Tilly to Saint-Contest, 23 December, 1752," *ibid.*, LXXVII, 304vo.

106. "Tilly to Saint-Contest, 26 December, 1752," *ibid.*, LXXVII, 316-316vo.

107. On the solution to the problem posed by Tilly see: "Saint-Contest to Tilly, 16 January, 1753," *ibid.*, LXXVIII, 35; "Tilly to Saint-Contest, 2 February, 1753," *ibid.*, LXXVIII, 91; "Tilly to Saint-Contest, 23 January, 1753," *ibid.*, LXXVIII, 48-48vo.

108. *AAE-CP-Palatinat,* LXXVIII, 26-26vo; "Louis XV to Elector Palatinate, 16 June, 1753," *ibid.*, LXXVIII, 27.

109. *AAE-CP-Palatinat,* LXXVIII, 45-47, 52-54; "Vergennes to Saint-Contest, 25 June, 1753," *ibid.*, LXXVIII, 59-59vo.

110. "Tilly to Saint-Contest, 23 January, 1753," *ibid.*, LXXVIII, 48-51.

111. "Letter Koch to Kaunitz, 17 June, 1752," Schlitter, *Correspondance Secrète,* 236.

112. "Vergennes to Saint-Contest, 25 January, 1753," *AAE-CP-Palatinat,* LXXVIII, 60.

113. See, for example, "Vergennes to Saint-Contest, 30 January, 1753," *ibid.*, LXXVIII, 67.

114. "Louis XV to Elector Palatinate, 16 January, 1753," *ibid.*, LXXVIII, 28.

115. "Vergennes to Saint-Contest, 21 February, 1753," *ibid.*, LXXVIII, 144-145.

116. Louis Bonneville de Marsangy, *Le Chevalier de Vergennes; son ambassade à Constantinople* (Paris, 1894), I, 105-107.

117. *Ibid.*, 109.

118. *AAE-CP-Palatinat,* LXXVIII, 155-157.

119. "Saint-Contest to Tilly, 23 March, 1753," *ibid.*, LXXVIII, 193.

120. "Wrede to Saint-Severin, 7 April, 1753," *ibid.*, LXXVIII,233.

121. *Ibid.*, 244.

122. "Extrait d'un rescript de l'Électeur Palatinat..., 13 April, 1753," *ibid.*, LXXVIII, 245.

123. *AAE-CP-Palatinat,* LXXVIII, 281-282vo.

124. "Mémoire pour servir d'instruction au sieur Baron de Zuckmantel..., le 2 August, 1753," printed in André Lebon, editor, *Recueil des Instructions données aux ambassadeurs et ministres de France depuis les traités de Westphalie jusqu' à la Révolution* (Paris, 1889), VII, 458-468; *Gazette de France,* 23 June, 27 October, 1753," 299, 508.

125. "Vergennes to Saint-Contest, 4, 25 October, 1753," *AAE-CP-Trèves.* XVIII, 86. 87.

126. "Vergennes to Saint-Contest, 25 November, 1753," *ibid.*, XVIII, 100-103vo, 123-126vo.

127. *AAE-CP-Trèves.* XVIII, 240; *Gazette de France,* 20 July, 3 August, 25 December, 1754, 341, 364-366, 603-604.

128. "Vergennes to Saint-Contest, 25 November, 1753," *AAE-CP-Trèves,* XVIII, 123vo-124vo.

129. "Vergennes to Saint-Contest, 28 February, 1754," *ibid.*, XVIII, 155.

130. "Vergennes to Rouillé, 31 October, 1754," *ibid.*, XVIII, 269.

131. "Rouillé to Vergennes, 28 November, 12 December, 1754," *ibid.*, XVIII, 273; 277-278vo.

132. "Newcastle to Saint-Contest, 29 October, 1752," *AAE-CP-Brunswick-*

Hanovre, LI, 568-568vo.

133. Bourge, "Le comte de Vergennes, ses débuts . . .," 166.

134. George II left Hanover the 8th of November, 1752, *Gazette de France,* 25 November, 1752, 575-576, 578.

135. Charles de Chambrun, *À l'école d'un diplomate,* 53.

Chapter 4. Constantinople

1. K. Waliszewski, *La dernière des Romanovs: Elizabeth Ire; 1741-1762* (Paris, 1902), 130-139.

2. On the general problem of Russia and Eastern Europe in the eighteenth century see: Emil Bourgeois, *Manuel historique de politique étrangère* (Paris, 1893), I, 389-453.

3. Des Alleurs died the 23rd of November, 1754. *Gazette de France,* 18 January, 1755, 25; See also: *AAE-CP-Turquie,* CXXVIII, 24.

4. "Sir Thomas Robinson to Albermarle, 15 August, 1754," L.G.W. Legg, *British Diplomatic Instructions,* VII, 47.

5. On the *secret du roi* see: D. Ozanam and M. Antoine, *Correspondance secrète du comte de Broglie avec Louis XV* (1756-1784) (Paris, 1956-61), 2 volumes; Edgar Boutaric, *Correspondance secrète inédite de Louis XV* (Paris, 1866), 2 volumes; Duc de Broglie, *Le secret du roi* (Paris, 1870), 2 volumes; Jacques de Broglie, *Le Vainqueur de Bergen et le secret du roi* (Paris, n.d.).

6. D. Ozanam and M. Antoine, *Correspondance secrète,* I, xx-xxv.

7. *Ibid.,* xxvii fn.

8. See: "Rouillé to Le Dran, 6 January, 1755," "Le Dran to Rouillé, 7 January, 1755," *AAE-CP-Turquie,* CXXVIII, 6, 16-16vo.

9. The author of the biographical article on Vergennes in Michaud's *Biographie Universelle; Ancienne et Moderne* (Paris, 1827), XLVIII, 180-181, suggested, but apparently did not completely accept, the hypothesis that Chavigny encouraged the appointment of Vergennes as minister extraordinary or plenipotentiary, in order to use the difference between Vergennes' salary and the ambassadorial one to pay off the debts left by the dead ambassador.

10. *AAE-Documents personnels,* LXVIII, 7-9; Le Baron de Besenval, *Mémoires* (Paris, 1805), II, 218-220. Besenval gives to Chavigny the credit for Vergennes' appointment.

11. Duc de Luynes, *Mémoires sur la cour de Louis XV* (Paris, 1864), XIV, 16.

12. "Rouillé to Le Dran, 13 January, 1755," *AAE-CP-Turquie,* CXXVIII, 34.

13. On the question of the alternative routes to Constantinople see "Mémoires sur le voyage du Ministre de Sa Majesté à Constantinople, 8 January, 1755," *ibid.,* CXXVIII, 7-9vo.

14. "M. Gautier to Rouillé, 21 January, 1755," *ibid.,* CXXVIII, 57-58; "Pièces justificatives du comptes de M. Gautier pour l'armement du vaisseau *L'heureux* qui a porté M. le Chevalier de Vergennes à Constantinople, *ibid.,* CXXIX, 439ff.

15. "Rouillé to Gautier, 15 January, 1755," *ibid.,* CXXVIII, 40.

16. "Vergennes to Rouillé, 21 January, 1755," *ibid.,* CXXVIII, 59-59vo.

17. For details on the gifts Vergennes took with him to Constantinople, see: "État de présents de M. le Chevalier de Vergennes pour le Grand Seigneur, le Grand Vizir, le Capitan Pacha et autres seigneurs et officiers de la Porte," *AAE-DP* - LXVIII, 16-17; *AAE-CP-Turquie,* CXXVIII, 116-128.

18. "Vergennes to Rouillé, 25 January, 1755," *ibid.,* CXXVIII, 100.

19. *Gazette de France,* 25 January, 1755, 35; "Rouillé to Peysonnel, 23 January, 1755," *AAE-CP-Turquie,* CXXVIII, 93.

20. "Rouillé to Peyrotte, 27 February,1755," *ibid.,* CXXVIII, 182.

21. "Chavigny to Rouillé, 15 February, 1755," quoted in Marsangy, *Vergennes à Constantinople,* I, 129-130.

22. "Chavigny to Rouillé, 1 March, 1755," *ibid.,* I, 130.

23. "Chavigny to Rouillé, 8 March, 1755," *ibid.;* "Tott to Rouillé, 24 March, 1755," *AAE-CP-Turquie,* CXXVIII, 226.

24. "Vergennes to Rouillé, 24 March, 1755," *ibid.,* CXXVIII, 228; "Tott to Rouillé, 24 March, 1755," *ibid.,* CXXVIII, 226.

25. Vergennes arrived at Constantinople the 23rd of May, 1755 after a voyage of 52 days. See: "Vergennes to Rouillé, 24 May, 1755," *ibid.,* CXXVIII, 358; "Gautier to Rouillé, 4 April, 1755," *ibid.,* CXXIX, 493-493vo; The Baron de Tott stated they set sail "dans les premiers d'avril, 1755," *Mémoires sur les Turcs et les Tartars* (Amsterdam, 1784), I, 1; Also: *AAE-CP-Turquie,* CXXIX, 439.

26. "Vergennes to Rouillé, 16 April, 1755," *ibid.,* CXXVIII, 274vo.

27. *Gazette de France,* 3 May, 1755, 216; "Vergennes to Rouillé, 6 April, 1755," *AAE-CP-Turquie,* CXXVIII,257.

28. "Vergennes to Rouillé, 16 April, 1755," *ibid.,* CXXVIII, 274.

29. Wenck, *Codex juris gentium recentissimi (1735-1772),* (Leipzig, 1781-95), Vol. I, 538.

30. *AAE-CP-Turquie,* CXXVIII, 18ff; Vergennes' "Instructions" are also printed in Louis Bonneville de Marsangy, *Le Chevalier de Vergennes;son ambassade à Constantinople* (Paris, 1894), I, 197-200. See also: "Points à décidés pour former l'Instruction de M. le chevalier de Vergennes, 8 January,1755," *AAE-CP-Turquie,* CXXVIII, 10-14. The difficulty of trying to comprehend the elements conditioning Turkish policy was complicated by the fact that "every Turkish minister has himself for its (Turkish policy's) first object. They study solely their own security and permanence in office." Sir James Porter, *Turkey: its History and Progress* (London, 1854), I, 270,

31. *AAE-CP-Turquie,* CXXVIII, 18vo-19.

32. *Ibid.*

33. *Ibid.,* 19.

34. A translated copy of the treaty of peace (the Treaty of Kurdan) is in J.C. Hurewitz, editor, *Diplomacy in the Near and Middle East; a Documentary Record: 1535-1914* (Princeton, 1956), I, 51-52.

35. *AAE-CP-Turquie,* CXXVIII, 19.

36. *Ibid.,* 19-19vo.

37. *Ibid.,* 19vo.

38. *Ibid.*

39. *Ibid.,* 20.

40. *Ibid.,* 20-20vo. See also: "Mémoire de M. de Vergennes sur la Porte Ottomane," L.P. Ségur, *Politique de tous les cabinets de l'Europe pendant les regnes de Louis XV et de Louis XVI* (Paris, 1801), III, 114-115.

41. Charles Joseph Mayer, *Vie publique et priveé de Charles Gravier, Comte de Vergennes* (Paris, 1789), 41.

42. Ségur, *Politique de tous les cabinets . . .,* I, 69; D.Ozanam and M. Antoine, editors, *Correspondance secrète du comte de Broglie avec Louis XV* (Paris, 1956), I, xxix.

43. "Copie de l'ordre du Roi adressé au Sr. Perrault, 20 February, 1755," *AAE-*

CP-Turquie, CXXX, 41-42.

44. "Instructions particulières du Roi pour M. de Vergennes, 22 February, 1755," *ibid.*, CXXX, 45-47vo.

45. *Ibid.*, 45-45vo.

46. "Vergennes to Louis XV, 18 January, 1756," *ibid.*, CXXX, 97; Ozanam and Antoine, editors, *Correspondance secrète,* (Paris, 1965), I, xii, xxiv-xxv.

47. Marsangy, *Vergennes á Constantinople,* I, 122-123, 367-370; Also: *AAE-CP-Turquie,* CXXVIII, 60.

48. See, for example, Marsangy, *Vergennes à Constantinople,* 122-123; Marcus Cheke, *The Cardinal de Bernis* (New York, 1959), 231-232. See also the description of the entourage of the French ambassador to Russia, L'Hôpital, on his way to his post in *Gazette d'Amsterdam et d'Utrecht,* 19 December, 1756.

49. Marsangy, *Vergennes à Constantinople,* I, 123.

50. Comte de Saint-Priest, *Mémoires* (Paris, 1929), I, 104.

51. Marsangy, *Vergennes à Constantinople,* I, 181 and "Mémoire sur la situation des affaires du feu M. le Comte des Alleurs," *AAE-CP-Turquie,* CXVIII, 512-521.

52. The phrase is Peyrotte's: *ibid.*, CXXVIII, 64; See also: "Peyrotte to Rouillé, 22 May, 1755," *ibid.*, CXXVIII, 342.

53. "Mémoire pour servir d'Instruction au Sr. de Tott allant à Constantinople avec le Chevalier de Vergennes, 21 February, 1775," *ibid.*, CXXVIII, 155-160; See also: "Tott to Rouillé, 2 June, 1775," *ibid.*, CXXVIII, 369vo.

54. Baron de Tott, *Mémoires sur les Turcs et les Tartars* (Amsterdam, 1784), I, 2-3.

55. *Ibid.*, 3-4; *Gazette de France,* 12 July, 1755, 325. In a dispatch dated 11 June, 1755, Vergennes stated he arrived at Constantinople the "22 May vers midi." "Vergennes to Rouillé, 11 June, 1755," *AAE-CP-Turquie,* CXXVIII, 385. This date is confirmed by Vergennes' colleague, Peysonnel: 'Peysonnel to Rouillé, 3 June, 1755," *ibid.*, CXXVIII, 373. Tott's statement in his *Mémoires,* I, 3-4 that they arrived on the 21st is in error.

56. *Ibid.*, I, 7-8,

57. *Ibid.*, I, 15. Marsangy, *Vergennes à Constantinople,* I, 267 fn; *Gazette de France,* 5 July, 1755, 313.

58. Foreigners were terrified by the Sultan's brutal treatment of his subjects and foreigners. On this see: Tott, *Mémoires,* I, 24, 27; Sir Harold Gibb and Harold Bowen, *Islamic Society and the West* (New York, 1950), I, pt, I, 45; Such cruel treatment of public servants extended all the way down the ranks to the *drogman.* See Sir James Porter, *Turkey: its History and Progress,* I, 298-299; "Mémoire de M. de Vergennes, sur la Porte Ottomane," Ségur, *Politique de tous les Cabinets,* III, 106.

59. Albert Flamant, "En Rèvant dans le Grand Serail," *Revue de Deux-Mondes* (1931), II, 666.

Chapter 5. Ceremony and Debts at the Court of the Sultan

1. "Vergennes to Rouillé, 25 May, 1755," *AAE-CP-Turquie,* CXXVIII, 348.

2. *Ibid., Gazette de France,* 5 July, 1755, 313.

3. H.A.R. Gibb and H. Bowen, *Islamic Society and the West,* New York, 1950 I, Pt. I, 123-124 describe the office and function of the *Re'is Efendi.*

4. "Vergennes to Rouillé, 11 June, 1755," *AAE-CP-Turquie,* CXXVIII, 389-389vo.

5. *Ibid.*, 389vo.
6. *Ibid.*, 387.
7. *Ibid.*
8. *Ibid.*, 387-388vo.
9. *Ibid.*, 389vo-390.
10. *Ibid.*, 391-392.
11. *Ibid.*, 392-394.
12. *Gazette de France,* 29 April, 1758, 201-202.
13. "Vergennes to Rouillé, 11 June, 1755," *AAE-CP-Turquie,* CXVIII, 394-394vo.
14. "Discours prononcé à l'audience du grand vizir, le 31 May, 1755," *AAE-CP-Turquie,* CXXVIII, 353-353vo.
15. "Vergennes to Rouillé, 11 June, 1755," *ibid.*, 396vo-397.
16. *Ibid.*, 397-398.
17. "Mémoire de M. de Vergennes sur la Porte Ottomane," Ségur, *Politique de tous les Cabinets,* III, 111.
18. "Peyrotte to Rouillé, 1 January, 1755," *AAE-CP-Turquie,* CXXVIII, 2vo.
19. *Ibid.*, 2vo-3.
20. "Peyrotte to Rouillé, 22 January, 1755." *ibid.*, CXXVIII, 64.
21. "Mémoire de M. de Vergennes sur la Porte Ottomane," Ségur, *Politique de tous les Cabinets,* III, 111.
22. Marsangy, *Vergennes à Constantinople,* I, 162-172; *AAE-CP-Turquie,* CXX-VIII, 398-401vo, 405-406; Albert Flamant, "En Rèvant dans le Grand Serail," *Revue des Deux-Mondes* (1931), II, 669; Tott, *Mémoires,* I, 22-25; Duc de Luynes, *Mémoires du duc de Luynes sur la cour de Louis XV* (Paris, 1864), XIV, 217-218: Vergennes' ordeal of the audience with the Sultan is similar to that experienced by the other European ambassadors at the Porte. See: Sir James Porter, *Turkey: its History and Progress,* I, 290-293. See, also, Edwin Pears' review article of Porter's book in *The English Historical Review* (1894), IX, 799-804.
23. *Gazette de France,* 26 July, 1755, 349.
24. Gibb and Bowen, *Islamic Society and the West,* I, Pt. I, 35-36.
25. Sir James Porter, *Turkey: its History and Progress,* I, 290-292.
26. "Vergennes to Rouillé, 11 June, 1755," *AAE-CP-Turquie,*CXXVIII, 399vo.
27. When Lord Winchelsia, the British ambassador to the Porte (1661-1669), failed to show what the Turkish attendants to the Sultan felt was the proper obeisance, they put their hands on his head and shoved it to the ground. Edwin Pears, "Review of Marsangy's *Le Chevalier de Vergennes, son ambassade à Constantinople," English Historical Review* (1894), IX, 799-804.
28. *AAE-CP-Turquie,* CXXVIII, 372-372vo. Vergennes' discourse is also printed in Marsangy, *Vergennes à Constantinople,* I, 169-170.
29. "Vergennes to Rouillé, 11 June, 1755," *AAE-CP-Turquie,* CXXVIII, 401.
30. *Ibid.*, 401-401vo.
31. *Ibid.*, 401vo; "Vergennes to Rouillé, 4 June, 1755," *ibid.*, CXXVIII, 375.
32. "Vergennes to Rouillé, 11 June, 1755," *ibid.*, CXXVIII, 385.
33. "Vergennes to Rouillé, 11 July, 1755," *ibid.*, CXXVIII, 508.
34. *Ibid.*
35. "Vergennes to Louis XV, 1 July, 1755," *ibid.*, CXXX, 62.
36. "Vergennes to Rouillé, 15 June, 1755," *ibid.*, CXXVIII, 411vo.
37. "Vergennes to Rouillé, 11 July, 1755," *ibid.*, CXXVIII, 508-508vo.
38. *Ibid.*

39. *Ibid.,* 510-510vo; Also: "Vergennes to Rouillé, 25 May, 1755," *ibid.,* CXXVIII, 349.

40. "Rouillé to Vergennes, 11 October, 1755," *ibid.,* CXXIX, 228-228vo.

41. *Ibid.,* 228vo-230.

42. *Ibid.,* 230-230vo.

43. *Ibid.,* 232-232vo.

44. *Ibid.,* 234.

45. Marsangy, *Vergennes à Constantinople,* I, 189fn; On the liquidation of des Alleurs' debts see: *AAE-CP-Turquie,* CXXXI, 323-327; "Rouillé to Vergennes, 23 May, 1756, *ibid.,* CXXXII, 41-43vo; "Compte de la liquidation de la succession de feu M. le Comte Desalleurs," *ibid.,* CXXXII, 128, 129vo-132; "Vergennes to Rouillé, 19 July, 1756," *ibid.,* 120-127.

46. "Vergennes to Rouillé, 17 July, 1755," *AAE-CP-Turquie,* CXXVIII, 531-531vo.

47. "Vergennes to Rouillé, 10 February, 1756, *ibid.,* CXXXI, 170 vo.

48. *Ibid.,* 170-717.

49. "Rouillé to Vergennes, 25 May, 1756," *ibid.,* CXXXII, 45-45vo.

50. "Vergennes to Rouillé, 10 July, 1755," *ibid.,* CXXVIII, 505-505vo. Inflation caused by famine was a recurring problem at Constantinople. See *Gazette de France,* 27 May, 1758, 251.

51. "Vergennes to Rouillé, 10 July, 1755," *AAE-CP-Turquie,* CXXVIII, 505.

52. The duc de Luynes said that Vergennes received 93,000 *livres* as his "appointments", but undoubtedly he was counting all of the extra "gratifications." My own figures come from *AAE-DP*-LXVIII, 7-8. The duc de Luynes also reported that Vergennes received 40,000 *livres* for his *establishment,* but the request for the *ordonnance* to cover this expense gave the figure at 34,350 *livres. AAE-DP*-LXVIII, 12; Duc de Luynes, *Mémoires,* XIV, 27.

53. *AAE-DP*-LXVIII, 9. Undoubtedly the 20,000 *écus* for gifts mentioned by Marsangy, *Vergennes à Constantinople,* I, 128, were *écus d'argent* worth about 3 *livres* each. See also: *ibid.,* I, 367-370.

54. "Vergennes to Rouillé, 10 July, 1755," *AAE-CP-Turquie,* CXXVIII, 505-505vo.

55. *Ibid.,* 506.

56. "Vergennes to Rouillé, 10 February, 1756," *ibid.,* CXXXI, 166-168.

57. On the reputation of the embassy at Constantinople as a lucrative post, see: Duc de Luynes, *Mémoires,* XIV, 13: Saint-Priest, *Mémoires,* I, 104.

58. "Vergennes to Rouillé, 10 July, 1755," *AAE-CP-Turquie,* CXXVIII, 506-506vo.

Chapter 6. 1755—Turkish Declaration to Russia

1. "Rouillé to Vergennes, 11 May, 1755," *Archives des Affaires Étrangèrs—Correspondance Politique-Turquie,* CXXVIII, 309-310. Hereafter referred to as *AAE-CP-Turquie.* See also Pierre Rain, *La diplomatie française, d'Henri IV à Vergennes* (Paris, 1945), 228-229; V.H.H. Green, *The Hanoverians;* 1714-1815 (London, 1848), 178, 190-199.

2. "Vergennes to Louis XV, 1755," *AAE-CP-Turquie,* CXXX, 62.

3. On the competence of Peyrotte see *ibid.,* CXXVIII, 35-36; CXXX, 45-47, 48-51. Peyrotte retired in 1766. See "Vergennes to Tott, 13 October, 1766," *Archives*

de la Famille Vergennes. Hereafter cited as *AFV*.

4. Sir James Porter, *Turkey; Its History and Progress* (London, 1854), I, 298-299.

5. Fonton translated several Persian novels into French, including "Aventures de Zélide et de Féraunes." He is also the author of "Essai sur la musique orientale comparée à la musique Européane."

6. *Essai sur les troubles actuel de Perse et de Georgie* (Paris, 1754); *Observations historiques et géographiques sur les peuples barbares qui ont habité les bords du Danube et du Pont-Euxin* (Paris, 1756).

7. "Rouillé to Lancey, 13 August, 1755," *AAE-CP-Turquie*, CXXX, 39; "Rouillé to Vergennes 28 October, 1755," *ibid.*, CXXXIX, 314-314vo.

8. *Archives des Affaires Étrangères - Documents Personnels* LXIX, 35-54vo. Hereafter referred to as *AAE-DP*.

9. André Michel, *Histoire de l'Art, depuis les premiers temps chrétiens jusqu'à nos jours* (Paris, 1924), VII, 2e partie, 539.

10. On Antoine Favray See: *Neptunia* (1960), 4e trimestre. 16-21; J. Watelet, *L'Orient dans lÁrt Français:* Études d'Art (Alger, 1959); A. Boppe, *Les Peintres du Bosphore au XVIIIe siècle* (S.L., 1911); Jean Houel, *Voyage Pittoresque de Sicili et de Malte* (S.L. 1787).

11. Vergennes' opinions of Favray's art are contained in his letters to the young Tott. See "Vergennes to Tott, 24 June, 1764, 11 May, 1765, 12 March, 1766," *AFV*.

12. "Vergennes to Tott, 15 May, 1767." *ibid.*

13. See, for example, "M. Lincoln to Vergennes, 16 November, 1755," *Bibliothèque Nationale, Salle des Manuscripts, fonds français, n.a.* 12276, fols. 378-379. Hereafter referred to as *BNFF*.

14. Porter, *Turkey: Its History and Progress,* I, 302-303.

15. Vergennes' correspondence with his contacts in Moldavia and to the princes of Wallachia and Moldavia, are contained in the Collection, *Bibliothèque Nationale, Salle des Manuscrits,* fonds Francais, n.a. 12276.

16. *AAE-CP-Turquie,* CXXVIII, 55-56, 104-111 vo; "Tott to Rouillé, 2 June, 1755," *ibid.*, CXXVIII, 369vo.

17. Tott, *Mémoires sur les Turcs et les Tartars* (Amsterdam, 1784), I, 1; also "Mémoire" dated 6 May, 1766, *AAE-DP,* LXVII, 10.

18. *AAE-DP,* LXVII, 12.

19. Vicq-D'Azyr, *Éloge de M. le Comte de Vergennes* (Paris, 1788), 18; on the younger Tott's activities in the Levant, see *AAE-DP,* LXVII, 1-52vo.

20. "Vergennes to Choiseul, 30 July, 1767," *AAE-CP-Turquie* CXLIV, 32vo-37; "Vergennes to Tott, 13 October, 1766," *AFV*.

21. See "Extrait" of a letter from M. d'Aubiterre to Rouillé, 22 January, 1755, *AAE-CP-Turquie,* CXXVIII, 61-61vo.

22. "Mémoire pour servir d'Instructions au Sr. de Tott allant à Constantinople avec le Chevalier de Vergennes." Read to Tott, 21 February, 1755, *ibid.*, CXXVIII, 155ff.

23. "Vergennes to Rouillé, 26 July, 1755," *ibid.*, CXXVIII, 560vo.

24. "Comte Michel Czaki to Louis XV, Rodosto, 17 August, 1755," *ibid.*, CXXIX, 40-41.

25. See letter from Bercheny, 23 August, 1755, *ibid.*, CXXIX, 122.

26. "Tott to Rouillé, 18 September, 1755," *ibid.*, CXXIX, 194-201.

27. "Vergennes to Rouillé, 20 October, 1755," *ibid.*, CXXIX, 241-242vo.

28. "Rouillé to Tott, 31 October, 1755, *ibid.*, CXXIX 346-351; "Rouillé to Tott, 25 December, 1755," *ibid.*, CXXIX, 423.

29. "Rouillé to Vergennes, 30 December, 1755," *ibid.*, CXXIX, 437-438.
30. "Rouillé to Vergennes, 11 May, 1755," *ibid.*, CXXVIII, 311.
31. R. Nesbit Bain, *The Daughter of Peter the Great* (Westminster, 1899), 172 and fn.
32. D.B. Horn, *Sir Charles Hanbury Williams and European Diplomacy (1747-1758),* (London, 1930), 181.
33. "Rouillé to Vergennes, 11 May, 1755," *AAE-CP-Turquie,* CXXVII, 311. See also: D.B. Horn, *Sir Charles Hanbury Williams,* 179; R. Nesbit Bain, *The Daughter of Peter the Great,* 175; R. Waddington, *Louis XV et le renversement des alliances* (Paris, 1896), 125.
34. Albert Vandal, *Louis XV et Elizabeth de Russie* (Paris, 1882), 262.
35. *Ibid.*, 184.
36. "Rouillé to Vergennes, 11 May,1755," *AAE-CP-Turquie,* CXXVIII, 311.
37. On French attempts to discover the details of the Anglo-Russian agreement see: L. Jay Oliva, *Misalliance: A Study of French Policy in Russia During the Seven Years' War* (New York, 1964), 12-27.
38. "Rouillé to Vergennes, 11 May, 1755," *AAE-CP-Turquie,* CXXVIII, 311; "Vergennes to Louis XV, 14 August, 1755," *ibid.*, CXXX, 64vo; Also, Albert Vandal, *Louis XV et Elizabeth de Russie,* 244-247.
39. "Instructions Particulières du roi pour le Sr. de Vergennes . . . ., 22 February, 1755," *AAE-CP-Turquie,* CXXX, 45-47; "Vergennes to Louis XV, 14 August, 1755," 18 January, 1756, *ibid.*, CXXX, 64vo. 90.
40. "Rouille to Vergennes, 11 May, 1755," *ibid.*, CXXVIII, 312.
41. *Ibid.*, 312-314.
42. *Ibid.*, 314-314vo. "Mémoire, 17 May, 1755," *ibid.*, CXXVIII, 328-329; "Marmontel's Note of 20 May, 1755," *ibid.*, CXXVIII, 333-334; and 9 June, 1755, *ibid.*, CXXVIIII, 318-388; "Memo" of 15 June, 1755, *ibid.*, CXXVIII, 402-416; Also: "Rouillé to Vergennes, 27 June, 1755," *ibid.*, CXXVIII, 487-488vo, and "Marmontel note of 4 July,1755," *ibid.*, CXXVIII, 494.
43. "Rouillé to Vergennes, 11 May, 1755," *ibid.*, CXXVIII, 314vo-315.
44. "Rouillé to Vergennes, 13 May, 1755," *ibid.*, CXXVIII, 319-319vo,
45. "Vergennes to Rouillé, 10 August, 1755," *ibid.*, CXXIX, 13-13vo.
46. "Instructions particulières du Roi pour le Sr. de Vergennes. à Versailles, le 22 February, 1755," *ibid.*, CXXX, 45.
47. *Ibid.;* "Vergennes to Louis XV, 1 July, 1755," *ibid.*, CXXX 59.
48. *Ibid.*, 58.
49. "Instructions particulières du Roi pour le Sr. de Vergennes," *ibid.*, CXXX, 45vo.
50. "Vergennes to Louis XV, 1 July, 1755," CXXX, 59-60vo.
51. *Ibid.*, fol. 63.
52 ."Vergennes to Rouillé, 17 August, 1755," *ibid.*, CXXIX, 46-49vo; "Vergennes to Louis XV, 22 October, 1755," *ibid.*, CXXX, 65-65vo.
53. "Vergennes to Rouillé, 17 August, 1755," *ibid.*, CXXIX, 50vo-53vo.
54. *Ibid.*, 54.
55. *Ibid.*, 54vo-56vo; "Vergennes to Louis XV, 1 July, 1755," *ibid.*, CXXX, 60vo.
56. "Vergennes to Rouillé, 17 August, 1755," *ibid.*, CXXIX, 56vo-58vo; "Vergennes to Louis XV, 1 July, 1755," *ibid.*, CXXX, 59-59vo.
57. "Vergennes to Rouillé, 17 August, 1755," *ibid.*, CXXIX, 59-63.
58. *Ibid.*, 66.

59. *Ibid.*, 67-69; Also, 182-182vo.

60. D.B. Horn, *Sir Charles Hanbury Williams,* 192-193; Sir James Porter, *Turkey: Its History and Progress,* I, 311.

61. On Vergennes' intelligence-gathering on Russian military activities, see: "Prince of Wallachia to Vergennes, 31 August, 1755;" "Lincoln to Vergennes, 22 September, 2 November, 16 November, 1755," *BNFF* n.a. 12276, 326-329; 339-342; 361-366; 378-379.

62. "Vergennes to Louis XV, 22 October, 1755," *AAE-CP-Turquie,* CXXX,66.

63. "Vergennes to Rouillé, 14 September, 1755," *ibid.*, CXXIX, 171-175.

64. "Vergennes to Rouillé, 18 September, 1755," *ibid.*, CXXIX, 177vo-181.

65. *Ibid.*, 184 vo.

66. "Vergennes to Rouillé, 21 October, 1755," *ibid.*, CXXIX, 245vo-246.

67. Gautier was undoubtedly the same French merchant at Marseille who secured the merchant ship Vergennes used to travel to Constantinople. See "Gautier to Rouillé, 3 January, 1755," *ibid.*, CXXVIII, 133-133vo. On Gautier, see "Rouillé to Vergennes, 22 August, 1755,"*ibid.*, CXXIX, 116.

68. "Vergennes to Rouillé, 21 October, 1755," *ibid.*, CXXIX, 246vo-247.

69. *Ibid.*, 247-247vo.

70. *Ibid.*, 248-248vo.

71. *Ibid.*, 248vo-249.

72. *Ibid.*, 250-250vo.

73. *Ibid.*, 252vo.-253.

74. *Ibid.*, 254-254vo.

75. *Ibid.*, 258; on Malszewski's relations with the French, see "Prince of Wallachia to Vergennes, 16 July, 31 August, 1755," *BNFF* n.a. 12276, 311, 327.

76. "Vergennes to Louis XV, 22 October, 1755," *AAE-CP-Turquie,* CXXX, 67vo.

77. "Vergennes to Rouillé, 21 October, 1755," *ibid.*, CXXIX, 255-262vo.

78. "Vergennes to Louis XV, 22 October, 1755," *ibid.*, CXXX, 66vo.

79. "Vergennes to Rouillé, 21 October," *ibid.*, CXXIX, 270-270vo.

80. *Ibid.*, 270vo-271vo.

81. On Rouillé's position on a French treaty with Constantinople see "Mémoire sur un traité à faire entre sa Majesté et le grand Seigneur." And, "Rouillé to Vergennes, 29 December, 1755," both in *ibid.*, CXXIX, 425-437vo.

82. "Vergennes to Rouillé, 29 October, 1755," *ibid.*, CXXIX, 162vo-265vo.

83. "Rouillé to Vergennes, 29 December, 1755," *ibid.*, CXXX, 111vo.

84. "Vergennes to Louis XV, 29 February, 1756," *ibid.*, CXXX, 111vo.

85. "Vergennes to Louis XV, 18 January, 29 February, 1756," *ibid.*, CXXX, 104-104vo; 107-107vo.

86. "Vergennes to Louis XV 28 October, 1755," *ibid.*, CXXX, 69-69vo. On the question of the cruelties of the Sultan towards his minister, see: Sir Hamilton Gibb and Harold Bowen, *Islamic Society and the West* (New York, 1950), Vol. I, Pt. I, 120-121.

87. *AAE-CP-Turquie,* XXX, 70.

88. "Vergennes to Rouillé, 22 November, 1755," *ibid.*, CXXIX, 375-381vo.

89. "Vergennes to Louis XV, 18 January, 1755," *ibid.*, CXXX, 97, 99.

90. "Vergennes to Rouillé, 29 January, 1756," *ibid.*, CXXXI, 77-90vo.

91. *Ibid.*, 90vo-93.

92. "Vergennes to Louis XV, 18 January, 1756," *ibid.*, CXXX, 100.

93. "Vergennes to Rouillé, 22 February, 1756," *ibid.*, CXXXI, 264vo-265;

"Éxtrait des lettres du Dr. Peysonnel consul au Crimée, 8 March, 1756," *ibid.*, CXXXI, 335; "Vergennes to Louis XV, 18 January, 1755," *ibid.*, CXXX, 104vo-105vo.

94. "Vergennes to Rouillé, 2 April, 1756," *ibid.*, CXXXI, 355-356.

95. "Vergennes to Rouillé, 17 August, 1755," *ibid.*, CXXIX 69vo-71; On the question of the effectiveness of money in diplomatic affairs, see also the comments of Vergennes' successor at Constantinople, the Comte de Saint-Priest, *Mémoire sur l'ambassade de France en Turquie* (Paris, 1877), 151; Also Sir Harold Nicolson, *Diplomacy* (London,1963), 61-63.

96. "Rouillé to Vergennes, 17 November, 1755," *ibid.*, CXXIX, 368-369. The promotion was announced in the *Gazette de France,* 28 February, 1756, 97. See also: *ibid.*,27 March, 1756, 145.

Chapter 7. The Diplomatic Revolution

1. Sir Richard Lodge, *Great Britain and Prussia in the 18th Century* (Oxford, 1932), l.

2. Émile Bourgeois, *Manuel historique de politique Étrangère* (Paris, 1893), I, 350.

3. Lodge, *Great Britain and Prussia,* 79.

4. André Castelot, *Queen of France* (New York, 1957), 8.

5. J.O. Lindsay, editor, *The Old Régime: 1713-1763* in *The New Cambridge Modern History* (Cambridge, 1957), VII, 441.

6. Lodge, *Great Britain and Prussia,* 80.

7. *Ibid.,* 74-106; See also Pierre Muret, *La Prépondérance anglaise* (1715-1763) (Paris, 1942), 465-520; J.O. Lindsay, editor, *op. cit.,* 440-464.

8. *Ibid.,* 448.

9. R. Waddington, *Louis XV et le renversement des alliances* (Paris, 1896), 152.

10. "The Treaty of St.Petersburg, 30 September, 1755," in D.B. Horn and Mary Ransome, editors, *English Historical Documents: 1714-1783* (London, 1957), X, 930-934; Lodge, *Great Britain and Prussia,* 82.

11. *Ibid.,* 82.

12. Horn and Ransome, *English Historical Documents,* X, 934-936.

13. C.P. Duclos, *Mémoires Secrètes sur les règnes de Louis XIV et de Louis XV* (Lausanne, 1791), II, 399.

14. Constantin de Grunwald, *Troi siècles de diplomatie* (Paris, 1945), 82.

15. R. Waddington, *Louis XV et le renversement des alliances,* 224-226.

16. *Ibid.,* 350-351.

17. "Convention de neutralité entre S.M. Très Chrétienne et S.M. 1'Imp. Reine de Hongrie et de Boheme Signé à Versailles, 1 May, 1756," Frederick August W. Wenck, *Codex juris gentium*. . .(Lipsiae, 1781-95), III, 139-141; "Traité d'amitié et d'alliance," *ibid.,* III, 141-147; "Cinq articles séparés," in Christophe G. Koch, *Recueil du Traités et actes diplomatiques* (Basle, 1802), II, 11-16.

18. Lindsay, *The Old Régime: 1713-1763,* 454.

19. "Mémoire de M. de Vergennes sur la Porte Ottomane," L.P. Ségur, *Politique de tous les cabinets de l'Europe* (Paris, 1801), III, 119.

20. *Gazette de France,* 29 May, 253.

21. "Rouillé to Vergennes, 18 February, 1756," *AAE-CP-Turquie,* CXXXI, 206vo-210vo; Also, "Rouillé to Vergennes, 3 December, 1755," *ibid.,* CXXIX, 433-434; Louis to Vergennes: "Instructions Particulière," dated 22 February, 1755,

ibid., CXXX, 111vo-112.

22. "Vergennes to Rouillé, 6 April, 1756," *ibid.*, CXXXI, 263-263vo, 259-259vo; "Vergennes to Louis XV, 5 April, 1756," *ibid.*, CXXX, 113vo.

23. "Rouillé to Vergennes, 2 May, 1756," *ibid.*, CXXXII, 2-9vo.

24. "Vergennes to Rouillé, 14 June, 1756," *ibid.*, CXXXII, 67-69.

25. Certainly Vergennes later saw the dangers to his position in the new alliances. See "Mémoire de M. de Vergennes sur la Porte Ottomane." Ségur, *Politique de tous les Cabinets,* III, 119.

26. "Vergennes to Rouillé, 14 June, 1756," *AAE-CP-Turquie,* CXXXII, 70.

27. "Rouillé to Vergennes, 1 June, 1756," *ibid.*, CXXXII, 56vo.

28. *Ibid.*, 56-61.

29. "Vergennes to Louis XV, 6 July, 1756," *ibid.*, CXXX, 118-118vo.

30. "Vergennes to Louis XV, 20 July," *ibid.*, CXXX 124-124vo; also "Vergennes to Louis XV, 6 July, 1756," *ibid.*, CXXX, 120.

31. Ségur, *Politique de tous les cabinets,* II, 12-13fn.

32. "Rouillé to Vergennes, 26 June, 1756," *AAE-CP-Turquie,* CXXXII, 77-82vo; "Rouillé to Vergennes, 17 July, 1756," *ibid.*, CXXXII, 106-106vo; "Vergennes to Rouillé, 17 August, 1756," *ibid.*, CXXXII, 188-207vo.

33. "Vergennes to Rouillé, 22 July, 1756," *ibid.*, CXXXII, 159vo. "Communiqué à la Porte le 19 July, 1756," *ibid.*, CXXXII, 144-150vo.

34. Comte de Saint-Priest, *Mémoire sur l'ambassade de France de Turquie* (Paris, 1877), 152-153.

35. "Note Tirée des anecdotes du chevalier Porter," *AAE-CP-Turquie,* CXXXII, 90-91; Duc de Broglie, *The King's Secret* (London, s.d.), II 250; "Vergennes to Rouillé, 22 July, 1756," *AAE-CP-Turquie,* CXXXII, 161.

36. "Vergennes to Rouillé, 22 July, 1756," *ibid.*, CXXXII, 158vo-159; "Vergennes to Louis XV, 20 July, 1756," *ibid.*, CXXX, 121-121vo.

37. "Vergennes to Louis XV, 20 July, 1756," *ibid.*, CXXX, 122vo.

38. "Rouillé to Vergennes, 27 June, 1756," *ibid.*, CXXXII, 83-88vo. See also the account of this *rapprochement* in L. Jay Oliva, *Misalliance: A Study of French Policy in Russia during the Seven Years' War* (New York, 1964), 30-46.

39. "Rouillé to Vergennes, 27 June, 1756," *AAE-CP-Turquie,* CXXXII, 83-84.

40. "Vergennes to Louis XV, 5 September, 1756," *ibid.*, CXXX, 137.

41. "Rouillé to Vergennes, 27 June, 1756," *ibid.*, CXXXII, 84vo.

42. "Traité d'alliance entre la Grand Bretagne et la Russie 30 September," *Recueil des Traités et actes diplomatiques,* II, 1-10.

43. "Rouillé to Vergennes, 27 June, 1756," *AAE-CP-Turquie,* CXXXII, 85-86vo: L. Jay Oliva, *Misalliance: A Study of French Policy in Russia During the Seven Years War* (New York, 1964), pp. 46-69.

44. "Vergennes to Rouillé, 18 August, 1756," *AAE-CP-Turquie,* CXXXII, 208-209vo.

45. *Ibid.*, 210-211vo.

46. *Ibid.*, 212vo.

47. "Vergennes to Louis XV, 5 September, 1756," *ibid.*, CXXX, 137-vo-138.

48. "Vergennes to Rouillé, 30 August, 1756," *ibid.*, CXXXII, 215-224; "Vergennes to Louis XV, 5 September, 1756," *ibid.*, CXXX, 142.

49. "Acte d'accession de la Russie au traité de Versailles du 1 May, 1756, entre la France et l'Autriche," George F. Martens, *Supplément au Recueil des principaux traités* (Gottinque, 1807), III, 33-36; The secret declaration dated January 11, 1757 is in *AAE-CP-Russie,* Supplement IX, 79-81.

50. K. Waliszewski, *La dernière des Romanovs: Elizabeth 1re Impératrice de Russie: 1741-1762* (Paris, 1902), 426; Oliva, *Misalliance,* 57-61.

51. "Convention entre la France, l'Impératrice Reine et la Suède sur l'exercise de la garantie de la paix de Westphalie," Koch, *Recueil des traités et actes diplomatiques,* II, 33-39.

52. Austro-Russian treaty dated January 22, 1757, Martens, *Recueils des traités et conventions conclus par la Russie avec les puissances é trangères* (St. Petersburg, 1874-1909), IX, 352ff.

53. "Traité d'Union et d'amitié défensif entre la France et l'Autriche," Koch, *Recueil des traités et actes diplomatiques,* II, 43-81.

54. Comte de Saint-Priest, *Mémoires,* 153.

55. For a detailed and scholarly discussion of the Franco-Russian *rapprochement* see L. Jay Oliva, *Misalliance: A Study of French Policy in Russia During the Seven Years' War* (New York, 1964).

Chapter 8. Trade Treaties with Porte

1. "Rouillé to Vergennes, 22 March, 1775," *AAE-CP-Turquie,* CXXVIII, 224-225.

2. "A. F. Eichel to Graf Podewils, 9 January, 1775," Friedrich des Grossen, *Politische Correspondenz* (Berlin, 1883), XI, 7-8, Also: "A. F. Eichel to Graf Podewils, 14 January, 1775," *ibid.,* XI, 14-16; "Postscriptum Secundum, 18 January, 1755," *ibid.,* XI, 21-24.

3. *AAE-CP-Turquie,* CXXVIII, 452.

4. "Rouillé to Vergennes, 9 May, 1755," *ibid.,* CXXVIII, 307-308.

5. "Instructions particulières . . . ." *ibid.,* CXXX, 45vo; "Vergennes to Louis XV, 14 August, 1755," *ibid.,* CXXX, 64.

6. "Rouillé to Vergennes, 9 May, 1755," *ibid.,* CXXVIII, 307-308.

7. "Vergennes to Louis XV, 22 October, 1755," *ibid.,* CXXX, 68; "Vergennes to Louis XV, 18 January, 1756," *ibid.,* CXXX, 106.

8. "Vergennes to Louis XV, 12 October, 1756," *ibid.,* CXXX, 155-155vo.

9. *Ibid.,* 156-156vo.

10. "Vergennes to Rouillé, 31 July, 1755," *ibid.,* CXXVIII, 570-572; "Rouillé to Vergennes, 22 December, 1755," *ibid.,* CXXIX, 420-420vo; "Vergennes to Rouillé, 14 August, 1755," *ibid.,* CXXIX, 21-23vo; "Vergennes to Louis XV, 1 July, 12 October, 12 November, 1756," *ibid.,* CXXX, 60vo; 156-156vo; 169.

11. "Rouillé to Vergennes, 22 December, 1755," *ibid.,* CXXIX, 420-420vo; "Vergennes to Louis XV, 18 January, 1756," *ibid.,* CXXX, 106.

12. *Politische Correspondenz,* XI, 176; "Vergennes to Louis XV, 1 July, 1755," *AAE-CP-Turquie,* CXXX, 58vo.

13. "Copie de la lettre du Roi de Prusse à M. l'envoyé Suède à la Porte," *ibid.,* CXXVIII, 455-460; "A.F. Eichel to Graf Podewils, 14 January, 1755," *Politische Correspondenz,* XI, 14-16; A l'envoyé de Suède de Celsing à Constantinople, 18 January, 1755," *ibid.,* XI, 24-25.

14. "Vergennes to Rouillé, 24 June, 1755," *AAE-CP-Turquie,* CXXVIII, 427-433vo.

15. "A.F. Eichel to Podewils, 14 March, 1755," *Politische Correspondenz* XI, 83-84.

16. See: "Frederick to Baron de Knyphausen, 12 August, 1755," *ibid.,* XI, 257-

258.

17. See: *ibid.*, XI, 176-178; "Vergennes to Louis XV, 1 July, 1755," *AAE-CP-Turquie*, CXXX, 62.

18. He returned to Potsdam the 4th of November, 1755, "Frederick to Celsing, 8 November, 1755," *Politische Correspondenz*, XI, 367.

19. "Vergennes to Rouillé, 24 June, 1755," *AAE-CP-Turquie*, CXXVIII, 434-435.

20. "Rouillé to Vergennes, 13 May, 1755," *ibid.*, CXXVIII, 320vo-321.

21. "Rouillé to Peysonnel, 22 December, 1755," *ibid.*, CXXIX, 421-422. "Frederick to Vergennes, 8 December, 1755," *Politische Correspondenz*, XI, 423-424.

22. "Rouillé to Vergennes, 30 December, 1755," *AAE-CP-Turquie*, CXXIX, 433-434.

23. "Vergennes to Louis XV, 29 February, 1756," *ibid.*, CXXX, 111vo-112.

24. "Frederick to Secretary Mitchell at London, 8 June, 1756," *Politische Correspondenz*, XII, 389-392; "Frederick to Vargennes, 27 June, 1756," *ibid.*, 470-471.

25. "Podewils to A.F. Eichel, 25 August, 1756," *ibid.*, XIII, 277.

26. L. Jay Oliva, *Misalliance: A Study of French Policy in Russia During the Seven Years War* (New York, 1964), 48-51, 66-67.

27. "Broglie to Louis XV, 28 February, 1759," Didier Ozanam and Michael Antoine, *Correspondance secrète du comte de Broglie avec Louis XV: 1756-1774* (Paris, 1956), I, 93.

28. The Poles did complain to the Turks, but nothing came of it. See: "Frederick to Secretary Benôit at Warsaw, 20, 25 May, 1761," *Politische Correspondenz*, XX, 405-406, 417.

29. "Vergennes to Rouillé, 24 January, 1757," *AAE-CP-Turquie*, CXXXIII, 145.

30. "Vergennes to Duc de Choiseul, 16 March, 1761," *ibid.*, CXXXVII, 125vo.

31. "Vergennes to Louis XV, 5 September, 12 October, 1756; 12 January, 23 March, 27 April, 10 June, 1757," *ibid.*, CXXX, 137vo-140, 154vo,173, 189vo, 202-202vo, 221. See also the untitled "Mémoire," fols. 204-208vo.

32. "Frederick to Rexin, 10 February, 4 April, 1758," *Politische Correspondenz*, XVI, 237-351.

33. "Frederick to Rexin, 4 April, 1758", *ibid.*, 351; Also: "Vergennes to Bernis, 15 January, 1758," *AAE-CP-Turquie*, CXXXIV, 39-40.

34. "Vergennes to Louis XV, 23 March, 1757," *ibid.*, CXXX, 191-191vo.

35. Comte Charles de Chambrun, *À l'école d'un diplomate: Vergennes* (Paris, 1944), 118-119. Frederick, of course, knew of the Turk's admiration for military prowess. See his letter to Rexin, 12 January, 1761, *Politische Correspondenz*, XX, 188. Vergennes also recognized the bad effects at Constantinople of French defeats. See: "Vergennes to duc de Choiseul, 2 April, 1761, *AAE-CP-Turquie*, CXXXVII, 133-134vo.

36. M. Cheke, *The Cardinal de Bernis* (New York, 1958), 110.

37. "Rouillé to Vergennes, 29 June, 1757," *AAE-CP-Turquie*, CXXIII, 227.

38. Cheke, *The Cardinal de Bernis*, 137.

39. *ibid.*, 21.

40. *ibid.*, 38.

41. "Vergennes to Bernis, 15 August, 1757," *AAE-CP-Turquie*, CXXXIII, 264.

42. "Vergennes to Bernis, 16 September, 1, 15, October, 1757," *ibid.*, CXXXIII, 316-316vo, 320-321, 338.

43. "Vergennes to Bernis, 30 October, 1757," *ibid.*, CXXXIII, 345; *Gazette de France*, 3 December, 1757, 609.

44. *Gazette de France*, 11 March, 5 August, 1758, 117, 369.

45. "Vergennes to Bernis, 15 January, 1758," *AAE-CP-Turquie,* CXXIV, 33-34. See also: "Vergennes to Bernis, 15 November, 1757," "Vergennes to Bernis, 15 December, 1757," "Bernis to Vergennes, 27 November, 1757," on attempts by England, Prussia and France to influence Turkish policy." *ibid.,* CXXXIII, 352-363, 407vo-408, 390-390vo.

46. "Vergennes to Louis XV, 28 May, 14 July, 1 August, 9 October, 1758," *ibid.,* CXXX, 259vo, 262, 273vo, 291vo; "Vergennes to Choiseul, 15 February, 1760," *ibid.,* CXXXVI, 411.

47. The problem of keeping the Turks neutral really boiled down to the problem of allaying Turkish suspicions of Austria and Russia. On this, see: *Gazette de France,* 18 February, 1758, 81.

48. "Vergennes to Bernis, 1 December, 1757," *AAE-CP-Turquie,* CXXXIII, 394-395vo.

49. "Bernis to Vergennes, 29 November, 1757," *ibid.,* CXXXIII, 386-388; "Vergennes to Louis XV, 12 March, 1758," *ibid.,* CXXX, 241.

50. "Bernis to Vergennes, 31 December, 1757," *ibid.,* CXXXIII, 429-429vo.

51. *Ibid.,* 429. See Bernis' pessimistic estimate of France's diplomatic and military position, also, in "Bernis to l'Hôpital, 31 December, 1757," *AAE-CP-Russie,* LIV, 436.

52. "Bernis to Choiseul, 26 August, 1758," *AAE-MD-France,* CCCCCLXXI, 189; *Gazette de France,* 11 November, 1758, 569.

53. *Gazette de France,* 2 December, 1758, 605-606.

54. Louis Dollot, "Conclaves et diplomatie française au XVIIIe siècle," *Revue d'histoire diplomatique* (1961), 132-135.

55. Paget Toynbee, *Letters of Horace Walpole* (Oxford, 1904), VIII, 44.

56. Letter dated 30 November, 1758, *AAE-CP-Turquie,* CXXXIV, 369-370vo.

57. "Vergennes to Choiseul, 2 January, 1759," *ibid.,* CXXXV, 5-5vo.

58. "Choiseul to Vergennes, 20 January, 1759," *ibid,* CXXXV, 23-24.

59. Reinhold Köser, *König Friedrich der Grossen.* (Stuttgart and Berlin, 1893-1905), II, 297-300; On Frederick's relations with the Porte during the critical period. See: *Politische Correspondenz,* Vol. XIX, XX. *passim.*

60. "Vergennes to Choiseul, 1 April, 1759," *AAE-CP-Turquie,* CXXXV, 109-111vo; "Vergennes to Louis XV, 27 March, 1759," *ibid.,* CXXX, 324.

61. "Mèmoire de M. de Vergennes sur la Porte Ottomane," L.P. Ségur, *Politique de tous les Cabinets de l'Europe pendant les règnes de Louis XV et de Louis XVI* (Paris, 1801), III, 123.

62. "Vergennes to Choiseul, 1 May, 1759," *AAE-CP-Turquie,* CXXXV, 149-150.

63. "Vergennes to Choiseul, 1 April, 1759," *ibid.,* CXXXI, 115-115. "Frederick to Comte de Finckenstein, 14 March, 1761," *Politische Correspondenz,* XX, 269.

64. Sir James Porter, *Turkey: Its History and Progress,* edited by Sir George Larpent (London, 1854), I, 288-299.

65. "Vergennes to Choiseul, 1 May, 1759," *AAE-CP-Turquie,* CXXXV, 150-150vo; "Vergennes to Louis XV, 27 March, 17 April, 1759," *ibid.,* CXXX, 324, 327-329.

66. "Choiseul to Vergennes, 11 June, 1759," *ibid.,* CXXXV, 173-173vo.

67. "Vergennes to Choiseul, 24 July, 1759," *ibid.,* CXXXV, 198-199.

68. "Mémoire du Chevalier de Vergennes a la Porte, 15 August, 1759," *ibid.,* CXXXV, 212-215.

69. "Réponse de la Porte au mémoire de M. de Vergennes, 17 August, 1759," *ibid.,* CXXXV, 216-217vo.

70. "Vergennes to Choiseul, 1 September, 1759," *ibid.*, CXXXV, 223-228.

71. "Vergennes to Choiseul, 30 September, 1759," *ibid.*, CXXXV, 239vo-242vo.

72. "Choiseul to Vergennes, 11 November, 1759," *ibid.*, CXXXV, 300.

73. "Vergennes to Choiseul, 3 April, 1761," *ibid.*, CXXXVII, 139-141; "Vergennes to Louis XV, 7 April, 1761," *AAE-CP-Suède*, Supplément, XII, 102-105vo; *Politische Correspondenz*, XX, 261-262, 399-404, 418-420, 433. The treaty was ratified the 27th of July, 1761, *AAE-CP-Turquie*, CXXXV II, 264vo-265.

74. "Frederick to Secretary Benoît at Warsaw, 20 May, 1761;" "Frederick to Comte de Finckenstein, 21 May, 4 June, 1761," *Politische Correspondenz*, XX, 405-407, 438-439; "Vergennes to Choiseul, 1 September, 1761," *AAE-CP-Turquie*, CXXXVII, 282-283vo.

75. "Vergennes to Choiseul, 1 May, 1761," *ibid.*, CXXXVII, 171vo.

76. "Vergennes to Choiseul, 3 July, 1761," *ibid.*, CXXVIII, 229-233.

77. Koser, *König Friedrich der Grosse*, II, 297. See also: "Mémoire de M. de Vergennes sur la Porte Ottomane," Ségur, *Politique de tous le cabinets*, III, 123; "Vergennes to Choiseul, 3 July, 1761, *AAE-CP-Turquie*, CXXXVII, 232-234; "Vergennes to Choiseul, 16 January, 1762," *ibid.*, CXXXVIII, 13-15; "Extrait de principaux articles du mémoire présenté au grand sultan par M. Rexin," *ibid.*, Supplément, XVI, 102-103vo. On Frederick's hopes to bring the Turks into the war on his side, see, for example: *Politische Correspondenz*, XXI, 3-5, 28-29, 42, 48-50, 54-56, 59, 60, 62, 64, 71, 96-100, 111-113, 115-120, 123-127, 144-151, 156-157, 160-161, 172, 176-177, 191, 201, 255. When Peter III became Czar of Russia and established friendly relations with Frederick, the latter denied he had ever considered bringing the Turks into the war against Russia. He encouraged them only to attack Austria, he told Peter. All the hostile maneuvers of the Tartars against Russia were not his doing, he explained, they were the work of the French ambassador, Vergennes, who wanted the Tartars to invade Russia. See: "Au Colonel Baron de Golitz à Saint Petersburg, 10 April, 1762," *ibid.*, XXI, 361.

Chapter 9. Matters of Prestige

1. "Vergennes to Choiseul, 17 November, 1760;" "Mémoire amical de son Altesse le Grand Vizir," *AAE-CP-Turquie*, CXXXVI, 252-256, 274-277.

2. "Vergennes to Choiseul, 2 July, 3 July, and enclosures," *ibid.*, CXXXVI, 138-144.

3. "Vergennes to Choiseul, 2 July, 1 October, 1760," *ibid.*, CXXXVI, 138-139, 203vo-204vo.

4. "Vergennes to Choiseul, 1 October, 1760," *ibid.*, CXXXVI, 139.

5. *Gazette de France*, 22 November, 1760," 564-565; "Vergennes to Choiseul, 16 November, 1760," *AAE-CP-Turquie*, CXXXVI, 243-243vo.

6. "Vergennes to Choiseul, 15 December, 1760," *ibid.*, CXXXVI, 294.

7. "Vergennes to Choiseul, 17 November, 1760," *ibid.*, CXXXVI, 246vo;

8. *Ibid.*, 245vo-246; Comte de Saint-Priest, *Mémoires: Règnes de Louis XV et de Louis XVI* (Paris, 1929), I, 11.

9. "Vergennes to Choiseul, 17 November, 1760," *AAE-CP-Turquie*, 136, 247vo-248.

10. *Ibid.*, 249.

11. "Vergennes to Choiseul, 26 November, 1760," *ibid.*, CXXXVI, 265vo-267vo.

12. *Ibid.*, 273.

13. "Choiseul to Vergennes, 6 January, 1761," *ibid.*, CXXXVII, 20.

14. *Ibid.*, 20 vo.

15. *Ibid.*, 20vo-21vo. Actually the Maltese gave the ship to Louis XV. See: "Vergennes to Choiseul, 14 July, 1761," *ibid.*, CXXXVII, 249vo-250.

16. "Choiseul to Vergennes, 6 January, 1761," *ibid.*, CXXXVII, 22-22vo.

17. "Réponse au mémoire de la pacte du Grand Vizir à l'ambassadeur du roi à Constantinople," *ibid.*, CXXXVII, 18-19vo.

18. *Ibid.*, CXXXVII, 82-82vo.

19. "Vergennes to Choiseul, 16 February, 1761," *ibid.*, CXXXVII, 58-74.

20. *Ibid.*, 88-88vo; Also "Vergennes to Tott, 22 April, 1768," Papiers Vergennes: Lettres autographes à Tott. *AFV*.

21. "Vergennes to Choiseul, 16 March, 1761," *AAE-CP-Turquie*, CXXXVII, 122-122vo.

22. "Choiseul to Vergennes, 19 April, 1761," *ibid.*, CXXXVII, 151.

23. "Choiseul to Vergennes, 30 May, 1761," *ibid.*, CXXXVII, 198-198vo.

24. "Choiseul to Vergennes, 13 June, 1761," *ibid.*, CXXXVII, 205-205vo.

25. *Ibid.*, 205.

26. "Mémoir du grand Vizir au très honoré ambassadeur de France," with Vergennes' dispatch of 20 May, 1761, *ibid.*, CXXXVII, 194-195. Also: "Vergennes to Duc de Choiseul, 5 February, 1761," *ibid.*, 46-47.

27. The description of the arrival is by Vergennes. Dispatches and Bulletins, dated 31 January, 1762, *ibid.*, CXXXVIII, 21-31, 36; "Note" dated 1 November, 1761, Order of Louis XV to ship at Toulon to tow Turkish vessel to Constantinople. *ibid.*, CXXXVII, 327, 337-337vo, 356. On the flying of the Turkish flag, see: "Vergennes to Choiseul, 16 November, 1761," *ibid.*, CXXXVII, 347-349vo; and "Choiseul to Vergennes, 10 January, 1762," *ibid.*, CXXXVIII, 8.

28. *Gazette de France*, 19 March, 1762, 99.

29. *Ibid.*, 2, 26 April, 1762, 115, 143.

30. "Vergennes to Choiseul, 13 March, 1762," *AAE-CP-Turquie*, CXXXVIII, 85-86.

31. "Choiseul to Vergennes, 27 April, 1762," *ibid.*, CXXXVIII, 153-153vo.

32. "Vergennes to Comte de Choiseul, 1 June, 1762," *ibid.*, CXXXVIII, 190-191.

33. "Extrait des lettres de M. de Vergennes, 7 March, 1759," *ibid.*, CXXXV, 78-82; "Vergennes to Choiseul, 7 March, 1759," *ibid.*, CXXXV, 54-59; "Conclusion de la Requête presenté par les Grecs en 1757," *ibid.*, CXXXV, 60-60vo; "Choiseul to Vergennes, 14 December, 1759," *ibid.*, CXXXV, 282-282vo; "Traduction du Nichan ou Brevet expédié avec Khatt cherif sous le Règne de Sultan Osman III;" *ibid.*, CXXXV, 61-64; "Traduction d'un Sermon avec Khatt cherif adressé au Kady de Jerusalem . . .," *ibid.*, CXXXV, 65-68; "Notes sur le Commandement accordé aux Grecs pour diverses possessions de la Terre Sainte," *ibid.*, CXXXV, 70-75; "Traduction d'un Sermon addressé au Kady de Jerusalem, et à Mounis Effendy des Khodjaghian . . .," *ibid.*, CXXXV, 76-77vo.

34. "Au roi," *ibid.*, CXXXVI, 11-11vo.

35. "Vergennes to Choiseul, 13 February, 1761," *ibid.*, CXXXVII, 48-54vo.

36. *Ibid.*, 50.

37. "Vergennes to de la Ville, 14 February, 1761," *ibid.*, CXXXVII, 53-55.

38. "Choiseul to Vergennes, 21 March, 1761," *ibid.*, CXXXVII, 129vo.

39. "Vergennes to Choiseul, 1 May, 1761," *ibid.*, CXXXVII, 173vo-174.

40. "Vergennes to Comte de Choiseul, 3 December, 1761," *ibid.*, CXXXVII, 365-369.

41. *Ibid.*, 366.
42. *Ibid.*, 366vo-367.
43. *Ibid.*
44. *Ibid.*, 370-373; also 367-368.
45. *Ibid.*, 367vo.
46. *Ibid.*, 368vo.
47. "Vergennes to Comte de Choiseul, 15 December, 1761," *ibid.*, CXXXVII, 374-376vo.
48. *Ibid.*, 377.
49. *Ibid.*, 377-377vo.
50. "The Comte de Choiseul to Vergennes, 24 January," *ibid.*, CXXXVIII, 20.

Chapter 10. 1764—The Election of the King of Poland

1. J.O. Lindsay, editor, *The New Cambridge Modern History* (Cambridge, 1957), VII, "The Old Régime: 1713-1763," 467, 471, 473-474, 477.
2. Vergennes was notified of Elizabeth's death in a dispatch dated 14 January, 1762, *AAE-CP-Turquie,* CXXXVIII, 42.
3. L. Hauser, "Zur Geschichte Friedrichs II und Peter III," *Forschungen zur deutschen Geschichte* (Munich, 1864), IV, 3, 6. Also: "Comte de Choiseul to Vergennes, 21 March, 1762," *AAE-CP-Turquie,* CXXXVIII, 111vo.
4. "Traité paix entre les cours de Prusse et Russie, 3 May, 1762," Wenck, *Codex Juris Gentium* . . .III, 299ff. See also: Frederick's "Instructions" to Baron von Goltz, his envoy to St. Petersburg, in Kurt Treusch von Buttlar and Otto Herrmann, editors, *Politische Correspondenz Friedrich's der Grossen* (Berlin, 1894), XXI, 234-236; "Frederick to Prince Henri, 20 May, 1762", "Frederick to L'Empéreur de Russie, 21 May, 1762," "Frederick to Baron de Goltz, 21 May, 1762," *ibid.*, XXI, 448, 451, 455; Hauser, *op. cit.*, IV, 8.
5. "Frederick to Baron de Goltz, 1 May, 1762," "Frederick to Peter III, 1 May, 1762," *Politische Correspondenz,* XXI, 407-409, 409-413.
6. Georg F. Martens, *Recueil des principaux traités d'alliance de paix, de trève . . .etc.,conclu par les puissances de l'Europe* (Göttingen, 1791), I, 12-14.
7. "Frederick to Baron de Knyphausen, 25 May, 1762;" "Frederick to Prince Henri, 27 May, 1762," *Politische Correspondenz,* XXI, 469-470.
8. "Frederick to Baron de Goltz, 23 March, 1762," *ibid.*, XXI, 313; Peter III's and Frederick's peace was described by one observer as "more like a declaration of love than one of alliance between two sovereigns." Duc de Broglie, editor, *The King's Secret: Being the Secret Correspondence of Louis XV with his Diplomatic Agents* (New York, s.d.) 9.
9. "Frederick to Prince Henri, 20 May, 1762;" Also: "Frederick to Peter III, 23 March, 1762," *Politische Correspondenz,* XXI, 448, 314.
10. "Vergennes to Comte de Choiseul, 16 April, 1762," *AAE-CP-Turquie,* CXXXVIII, 142vo-143.
11. The Comte de Broglie, the chief of Louis XV's secret diplomacy did indeed charge Vergennes with the task of inciting the Turks to war through two of his agents, Saint-Foy and La Vergne. See: "D.Ozanam and M. Antoine, *Correspondance secrète du Comte de Broglie avec Louis XV* (Paris, 1956), I, Liv fn
12. "Comte de Choiseul to Vergennes, 30 March, 1762," *AAE-CP-Turquie,* CXXXVIII, 115-120.

13. "Vergennes to Comte de Choiseul, 16 April, 30 April, 14 May, 1762;" "Comte de Choiseul to Vergennes, 27 April, 1762," *ibid.*, CXXXVIII, 146vo-147, 157-164, 166-167vo, 153vo-155vo Also: folios. 178-179.

14. "Mémoire envoyé la Porte Ottomane le 28 juin, 1762," *ibid.*, CXXXVIII, 225-229vo. See also the "Mémoires" dated 7 July, and 10 July, 1762, *ibid.*, CXXXVIII, 256-259, 266-269vo.

15. "Vergennes to Comte de Choiseul, 1 July, 1762." *ibid.*, CXXXVIII, 230.

16. The Sultan's daughter died the second of July, 1762. *Gazette de France,* 9 August, 1762, 285.

17. "Note remise à la Porte, 10 July, 1762," *AAE-CP-Turquie,* CXXXVIII, 266-269vo.

18. "Vergennes to Comte de Choiseul, 10 July, 1762," *ibid.*, CXXXVIII, 263.

19. Reinhold Köser, *König Friedrich der Grosse* (Stuttgart and Berlin, 1893-1905), II, 314.

20. "Vergennes to Comte de Choiseul, 10 July, 16 July, 1762," *AAE-CP-Turquie,* CXXXVIII, 264-264vo, 276-278.

21. *Gazette de France,* "Supplément," 2 August, 1762.

22. Le comte D'Angeberg [pseudonym of J. L. Chodzko], editor, *Recueil des traités, conventions et actes diplomatiques concernant la Pologne, 1762-1862* (Paris, 1862), 1-2; "Frederick to Catherine II, 18 July, 1762," "Catherine to Frederick, 24 July, 1762," *Russkoe istorecheskoe obshchesto Sbornik* (St. Petersburg, 1877), XX, 151-152. Hereafter referred to as: *Sbornik.* See also: K. Rahbek Schmidt, "Wie is Panins Plan zu enien Nordischen System enstaden?" *Zeitschuft fur Slawistk* (Berlin, 1957), II, No.3, 414-415.

23. "Catherine to Frederick II, 17 November, 1762," *Sbornik,* XX, 152-155; "Unterredungen des Königs mit dem Gross Britannischer Gesandten Mitchell, 1, 2, August, 1762," *Politische Correspondenz,* XXII, 101-102.

24. "Frederick to Etatminister Schlabrendorff, 19 July, 1762," "Frederick to General Herzog von Braunschweig-Bevern, 19 July, 1762," "Frederick to Comte de Finckerstein, 20 July, 1762," *Politische Correspondenz,* XXII, 48, 49, 51.

25. "The Comte de Choiseul to Vergennes, 31 July, 1762," *AAE-CP-Turquie,* CXXXVIII, 290-291.

26. "Vergennes to Comte de Choiseul, 16 August, 1762," *ibid.*, CXXXVIII, 310-310vo.

27. "Vergennes to Comte de Choiseul, 30 August, 1762," *ibid.*, CXXXVIII, 331-340vo.

28. *Ibid.*

29. "Comte de Choiseul to Vergennes, 19 September, 1762," *ibid.*, CXXXVIII, 362.

30. "Vergennes to Comte de Choiseul, 21 October, 1762," *ibid.*, CXXXVIII, 395-395vo.

31. "Comte de Choiseul to Vergennes, 6 November, 1762," *ibid.*, CXXXVIII, 403-404.

32. *Ibid.*, 404.

33. "Vergennes to Choiseul-Praslin, 2 January, 1763," *Sbornik,* XX, 1722.

34. "Catherine to Frederick, 27 September, (o.s.), 1763," *Sbornik,* XX, 1722.

35. "Traité d'alliance entre l'Impératricede toutes les Russies et le roi de Prusse à Petersburg, 11 April, 1764," Georg F. Martens, *Recueil des Traites,* etc., I, 89-94; "Catherine to Frederick, 6 April, 1764," "Frederick to Catherine, 5, 12, May, 1764," *Sbornik,* XX, 200, 202-203; Louis XV knew of the secret articles of this treaty. See:

"Broglie to Louis XV, 25 May, 1764," D. Ozanam and M. Antoine, *Correspondance secrète,* I, 235-239.

For general background to this important treaty and the Polish election, see also: *Sbornik,* Volumes XII, XX, XXII, XLVIII, LI, CIX; *Politische Correspondenz,* XXII, 210ff, 328ff, 371-372, 417-418, 428, 503-504, 517, 519-520, 524-525, XXIII, 4-5, 5-6; Herbert H. Kaplan, *The First Partition of Poland* (New York, 1962), 24-25.

36. "Frederick to Catherine, 7 November, 1763," *Sbornik,* XX, 184.

37. "Catherine to Frederick, 6 October, 1763," *Sbornik,* XX, 177, See also: *ibid.,* XLVI, 11ff, 89ff, 505; XLVIII, 298-313, 557, 560, 568-569; K.R. Schmidt, "Problems Connected with the Last Polish Royal Election," *Scando-Slavica* (1956), II, 134-148.

38. "Frederick to Prince Henri, 9 October, 1763," Friedrich II, *Oeuvres de Frédéric le Grand* (Berlin, 1847-57), XXVI, 288; "Choiseul-Praslin to Vergennes, 18 September, 1763," *AAE-CP-Turquie,* CXXXIX, 221-222. Also: *ibid.,* folios, 237-240vo; "Hennin to Vergennes, 13 October, 1763," in "Correspondance de M.Hennin résident de France en Pologne avec M. le Chevalier de Vergennes ambassadeur à Constantinople. . .1763-1764," *Bibliothèque de l'"Institut,* M.S. 1233, 117.

39. Frederick really did not care who became King of Poland as long as it was not a prince of the House of Austria. See: "Frederick to Baron Von Goltz, 12 September, 1762;" "Frederick to the Empress of Russia, 15 February, 1763," *Politische Correspondenz,* XXII, 211, 525.

40. "Mémoire pour servir d'instruction au sieur marquis de Paulmy . . . allant à Varsovie en qualité d'ambassadeur de S.M. près le roi et le Republique de Pologne, 7 April, 1760," Louis Farges, *Recueil des instructions donneés aux ambassadeurs et ministres de France depuis les traités de Westphalie jusqu'à la revolution française* (Paris, 1888), "Pologne," V, 216-229; Herbert H. Kaplan, *The First Partition of Poland* (New York,1962), pp. 1-46; L. Jay Oliva, *Misalliance, A Study of French Policy in Russia During the Seven Years' War* (New York, 1964), pp. 95-108, 155-159.

41. "Hennin to Vergennes, 20 October, 1763," "Correspondance Hennin, "Bibliothèque de l'Institut, MS 1233, 123-129.

42. D. Ozanam and M. Antoine, *Correspondance secrète du Comte de Broglie avec Louis XV* (Paris, 1956), I, xl-xli, lvi. "Hennin to Vergennes, 20 October, 1763," "Correspondance Hennin," Bibliothèque de l'Institut,MS 1233, 123-129.

43. "Hennin to Vergennes, 29 December, 1763," "Vergennes to Hennin, 1 December, 1763,"[1764?], "Hennin to Vergennes, 16 February, 1764," "Correspondance Hennin," Bibliothèque de l'Institut, MS 1233, 160-160vo, 169-169vo, 190vo-191.

44. "Broglie to Louis XV, 27 July, 1763," D. Ozanam and M. Antoine, *Correspondance secrète,* I, 173-173.

45. "Choiseul-Praslin to Vergennes, 18 October, 1763," *AAE-CP-Turquie,* CXXXIX, 237vo-238; "Louis XV to Tercier, 17 March, 1763," E.Boutaric, *Correspondance secrète inédite de Louis XV sur la politique étrangère* (Paris, 1866), I, 290; "Instructions secrète et particulière pour le Baron de Breteuil . . . allant à Petersburg en qualité de ministre plenipotentiaire . . .1 April,1760," Alfred Rambaud, editor, *Recueil des instructions données aux ambassadeurs et ministres de France depuis les traités de Westphalie jusqu'à la révolution française* (Paris, 1890), IX, "Russie," 145-146. "Hennin to Vergennes, 20 Octover, 1763," "Vergennes to Hennin, 18 November, 1763," "Vergennes to Hennin, 1 December, 1764 [63?]" in "Correspondance de M. Hennin résident de France en Pologne avec M. le chevalier de Vergennes ambassadeur à Constantinople ... 1763-1764," *Bibliothèque de*

l'Institut, MS 1233, 129, 162vo, 169.

46. On the attitude of France's allies, see Duc de Broglie, editor, *The King's Secret,* II, 216-217; England's hands-off policy is stated clearly in "Lord Halifax to the Earl of Hertford, 8 November, 1763," and "George III to Elector of Saxony, 25 October, 1763," L. G. Wickham Legg, *British Diplomatic Instructions,* 1689-1789 (London, 1934), VII, "France," 91-92.

47. "Louis XV to Tercier, 17 March, 1763, "E. Boutaric, *Correspondance secrète inédite de Louis XV sur la politique étrangère* (Paris, 1866), I, 290.

48. "Louis XV to Tercier, 19 May," *ibid.,* I, 293.

49. "Mémoire sur l'interêt qu'à la France à l'election d'un roi de Pologne," read by duc de Praslin in Council May 8, 1763. *AAE-CP-Pologne,* CCLXXV, 21-32.

50. See Choiseul's "Instructions" to Vergennes on death of King of Poland, *AAE-CP-Turquie,* CXXXIX, 237vo; "Vergennes to Hennin, 18 November, 1763," "Hennin to Vergennes, 2 June, 1763," "Correspondance Hennin," Bibliothèque de l'Institut, MS 1233, 161vo.

51. "Broglie to Louis XV, 27 July, 1763," D. Ozanam and M. Antoine, *Correspondance secrète du comte de Broglie avec Louis XV* (Paris, 1956), I, 173-174.

52. "Hennin to Vergennes, 14 November, 1763," "Correspondance Hennin," Bibliothèque de l'Institut, MS 1233, 152vo; See also: "Hennin to Vergennes, 2 June, 1763," *ibid.,* 37.

53. "Hennin to Vergennes, 26 January, 1764," *ibid.,* 186.

54. The agent was General Monet. See "Tercier to Broglie, 24 November, 1763." *AAE-CP-Pologne,* CCLXXVIII, 472-473. Also, "Duc de Choiseul-Praslin to Hennin, 20 October, 1763," *ibid.,* CCLXXVI, 67-69.

55. "Tercier to Broglie, 24 November, 1763," *ibid.,* CCLXXVIII, 471-480; "Louis XV to Tercier, 22 March, 1764," Boutaric, *Correspondance secrète,* I, 313; "Broglie to Louis XV, 14 April, 1764," D. Ozanam and M. Antoine, *Correspondance secrète,* I, 220.

56. "Déclaration du Roy au sujet de la vacance du trône de Pologne," *AAE-CP-Turquie,* CXL, 111-114vo; also: "Déclaration de S.M.T.C. à propos de l'élection future du roi de Pologne, 24 February, 1764," *AAE-CP-Pologne,* CCLXXIX, 309-312. Duc de Broglie, *Le secret du Roi; Correspondance secrète de Louis XV avec ses agents diplomatiques 1752-1774* (Paris, 1878), II, 247.

57. "Choisèul-Praslin to Vergennes, 18 October, *AAE-CP-Turquie,* CXXXIX, 237-240vo.

58. On the attitude of secret diplomacy see: "Hennin to Vergennes 2 June, 1763," "Paulmy to Vergennes, 6 June, 23 July, 1763," "Vergennes to Paulmy, 3 June, 1763," Correspondance Hennin," *Bibliothèque de l'Institut,* MS 1233, 37-38vo, 40-41, 74, 52vo-53.

59. "À notre très honoré ami l'ambassadeur de France," "Vergennes to Choiseul-Praslin, 1763," *AAE-CP-Turquie,* CXXXIX, 304vo-390vo.

60. "Vergennes to Choiseul-Praslin, 2 November, 1763," *ibid.,* CXXXIX, 241-243vo.

61. "Hennin to Vergennes. 7 November, 1763," "Paulmy to Vergennes, 7 November, 1763." "Correspondance Hennin," MS 1233, 146-146vo, 147.

62. *Ibid.,* 146vo.

63. "Hennin to Vergennes 14 November, 1763," *ibid.,* 152-152vo.

64. "Choiseul-Praslin to Vergennes 15 January, 1764," *AAE-CP-Turquie,* CXL, 33-35.

65. "Duc de Choiseul-Praslin to Vergennes, 18 October, 1763," *ibid.,* CXXIX,

237vo-240vo.

66. "Choiseul-Praslin to Vergennes, 15 January, 1764," *ibid.*, CXL, 34-35.

67. "Vergennes to Choiseul-Praslin, 23 December, 1763," *ibid.*, CXXIX, 304vo-309vo; "Vergennes to Choiseul-Praslin, 2 January, 1764," *ibid.*, CXL, 8-10vo.

68. D. Ozanam and M. Antoine, *Correspondance secrète*, I, xxix.

69. "Vergennes to Choiseul-Praslin, 30 June, 1764," *AAE-CP-Turquie*, XL, 277.

70. "Choiseul-Praslin to Vergennes, 15 January, 1764," *ibid.*, XL, 33.

71. "Vergennes to Choiseul-Praslin, 2, 14 January, 1764," *ibid.*, XL, 3-5, 15vo-18vo; "Hennin to Vergennes, 14 November, 1763," "Correspondance Hennin," Bibliothèque de l'Institut, MS 1233, 152vo.

72. "Traduction de l'extrait d'une lettre écrite de Constantinople, datté du 16 January, 1764," *AAE-cp-Turquie*, XL, 36-36*vo*.

73. Ibid., XL, 37-38vo.

74. "Traduction de extrait d'une lettre écrite de Constantinople, datté du 16 January, 1764," *ibid.*, XL, 48vo.

75. On Russian activities at Constantinople see: *Sbornik*, XX, 189-192.

76. "Traduction d'une note remise par la Porte Ottoman, 16 January," *AAE-CP-Turquie*, CXL, 37-37vo; "Traduction d'une mémoire amical pour le très honorable Ambassadeur de France, *ibid.*, CXL, 38-38vo.

77. "Vergennes to Choiseul-Praslin, 31 January, 1764," *ibid.*, CXL, 48vo.

78. *Ibid.*, 47-49.

79. "Note remise à la Porte de la part de M. de Vergennes," *ibid.*, CXL, 45. Frederick II of Prussia certainly had no illusions that the Turks' policy followed that of France. See "Frederick to Catherine, 19 January, 1764," *Sbornik*, XX, 197.

80. *AAE-CP-Turquie*, CXL, 54-55.

81. *Ibid.*, 55-55vo.

82. "Vergennes to Choiseul-Praslin, 14 September, 1764," *ibid.*, CXL, 356vo.

83. "Choiseul-Praslin to Vergennes, 2 February, 1764," *ibid.*, 56-56vo.

84. "Louis XV to Tercier, 21 July, 1764," and "Louis XV to Comte Broglie, 8 January, 1768," Boutaric, *Correspondance secrète*, I, 326, 360.

85. "Broglie to Louis XV, 25 May, 1764," D. Ozanam and M. Antoine, *Correspondence secrète*, I, 237.

86. "Vergennes to Choiseul-Praslin, 14 September, 1764," *AAE-CP-Turquie*, CXL, 350-350vo; "Vergennes to Hennin, 13 September, 1764," "Correspondance Hennin," *Bibliothèque de l'Institut*, MS 1233, 305vo

87. Saint-Priest, *Mémoire sur l'ambassade de France en Turquie* (Paris, 1877), 159; Adolf Beer, *Die erste Theilung Polens* (Vienna, 1873), I, 156ff.

88. See, for example, Branicki letters to Colonel Stankiewitz, 2 July, 17 August, 1764, *AAE-CP-Turquie*, CXL, 282, 331-332vo; Also: *Gazette de France*, 12 December, 1763, 425; 2, 16 March, 27 May, 1765, 113, 137, 165.

89. "Vergennes to Choiseul, 30 September, 1764," *AAE-CP-Turquie*, CXL, 363vo-366vo.

90. "Vergennes to Choiseul-Praslin, 15 August, 30 September, 1764," *ibid.*, CXL, 322-327, 363-364; Also: "Mémoire de M. de Vergennes sur la Porte Ottomane," L.P. Ségur, *Politique de tous les cabinets de l'Europe* (Paris, 1801), III, 125.

91. *Gazette de France*, 5 November, 1764, 355.

92. "Vergennes to Choiseul-Praslin, 6 October, 1764," *AAE-CP-Turquie*, CXL, 386vo-398. The essentials of this significant conversation between Vergennes and the Reîs Efendi are printed in Bonneville de Marsangy, *Le Chevalier de Vergennes; son ambassade à Constantinople* (Paris, 1894) II, 277-286.

93. "Choiseul-Praslin to Vergennes, 6 November, 1764," *AAE-CP-Turquie,* CXL, 432-433vo.

94. *Ibid.,* 433vo-435.

95. *AAE-CP-Pologne,* CCLXXXVIII, 283-284, 379, 383, 417, 430; "Instructions à M. de Conflans . . . etc.," Louis Farges, *Recueil des Instructions,* "Pologne," V, 255-258; "Choiseul to Vergennes, 14 May, 1766," "Vergennes to Choiseul, 31 July, 1766," *AAE-CP-Turquie,* CXLII, 73-73vo 188-193.

96. "Hennin to Vergennes, 14 June, 1764," "Correspondance Hennin," *Bibliothèque de l'Institut,* MS 1233, 240.

97. "Hennin to Vergennes, 28 June, 1764," *ibid.,* 242vo.

98. "Vergennes to Hennin, 1, 20 December, 1764 [63?];" "Hennin to Vergennes, 14 November, 1763, 22 March, 1764," *ibid.,* 169, 177vo, 152vo-, 224.

99. "Vergennes to Hennin, 4 May, 1764," *ibid.,* 221vo-222.

100. "Vergennes to Hennin, 18 November, 1763," *ibid.,* 161vo.

101. "Vergennes to Hennin, 13 September, 1764," *ibid.,* 307.

Chapter 11. War

1. "Choiseul to Vergennes, 21 April, 1766," *AAE-CP-Turquie,* CXLII, 82-84

2. *Ibid.,* 82; England's policy and the Russo-Turkish war is discussed in : M.S. Anderson, "Great Britain and the Russo-Turkish War of 1768-74," *English Historical Review,* LXIX, 47.

3. "Choiseul to Vergennes, 21 April, 1766," *AAE-CP-Turquie,* CXLII, 82vo, 84, 83. (*Sic:* the folios are misnumbered). Choiseul's policies and his role as "Mustapha's prompter" are discussed at length in Albert Sorel's *The Eastern Question in the Eighteenth Century* (London, 1898).

4. "Vergennes to Choiseul, 28 May, 1766," *AAE-CP-Turquie,* CXLII, 86-101vo.

5. *Ibid.,* 88-93vo.

6. *Ibid.,* 95-95vo.

7. *Ibid.,* 96-96vo.

8. *Ibid.,* 96vo -97vo.

9. *Ibid.,* 99.

10. *Ibid.,* 100-100vo.

11. "Choiseul to Vergennes, 19 June, 1766," *ibid.,* CXLII, 128-128vo.

12. *Ibid.,* 129-130vo.

13. *Ibid.,* 132vo

14. *Gazette de France,* 4 July, 1766. 213-214; "Relation du tremblement de terre arrivé à Constantinople," *AAE-CP-Turquie,* CXLII, 104-105vo.

15. "Vergennes to Choiseul, 14 July, 1766," *ibid.,* CXLII, 168vo.

16. *Ibid.,* 165-187.

17. "Vergennes to Louis XV, 18 February, 1767," *ibid.,* Supplément XVIII, 4-7vo.

18. "Vergennes to Louis XV, 21 April, 1767," *ibid.,* Supplément XVIII, 9-9vo. Also: "Vergennes to Louis XV, 8 July, 1767," *ibid.,* Supplément XVIII, 16-18vo.

19. "Vergennes to Broglie, 21 April, 1767," *ibid.,* Supplément XVIII, 10-10vo.

20. "Louis XV to Vergennes, 23 April, 1767," *ibid.,* XVIII, 11-11vo.

21. "Vergennes to Louis XV, 20 August, 1767," *ibid.,* Supplément XVIII, 19-19vo. Also: "Vergennes to Louis XV, 2 December, 23 January, 1767, 1768," *ibid.,* XVIII, 22vo -23, 91-91vo.

22. "Extraits des lettres de M. de Vergennes et du Sr Fort, Vice Consul d'Alex-

andria concernant l'arrêt du Sr Roboli, premier Drogman du Consulat." CXLV, 45-49vo.

23. "Vergennes to Choiseul-Praslin, 14 December, 1767," *ibid.*, CXLIV, 264.

24. "Choiseul-Praslin to duc de Choiseul, 13 February, 1768," *ibid.*, CXLV, 38-40; "Choiseul to Vergennes, 8 February, 1768," *ibid.*, CXLV, 50. Also: "Choiseul-Praslin to Choiseul, 15 February, 1768," *ibid.*, CXLV, 60-60vo.

25. "Vergennes to Choiseul, 29 March, 1768," *ibid.*, CXLV, 105-110; "Vergennes to Choiseul, 14 April, 1768," *ibid.*, CXLV, 127-128.

26. "Vergennes to Choiseul, 15 April, 1768," *ibid.*, CXLV, 129.

27. "Choiseul to Vergennes, 13 October, 1766," *ibid.*, CXLIII, 302.

28. "Choiseul to Vergennes, 30 April, 1767," *ibid.*, CXLIII, 156-156vo.

29. "Vergennes to Choiseul, 14 July, 1767," *ibid.*, CXLIV, 4-6.

30. "Choiseul to Vergennes, 25 April, 1768," *ibid.*, CXLV, 135. Also: "Vergennes to Tott, 29 May, 1768," Papiers Vergennes, Lettres autographes à Tott, 1761-1775, *AFV*. Vergennes' letter of recall was dated 25 April, 1768. See: Papiers Vergennes, Constantinople, Correspondance et Documents, *AFV*.

31. Saint-Priest's nomination is dated 22 April, 1768 and is in *AAE-CP-Turquie,* CXLV, 132.

32. "Vergennes' response to Choiseul's letter of recall is dated 31 May, 1768," *ibid.*, CXLV, 187-188vo.

33. Herbert H. Kaplan, *The First Partition of Poland* (New York, 1962), 91-94.

34. *Ibid.*

35. The names and activities of some of these agents can be found in John Francis Cough, translator and editor, *The Private Letters of Baron de Viomenil on Polish Affairs* (Jersey City, 1936), *Passim*.

36. "Lettre d'un agent secrèt à Vienne, January, 1768," *AAE-CP-Turquie,* Suplément, XVIII, 157-159; See also other letters from the same agent, *ibid.*, 97-98vo, 99-100vo, 101-106vo, 148-149vo, 151-152vo, 155-156, 160-161vo.

37. Kaplan, *The First Partition of Poland,* 99-100.

38. *Gazette de France,* 12 September, 1768, 301.

39. *AAE-CP-Turquie,* Supplément, XVIII, 157-159; Also: "Vergennes to Louis XV, 8 October, 1768," *ibid.*, Supplément XVIII, 153-154.

40. "Mémoire de M. de Vergennes sur la Porte Ottomane," L.P. Ségur, *Politique de tous les Cabinets de l'Europe pendant les règnes de Louis XV et de Louis XVI* (Paris, 1801), III, 137; "Rehd to Frederick, 2 November, 1768," Frederick II, *Politische Correspondenz Friedrich des Grossen* (Berlin, 1879-1939), XXVII, 419-420; "Catherine II to Frederick II, 14 November, 1768," *Russkoe istorecheskoe obshchesto Sbornik* (St. Petersburg, 1877), XX, 243. Hereafter referred to as *Sbornik; Gazette de France* 7, 14 November, 1768, "Supplément," 19 December, 1768, 365, 373,; 417-418.

41. "Choiseul to Vergennes and Saint-Priest, 14 November, 1768," *AAE-CP-Turquie,* CXLVII, 32vo.

42. "Saint-Priest to Vergennes, 17 November, 1772," Papiers Vergennes: Constantinople et Stockholm *AFV;* Saint-Priest, *Mémoires,* I, 136-137.

43. Émile Bourgeois, *Manuel historique de politique étrangère* (Paris, 1878), I, 434; See also: Frederick II to Catherine II, 26 July, 1769," "Catherine II to Frederick II, 13 October, 1769," *Sbornik,* XX, 265, 269; Saint-Priest, *Mémoires* (Paris, 1929), I, 130, 133, 139.

44. Kaplan, *The First Partition of Poland,* 115; "Frederick II to Rehd, 8 February, 1 and 12 March, 1769," *Politische Correspondenz,* XXVII, 97, 152, 176.

45. Kaplan, *The First Partition of Poland,* 119ff.

46. Frederick never told Catherine he feared an upset of the balance of power. He told her only that Vienna feared it. See his "Mémoire, 4 January, 1771," *Sbornik,* XX, 290-295.

47. "The Treaty of Peace (Kucuk Kainarji): Russia and the Ottoman Empire; 10/21 July, 1774," J.C. Hurewitz, *Diplomacy in the Near and Middle East* (New York, 1956), I, 54-61.

48. Charles Joseph Mayer, *La vie privée et publique de Charles Gravier de Vergennes* (Paris, 1789), 42.

49. Frederick II, "Considérations sur l'état politique de l'Europe," *Die Politischen testamenten Friedrichs des Grossen* (Berlin, 1920); "Frederick II to Catherine II, 15 December, 1769," *Sbornik,* XX, 248-250.

50. Both Catherine and Frederick held Choiseul responsible for the Turkish war. See their correspondance. *Sbornik,* XX, 251, 259, 263, 266.

51. Saint-Priest, *Mémoires,* II, 106.

52. Pierre Rain, *La diplomatie française d'Henri IV à Vergennes* (Paris, 1945), 277.

53. See the comments of Louis Philippe de Ségur who argued that France had accelerated the ruin of the Turks by encouraging them to war. *Politique de tous les cabinets,* II, 154.

54. *Ibid.*

55. "Mémoire de M. de Vergennes sur la Porte Ottomane," *ibid.,* III, 140.

56. "Prince Selim to Vergennes; translation received by Vergennes, 3 December, 1786," Printed in Louis XVI et le Sultan Selim III," *Revue d'histoire diplomatique* (Paris, 1912), XXVI, 526-529.

57. "Louis XVI to Prince Selim, 23 May, 1787," *ibid.,* 532.

Chapter 12. Recall

1. "Vergennes to Choiseul, 31 May, 1768," *AAE-CP-Turquie,* CXLV, 189-190vo; also folio 203; "Vergennes to Tott, 29 May, 1768," Papiers Vergennes, Lettres Autographes à Tott, 1761-1775, *AFV.* Actually, Vergennes' replacement came by the Continental route. See: Saint-Priest, *Mémoires,* I, 114-119; *Gazette de France,* 26 September, 30 December, 1768, 318, 427.

2. "Vergennes to Choiseul, 31 May, 1768," *AAE-CP-Turquie,* CXLV, 189vo-190.

3. "Contrat de mariage de Charles Gravier de Vergennes et d'Anne Vivier," *Archives de Seine-et-Oise,* Versailles, E. 1097.

4. *Ibid.*

5. *Ibid.*

6. *Ibid.*

7. "M. de Lancey to M. Tercier, 8 March, 1756," Printed in Bonneville de Marsangy, *Le Chevalier de Vergennes; son ambassade à Constantinople* (Paris, 1894) I, 192-193fn.

Vergennes' reputation with the ladies seems to have spread far enough so that two historian-biographers of Mme. d'Épinay have found it entirely plausible that Vergennes was the mysterious "Chevalier de V . . ." with whom Madame d'Épinay's sister-in-law, Madame de Jully was so passionately in love that is, after her love for her husband *"adoré"* and the *"toujours Amoureux"* singer, Jelyotte, had failed to satisfy her. The romance, as spun by Madame d'Épinay's biographers, is so sentimental and touching that only a misanthrope would question it. But the facts have a way of souring the romance. The only time Madame de Jully could possibly have loved someone other than her husband or her singer (that is to say, the only time when she was not either just married, pregnant, or dying from smallpox), Vergennes was in Germany on a mission. The day she died (10 December 1752) he was indeed in France, but, according to Madame d'Epinay, on that sad day Madame Jully's lover was at Constantinople. Madame Louis Florence Pétronille Tardieu d'Esclavelles d'Épinay, *Mémoires et Correspondance* (Paris, 1818), II, 915; Clara Adèle Luce Herpin and Gaston Mangras, *La jeunesse de Madame d'Épinay* (Paris, 1882) 396ff.

8. "fait au Palais de France à Pera de Constantinople, le 22 janvier, mil sept cent soixante," Papiers Vergennes: certificats de mariages, 1760-1767. *AFV*.

9. "Contrat de mariage de Charles Gravier de Vergennes et d'Anne Viviers," *Archives de Seine-et-Oise,* Versailles, E. 1097; See also: the birth certificate of Anne Viviers dated 28 January, 1730: "Extractum e Registris Capella Regia Gallicae et Porschialis Ste Ludovici Constantinopleos;" "Pardevant nous notaires á St. Germain enlaye soussigné présence les témoins cy après nommés et aussi soussignés, dated 6 December, 1792. *AFV*.

10. Marsangy, *Vergennes à Constantinople,* II, 359.

11. "Déclaration de M. de Viviers," *AAE-DP*-LXVIII, 43. See also: "Brevet d'assurances de deux pensions . . .etc.," *AAE-DP*-LXVIII, 45; "Dossier Personnel," Archives Nationales, F4 19655.

12. Paul Dimoff, *La vie et l'oeuvre d'André Chenier, jusqu'à la Révolution française 1769-1790* (Paris, 1936), I, 28.

13. "Vergennes to M. de Tott, 3 September, 1767," Papiers Vergennes: Lettres autographes à Tott, *AFV*.

14. "Choiseul to Vergennes, 3 May, 1767," Papiers Vergennes, Correspondance politique et particulières, ministres de Louis XV, *AFV*.

15. "Vergennes to Choiseul, 14 March, 1767," *AAE-CP-Turquie,* CXLIII, 78-93vo.

16. "Choiseul to Vergennes, 3 May, 1767," Papiers Vergennes, Correspondance politique et particulières, ministres de Louis XV, *AFV*.

17. "Vergennes to Choiseul, 30 June, 1768," *AAE-CP-Turquie,* CXLV, 209vo-210; "Vergennes to Tott, 17 July, 1768," Papiers Vergennes, Lettres autographes à Tott, 1761-1775", *AFV*.

18. S.R. Nicolas de Chamfort, *Maximes, pensées, anecdotes, charactères et dialogues* (Bruxelles, 1857), 187.

19. "Louis XV to Vergennes, 26 May, 1768," printed in Marsangy, *Vergennes à Constantinople,* II, 367; Also: "Louis XV to Vergennes, 31 July, 1768," Papiers Vergennes, Constantinople, Correspondance et documents, *AFV*.

20. "Louis XV to Vergennes, 26 May, 1768," Marsangy, *Vergennes à Constantinople* II, 367.

21. *Ibid.,* Also: "Saint-Priest, *Mémoires,*" I, 61, 104.

22. My interpretation agrees with that of Vergennes' contemporaries, Vicq-d'Azyr, *Éloge de Vergennes* (Paris, 1788), 23; Jean-Louis Soulavie, *Mémoires historique et politique du règne de Louis XVI,* (Paris, 1801), 2; Saint-Priest, *Mémoires,* I, 121, 141; Also see: Frederick Bulau, *Personnages Énigmatiques: Histoires Mystérieuses* (Paris, 1861), 281fn.

23. "Vergennes to Comte de Broglie, 19 July, 1768," *AAE-CP-Turquie,* Supplément XVIII, 142; See also: "Vergennes to Comte de Broglie, 26 November, 1786, *ibid.,* 169.

24. "Vergennes to Louis XVI, 23 February, 1776," Correspondance de M. le

Comte de Vergennes: 1774-1787, Archives Nationales, K164.

Chapter 13. To Stockholm

1. "Vergennes to Tott, 29 May, 1768," Papiers Vergennes: Lettres autographes à Tott, 1761-1775; "Vergennes to Duc de Praslin, 30 January, 1769," Papiers Vergennes, Correspondance Politique et particulière; ministres de Louis XV. *Archives de la famille Vergennes*. Hereafter cited as *AFV*.

2. "Vergennes to Tott, 17 July, 1768," Papiers Vergennes: Lettres autographes à Tott, 1761-1775, 1761-1775. *AFV*.

3. "Vergennes to Tott, 9 September, 1771." *ibid.*,

4. *Gazette de France,* 24 February, 1769, 65; Also: *ibid.*, 28 November, 1768, 389; Saint-Priest, *Mémoires sur l'ambassade de France en Turquie* (Paris, 1877), 268.

5. "Choiseul to Vergennes, 29 May, 1769;" Vergennes to Choiseul, 31 May, 1769," Papiers Vergennes, Correspondance politique et particulière; ministres de Louis XV. *AFV*. Also: "Gaudin to Vergennes, 29 May, 1769," Papiers Vergennes: Constantinople; correspondance et documents. *AFV*.

6. Bonneville de Marsangy, *Le comte de Vergennes; son ambassade en Suède 1771-1775* (Paris, 1898), 49.

7. Charles Joseph Mayer, *Vie publique et privée de Charles Gravier, Comte de Vergennes* (Paris, 1789), 69.

8. "Vergennes to Constantin, 1 June, 1769," Lettres autographes: Vergennes à Constantin, *AFV*.

9. "Vergennes to Constantin, 5 December, 1769," *ibid.*

10. *Ibid.*

11. "Vergennes to Constantin, 24 December, 1769," *ibid.*

12. "Vergennes to Constantin, 10 December, 1770," *ibid.*

13. *Ibid.*

14. "Vergennes to Constantin, 7 January, 1770," *ibid.*

15. "Vergennes to Constantin, 2 January, 1771," *ibid.*

16. See, for example, Vergennes' letters to Constantin, dated 25 October, 10 December, 1770, and 2 January, 24 April, 1771, *ibid.*

17. "Vergennes to Louis XV 1768," *AAE-CP-Turquie,* Supplément, XVIII, 138.

18. "Vergennes to Choiseul, 8 February, 1770," *AAE-DP-* LXVIII, 24-24vo.

19. "Choiseul to Vergennes, 15 February, 1770," *ibid.*, LXVIII, 25; This letter and the above cited are also in: Papiers Vergennes, Correspondance politique et particulière; ministres de Louis XV, *AFV*. See also: "Vergennes to Choiseul, 8 March, 1770," *ibid.*

20. "Vergennes to Choiseul, 4 May, 1770" Documents originaux, autographes, Bibliothèque de Versailles; "Duc de Praslin to Vergennes, 9 April, 21 May, 1770;" "Vergennes to Praslin, 17 April, 4 May, 1770," Papiers Vergennes: Correspondance politique et particulière; ministres de Louis XV. *AFV*.

21. See, for example, "Vergennes to Duc de Praslin, 30 January, 1769;" Duc de Praslin to Vergennes, 3 April, 10 July, 1769;" "Vergennes to Choiseul," sans date, and "Choiseul to Vergennes, 16 October, 1769." *ibid.*

22. "Comte de Broglie to Louis XV, 10 January, 26 January, 2 February, 16 February, 1770." D. Ozanam and M. Antoine, *Correspondance secrète du comte de Broglie avec Louis XV* (Paris, 1961) II, 208-212; 214-215.

23. "Vergennes to Tott, 11 May, 28 June, 1764," Papiers Vergennes: Lettres

autographes à Tott, 1761-1767, *AFV*.

24. "Procès-Verbal de l'état du château de Toulongeon fait par Claude Philippe Delaloge de Broindon, Conseillier au Parlement de Dijon ... etc." dated 26 May, 1757. *AFV*.

25. "Procès-Verbal de l'état du château de Toulongeon pour l'érection de la seigneurie du dit en comte," dated 21 May, 1765, *AFV*.

26. Marsangy, *Vergennes en Suède*, 50.

27. *Ibid*.

28. My description of the château and surrounding gardens is drawn from the two letters patent raising the property to a comté, dated 26 May, 1757 and 21 May, 1765, *op. cit., AFV*.

29. A. Geffroy, *Gustave III et la cour de France* (Paris, 1867), I, 9-13; Marsangy, *Vergennes en Suède*, 66-67.

30. A.W. Ward, G.W. Prothero, and Stanley Leathes, *The Cambridge Modern History: The Eighteenth Century* (New York, 1934), VI, 758-759.

31. A. Geffroy, *op. cit.*, I, 13.

32. James Frederick Chance, editor, *British Diplomatic Instructions 1689-1789: Sweden, 1727-1789* (London, 1928), V, xii-xiii.

33. *Ibid.*, V, xiv.

34. A.W. Ward, G.W. Prothero, and Stanley Leathes, *op. cit.*, VI, 765. A. Geffroy, *op. cit.*, I, 20-21.

35. Quoted in A.W. Ward, G.W. Prothero and Stanley Leathes, *op. cit.*, VI, 762-763.

36. A. Geffroy, *op. cit.*, I, 97, 99-100.

37. *Ibid.*, I, 76, 94-96.

38. "Vergennes to Aiguillon, 23 March, 1772," *AAE-CP-Suède*, Vol. 261, fol. 98.

39. Posselt, *Histoire de Gustave III*, trans. by J-L M. (Genève, 1807). Quoted in Marsangy, *Vergennes en Suède*, 19; On the peculiar physiognomy of Gustavus' head, see also Marquis de Bouillé *Mémoires sur la Révolution Française* (Paris, 1821), I, 339.

40. L. Léouzon, le duc de, *Gustave III; roi de Suède*, 1746-1792 (Paris, 1861), 25; A. Geffroy, *op.cit. France* (Paris, 1867), I, 127-129, Marsangy, *Vergennes en Suède*, 76-78.

41. Bouillé, *op.cit.*, I, 339-340.

42. L. Léouzon, le duc, *op.cit.*, I, 340.

43. Bouillé, *op.cit.*, I, 340.

44. A. Geoffroy, *op.cit.*, I, 31-44; duc de Broglie, *Le Secret du roi: Correspondance secrète de Louis XV avec ses agents diplomatiques*, 1752-1774 (Paris, 1878), II, 276-277.

45. Geffroy, *op.cit.*, 35-36, 42-44.

46. A.W. Ward, G.W. Prothero and Stanley Leathes, *op.cit.* VI, 765.

47. *Ibid.*, 766.

48. Rexis de Flassan, *Histoire générale et raisonneé de la Diplomatie Française*, . . .(Paris, 1811), VI, 565-569.

49. *Ibid.*, II, 311-312.

50. Geffroy, *op.cit.*, I, 109.

51. *Ibid*.

52. *Ibid.*, I, 110.

53. *Gazette de France*, 28 December, 1770, 422.

54. "Letter of 8 March, 1771" Quoted in Geffroy, *Gustave III*, I, 121.

55. The best book available on the relations between Gustavus III and the Comtesse d'Egmont is still La Comtesse d'Armaille, *La Comtesse d'Egmont, fille du Maréchal de Richelieu: 1740-1773* (Paris, 1899), 140ff.

56. *Gazette de France,* 29 March, 1771.

57. Geffroy, *op.cit.*, I, 123-124.

Chapter 14. Coup d'etat

1. "Comte de Broglie to Louis XV, 6 March, 1771," D. Ozanam et M. Antoine (ed.), *Correspondance secrète du Comte de Broglie avec Louis XV* (Paris, 1961), II, 258-259, *ibid.*, 259-260.

2. Saint-Priest, *Mémoires* (Paris, 1929), I, 141-142.

3. *Ibid.*, 47. Vergenne's separation from his family was one of the most difficult sacrifices he had to make as Ambassador to Sweden. See his personal letters to his son Constantine dated 4, 24 April and 6 May, 1771 in the private archives of the Vergennes family, *AFV*.

4. "Mémoire pour servir d'instruction au sieur Comte de Vergennes allant en Suède pour y résider en qualité -- d'ambassadeur du roi, 5 mai, 1771," *AAE-CP-Suède,* CCLIX, 203-210; The entire text of these instructions is in Marsangy, *Vergennes en suède,* 435-440.

5. *Ibid.*, 437.

6. *Ibid.*, 438.

7. *Ibid.*, 438-439.

8. "Vergennes to duc d'Aiguillon, 7 October, 1771," *AAE-CP-Suède,* Vol. CCLX, 243.

9. "Vergennes to Saint-Priest, 29 July, 1771," "Vergennes to Sabatier de Cabre, 18 June, 1771;" *AFV;* "Vergennes to duc de Vrillière, 17 June, 1771," Monthérot, "Decuments inédits sur la Révolution en Suède en 1772," *Mémoires de l'Académie Impériale des Sciences, Belles-Lettres et Arts de Lyon* (Lyon, 1857-1858), 2e Serie, tome 6, 31-36.

10. Letter "Vergennes to duc de Vrillière, 30 April, 1771," *AAE-CP-Suède,* CCLIX, 185-186vo ; On the question of the venality of Swedish politicians see "Vergennes to Vrillière, 17 June, 1771," Monthérot, "Documents inédits sur la Révolution en Suède en 1772" *Mémoires de l'Académie Impériales des Sciences, Belles-Lettres et Arts de Lyon,* 2e Serie, tome 6, 31-36.

11. Duc de Broglie, *The King's Secret* (New York, n.d,), II, 310-311. Saint-Priest at Constantinople said he received no instructions for six months because of the change of ministries: Saint-Priest, *Mémoires,* I, 140.

12. *Ibid., II, 297-311;* Marsangy, *Vergennes en Suède,* 88.

13. "Duc d'Aiguillon to Vergennes, 16 June, 1771," *AAE-CP-Suède,* CCLIX, 290.

14. "Vergennes to Aiguillon, 28 June, 1771," *AAE-CP-Suède,* CCLIX, 338-338vo. Also, 340-341vo ; See also: "Vergennes to Aiguillon, 23 June, 1771," *ibid.*, CCLIX, 323vo-324.

15. Charles Francis Sheridan, *History of the Late Revolution in Sweden* (London, 1778), 260-261; Marsangy, *Vergennes en Suède,* 132-133.

16. "Vergennes to Aiguillon, 2 August, 1771," *AAE-CP-Suède,* CCLX, 3-5; "Vergennes to Aiguillon, 9 August, 1771," CCLX, 18vo-23vo, see also: *AAE-CP-Suède,* CCXXVI, 74-115vo.

17. Letter: "Vergennes to Aiguillon, 9 August, 1771," *AAE-CP-Suède,* CCLX, 23-24.

18. "Réponse du Roi de Suède inseré au protocole du Sénat . . ." *AAE-CP-Suède,* CCLX, 131.

19. "Aiguillon to Vergennes, 27 November, 1771," *AAE-CP-Suède,* CCLX, 331-332; "Vergennes to Aiguillon, 12 Dec., 1771," *ibid.*, CCLX, 364-368.

20. "Extraits des Registres du Sénat du jeudi, 28 November, 1771 du matin," *AAE-CP-Suède,* CCLX, 333-334*vo*.

21. *Ibid.*, 335-336*vo*; "Vergennes to Sabatier de Cabre, 10 December, 1771," *AFV*.

22. "Vergennes to Aiguillon 29 November, 5 December, 1771," *AAE-CP-Suède,* CCLX, 337-343*vo*, 334-356*vo*.

23. "Vergennes to Sabatier de Cabre, 4 January, 1772," *AFV*.

24. "Vergennes to Aiguillon, 20 December, 1771," *AAE-CP-Suède,* CCLX, 337-380; "Vergennes to Aiguillon 20 December, 1771, Lettre particulière," *ibid.*, CCLX, 385-392*vo*, "Aiguillon to Vergennes, 12 December, 1771," *ibid.*, CCLX, 364-365*vo*.

25. "Vergennes to Aiguillon, 20 December, 1771, Lettre particulière," ibid., CCLX, 384-386*vo*, 390-392*vo* "Comte de Scheffer to Comte de Crentz, 21 December, 1771," *ibid.*, CCLX, 393-396, 405-408*vo*; Also: "Comte de Scheffer to duc d'Aiguillon, 23 December, 1771," *ibid.*, Supplément XII, 108-109.

26. "Aiguillon to Gustavus III, 10 December, 1771," *ibid.*, Supplément XII, 106-106*vo*.

27. *Ibid.*, 106-106*vo*. This note was apparently unknown to Vergennes. See also the cryptic letter of "Louis XV to Gustavus, 12 January, 1772," *ibid.*, CCLXI, 8.

28. "Aiguillon to Vergennes, 25 January, 1772," *ibid.*, CCLXI, 22. See also: "Aiguillon to Vergennes, 20 May, 1772," *ibid.*, CCLXI, 218-218*vo*.

29. "Vergennes to Sabatier de Cabre, 5 April, 1772," *AFV*. Also: Vergennes to Aiguillon, 24 January, 1772," *AAE-CP-Suède,* CCLXI, 17*vo*-20.

30. *Ibid.*, 20; See also: "Vergennes to Aiguillon, 14 February, 1771," *ibid.*, CCLXI, 44*vo*-47.

31. *Ibid.*, 46-47*vo*.

32. Marsangy, *Vergennes en Suède,* 180fn, 183.

33. "Vergennes to Aiguillon 24, 31 January, 1772," *AAE-CP-Suède,* CCLXI, 18-19, 24*vo*-29*vo*.

34. "Vergennes to Aiguillon, 3 February, 1772," *ibid.*, CCLXI, 32-36*vo*.

35. "Aiguillon to Gustavus III, 12 January, 1772," *ibid.*, Supplément XII, 113-113*vo*.

36. "Broglie to Louis XV, 17 February, 1772," D. Ozanam and M. Antoine, *op. cit.*, II, 330-331.

37. "Aiguillon to Vergennes, 23 February, 1772," *AAE-CP-Suède,* CCLXI, 55-56; Also: "Aiguillon to Vergennes, 1, 15 March, 1772," *ibid.*, CCLXI, 61-62, 75.

38. "Vergennes to Aiguillon, 6 March, 1772," *ibid.*, CCLXI, 63-64.

39. "Vergennes to Aiguillon, 9 March, 8 May, 1772," *ibid.*, CCLXI, 66-69*vo*, 192-194*vo*; "Aiguillon to Vergennes, 16 April, 31 May, 1771," *ibid.*, CCLXI, 158-159*vo*, 244-244*vo*; "Gustavus to Louis XV, 8 May, 1772," *ibid.*, CCLXI, 201-201.

40. "Vergennes to Aiguillon, 11 June, 1772," *ibid.*, CCLXI, 259-260.

41. "Vergennes to Aiguillon, 21 May, 1772," *ibid.*, CCLXI, 219-221*vo*. Also printed in Monthérot, "Documents inédits sur la révolution en Suède," 37-39.

42. "Vergennes to Aiguillon, 21 May, 1772," *AAE-CP-Suède,* CCLXI, 221*vo*-223.

43. "Gustavus to Vergennes, 21 May, 1772," *ibid.*, CCLXI, 226-227*vo*.

44. "Vergennes to Aiguillon, 5 June, 1772," *ibid.*, CCLXI, 254-254vo ; "Vergennes to Sabatier de Cabre, 15 June, 1772," *AFV*.
45. "Discours du Roy de Suède aux États assemblés devant luy le 1 juin, 1772 . . .," *AAE-CP-Suède*, CCLXI, 246-253. The speech is printed in Marsangy, *Vergennes en Suède*, 217-219.
46. "Vergennes to Aiguillon, 11 June, 1772," *AAE-CP-Suède*, CCLXI, 261vo -262.
47. "Gustavus to Louis XV, 17 June, 1772," *ibid.*, CCLXI, 271-271vo.
48. "Aiguillon to Vergennes, 11 June, 1772," *ibid.*, CCLXI, 267.
49. "Vergennes to Sabatier de Cabre, 5 April, 15 June, 1772," "Vergennes to Saint-Priest, 18 June, 1771," *AFV*.
50. Charles Francis Sheridan, *op. cit.*, 28.
51. George Georgeson Stahlberg, *An History of the Late Revolution in Sweden* (Edinburgh, 1776) 179-181; A. Geffroy, *Gustave III et la cour de France* (Paris, 1867), I, 160.
52. Charles Francis Sheridan, *op.cit.*, 284-285.
53. The English penetrated the secret sometime during the early summer of 1772. See "Vergennes to Saint-Priest, Stockholm, 30 August, 1772," *AFV*.
54. "Vergennes to Aiguillon, 25 June, 1772," *AAE-CP-Suède*, CCLXI, 285.
55. "Vergennes to Aiguillon, 9 July, 1772," *ibid.*, CCLXI, 293.
56. *Ibid.*, 296-296vo.
57. "Vergennes to Aiguillon, 6 August, 1772," *ibid.*, CCLXII, 9vo -10.
58. "Aiguillon to Vergennes, 9 August, 1772," *ibid.*, CCLXII, 11.
59. "Aiguillon to Vergennes, 13 August, 1772," "Vergennes to Aiguillon, 13 August, 1772," *ibid.*, CCLXII, 16, 17.
60. "Vergennes to Aiguillon, 16 August, 1772," *ibid.*, CCLXII, 26, 29-29vo.
61. The manifesto, dated 12 August, 1772, is printed in Marsangy, *Vergennes en Suède*, 233-234.
62. "Vergennes to Aiguillon, 18 August, 1772," *AAE-CP-Suède*, CCLXII, 34-35; "Relation de ce quest arrivé à Stockholm le 19 août, 1772, *ibid.*, CCLXII, 46-46vo ; Charles Francis Sheridan, *op.cit.*, 286-287; George Georgeson Stahlberg, *op.cit.*, 183; L. Léouzon, le duc, *Gustave III, Roi de Suède: 1746-1792* (Paris, 1861), 57-59.
63. Charles Francis Sheridan, *op.cit.*, (London, 1778), 288.
64. A Geffroy, *Gustave III et la cour de France* (Paris, 1867), I, 163; See also: "Letter #11, Queen of Sweden to her sister Princess Wilhelmina Carolina," *Letters of the Swedish Court* (London, 1809), 96-98.
65. *Ibid.*, 98.
66. "Vergennes to Aiguillon, 16 août, 1772," *AAE-CP-Suede*, CCLXII, 26vo ; "Relation de ce quest arrivé à Stockholm le 19 août, 1772," *ibid.*, CCLXII, 46vo-47vo.
67. *Ibid.*, 29.
68. "Letter #10 Queen of Sweden to her sister Princess Wilhelmina Carolina," *Letters of the Swedish Court* (London, 1809), 90; L. Léouzon, *le duc de, Gustave III; Roi de Suède: 1746-1792* (Paris, 1861), 63.
69. Apparently Gustavus had regularly patrolled the streets with the militia in order to gain the affection of the militia. See Letter #10 from the Queen of Sweden to her sister Princess Wilhelmina Carolina," *Letters of the Swedish Court* (London, 1809), 86.
70. Marsangy, *Vergennes en Suede*, 242.
71. "Vergennes to Aiguillon, 18 August, 1772," *AAE-CP-Suède*, CCLXII, 34-35.
72. "Gustavus III to Vergennes, 18 August, 1772," *ibid.*, CCLXII, 38-38d[vo].
73. Marsangy, *Vergennes en Suède*, 241.

74. Charles Francis Sheridan, *op.cit.*, 294; "Relation de ce qu'est arrivé a Stockholm le 19 août, 1772," *AAE-CP-Suède*, CCLXII, 48-48vo.

75. Charles Francis Sheridan, *op.cit.*, 294-295; "Letter #10, The Queen of Sweden to her sister Princess Wilhelmina Carolina," *Letters of the Swedish Court*, 87; Marsangy, *Vergennes en Suède*, 243.

76. "Relation de ce quest arrivé à Stockholm le 19 août, 1772," *AAE-CP-Suède*, CCLXII, 48vo.

77. Marsangy, *Vergennes en Suède*, 243.

78. "Relation de ce quest arrivé à Stockholm le 19 août, 1772," *AAE-CP-Suède*, CCLXII, 49.

79. Marsangy, *Vergennes en Suède*, 246-247.

80. George Georgeson Stahlberg, *op.cit.*, 187-188; "Letter #11, Queen of Sweden to her sister Princess Wilhelmina Carolina," *Letters of the Swedish Court*, 94.

81. "Vergennes to Aiguillon, 21 August, 1772," *AAE-CP-Suède*, Supplément XII, 188-189.

82. Marsangy, *Vergennes en Suède*, 263.

83. *AAE-CP-Suède*, CCLXII, 44; Also: 61-66vo.

84. "Vergennes to Aiguillon, 21 August," *ibid.*, CCLXII, 57-60vo; "Vergennes to Sabatier de Cabre, 21 August, 7 September, 1772," *AFV*.

85. "Relation de ce quest arrivé à Stockholm le 19 août, 1772," *AAE-CP-Suède*, CCLXII, 51vo-53.

86. "Vergennes to Aiguillon, 21 August, 1772," *ibid.*, CCLXII, 58.

87. "Vergennes to Aiguillon, 20 August, 1772," *ibid.*, CCLXII, 56-56vo.

88. "Vergennes to Saint-Priest, Stockholm, 30 August, 1772," "Gustavus to Vergennes, Stockholm, 30 October, 1772," "Comte de Lacy to Vergennes, Stockholm, 11 September, 1772," Papiers Vergennes: Stockholm, Correspondance et documents, *AFV*.

89. "Vergennes to Aiguillon, 28 August, 1 September, 1772, *AAE-CP-Suède*, CCLXII, 112, 123-124; Also "Vergennes to Aiguillon, 16 August, 1772," *ibid.*, 26vo-27, 29vo.

90. "Vergennes to Aiguillon, 21 August, 1772," *ibid.*, Supplément XII, 188vo-189.

91. As early as July, 1772, English agents passed on, to the Caps of the Estates, intelligence which caused them to suspect Gustavus was plotting a *coup d'etat*. See: A. Geffroy, *Gustave III et la cour de France* (Paris 1867), I, 159. Also: "Rochfort to Goodricke, 3, 7, 14 July, 1772," State Papers: Foreign office 95/120, 179-184; W. Bodham Donne, *Correspondence of George the Third with Lord North from 1768-1783*. (London, 1867), II, 363-366.

92. "Vergennes to Aiguillon, 28 August, 1772,' *AAE-CP-Suède*, CCLXII, 111-111vo.

93. "Comtesse d'Egmont to Gustavus III, 2 September, 1772," printed in La Comtesse d'Armaillé, *La Comtesse D'Egmont* (Paris, 1890), 258-259.

94. "Aiguillon to Vergennes, 10 September, 1772," *AAE-CP-Suède*, CCLXII, 147-148.

95. "Maupeou to Vergennes, 5 September, 1772," Papiers Vergennes: Correspondance politique et particulière: ministres de Louis XV, *AFV*.

96. The portrait now hangs in the home of M. et Mme Pierre de Tugny now living at Marly le Roi, France.

97. "Aiguillon to Vergennes, 10 September, 1772," *AAE-CP-Suède*, CCLXII, 147. For the opinion of the French public concerning Vergennes' role in the Swedish *coup d'état*, see Charles Joseph Mayer, *La vie publique et privée de Charles Gravier de*

Vergennes, ministre de l'État (Paris, 1789), 73 and 73-74fn; Anonymous, *Portrait du Comte de Vergennes* (1788), 6, 68; Felix Vicq-d'Azyr, *Éloge, de M. le Comte de Vergennes* (Paris, 1786), 29; "Saint-Priest to Vergennes, 3 November, 1772," Papiers Vergennes, *AFV*.

98. "Vergennes to Aiguillon, 1 October, 1772," *AAE-CP-Suède*, CCLXII, 210.

99. The French government had printed and distributed "La Relation de ce qu'est arrivé à Stockholm depuis le 19 jusqu'au 21 du mois dernier," which admitted nothing concerning France's role in the *coup d'éat*. See: *Mémoires secrètes de Bachaumont* (London, 1781-1789), IV, 40, 44. The silence of the French government, however, did not prevent many contemporaries from rightly concluding that Louis XV was deeply involved in the *coup d'état*. See: duc de Lévis, *Souvenirs et Portraits 1780-1789* (Paris, 1815), 113.

100. Gustave III, *Collection des Écrits politiques et Littéraires de Gustave III* (Stockholm, 1805), IV, 52.

101. "Duc de Broglie to duc d'Aiguillon, 5 September, 1772," *AAE-CP-Suède*, Supplément XII, 198.

Chapter 15. From Stockholm to Versailles

1. E. Amburger, *Russland und Schweden, 1762-1772* (Berlin, 1934), 266.

2. "Frederick to Gustavus III, 6 September, 1772," Friedrich des Grossen, *Politische Correspondenz* (Berlin, 1879-1919), XXXII, 455.

3. See the collection of letters in Papiers Vergennes, Stockholm, Correspondance politique:1) Collèque à Constantinople, 2) Collèque à St. Petersburg, 3) Collèque à Vienna. *AFV*. "Vergennes to Aiguillon, 18 September," *AAE-CP-Suède*, Supplément XII, 210vo-211.

4. "Vergennes to Aiguillon, 30 September, 9, 14 November, 1772," *ibid.*, CCLXI, 200vo-202, 281, 297-298.

5. For a thorough discussion of the intricacies of the British response to the *coup d'état*, see the excellent article by Michael Roberts, "Great Britain and the Swedish Revolution, 1772-1773," *The Historical Journal* (1964), VII, No. 1, especially 12, 18-19.

6. *Ibid.*, 19.

7. *Correspondance inédite du Général-Major de Martange* (Paris, 1898), 525-528.

8. "Aiguillon to Vergennes, 10 September, 8 December, 1772," *AAE-CP-Suède*, CCLXII, 147, 362.

9. "Aiguillon to Vergennes, 10 September, 5, 15 November, 1772," *AAE-CP-Suede*, CCXLII, 147, 271vo-272vo, 304-305.

10. "Louis XV to Général Monet, 23 October, 1772," D. Ozanam and M. Antoine, editor, *Correspondance secrète inédite de Louis XV et du général Monet, 1767-1772* (Paris, 1955), 47.

11. "Louis Ulrike to Frederick, 25 August, 1772;" "Frederick to Louise Ulrike, 30 August, 1772;" "Frederick to Prince Henry of Prussia, 30 August, 1772;" "Frederick to Baron D'Edelsheim, 1 September, 1772," *Politische Correspondenz*, XXXII, 431-433, 433-434, 440.

12. "Frederick II to Gustavus III, 6 September, 1772," "Frederick to Count de Donhoff, 4 September, 1772," *ibid.*, XXXII, 455, 433; "Frederick to Louis XV, 23 January, 1773," *AAE-CP-Suède*, CCLXIII, 59-60. See also: *ibid.*, fols. 208-208vo.

13. "Frederick II to Louise Ulrike, 30 August, 1772," *Politische Correspondenz*

XXXII, 432-433.

14. "Frederick to Louise Ulrike,11 September, 1772," *ibid.*, XXXII, 474-475.

15. "Gustavus III to Prince Henry, n.d. 1772," quoted in Marsangy, *Vergennes en Suède,* 312.

16. For English estimates of Russian weakness see: "Rochfort to Stormont, 18 March, 26 August, 1774," L.G. Wickham Legg, *British Diplomatic Instructions: 1689-1789* (London, 1934), VII, France, 138-139, 144; "Frederick to Prince Henry, 18 September, 1772," *Politische Correspondenz,* XXXII, 494-495, 508 fn. #2; "Catherine II to Gustavus III, 15 September, 1772," *AAE-CP-Russie,* XC, 231vo-232vo. See also: Louis-Philippe Ségur, *Politique de tous les cabinets de l'Europe* (Paris, 1793), I, 197.

17. "Frederick to Comte de Solms at Saint Petersburg, 4, 13 September, 1772;" "Frederick to Comte de Donhoff at Stockholm 4 September, 1772," *Politische Correspondenz* XXXII, 446-447, 482, 443.

18. "Goodricke to Suffolk, 37, 30 October, 1772," *Public Records Office,* London, England, State Papers; Foreign Office 95/122, 131-5, 138-140.

19. See, for example, "Vergennes to Aiguillon, 3 September, 1772," *AAE-CP-Suède,* CCLXII,127-132vo.

20. "Vergennes to Aiguillon,21, 28 August, 30 September, 1772," *ibid.*, CCLXII, 57, 113, 200; "Vergennes to Aiguillon, 19 January, 1773," *ibid.*, Supplément XII, 253vo; "Marquis de Blosset, French Ambassador to Copenhagen to Vergennes, 23 August, 1772," Papiers Vergennes, *AFV;* "Aiguillon to Vergennes, 5, 15, 26 November, 1772," *AAE-CP-Suède,* CCLXII, 271,304-5, 325-326.

21. "Vergennes to Aiguillon, 9 March, 1773," *AAE-CP-Suède,* CCLXIII, 162vo.

22. In a mémoire written by the Comte de Broglie and Favier and presented to Louis XV just before the latter's death, the question of a Swedish attack was raised and rejected on the grounds that it would only lead to failure. Louis-Philippe de Ségur, *Politique de tous les cabinets,* I, 306-309. See also: *AAE-CP-Suède* CCLXIII, 161-166; "Gunning to Suffolk 14/25 September, 1772," *Public Records Office,* London, England, State Papers; Foreign Office, 91/91, 72.

23. *AAE-CP-Suède,* CCLXIII,163vo.

24. "Vergennes to Constantin, 4 November, 1771," Papiers Vergennes; Lettres autographes à Constantin, 1769-1786, *AFV.*

25. "Vergennes to Constantin, 6 May, 1771," Also: 24 April, 1771, *ibid.*

26. "Vergennes to Constantin, 22 June, 1771," *ibid.*

27. "Vergennes to Constantin, 7 January, 1770," *ibid.*

28. "Vergennes to Constantin, 2 January, 1771," *ibid.*

29. "Vergennes to Constantin, 22 June, 1771," *ibid.*

30. "Vergennes to Aiguillon, 26 January, 1773," *AAE-CP-Suede,* CCLXIII, 63-70.

31. "Vergennes to Marquis de Noailles, 18 April, 1774," "Marquis de Blosset to Vergennes, 10 March, 1774," Papiers Vergennes, *AFV;* "Vergennes to Aiguillon 14 February, 1773,"*AAE-CP-Suède,* Supplément XII, 257vo.

32. "Vergennes to Aiguillon, 17 February, 1773," *AAE-CP-Suède,* CCLXIII, 109-109vo.

33. *Gazette de France,* 9 June, 21 July, 1774, 209, 263.

34. Bachaumont, *Mémoires sécrèts,* XXVII, 19th July, 1774, 304.

35. André Castelot, *Queen of France; A biography of Marie Antoinette* (New York, 1957), 79.

36. L.G. Wickham Legg, *British Diplomatic Instructions: 1689-1789* (London,

1934), Vol. VII, France, xxi; See also "Rochfort to Viscount Stormant, 17 June, 1774," *ibid.*, 142.

37. Charles Joseph Mayer, *La vie publique et privée de Charles Gravier de Vergennes, ministre de l'Etat* (Paris, 1789), 91.

38. Anonymous, *Portrait du Comte de Vergennes* (Bruxelles or Liège, 1788), 7-8.

39. Mayer, *Vie Publique*, 91.

40. On this point see, Bachaumont, *Mémoires secrèts*, VIII, 21 June, 1775, 97.

41. "Resumé des opérations ministères de M. le Comte de Vergennes," *AAE-MD-France*, CCCCXLVI, 358-358vo.

42. "Liste de plusieurs personnages recommandé par M. le dauphin, à celui de ses enfants qui succédera à Louis XV," Jean-Louis Soulavie, *Mémoires historiques et politiques* (Paris, 1801), I, 282-287, also 45.

43. "Le Mulier to Vergennes, 14 June, 1774," Papiers Vergennes; lettres divers, 1774, *AFV*.

44. "Langeron to Vergennes, s.d. 1774," *ibid.*

45. "Duc de Noailles to Vergennes, 17 July, 1774;" "Marquis de Noailles to Vergennes, 29, 30 August, 1774," "Sabatier de Cabre to Vergennes, 16 June, 1774," "Comte de Chatelet to Vergennes, 30 August, 1774," "Choiseul to Vergennes, 1774," *ibid.*

46. "Duc de Noailles to Vergennes, 17 July, 1774," "Marquis de Noailles to Vergennes, 29, 30 August, 1774," *ibid.*

47. "Zuckmantel to Vergennes, 13 August, 1774," *ibid.*

48. "Comte de Chatelet to Vergennes, 30 August, 1774," *ibid.*

49. "Gravier de Lagellière, 1 July, 1774," *ibid.*

50. "Marie Antoinette to Vergennes, 1774," *ibid.*

Chapter 16. The Past, Present, and Future in 1774

1. "Vergennes to [unknown] 14 September, 1769," *Documents originaux*, No.1. Bibliothèque de Versailles.

2. Simon Nicolas Henri Linguet, *Lettre de M. Linguet à M. le Comte de Vergennes, Ministre des Affaires Étrangères en France*, (London, 1777), p. 53.

3. Pierre Rain, *La diplomatie française de Henri IV a Vergennes* (Paris, 1945), p. 251.

4. Quoted in *ibid.*, p. 257.

5. "Instructions, Bernis à Comte de Stainville, 1757," *AAE-MD-France* XLII; Albert Sorel, *Recueil des Instructions données aux ambassadeurs et ministres de France* .... (Paris, 1884), I, Autriche, p. 356.

6. "Mémoire de M. de Vergennes à Louis XVI sur la situation politique de la France relativement aux différentes puissances." 1774, Kl64 no.2. Archives Nationales. Unless otherwise indicated, the quotations in this chapter are from this *mémoire*.

7. "Vergennes to Sabatier de Cabre, 4 November, 1772," *Archives de la Famille de Vergennes*. Hereafter referred to as *AFV*.

8. "Mémoire à Louis XVI en 1777," quoted in M. Flasson, *Histoire générale et raisonné de la diplomatie française* (Paris, 1809), V, p.127; See also the "Mémoire du Comte de Broglie, given to Louis XVI, 1 March, 1775," in Louis Philippe de Ségur, *Politique de tous le cabinets de l'Europe* (Paris, 1793), I, 171, 175 .

9. "Vergennes to Constantin, 28(?) February, 1772," *AFV*.

10. "Mémoire sur la politique extérieure de la France depuis 1774 adressé au Roi par le Sr. de Vergennes," 1782, *AAE-MD-France,* Tome 446.

11. "Vergennes to Louis XVI, 12 April, 1777," *AAE-MD-France,* Tome 1897, fol. 77vo.

12. On this definition of the term "balance of power" see: Martin Wight, "The Balance of Power," in *Diplomatic Investigations,* edited by Herbert Butterfield (London, 1966), pp. 148-175.

13. "Vergennes to Noailles, 7 December, 1776," *AAE-CP-Angleterre,* Tome 509, fol. 73; For detailed study of the build-up of the French navy under the administration of Sartine see the excellent study by Jonathan Dull, *The French Navy and American Independence: A Study of Arms and Diplomacy, 1774-1780.* (Princeton, N.J., 1975).

14. "Mémoire ou plan des mesures à concerter avec l'Espagne contre les entreprises qu'on peut supposer à l'Angleterre, December, 1776," Printed in Henri Doniol, *Histoire de la Participation de la France à l'établissement des États-Unis d'Amérique* (Paris, 1886), II, 164.

15. On the French navy and its relation to French foreign policy, see Jonathan Dull, *op. cit.,* Also, Maurice Loir, *La Marine Royale en 1789* (Paris, 1892); Lacour-Gayet, *La Marine Militaire de la France sous le règne de Louis XVI* (Paris, 1905); Alexandre Lambert de Sainte-Croix, *Essai sur l'administration de la Marine, 1689-1792* (Paris, 1892).

16. Jonathan Dull, *op. cit., passim.*

17. "Vergennes to Comte d'Aranda, 5 November, 1776," Printed in Doniol, *Histoire,* I, pp. 684-685

18. "Vergennes to Ossum, 12 April, 1777," *ibid.,* II, 260. See also: *ibid.,* I, 691; II, III.

19. Jonathan Dull, *op. cit., passim.*

Chapter 17. The Spanish Temptation

1. F. Rousseau, *La Règne de Charles III,* (Paris, 1907), vol. 11, 71-72; Francis P. Renaut, *Le Pacte de Famille et l'Amérique* (Paris, 1922), 174-204.

2. Henri Doniol, *Histoire de la participation de la France à l'établissement des États-Unis d'Amérique* (Paris, 1886), I. pp. 19-20.

3. "Ossun to Bertin, 7 July, 1774," *AAE-CP-Espagne,* 573, fols. 478-480.

4. Doniol, *Histoire,* I, 27; Also: Renaut, *Le Pacte de Famille,* 227-239.

5. "Garnier to Vergennes, 2 Nov. 1774," *AAE-CP-Angleterre,* 507, fol. 26; "Vergennes to Ossun, 10 October, 1774," *AAE-CP-Espagne,* 574, fol. 201.

6. "Vergennes to Louis XVI, 4 May, 1775," *AAE-MD-France,* 1897, fol. 40.

7. "Ossun to Vergennes, 20 February, 1775," *AAE-CP-Espagne,* 574, fols. 170vo-173vo; "Ossun to Vergennes, 20 May, 1775," *ibid.,* 576, fols. 112vo-114; "Vergennes to Ossun, 20 June, 1775," *ibid.,* fols. 201-202.

8. "Vergennes to Louis XVI, 4 May, 1775," *AAE-MD-France,* 1897, fol. 40.

9. *Ibid.*

10. "Vergennes to Ossun, 31 October, 1774," *AAE-CP-Espagne,* 574, fols. 289-290. On France's need for peace see also: Vergennes' dispatch to Ossun 29 November, 1774, *ibid.,* 574, fols. 390-390vo. "Vergennes to Louis XVI, 8 August, 1775," *AAE-MD-France,* 1897, fol. 45. To implement his wish to stay out of the war, Vergennes urged again and again that France try to mediate the Portuguese-Spanish dispute.

11. A. Morel-Fatio et H. Léonardin, *Recueil des Instructions données aux ambassadeurs et ministres de France depuis les traités de Westphalie jusqu'à Révolution Française* (Paris, 1899), XII bis, Espagne, Tome III, p. 344.
12. "Vergennes to Ossun, 13 September, 1774," *AAE-CP-Espagne*, 574, fols. 129vo-131.
13. "Vergennes to Ossun, 13 September, 1774," *ibid.*, 574, fols. 131.
14. "Vergennes to Ossun, 31 October, 1774," *ibid.*, 574, fol. 288vo.
15. *Ibid.*, fols. 288[vo]-289.
16. "Garnier to Vergennes, 27 January, 1775," *AAE-CP-Angleterre*, 508 fols. 133-134[vo].
17. "Garnier to Vergennes, 8 June, 1775," *ibid.*, 510 fol. 225[vo]; "Garnier to Vergennes, 13 June, 1775," *ibid.*, fols. 264-264vo; "Ossun to Vergennes," 3 July, 1775, *AAE-CP-Espagne*, 576, fol. 235.
18. "Vergennes to Ossun, 20 August, 1775," *ibid.*, 577, fols. 114-117vo; See also Juan F. Yela Utrilla, *Espana ante la independencia de los Estados Unidos* (Lérida, 1925), I, 56-61.
19. "Grimaldi to Aranda, 18 October, 1775," *AAE-CP-Espagne*, 578, fols. 70-75vo. Italics my own.
20. "Vergennes to Aranda, 25 November, 1775," *AAE-CP-Espagne*, 578, fols. 255-260.
21. *Ibid.*, fol. 257.
22. "Vergennes to Aranda, 25 November, 1775," *ibid.*, fol. 259.
23. "Vergennes to Ossun, 28 November, 1775," *ibid.*, 578, fol. 276.
24. "Vergennes to Ossun, 16 December, 1775," *ibid.*, 578, fols. 420vo-421.
25. *AAE-MD-Portugal*, 3 September, 1775, Tome I, fol. 294ff; Le Vte de Caix de Saint-Aymour. *Recueil des Instructions données aux ambassadeurs et ministres de France depuis les traités de Westphalie jusqu'à la Révolution Française.* (Paris, 1886), VII, Portugal, 371-380.

Chatper 18. The Revolution in America

1. "Guines to Vergennes, 1 July, 1775," *AAE-CP-Angleterre*, 511, 12-12vo.
2. "Vergennes to Guines, 10 July, 1775," *ibid.*, 511, fols. 78-81. Dallas D. Irvine, "The Newfoundland Fishery: a French Objective in the War of American Independence," *Canadian Historical Review* (September, 1932), vol. 13, pp. 276-277.
3. "Vergennes to Guines, 27 August, 1775," *AAE-CP-Angeleterre*, 511, fol. 317-317[vo].
4. "Guines to Vergennes, 1 July, 1775," *ibid.*, 511, fols. 16-17.
5. "Guines to Vergennes, 28 July, 1775," *ibid.*, 511, fols. 178-182[vo].
6. "Vergennes to Guines, 7 August, 1775," *ibid.*, 511, fol. 227.
7. Joseph Hamon, *Le Chevalier de Bonvouloir* (Paris, 1953) p. 25; "Guines to Vergennes, 8 September, 1775," *AAE-CP-Angleterre*, 511, fol. 369vo.
8. Doniol, *Histoire*, vol. l, pp. 266, 291.
9. John Meng. *Dispatches and Instructions of Conrad Alexander Gérard: 1778-1780* (Paris, 1939), p. 46.
10. Doniol, *Histoire*, vol. 1, p. 171.
11. "Guines to Vergennes, 29 September, 1775," *AAE-CP-Angleterre*, 512, fol. 33vo.
12. "Vergennes to Guines, 27 August, 1775," *AAE-CP-Angleterre*, vol. 511, folio

316vo.

13. John Durand, *New Materials for the History of the American Revolution* (New York, 1889), p. 49.

14. Jared Sparks, *The Writings of George Washington* (Boston, 1858),vol. 3, pp. 493-94.

15. Christopher Ward, *The War of the Revolution* (New York, 1952), vol. 1, p. 163 ff, 672; Peter Force, ed., *American Archives* (Washington, D.C., 1837-46), vol. 5, pp. 845-46; Douglas S. Freeman, *George Washington: Leader of the Revolution* (New York, 1952), vol. 4, pp. 81-82.

16. "Vergennes to Aranda, 25 November, 1775," *AAE-CP-Espagne,* 578, fol. 255-260.

17. "Vergennes to Louis XVI, 25 January, 1776," *AAE-MD-France,* 1897, fol. 55.

18. Doniol, *Histoire,* vol. 1, p. 242.

19. *AAE-CP-Angleterre,* vol. 515, fols. 389-392.

20. *Ibid.*, vol. 515, fol. 14.

21. *Ibid.*, vol. 515, fol. 17.

22. *AAE-Mémoires et Documents-États-Unis,* Hereafter referred to as *AAE-MD-Etats Unis,* vol. 1, fol. 105.

23. *Ibid.*, vol. 1, fol. 83.

24. Wharton, vol. 2, p. 65.

25. *AAE-CP-Angleterre,* "Supplément," vol. 18, folio 56; on the dating, and significance of this document see John J. Meng, "A Footnote to Secret Aid in the American Revolution," *American Historical Review* (July, 1938), vol. 43, pp.791-795.

26. Doniol, *Histoire,* vol. 1, 421 fn.

27. "Ossun to Vergennes, 25 April, 1776," *AAE-CP-Espagne,* 580, fols. 138-141. On Anglo-French mediation attempts see *AAE-CP-Angleterre,* 513, fols. 10-12; also fols. 20-22.

28. "Ossun to Vergennes, 25 April, 1776," *AAE-CP-Espagne,* 580 fols. 147-147vo.

29. "Vergennes to Ossun, 30 April, 1776," *ibid.*, 580, fol. 158vo.

30. "Vergennes to Ossun, 14 May, 1776," *ibid.*, 580, fol. 228vo.

31. "Ossun to Vergennes, 27 May, 1776," *ibid.*, 580, fol. 294vo.

32. "Aranda to Vergennes, 16 May, 1776;" "Vergennes to Ossun, 17 May, 1776," "Ossun to Vergennes, 30 May, 1776," *AAE-CP-Espagne,* 580, fol. 238-239vo, 246-248, 315-318.

33. "Vergennes to Ossun, 29 June, 1776," *ibid.*, 580, fol. 462-464vo.

34. *Ibid.*

35. *AAE-MD-France,* 584, fols. 306-308, dated July 7, 1776.

36. "Beaumarchais to Vergennes, 8 May, 1776," Doniol, *Histoire,* vol. 1, p. 515.

37. *AAE-CP-Angleterre,* vol. 516, fol. 26.

38. Doniol, *Histoire,* vol. 1, pp. 567-577.

39. "Grimaldi to Vergennes, 8 October, 1776," *AAE-CP-Espagne,* 582, fols. 65vo-67vo.

Chapter 19. Gates and Washington: Saratoga and Germantown

1. *AAE-CP-Angleterre,* vol. 518, fol. 66.
2. Doniol, *Histoire,* vol. 1, p. 615-616.
3. *AAE-CP-États-Unis,* vol. 1, fol. 261.

4. *AAE-CP-Angleterre,* vol. 519, fols. 99-103; Also, "Vergennes to Louis XVI, 17 October, 1776," *AAE-MD-France,* 1897, fol. 70.

5. Renaut, *Le Pacte de Famille et l'Amérique,* 243, 246-248.

6. Doniol, *Histoire,* vol. 1, 448-449.

7. *Ibid.,* 451-452. See also Vergennes' note to Garnier on this subject in *ibid.,* 461-462. And Garnier's dispatch of June 6, 1776, *ibid.,* 464.

8. Deane concluded his arrangements with the Roderique Hortelez and Company on the 15th of October, 1776. See Elizabeth S. Kite, "The Continental Congress and France: Secret Aid and the Alliance 1776-1777," *Records of the American Catholic Historical Society of Philadelphia* (1928), vol. 39, pp. 166-167.

9. *Journals of the Continental Congress* (Washington, 1906), vol. 6, p. 884; Francis Wharton, *Revolutionary Diplomatic Correspondance* (Washington, D.C. 1889) vol. 2. pp. 172-162.

10. Wharton, vol. 2, pp. 239; 244, 247; 248.

11. See Vergennes' "Réflexions" of November 5, 1776, Printed in Doniol, *Histoire,* I, 680-682.

12 . "Memo Concerning the Present State of the Late British Colonies in America," *AAE-CP-États-Unis,* vol. 2, fol. 20-21.

13. *Ibid.,* vol. 2, fols. 109-110.

14. Doniol, *Histoire,* vol. 2, p. 37.

15. "Deane to Vergennes, 22 March, 1777," *AAE-CP-États-Unis,* vol. 2, fol. 141.

16. "Deane to Vergennes, 12 May, 1777," *ibid.,* vol. 2, fol. 197.

17. "Deane to Vergennes, 5 April, 1777," *ibid.,* vol. 2, fol. 167; "7 April, 1777," *ibid.,* vol. 2, fols. 171-172.

18. Samuel Flagg Bemis, *Diplomacy of the American Revolution* (New York, 1925), p. 55; Meng, *op. cit.,* p. 74; Doniol, *Histoire,* vol. 2, p. 468.

19. See: "Vergennes to Noailles, 27 September, 1777," *AAE-CP-Angleterre,* vol. 525, fol. 29-32; "Noailles to Vergennes, 7 October, 1777," *ibid.,* vol. 525, fols. 72-72vo; "Vergennes to Noailles, 11 October, 1777," *ibid.,* vol. 525, fol. 98; On French policy during this critical period, see also Brian Morton, "Roderique Hortelez' to the Secret Committee: A Unpublished French Policy Statement of 1777," *The French Review,* vol. L, no. 6 (May, 1977), pp. 875-890.

20. "Mémoire sur les fonds nécessaire pour le service de la marine et des colonies pendant l'année 1776," Archives de la Marine, B'81, quoted in Lacour-Gazet, *La Marine Militaire de la France sous le règne de Louis XVI* (Paris, 1905), p. 59.

21. "État sommaire des archives de la marine antérieure à la Révolution," quoted in *ibid.,* p. 60; See also: M. Loir, *La Marine Royale en 1789* (Paris, 1892), p. 277.

22. 'Noailles to Vergennes, October, 7, 1777," *AAE-CP-Angleterre,* vol. 525, fols. 71-72.

23. "Noailles to Vergennes, October 10, 1777," *ibid.,* fol. 81.

24. *Ibid.,* fol. 86.

25. "Vergennes to Noailles, October 18, 1777," *ibid.,* fols. 129-130.

26. "Noailles to Vergennes, October 25, 1777," *ibid.,* fols. 194-195.

27. *Ibid.,* fols. 182-189.

28. "Noailles to Vergennes, November 4, 1777," *ibid.,* fols. 276-284.

29. *Ibid.,* fol. 285.

30. Henri Doniol, *Histoire,* II, 620.

31. "Noailles to Vergennes, November 14, 1777," *AAE-CP-Angleterre,* vol. 525, fols. 361-367.

32. "Vergennes to Noailles, November 21, 1777," *ibid.,* vol. 526, fols. 32-33.

33. "Instructions verbals donnée à M. Holker le 25 Novembre, 1777," *AAE-CP-États-Unis,* vol. 2, fols. 266-269.

34. *AAE-CP-Angleterre,* vol. 525, fols. 160-168.

35. An English translation of the dispatch appears in E.E. Hale, *Franklin in France* (Boston, 1887), 159ff.

36. Christopher Ward, *The War of the Revolution* (New York, 1952), I, 370-371.

37. *AAE-CP-Angleterre,* vol. 525, fols. 160-168.

38. *AAE-CP-États-Unis,* vol. 2, fol. 279.

39. *AAE-CP-Angleterre,* vol. 526, fols. 142-144.

40. "James Lowry to M. St. Pierre, chez M. Grand," *AAE-CP-États-Unis,* vol. 2, fols. 283-286. It is impossible to say definitely who M. St. Pierre was. The name might have been another alias for Dr. Bancroft, the British spy and confidant of Silas Deane.

41. "Noailles to Vergennes, Dec. 5, 1777," *AAE-CP-Angleterre,* vol. 526, fols. 157-174.

42. "Noailles to Vergennes, Dec. 2, 1777," *ibid.,* fols. 117-123.

43. *Ibid.,* fols. 157-174.

44. See the report by a French soldier on the American military, "copie d'un mémoire d'un officiers français passé en Amérique avec le marquis de Lafayette arrivé en France dans les premiers jours de décembre et parti de Philadelphie le 12 Septembre, 177," *AEE-CP-États-Unis,* vol. 4, fols. 425-428.

45. Doniol, *Histoire,* II, 623 (note).

46. "Vergennes to Noailles, Dec. 6 1777," *AAE-CP-Angleterre,* vol. 526, fols. 181-182.

47. *Ibid.,* fol. 183.

48. "Vergennes to Noailles, Jan. 17, 1778," *ibid.,* vol. 528, fols. 124-125.

49. "Letter to member of the Continental Congress, July 23, 1778," Francis Wharton, *op.cit.,* II, 664.

50. "Louis XVI to Charles III, 8 January, 1778," *AAE-MD-France* 1897, fols. 83-83.

Chapter 20. The Decision to Intervene

1. "Vergennes to Montmorin, 8 January 1778," quoted in Philippe Erlanger, "Louis XVI fondateur des États-Unis," *Revue de Paris* (1952), III, p. 78.

2. "Mémoire sur la politique extérieure, 1782," *AAE-MD-France,* vol. 446, fol. 355.

3. Louis Gottschalk, "The American Revolution in the Causal Pattern of the French Revolution," *Publications of the American Friends of Lafayette* (Easton, Penn., 1948), 19-20.

4. Saul Padover, *The Life and Death of Louis XVI* (New York, 1939), pp. 54-55.

5. Jonathan R. Dull, *The French Navy and American Independence,* (Princeton, 1975), 108, 255-256.

6. See, for example, L. H. Labandu, *Un diplomate Français à la cour de Catherine II, 1775-1780* (Paris, 1901), vol. I, xli-xlii.

7. "Mémoire sur la politique extérieure, 1782," *AAE-MD-France,* vol. 446, fol. 351.

8. Vergennes believed with almost a mathematical certainty that war was inevitable. As early as 1774, Vergennes told Louis XVI in a *mémoire* in which he recom-

mended a build-up of French armaments that the longer peace lasted the less likely it was to continue to last. "Mémoire de M. de Vergennes à Louis XVI sur la situation politique de la France relativement à différentes puissances, 1774," *Archives Nationales,* K164 no. 2[2]. See also Vergennes' "Considération sur le parti qu'il convient à la France de prendre vis à vis de l'Angleterre dans la circonstance actuelle," dated 31 August, 1776. Printed in Henri Doniol, *Histoire de la participation de la France à l'éstablissement des États-Unis d'Amérique* (Paris, 1886), vol. I, 567-577. Also, "Considérations sur l'affaire de colonies anglaises de l'Amérique, March, 1776," *AAE-CP-Angleterre,* Supplément, vol. XVIII, fols. 115-121.

9. Charles Gomel, *Les causes financières de la révolution française* (Paris, 1892), I, pp. 1-2.

10. Quoted in *ibid.,* pp. 7-8.

11. Gustave Schelle, *Oeuvres de Turgot . . .* (Paris, 1923), V, 406.

12 . L. A. Boiteaux, *Un mémoire prophétique de Turgot sur la révolution d'Amérique* (Paris, 1958), pp. 2 ff.

13. See, for example, C. J. Gignoux, *Turgot,* (Paris, 1945), 121ff.

14. Gustave Schelle, *loc. cit.*

15. Peter Mathias and Patrick O'Brien, "Taxation in Britain and France, 1715-1810: A Comparison of the Social and Economic Incidence of Taxes Collected for the Central Governments," *Journal of European Economic History* (1976), vol. 5, pp. 601-650.

16. "Vergennes to La Luzerne, 9 March, 1781," *AAE-CP-États-Unis,* vol. 15, fols. 341-344vo; "Vergennes to Montmorin, 17 December, 1779," *AAE-CP-Espagne,* vol. 596, fol. 182; Marquis d'Argenson, *Considérations sur la gouvernement ancienne et présent de la France* (Amsterdam, 1765), p. 18; on Vergennes' hairbrained notion that the war might help solve the problem of the state debt, see his elaboration of the idea in "Vergennes to Ossun, 14 June, 1776," *AAE-CP-Espagne,* vol. 580, fol. 389.

17. J.F. Bosher, *French Finances: 1770-1795* (Cambridge, England, 1970), pp. 142-182. Robert D. Harris, *Necker: Reform Statesman of the Ancien Regime* (Berkeley, 1979), pp. 145-146.

18. Doniol, *Histoire,* vol. I. p. 570.

19. "Vergennes to Aranda, 25 November, 1775," *AAE-CP-Espagne,* vol. 578, fol. 257.

20. Jonathan Dull, *The French Navy and American Independence* (Princeton, 1975)

21. "The Danish envoy to Spain, St. Saphorin, to his superior, Bernstorff, 9 and 30 Jan., 1777," *AAE-CP-Danemark,* 161, fols. 13-13[vo]. Also, "Bernstorff to Baron de Blome, envoy extraordinary of Denmark, 21 Jan., 1777," *ibid.,* 161, fol. 25.

22. On the significance of commerce in the making of French policy see: Robert R. Crout, "The Diplomacy of trade: The Influence of Commercial Considerations on French Involvement in the Anglo-American War of Independence, 1775-78," (Ph.D. Thesis, University of Georgia, 1977). See especially pp. 3, 93, 170, 214, 270-274. For a different interpretation, see: Doniol, *Histoire,* III, 140; Edward Corwin, *French Policy and the American Alliance* (Hamden, Conn., 1962), pp. 13-14.

23. "Vergennes to Ossun, 13 Sept., 1774," *AAE-CP-Espagne,* 574, fol. 131.

24. *AAE-Mémoires et Documents-Portugal,* 3 Sept., 1775, vol. I, fol. 294ff.

25. Corwin, *French Policy and the American Alliance of 1778,* p. 18.

26. "Vergennes to Aranda, 25 November, 1775," *AAE-CP-Espagne,* vol. 578, fol. 259.

27. G. Chinard, editor, *The Treaties of 1778* (Baltimore, 1928), p. 51.

28. S.F. Bemis, *The Diplomacy of the American Revolution,* (Bloomington, Indiana, 1957), p. 66.

29. "Mémoire" dated December, 1777, in Doniol, *Histoire,* II, p. 160.

30. "Bernstorff to Blome, 28 March, 1778," *AAE-CP-Danemark,* 161, fol. 281. "Vergennes to Breteuil, 10 March, 1778." *AAE-CP-Autriche,* 333, fol. 203; See also "Note" by M. Barthélemy, *ibid.,* 216.

31. "Dieyer to Schultz, London, 31 March, 1778," *AAE-CP-Danemark,* 161, fol. 181vo.

32. "Calliard to Vergennes, 31 March, 1778," *ibid.,* fol. 283.

33. "Breteuil to Vergennes, 17 April, 1778," *AAE-CP-Autriche,* 333, fol. 255-255vo.

34. "Vergennes to Breteuil, 22 June, 1778," *ibid.,* 335, fols. 61-62; "Vergennes to Breteuil, 11 July, 1778," *ibid.,* fols. 89-89[vo]. "Vergennes to Breteuil, 20 August, 1778," *ibid.,* 335, fols. 148-149[vo]. The British naval historian, W. Laird Clowes, concluded that, in the attack on the *Belle Poule,* Britain was technically the aggressor but that the behavior of the *Belle Poule,* and her sister ship was "so unfriendly" as to justify the attack. W. Laird Clowes *The Royal Navy: A History from the Earliest Times to the Present* (London, 1897-1903), vol. IV, pp. 13ff.

35. "Vergennes to Breteuil, 26 July, 1778," *AAE-CP-Autriche,* 335, fol. 102.

36. "Vergennes to Breteuil, 26 July, 1778," *ibid.,* 335, fol. 101.

37. "Le Baron de Blome to Comte Bernstorff, 19 Dec., 1776," *AAE-CP-Danemark,* 160, fols. 487[vo]; 498; S. F. Bemis, *op. cit,* p. 65.

38. "St. Saphorin to Bernstorff, Madrid, 30 January, 1777," *AAE-CP-Danemark,* 161, fol. 48[vo].

39. "Le Baron de Blome to Bernstorff, 15 March, 1778," *ibid.,* 161, fol. 268.

40. "Calliard to Vergennes, 28 July, 1778," *ibid.,* 161, fol. 296[vo]-298[vo].

41. "Breteuil to Vergennes, 24 March, 1778," *AAE-CP-Autriche,* 333, fol. 222.

42. "Vergennes to Guines, 23 June, 1775," *AAE-CP-Angleterre,* 510, fols. 297-297[vo]; "Vergennes to Guines, 27 Aug., 1775," *ibid.,* 511, fols. 317-317[vo].

43. "Vergennes to Noailles, 24 January, 1778," Printed in Doniol, *Histoire,* II, 792-793.

44. S. F. Bemis, "British Secret Service and the Franco-American Alliance," *American Historical Review,* XXIX, 474-475; Bemis, *Diplomacy of the American Revolution,* 65-66.

45. "Bernstorff to Baron do Blome, 21 January, 1777," *AEE-CP-Danemark,* 161, fol. 35.

46. "St. Saphorin to Bernstorff, 30 January, 1777," *ibid.,* fol. 48[vo].

47. "Louis XVI to Charles III, 9 March, 1778," Archives Nationales, K164#3.

48. "Vergennes to Louis XVI, 12 April, 1777," *AAE-MD-France,* 1897, fol. 77[vo]. In referring to Joseph II's diplomacy, Vergennes wrote to Louis XVI: "It is easy to make a war without being, materially, the aggressor."

49. Alexandre Tratchevsky, "La France et l'Allemagne sous Louis XVI," *Revue Historique* (Paris, 1881), vol. XIV, p. 257.

50. "Vergennes to Monteil, 14 September, 1779," *AAE-CP-Genoa,* vol. 160, fol. 330.

51. *AAE-MD-États-Unis,* vol. I, fols. 289-295; Gottschalk, *Lafayette and the Close of the American Revolution,* p. 61.

52. Lee Kennett, *The French Forces in America, 1780-1783* (Westport, Conn. 1977) pp. 6-9.

Chapter 21. Spain Enters the War

1. Henri Doniol, *Histoire de la participation à l'établissement des États-Unis d'Amérique* (Paris, 1886), Vol. I, pp. 308-9, 315; Stetson Conn, *Gibraltar in British Diplomacy in the 18th Century* (New Haven, 1942), pp. 181-182.
2. Francis P. Renaut, *Le Pacte de Famille et l'Amérique* (Paris, 1922), pp. 262-267.
3. *Ibid.*, p. 266.
4. "Montmorin to Vergennes, 28 January, 10 April, 1778," *AAE-CP-Espagne*, 588, fol. 135; 589, fols. 43-64. Doniol, *Histoire*, III, 575-576, 753; Edward S. Corwin, *French Policy and the American Alliance* (Hamden, Conn., 1962), pp. 176-198.
5. Doniol, *Histoire*, III, p.20.
6. Renaut, *op. cit.*, p. 277.
7. "Montmorin to Vergennes, 28 January, 2 February, 1778," *AAE-CP-Espagne*, Vol. 588, fols. 135-151; 218-220.
8. Conn. *Gibraltar*, p. 181; Renaut, *op. cit.*, pp. 273-274.
9. *Ibid.*, 276.
10. "Louis XVI to Charles III, 9 March, 1778," Archives Nationales K 164, No. 3.
11. "Charles III to Louis XVI, 22 March, 1778," *ibid.*, fol. 17.
12. Doniol, *Histoire*, III, p. 22-24
13. "Floridablanca to Aranda, 13 January, 1778," *AAE-CP-Espagne* Vol. 588, fols. 65-74; Doniol, *Histoire*, II, pp. 775-780.
14. "Projet de réponses à faire aux différentes questions de l'Espagne," approved by Louis XVI, 28 January, 1778, *AAE-CP-Espagne*, Vol. 588, fols. 152-160.
15. Doniol, *Histoire*, III, p. 18-20, 25.
16. "Floridablanca to Aranda, 13 January, 1778," J.F. Yela Utrilla, *Espana ante la independencia de los Estados Unidos* (Lerida, 1925), II, 188-195; I, 269-304.
17. "Floridablanca to Aranda, 9 March, 1778," *AAE-CP-Espagne*, Vol. 588, fol. 342.
18. "Montmorin to Vergennes, 9 February, 1778," *AAE-CP-Espagne*, Vol. 588, fol. 253.
19. Yela Utrilla, *Espana ante la independencia de los Estados Unidos*, I, pp. 269-304, 342; Francis P. Renaut, *Le Pacte de Famille*, p. 263, 276; Samuel Flagg Bemis, *The Diplomacy of the American Revolution* (Bloomington, 1957), p. 76; Stetson Conn, *Gibraltar*, pp. 181-182.
20. "Grimaldi to Aranda, 8 October, 1776," *AAE-CP-Espagne*, Vol. 582, fol. 34.
21. "Réflexions sur la conduite à tenir dans les circonstances présentes relativement à 1'Espagne," printed in Doniol, *Histoire*, III, p. 160; also, Bemis, *op. cit.*, p. 76.
22. "Montmorin to Vergennes, 30 March, 1778," *AAE-CP-Espagne*, Vol. 588, 439-444.
23. Renaut, *Le Pacte de Famille*, p. 36.
24. My conclusions concerning Vergennes and French naval policy are drawn primarily from the excellent study by Jonathan Dull, *op. cit.*, p. 103; see also Doniol, *Histoire*, III, p. 160ff.
25. Dull, *op. cit.*, 104; Also see: "Vergennes to Montmorin, 22 June, 1778," printed in Doniol, *Histoire*, III, p. 479.
26. S.F. Bemis, *The Diplomacy of the American Revolution*, p. 77; Doniol, *Histoire*, III, 13-14, 21.
27. "Montmorin to Vergennes, 20 March, 1778," *AAE-CP-Espagne*, fols. 401-408.

28. Stetson Conn, *Gibraltar,* p. 182.
29. *Ibid.*
30. "Montmorin to Vergennes, 27 April, 1778," *AAE-CP-Espagne,* Vol. 589, fols. 104-110; Bemis, *op. cit., American Revolution,* p. 77; Stetson Conn, *Gibraltar,* pp. 182ff.
31. *Ibid.,* 182-183; D. Manuel Danvila Y Collado, *Reinado de Carlos III,* (Madrid, 1896), V. pp. 7-9; Also: Conn, *Gibraltar,* pp. 184-185; "Almodovar to Floridablanca, 18 September, 1778," Danvila, *Reinado de Carlos III,* V, p. 23.
32. "Réflexions sur la conduite à tenir dans les circonstances présentes relativement à l'Espagne, 20 June, 1778," Doniol, *Histoire* and "Vergennes to Montmorin, 20 June, 1778," *AAE-CP-Espagne,* Vol. 589, fols. 310-317, 321-26; See also: "Montmorin to Vergennes, 26 May, 1778," *ibid.,* Vol. 589, fols. 227-236.
33. Paul del Perugia, *La tentative d'invasion de l'Angleterre,* (Paris, 1939), p. 36; Rénaut, *Le Pacte de Famille,* p. 279.
34. See Floridablanca's official dispatch and confidential letter to Almodovar, 25 August, 1778, Danvila, *Reinado do Carlos III,* Vol. 5, pp. 19-21, Bemis, *Diplomacy of the American Revolution,* p. 78-79.
35. Danvila, *Reinado de Carlos III,* V, p. 33; Bemis, *Diplomacy of the American Revolution,* p. 79.
36. Conn, *Gibraltar,* pp. 184-185; "Almodovar to Floridablanca, 18 September, 1778," Danvila, *Reinado de Carlos III,* V, p. 23.
37. "Vergennes to Montmorin, 9, 17, October, 1778," *AAE-CP-Espagne,* Vol. 291, fols. 38-41; 60-72; Danvila, *Reinado de Carlos III,* V, pp. 26-30.
38. "Floridablanca to Almodovar, 25 August, 1778," *ibid.,* V, p. 20; Bemis, *Diplomacy of the American Revolution,* p. 79.
39. "Floridablanca to Vergennes, 20 November, 1778," *AAE-CP-Espagne,* Vol. 591, fols. 219-220; Doniol, *Histoire,* III, 619-621.
40. "Projet de Guerre, 24 December, 1778," *AAE-CP-Espagne,* Vol. 591, fols. 419-425; Doniol, *Histoire,* III, pp. 604-606, 635-637.
41. France, according to Vergennes' figures, had 62 ships of the line and Spain had 45. "Projet de Guerre," *op cit.,* Vol, 591, fols. 419-425.
42. Renaut, *Le Pacte de Famille,* p. 287.
43. *Ibid.,* p. 286.
44. Conn, *Gibraltar,* pp. 186-187. See also, Renaut, *Le Pacte de Famille,* pp. 284-85.
45. "Montmorin to Vergennes, 22 June, 1778," *AAE-CP-Espagne,* Vol. 589, fols. 341-342.
46. "Traduction de 1a Note remise à l'ambassadeur de France par M. 1e Comte de Floridablanca," 11 August, 1778; Doniol, *Histoire,* III, 536-544.
47. *Ibid.*; and "Montmorin to Vergennes, 18 August, 1778," *AAE-CP-Espagne,* Vol. 590, fols. 218-239.
48. "Vergennes to Montmorin, 24 December, 1778," *ibid.,* Vol. 591, fols. 428-430.
49. *Ibid.,* Vol. 590, fols. 186-215.
50. "Montmorin to Vergennes, 31 August, 1778," *ibid.,* Vol. 590, fols. 303-316.
51. Renaut, *Le Pacte de Famille,* p. 294; also: "Floridablanca to Vergennes, 11 June, 1779," *AAE-CP-Espagne,* Vol. 594, fols. 225-226.
52. "Vergennes to Montmorin, 19 March, 1779," Doniol, *Histoire,* III, pp. 691-695.
53. "Vergennes to Louis XVI, 5 December 1778," *AAE-MD-France,* Vol. 1897,

fol. 94.

54. "Montmorin to Vergennes, 12 and 13 January, 1778," quoted in Doniol, *Histoire,* III, pp. 642-643.

55. "Montmorin to Vergennes, 14 January, 1778," *ibid.*, p. 643 and footnote.

56. "Vergennes to Montmorin, 22 January, 1779," printed in part in Doniol *Histoire,* III, p. 644.

57. "Montmorin to Vergennes, 1, 8, February, 1779," the letter of 1 February is cited in *ibid.*, p. 645. The letter of 8 February, 1779 is printed in part, *ibid.*, p. 645 and footnote.

58. Articles I and II; the entire draft of the Convention is printed in *ibid.*, III, pp. 803-810.

59. "Projet de Guerre, Vergennes to Montmorin, 24 December, 1778," *AAE-CP-Espagne,* Vol. 591, fols. 419-425.

60 "Vergennes to Montmorin, 12 February, 1779," "Vergennes to Floridablanca, 12 February, 1779," *AAE-CP-Espagne,* Vol. 592, fols. 233vo-235, 245-246, 247-248.

61. "Montmorin to Vergennes, 12 January, 1779," *ibid.*, Vol. 592, fols. 37-45.

62. "Vergennes to Montmorin, 19 March, 1779," *ibid.*, Vol. 593, fols. 92-109. There are two good secondary studies of this campaign of 1779: A. Temple Patterson, *The Other Armada,* (Manchester, 1960), written from the British point of view, and Paul del Perugia, *La tentative d'invasion de l'Angleterre de 1779* (Paris, 1939), written from a French viewpoint. I have used both extensively.

63. "Vergennes to Floridablanca, 12 February, 1779," *AAE-CP-Espagne.*, fol. 247-247vo; also "Montmorin to Vergennes, 31 July, 1779," *ibid.*, Vol. 594, fol. 505.

64. Both the Irish and Isle of Wight expedition plans are described in Paul del Perugia, *La tentative d'invasion de l'Angleterre de 1779* (Paris, 1939), pp. 41-73.

65. *Ibid.*, pp. 65-66. The author of Vergennes' plan was not Broglie, however, but an officer by the name of Hamilton.

66. "Montmorin to Vergennes, 7 September, 1778, 7 December, 1778," *AAE-CP-Espagne,* Vol. 590, fol. 355; Vol. 591, fol. 318.

67. "Vergennes to Montmorin, 24 December, 1778," *ibid.*, Vol. 591, fol. 417.

68. "Vergennes to Montmorin, 21 September, 1778," *ibid.*, Vol. 590, fol. 418; Paul del Perugia, *La tentative d'invasion,* pp. 26-28.

69. Patterson, *The Other Armada,* pp. 47ff; later the number of French troops was raised to 30,000.

70. "Vergennes to Montmorin, 31 July, 1778," *AAE-CP-Espagne.*, Vol. 590, fol. 141.

71. "Vergennes to Montmorin, 12 February, 1779," printed in full in Doniol, *Histoire,* III, pp. 685-687.

72. Article IV, *ibid.*, III, p. 806.

73. Articles V to X, *ibid.*, III, pp. 807-809.

74. Article XI, *ibid.*, III, p. 810.

75. Article XII, III, *ibid.*

76. "Vergennes to Montmorin, 12 February, 1779," printed in full in *ibid.*, III, pp. 650-654.

77. *Ibid.*, III, p. 654, and "Vergennes to Montmorin, 12 February, 1779," printed in part in *ibid.*, pp. 655-658.

78. "Montmorin to Vergennes, 22 February, 1779," printed in part in *ibid.*, III, p. 660 and footnote.

79. *Ibid.*, III, p. 661.

80. "Montmorin to Vergennes, 28 February, 1779," printed in full in *ibid.*, III, pp.

665-667.

81. *Ibid.*, III, p. 666.

82. "Montmorin to Vergennes, 28 February, 1779," *ibid.*, III, pp. 665-667.

83. "Vergennes to Montmorin, 8 March, 1779," printed in part in *ibid.*, III, pp. 668-669 and footnote.

84. "Vergennes to Montmorin, 19 March, 1779," printed in full in *ibid.*, III, pp. 670-672.

85. "Vergennes to Montmorin, 19 March, 1779," and "Réponse à l'écrit de l'Espagne sur la négotiation qui se suit par 1a médiation de S.M.C. en Angleterre, et sur la jonction projetée des flottes françaises et espagnoles, pour l'expédition contre l'Angleterre," dated also 19 March, 1779. Both printed in full in *ibid.*, III, pp. 691-695; 696-700.

86. "Montmorin to Vergennes, 28 February, 1779," *ibid.*, III, p. 644.

87. "Montmorin to Vergennes, 22 March, 1779," printed in full in *ibid.*, 746 and footnote.

88. A French version of the British reply of 16 March is printed in *Exposé des motifs de la conduite du Roi très chrétien, relativement à l'Angleterre accompagné d'un pareil Exposé de ceux qui ont determiné le Roi d'Espagne, dans le parti qu'il a pris à l'égard de la même Puissance,* (Paris, 1779). Printed in full in *ibid.*, III, pp. 824-856.

89. *Ibid.*, III, 748.

90. "Montmorin to Vergennes, 29 March, 1779," *ibid.*, III, pp. 799-800.

91. *Ibid.*, III, pp. 850-853.

92. *Ibid.*, p. 853.

93. *ibid.*, III, p. 750; "Vergennes to Floridablanca, 29 April, 1779," *ibid.*, III, p. 764 and footnote.

94. "Vergennes to Montmorin, 12 April, 1779," *ibid.*, III, pp. 801-803.

95. "Vergennes to Montmorin, 29 April, 1779," printed in large part in *ibid.*, III, pp. 767-769.

96. Quoted in *ibid.*, III, p. 792.

97. "Montmorin to Vergennes, 13 April, 1779," *ibid.*, III, pp. 755-759.

98. *Ibid.*, III, p. 806.

99. "Montmorin to Vergennes, 30 March, 1779," *ibid.*, III, pp. 753-754 and footnote.

100. *Ibid.*, III, p. 810.

101. "Montmorin to Vergennes, 17 May, 1779," printed in part in *ibid.*, III, p. 771.

102. S.F. Bemis, *Diplomacy of the American Revolution*, p. 83.

103. "Mémoire sur les opérations aux quelles on pourrait employer nos forces navales contre l'Angleterre, January, 1778," *AAE-CP-Espagne*, Vol. 588, fols. 212-215; J. Dull, *The French Navy and American Independence*, pp. 116-135.

104. *Ibid.*, p. 149; "Montmorin to Vergennes, 7 September, 7 December, 1778," *AAE-CP-Espagne*, Vol. 590, fol. 355; Vol. 591, fol. 318.

105. Paul del Perugia, La tentative d'invasion de l'Angleterre de 1779, p. 33.

106. "Vergennes to Montmorin, 5 May, 1778," *AAE-CP-Espagne* 589, fol. 589; Perugia, *La tentative d'invasion de l'Angleterre de 1779*, pp. 52-56.

107. *Ibid.*, p. 84.

108. "Mémoire du Roi pour servir d'instruction au Comte d'Orvilliers à l'île Sissargas, 29 May, 1779," *AAE-CP-Espagne*, Vol. 594, fol. 152ff.

109. See: "Montmorin to Vergennes, 3, 5, July, 1779," *AAE-CP-Espagne*, Vol. 594, fols. 369, 372-376.

110. Reports of the French Officer Bessières to Vergennes, cited in Perugia, *La tentative d'invasion,* p. 94-95.

111. *Ibid.*, p. 97.

112. *Ibid.*, p. 99.

113. "Beaumarchais to Vergennes, 31 August, 1779," *AAE-CP-Espagne,* Vol. 538, fol. 90.

114. Quoted in Perugia, *La tentative d'invasion,* p. 142.

115. "Mémoire" by Aranda dated 21 June, 1779. Also "Aranda to Vergennes, 4 August, 1779," *AAE-CP-Espagne,* Vol. 594. fols. 287-290; Vol. 595,fols. 13-21.

116. "Comte d'Orvilliers to Vergennes, 2 September, 1779," *AAE-CP-Espagne,* Vol. 595, fol. 276.

117. Perugia, *La tentative d'invasion de l'Angleterre,* p. 160.

118. *Ibid.*, p. 161-162.

119. *Ibid.*, p. 176.

120. Jonathan Dull, *The French Navy and American Independence,* p. 158.

Chapter 22. Dutch Neutrality: 1776-1782

1. On Dutch politics and diplomacy in the latter part of the 18th century see: Robert R. Palmer, *The Age of the Democratic Revolution* (Princeton, 1959), Vol. I; Henry de Peyster, *Les Troubles de Hollande, 1780-1795* (Paris, 1905); Alfred Cobban, *Ambassadors and Secret Agents,* (London, 1954); Alice Clare Carter, *The Dutch Republic in Europe in the Seven Years War* (Coral Gables, 1971).

2. *AAE-CP-Russie,* Supplément, Vol. 16, fol. 9; declaration printed in Francis P. Renaut, *Les Provinces-Unies et la guerre d'Amérique* (1775-1784), Vol. I, pp. 323-333; and J.B. Scott, *The Armed Neutrality of 1780 and 1800,* p. 274.

3. Paul Fauchille, *La diplomatie française et la ligue des neutres de 1780,* pp. 210-211.

4. See, for example: Arts. XXVI and XXVII, Elbert Chinard, editor, *The Treaties of 1778 and Allied Documents* (Baltimore, 1928), pp. 40-43. However, the Franco-American treaty, unlike the conventions relative to the armed neutrality, explicitly listed naval stores as non-contraband, *ibid.*, p. 42.

5. Paul Fauchille, *La diplomatie française et la ligue des neutres de 1780,* p. 380.

6. Francis P. Renaut, *op.cit.*, Vol. I, pp. 338-339.

7. "La Vauguyon to Vergennes, 2 June, 1780," *AAE-CP-Hollande,* Vol. 541, fol. 122.

8. "Vergennes to La Vauguyon, 3 May, 1780," *ibid.*, Vol. 541, fol. 14.

9. Francis P. Renaut, *op. cit.*, (1775-1784), Vol. I, p. 362.

10. According to the British ambassador at The Hague, Sir Joseph Yorke, the hope of forming a neutral league with the northern states was a "very seducing phantom" in Dutch heads months before Catherine issued her declaration. See *ibid.*, p. 346.

11. "Vergennes to LaVauguyon, 29 June, 1780," *AAE-CP-Hollande,* Vol. 541, fol. 334; "LaVauguyon to Vergennes, 21 July, 1780," *ibid.*, Vol. 541, fol. 329.

12. Francis P. Renaut, *op. cit.*, Vol. I, p. 351.

13. *Ibid.*, p. 350.

14. "LaVauguyon to Vergennes, 2 May, 1780," *AAE-CP-Hollande,* Vol. 541, fols. 5-6.

15. "LaVauguyon to Vergennes, 30 May, 1780," "LaVauguyon to Vergennes,

6 June, "LaVauguyon to Vergennes, 1 August, 1780," *ibid.*, Vol. 541, fols. 107-110; 126-130; 382vo -383.

16. "Vergennes to LaVauguyon, 19 June, 1780," *AAE-CP-Hollande*, Vol. 541, fol. 223.

17. "Vergennes to LaVauguyon, 18 June, 1780," *ibid.*, Vol. 541, fol. 179.

18. *Ibid.*, fols. 179vo -180.

19. "LaVauguyon to Vergennes, 30 June, 1780," *ibid.*, Vol. 541, fol. 230.

20. "LaVauguyon to Vergennes, 4 July, 1780," *ibid.*, Vol. 541, fols. 273vo-274.

21. "LaVauguyon to Vergennes, 7 July, 1780," *ibid.*, Vol. 541, fols. 282-284.

22. "Vergenees to LaVauguyon, 13 July, 1780," *ibid.*, Vol. 541, fols. 296vo -297.

23. "Vergennes to LaVauguyon, 13 July, 1780," *ibid.*, Vol. 541, fols. 298-299vo.

24. *Ibid.*

25. *Ibid.*

26. "Vergennes to LaVauguyon, 29 June, 1780," *ibid.*, Vol. 541, fol. 224.

27. "LaVauguyon to Vergennes, 14 July, 1780," *ibid.*, Vol. 541, fols. 304-305.

28. "Vergennes to LaVauguyon, 16 July, 1780," *ibid.*, Vol. 541, fols. 309-310.

29. "Vergennes to LaVauguyon, 27 July, 1780," *ibid.*, Vol. 541, flos. 363-369.

30. "Vergennes to LaVauguyon, 19 August, 1780," *ibid.*, Vol. 541, fols. 468-471.

31. "LaVauguyon to Vergennes, 28 July, 1780," "LaVauguyon to Vergennes, 1 August, 1780," *ibid.*, Vol. 541, fol. 372, 381-382.

32. "Vergennes to LaVauguyon, 6 August, 1780," *ibid.*, Vol. 541, fols. 410.

33. "Extract d'une lettre de St. Eustache du 11 Aout, 1780," *ibid.*, Vol. 541, fols. 421-421vo.

34. "Vergennes to LaVauguyon, 24 August, 1780," *ibid.*, Vol. 541, fols. 486vo -487.

35. For the Dutch plenipotentiaries' instructions see: F. Edler, *The Dutch Republic and the American Revolution,* p. 146; Isabel de Madariaga, *Britain, Russia and the Armed Neutrality of 1780,* (New Haven, 1962), p. 231. My discussion of British and Russian policies regarding the Armed Neutrality is heavily indebted to this excellent study.

36. "LaVauguyon to Vergennes, 3 October, 1780," *AAE-CP-Hollande*, Vol. 541, fols. 121vo -124.

37. "LaVauguyon to Vergennes, 10 October, 13 October, 1780," *ibid.*, Vol. 541, fols. 136-138vo ; 149-150vo.

38. Isabel de Madariaga, *Britain, Russia and the Armed Neutrality of 1780,* pp. 234-235; Samuel F. Bemis, *The Diplomacy of the American Revolution,* p. 156.

39. Samuel Flagg Bemis, *Diplomacy of the American Revolution,* pp. 144-145.

40. See "Necker to Vergennes, 1 May, 1780," and "Vergennes to LaVauguyon, 4 May, 1780," *AAE-CP-Hollande,* Vol. 541, fols. 3, 13.

41. "LaVauguyon to Vergennes, 9 May, 1780," *ibid.*, Vol. 541, fols. 27-32.

42. Francis P. Renaut, *op. cit.*, Vol. I, p. 363.

43. "Vergennes to LaVauguyon, 1 June, 1780," *AAE-CP-Hollande,* Vol. 541, fol. 114vo.

44. "Sartine to Vergennes, 9 June, 1780," *ibid.*, Vol. 541, fol. 146.

45. "Sartine to Vergennes, 16 June, 1780," *ibid.*, Vol. 541, fol. 166.

46. See: *ibid.*, Vol. 541, fol. 188.

47. "LaVauguyon to Vergennes, 6 August, 11 August, 1780," *ibid.*, Vol. 541, fols. 414-415vo ; 425; also: 426-429; "LaVauguyon to Vergennes, 18 September, 1780," *ibid.*, Vol. 542, fols. 88-89vo.

48. "LaVauguyon to Vergennes, 9 February, 13 February, 17 February, 1781,"

ibid., Vol. 543, fols. 290vo; 293-293vo.

49. Francis P. Renaut, *op. cit.*, Vol. I, 364; Sartine, the French Minister of the Navy, was aware that the British had learned about the new supply system. See "Sartine to Vergennes, 18 August, 1780," *AAE-CP-Hollande*, Vol. 541, fol. 465-465vo.

50. Renaut, *op. cit.*, p.364.

51. Hunt, Ford, Fitzpatrick and Hill, editors, *Journal of the Continental Congress* (Washington, 1903-1931), Vol. 1779, pp. 1167-1168; 1180; 1197-1198; 1236.

52. D. D. Wallace, *The Life of Henry Laurens* (New York, 1915), pp. 355-359.

53. *Ibid.*, pp. 355-359.

54. Francis P. Renaut, *op. cit.*, Vol. I, 375-378.

55. "LaVauguyon to Vergennes, 30 October, 1780," *AAE-CP-Hollande*, Vol. 542, fol. 230; also, Yorke, Mémoir to "Leurs Hautes et Puissances Seigneurs," *ibid.*, fols. 271-272. Also: I.R. Christie, *The End of North's Ministry, 1780-1782* (London, 1958), p. 246; Samuel Flagg Bemis, *The Diplomacy of the American Revolution*, p. 160.

56. "LaVauguyon to Vergennes, 17 November, 1780," *AAE-CP-Hollande*, Vol. 542, fols. 323-323vo.

57. *Ibid.*, fols. 323vo -324. Francis P. Renaut, *op. cit.*, Vol. I, 385.

58. *Ibid.*

59. *Ibid.*, 386.

60. "Extraits des Résolutions des États du Hollande et Quesfrise, 23 November, 1780;" "Extraits des Résolutions du Conseil de la ville d'Amsterdam, 21 November, 1780," *AAE-CP-Hollande*, Vol. 542, fols. 351-356; "LaVauguyon to Vergennes, 24 November, 1 December, 1780," *ibid.*, fols. 357-365; 387-387vo.

61. The opinion is that of LaVauguyon; "LaVauguyon to Vergennes, 24 November, 1780," *ibid.*, Vol. 542, fols. 371-371vo.

62. Madariaga, *op. cit.*, p. 236.

63. "Béranger to Vergennes, 19 December, 1780," *AAE-CP-Hollande*, Vol. 542, fols. 429vo-430.

64. Francis P. Renaut, *op. cit.*, Vol. I, p. 384.

65. "LaVauguyon to Vergennes, 21 November, 1780," *AAE-CP-Hollande*, Vol. 542, fols. 340-342vo; See also: fols. 333-334vo; 335-336vo; 337-338vo.

66. Renaut, *op. cit.*, pp. 399-400.

67. Madariaga, *op. cit.*, pp. 200; 203, Renaut, *op. cit.*, pp. 339-340.

68. "Lord Stormont to George III, December 18, 1780," in John Fortescue, *The Correspondence of King George III from 1760 to December, 1783*, (London, 1927-28), Vol. V, pp. 14, 166; Francis Piggott and G.W.T. Omond, *Documentary History of the Armed Neutralities of 1780 and 1800* (London, 1919), pp. 288ff; A copy of the Manifesto is in *AAE-CP-Hollande*, Vol. 542, fols. 435-436.

69. Francis P. Renaut, *op. cit.*, Vol. I, pp. 390-407.

70. Alice Clare Carter, *The Dutch Republic in Europe in the Seven Years War*, *passim;* Francis P. Renaut, *op. cit.*, Vol. I, p. 409.

71. *Ibid.*, pp. 414-417.

72. Samuel F. Bemis, *The Diplomacy of the American Revolution*, p. 162.

73. Madariaga, *Britain, Russia and the Armed Neutrality of 1780* pp. 195-216, 231, 232, and *passim*.

74. *Ibid.*, 200, 225.

75. "Letter Frederick to Princess of Orange, 7 February, 1780," printed in Henry de Peyster, *Les Troubles de Hollande, 1780-1795*, p. 66, fn. #1.

Chapter 23. The Bavarian Crisis: I

1. "Breteuil to Vergennes, 10 March, 1778," *AAE-CP-Autriche,* vol. 333, fol. 173vo.

2. "LaLuzerne to Vergennes, 23 December, 1777," *ibid.*, vol. 333, fol. 16vo.

3. "Mémoire pour servir d'instruction au sieur chevalier de la Luzerne, . . . allant à Munich en qualité d' envoyé extraordinaire du Roi près de l'électeur de Bavière, Dec., 1776," *AAE-CP-Bavière,* Supplément IX, printed in André Lebon, *Recueil des instructions donneés aux ambassadeurs et ministres de France depuis les traités de Westphalie jusqu'à la Révolution Française* (Paris), VIII, Bavière, Palatinat, Deux-Ponts, p. 368.

4. Paul Oursel, *La diplomatie de la France sous Louis XVI* (Paris, 1921), pp. 25-27.

5. Gustave Fagniez, *La politique de Vergennes et la diplomatie de Breteuil* (Paris, 1922), p. 21.

6. "Mémoire de M. de Vergennes à Louis XVI sur la situation politique de la France relativement à différentes puissances, 1774," Archives Nationales K 164no 2^2 ; See also: Breteuil's statement on Joseph's ambitious character in "Mémoire de Breteuil sur la Hollande, 11 November, 1784," and "Mémoire de Breteuil sur la Bavière, 2 January, 1785," Archives Nationales K 164.

7. Emil Bourgeois, *Manuel Historique de politique étrangerè* (Paris, 1893), I, 383.

8. "Mémoire pour servir d'instructions au sieur Baron de Breteuil allant résider à Vienne en qualité d'ambassadeur extraordinaire du roi près leurs majestés impériales et royales apostaliques, 28 Dec., 1774," Printed in Albert Sorel, *Recueil des instructions* . . . etc., (Paris, 1884), I, Autriche, 454, 486.

9. Ernest Lavisse, *Histoire de France depuis les origines jusqu'à la Révolution* (Paris, 1911), IX, 97.

10. "Mémoire pour servir d'instruction au sieur chevalier de la Luzerne, . . . Bavière, Dec., 1776," Lebon, *Receuil des instructions,* VII, 366.

11. Paul Oursel, *La diplomatie de la France,* 39; "Marie Thérèse to Mercy, 30 Juin, 31 juillet, 1777," "Mercy to Marie Thérèse, 15 April, 1777; Alfred R. von Arneth and A. Gelfsoy, *Correspondance secrète entre Marie Thérèse et le Comte de Mercy d'Argenteau* (Paris, 1874), vol. III, pp. 88-99, 106.

12. "Vergennes to Louis XVI, 12 April, 1777." *AAE-MD-France,* 1897, fols. $76\text{-}76^{vo}$.

13. *Ibid.*, fols. 77vo -78.

14. *Ibid.*, fols. $78\text{-}78^{vo}$.

15. *Ibid.*, fols. 78vo -79.

16. Ernest Lavisse, *Histoire de France,* IX, 94

17. Oursel, *La diplomatie de la France,* 76; on the different points of view about the Austrian alliance, see: L.P. Ségur, *Politique de tous les cabinets de L'Europe pendant les règnes de Louis XV et de Louis XVI* (Paris, 1801), vol. III, pp. 158-171; 251ff.

18. "Mémoire pour servir d'instruction au sieur Baron de Breteuil" . . . . Albert Sorel, *Recueil des instructions,* Autriche, 463.

19. "Pons to Vergennes, 23 December, 1775," *AAE-CP-Prusse* 193. See also *AAE-MD-Prusse,* VIII, fols. 82-196.

20. Letter of Goussen to Vergennes, 31 Jan., 1778, quoted in Oursel, *La diplomatie de la France,* 118.

21. "Mémoire pour servir d'instructions au Sieur Baron de Breteuil" . . . Albert Sorel, *Recueil des instructions,* Autriche, 494.

22. Ernest Lavisse, *Histoire de France,* IX, 96.

23. "Mémoire de M. de Vergennes à Louis XVI, sur la situation politique de la France relativement à différentes Puissances," 1774, Archives Nationales K 164no 2^{2}; "Mémoire pour servir d'instructions au Sieur Baron de Breteuil . . .", Albert Sorel, *Recueil des instructions,* Autriche, 494.

24. "Breteuil to Vergennes, 10 Jan., 1778, 13 Jan., 1778, 17 Jan., 1778, 20 Jan., 1778, 21 Jan. 1778," *AAE-CP-Autriche,* 333, fols. 36-37vo; 42-46; 49vo -50vo; 52vo -55; "La Luzerne to Vergennes, 3 Jan., 1778, 12 Jan., 1778, 18 Jan., 1778;" *ibid.,* 333, fol. 32vo -32; 47-49; 52.

25. "Breteuil to Vergennes, 5 Feb., 1778," *ibid.,* 333, fol. 71-71vo.

26. "Marie Thérèse to Marie Antoinette, 1 Feb., 1778, 19 Feb., 1778, 6 March, 1778, 14 March, 1778," A. von Arneth, *Maria Theresa und Marie Antoinette; Ihr Briefwechsel* (Paris, 1875), pp. 219ff. "Breteuil to Vergennes, 10 Jan., 1778," *AAE-CP-Autriche,* 333, fol. 39; Oursel, *La diplomatie de la France,* 54.

27. "La Luzerne to Vergennes, 12 Jan., 1778," *AAE-CP-Autriche,* 333, fol. 48vo.

28. "Mémoires de la guerre de 1778," Frederick II, *Oeuvres* (s.L. 1790), vol. 4, pp. 313-316; "La Luzerne to Vergennes, 24 Jan., 1778," *AAE-CP-Autriche,* 333, fol. 60.

29. "La Luzerne to Vergennes, 27 Jan., 1778," *ibid.,* 333, fol. 62.

30. "Marie Thérèse to Marie Antoinette, 2 Aug. 1780," A. von Arneth, *Maria Theresa und Marie Antoinette; Ihr Briefwechsel,* p. 321.

31. Oursel, *La diplomatie de la France . . .,* 112.

32. "Mémoire de la guerre de 1778," Frederick II, *Oeuvres,* vol. 4, pp. 314-316; on Frederick's relations with Deux-Points, see: Le Comte de Goertz, *Mémoire historique relative aux Négociations qui eurent lieu en 1778 pour la Succession de Bavière . . . .* (Paris, 1812), *passim.*

33. "La Luzerne to Vergennes, 1 February, 1778, 14 March, 1778," *AAE-CP-Autriche,* 333, fols. 78vo -80vo; 194; "Traduction d'une déclaration faite par le Baron de Schwartzenau, Ministre de S.M. Prussienne à la Diète de l'Empire, 16 March, 1778," *ibid.,* 333, fols. 194-195. See also: Frederick's "Mémoire" to Duke of Deux-Ponts, *ibid.,* 333, fols. 80vo -89vo.

34. "Vergennes to Breteuil, 5 Feb., 1778," *ibid.,* 333, fol. 90-92, 95; "Vergennes to Breteuil, 9 March, 1775," quoted in Charles de Chambrun, *A l'école d'un diplomate: Vergennes* (Paris, 1944), p. 264.

35. "Vergennes to Breteuil, 10 March, 1778," *AAE-CP-Autriche,* 333, fols. 194vo-199. "Vergennes to Breteuil, 4 April, 1777," *ibid.,* 333, fols. 252vo

36. "Vergennes to Breteuil, 4 April, 1778," *ibid.,* 333, fols. 249vo.

37. "Mémoire de la guerre de 1778," Frederick II, *Oeuvres,* vol. 4, pp. 317-318.

38. "Vergennes to Breteuil, 5 February, 1778," *AAE-CP-Autriche,* 333, fols. 91-92,

39. *Ibid.,* 333, fols. 94-94vo.

40. "Breteuil to Vergennes, 18 Feb., 1778," *ibid.,* 333, fols. 98-99vo.

41. "Breteuil to Vergennes, 18 Feb., 1778," *ibid.,* 333, fols. 110vo -111vo.

42. "Breteuil to Vergennes, 18 Feb., 1778, *ibid.,* 333, fols. 111-111vo.

43. "Vergennes to Breteuil, 23 Feb., 1778," *ibid.,* 333, fols. 149-150.

44. "Vergennes to Breteuil, 8 June, 1778," *ibid.,* 335, fol. 26.

45. "Vergennes to Breteuil, 5 Feb., 1778," *ibid.,* 333, fols. 95vo -96.

46. "Traduction d'une déclaration faite par le Baron de Schwartzenau, Ministre de S.M. Prussienne à la Diète de l'Empire, 15 March, 1778," *AAE-CP-Autriche,* 333, fols. 194-195; See also: Frederick's exchange of letters with Joseph in April, 1778, "Correspondance de l'empéreur et de l'impératrice-reine avec le Roi . . . ." Fre-

derick II, *Oeuvres,* vol. 4, pp. 365-380.

47. "La Luzerne to Vergennes, 10 Feb., 1778," *AAE-CP-Autriche,* 333, fol. 80.

48. "Vergennes to Breteuil, 10 March, 1778," *ibid.*, 333, fols. 196-197. See also: A. Unzer, *Du Friede von Tëschen* (Kiel, 1903), pp. 55-56; Oursel, *La diplomatie de la France,* pp. 130-131.

49. "Breteuil to Vergennes, 24 March, 1778," *AAE-CP-Autriche,* 333, fol. 219.

50. "Breteuil to Vergennes, 17 April, 1778," *ibid.*, 333, fols. 243-246.

51. "Vergennes to Breteuil, 26 April, 1778," *ibid.*, 333, fol. 284-284vo.

52. "Vergennes to Breteuil, 3 May, 1778," *ibid.*, 333, fols. 306vo -307.

53. "Breteuil to Vergennes, 10 March, 1778," *ibid.*, 333, fols. 176-176vo ; "Vergennes to Breteuil, 25 February, 1778," *ibid.*, 333, fols. 177-177vo.

54. "Breteuil to Vergennes, 18 March, 23 April, 1778," *ibid.*, 333, fols. 180vo -181; 267vo.

55. "Vergennes to Breteuil, 3 May, 1778," *ibid.*, 333, fol. 306vo.

56. "Vergennes to Breteuil, 3 May, 1778," *ibid.*, 333, fol. 307.

57. "Breteuil to Vergennes, 9 July, 1778," *ibid.*, 335, fols. 62-65.

58. "Vergennes to Breteuil, 20 Juillet, 1778," *ibid.*, 335, fols. 100vo-103; "Breteuil to Vergennes, 29 Juillet, 1778," *ibid.*, 335, fols. 100-105vo ; "Vergennes to Breteuil 20 Aout, 1778," *ibid.*, 335, fol. 149.

Chapter 24. The Bavarian Crisis: II

1. "Copie de la lettre de S.M. l'impératrice-reine, envoyé par le Sr. Thugut," in Frederick II, *Oeuvres,* (s. l. 1790), Vo. 4, pp. 381-382; "Breteuil to Vergennes, 14 July, 1778," *AAE-CP-Autriche,* Vol. 335, fol. 67; "Propositions de S.M. l'impératrice-reine, 17 July, 1778," *ibid.*, Vol. 335, fols. 68-69vo; also in Frederick II, *Oeuvres,* Vol. 4, p. 383; "Louis XVI to Vergennes, 22 July, 1778," *AAE-MD-France,* 1897, fol. 89.

2. "Lettre du Roi de Prusse à l'impératrice-reine, 17 July, 1778," *AAE-CP-Autriche,* fols. 70-72; also 96vo-97vo; Frederick II, *Oeuvres,* Vol. 4, pp. 384-385.

3. "Breteuil to Vergennes, 29 July, 1778," *AAE-CP-Autriche,* Vol. 335, fols. 90-90vo; Paul Oursel, *La diplomatie de la France sous Louis XVI* (Paris, 1921), pp. 210-212.

4. "Breteuil to Vergennes, 5 August, 1778," *AAE-CP-Autriche,* Vol. 335, fol. 115.

5. Frederick II, *Oeuvres,* Vol. 4, pp. 392-394; 398; also see: "Contre proposition, 6 August, 1778," *AAE-CP-Autriche,* Vol. 335, fols. 116, 120; "Réponse de ministres Prussiens aux propositions de M. le Baron de Thugut," *ibid.*, Vol. 335, fol. 128vo ; Breteuil to Vergennes, 31 August, 1778," *ibid.*, Vol. 335, fol. 138vo.

6. "Breteuil to Vergennes, 29 July, 1778," *ibid.*, 335, fols. 90vo -91.

7. "Traduction d'une déclaration faite par le Baron de Schwartzenau, Ministre de S.M. Prussienne à la Diète de l'Empire, 16 March, 1778," *ibid.*, 333, fols. 194-195.

8. "M. le Marquis de Bombelle to Vergennes, 17 July, 1778," *ibid.*, 335, 75vo -76.

9. "Breteuil to Vergennes, 29 July, 1778," *ibid.*, 335, fol. 96.

10. "Breteuil to Vergennes, 6 August, 1778," *ibid.*, 335, fols. 116-117vo.

11. "Breteuil to Vergennes, 6 August, 1778," *ibid.*, 335, fols. 117-118.

12. "La Luzerne to Vergennes, 20, 29 Feb., 1 March, 11 April, 2 June, 1778," *ibid.*, 333, fols. 115-116, 139-140, 145-146, 235-236vo; vol. 335, fols. 13-13vo; "Breteuil to Vergennes, 9 July, 1778; 12 August, 1778," *ibid.*, 335, fols. 63; 124vo.

13. "Breteuil to Vergennes, 29 July, 1778," *ibid.*, 335, fols. 98vo-99.

14. "Vergennes to Breteuil, 20 July, 1778," *ibid.*, 335, fols. 104-104vo. "Breteuil to Vergennes, 29 July, 1778," *ibid.*, 335, 105vo.

15. "Breteuil to Vergennes, 15 May, 1778, 6 August, 1778," *ibid.*, 333, fols. 312-312vo; 335, 119. "Breteuil to Vergennes, 29 July, 1778," *ibid.*, 335, fols. 92vo. "Vergennes to Breteuil, 8 June, 1778," *ibid.*, 335, fol. 29vo.

16. "Vergennes to Breteuil, 26 July, 1778," *ibid.*, 335, fol. 101; "Breteuil to Vergennes, 31 August, 1778," *ibid.*, 335, fols. 140-141; "Vergennes to Breteuil, 20 August, 1778," *ibid.*, 335, fols. 142-142vo; "Vergennes to Breteuil, 20 August, 1778," *ibid.*, 335, fols. 148vo-149.

17. "Vergennes to Breteuil, 27 November, 1778," *ibid.*, 335, fol. 242.

18. "Vergennes to Breteuil, 9 September, 1778," *ibid.*, 335, fol. 160vo.

19. F.F. Martens, "Actes diplomatiques concernant la Hongrie de Teschen de 1779," *Russkoe istoricheskoe obschesto Sbornik* (St. Petersburg, 1888), Vol. LXV, p. iii, hereafter referred to as *Sbornik;* also, A. Unser, *Der Friede von Teschen* (Kiel, 1903), pp. 188ff.

20. *Sbornik*, iv.

21. *Ibid.*, 37-39

22. For Catherine's summary of and views of the Bavarian Crisis see her "Rescrit de S.M. l'Impératrice Catherine II au Prince Repnine 22 Octobre, 1779," *ibid.*, Vol. LXV, pp. 30-43.

23. "Breteuil to Vergennes, 18 February, 1778," *AAE-CP-Autriche,* 333, fols. 102-102vo.

24. "Breteuil to Vergennes, 27 June, 1778," *ibid.*, 335, fol. 46vo; On the moderation of the threat of a Russo-Turkish War, see: J.W. Zinkeisen, *Geschichte des osmanischen Reiches* (Gotha, 1859), Vol. 6, pp. 208ff.

25. "Vergennes to Breteuil, 20 August, 1778," *AAE-CP-Autriche,* 335, fol. 143.

26. "Vergennes to Breteuil, 7 November, 1778," *ibid.*, 335, fol. 227.

27. "Vergennes to Breteuil, 7 November, 1778," *ibid.*, 335, fol. 227. "Breteuil to Vergennes, 22 July, 1778," *ibid.*, 335, fol. 75vo.

28. "Vergennes to Corberon, 24 October, 1778," *ibid.*, 335, 208vo. On Corberon's role in the succeeding negotiations, see L.H. Labande, editor, *Un diplomate Français à la cour de Catherine II, 1775-1780; Journal intime du chevalier de Corberon* (Paris, 1901), II. 194ff. Unfortunately, for the critical year 1778, Corberon's Journal is useless.

29. "Representation," *Sbornik,* pp. 15-17; "Representation of Catherine to Vienna," *AAE-CP-Autriche,* 335, fols. 220vo-224. See also: "Rescrit de S.M. l'impératrice Catherine II au Prince Repnine du 22 Octobre, 1778," *Sbornik,* pp. 33-35.

30. *Ibid.*, p. 35.

31. *AAE-CP-Autriche,* 335, fol. 224.

32. "Vergennes to Corberon, 6 November, 1778," *ibid.*, 335, fols. 225-225vo.

33. "Breteuil to Vergennes, 23 November, 1778," *ibid.*, 335, fol. 230-230vo.

34. "Vergennes to Breteuil, 7 November, 1778," *ibid.*, 335, fols. 226vo-227.

35. "Breteuil to Vergennes, 23 November, 1778, 3 January, 1779," *ibid.*, Vol. 335, fols. 231vo, 330vo.

36. Oursel, *La Diplomatie de la France sous Louis XVI,* pp. 270ff; See also: "Convention entre la Russie et la Prusse, conclue le 10 février, 1772," *Sbornik,* pp. 26-29; "Note Secrète du Prince Repnine, adressé au Ministre du Prusse le Comte Finkenstein, du 8 (19) December, 1778," *ibid.*, pp. 97-98; 110-113; "Projet d'une Convention secrète," *ibid.*, 113-119.

37. "Breteuil to Vergennes, 23 November, 1778," *AAE-CP-Autriche,* 335, fol. 231vo.

38. Art. III, "Traité de paix entre Sa Majesté l'impératrice de Hongrie et de Bohême, et Sa Majesté le Roi de Prusse, conclu et signé à Teschen le 13 May, 1779...," in George Frederick von Martens, *Recueil de Traités*... (Gottingen, 1817), Vol. II, pp. 663-664.

39. Arts. I, IV, "Convention entre Sa Majesté l'Impératrice-Reine et S. A. A. Électorale Palatine," *ibid.,* pp. 669-671.

40. Arts, I, III, "Convention entre leurs Altesses Sérénis-simes l'Électeur Palatin et l'Électeur de Saxe...," *ibid.,* pp. 675-676.

41. Art. XV, "Traité de paix entre Sa Majesté l'Impératrice de Hongrie et de Bohême et Sa Majesté le Roi de Prusse, conclu et signé à Teschen le 13 May, 1779...," *ibid.,* p. 667.

42. "Acte d'Accession de Monsieur le Duc des Deux-Ponts à la Convention signée dans la Ville de Teschen, par les ministres Plénipotentiaires de Sa Majesté l'Impératrice-Reine de Hongrie et de Bohême et du Sérénissime Électeur Palatin...," *ibid.,* 673-674.

43. Art. X, "Traité de paix entre S.M. l'Impératrice... et S.M. le Roi de Prusse, conclu et signé à Teschen, le 13 May, 1779...," *ibid.,* pp. 665-666. "Vergennes to Breteuil, 16 November, 1778," *AAE-CP-Autriche,* 335, fols. 239vo-240. "Vergennes to Corberon, 20 November 1778," *ibid.,* 335, fol. 244.

44. Frederick II, *Politische Correspondenz* (Leipzig, 1931), XLII, 420.

45. L.H. Labande, editor, *Un diplomate français à la cour de Catherine II,* Vol. I, xxxviii.

46. *Ibid.,* xxxviii-xxxix.

47. Vincent-Félix Brun, *Guerres Maritimes de la France. Port de Toulon, ses armements, son administration depuis son origine jusqu'à nos jours* (Paris, 1861), I, 534.

48. L.H. Labande, *Loc cit.*

Chapter 25. Mogilev

1. "Abenzel to Kaunitz, 4 June, 1780," quoted in Robert Salomon, *La politique orientale de Vergennes (1780-1784)* (Paris, 1935), 46.

2. *Ibid.,* 37.

3. Svetlana Kluge, "Vergennes and the Franco-Russian Rapprochement," (Unpublished M.A. thesis, Columbia University, New York), 80.

4. "Catherine to Galitzin, 13 Feb., 1780," Salomon, *op. cit.,* 37.

5. Alfred von Arneth, *Geschichte Maria-Theresia* (Vienna, 1879), X, 664.

6. Salomon, *op. cit.,* 40-41.

7. "Réflexions sur l'entrevue Prochaine de Sa Majesté l'Empéreur avec l'Impératrice de Russie Dictées par Son Altesse le Prince de Kaunitz le 23 Avril, 1780," printed in full in *ibid.,* Annexe #1. Vergennes heard of all of this in a letter from "Barthélemy to Vergennes 28 March, 1780," *AAE-CP-Autriche,* 341, fols. 109; Joseph left for Mogilev on the 26th of April, 1780.

8. "Joseph to Maria Theresa, 12 July, 1780," in Alfred von Arneth, *Maria Theresia and Joseph II* (Vienna, 1868), III, 250.

9. "Joseph to Maria Theresa, 12 July, 1780," *Loc. cit.*

10. "Joseph to Maria Theresa, 18 July 1780," *ibid.,* III, 281; Comte de Saint-

Priest, *Mémoires: Règnes de Louis XV and Louis XVI* (Paris, 1929), Vol. I, p. 163.

11. "Breteuil to Vergennes, 5 October 1780," *AAE-CP-Autriche,* 341, fols. 297-308vo; 310-320.

12. In 1783 when Vergennes instructed his new ambassador to Vienna, the Marquis de Noailles, he told him that "nothing is more uncertain than the present alliance subsisting between the two courts [Vienna and Versailles]," Pierre Rain, *La diplomatie française d'Henri IV à Vergennes* (Paris, 1945), p. 309.

13. *Ibid.*, p. 311.

14. *Ibid.*

15. "Vergennes to Breteuil, 18 November 1780," *AAE-CP-Autriche,* 341, fols. 345-347.

16. "Maria Theresa to Mercy, 31 July 1777," Alfred von Arneth and A. Geoffroy, *Marie Antoinette: Correspondance sécrète entre Maria-Thérèse et le Comte de Mercy d'Argenteau* (Paris, 1874), 99-100.

17. "Kaunitz to Cobenzl, 22 August 1780," Salomon, *La Politique Orientale de Vergennes,* p. 55.

18. On these negotiations see "Projet du Traité d'Union d'Amitié et de Garantie signé Entre sa Majesté-L'Empéreur . . . et sa Majesté L'Impératrice de toutes les Russies," *ibid.*, Annexe #3. On the secret provisions of the projected treaty, see: *ibid.*, Annexes #4 and #5.

19. Bernard Fay, *Louis XVI ou La Fin d'un Monde* (Paris, 1955), p. 210.

20. Pierre Rain, *La diplomatie française,* 310; Philippe Sagnac, *La Fin de l'Ancien Régime et la Révolution Américaine* (1763-1789) (Paris, 1952), 537; Salomon, *op. cit.*, 118-119.

21. "Breteuil to Vergennes, 21 February 1782," *AAE-CP-Autriche,* 345, fol. 68.

22. Reinhold Köser, *König Friedrich der Grosse,* II, 519, 605-606.

23. *Ibid.*, 609.

24. *Ibid.*, 610-611.

25. *Ibid.*,

26. "Breteuil to Vergennes, 10 August, 1782," *AAE-CP-Autriche,* 345, fol. 330-331.

27. Charles-Roux, "La Politique Française en Egypte à la fin du XVIII siècle," *Revue Historique* (1906), XCI, 2-7, 225-226.

28. *Ibid.*, 8.

29. "Mémoire du Comte de Saint-Priest sur son ambassade, 1768-1784," *ibid.*, 8.

30. "Mémoire presenté par le Comte de Saint-Priest pendant son séjour en France, 1777-1778," *ibid.*, 9.

31. *Ibid.*, 17-18.

32. *Ibid.*, 9-10.

Chapter 26. Peace Appears Trailing Clouds of Ambitions

1. Sir Harold Nicolson, *The Congress of Vienna: A Study in Allied Unity: 1812-1822* (Compass Books Edition, New York, 1961), 260, 51.

2. "Vergennes to LaLuzerne, April 9, 1782," J. B. Scott, *American Secretaries of State* (New York, 1927), I, 56; E. E. Hales, *Franklin in France* (Boston, 1887), II, 52.

3. "Vergennes to LaLuzerne, June 28, 1782," J.B. Scott, *American Secretaries of State,* I, 306-307; Hales, *Franklin in France,* II, 153.

4. On the British attempts to conclude separate settlements with France and her

allies, see: Doniol, *Histoire,* V, 26; "Franklin to David Hartley, January 15, 1782," A. H. Smyth, *The Writings of Benjamin Franklin* (New York, 1906), VIII, 358.

5. "LaVauguyon to Vergennes, 18 April, 1782," *AAE-CP-Hollande,* Vol. 548, fols. 318-319vo.

6. Bemis, *Diplomacy of the American Revolution,* (Bloomington, Ind., 1957), 195. Francis Wharton, *Diplomatic Correspondence of the American Revolution* (Washington, D.C., 1889), V, 271, 298; Doniol, *Histoire,* V, 40.

7. "Shelburne to General Carleton and Admiral Digby, May, 1782," E.G.P. Fitzmaurice, *Life of Shelburne,* (London, 1875-76), III, 199-201.

8. W.C. Ford, *et. al., Journals of the Continental Congress, 1774-1789* (Washington, D.C., 1904-1937), May 14, May 31, 1782; Bemis, *Diplomacy of the American Revolution,* 202.

9. *Ibid.,* 204; Sir John Fortescue, *Corerespondence of George III* (London, 1927-28), Vol. I, 40-41.

10. Doniol, *Histoire,* V, 96.

11. On Necker's private attempts to open peace negotiations, see: Richard B. Morris, *The Peace Makers* (New York, 1965), Chapter V, pp. 88-111; Baron Jehan de Witte, editor, *Journal de l'Abbé de Veri* (Paris, 1928-30), Vol. II, pp. 381, 386, 398.

12. *Ibid.,* II, 386, 398; Richard B. Morris, *The Peace Makers,* p. 96.

13. *Ibid.,* p. 97.

14. *Ibid.,* pp. 101-103.

15. *Ibid.,* p. 104.

16. "Count Mercy d'Argenteau to Kaunitz, January 21, 1781," Quoted in Richard B. Morris, *op. cit.,* p. 107.

17. "Journal of Maréchal de Castries," p. 87, cited in Duc de Castries, *Le Testament de la Monarchie* (Paris, 1958-59), 261.

18. See, for example: "Dupont to Vergennes, January 4, 1782," "De Lessait to Vergennes, June 12, 1782," "La Toul to Vergennes, August 29, 1782," *AAE-CP-Angleterre,* Vol. 536, fol. 13ff; Vol. 537, fols. 234ff; 285ff.

19. Duc de Castries, *Le Testament de la Monarchie,* pp. 259ff.

20. On the question of the court rumors about replacing Vergennes, see: Louis Petit Bachaumont, *Mémoires secrets pour servir à l'histoire de la République des lettres en France* (Bruxelle, 1871), Vol. XXIII, pp. 275-276.

21. "LaVauguyon to Vergennes, 11, 14, 26 June, 16 August, 1782," "Vergennes to LaVauguyon, 20 June, 1782," *AAE-CP-Hollande,* Vol. 549, fols. 289vo-290, 293vo-294; 317-320; 378; 348-349; Vol. 550, fols, 313-314vo.

22. L.H. Butterfield, editor, *Diary and Autobiography of John Adams* (Cambridge, Mass., 1961), III, pp. 82-88.

23. "Vergennes to LaVauguyon, 10 and 17 October, 1782," *AAE-CP-Hollande,* Vol. 551, fols. 192; 231vo.

24. "Projet d'instruction," *AAE-CP-Hollande,* Vol. 550, fols. 62-63vo.

25. "Vergennes to LaVauguyon, 5,12, May, 1782," *AAE-CP-Hollande,* Vol. 549, fols. 27-27vo; 69-70vo.

26. "Vergennes to LaVauguyon, 12 May, 1782," *ibid.,* Vol. 549, fol. 71.

27. "LaVauguyon to Vergennes, 28 May, 1782;" "Vergennes to LaVauguyon, 30 May, 1782," *ibid.,* Vol. 549, fols. 193-194; 203vo-204vo.

28. "Vergennes to LaVauguyon, 8 August, 1782;" "LaVauguyon to Vergennes, 13 August, 1782," *ibid.,* Vol. 550, fols. 268vo-269vo ; 298-301vo.

29. "LaVauguyon to Vergennes, 13 August, 1782," *ibid.,* Vol. 550, fols. 298-301vo.

30. J.B. Scott, *American Secretaries of State* (1927-29), Vol. I, 65.
31. C.F. Adams, editor, *Works of John Adams,* (Boston, 1850-1856), IX, 472.
32. L.H. Butterfield, *The Adams Papers* (Cambridge, Mass., 1961), II, "Diary", 302, 319; and *ibid.,* IV, "Autobiography," 92.
33. Bernard Bailyn, "Butterfield's Adams: Notes for a Sketch," *The William and Mary Quarterly* (April, 1962) XIX, no. 2, 244-245. See also: Peter Shaw's very perceptive *The Character of John Adams* (Chapel Hill, 1976), Chapters V, VI, VII.
34. Butterfield, *Adams Papers,* II, 305, IV, p. 107, 111-112.
35. *Dictionary of American Biography* (New York, 1933), X, 5.
36. S.F. Bemis, *Pinckney's Treaty,* (New Haven, 1960), 29-30; on Jay's isolation at Madrid, see: Frank Monaghan, *John Jay* (New York, 1935) pp. 152ff.
37. *Dictionary of American Biography,* X, 6.
38. L.G.W. Legg, editor, *British Diplomatic Instructions* - 1745-1789, Vol. VII, France, 178; Lord John Russell, *Memorials and Correspondence of Charles James Fox* (London, 1857), IV.
39. *Dictionary of National Biography,* Vol. XIX, 167. The critic was Lord Malmesbury.
40. "Charles III to Count d'Aranda, 26 August, 1782," *Archivo Historico Nacional, Estado,* Vol. 4215, #2, p. 4.
41. On the Spanish notion of such a truce based on *uti possidetis* see: Samuel Flagg Bemis, *Hussey-Cumberland Mission and American Independence* (Princeton, 1931), pp. 29-30, 101, 103, 107, 108, 113, 115, 118, 124, 129.
42. "Vergennes to Louis XVI, 27 September, 1780," *Archives Nationales,* K 164, no. 3; Doniol, *Histoire,* IV, 488.
43. Bemis, *Diplomacy of the American Revolution,* p. 181.
44. "Adams to Vergennes, July 13, 1781," C.F. Adams, *The Works of John Adams,* VII, 438.
45. *Ibid.,* VII, 452fn.

Chapter 27. The Crisis of 1783

1. Comte de Saint-Priest, *Mémoires: Règnes de Louis XV and de Louis XVI* (Paris, 1929), Vol. I, p. 178.
2. "Treaty of Peace (Küçük Kaynarji): Russia and the Ottoman Empire 10/21 July 1774," in *Diplomacy in the Near and Middle East: A Documentary Record: 1535-1914,* edited by J.C. Hurewitz (Princeton, 1956), I, 55.
3. "Saint-Priest to Vergennes, 26 August, 10 September, 1782," *AAE-CP-Turquie,* Vol. 168, fols. 180-180vo, 189vo-190.
4. "Vérac to Vergennes, 10 September 1782," *AAE-CP-Russie,* Vol. 109, fols. 167-167vo.
5. Robert Salomon, *La Politique Orientale de Vergennes (1780-1784),* (Paris, 1935), pp. 129-133.
6. "Dispatch of Mercy, 28 December, 1782," *ibid.,* p. 142.
7. Svetlana Kluge, "Vergennes and the Franco-Russian Rapprochement: 1774-1787," (unpublished thesis, Columbia University), 90-91.
8. Salomon, *La Politique Orientale de Vergennes,* 149-151; See also: Annexe #6, *ibid.,*; also Alfred R. von Arneth, *Joseph II and Katherina von Russland: Ihre Briefwechsel* (Vienna, 1869), p. 197.
9. *Ibid.,* 154-156.
10. "Vergennes to Saint-Priest, 25 February 1783," *AAE-CP-Turquie,* Vol. 168,

fol. 326vo.

11. "Saint-Priest to Vergennes, 8 March 1783," *ibid.*, Vol. 168, fols. 337-341vo ; also, Alexandre Tratchevsky, "La France et l'Allemagne sous Louis XVI," *Revue historique* (1881), Vol. XIV, p. 283.

12. "Breteuil to Vergennes, 28 March, 1783," *AAE-CP-Autriche,* Vol. 344, fol. 324-328.

13. "Mercy to Kaunitz, 19 April 1783," Salomon, *La Politique Orientale de Vergennes,* p. 164.

14. "Joseph to Catherine, 19 May 1783," Alfred von Arneth, *Joseph II und Katherina von Russland: Ihr Briefwechsel* (Vienna, 1869), 202.

15. Salomon, *La Politique Orientale de Vergennes,* p. 167.

16. *Ibid.*, p. 174.

17. *Ibid.*, p. 175.

18. The details of this very important series of meetings between Mercy and Vergennes are found in "Dépèche d'Office from Mercy to Kaunitz, 17 June 1783," and are summarized in Salomon, *La Politique Orientale de Vergennes,* pp. 179-189.

19. *Ibid.*, p. 188.

20. *Ibid.*

21. *Ibid.*, p. 189.

22. "Vergennes to Montmorin, 20 June 1783," *AAE-CP-Espagne,* Vol. 610, fols. 599-600.

23. Salomon, *La Politique Orientale de Vergennes,* pp. 194-195.

24. "Letter to Berten, 11 July 1783," Bibliothèque Nationale fonds françaises, n.a. 6498.

25. Salomon, *La Politique Orientale de Vergennes,* pp. 198-199.

26. *Ibid.*, p. 201.

27. *Ibid.*, p. 204.

28. "Vergennes to Montmorin, 20 June 1783," and "Montmorin to Vergennes, 22 June, 7 July," *AAE-CP-Espagne,* Vol. 610, fols. 599-602vo ; 626-628.

29. "Vergennes to Vérac, 18 June 1783," *AAE-CP-Russie,* Vol. 110, fols. 411vo-413vo ; also, "Office verbal pour la cour de Russie", *ibid.*, Vol. 110, fols. 414-415vo.

30. "Négociations at Constantinople," Archives Nationale, K1348, No. 50; Salomon, *La Politique Orientale de Vergennes,* pp. 210-211.

31. "Mercy to Joseph, 17 August, 1783," *ibid.*, p. 221.

32. *Ibid.*, p. 211.

33. "Joseph to Kaunitz, 5 July 1783," A. Beer, *Joseph II, Leopold II und Kaunitz: Ihr Briefwechsel* (Vienna, 1873), p. 134.

34. "Barthélemy to Vergennes, 12 September 1783," *AAE-CP-Autriche,* Vol. 344, fols. 411-416vo.

35. Salomon, *La Politique Orientale de Vergennes,* p. 228.

36. Henri Valloton, *Catherine II* (Paris, 1935), p. 188.

37. "Joseph to Mercy, 30 October, 1783," Arneth and Flammermont, *Correspondance Secrète du Comte de Mercy d'Argenteau avec l'Empéreur Joseph II et le Prince de Kaunitz* (Paris, 1889), I, 220.

38. "Instructions to Noailles, 4 October 1783," Albert Sorel, ed., *Recueil des Instructions données aux ambassadeurs et ministres de France* (Paris, 1884), I, 528.

39. "Exposé succinct sur la situation politique de la France relativement à différentes puissances," dated December 8, 1774, in Henri Doniol, *Histoire de la participation de la France à l'établissement des États-Unis d'Amérique* (Paris, 1886-92), Vol. I, p. 14.

40. The idea of a Franco-Russian commercial agreement to share the profits of the Black Sea and Eastern Mediterranean trade was not new. In fact, in 1762, when Vergennes was still ambassador to Constantinople, one of his subordinates recommended it in a memoir submitted to Vergennes. See Peyssonel, *Traité sur le commerce de la mer noire* (Paris, 1787); and Svetlana Kluge, "Vergennes and the Franco-Russian Rapprochement: 1774-1787," (unpublished Thesis, Columbia University), 13-14.
41. *Ibid.*, p. 109.
42. Charles Joseph de Mayer, *Vie publique et privée de Charles Gravier, Comte de Vergennes* (Paris, 1789), p. 167.
43. "Mémoire au Roi, 29 April 1784," Archives Nationale, K161.

Chapter 28. The Vergennes Family

1. H. De Goutel, *Vergennes et l'indépendance Américaine: Vergennes et Wilson,* (Paris, 1918), pp. 19-20.
2. Anonymous, *Portrait du Comte de Vergennes ministre et Secrétaire d'État au département des Affaires Étrangères* (S.I., 1788) p. 44.
3. Claude C. Rulhière, *"Le Comte de Vergennes; première cause des États Généraux,"* in *Oeuvres,* Vol. I, pp. 165fn, 164, 148. The authorship of this work is not certain: Anonymous, *Portrait du Comte de Vergennes ministre et Secrétaire d'état* . . . (s. l., 1788) p. 29; Charles Joseph Mayer, *Vie publique et privée de Charles Gravier de Vergennes, ministre de l'État* (Paris, 1789), p. 148; Alexandre Tratchevsky, "La France et l'Allemagne sous Louis XVI," *Revue Historique* (Paris, 1881), vol. XIV, pp. 255-256.
4. J.L. Soulavie, *Mémoires historiques et politiques du règne de Louis XVI* (Paris, 1801), pp. 14-15; "Vergennes to Louis XVI, 29 Dec., 1774," K164 no. 3, *Archives Nationales.*
5. J.N. Moreau, *Mes Souvenirs* (Paris, 1898-1901) Vol. II, pp. 318-319, 333, 366.
6. "Lettres autographes à Constantin, 1769-1786," 4 Nov., 1771, *AFV.* Letter "Vergennes à Comtesse, 30 August, 1774," printed in Charles J. Mayer, *Vie Publique et privée de . . . Vergennes . . .*, p. 166. Also, pp. 167-170.
7. "Lettres autographes à Constantin, 1769-1786, 16 Sept., 1779, 8 Feb. 1781, 3 March, 1781," *AFV.* "Lettres autographes à son épouse, 1774, 1782," *ibid.,;* Mayer, *Vie publique et privée . . . de Vergennes . . .*, 170.
8. *Ibid.*, 157.
9. *Ibid.*, 158.
10. *Ibid.*, 176.
11. On this point see: Anon., *Portrait du comte de Vergennes ministre et Secrétaire d'état,* p. 32.
12. Mayer, *Vie publique et privée de . . . Vergennes . . .*, 186-187.
13. Moreau, *Mes Souvenirs,* II, p. 333. Morganatic marriages were not uncommon in France. According to the French concept of heredity, the status of the woman was immaterial. Ordinarily, however, this type of marriage was used to "manure the land" of the poor nobleman. Pierre Goubert, *The Ancien Régime* (New York, 1969), pp. 160-161.
14. "Érection en comté de la terre de Toulongeon en faveur de M. Gravier de Vergennes," Archives départementales de la Côte d'Or, Série B. 67.
15. Mayer, *Vie publique et privée,* p. 192.

16. J.A. LeRoi, *Histoire de Versailles* (Versailles, s.d.), II, 453.
17. "Vergennes to Louis XVI, 20 Oct., 1775," K164, No.[3] , AN.
18. "Mémoire envoyé par M. d'Ormesson au Comte de Vergennes relatif aux terres de Fravenberg et Welferding, Fontainebleau, 14 Nov., 1783," *AFV*. "Lettres-patentes du Roi en forme d'édit, August, 1787," *ibid.*
19. For a lengthy discussion of Vergennes' wealth see: Mayer, *Vie publique et privée,* 188ff.
20. *Ibid.*, 192. The annual revenue of one of the "Grand" noblemen ranged between 100,000 and 500,000 *livres*.
21. A summary of Vergennes' testament will of 1784 is printed in the "Appendix" of Charles de Chambrun, *À l'école d'un diplomate: Vergennes* (Paris, 1944).
22. Jean Meyer, "Un problème mal posé: la noblesse pauvre: l'exemple breton au XVII siécle," *Revue d'Histoire Moderne et Contemporaire,*" tome XVIII, April-June, 1971, pp. 171ff.
23. "Letter, Vergennes to Duc d'Aiguillon, 18 July, 1771," *Archives des Affaires Étrangères - Dossiers Personnels,* Vol. 68, fols. 61-61vo.
24. "Gojard to Louis XVI, 1 July, 1787," Archives Nationales "Dossier personnel," F4 1965[5]
25. *Ibid.*, Also. *AEE-DP,* Vol. 68, fols. 38-39.
26. "Letter, Vergennes to Louis XVI, 10 Nov., 1783," *AAE-MD-France,* Vol. 1897, fol. 120.
27. Mayer, *Vie publique et privée,* pp. 156-157; Rulhière, *Oeuvres,* I, pp. 149-150; Anon., *Portrait du comte de Vergennes ministre et secrétaire' d'état.* p. 53.
28. Alfred Ritter von Arneth, *Maria Theresa und Marie Antoinette; ihr Briefwechsel,* 1770-1780 (Paris, Vienna, 1865), Vol. I, pp. 124, 128.
29. Alfred Ritter von Arneth, *Correspondance secrète entre Marie Thérèse et le Cte de Mercy d' Argenteau* (Paris, 1874) Vol. II, pp. 243, 266, 271.
30. *Ibid.*, 271.
31. *Gazette de France,* Année, 1774, p. 410.
32. "Comte de Vergennes à sa femme, Lundi (?), 1782" *AFV; Gazette de France,* Année 1782, 203; A. Castelot, *Queen of France: A Biography of Marie Antoinette* (New York, 1957), p. 169.
33. René de la Croix, duc de Castries, *Le Testament de la monarchie* (Paris, 1958), p. 332.
34. "Vergennes to Madame de Vergennes, 3 June, 1774," *AFV*.
35. "Vergennes to Constantin, 5 December, 1769," *ibid.*
36. "Vergennes to Constantin, 26 February, 1774," *ibid.;* J. Baltreau, M. Barroux et M. Prevost, *Dictionnaire de Biographie Française* (Paris, 1941) Vol. 4, 1508.
37. "Vergennes to Madame de Vergennes, 3 June, 1774," *AFV*.
38. Louis Petit de Bachaumont, *Mémoires secrète pour servir à l'histoire de la République des lettres en France* (Bruxelle, 1784) Vol. IX, Jan. 20, 1776. On the authorship of the *Mémoires secrets* see: Robert S. Tate, "Petit de Bachaumont: his circle and the *Mémoires secrets*" in *Studies on Voltaire and the Eighteenth Century,* Vol. LXV, pp. 175-177. I am indebted to Ms. Svetlana Kluge for this latter reference.
39. M. Michaud, *Biographie Universelle* (Paris, n.d.), Vol. XXXVII, pp. 172-173.
40. See, for example, his *Abregé historique de la vie de Marie Thérèse* . . . (Paris, 1773); and *Citations curieuses, dignes de l'attention des penseurs et des riches propriétaires* (Metz, 1814).
41. M. le Dr. Hoefer, *Nouvelle Biographie Général* (Paris, 1863), XLVI, 959 fn.
42. "Vergennes to Madame de Vergennes, 3 June, 1774," *AFV*.

43. "Vergennes to Louis XVI, 20 October, 1775," *AAE-MD-France,* 1897, fol. 50-50vo.
44. "Vergennes to Louis XVI, 21 November, 1776," *ibid.*, vol. 1897, fol. 72.
45. Bachaumont, *Mémoires,* XXXIV, 31 March, 1787, 342-343.
46. G. Cottreau, "Les Gardes de la Porte du Roi et leur denier Capitaine-Colonel le Vicomte de Vergennes en 1783," *Carnet de la Sabretache: Revue Militaire Retrospective* (Paris, 1903) 2ème Série, 2ème Volume, p. 195.
47. *Ibid.*, 193-196.
48. "Vergennes to Constantin, 19 March, 1777," *AFV.*
49. "Vergennes to Constantin, 3 March, 1781," *ibid.*
50. "Vergennes to Constantin , n.d., 1777. *ibid.*
51. 24 June, 1786, *AFV.* "Vergennes to Durfort, French Minister to Tuscany, 8 February, 1785," *AAE-CP-France,* 141 bis, fols. 40-40[vo].
52. Such denials meant very little since Vergennes had used Constantin for diplomatic tasks several times when the lad was much younger. "Vergennes to Louis XVI, 2 May, 1776," *AAE-MD-France,* 1897, fol. 63.
53. "Vergennes to Constantin, 24 June, 19 July, 1786," *AFV.*
54. "Vergennes to Constantin, 19 July, 1786," *ibid.*
55. "Vergennes to Constantin, 6 September, 1786," *ibid.*
56. "Vergennes to Constantin, 30 September, 1786," *ibid.*
57. "Vergennes to Constantin, 30 September, 1786," *ibid.*
58. "Vergennes to Constantin, 30 September, 1786," *ibid.*
59. "Vergennes to Constantin, 19 September, 1786," *ibid.*
60. "Vergennes to Constantin, 19 September, 1786," *ibid.*
61. "Vergennes to Constantin, 13 August, 1786," *ibid.*
62. "Vergennes to Constantin, 31 July, 1786," *ibid.*
63. "Vergennes to Constantin, 30 September, 1786," *ibid.*

Chapter 29. Gibraltar

1. Printed Résumés of the Seven Conferences between Vergennes and Grenville are found in Doniol, *Histoire,* V, pp. 112-118.
2. *Ibid.*, pp. 114-115; also, John Russell, *Memorials and Correspondence of Charles James Fox* (London 1857), Vol. IV, pp. 194-198; on the wishes of Vergennes regarding mediation see also L.G.W. Legg, editor, *British Diplomatic Instructions,* (London, 1922-1934), Vol. VII, p. 191.
3. Doniol, *Histoire,* V, pp. 116-117.
4. "Mr. Fox to George III, 18 May, 1782," Sir John Fortescue, editor, *Correspondence of King George III,* (London, 1928), Vol. VI, p. 31.
5. Doniol, *Histoire,* V, pp. 84; 116-117.
6. See the "Projet Préliminaire proposé par le ministre de la cour Britannique au mois d'aout, 1782," *Archivo Historico Nacional Estado,* Vol. 4203, page 36, Library of Congress, Manuscript Division.
7. "Shelburne to Fitzherbert, 23 September 1782," *British Diplomatic Instructions,* Vol. VII, pp. 188-189.
8. "George III to Shelburne, 14 September, 1782," Fortescue, *Correspondence of King George III,* VI, p. 126.
9. "Shelburne to Fitzherbert, 23 September, 1782," Legg, *British Diplomatic Instructions,* Vol. VII, pp. 189-190.

10. Doniol, *Histoire,* V, p. 143.

11. "Shelburne to Fitzherbert, 23 September, 1782," Legg, *British Diplomatic Instructions,* pp. 187-188. See also: "Projet Préliminaire proposé par le ministre de la cour Britannique au mois d'aout, 1782," *Archivo Historico Nacional Estado,* Vol. 4203, p. 36, *LCMD.*

12. Legg, *British Diplomatic Instructions,* p. 190.

13. "George III to Shelburne, 14 September, 1782," Fortescue, *Correspondence of King George III,* p. 126.

14. Art. IX, X, Georg. F. Martens, *Recueil de traités d'Alliance, de paix, de Trève, de Neutralité, de commerce, de limites, d'éxchange . . . des Puissances et états de l'Europe* (Gottingue, 1818), III, 524.

15. Art. XI, XII, *ibid.*

16. Art. VII, *ibid.,* p. 523.

17. Art. XIII, XIV, XV, and "Declaration," *ibid.,* p. 525, 530.

18. Art. XVII, *ibid.,* p. 526.

19. Art. XIX, *ibid.,* p. 526.

20. Art. XXI, *ibid.,* p. 527.

21. The best account of the Hussey-Cumberland negotiations is still Samuel Flagg Bemis, *The Hussey-Cumberland Mission and American Independence* (Princeton, 1931). See also: Stetson Conn, *Gibraltar in British Diplomacy in the Eighteenth Century* (New Haven, 1942), pp. 190-197. Conn makes use of several sources not available to Bemis.

22. *Ibid.,* pp. 194-195.

23. S. F. Bemis, *The Hussey-Cumberland Mission,* pp. 32-33; Danvila y Collado, *Reinado de Carlos III* (Madrid, 1893-1896), V, p. 155.

24. S.F. Bemis, *The Diplomacy of the American Revolution* (Bloomington, Ind, 1957) p. 183 and footnote.

25. *Ibid.* On Vergennes' views of mediation by the Imperial powers see: "Vergennes to Montmorin, 22 January, 1781," Printed in Doniol, *Histoire,* IV, pp. 524-528.

26. Danvila y Collado, *Reinado de Carlos III,* V, pp. 197-198.

27. M. de Flassan, *Histoire général et raisonnée de la diplomatie française* (Paris, 1811), Vol. V, p. 293; Alfred Arneth, *Joseph II und Katherine von Russland; Ihr Briefwechsel* (Vienna, 1869), p. 35; Francis Wharton, *Revolutionary Diplomatic Correspondence of the United States* (Washington, 1889), Vol. IV, p. 861; Aranda's conferences with Vergennes during this period are summarized in his "Journal" of May 2 to 16, 1781 in *Archivo Historico Nacional Estado,* Vol. 4203, pages 4-27, *LCMD.*

28. "Vergennes to LaVauguyon, 31 May, 1781," *AAE-CP-Hollande,* Vol. 544, fol. 104.

29. S.F. Bemis, *The Diplomacy of the American Revolution,* pp. 186-187; "Adams to Vergennes, 13 July, 1781," C. F. Adams, *The Works of John Adams* (Boston, 1850-1856), Vol. VII, pp. 436-439; Wharton, *Revolutionary Diplomatic Correspondence* IV, 860-867.

30. Danvila y Collado, *Reinado de Carlos III,* V, pp. 345-358.

31. "Propositions formelles de l'Espagne remises à Mr de Fitzherbert le 7 October, 1782," *Archivo Historico Nacional Estado,* Vol. 4203, p. 46, *LCMD.* In May 1782 Floridablanca had sent Aranda guidelines to follow in negotiating with the English. Floridablanca stressed the importance of Gibraltar: "Floridablanca to Aranda, May 24, 1782," *ibid.,* Vol. 4215, p. 54. *LCMD.* See also, the Spanish response to the British "Projet Préliminaire," in *ibid.,* Vol. 4203, p. 40-42, *LCMD.*

32. Danvila y Collado, *Reinado de Carlos III,* V, p. 385, "Aranda to Shelburne, 17 Dec. 1782," *Archivo Historico Nacional Estado,* Vol. 4203, p. 91, *LCMD.*

33. "Vergennes to Montmorin, August 18, 1782," *AAE-CP-Espagne,* Vol. 608, fol. 206.

34. "Précis de mes entretiens avec les ministres anglais concernant l'Espagne, 30 Sept, 1782," *Archivo Historico Nacional Estado,* Vol. 4215, pp. 341-342, *LCMD.*

35. *Ibid.*, p. 343.

36. "Lord Shelburne to George III, 13 September, 1782," George III to Lord Shelburne, 16 September, 1782," Fortescue, *The Correspondence of King George III, 1760-1783,* Vol. VI, pp. 123; 129.

37. "Rayneval to Vergennes, 18 September, 1782," *AAE-CP-Angleterre,* Vol. 538, fol. 34-36. Also, "Précis de mes entretiens avec les ministres anglais, 30 Sept. 1782," *Archivo Historico Nacional Estado,* Vol. 4215, pp. 354-357, *LCMD.*

38. "Grantham to Fitzherbert, 23 September, 1782," Legg, *British Diplomatic Instructions*, Vol. VII, France, pp. 186-190.

39. *Archivo Historico Nacional Estado,* Vol. 4215, pp. 470-473, 517-519, 530-533, *LCMD.*

40. Conn, *Gibraltar in British Diplomacy,* p. 210; Charles III still believed that Gibraltar could be conquered, "Floridablanca to Aranda, 11 Nov. 1782," *Archivo Historico Nacional Estado,* Vol. 4215, pp. 613-619, *LCMD.*

41. "Vergennes to Aranda, 30 Sept. 1782," *Archivo Historico Nacional Estado,* Vol. 4215, p. 364, *LCMD.*

42. "Grantham to Fitzherbert, October 21, November 9, 1782," Legg, *British Diplomatic Instructions,* VII, pp. 193-195; 195-199.

43. "Réponse de l'angleterre aux propositions de l'Espagne, 9 November, 1782," *Archivo Historico Nacional Estado,* Vol. 4203, p. 62, *LCMD.;* "Grantham to Fitzherbert, 9 November, 1782," Legg, *British Diplomatic Instructions,* VII, pp. 195-199.

44. Danvila y Collado, *Reinado de Carlos III* , V, p. 375; Also "Floridablanca to Aranda, 11 Nov. 1782," *Archivo Historico Nacional Estado,* Vol. 4215, pp. 613-619. *LCMD.*

45. "Proposition de l'Espagne .... 7 Nov. 1782, *Archivo Historico Nacional Estado,* Vol. 4203, pp. 54-57; *LCMD;* "Aranda to Vergennes, 7 Nov. 1782," *ibid.*, 4215, pp. 685-689, *LCMD;* Also, "Floridablanca to Aranda, 11 Nov. 1782," *ibid.*, 4215, pp. 618-619.

46. "Vergennes to Montmorin, November 12, 1782," *AAE-CP-Espagne,* Vol. 610; *Archivo Historico Nacional Estado,* Vol. 4215, pp. 622-627, *LCMD.*

47. *Ibid.*, p. 624-627; Conn, *Gibraltar in British Diplomacy,* p. 212.

48. "Réponse de l'Angleterre aux propositions de l'Espagne, 9 Nov. 1782," *Archivo Historico Nacional Estado,* Vol. 4203, p. 64, *LCMD.*

49. "Montmorin to Vergennes, 24 October, 1782," *AAE-CP-Espagne,* Vol. 609.

50. Conn, *Gibraltar in British Diplomacy,* p. 213fn; See also: "Vergennes to Montmorin, 12 Nov. 1782," *Archivo Historico Nacional Estado,* Vol. 4215, p. 628, *LCMD.*

51. "Carmichael to Livingston, 29 September, 1782," Wharton, *Revolutionary Diplomtic Correspondence,* V, pp. 783-785.

52. "Lord Grantham to George III, November 3, 1782," Fortescue, *Correspondence of King George III,* Vol. VI, p. 150.

53. "Rayneval to Vergennes, December 4, 1782," *AAE-CP-Angleterre,* Vol. 539.

54. The Spanish ultimatum, dated 28 November, 1782 is in *Archivo Historico*

Nacional Estado, Vol. 4203, pp. 66-67, *LCMD*. The ultimatum is also printed in Conn, *Gibraltar in British Diplomacy,* p. 219.

55. Conn, *Gibraltar in British Diplomacy,* 220fn; "George III to Shelburne, 2 December, 1782," "George III to Grantham, 3 December, 1782," "Fortescue, *Correspondence of King George III,* VI, pp. 168; 169.

56. "Réponse aux propositions de l'ambassadeur d'Espagne..., *Archivo Historico Nacional Estado,* Vol. 4203, p. 72, *LCMD;* "Rayneval to Vergennes, December 4, 1782," *AAE-CP-Angleterre,* Vol. 539.

57. "Floridablanca to Aranda, 23 November, 1782," *Archivo Historico Nacional Estado,* Vol. 4215, pp. 748-751, *LCMD*. Conn, *Gibraltar in British Diplomacy,* p. 223.

58. "Vergennes to Rayneval, 7 December, 1782," *AAE-CP-Angleterre,* Vol. 539 fol. 217.

59. "Floridablanca to Aranda, 23 November, 1782," *Archivo Historico Nacional Estado,* Vol. 4215, pp. 751-758, *LCMD;* "Vergennes to Montmorin, December, 1782," *ibid.*, pp. 809-816.

60. Conn, *Gibraltar in British Diplomacy,* p. 223.

61. "Vergennes to Aranda, 8 Dec. 1782," *Archivo Historico Nacional Estado,* Vol. 4215, pp. 841-842, *LCMD*.

62. "Résumé des observations faites par Monsieur de Rayneval," Legg, *British Diplomatic Instructions,* VII, pp. 202-203fn.

63. "George III to Grantham, 11 December, 1782," "George III to Shelburne, 11 December, 1782," Fortescue, *The Correspondence of King George III,* VI, pp. 182-183; 183-184; "Rayneval to Vergennes, 12 December, 1782," *AAE-CP-Angleterre,* Vol. 539, fol. 285.

64. "Grantham to Fitzherbert, 11, 12, December, 1782," Legg, *British Diplomatic Instructions,* VII, pp. 201-202; Rayneval, "Réflexion sur l'état actuel des négotiations," *AAE-CP-Angleterre,* Supplément, Vol. 19, fols. 303-364.

65. "Shelburne to George III, 14 December, 1782," Fortescue, *Correspondence of King George III,* VI, pp. 185-186.

66. "Vergennes to Aranda, 15 December, 1782," *Archivo Historico Nacional Estado,* Vol. 4215, p. 900, *LCMD*.

67. "Vergennes to Rayneval, 16 December, 1782," *AAE-CP-Angleterre,* Vol. 539, fol. 245.

68. "Aranda to Floridablanca, 18 December, 1782," *Archivo Historico Nacional Estado,* Vol. 4215, pp. 876-899, *LCMD*.

69. "George III to Grantham, 19 December, 1782," Fortescue, *Correspondence of King George III,* VI, p. 192.

70. Conn, *Gibraltar in British Diplomacy,* p. 232; Arts. VII, VIII, "Traité définitif de paix entre la Grande Bretagne et la France, 3 September, 1783," Georg F. Martens, *Recueil de traités d'alliance, de paix, de trève, de neutralité, de commerce, de limites* ... [etc.,], *des puissances et états de l'Europe* (Gottingen, 1818), III, pp. 523-524.

71. Conn, *Gibraltar in British Diplomacy,* p. 232.

72. Arts. IV, V, "Traité définitif de paix entre S.M. Britannique et le Roi d'Espagne, 3 September, 1783," Martens, *Recueil des Traités,* III, 544.

73. "George III to Shelburne, 11 December, 1782," "George III to Grantham, 19 December, 1782," Fortescue, *Correspondence of King George III,* VI, pp. 183-184; 192.

74. "Montmorin to Vergennes, 1 December, 1782," *AAE-CP-Espagne,* Vol. 609,

fol. 334.

75. Art. IV, "Article préliminaire de paix, entre le Roi de l'Espagne et le Roi de la Grande Bretagne, 20 January, 1783," Martens, *Recueil des Traités,* III, 511-512. See also: "Aranda to Grantham, 17 December, 1783," *Archivo Historico Nacional Estado,* Vol. 4203, pp. 77-81; "Grantham to Aranda, 26 Dec. 1782," *ibid.*, pp. 84-89; "Fitzherbert to Aranda, 2 February, 1783," *ibid.*, pp. 135-136; "Aranda to Fitzherbert, 2 February, 1783," *ibid.*, pp. 137-138, *LCMD.*

76. "Fox to George Montagu, 10 June, 2 July, 20 July, 1783," Legg, *British Diplomatic Instructions,* Vol. VII, 237-238; 239-241; 242-244. Even before Fox entered the picture, Aranda and Fitzherbert had begun the task of defining more precisely the rights and extent of the British settlement in Honduras. See "Aranda to Fitzherbert, 4 March, 1783," *Archivo Historico Nacional Estado,* Vol. 4203, pp. 142-143, *LCMD*. The final compromise was arranged at a meeting between Aranda and Fitzherbert at which Vergennes and Rayneval mediated. *ibid.*, pp. 145-165.

77. Art. VI, Martens, *Recueil des traités,* III, 545-546.

78. Arts. VII, VIII, IX, *ibid.*, III, 547.

79. Conn, *Gibraltar in British Diplomacy,* p. 236.

80. "Vergennes to Montmorin, 12 Nov. 1782," *Archivo Historico Nacional Estado,* Vol. 4215, p. 628, *LCMD.*

Chapter 30. The Right to Catch Fish

1. Francis Gardiner Davenport, ed., *European Treaties bearing on the History of the United States and its Dependencies* (4 vols., Washington, D.C., 1917-37), IV, art. 5, 93-4; Harold Innis, *The Cod Fisheries* (New Haven, 1940), p. 179.

2. Innis, *Cod Fisheries,* p. 185.

3. Dallas D. Irvine, "The Newfoundland Fishery: A French Objective in the War of American Independence," *Canadian Historical Review* XIII (1932), 269; Francis P. Renaut, *Le Pact de famille et l'Amérique: la politique coloniale franco-espagnole de 1760 à 1792* (Paris, 1922), p. 347; "Réflexions," in Henri Doniol, *Histoire de la participation de la France à l'établissement des États-Unis Amérique;* correspondance et documents (5 vols., Paris, 1886-92), I, 243-9. For the dating of this document, see John J. Meng, "A Footnote to Secret Aid in the American Revolution," *American Historical Review,* XLIII (July, 1938), 791-5. Charles de la Morandière, *Histoire de la pêche française de la morue dans l'Amérique septentrionale* (2 vols., Paris, 1962), II, 937-40, has given conclusive evidence that Vergennes contemplated a new distribution of the area where Englishmen and Frenchmen could fish as early as 1775.

4. Irvine, "The Newfoundland Fishery," *Canadian Historical Review,* pp. 282-4

5. "Vergennes to Garnier, 12 April, 1775," *AAE-CP-Angleterre,* vol. 509, f. 328ff.; La Morandière, *Histoire de la pêche française,* II, 937. The italics are my own.

6. Gilbert Chinard, ed., *The Treaties of 1778 and Allied Documents* (Baltimore, 1928), p. 29.

7. *Ibid.*, pp. 29-30. The italics are my own.

8. L. H Butterfield, ed., *Diary and Autobiography of John Adams* (Cambridge, Mass., 1961), IV, 187-91.

9. "Treaty of Neutrality in America between Great Britain and France, concluded at Whitehall, Nov. 6/16, 1686," in Davenport, ed., *European Treaties,* II, 320.

10. "Treaty of Peace between Great Britain and France, concluded at Utrecht, March 31/April 11, 1713," *ibid.*, III, Art. 13, p. 212.

11. E.T. Daubigny, *Choiseul et la France d'outre-mer* (Paris, 1892), p. 306.

12. "Treaty of Peace between Great Britain, France, and Spain, concluded at Paris, February, 10, 1763," in Davenport, ed., *European Treaties,* IV, Articles 2 and 5, pp. 92, 93-4.

13. La Morandière, *Histoire de la pêche française,* II, 851-71; also Daubigny, *Choiseul et la France d'outre-mer,* p. 297 ff.

14. "Sartine to Vergennes, 2 mai 1775," *Archives Nationales, Colonies,* C^{11F}, t. 2, f. 126.

15. John Bassett Moore, ed., *Digest of International Law* (8 vols., Washington, D.C., 1906), I, 779-80n; George Chalmers, *Opinions of Eminent Lawyers* (Burlington, 1858) pp. 625, 628-9, 638.

16. Felix Gilbert, "The New Diplomacy of the Eighteenth Century," *World Politics,* IV (1951-52), 24-5.

17. When the British diplomat, Fitzherbert, pointed out to Adams that the United States had in effect sided with France when she signed the Treaty of 1778, Adams replied, "I said perhaps not, for the whole [the Treaty] was to be conformable to the true Construction of the Treaties of Utrecht and Paris, and that if the English did not now admit the exclusive Construction they could not contend for it vs. Us." Butterfield, ed., *Diary and Autobiography of John Adams,* III, 76.

18. Percy Thomas Fenn, *The Origins of the Rights of Fishing in Territorial Waters* (Cambridge, 1926), p. 135ff.

19. "Livingston to Franklin, Jan. 7, 1782," in Francis Wharton, ed., *The Revolutionary Diplomatic Correspondence of the United States* (6 vols., Washington, D.C., 1889), V, 91.

20. See *ibid.*, III, 304, for the Americans' elaboration of this point.

21. Francis Wharton, comp., *A Digest of the International Law of the United States* (3 vols., 2nd ed., Washington, D.C., 1887), III, 892.

22. C. B. Elliott, *The United States and the Northeastern Fisheries* (Minneapolis, 1887), p. 25.

23. C. F. Adams, ed., *The Works of John Adams* (10 vols., Boston, 1850-56), III, 47

24. "Silas Deane to Vergennes, March 18, 1777," in B. F. Stevens, ed., *Fascimiles of Manuscripts in European Archives Relating to America, 1773-1783* (25 vols., London, 1889-95), VII, 659[2].

25. "Vergennes to Montmorin, 13 Dec., 1777," *ibid.*, XX, 1774[4].

26. "Shelburne to Fitzherbert, 9 November, 1782," L.G. Wickham Legg, *British Diplomatic Instructions: 1689-1789* (London, 1934), Vol. VII, France, p. 196.

27. "Dr. Bancroft to Mr. Wentworth, May 2, 1777," B.F. Stevens, *Facsimiles of Manuscripts,* III, 254[2].

28. "Chief Justice William Smith to William Eden, Aug. 3, 1780," *ibid.*, VII, 729[3] "Mr. Heron's Information at a Conversation in New York, Sept. 4, 1780," *ibid.*, VII, 733[2].

29. Wharton, ed., *Revolutionary Diplomatic Correspondence,* III, 225, 234, 237.

30. *Ibid.*, III, 302, dated Aug. 14, 1779.

31. *Ibid.*, III, 293-9.

32. Adolphe de Circourt, *Histoire de l'action commune de la France et de l'Amérique pour l'indépendence des États-Unis* (Paris, 1876), III, 276-7

33. Elliott, *The United States and the Northeastern Fisheries,* p. 27.

34. *Ibid.*

35. LaLuzerne reported his discussions to Vergennes on Jan. 1, 5, 11, 18, 25, and

28, 1782. Doniol, *Histoire,* V, 62-4.

36. "Vergennes to LaLuzerne, 23 Mars 1781," *ibid.*, V, 69.

37. "Vergennes to LaLuzerne, 12 Août 1781, *ibid.*, V. 69.

38. Wharton, ed., *Revolutionary Diplomatic Correspondence,* V, 238-41.

39. Samuel Flagg Bemis, *The Diplomacy of the American Revolution* (Bloomington, 1957). pp. 220-3.

40. "Jay to Livingston, 17 Nov. 1782," Wharton, ed., *Revolutionary Diplomatic Correspondence,* VI, 29; see, for example: Bemis, *The Diplomacy of the American Revolution,* pp. 220-1; John Richard Alden, *The American Revolution,* 1775-1783 (New York, 1954), pp. 259-60; Merrill Jensen, *The New Nation; A History of the United States During the Confederation, 1781-1789* (New York, 1950), p. 14.

41. Articles IV and V, "Traité définitif de paix et d'amitié entre le Roi de la Grande Bretagne et le Roi Très Chrétien, 3 Septembre, 1783," Martens, *Recueil de Traités,* Vol. III, pp. 522-523.

42. Article III, "Traité définitif de paix et d'amitié entre S.M. Britannique et les États-Unis de l'Amérique, 3 Sept., 1783," *ibid.*, Vol. III, pp. 556-557.

Chapter 31. The Mississippi Boundary

1. D. Hunter Miller, *Treaties and Other International Acts of the United States of America* (Washington, 1931), II, 39.

2. John Adams: His country was "destined to be the greatest power on earth." "The Politics of John Adams," Anson D. Morse, *American Historical Review* (1898-1899) Vol. 4, 301.

3. The phrase is Franklin's; see "Benjamin Franklin to Robert R. Livingston, 12 August, 1782," Francis Wharton, *Revolutionary Diplomatic Correspondence* (Washington, D.C., 1889), V, 657. The fear that Americans might have been "cooped up" between the Atlantic Ocean and the Appalachian Mountains has haunted American historians. See Richard B. Morris, *The Peace Makers,* (New York, 1965), 290, 306, 308.

4. For Americans' arguments for their claims to the Mississippi territory, see: W.C. Ford and Gaillard Hunt, *Journals of the Continental Congress* (Washington, 1904-1937), XVIII, p. 900-2, 935-947; William T. Hutchinson and William M.E. Rachal, editors, *The Papers of James Madison* (Chicago, 1962), II, 114-117. The French position is outlined in several places. See: "Gérard to Vergennes, 28 Jan., 1779." *AAE-CP-États-Unis,* Vol. VII, fols. 129-135; "Barbé-Marbois to Vergennes, September 30, 1780,"*ibid.*, XIII, fols. 211ff; also, P.C. Phillips, *The West in the Diplomacy of the American Revolution,* (New York, 1967), 177-178; and the perceptive discussion in William Stinchcombe, *The American Revolution and the French Alliance* (Syracuse, 1969), pp. 33-37.

5. "Livingston to Franklin, January 7, 1782," Wharton, *Revolutionary Diplomatic Correspondence* V, 87-88.

6. "Proclamation of 1763 (7 October, 1763)," Merrill Jensen, editor, *English Historical Documents* (London, 1955), IX, 642. Also "Letter of Earl of Hillsborough to General Gage, 15 April, 1768," *ibid.*, 706.

7. D. Pickering, editor, *Statutes at Large, From Magna Carta to 1806* (Cambridge, 1762-1807), XXX, 549; for a discussion of the background of the Quebec Act, see: C.W. Alvord, *The Mississippi Valley in British Politics* (NewYork, 1959), Vol. II, pp. 209-251.

8. "The Treaty of Paris, 10 February, 1763," D. B. Horn and Mary A. Ransome, editors, *English Historical Documents: 1714-1783* (London, 1957) X, 937-939. See also: "Notes on Observations of Barbé-Marbois on Western Boundary of United States," James Madison, *Papers,* II, 115.

9. "Gérard to Vergennes, 4 March, 1779," *AAE-CP-États-Unis,* VII, fols. 328, 336; "Notes on Observations of Barbé-Marbois on Western Boundaries of the United States," James Madison, *Papers,* II, 116.

10. Samuel Flagg Bemis, *Diplomacy of the American Revolution* (Bloomington, Ind. 1957), p. 104.

11. Some Americans recognized the difficulties involved in claims based on conquest. See: "LaLuzerne to Vergennes, 11 June, 1780," *AAE-CP-États-Unis,* XII, fol. 74.

12. "Gérard to Vergennes, 4 March, 1779," *ibid.*, VII, fol. 328. 350, 336. "Livingston to Franklin, January 7, 1782," Wharton, *Revolutionary Diplomatic Correspondence*, V, 88-9; *Journals of the Continental Congress, 1774-1789.* (Washington, 1904-1937), XVIII, 936-7; New York State Historical Society, *Collection of N.Y. State Hist. Soc.* (1878), 134-139, 146; Gerald Stourzh, *Benjamin Franklin,* (Chicago, 1954), 201, P.C. Phillips, *op. cit.*, 186.

13. *Collections of New York State Historical Society* (1878), p. 149.

14. John Jay III, *Peace Negotiations of 1782 and 1783,* (New York, 1884), Appendix, p. 150.

15. "LaLuzerne to Vergennes, 11 February, 1780," *AAE-CP-États-Unis,* XI, fol. 190; P.C. Phillips, *op. cit.*, 160-161.

16. Doniol, *Histoire,* IV, 555-556.

17. "Vergennes to LaLuzerne, June 3, 1789," quoted in P.C. Phillips, *op. cit.*, 163; also "Vergennes to LaLuzerne, August 12, 1781," *ibid.*, 200; also "Vergennes to LaLuzerne, 7 August 1780," Doniol, *Histoire,* IV, 429.

18. "Vergennes to Montmorin, August 12, 1781," *AAE-CP-Espagne,* 603; also Renaut, *Le Pacte de Famille et l'Amerique,* 329.

19. Samuel Flagg Bemis, *The Rayneval Memoranda of 1782 on Western Boundaries and some Comments on the French Historian Doniol,* published by the American Antiquarian Society (Worcester, Mass. 1938), 13. On conversations between Aranda, Jay, Vergennes, and Rayneval on the Mississippi boundary, see also: Aranda's *Diary* in Yela Utrilla, *Espana ante la independencia de los Estados Unidos,* (Lerida, 1922), II, pp. 355.364.

20. S.F. Bemis, *The Rayneval Memoranda,* p. 14.

21. *Ibid.*, Yela Utrilla, *op. cit.*, Vol. I, 462.

22. S.F. Bemis, *The Rayneval Memoranda,* p. 15; Utrilla, *op. cit.*, I, p. 463.

23. Bemis, *The Rayneval Memoranda,* 14-16.

24. Wharton, *Revolutionary Diplomatic Correspondence,* VI, 23.

25. Bemis, *Rayneval Memoranda,* 17.

26. *Ibid.*, 17-18.

27. Wharton, *Revolutionary Diplomatic Correspondence,* VI, 26-27; For the background on Rayneval's compromise proposal see "Mémoire," *AAE-CP-Etats-Unis,* XXII, fols. 309-317. A complete and accurate copy of this memo can be found in Bemis, *Rayneval Memoranda,* 30-67; Yela Utrilla, *op. cit.*, Vol. I, p. 473. See also: *AAE-CP-Etats-Unis,* Vol. XXV, fols. 63-71.

28. There is an easily available map opposite page 218, in Bemis' 1935 edition of *Diplomacy of the American Revolution.*

29. Bemis, *Rayneval Memoranda,* 63-64.

30. "Rayneval to John Jay, Sept. 6, 1782," Wharton, *Revolutionary Diplomatic Correspondence, VI, 26.*

31. *Ibid.*, VI, 29.

32. *Ibid.*, VI, 29.

33. On Shelburne's desire for peace see: L.G. Wickham Legg, *British Diplomatic Instructions* (1689-1789) France, Part IV, 1745-1789 (London, 1934), III, 198.

34. "Projet des préliminaires remis le 17 Aout, 1782, par M. le Comte de Grasse comme le résultat de ses conversations avec M. le Comte de Shelburne et des dispositions qu'il lui a manifestées," Doniol, *Histoire,* V, 104.

35. The puzzle of Shelburne's intentions was further complicated by the fact that the Englishman seemed willing to by-pass completely his representatives in Paris, Allyne Fitzherbert and Richard Oswald. Sir John Fortescue, *The Correspondence of King George III (1760-1783),* (London, 1928), VI, 127.

36. *Ibid.*, V, 40.

37. "Conférences de M. de Rayneval avec les ministres anglais," Doniol, *Histoire,* V, 603-626; See also *ibid.*, V, 123, 140.

38. Doniol, *Histoire,* V, 123.

39. *Ibid.*, 140.

40. Edward S. Corwin, *French Policy and the American Alliance* (Princeton, 1916), 335.

41. Doniol, *Histoire,* V, 140.

42. *Ibid.*, 619.

43. *Ibid.*

44. The French dispatches relative to Rayneval's secret meeting with Shelburne can be found at the end of Volume V, in Doniol, *Histoire.* For a different treatment of the thesis that Rayneval's mission did not constitute an attempt to betray the United States, see: J.B. Perkins, *France in the American Revolution* (Boston and New York, 1911), p. 475. and *passim.*

45. Fitzmaurice, *Life of William, Earl of Shelburne 1776-1805* (London, 1876), III, 266; 142; see also Vergennes' response to this meeting, *ibid.*, 132.

46. Fitzmaurice, *Shelburne,* III, 292. See also 286.

47. For evidence of George III's suspicions of speculators and his attempts to curb their activities, see: *ibid.*, 311. Sir John Fortescue, *The Correspondence of King George III* (London, 1928), III, 154, 160, and 532.

48. Doniol, *Histoire,* V, 614.

49. Fitzmaurice, *Shelburne, 1776-1805* (London, 1976), III, 286.

50. See: Silas Deane, *The Deane Papers . . . 1774-1790* (New York, 1887-90), IV, 63-65; B.F. Stevens, *Facsimiles of Manuscripts in European Archives Relating to America* (London, 1889-95), 492, 301, 240, 335, 289; Fortescue, *Correspondence of George III,* III, 532.

51. Fitzmaurice, *Shelburne,* III, 267.

52. John Jay, *The Diary of John Jay During the Peace Negotiations of 1782* (New Haven, 1934), edited by Frank Monaghan, p. 12.

53. Wharton, *Revolutionary Diplomatic Correspondence,* I, 647.

54. Fortescue, *Correspondence of George III,* III, 193.

55. John Jay, *The Diary of John Jay During the Peace Negotiations of 1782,* p.12.

56. Matthew Ridley, *Diary,* quoted in L.H. Butterfield, *Diary and Autobiography of John Adams* (Cambridge, Mass. 1961), III, 40 fn.

57. *Ibid.*, III, 39.

58. John Jay, *Diary of John Jay During the Peace Negotiations,* 12.

59. Butterfield, *Diary and Autobiography of John Adams,* III, 82.
60. *Ibid.*
61. Louis Bonneville de Marsangy, *Le Comte de Vergennes; son ambassade en suède* (Paris, 1898), Chapters VII-XIII.
62. François de Collières, *The Practice of Diplomacy,* trans. A.F. Whyte (London, 1917), 31-32.

Chapter 32. The Legacy of the American War

1. Charles de Chambrun, *À l'école d'un diplomate: Vergennes* (Paris, 1944), p. 392.
2. Baron Pierre Victor de Besenval, *Mémoires . . . écrits par lui-même* (Paris, 1805), Vol. III, p. 54.
3. Jean Louis Campan, *Mémoires de la vie privée de Marie Antoinette* (Paris, 1822), I, pp. 233-234; see, also: *AAE-CP-Autriche,* Vol. 333, fol. 216.
4. "Montmorin to Vergennes, 28 January, 10 April, 1778," *AAE-CP-Espagne,* Vol. 589, fols. 135, 43-64.
5. Duc de Castries, *Le Maréchal de Castries* (Paris, 1956), pp. 108-109 and *passim.*
6. Chambrun, *Vergennes,* p. 395.
7. Samuel Flagg Bemis, *The Diplomacy of the American Revolution* (Bloomington, Indiana, 1957), pp. 13-15 and *passim.*
8. René Pinon, *Histoire de la Nation française* (Paris, 1929), Vol. IX, "Histoire diplomatique," p. 336; See, also: Chambrun, *Vergennes,* p. 3; Arthur Hassell, *The Balance of Power* (London, 1950), pp. 339-340; Ernest Lavisse, *Histoire de France* (Paris, 1911), Vol. IX, p. 91.
9. Chambrun, *Vergennes,* p. 3.
10. "Mémoire presenté au Roi par le Cte de Vergennes, 29 March, 1784," *AAE-MD-France,* Vol. 587, fols. 207-225. Also Archives Nationales, K164#3.
11. See: "Dupont to Vergennes, 4 Jan. 1782." "DeLessait to Vergennes, 12 June, 1782." "LaToul to Vergennes, 29 August, 1782," *AAE-CP-Angleterre,* Vol. 536, fols. 13ff; Vol. 537, fols. 234ff; 285 ff.
12. Duc de Castries, *Le Testament de la Monarchie* (Paris, 1958-59), pp. 259-261.
13. "Mémoire presenté au Roi par le Cte de Vergennes, 29 March, 1784," *AAE-MD-France,* vol. 587, fol. 207.
14. *Ibid.,* fols. 210-211.
15. *Ibid.,* fols. 211-211vo.
16. *Ibid.,* fols. 223vo-224.
17. *Ibid.,* fol. 223vo.
18. *Ibid.,* fol. 224.
19. *Ibid.,* fol. 224vo.
20. "Vergennes to Montmorin, 12 Nov. 1782," *Archivo Historico Nacional Estado,* Vol. 4215, p. 628. *LCMD;* "Mémoire presenté au Roi par le Cte de Vergennes, 29 March, 1784," *AAE-MD-France,* Vol. 587, fol. 224.
21. Robert D. Harris, "French Finances and the American War," *Journal of Modern History* (1976) vol. 48, no. 2, p. 236.
22. Robert D. Harris, "Necker's *Compte Rendu* of 1781; a Reconsideration," *Journal of Modern History* (1970) Vol. 42, no. 2, pp. 161-183
23. Harris, "French Finances and the American war," *op. cit.,* p. 242.
24. See, for example *ibid.,* pp. 233-258. James Riley's reviews of Harris' *Necker:*

Reform Statesman of the Ancien Régime and Françoise Mosseu's *Les intendants des finances au XVIIIe siecle*...in *Eighteenth Century Studies* (1980), Vol. 14, no. 1, pp. 97-103.

25. Guéry, Alain, "Les finances de la monarchie française sous l'ancien régime," *Annales, economies, sociétés, civilisations* (1978), vol. 33, no. 2, p. 231.

26. On the Geneva uprising and diplomacy, see: E Chapuisat, *La prise d'armes de 1782 à Génève* (Geneva, 1932).

27. J. Soulavie, *Mémoires historiques et politiques du règne de Louis XVI* (Paris, 1801), V, p. 275. Soulavie also suggests that Vergennes actually feared the influence in France of the revolutionaries in Geneva. *ibid.*, p. 245, 250.

28. Louis Gottschalk, "The Place of the American Revolution in the Causal Pattern of the French Revolution," (Publication of the American Friends of Lafayette, Easton, Penn., 1948).

29. "Jefferson to Dr. Richard Price, 8 January, 1789," Julian Bond, editor, *The Papers of Thomas Jefferson,* (Princeton, 1958), XIV, p. 420.

30. Alphonse Aulard, "La Révolution française et la Révolution américaine," *Études et leçons sur la Révolution Française* (Paris, 1921), pp. 59-139; Gilbert Chinard, "Notes on the French Translations of the 'Forms of Government or Constitutions of the Several United States', 1778 and 1783," *Year Book of the American Philosophical Society* (Philadelphia, 1943), pp. 88-106; A. Schalck de la Faverie, "La Révolution Américaine et la Révolution Française," *Journal de la Société des Américanistes de Paris* (1914-1919), #11, pp. 385-401; Godechet, J. "Les Combattants de la guerre de l'Indépendance des États-Unis et les troubles agraires en France de 1789 a 1792," *Annales historiques de la Révolution française* (Paris, 1956), July-Sept., 1956; Bernard Fay, *L'esprit révoltionnaire en France et aux États-Unis a la fin du XVIIIe siècle* (Paris, 1925); Durand Echeverria, *Mirage in the West* (Princeton, 1957).

31. "Vergennes to Montmorin, 24 December, 1779," *AAE-CP-Espagne*, 591, fol. 422.

32. J.F. Bosher, *French Finances: 1770-1795; from Business to Bureaucracy* (Cambridge, 1970), p. 304.

33. L'abbé de Véri, *Journal* (Paris, 1928-29), Vol. I, pp. 157-158.

34. Aline Logette, *Le comité contentieux des finances près le conseil du Roi (1777-1791),* (Nancy, 1964), p. 5.

35. Besenval, *Mémoires,* Vol. II, pp. 114ff; Duc de Castries, *Le Maréchal de Castries* (Paris, 1956), pp. 105-106.

36. Logette, *op. cit.*, 7-8.

37. Bosher, *op. cit.*, 166-182.

38. Eugène Lavaquéry, *Necker, Fourrier de la révolution,* (Paris, 1933) p. 193; Bosher, *op. cit.*, p. 63.

39. Lavaquéry, *op. cit.*, 198; Bosher, *op. cit.*, p 65; Robert D. Harris, *Necker, Reform Statesman of the Ancien Regime* (Berkeley, 1979) pp. 237-238.

40. Bosher, *op. cit.*, 26.

41. "Commission de chef du Conseil Royal des Finances pour le Sieur Comte de Vergennes," dated 20 February, 1783. *AFV.* Also letter, "M. de Nicolai to Vergennes, 7 March, 1783," *ibid.*

42. Bachaumont, *Mémoires Secret,* XXII, p. 110.

43. *Ibid.*, 110; See also the "Commission...." cited above, which stipulates that Vergennes was the chief of all "Superior officers" of Louis XVI's finances.

44. Bosher, *op. cit.*, 26, 28.

45. Michel Antoine, "Les conseils des finances sous le règne de Louis XV," *Revue d'histoire moderne et contemporaire* (1958), p. 184.

46. See, for example: "DuPont de Nemours to Vergennes, 4 January, 23 November, 1782," *AAE-CP-Angleterre,* Vol. 536, fols. 13-14vo; Vol. 539, fols. 21-22vo. Also, the important six memoirs written in 1786, *AAE-Mémoires et Documents - Angleterre,* Vol. 65, fols. 3-8, 9-21, 24-175vo, 199-223, 226-234vo.

47. Pierre Jolly, *Calonne: 1734-1802* (Paris, 1949), pp. 145-146.

48. *Ibid.,* 149.

49. M. Cheke, *The Cardinal de Bernis* (New York, 1958), p. 279.

50. D. Dakin, "The Breakdown of the Old Regime in France," in A Goodwin, *The New Cambridge Modern History* (Cambridge, 1965), Vol. VIII, pp. 614-615.

51. "Maréchal de Castries to Louis XVI, 30 December, 1786," printed in Duc de Castries, *Le Maréchal de Castries* (Paris, 1956), pp. 144-145.

52. Pierre Jolly, *Calonne,* 150.

53. Dakin, *op. cit.,* 614-615.

Chapter 33. The Scheldt River Dispute: 1780-1785

1. "LaVauguyon to Vergennes, 2 May, 1780;" "LaVauguyon to Vergennes, 18 July, 1780," *AAE-CP-Hollande,* Vol. 541, fols. 5-6; 319-319vo.

2. The Treaty of Westminster, March 3, 1678 provided for mutual assistance in case either party should be attacked. An attack on the United Provinces obliged England to lend the Dutch 10,000 men. The Dutch were obliged to assist the English with 6,000 men and 20 men-of-war in case the latter were attacked. *Collection of all the Treaties of Peace, Alliance and Commerce between Great Britain and other Powers, 1648 ... 1783* (London, 1785), I, 213; Georg Frederick Martens, *Supplément au recueil des principaux traités...,* (Göttingen, 1802-1828), Vol I, 125.

3. George Grosjean, *La politique Rhénane de Vergennes* (Paris, 1925), 96.

4. *Ibid.*

5. "Béranger to Vergennes, 27 January, 1784," *AAE-CP-Hollande,* Vol. 557, fols. 98vo-99vo.

6. "Noailles to Vergennes, 17 May, 1784," *AAE-CP-Autriche,* Vol. 547, fols. 283-284; "Apprédiris [Louis XVI's minister to Brussels] to Vergennes, 21 April, 1784," Eugène Hubert, *Correspondance des ministres de France accrédités à Bruxelles de 1780 à 1790* (Bruxelles, 1920), Vol. I, p. 63.

7. "Noailles to Vergennes, 19 May, 1784," *AAE-CP-Autriche,* Vol. 547, fol. 286vo; "Joseph II to Mercy, 15 May, 1784," in A. von Arneth et J. Flammermont, *Correspondance secrète du comte Mercy d'Argenteau avec l'Empéreur Joseph II et le prince Kaunitz* (Paris, 1889-1891), I, p. 263.

8. "Tableau Sommaire des droits et prétentions de Son Majesté l'Empéreur et Roi à la charge de Leur Hautes Puissances les Seigneurs États-Généraux des Provinces Unies." *AAE-CP-Hollande,* Vol. 558, fols. 26-30vo; for a detailed account of Joseph's policies regarding the Scheldt, see: F. Magnette, *Joseph II et la liberté de l'Escaut* (Paris, 1897), 35-36.

9. "LaVauguyon to Vergennes, 7 May, 1784," *AAE-CP-Hollande,* Vol. 558, fols. 35-36. Apparently the English offered their support to the United Provinces, but it was refused. See: Pierre Rain, *La Diplomatie française d'Henri IV à Vergennes* (Paris, 1945), p. 316.

10. "Vergennes to Noailles, 21 May, 1784," *AAE-CP-Autriche,* Vol. 547, fol. 294;

"Vergennes to Comte d'Andlaw [Louis XVI's minister at Brussels] 27 May, 1784"; Eugène Hubert, *Correspondance des ministres de France*. . .*à Bruxelles,* pp. 69-71.

11. "Vergennes to Noailles, 21 May, 1784," *AAE-CP-Autriche,* Vol. 547, fols. 295-295vo.

12. "Vergennes to Noailles, 22 July, 1784," *ibid.*, fols 394-394vo; "Béranger to Vergennes, 18 June, 1784," *AAE-CP-Hollande,* Vol. 558, fol. 247.

13. "Noailles to Vergennes, 23 June, 1784," *AAE-CP-Autriche,* Vol. 547, fol. 345vo-346.

14. *Ibid.*, fols. 394-394vo.

15. "Vergennes to Noailles, 1 October, 1784," *ibid.*, Vol. 548, fols. 122-124; "Béranger to Vergennes, 8 June, 1784," *AAE-CP-Hollande,* Vol. 558, fols. 205-206.

16. "Béranger to Vergennes, 11 June, 1784," *ibid.*, fols 217vo-219vo; "Vergennes to Béranger, 1 July, 1784," *ibid.*, fol. 299. "Andlaw to Vergennes, 24 June, 1784," Eugène Hubert, *Correspondance des ministres de France . . . à Bruxelles*. . ., Vol. I, pp. 78-79.

17. "Noailles to Vergennes, 16 October, 1784," *AAE-CP-Autriche,* Vol. 548, fols. 152-153.

18. "Vergennes to Béranger, 1 July, 1784," *AAE-CP-Hollande,* Vol. 558, fol. 299.

19. "Noailles to Vergennes, 20 October, 1784," *AAE-CP-Autriche,* Vol. 548, fol. 157; "Vergennes to Béranger, 17 October, 1784," *AAE-CP-Hollande,* Vol. 559, fol. 372vo; "Apprédiris to Vergennes, 9 October, 1784," Eugène Hubert, *Correspondance des ministres*. . ., Vol. 3, pp. 82-84; A. Cauchie, *Le Comte 1.-c.-M Barbiano de Belgiojoso et ses papiers d'États conservé à Milan* (Bulletin de la commission royale d'histoire de Belgique, 1912), Vol. LXXXI, p. 184.

20. "Apprédiris to Vergennes, 5 November, 1784," Eugène Hubert, *Correspondance des ministres*. . ., Vol. 1, pp. 90-91; "Kaunitz to Mercy, 21 October, 1784," A. von Arneth and J. Flammermont, *Correspondance secrète du comte de Mercy d'Argenteau avec l'empéreur Joseph et le Prince de Kaunitz,* Vol. I, pp. 309-310.

21. "Joseph II to Marie Antoinette, 29 October, 1784," A. von Arneth, *Marie Antoinette, Joseph II und Leopold II, Ihr Briefwechsel* (Leipzig, 1866), p. 43.

22. "Noailles to Vergennes, 24 October, 1784," *AAE-CP-Autriche,* Vol. 548, fol. 164.

23. "Vergennes to Béranger, 17 October, 1784," *AAE-CP-Hollande,* Vol. 559, fols. 372vo-373vo.

24. Cauchie, *Le comte L.-C.-M. Barbiano di Belgiojoso et ses papiers d'Etats*. . ., p. 184.

25. "Observations de M. de Vergennes sur le coup de canon tiré sur l'Escaut le 8 October, 1784," *AAE-MD-France,* Vol. 1897, fol. 130.

26. *Ibid.*, fol. 131.

27. *Ibid.*

28. *Ibid.*, fol. 133.

29. "Barthélemy to Vergennes, 14 September, 1784," *AAE-CP-Angleterre,* Vol. 550, fol. 44; "D'Adhémar to Vergennes, 1 December, 1784," *ibid.*, Vol. 550, fol. 291.

30. Perhaps, on the other hand, Vergennes already knew that Calonne would support him. See Georges Grosjean, *La Politique Rhénane de Vergennes,* (Paris, 1925), 103.

31. "Observations de M. de Vergennes. . .le 8 Octobre, 1784," *AAE-MD-France,* 1897, fol. 135.

32. "Vergennes to Louis XVI, 5 November, 1784," *ibid.*, fol. 138.

33. Grosjean, *La Politique Rhénane*..., 103-106; Alexandre Tratchevsky, "La France et l'Allemagne sous Louis XVI," *Revue historique*, Vol. XV, p. 7-8.

34. "Vergennes to Béranger, 17 October, 1784," *AAE-CP-Hollande*, Vol. 559, fols. 372vo-373.

35. "Vergennes to Béranger, 19 August, 1784," *ibid.*, fols. 64-64vo.

36. "Résultats du Conseil de Guerre tenue 2 Novembre, 1784," with "Noailles to Vergennes, 10 November, 1784," *AAE-CP-Autriche*, Vol. 548, fols. 204-206vo.

37. "Noailles to Vergennes, 17 November, 1784," *ibid.*, fols. 217-218vo.

38. Henry Peyster, *Les Troubles de Hollande à la veille de la Révolution française 1780-1795* (Paris, 1905), p. 124.

39. "Déclaration arretée au conseil d'État, 17 Novembre, et expediée à Vienne, le 20 Novembre, 1784," *AAE-CP-Autriche*, Vol. 548, fols. 225-226.

40. "Vergennes to Noailles, 18 November, 1784," *ibid.*, 228-229.

41. *Ibid.*

42. "Vergennes to Noailles, 20 November, 1784," *ibid.*, fol. 236.

43. "Noailles to Vergennes, 24 November, 1784," *ibid.*, fols. 246vo-247; also, "Noailles to Vergennes, 25 December, 1784," *ibid.*, fol. 335vo.

44. "Insinuation faite par M. le Comte de Mercy dans la conférence du 30 Novembre, 1784," *ibid.*, fols. 254-256; "Joseph II to Mercy, 1 August, 1784," A. von Arneth et J. Flammermont, *Correspondance secrète du comte de Mercy d'Argenteau avec l'empéreur Joseph II et le prince de Kaunitz* (Paris, 1889-1891), Vol. I, p. 275. See also the dispatches of 2, 16 August: 1, 4, 25 September; 16, 29 October; 6, 19 November; 3, 17 December, 1784; 17 January, 1785.

45. "Insinuation faite par M. le Comte Mercy....," *AAE-CP-Autriche*, Vol. 548, fol. 255.

46. "Joseph II to Louis XVI, December, 17, 1784," Alfred von Arneth, *Marie Antoinette, Joseph II und Leopold II, Ihr Briefwechsel* (Leipzig, 1866), p. 58-59.

47. "Louis XVI to Joseph II, 6 January, 1785," Archives Nationales, Series K4418, K161 no. 27 bis 2, also printed in *ibid.*, pp. 65-68.

48. "Louis XVI to Joseph II, 6 January, 1785," Archives Nationales, series K 4418, K 161 no. 27 bis 2.

49. "Noailles to Vergennes, 30 November, 1784," *AAE-CP-Autriche*, Vol. 548, fols. 258vo.

50. Henry de Peyster, *Les Troubles de Hollande*, 124-125; A. Tratchevsky, "La France et l'Allemagne sous Louis XVI," *Ravue historique*, Vol. XV, p. 10.

51. "Noailles to Vergennes, 18 December, 1784," *AAE-CP-Autriche*, Vol. 548, fols. 305vo-306.

52. "Vergennes to Béranger, 30 December, 1784," *AAE-CP-Hollande*, Vol. 560, fol. 361vo.

53. *Ibid.*, also, "Louis XVI to Joseph, n.d. 1785," Archives Nationales, Series K 4418 K 161 27 bis 2.

54. "Vergennes to Béranger, 30 December, 1784," *AAE-CP-Hollande*, Vol. 560, fol. 362; "Louis XVI to Joseph II, 5 February, 1785," Archives Nationales, Series K 4418 K 161 27 bis 3.

55. "Marie Antoinette to Joseph II, 22 September, 5 November, 1784," A. von Arneth, *Marie Antoinette, Joseph II and Leopold II, Ihr Briefwechsel* (Leipzig, 1866), pp. 40, 46; Pierre Rain, *La diplomatie française d'Henri IV à Vergennes* (Paris, 1946), p. 316.

56. To Saxony and Hanover were later added Saxe-Weimar, Saxe-Gotha, Palati-

nate-Deux-Ponts, Brunswick, Boden, Hesse-Kassel, Anhalt, Ansbach, Mecklenburg, Mainz and other small states.

57. "Noailles to Vergennes, 18 December, 1784," *AAE-CP-Autriche,* Vol. 548, fol. 305-307vo.

58. "Vergennes to Béranger, 30 December, 1784," *AAE-CP-Hollande,* Vol. 560, fol. 361vo.

59. "Joseph II to Louis XVI, 21 February, 1785," A. von Arneth, *Marie Antoinette, Joseph II and Leopold II, Ihr Briefwechsel,* p. 81.

60. "Louis XVI to Joseph II, 3 December, 1784," Archives Nationales, Series K 4418 K 161 no. 27 bis 1.

61. *Ibid.*

62. "Joseph II to Louis XVI, 19 January, 1785," A. von Arneth, *Marie Antoinette,* . . ., p. 71; "Vergennes to Béranger, 20 December, 1784," *AAE-CP-Hollande,* Vol. 560, fol. 362.

63. Art. XV, "Traité d'accord définitif entre S.M. Impériale et Royale Apostolique et L.H.P. Seigneurs États-Générals des Provinces-Unies; Signé à Fontainebleau le 8 Novembre, 1785," Georg Martens, *Recueil de Traités . . . des Puissances et états de l'Europe* . . . . (Göttingen, 1818), Vol. IV, p. 58.

64. Art. V, *ibid.*, p. 56.

65. Arts. VIII, IX, *ibid.*, p. 57.

66. Arts. IV, XIII, XXIV, XXV, XXVI, *ibid.*, pp. 55, 57, 60.

67. Arts. XI, XII, XIV, XVIII, XIX, XX, XXII, XXIII, *ibid.*, pp. 57, 58, 60.

68. Art. XV *ibid.*, p. 58.

69. Art. VII, *ibid.*, p. 56.

70. Art. VII, Art. II, *ibid.*, pp. 55-56.

71. Art. XXVIII, *ibid.*, pp. 61-62.

72. "Vergennes to Vérac, November 3, 1785," *AAE-CP-Hollande.* Vol. 565, fols. 9-13.

73. "Vérac to Vergennes, 22 November, 1785," *ibid.*, fol. 145.

74. "Vergennes to Vérac, 28 November, 1785," *ibid.*, fols. 160-162.

75. Some secondary sources imply that the question of how much France would pay was settled before the Treaty of Fontainebleau was signed. See: Pierre Rain, *La diplomatie française d'Henri IV à Vergennes* (Paris, 1945), p. 319. While the sources are not altogether clear, my reading of them is that the issue was postponed until after the signatures. How much did France pay? Again, scholars have reached different conclusions: Pierre Rain, *ibid.*, p. 319, says France paid four million florins; George Grosjean, *La politique Rhénane de Vergennes* (Paris, 1925), p. 136, says four and one-half million; and Henry de Peyster, *Les Troubles de Hollande à la veille de la Révolution française 1780-1795* (Paris, 1905), p. 144, cites five million florins as the figure. My conclusion is that Louis XVI agreed to pay one-half the indemnity of 9,500,000 florins.

76. "Joseph to Marie Antoinette, 20 February, 1785," A. von Arneth, *Marie Antoinette,* . . . ., p. 77.

77. "Marie Antoinette to Joseph II, 10 November, 1785," *ibid.*, p. 100.

78. "Marie Antoinette to Joseph II, 31 December, 1785," *ibid.*, p. 102.

79. *Ibid.*, p. 103.

80. "Marie Antoinette to Joseph, 16 May, 1785, 22 September, 1784," *ibid.*, pp. 87, 39.

81. "Marie Antoinette to Joseph II, 4 February, 1785," *ibid.*, p. 72.

82. "Marie Antoinette to Joseph, 26 November, 1785," *ibid.*, p. 51.

83. "Marie Antoinette to Joseph II, 4 February, 1785," *ibid.*, p. 72.
84. "Marie Antoinette to joseph II, 31 December, 1785," *ibid.*, p. 102.
85. "Mercy to Joseph II, 31 December, 1784," "Marie Antoinette to Joseph II, 31 December, 1784," *ibid.*, pp. 64-65.
86. George Grosjean, *La politique Rhénane de Vergennes* (Paris, 1925), 185-187.
87. *Ibid.*, p. 188.
88. *Ibid.*, p. 192.

Chapter 34. Relations with Italy: 1774-1787

1. "Mémoire pour servir d'instructions au sieur Baron de Breteuil allant résider à Vienne en qualité d'ambassadeur extraordinaire du roi près leurs majestés impériales et royales apostolique, 28 December, 1774," *AAE-CP-Autriche,* Vol. 326; printed in Albert Sorel, *Recueil de Instructions données aux ambassadeurs et ministres de France* . . . (Paris, 1884), Vol. 1, Autriche, 466ff.
2. *Ibid.*, 467; 481.
3. "Projet de traité entre le roi et la République de Gênes, 15 May 1768," Edward Driault, *Recueil des instructions données aux ambassadeurs et ministres de France, Florence, Modène et Gênes* (Paris, 1912) XIX, 370-375.
4. "Point de Vue Politique sur la Corse, 1777," *Archives des Affaires Étrangères—Mémoires et Documents—Corse,* 1539, fol. 11. Hereafter referred to as *AAE-MD-Corse;* See also: "Mémoire politique et raisonné sur les Îles situées dans le détroit qui sépara la Corse de la Sardaigne," *AAE-CP-Gênes,* Vol. 159, fols. 349-76.
5. Article IX of the Treaty, Driault, *op. cit.*, pp. 370-375. Also, see: "Boyer to Vergennes, 10 July, 1775," *AAE-CP-Gênes,* Vol. 158, fol. 174.
6. "Comte de Muy to Vergennes, 17 March, 1775," *ibid.*, fols. 106-107; See also: "Boyer to Vergennes, 3 April, 1775," *ibid.*, fols. 115vo -116; "Vergennes to Boyer, 9 May, 1775," *ibid.*, fol. 140.
7. "Vergennes to Monteil, 13 October, 10 November, 1778," *ibid.*, Vol. 160, fols. 173, 186.
8. Of the numerous reports on English ship activity see, for example: *ibid.*, Vol. 160, fols. 159, 163, 171, 203.
9. *Ibid.*, fols. 95-99vo, 115, 249, 250-251vo, 252vo, 260-262; "Extract of letter by Sartine, 15 February 1778," *ibid.*, fols. 241-244vo and ff.
10. "Vergennes to Monteil, 14 September, 1779," *ibid.*, fols. 330vo -331; "Letter of Sartine of September, 1779," fol. 327.
11. Le Comte Horric de Beaucaire, *Recueil des instructions données aux ambassadeurs et ministres de France* (Paris, 1898), XIV, Savoie-Sardaigne et Mantoue, Tome I, p. lxxxii.
12. "Chauvelin to Duc de Choiseul, 13 December 1758," *AAE-CP-Turin-Sardaigne,* Vol. 230, fol. 101.
13. *Ibid.*, and Beaucaire, *Recueil des instructions* . . ., p. xcv.
14. "Observations de M. de Vergennes sur le coup de canon tiré sur l'Escault le 8 Octobre 1784," *AAE-MD-France,* Vol. 1897, fols. 133.
15. "Vergennes to Flavigny, 24 October 1774," *AAE-CP-Parme,* Vol. 39, fols. 250-250vo.
16. "Mémoire pour servir d'instruction au Sieur Baron de Zuckmontel . . . allant à Venise pour y résider en qualité d'ambassadeur de S.M. 15 Septembre, 1771, *AAE-MD-Venise,* Vol. 36, fols. 96-105; Pierre DuParc, *Recueil des instructions données*

aux ambassadeurs et ministres de France . . . (Paris, 1958), XXVI, Venise, 263-265.

17. "Mémoire pour servir d'instructions au Sieur Marquis de Vergennes allant à Venise pour y résider en qualité d'ambassadeur de S.M., 21 March 1779," *AAE-MD-Venise,* Vol. 36, 149-160; DuParc, *Recueil des instructions* . . ., pp. 275-277.

18. "Louis XVI to Vergennes, 11 April, 1775," *AAE-MD-France,* Vol. 1897, fol. 37.

19. Pierre DuParc, *Recueil des instructions* . . ., p. ix.

20. "Mémoire pour servir d'instructions au Sieur Marquis de Vergennes . . ." *AAE-MD-Venise,* Vol. 36, fol. 149-160.

21. *Ibid.*, fols. 149-160.

22. DuParc, *Recueil des instructions* . . ., p. xxiv.

23. Louis de Laique, "Le comte de Froullay, ambassadeur à Venise," (1733-1743) *Revue d'histoire diplomatique* (Paris, 1913), 27e année, pp. 85-89.

24. "Letter from Bernis 25 November 1752," *AAE-CP-Venise,* Vol. 214, fols. 118-119.

25. "Mémoire pour servir de supplément aux instructions du Sieur Marquis de Vergennes retournant à Venise en qualité d'ambassadeur du Roi, 15 September 1783," *AAE-MD-Venise,* Vol. 22, fols. 86-88.

26. Gabriel Hanotaux, *Recueil des instructions données aux ambassadeurs* . . . (Paris, 1913), XX, Rome, tome III (1724-1791), x-xi.

27. "Mémoire pour servir d'instruction au Sieur du de Nivernois . . . allant à Rome en qualité d'ambassadeur extraordinaire . . ., 10 November 1748," *AAE-CP-Rome,* Supplémentaire, 18, fol. 126; see also, Robert A. Graham, S.J., *Vatican Diplomacy* (Princeton, 1959), pp. 161-163.

28. "Louis XVI to King of Spain, 10 October 1774," *AAE-MD-France,* Vol. 1897, fol. 13.

29. Hanotaux, *Recueil des instructions* . . . ., p. xxx, Rome, tome III, 471-472; A. Morel-Fatio et H. Leonardon, *Recueil des instructions* . . . ., III, bis, Espagne, tome II, xxxiii-xxxiv; 344-345.

30. "Mémoire sur le conclave," *AAE-CP-Rome,* Vol. 868, fol. 251.

31. *AAE-CP-Rome,* Vol. 868, fol. 213; fol. 251; on the Spanish-French cooperation, see also: the additional correspondence in *AAE-CP-Espagne,* Vols. 574, 575; "Vergennes to Ossun, 31 October 1774;" "Floridablanca to Grimaldi, 15 September 1774," *ibid.*, Vol. 574, fols. 286vo, 138-158vo.

32. A. Theiner, *Histoire du Pontificat de Clément XIV,* II, 521.

33. *Ibid.*, 521.

34. "Mémoire presenté par les cardinaux de Bernis et Orsini au doyen du Sacré Collège," *AAE-CP-Rome,* Vol. 869, fols. 95-96.

35. "Copie du billet au Cardinal Jean-Francois Albani, 11 November 1774," *ibid.*, Vol. 869, fols. 193-193vo; "Mémoire pour servir d'instruction à M.M. les Cardinaux de Luynes et de Bernis qui assistent au présent Conclave 24 October, 1774," *ibid.*, fols. 106ff.

36. Hanotaux, *Recueil des instructions* . . . ., XX, Rome, tome III, 598; "l'Abbé Georgel à Vergennes, 15 October 1774," *AAE-CP-Autriche,* Vol. 324, fol. 122; "Vergennes à l'Abbé Georgel, 31 Octobre 1774," *ibid.*, Vol. 324, fol. 154.

37. "Journal du Conclave," *AAE-CP-Rome,* 869-872.

38. "Journal du Conclave, 13-14 February 1775," *ibid.*, 872, fol. 137.

39. "Mémoire pour servir d'instruction au Sieur Baron de Talleyrand-Périgord . . . allant à Naples pour y résider en qualité d'ambassadeur extraordinaire et plénipotentaire du roi auprès du roi des Deux-Sicilies, 3 April 1785," *AAE-CP-Naples,*

Vol. 112, 251vo; on Talleyrand's appointment, see also: *AAE-MD-France*, 1897, fols. 68-69; Joseph Reinach, *Recueil des Instructions données aux ambassadeurs et ministres de France depuis les traités de Westphalie jusqu'à la révolution française* (Paris, 1893), 10, Naples et Parme, 123.

40. *Ibid.*, pp. 10, 105.

41. "Mémoire pour servir d'instruction au Sieur Baron de Talleyrand-Périgord . . . allant à Naples pour y résider en qualité d'ambassadeur extraordinaire et plénipotentiare du roi auprès du roi des Deux-Sicilies, 3 April 1785," *AAE-CP-Naples*, Vol. 112, 245vo -246vo.

42. "Mémoire pour servir d'instruction au Sieur Baron de Breteuil . . . allant à Naples pour y résider en qualité d'ambassadeur extraordinaire de S.M. auprès du roi des Deux Sicilies, 1 May 1772," *ibid.*, Vol. 94, fols. 294-294vo.

43. *Ibid.*, fols 299-299vo. Reinach, *Recueil des instructions* . . ., 108-110.

44. "Mémoire pour servir d'instruction au Sieur Baron de Talleyrand-Périgord . . ., 3 April 1785," *AAE-CP-Naples*, Vol. 112, fol. 246vo.

45. "Vergennes to Billerey, 8 June 1784," *AAE-CP-Toscane*, Vol. 141A. fol. 59. Also "Billerey to Vergennes, 25 June 1784," *ibid.*, fols. 69-69vo.

46. *AAE-MD-Corse*, Vol. 1439, fol. 70.

47. "Vergennes to Durfort, 18 January 1785," *AAE-CP-Toscane*, Vol. 141A, fol. 255.

48. "Vergennes to Durfort, 14 December 1784," *ibid.*, fols. 205-205[vo].

49. "Vergennes to Durfort, 21 December 1784," *ibid.*, 214.

50. "Durfort to Vergennes, 7 January 1785," *ibid.*, fol. 236.

51. *Ibid.*, fols. 236vo-237.

52. "Vergennes to Durfort, 18 January 1785," *ibid.*, fol. 255.

53. "Durfort to Vergennes, 3 December 1785," *ibid.*, fol. 195.

54. "Coup d'oeil rapide et apperçu préliminaire sur la législation de la Toscane," *ibid.*, fols. 262-271.

55. "Durfort to Vergennes, 31 December 1784," *ibid.*, fol. 228vo.

56. "Vergennes to Billerey, 11 May 1785," *ibid.*, fol. 51.

57. "Vergennes to Durfort, 18 January 1785," *ibid.*, fol. 255.

58. "Vergennes to Louis XVI, 29 March 1784," *Archives Nationales*, K161; Printed also in L.P. Ségur, *Politique de tous les cabinets de l'Europe* . . . . (Paris, 1801), Vol. 3, pp. 213-214.

59. D.H. Horn, *Great Britain and Europe in the 18th Century*, (Oxford 1967), pp. 344-349.

60. "Vergennes to Durfort, 1 March 1785," *AAE-CP-Toscane*, Vol. 141A. fol. 33-33vo.

Chapter 35. Commerce and Diplomacy: I

1. Reginald E. Rabb, *The Role of William Eden in William Pitt's Liberal Trade Policy*, (New York, 1942), p. 36.

2. DuPont de Nemours, "Réflexions sur le bien que peuvent se faire réciproquement la France et l'Angleterre," *AAE-MD-Angleterre*, 65, folios 3-8. That the English recognized this motive behind Vergennes' actions is clearly demonstrated; see: "Hailes to Carmarthen, 25 October, 1786," printed in J. Holland Rose, *William Pitt and National Revival* (London, 1911), p. 344.

3. Oscar Browning, "The Treaty of Commerce Between England and France in

1786," *Transactions of the Royal Historical Society* (London, 1885), II, New Series, pp. 357-360.

4. See Vergennes' opinion, which is similar to that of Rayneval, in "Mémoire de M. de Vergennes à Louis XVI sur la situation politique de la France relativement aux différentes puissances, 1774," Archives Nationales, K 164 No. 2^2.

5. "Eden to Carmarthen, 6 April 1786," *The Journal and Correspondence of William Eden,* Lord Auckland (London, 1861-62), I, p. 97. Hereafter referred to as *Auckland Papers.*

6. "Eden to Carmarthen, 17 April 1786," William Eden, "Letters and Papers from Mr. Eden relative to the negotiation of the Anglo-French Commercial Treaty of 1786 to the British Secretary of State," folios 21-22, (Originals, *Public Records Office,* London, England, State Papers, Foreign Office, France). I consulted the microfilm copies of these documents at *Eleutherian Mills Historical Library,* Wilmington, Delaware, Accesson #456; see also "Eden to Carmarthen, 6 June 1786," (Most Secret), *ibid.,* folios 116-116vo. Hereafter referred to as the *Eden Papers.*

7. "Vergennes to Louis XVI, 26 September 1786," *Archives Nationales,* K 164$^{no\,3}$. The idea of a *rapprochement* was not new to Vergennes. As early as 1775, his former chief of Louis XV's "secret" diplomacy suggested it. See: "Mémoire du Comte de Broglie, 1 March 1775," Louis Phillippe de Ségur, *Politique de tous les cabinets de l'Europe pendant les règnes de Louis XV et de Louis XVI.* (Paris, 1793), I, pp. 172-173.

8. Oscar Browning, *op. cit.,* p. 349.

9. Quoted in John Ehrman, *The British Government and Commercial Negotiations with Europe:* 1783-1793 (Cambridge, England, 1962), p. 28.

10. *Ibid.,* p. 1.

11. See: Pitt's "House of Commons Speech, May 5, 1786," cited in Oscar Browning, *op. cit.,* p. 356.

12. "Pitt to William Eden, 31 May 1786," *Auckland Papers,* I, p. 119.

13. "Treaty of Versailles, September 3, 1783," Hansard, *The Parliamentary History of England From the Earliest times to the Year 1803* (London, 1814), XXIII, Series I, 1782-1783, p. 1166.

14. Oscar Browning, *op. cit.,* p. 349.

15. J. Holland Rose, "The Franco-British Commercial Treaty of 1786," *English Historical Review* (1908), XXIII, p. 714; Léon Cahen, "Une Nouvelle interprétation du traité Franco-Anglais de 1786-1787," *Revue Historique* (1939), CLXXXV, p. 258; a very good recent study of this treaty is Marie M. Donaghay, "The Anglo-French Negotiations of 1786-1787," (Unpublished doctoral dissertation, University of Virginia, 1970).

16. Oscar Browning, *op. cit.,* p. 351.

17. *Ibid.,* pp. 350-351.

18. "Carmarthen to Craufurd, 5 August, 1785," *Public Records Office,* London, England, State Papers, Foreign Office, (France) 27/16; printed in J. Holland Rose, "The Franco-British Commercial Treaty of 1786," *English Historical Review,* XXIII, p. 713.

19. Léon Cahen, "Une nouvelle interprétation du traité Franco-Anglaise de 1786-1787," pp. 263-265.

20. Dispatch dated 26 February 1785, *AAE-CP-Angleterre,* tome 552, folio 252vo.

21. Cahen, *op. cit.,* pp. 265-266.

22. *Ibid.,* p. 266; J. Holland Rose, "The Franco-British Commercial Treaty of 1786," *English Historical Review,* XXIII, pp. 710-712.

23. "Vergennes to Adhémar de Grignan, 17 January 1785," *AAE-CP-Angleterre,* tome 552, folio 55.

24. See the note dated 21 June 1782 edited by Vergennes and given to Lord Shelburne, printed in Comte de Butenval, *Précis historique et économique du traité de Commerce entre la France et la Grande Brêtagne* (Paris, 1869), p. 16.

25. "Adhémar de Grignan to Vergennes, 25 January 1785," *AAE-CP-Angleterre,* tome 552, folios 85-86.

26. Ehrman, *op. cit.,* pp. 30-31.

27. J. Holland Rose, "The Franco-British Commercial Treaty of 1786," *English Historical Review,* XXIII, p. 711.

28. "Arrêt du Conseil d'État du Roi. Concernant les Marchandises étrangerèse, prohibées dans le Royaume . . .," 17 July 1785.

29. "Arrêt du Conseil d'État du Roi, Qui renouvelle les anciennes défenses d'introduire dans la Royaume, anciennes toiles de coton, et Mousselines venant de l'Étranger, autres que celles de l'Inde apportées par commerce nationale . . .," 10 July 1785, signed by Gravier de Vergennes.

30. Ehrman, *op cit.,* pp. 30-31.

31. "Carmarthen to Craufurd, 4 March 1785," *Public Records Office,* London, England, State Papers, Foreign Office (France), 27/16.

32. "Carmarthen to Craufurd, 5 August 1785," *Public Records Office,* London, England, State Papers, Foreign Office, (France), 27/16.

33. "Prohibition générale à toutes les entrés du Royaume par la décision du conseil d'État du 21 October 1785," *Eden Papers,* Vol. I, folios 95-96.

34. Ehrman, *op. cit.,* p. 32.

35. "Craufurd to Carmarthen, 10 March, 1785," *Public Records Office,* London, England, State Papers, Foreign Office, (France), 27/16.

36. *Ibid.*

37. "Hailes to Carmarthen, 4 August, 1785," *Public Records Office,* London, England, State Papers, Foreign Office, (France), 27/16; also printed in J. Holland Rose, "The Franco-British Commercial Treaty of 1786," *English Historical Review* XXIII, p. 712.

38. "Hailes to Carmarthen, 1 December 1785," cited in *ibid.,* p. 714.

39. J. Holland Rose, *William Pitt and National Revival* (London, 1911), p. 311.

40. J. Holland Rose, "The Franco-British Commercial Treaty of 1786," *English Historical Review,* XXIII, p. 715-716.

41. "Eden to Pitt, 13 April 1786," printed in *ibid.,* p. 717.

42. Léon Cahen, *op. cit.,* p. 269.

43. "Rayneval to Craufurd, 15 September 1785," *AAE-CP-Angleterre,* Vol. 554, folio 153vo.

44. "Louis XVI to DuPont de Nemours, 19 September 1774," the DuPont letters and manuscripts are found in the *Eleutherian Mills Historical Library,* Wilmington, Delaware, Winterthur MSS a/31 item #13, Section 32 pieces. Hereafter referred to as *WMSS;* "Vergennes to DuPont de Nemours, 4 February 1775," *WMSS* 2/9; "DuPont de Nemours to Vergennes, 2 April 1755," *WMSS* 2/1; "DuPont de Nemours to Vergennes, 2 April 1775," *WMSS* 2/1; "DuPont de Nemours to Vergennes, 6 November 1782," *WMSS* 2/1; "DuPont de Nemours to Vergennes, 30 May 1776," *AAE-CP-Angleterre,* folio 238; "DuPont de Nemours to Vergennes, 11 June 1781," *ibid.,* vol. 534, folio 97; See also: "DuPont de Nemours to Comte Chreptowicz, 25 December 1803," in "Lettres inédits de DuPont de Nemours," *Journal des Économistes* (Paris, 1907), 6e-Serie, Tome XIV, p. 15.

45. "DuPont de Nemours to Vergennes, 30 May 1776," *AAE-CP-Angleterre,* Vol. 516, folios 238-239vo; see, also: "DuPont de Nemours to Vergennes, 11 June 1781," *ibid.,* vol. 534, folio 97; "DuPont de Nemours to Vergennes, 17 October 1718," *ibid.,* vol. 534, folio 270.

46. Gustave Schelle, *DuPont de Nemours et l'école physiocratique* (Paris, 1888), p. 203.

47. "DuPont de Nemours to Vergennes, 14 August 1755," *WMSS* 2/1.

48. "DuPont de Nemours to Vergennes [c. July, 1782]," *ibid., WMSS* 2/1; "DuPont de Nemours to Vergennes, [c. July, 1782]," *WMSS* 2/1; "DuPont de Nemours to Villevault, 17 August 1782," *WMSS* 2/1; "DuPont de Nemours to Villevault, 8 September 1782," *WMSS* 2/1.

49. Gustave Schelle, *DuPont de Nemours,* pp. 224-225.

50. Boyetet, *Recueil de Divers Mémoires Relatifs au Traité de Commerce avec l'Angleterre. . . .*(Paris, 1789), p. 3, 18.

51. "Commissaires généraux du commerce . . .etc., 30 January 1785," *WMSS* 2/3 Item #24. "Extrait de L'arrêt du Conseil du 29 mars, 1785, Concernant la Balance du Commerce," *WMSS* 2/31, Item # 27.

52. B.G. DuPont, *DuPont de Nemours: 1739-1817* (Newark, Delaware, 1933), II, p. 142.

53. These six memoirs are in *AAE-MD-Angleterre,* tome 65, folios 3-8; 9-21; 24-175vo; 199-223; 226-234vo.

54. "Réflexions sur le bien que peuvent se faire réciproquement la France, et l'Angleterre," *AAE-MD-Angleterre,* tome 65, folios 3-8.

55. "Observations sur les motifs particuliers qui peuvent déterminer le traité de commerce," *AAE-MD-Angleterre,* tome 65, folios 9-21.

56. See, for example: "Observations sur la Note concernant la Base du Traité de Commerce, Communiqué par M. le Comte de Vergennes à M. Le Contrôleur Général, *ibid.,* tome 65, folios 24-175vo; "Remarques sur les Observations faites au Comité du 9 Aout 1786, relativement à la Lettre Confidentielle de M. Eden," *ibid.,* tome 65, folios 180-195vo; "Observations sur les avantages que trouvera la France dans la diminution des droites actuellement imposés à l'entreé des Marchandises Françaises en Angleterre, *ibid.,* tome 65, folios 199-223.

57. "Eden to Carmarthen, 6 April 1786," *Auckland Papers,* I, p. 98.

58. "Project," *Eden Papers,* Vol. I, folios 13-16; also in *Auckland Papers,* I, pp. 479-481.

59. Ibid.

60. "Pitt to Eden, 20 April 1786," *ibid.,* I, pp. 108-109.

61. "Pitt to Eden, 10 May 1786," *ibid.,* pp. 481-486; "Secret and Confidential memorandum, 20 April 1786," *Eden Papers,* I, folios 25-25[vo].

62. "Pitt to Eden, 20 April 1786," *Auckland Papers,* I, p. 107.

63. "Pitt to Eden, 10 May, 1786," *ibid.,* I, p. 485; on the question of admitting French silks into England, see also: "George Rose to William Eden, 31 May 1786," *ibid.,* pp. 120-121.

64. *Ibid.,* p. 486.

65. *Ibid.*

66. "Eden to Pitt, May 6, 1786," *ibid.,* I, p. 115.

67. *Ibid.,* p. 116.

68. Oscar Browning, "The Treaty of Commerce Between England and France in 1786," *Transactions of the Royal Historical Society,* (1885), II, New Series, p. 357.

69. "Draft of a Declaration proposed to be delivered by Mr. Eden, 31 May 1786,"

Eden Papers, Vol. I, folios 111-113vo.

70. "Eden to Carmarthen, 8 June 1786," *Eden Papers,* I, folio 120 and *Auckland Papers,* I, p. 124.

71. "Carmarthen to Eden, 10 June 1786," *Eden Papers,* I, folio 122-122vo.

72. Articles I, II, III in "Draft of Declaration proposed to be delivered by Mr. Eden," *Eden Papers,* I, folios 111-113.

73. "Contre-Déclaration," transmitted to Carmarthen with Eden's letter of 17 June 1786, *Eden Papers,* Vol. I, folios 130-131.

74. "Draft to Mr Eden, 18 July 1786," *Eden Papers,* Vol. I, folios 146-155vo.

75. *Ibid.*

76. "Eden to Pitt, 23 August 1786," *Auckland Papers,* I, p. 156, 494.

77. See, for example: "Answer of Ribbon Manufacturers concerning opening England to French Ribbon Trade," *Eden Papers,* I, folio 297.

78. *Ibid.*

79. "Eden to Carmarthen, 13 August 1786," *Eden Papers,* I, folios 207-211vo; "Eden to Carmarthen, 27 August 1786," *ibid.,* II, folios 1-5; "Observations sur la réplique confidentielle remise par M. Eden," dated 13 August 1786, *ibid.,* I, pp. 215-220.

80. *Ibid.*

81. "Rayneval to Eden, 13 August 1786," *Eden Papers,* I, 225-228vo; "Eden to Carmarthen, 17 August 1786," *ibid.,* 256-256vo.

82. "Carmarthen to Eden, 20 August 1786," *ibid.,* 266-286.

83. *Ibid.*

84. See: "Memorandum for instructions for Mr. Eden, 28 August 1786," and "Pitt to Eden, 21 September 1786," both printed in J. Holland Rose, "The Franco-British Commercial Treaty of 1786," *English Historical Review* (1908), Vol. 92, pp. 720-722.

85. "Eden to Pitt, 13 July 1786," and "Eden to Pitt, 25 July 1786," *Auckland Papers,* I, 143-145; 147-148; "Eden to Carmarthen, 13 August 1786," and "Eden to Carmarthen, 8 September 1786," *Eden Papers,* I, p. 221; II, folios 53-58vo.

86. "Eden to Carmarthen, 25 September 1786," "Rayneval to Eden, 25 September 1786," "Eden to Carmarthen, 27 September 1786," *Eden Papers,* II, folios 102-106vo; pp. 120-230.

87. "Traité de Navigation et de Commerce entre la Grande Brêtagne et la France, 26 September 1786," *ibid.*

88. "Eden to Carmarthen, 11 November 1786," *Eden Papers,* II, folio 312.

89. Léon Cahen, "Une Nouvelle interprétation du Traité Franco-Anglais de 1786-1787," *Revue Historique* (1939), Vol. 185, pp. 265-285.

90. *Ibid.,* pp. 273-274.

91. *Observations de la chambre de commerce de Normandie sur le Traité. . .entre la France et l'Angleterre* (Rouen, 1788); see also: Henri Sée, "The Normandy Chamber of Commerce and the Commercial Treaty of 1786," *Economic History Review* (1929-1930), II, pp. 308-313.

92. Anonymous, *Lettre à la Chambre de Commerce de Normandie* (Rouen et Paris, 1788).

93. *Ibid.,* 48, 54, 56, 170-171.

94. *Ibid.,* p. 33.

95. *Ibid.,* pp. 61-62.

96. *Ibid.,* p. 64.

97. *Ibid.,* pp. 64-65.

98. *Ibid.,* pp. 65-68.

99. Cahen, *op. cit.*, pp. 271-285.

100. Boyetet, "Deuxième Mémoire," in *Recueil de Divers Mémoires relatifs au traité de Commerce avec l'Angleterre* (Paris, 1789), p. 19.

101. Cliquot-Blervache, "Considérations sur le traité de commerce entre la France et la Grande-Brêtagne, du 26 September 1786," quoted in Jules de Vroil, "Le traité de commerce de 1786," *Journal des Économistes,* Vol. XVII, p. 57.

102. Boyetet, *Recueil de Divers Mémoires,* p. 18. On the French government's attempts to gather information and consult with various parties see Marie Donaghay, "Calonne and the Anglo-French Commercial Treaty of 1786," *The Journal of Modern History* (1978), Vol. 50, University Microfilms U-00038.

103. "Hailes to Carmarthen, 25 October 1786," printed in J. Holland Rose, *William Pitt and National Revival,* p. 344.

104. "Pitt to Eden, 16 December 1785," *Auckland Papers,* I, p. 90.

105. "Eden to Morton Eden, 27 January 1786," *ibid.*, I, p. 94.

106. Ehrman, *The British Government and Commercial Negotiations with Europe: 1783-1786,* p. 45.

107. *Ibid.*

108. Marie Donaghay, "The Maréchal de Castries and the Anglo-French Commercial Negotiations of 1786-1787," *The Historical Journal,* (1979), Vol. 22, no. 2, pp. 297-303.

109. On the negotiations for consular relations between England and France, see Marie Donaghay, "The Anglo-French Negotiations of 1786-1787," (Unpublished Doctoral dissertation, University of Virginia, 1970), p. 147. Also, Marie Donaghay, "The Maréchal de Castries and the Anglo-French Commercial Negotiations of 1786-1787; *op. cit.*, pp. 304-307.

110. *Ibid.*, 312.

111. Donaghay, "The Anglo-French Negotiations of 1786-1787," pp.154, 234-235.

Chapter 36. Commerce and Diplomacy: II

1. See: L. Jay Oliva, *Misalliance: A Study of French Policy in Russia During the Seven Years' War* (New York, 1965), 121-134; 165-167; 198-199; M. de Flassan, *Histoire générale et raisonnée; de la diplomatie française* (Paris, 1811), Vol. VII, 431-432; J.H. Castera, *The Life of Catherine II, Empress of Russia* (London, 1798), Vol. III, p. 260.

2. *Ibid.*, Vol. VII, p. 439; J.L. van Regemorter, "Commerce et Politique: préparation et négotiation du traité franco-russe de 1787," *Cahiers du Monde Russe et Soviétique* (July-September, 1967), Vol. III, no. 3, p. 233.

3. "Mémoire" by Michel, Beaujon, Raimbert and Goosen, dated January 1757, quoted in Oliva, *Misalliance,* p. 125.

4. Regemorter, *op. cit.*, p. 234; "Ségur to Vergennes, 4 March, 1786," *AAE-CP-Russie,* Vol. 117, fol. 134vo.

5. *Ibid.*

6. *Ibid.*

7. Chevalier de Corberon, *Un diplomate français à la cour de Catherine II (1775-1780), Journal intime* (Paris, 1901), Vol. II, p. 342; "Corberon to Sartine, 12 October, 1779," *Archives de la Marine,* B^{7}, 441, cited in Regemorter, *op. cit.*, p. 234; for Ségur's opinion of the French merchants in Russia, see: "Ségur to Vergennes, 4 March, 1786," *AAE-CP-Russie,* Vol. 117, fols. 134-138.

8. Frank Fox, "Negotiating with the Russians: Ambassador Ségur's Mission to Saint Petersburg, 1784-1789," *French Historical Studies* (Spring, 1971), Vol. VII, no. 1, pp. 52-53; Regemorter, *op. cit.*, 235-237.

9. Comte de Ségur, "Observations sur les moyens propres à encourager le commerce et la navigation de la France ... en Russie, 1788," *AAE-MD-France,* Vol. 2013, fo. 158.

10. "Instructions au Marquis de Beausset ..." in A. Rambaud, *Recueil des instructions données aux ambassadeurs et ministres de France* ... (Paris, 1890), Vol. II, Russie, p. 230.

11. "Calonne to Vergennes, 25 April, 1786," *Archives Nationales,* F^{12}, 1835.

12. Oliva, *op. cit.*, 126. See also: Flassan, *op. cit.*, Vol. VII, 431.

13. Comte de Broglie and Favier, "Conjectures raisonnées sur la situation actuelle de la France dans le systême politique de l'Europe," in Louis-Philippe de Ségur, *Politique de tous les cabinets de l'Europe* (Paris, 1793), Vol. I, p. 334.

14. "Antoine to Hennin, Jan. 16, 1786," "Raimbert to Vergennes, 9/20 January, 1786," *AAE-CP-Russie,* Vol. 117, fols. 52-53vo; 56; 59-60.

15. Raimbert, in his summary of trade for the port of Kersen for 1785, concluded also that France enjoyed an unfavorable balance of trade with Russia. "Raimbert to Vergennes 9/20 January, 1786," *ibid.*, Vol. 117, fol. 59.

16. "Vergennes to Ségur, 12 May, 1786," *ibid.*, Vol. 117, fol. 192.

17. "Réponse à la Note remise par Messieurs les plénipotentiaires Russes à M. le comte de Ségur," *ibid.*, Vol. 117, fol. 198vo.

18. Quoted in J.L. Regemorter, *op. cit.*, p. 246; see also: "Ségur to Vergennes, 3 February, 1786; 5 May, 1786," *AAE-CP-Russie,* Vol. 117, fol. 75; Vol. 118, fol. 10.

19. Quoted in Oliva, *Misalliance,* p. 165-166.

20. "Mackenzie Douglas to Jean Pierre Tercier, 22 May, 1757," *AAE-CP-Russie,* Vol. 52, fol. 432.

21. Peyssonnel, *Traité sur le commerce de la mer noire* (Paris, 1787); see also A. Rambaud, *Recueil des instructions* ..., Vol. II, Russie, pp. 319-320.

22. Louis-Philippe de Ségur, *Mémores ou souvenirs et anecdotes* (Paris, 1827), Vol. II, p. 328.

23. "Ségur to Vergennes, 16 April, 1785," *AAE-CP-Russie,* Vol. 113, fols. 179-180; Ségur, *Mémoires,* Vol. II, p. 296.

24. "Ségur to Vergennes, 3 February, 1786," *AAE-CP-Russie,* Vol. 117, fol. 76.

25. "Ségur to Vergennes, 4 March, 1786," "*ibid.*, Vol. 117, fol. 135.

26. Frank Fox, "Negotiating with the Russians," *French Historical Studies,* Vol. VII, p. 55

27. Louis-Philippe de Ségur, *Politique de tous les cabinets de l'Europe* (Paris, 1793), I, 289-290.

28. "Broglie to Louis XV, 16 April, 1773," Émile Boutaric, *Correspondance Secrète de Louis XV sur la politique étrangère* (Paris, 1866), II, 53-54; "Mémoire du Comte de Broglie, 1 March, 1775," printed in Louis-Philippe de Ségur, *Politique des tous les cabinets de l'Europe* (Paris, 1793),I, 168. See also *ibid.*, 329-346.

29. "Lord Rochford to Earl Harcourt, 21 February, 1772," L.G. Wickham Legg, *British Diplomatic Instructions, 1689-1789* (London, 1934), VII, France, 124.

30. "Mémoire de M. de Vergennes sur la Porte Ottomane," in Louis-Philippe de Ségur, *Politique de tous les cabinets de l'Europe* (Paris, 1801), II, 114-115; see also "Conjectures raisonnées sur la situation actuelle de la France dans le système politique de l'Europe ...," and "Ouvrage dirigé par le Comte de Broglie, exécuté par M. Favier, et remis à Louis XV dans les derniers mois de son règne" in *ibid.*, 7ff.

31. "Conjectures raisonnée sur la situation . . .," in *ibid.*, I, 320-321.
32. Dietrich Gerhard, *England und der Aufstieg Russlands* (Munich, 1933), 12.
33. "Stainville to l'Hôpital, 16 September, 1758," *AAE-CP-Russie*, Supplement, X, fol. 105.
34. Louis-Philippe de Ségur, *Politique* . . . (Paris, 1801), II, 117, 119fn.
35. "Mémoire pour servir d'instruction au sieur Comte de Ségur . . ., 16 December, 1784," in A. Rambaud, ed. *Recueil des instructions*, Vol. II, pp. 389-396.
36. "Ségur to Vergennes, 11 May, 1785," *AAE-CP-Russie*, Vol. 113, fol. 294.
37. Frank Fox, "Negotiating with the Russians . . .," *French Historical Studies*, VII, 51.
38. Comte de Ségur, *Mémoires*, II, 269ff.
39. "Bezborodko to S.R. Vorontsov, 24 October, 1785," O.S. in P. Bartenev ed. *Arkhiv Knyaza Vorontsova*, cited in Fox, "Negotiating with the Russians," *French Historical Studies*, VII, pp. 51-52.
40. "Note: Ségur to Vice-Chancelier Osterman, 13 July, 1785," *AAE-CP-Russie*, Vol. 114, fol. 91.
41. Réponse à la note remise par Messieurs les plénipotentiaires Russes à M. le comte de Ségur," *ibid.*, Vol. 117, fol. 196.
42. "Instructions d'Osterman à Simolin, 6 February, 1786," in Martens, *Recueil des traités*, Vol. XIII, p. 200; Ségur, "Observations sur les principes fundamentaux de la Russie dans ses traités de commerce, 15 July, 1785," *AAE-CP-Russie*, Vol. 114, fols, 114-115.
43. Regemorter, *op. cit.*, 246; A. Rambaud, *Recueil des instructions* . . ., Russie, II, pp. 405-407.
44. "Ségur a Vergennes, 19 October, 1785," *AEE-CP-Russie*, Vol. 115, fol. 80.
45. "Réponse à la Note remise par Messieurs les plénipotentiaires Russes à M. le comte de Sègur," *ibid.*, Vol. 117, fols. 196-196vo.
46. "Raimbert to Castries 12/23 Dec., 1785," *Archives Nationales*, Correspondance Consulat, St. Petersburg, 8 AE ss B' 989, fol. 199.
47. "Réponse à la *Gazette de Leyde*, 1785," *AAE-CP-Russie*, Vol. 113, fol. 375.
48. Ségur, *Mémoires*, II, 298.
49. A. Rambaud, *Recueil des instructions* . . ., Russie, Vol. II, 407.
50. "Ségur to Vergennes, 3 February, 22 September, 19 November, 1786," *AAE-CP-Russie*, 117, fols. 75-78; Vol. 119, fols. 77-78; 221; Ségur, Mémoires, II, 382ff. Also, *AAE-CP-Russie*, 117, fols. 169ff.
51. "Ségur to Vergennes, 19 November, 1786," *ibid.*, Vol. 119, fols. 224vo-225.
52. "Ségur to Vergennes, 5 May, 1786," *ibid.*, Vol. 118, fol. 10-10vo; "Ségur to Castries, 19 November, 1786," *Archives de la Marine*, B7 457.
53. "Réponse à la Note rémise par Messieurs les plénipotentiaires Russes à M. le comte de Ségur," *AAE-CP-Russie*, Vol. 117, fols, 199vo-200; "Ségur to Vergennes, 5 May, 1786," *ibid.*, Vol. 118, fol. 10vo.
54. "Ségur to Vergennes, 19 November, 1786," *ibid.*, Vol. 119, fol. 224.
55. Ségur to Vergennes, 19 November, 1786," *ibid.*, fols. 224-224vo; Ségur to Castries, 19 November, 1786," *Archives de la Marine*, B VII 457; Comte de Ségur, *Mémoires*, II, p. 419; Ségur to Vergennes, 25 November, 1786," *AAE-CP-Russie*, Vol. 119. fols. 240-41.
56. "Vergennes to Ségur, December 16, 1786," *ibid.*,, Vol. 119, fols. 373vo-394.
57. The treaty is printed: "Traité de navigation et de commerce entre Sa Majesté le Roi de France et Sa Majesté l'Impératrice de toutes les Russies; conclu à St. Petersburg, le 31 Décembre, 1786, 11 Janvier, 1787," Georg Martens, *Recueil de*

traités, Vol. IV, 197-219.

58. Frank Fox, "Negotiating with the Russians," *French Historical Studies,* VII, 70.

59. J. L. Regemorter, *op. cit.*, 248.

60. Fox, *op. cit.*, 70; Ségur, *Mémoires,* II, 84; Regemorter, *op. cit.*, 250.

61. *Ibid.*, 255.

62. See, for example: Georg Martens, *Recueil de traités* Vol. II, p. 282, 326, 632-652; Vol. IV, pp. 12-13.

63. "Traités de limites et de commerce entre la France et l'Evêque de Liège, 1772-1778," Georg Martens, *ibid.*, Vol. II, pp. 72-83.

64. "Convention entre le Roi de France et l'Électeur de Trèves, concernant plusiers échanges et des limites de leurs États respectifs. Conclus le 1 Juillet, 1778, avec les lettres patente du Roi données à Versailles le 22 Mars, 1780," *ibid.*, Vol. II, pp. 268-282.

65. "Procès verbal de limites entre la France et le canton de Berne signé le 15 November, 1774 et ratifiée par le Roi le 9 Avril, 1775," Georg Martens, *ibid.*, II, pp. 331-363.

66. "Traités de limites et d'échanges entre S.M. le Roi très chrétien et le Prince de Nassau-Weilbourg, à Nancy, le 24 Janvier, 1776, ratifiée par l'Empire, 1785," *ibid.*, II, 429-454,

67. "Traités de limites de l'île de St. Dominique conclu entre la France et l'Espagne le 3 juin, 1777, et ratifiée par le Roi 4 juillet, 1777," *ibid.*, II, pp. 519-543.

68. Convention entre la France et l'Espagne qui règle les fonctions des officiers des Amirautés et de consuls, pour la contrabande des navires appartenants aux sujets respectifs des nations du 27 December, 1774," *ibid.*, Vol. II, pp. 364-371; "Traités définitifs de limites entre la France et l'Espagne pour établir une ligne divisoire aux Aldudes ou Quint-Royal et Val-Carlos,et pour déterminer les limites des deux monarchies dans cette partie des Pyrénées. Signé à Elissonde, 27 Août, 1785, *ibid.*, II, 26-30.

69. *AAE-MD-France,* Vol. 548, fol. 98; "Traité d'Amitié de guarantie et de commerce conclu entre les Cours Royales d'Espagne et de Portugal, fait au Prado, le 1 mars, 1778, au quel la France a accedé 1783," George F. Martens, *Recueil de Traités,* IV, pp. 612-627.

70. "Traité de commerce entre S.M. le Roi de France et le Sérénissime Duc de Mecklenbourg - Schwerin, conclu à Hambourg le 18 Septembre, 1779," *ibid.*, Vol. II, 709-729.

71. "Pacte secrète d'amitié et d'union entre le Roi très chrétien et le Roi de Suède fait à Versailles le 19 juillet, 1784," *AAE-MD-France,* Vol. 1897, fols. 125-176vo; also: *ibid.*, Vol. 584, fol. 98; *Archives Nationales,* K 164 no. 2^4, 19 July, 1784.

72. Art. XXXI, "Traités de limites et de commerce entre la France et l'Evêque de Liege 1772-1778," Georg Martens, *Recueil de Traités,* Vol. II, p. 58.

73. "Abolition du droit d'Aubaine entre la France et 23 ville Impériales, Octobre, 1774," *ibid.*, Vol. II, 326-330.

74. "Convention pour l'abolition du droit d'aubaine entre la France et les États du Duc de Wurtemburg, 14 Avril, 1778," *ibid.*, Vol. II, 628-631.

75. Article XIII, "Treaty of Amity and Commerce, 1778," in James Scott Brown, *The Treaties of 1778* (Baltimore, 1928), p. 31.

76. "Convention pour l'abolition du Droit d'aubaine entre la France et les États du Landgrave de Hesse-Darmstadt, 27 juillet, 1779," *ibid.*, Vol. II, pp. 705-708.

77. Article II, "Traité de commerce entre Sa Majesté le Roi de France et le Sérénissime Duc de Mecklenburg-Scherwin, 18 September, 1779," Martens, *Recueil*, Vol. II, p. 710.

78. Article XVI, "Traité de navigation et de commerce entre Sa Majesté le Roi de France et Sa Majesté l'Impératrice de toutes les Russes," *ibid.*, Vol. II, 204-205.

79. See, for example: Articles XXII-XXIV in the treaty with Liège, *ibid.*, II, pp. 54-55; Article XII in treaty with Trèves, *ibid.*, II, 274.

80. Article XII, "Traité de commerce entre S. M. le Roi de France et le Sérénissime Duc de Mecklenbourg - Schwerin, conclu à Hambourg le 18 Septembre, 1779," *ibid.*, I, 714.

81. Article XIV, *ibid.*, 714.

82. Georges Livet, *Recueil des Instructions données aux ambassadeurs et ministres de France* . . . (Paris, 1962), Vol. XXVIII, États Allemands, tome I, p. xix-xxi.

83. Saint-Aymour, *Recueil des instructions,* VII, Portugal, p. xlviii.

84. *Ibid.*, xlviii-xlix.

85. W. R. Brock, "The effects of the loss of American colonies upon British policy," (Publication of the [English] Historical Assoc., London, 1957), p. 11; See also: A. Goodwin, *The New Cambridge Modern History* (Cambridge, 1965), Vol. VII, p. 562.

86. Richard B. Morris, *The Peace Makers* (New York, 1965), p. 455.

87. Marie M. Donaghay, "The Anglo-French Negotiations of 1786-1787," (Unpublished Doctoral dissertation, University of Virginia, 1970) pp. 229, 235.

88. W. O. Henderson, *The Genesis of the Common Market* (Chicago, 1962), p. 44-45.

Chapter 37. The Dutch Entanglement: 1783-1787

1. "Vergennes to LaVauguyon, 7 January, 1781," *AAE-CP-Hollande,* Vol. 543, fol. 37.

2. "Goertz to Frederick, 12 January, 1781," *Politische Correspondenz Friedrichs des Grossen* (Berlin, 1929-1939), Vol. 45, p. 208.

3. Madariaga, *Britain, Russia and the Armed Neutrality of 1780* (New Haven, 1962), pp. 290-291.

4. *Ibid.*, pp: 439-445.

5. "Vergennes to LaVauguyon, 7 January, 1781," *AAE-CP-Hollande,* Vol. 543, fol. 37vo.

6. "LaVauguyon to Vergennes, 12 January, 1781," *ibid.*, Vol. 543, fol. 71.

7. "LaVauguyon to Vergennes, 15 January, 1781," "Vergennes to LaVauguyon, 18 January, 1781," *ibid.*, Vol. 543, fols. 71; 125.

8. "LaVauguyon to Vergennes, 19 January, 1781," *ibid.*, vol. 543, fol. 129vo -132.

9. "LaVauguyon to Vergennes, 1 March, 1781," *ibid.*, Vol. 543, fols. 359-359vo. Madariaga, *Britain, Russia and the Armed Neutrality* of 1780, p. 292.

10. *Ibid.* 293.

11. Quoted in *ibid.*, 298.

12. *Ibid.*, 309.

13. *Ibid.*, p. 309.

14. *Ibid.*, 320.

15. "Vergennes to LaVauguyon, 18 January, 1781," *AAE-CP-Hollande,* Vol. 543, fol. 125.

16. "LaVauguyon to Vergennes, 26 January, 1781," *ibid.*, Vol. 543, fol. 154-160.

17. *Ibid.*, fols. 158-158vo.

18. "LaVauguyon to Vergennes, 26 January, 1781," *ibid.*, Vol. 543, fols. 159vo-165.

19. *Ibid.*, fol. 165vo.

20. "LaVauguyon to Vergennes, 2, 6 February, 1781," *ibid.*, Vol. 543, fols. 205-209; 227vo-228.

21. "Vergennes to LaVauguyon, 8, 17 February, 1781," *ibid.*, Vol. 543, fols. 264-265; also 268-269; 302-310.

22. Henry de Peyster, *Les troubles de Hollande à la veille de la Révolution française 1780-1795* (Paris, 1905), p. 66.

23. *AAE-CP-Hollande,* Vol. 543, fols. 345-349; 350-352.

24. "Joly de Fleury to Vergennes, 5, 19 March, 1782," *ibid.*, Vol. 548, fols. 29-29vo; 122; "Berkenwoode to Vergennes, 9 March, 1782," *ibid.*, fols. 63-63vo.

25. "LaVauguyon to Vergennes, 26 March, 1782," *ibid.*, Vol. 548, fols. 175vo-176.

26. "Vergennes to LaVauguyon, 4 April, 1782," *ibid.*, Vol. 548, fols. 224-225.

27. On the charges and complaints about these combined operations, see: *AAE-CP-Hollande,* Vol. 548, fols. 175vo-176; 224-225; 220-223; 236-240, 291; 315-315vo.

28. See Castries' note on Plettenberg, 13 April, 1782, *ibid.*, Vol. 548, fol. 291.

29. "Castries to Vergennes, 15 May, 1782," *ibid.*, Vol. 549, fols. 89-89vo.

30. "LaVauguyon to Vergennes, 21, 31 May, 4 June, 1782," *ibid.*, Vol. 549, fols. 127-128; 213-214; 227-228. "Vergennes to LaVauguyon, 25 May, 1782," *ibid.*, fol. 179.

31. "Vergennes to LaVauguyon, 6 June, 1782," *ibid.*, Vol. 549, fols. 246-246vo; "LaVaugyon to Vergennes, 14 June, 1782," *ibid.*, Vol. 549, fols. 314vo-317.

32. "Vergennes to LaVauguyon, 5 July, 1782," *ibid.*, Vol. 549, fol. 45-45vo.

33. "LaVauguyon to Vergennes, 8 July, 1782," *ibid.*, Vol. 550, fols. 60-60vo.

34. "Vergennes to LaVauguyon, 21 July, 1782," *ibid.*, Vol. 550, fols. 149-149vo.

35. "Vergennes to LaVauguyon, 1 August, 1782," *ibid.*, Vol. 550, fol. 226.

36. *Ibid.*, Vol. 550, fol. 243.

37. "Vergennes to LaVauguyon, 10,17 October, 2 November, 1782," *AAE-CP-Hollande,* Vol. 551, fols. 192, 231vo, Vol. 552, fols. 14, 164-165.

38. "Vergennes to LaVauguyon, 18 January,, 1783," *ibid.*, Vol. 553, fol. 84ff.

39. *Ibid.*

40. "Bérenger to Vergennes, 3 October, 1783," *ibid.*, Vol. 556, fol. 6.

41. "Vergennes to LaVauguyon, 2 November, 1782," *ibid.*, Vol. 552, fol. 10vo.

42. "Bérenger to Vergennes, 13 June, 1783," and "Propositions des plénipotentiaires Hollandais, 23 June, 1783," *ibid.*, Vol. 554, fols. 346 and ff; "Vergennes to Bérenger, 8, 17 July, 1783," *ibid.*, Vol. 555, fol. 25, 51-51vo.

43. L. André et E. Bourgeois, *Recueil des instructions aux ambassadeurs et ministres de France* ... (Paris, 1924), Vol. XXVI, pp. 331-332.

44. "Bérenger to Vergennes, 24 October, 1783," *AAE-CP-Hollande,* Vol. 556, fol. 76.

45. "Vergennes to Bérenger, 22 January, 1784;" see also: "Vergennes to Bérenger, 19, 29 February, 25 March, 1784," *AAE-CP-Hollande,* Vol. 557, fols. 74, 164vo, 195, 293.

46. "Bérenger to Vergennes, 23, 26 March, 1784," *ibid.*, Vol. 557, fols. 282ff and 298ff.

47. "LaVauguyon to Vergennes, 23, 27, 30 April, 1784," *ibid.*, Vol. 557, fols. 431ff, 443ff, 462ff.

48. "Vergennes to LaVauguyon, 6 May, 1784," *ibid.*, Vol. 558, fols. 22ff.

49. "Vergennes to Bérenger, 17 July, 1783," *ibid.*, Vol. 555, fol. 50.

50. "LaVauguyon to Vergennes, 7, 26 May, 1784," "Projet d'articles du traité," *AAE-CP-Hollande,* Vol. 558, fols. 36ff, 145, 39ff. Yet Bérenger also recognized that the credit of the Patriots could not be sustained in the United Provinces with the help and influence of Louis XVI. "Bérenger to Vergennes, 25 July, 1783," *ibid.*, Vol. 555, fols. 76vo-77.

51. See the mémoire on Breteuil's and Calonne's position, written after the events described, in *AAE-CP-Hollande,* Supplément, Vol. 21, fols. 103ff.

52. *Ibid.;* Alfred Cobban, *Ambassadors and Secret Agents* (London, 1954), p. 26.

53. *Ibid.*, p. 21-25.

54. "Mémoire sur la politique extérieure de la France depuis 1774 addressé au Roi par le Cte de Vergennes," *AAE-CP-France,* Vol. 446, fols. 351-358.

55. Alfred von Arneth and A. Geffroy, *Correspondance secrète entre Marie Thérèse et le Comte de Mercy d'Argenteau* (Paris, 1881), II, 299-300.

56. Duc de Castries, *Le Testament de la Monarchie* (Paris, 1958) 141; Louis Petit de Bachaumont, *Mémoires Secrets pour servir, à l'histoire de la république des lettres en France,* (London, 1781-1789), XXIII, pp. 275-276; Richard B. Morris, *The Peacemakers* (New York, 1965), pp. 88-111.

57. Cobban, *op. cit.*, p. 26.

58. "Maillebois to Vergennes, 27 March, 1786," Colenbrander, De Patriottentijd, hoofdzakeijk naar buitendsche bescheiden (Gravenhage, 1897-99), II, 164, fn. #3; Baron de Kinckel, *Mémoires et correspondance* (La Haye, 1857), Vol. I, pp. 130-131, fn. 1; Le chevalier de Corberon, *Un diplomate française à la cour de Catherine II, 1775-1780* (Paris, 1901), Vol. II, pp. 239fn, 358, 360.

59. "Madariaga, *Britain, Russia and the Armed Neutrality of 1780,* p. 439 and *passim.*

60. "Vérac's instructions, dated 4 January, 1785," *AAE-CP-Hollande,* Vol. 561, fols. 9-15.

61. Alfred Cobban, *op. cit.*, pp. 33-34.

62. *Ibid.*, 36.

63. Quoted in: A. Cobban, *op. cit.*, p. 34.

64. "Vergennes to Bérenger, 5 February, 1784," *AAE-CP-Hollande,* Vol. 557, fol. 125.

65. See, for example, his dispatches to Bérenger, 19 February, 25 March, 1784," *AAE-CP-Hollande,* Vol. 557, fols. 164vo-165; 283vo-294.

66. "Bérenger to Vergennes, 26 March, 1784," *ibid.*, Vol. 557, fols. 298-302.

67. "LaVauguyon to Vergennes, 27 April, 1784," *ibid.*, Vol. 557, fols. 444-445vo.

68. "LaVauguyon to Vergennes, 7 May, 1784," *ibid.*, Vol. 558, fols. 35-37; "Projet d'articles formant l'élément du traité-proposé," *ibid.*, fols. 39-40vo.

69. "Vergennes to Bérenger, 11, 13 July, 1784," "Bérenger to Vergennes, 2 July, 1784," *AAE-CP-Hollande,* Vol. 558, fols. 302-314, 346-346vo; also: fols. 376vo -378; 414, 424.

70. "Vergennes to Bérenger, 11 July, 1784," *ibid.*, Vol. 555, fols. 346-346vo.

71. *Ibid.*, Vol. 565, fols. 76ff.

72. Article II, "Traité d'alliance défensive entre sa Majesté le Roi Très-Chrétien et les États-Généraux des Provinces-Unies des Pays-Bas, à Fontainebleau, le 10 Novembre, 1785," Georg Martens, *Recueil de Traités ... des Puissances et états de l'Europe* ... (Gottingen, 1818), Vol. IV, pp. 65-66.

73. Article III, *ibid.*, p. 67.

74. Article IV, *ibid.*, p. 67.
75. Article Séparé II, *ibid.*, p. 71.
76. Article VIII, *ibid.*, pp. 68-69.
77. Article Séparé IV, *ibid.*, p. 71.
78. Alfred Cobban, *op. cit.*, (London, 1954), pp. 64-66.
79. "Vérac to Vergennes, 8 November, 1785," *AAE-CP-Hollande*, Vol. 565, fols. 42-45.
80. Cobban, *op. cit.*, p. 65.
81. "Vérac to Vergennes, 2 December, 1785," *AAE-CP-Hollande*, Vol. 565, fol. 186.
82. Cobban, *op. cit.*, p. 69.
83. "D'Esterno to Vergennes, 15 August, 1786," *AAE-CP-Prusse*, Vol. 205, fol. 289. "Vergennes to d'Esterno, 26 August, 1786," *ibid.*, Vol. 205, fol. 321.
84. "Mercy d'Argenteau to Kaunitz, 5 November, 1786," A. von Arneth and J. Flammermont, editors, *Correspondance secrète du comte de Mercy d'Argenteau avec l'Empéreur Joseph II et le Prince de Kaunitz* (Paris, 1889-1891), Vol. I, p. 56.
85. Mirabeau's report on these two missions is contained in H.G. Riquetti, *Comte de Mirabeau, Historie secrète de la cour de Berlin* (London, 1789), 2 vols.
86. *Ibid.*, Vol. I, 105, 128, Vol. II, 231.
87. "Frederick William to Prince of Orange, 3 September, 1786," F.J.K. Kramer, *Archives ou Correspondance inédite de la maison d'Orange-Nassau* (La Haye, 1835-1896), Vol. III 5e serie, pp. 405-406.
88. "Goertz to Frederick William II, 13 October, 1786," H.T. Colenbrander, *De Patriottentijd, hoofdzakeijk naar buitendsche bescheiden,* Vol. III, pp. 62-62; Cobban, *Ambassadors and Secret Agents,* p. 95.
89. "Frederick William II to Goertz, 27 October, 1786," in Johann von Goertz, *Historische und politische Denkwürdigkeiten des köneglich Preussischen Staatsminsters Johann Eustach Grafen von Goertz* (Stuttgart and Tubingen, 1827-28), p. 139.
90. "Finckenstein to Thulemeyer, 10 October, 1786," *ibid.*, p. 64.
91. Cobban, *op. cit.*, pp. 96-97.
92. For a discussion of the activities of the French agents, see: Alfred Cobban, *Ambassadors and Secret Agents,* pp. 37-47 and *passim.*
93. "Vergennes to Rayneval, December 14, 1786," *AAE-CP-Hollande*, Vol. 569, fols. 536-539.
94. "Vergennes to Rayneval, 5 January, 1787," *ibid.*, Vol. 571, fol. 99.
95. "Vergennes to Vérac, 3 August, 1786," *ibid.*, Vol. 568, fols. 178ff.
96. *Ibid.*
97. "Rayneval to Vergennes, 29 November, 1786,"; Colenbrander, *op. cit.*, III, p. 76.
98. "Rayneval to Vergennes, 27 December, 1786," *AAE-CP-Hollande,* fol. 570, fols. 437-441.
99. Henry de Peyster, *Les troubles de Hollande à la veille de la Révolution Française* (1780-1795) (Paris, 1905), p. 182.
100. Colenbrander, *op. cit.*, III, pp. 99-109.
101. Cobban, *op. cit.*, pp 104-105.
102. "Rayneval to Vergennes, 27 December, 1786," *AAE-CP-Hollande,* Vol. 570, fols. 437-441.
103. Cobban, *op. cit.*, p. 183.

Epilogue

1. Louis Petit de Bachaumont, *Mémoires secrets pour servir à l'histoire de la République de lettres en France* (Bruxelles, 1871), Vol. XXXIV, p. 24.
2. "État civil de Versailles paroisse de Notre Dame, 14 February, 1787," in *Souvenirs Franco-Américains à Versailles et en Seine-et-Oise,* p. 16, Archives de la Seine-et-Oise, Versailles.
3. Charles Joseph Mayer, *Vie publique et privée de Charles Gravier de Vergennes* (Paris, 1789), p. 180; Saul Padover, *The Life and Death of Louis XVI* (New York, 1939), p. 135.
4. *Souvenirs Franco-Américains,* pp. 14-16.
5. "Inventaire des objets d'art laissés chez M. de Vergennes, émigré (1793)," *Archives Nationales* F 17^{A} (1268) 17°, fol. 226.

Bibliography

The documentary sources for Vergennes' diplomatic career are exceedingly rich, both in unpublished material as well as in printed transcripts. And the secondary material is staggering. Fortunately, there are published guides, inventories and bibliographies that can help the scholar through the material in archives and libraries. And descendants of Vergennes, the late M. Odon de Vergennes of Paris and M. Pierre de Tugny of Marly le roi, France, were especially generous with their time in introducing this scholar to the family papers. Also, Ms. Svetlana Kluge has organised and made more usable to the scholar the Vergennes family papers. For this labor we all owe her a debt of gratitude. While the following bibliogrphy is by no means exhaustive, it constitutes those materials basic to the study of Vergennes' personal and professional career. I have not included here the vast amount of material relating to Vergennes' responsibilities for internal administration of the French provinces.

Guides, inventories and bibliographies

Aimée, Denise. "Vergennes: essai bibliographique, historique et critique." *Franco-American Review* 1 (1936–37), 149–59.

Bemis, Samuel Flagg, and Griffin, Grace Gordon. *Guide to the Diplomatic History of the United States 1775–1921*. Washington, D.C., 1935.

Bourgeois, Emile. *Manuel historique de politique étrangère*. Vol. 1. Paris, 1893.

Inventaire analytique des archives du Ministère des Affaires Etrangères: Correspondance politique. 8 vols. Paris, 1885–99.

Inventaire sommaire des archives du Département des Affaires Etrangères: Correspondance politique. 3 vols. Paris, 1903–19.

Inventaire sommaire des archives du Département des Affaires Etrangères: Mémoires et Documents. 3 vols. Paris, 1883–96.

Leland, Waldo; Meng, John J.; and Doysié, Abel. *Guide to Materials for American History in the Libraries and Archives of Paris*. Vol. 1, *Libraries*, Vol. 2, *Archives of the Ministry of Foreign Affairs*. Washington, D.C., 1943.

Préclin, Edmond, and Tapie, Victor-L. *Clio: le XVIIIe siècle*. Vol. 1, *La France et le monde de 1715 à 1789*, Vol. 2, *Les forces internationales*. Paris, 1952.

Thomas, Daniel, and Case, Lynn M. *Guide to the Diplomatic Archives of Western Europe*. Philadelphia, 1959.

Primary Sources: Unpublished

England: *Public Records Office State Papers: Foreign*
"Letters and Papers of Mr. Eden, relative to the negotiations of the Anglo-French Commercial Treaty of 1786."

France: *Archives des Affaires Etrangères*
Correspondance Politique
Documents: Personnel
Mémoires et Documents

Archives de la Côte d'Or
Series, B and C.

Archives de la famille Vergennes
I originally consulted these family papers in Paris through the courtesy of M. Odon de Vergennes. Later M. and Mme Pierre de Tugny, now at Marly le roi, allowed me to continue my research in the family papers. This collection contains materials of a political and diplomatic nature as well as a goodly number of personal letters and documents.

Archives Nationales
K series
F series

Archives de la Seine et Oise
"Etat-civil de Versailles, paroisse de Notre Dame" in "Souvenirs franco-américains."
E series

Bibliothèque de l'Arsenal
"Papiers de Dreux, secrétaire de Vergennes," manuscrits 6402–6403.
"Lettres: Vergennes à Gerault, 1763," manuscrit 7055.
"Receuil d'Observations de conseils et de Maximes adressé aux fils de M. le Comte de Vergennes . . .," manuscrit 2328.

Bibliothèque de l'Institut de France
"Correspondance de M. Hennin . . .," manuscrit 1233.
"Eloge du comte de Vergennes, avril, 1787" par M. P. M. Hennin, manuscrit 1226, no. 26.

Bibliothèque municipale de Versailles
"Documents originaux, autographes;
Comte de Vergennes," in "Collection, Panthéon Versailles."

Bibliothèque Nationale
Vergennes' political correspondence with French agents and the princes of Wallachia and Modavia. Salle des manuscrits, fonds français, nouvelles acquisitions 12276.
"Résumé des dépêches Vienne, 1766–1777," fonds français, nouvelles acquisitions 6949.
"Extraits de la correspondance d'Estaing/Vergennes 1777–1779," fonds français, nouvelles acquisitions 9429.

Spain: Archivo Histórico Nacional: Estado
Vols. 4203, 4215, 4199 bis

U.S.A.: Eleutherian Mills Historical Library, Wilmington, Del.
Library of Congress (Microfilm Division)
"Papers of the Continental Congress, 1774–1789."
Items 85–86, 111–114.

Primary Sources: Printed

Adams, C.F., editor, *Works of John Adams.* 10 vols. Boston, 1850–56.
Argenson, René-Louis de Voyer de Paulmy, marquis d'. *Mémoires et journal inédit du marquis d'Argenson.* 5 vols. Paris, 1857–58.
Arneth, Alfred von, ed. *Joseph II und Katerina von Russland. Ihr Briefwechsel.* Vienna, 1809.
——. *Marie Antoinette, Joseph II und Leopold II, Ihr Briefwechsel.* Leipzig, 1866.
——. *Marie Theresia und Joseph II, Ihre Correspondenz . . .* Leipzig, 1867.
——. *Maria Theresia und Marie Antoinette ihr briefwechsel.* Leipzig, 1866.
Arneth, Alfred von and Flammermont, J. *Correspondance secrète du Comte Mercy-Argenteau avec l'empereur Joseph et le Prince de Kaunitz.* 2 vols. Paris, 1889-91.
Arneth, Alfred von et Geoffroy, A., eds. *Marie Antoinette, correspondance secrète entre Marie Antoinette et le Comte de Mercy-Argenteau, avec les lettres de Marie Thérèse et de Marie Antoinette.* Paris, 1874–75.
Bachaumont, Louis Petit de. *Mémoires secrets pour servir à l'histoire de la république des lettres en France . . .* 36 vols. London, 1778–89.
Broglie, duc de. *Le secret du roi, correspondance secrète de Louis XV avec ses agents diplomatiques 1752–1774.* 2 vols. Paris, 1878.
Boutaric, Edgard. *Correspondance secrète inédite de Louis XV . . .* 2 vols. Paris, 1866.
Boyd, Julian, ed. *The Papers of Thomas Jefferson.* vols. 1–6. Princeton, 1950.
Butterfield, L.H., ed. *Diary and Autobiography of John Adams.* 4 vols. Cambridge, Mass., 1961.
Carolina, Wilhemina. *Letters of the Swedish Court, written chiefly in the early part of the reign of Gustavus III.* London, 1809.
Cauchie, A. *Le comte M. Barbiano de Belgiojoso et ses papiers d'Etat conservés à Milan* in *Bulletin de la Commission Royale d'histoire de Belgique.* Vol. 81. 1912.
Chance, James Frederick, ed. *British Diplomatic Instructions 1689–1789.* Vol. 5, *Sweden.* London, 1928.
Chinard, Gilbert, ed. *The Treaties of 1778 and Allied Documents.* Baltimore, 1928.
Chodzko, L.J.B. [Le comte d'Angeberg], ed. *Recueil des traités, conventions et actes diplomatiques concernant la Pologne 1762-1862.* Paris, 1862.
Colenbrander, H. T. *De Patriottentijd . . .* 3 vols. Gravenhoge, 1897–99.
Cough, John Francis, trans. and ed. *The Private Letters of Baron Vioménil on Polish Affairs.* Jersey City, 1935.
Davenport, Francis Gardiner, ed. *European Treaties Bearing on the History of the United States and Its Dependencies.* 4 vols. Washington, D.C., 1917–37.
Droysen, J.G.; Ducker, M.W.; Sybel, H. von; Volz, G.B. et al., eds. *Politische Correspondenz Friedrich's des Grossen.* 45 vols. Berlin, 1879–1937.
Dulcos, C.P. *Mémoires secrets sur les règnes de Louis XV et de Louis XVI.* 2 vols.

Lausanne, 1791.
Durand, John. *New Materials for the History of the American Revolution*. New York, 1889.
Fay, Bernard, "Correspondance intime de Gérard de Rayneval avec Hennin," *Franco-American Review I* (1936–37), 76–84.
Force, Peter, ed. *American Archives*. 4th series, 6 vols.; 5th series, 3 vols. Washington, D.C., 1837–53.
Ford, W.C. and Hunt, Gaillard, eds. *Journals of the Continental Congress*. 34 vols. Washington, D.C. 1904–37.
Fortescue, Sir John. *The Correspondance of George the Third from 1760 to December 1783* ... 6 vols. London, 1927–28.
Friedrich II, *Die Politischen testamenten Friedrich's des Grossen*. Berlin, 1920.
Friedrich II, *Oeuvres de Frédéric le Grand*. 31 vols. Berlin, 1846–57.
Horn, D.B. and Ransome, Mary. *English Historical Documents: 1714–1783*. 10 vols. London, 1957.
Hubert, Eugène, *Correspondance des Ministres de France accredités à Bruxelles de 1780 à 1790*. 2 vols. Bruxelles, 1920.
Hutchinson, William T., and Rachal, William M. E., eds. *The Papers of James Madison*. Vols. 1–6. Chicago, 1962.
Hurewitz, J.C. ed. *Diplomacy in the Near and Middle East: A Documentary Record: 1535–1914*. 2 vols. Princeton, 1956.
Jenkinson, C. *A Collection of All the Treaties of Peace, Alliance and Commerce between Great Britain and other powers, 1648 ... 1783*. 3 vols. London, 1785.
Jensen, Merrill. *English Historical Documents*. Vol. 10. London, 1955.
Koch, Christophe Guillaume de. *Table des traités entre la France et les puissances étrangères ... suivie d'un recueil de traités et actes diplomatiques* ... 2 vols. Basle, 1802.
Kramer, F. J. K. *Archives ou correspondance inédite de la maison d'Orange-Nassau*. The Hague, 1835–96.
Labande, L. H., ed. *Un diplomate français à la cour de Catherine II, 1775–1780: Journal intime du Chevalier de Corberon*. 2 vols. Paris, 1901.
Labaree, Leonard W. ed. *The Papers of Benjamin Franklin*. Vols. 1–21. New Haven, 1959.
Legg, L.G. Wickam, ed. *British Diplomatic Instructions, 1689–1789*. Vol. 7, *France*. London, 1934.
LePage, Auguste, ed. *Mémoire de l'élection de l'Empereur Charles VII ... en 1741*. Paris, 1870.
Lévis, Gaston P.M. duc de. *Souvenirs et Portraits; 1780–1789*. Paris, 1815.
Linguet, Simon N.H. *Lettre de M. Linguet à M. le Comte de Vergennes, Ministre des Affaires Etrangères en France*. London, 1777.
Lodge, Sir Richard, *Private Correspondence of Chesterfield and Newcastle: 1744–46*. Royal Historical Society Publications, Camden series, 3rd series, vol. 44. London, 1930.
Luynes, Duc de. *Mémoires du duc de Luynes sur la coùr de Louis XV*. 17 vols. Paris, 1860–65.
Martens, Georg F. *Recueil des principaux traités d'alliances de paix, de trève ... etc., conclu par les puissances de l'Europe*. 7 vols. Göttingen, 1791–1801.
Martens, Fedor F. *Recueils des traités et conventions conclus par la Russie avec les puissances étrangères*. 15 vols. St. Petersburg, 1874–1909.
Martens, Georg F. *Supplément au Recueil des principaux traités* ... 20 vols. Göt-

tingen, 1802–42.

Meng, John J. *Dispatches and Instructions of Conrad Alexander Gérard, 1778–1780.* Paris, 1939.

Miller, D. Hunter, *Treaties and Other International Acts of the United States of America.* Vols. 1–2. Washington, D.C., 1931.

Monaghan, Frank, ed. *The Diary of John Jay during the Peace Negotiations of 1782.* New Haven, 1934.

Montherot, J. P. "Documents inédits sur la Révolution en Suède en 1772." *Mémoires de l'Academie Impériale des Sciences Belles-Lettres et Arts de Lyon.* 2nd series, 6 (1857–58), 30–39.

Noailles, Duc de. *Mémoires du duc de Noailles.* Edited by Claude Bernard Petitot. 4 vols. These constitute volumes 71–74 of the *Collection Complète des mémoires relatifs à l'histoire de France.* Paris, 1819–26.

Ozanam, D. and Antoine, M. *Correspondance secrète du comte de Broglie avec Louis XV (1756–1784).* 2 vols. Paris, 1956–61.

Pickering, D., ed. *Statutes at Large, from Magna Charta to ... 1761.* 24 vols. Cambridge, Eng., 1762.

Piggott, Francis, and Ormond, G.W.T., eds. *Documentary History of the Armed Neutralities of 1780 and 1800.* London, 1919.

Recueil des instructions données aux ambassadeurs et ministres de France depuis les traités de Westphalia jusqu' à la Révolution française. Publiées sur les auspices de la commission des Archives Diplomatiques au Ministère des Affaires Étrangères. 28 vols. Paris 1884–1960.

Riquette, H.G., *Comte de Mirabeau. Histoire secrète de la cour de Berlin.* 2 vols. London, 1789.

Russell, John. *Memorials and Correspondence of Charles James Fox.* London, 1857.

Saint-Priest, Francois Emmanuel. *Mémoires.* Paris, 1929.

Saint-Priest, Francois Emmanuel, Comte de. *Mémoires sur l'ambassade de France en Turquie.* Paris, 1877.

Sbornik imperatorskago russkago istoricheskago obshcestva. Vols. 1, 9, 12, 15, 20, 22, 27, 45, 48, 51, 65, 109, 135, 145. St. Petersburg, 1867–1916.

Schelle, Gustave. *Ouevres de Turgot* ... 5 vols. Paris, 1913–23.

Schlitter, Hanns. *Correspondance secrète entre le Comte A.W. Kaunitz-Reitberg, Ambassadeur impériale à Paris et le Baron Ignaz de Koch, secrétaire de l'Impératrice Marie-Thérèse, 1750–1752.* Paris, 1899.

Segur, Louis Philippe. *Mémoires ou souvenirs et anecdotes.* 3 vols. Paris, 1827.

Soulavie, Jean Louis. *Mémoires historiques et politiques du règne de Louis XVI* ... 6 vols. Paris, 1801.

Sparks, Jared. *Diplomatic Correspondence of the American Revolution.* 12 vols. Boston, 1829–30.

Stevens, B.F., ed. *Facsimiles of Manuscripts in European Archives Relating to America, 1773–1783.* 25 vols. London, 1889–95.

Tott, Francois, Baron de. *Mémoires sur les Turcs et les Tartares.* 2 vols. Amsterdam, 1784.

Wenck, Frederick August. *Codex juris gentium* ... 3 vols. Leipzig, 1781–95.

Wharton, Francis, ed. *The Revolutionary Diplomatic Correspondence of the United States.* 6 vols. Washington, D.C., 1889.

Witte, Baron Jehan de, ed. *Journal de l'Abbé de Veri.* 2 vols. Paris, 1928–30.

Yorke, Philip C. *The Life and Correspondence of Philip Yorke, Earl of Hardwicke, Lord High Chancellor of Great Britain.* 3 vols. Cambridge, Eng., 1913.

Contemporary Newspapers

Affaires de l'Angleterre et de l'Amérique. 15 vols. Antwerp, 1776–79.
The Annual Register. Vols. 1–26. London, 1758–84.
Gazette de France. Paris, 1631–32. Appeared weekly until 1761, semiweekly after that date.

Secondary Sources: Books

Adelung, Johan Christoph. *Pragmatische Staatsgeschichte Europens von dem Ableben Kaiser Carls 6 an bis auf die gegenwartigen Zeiten*. 11 vols. Gotha, 1766.
Alden, John Richard. *The American Revolution 1775–1783*. New York, 1954.
Alvord, C.W. *The Mississippi Valley in British Politics*. New York, 1959.
Amburger, Erik. *Russland und Schweden 1762–1772*. Berlin, 1934.
Arneth, Alfred Von. *Maria Theresa nach dem Erbfolgekrieg 1748–1756*. Vienna, 1870. Vol. 4 of *Geschichte Maria Theresias*, 10 vols., Vienna, 1863–76.
Aulard, Francois-Alphonse. *Etudes et leçons sur la révolution française*. 2 vols. 1893–93.
Bain, R. Nesbit. *The Daughter of Peter the Great: A history of Russian Diplomacy*. New York, 1900.
——. *Gustavus III and His Contemporaries, 1746–1792* 2 vols. London, 1894.
Bancroft, George. *History of the United States of America from the Discovery of the Continent*. Vols. 3–6. Port Washington, N.Y., 1967.
Bartélémy, M de. *Histoire des relations de la France et du Danemark sous le ministere du Comte de Bernstorff*. Copenhagen, 1887.
Beer, Adolf. *Die erste Theilung Polens*. 3 vols. Vienna, 1873. Vol. 3 is a collection of documents.
Bemis, Samuel Flagg, ed. *The American Secretaries of State and Their Diplomacy*. Vol. 1. New York, 1927–29.
——. *Diplomacy of the American Revolution*. New York, 1925.
——. *The Hussey-Cumberland Mission and American Independence*. Princeton, 1931.
——. *Pinckney's Treaty: America's Advantage from Europe's Distress, 1783–1800*. New Haven, 1960.
——. *The Rayneval Memoranda of 1782 on Western Boundaries and Some Comments on the French Historian Doniol*. American Antiquarian Society, Worcester, Mass., 1938.
Bosher, J.F. *French Finances, 1770–1794: From Business to Bureaucracy*. Cambridge, Eng., 1970.
Broglie, Albert duc de. *Histoire et diplomatie*. Paris, 1889.
——. *Marie Thérèse Impératrice, 1744–1746*. 2 vols. Paris, 1888
Broglie, Jacques de. *Le Vainqueur de Bergen et le secret du roi*. Paris, n.d.
Bulau, Frédérick. *Personnages énigmatiques: histoires mystérieuses*. 3 vols. Paris, 1861.
Butterfield, Herbert. *Diplomatic Investigations*. London, 1966.
Callières, Francois de. *The Practice of Diplomacy*. Translated by A.F. Whyte. London, 1919.
Carter, Alice Clare. *The Dutch Republic in Europe in the Seven Years' War*. Coral Gables, 1971.

Castelot, André. *Queen of France: A Biography of Marie Antoinette.* New York, 1957.

Castera, J.H. *The Life of Catherine II, Empress of Russia.* 3 vols. London, 1798.

Castries, René de La Croix, duc de. *Le Maréchal de Castries (1727–1800).* Paris, 1956.

Chalmers, George. *Opinions of Eminent Lawyers on Various Points of English Jurisprudence*... Burlington, Vt., 1858.

Chambrun, Charles. *A l'école d'un diplomate.* Paris, 1944.

Chamfort, S.R. Nicolas de. *Penseés, maximes, anecdotes, dialogues*... Bruxelles, 1857.

Chapuisat, E. *La Prise d'armes de 1782 à Genève.* Geneva, 1932.

Cheke, Marcus. *The Cardinal de Bernis.* New York, 1959.

Christie, Ian, R. *The End of North's Ministry, 1780–1782.* London, 1958.

Circourt, Adolphe de, trans. *Histoire de l'action commune de la France et de l'Amérique pour l'indépendance des États-Unis.* 3 vols. Paris, 1876. A translation of George Bancroft's *History of the United States of America from the Discovery of the Continent,* vols. 10–12 of original edition.

Clowes, W. Laird. *The Royal Navy: A History from The Earliest Times to the Present.* 7 vols. London, 1897–1903.

Cobban, Alfred. *Ambassadors and Secret Agents.* London, 1954.

Conn, Stetson. *Gibraltar in British Diplomacy in The Eighteenth Century.* New Haven, 1942.

Corwin, Edward. *French Policy and the American Alliance.* Hamden, Conn., 1962.

Coxe, William. *Memoirs of the Administration of the Right Honorable Henry Pelham.* 2 vols. London, 1829.

Crout, Robert, "The Diplomacy of Trade: The Influence of Commercial Considerations on French Involvement in the Anglo-American War of Independence, 1775–1778." Ph.D. dissertation, University of Georgia, 1977.

Danvila y Collado, Manuel. *Reinado de Carols III.* 6 vols. Madrid, 1893–96.

Daubigny, E.T. *Choiseul et la France d'Outremer.* Paris, 1892.

Dimoff, Paul. *La Vie et l'oeuvre d'André Chenier, jusqu'à la révolution française.* 2 vols. Paris, 1936.

Donaghay, Marie. "The Anglo-French Negotiations of 1786–1787." Ph.D. dissertation, University of Virginia, 1970.

Doniol, Henri. *Histoire de la participation de la France à l'établissement des États-Unis d'Amérique.* 5 vols. Paris, 1886–99.

——. *Le Ministère des Affaires Etrangères en 1784.* Paris, 1893.

——. *Politique d'autre-fois; Le Cte de Vergennes et P.M. Hennin 1749–1787.* Paris, 1898.

Dull, Jonathan. *The French Navy and American Independence: A Study of Arms and Diplomacy 1774–1780.* Princeton, 1975.

Echeverria, Durand. *Mirage in the West.* Princeton, 1957.

Edler, Friedrich. *The Dutch Republic and the American Revolution.* Baltimore, 1911.

Elliott, Charles B. *The United States and the Northeastern Fisheries.* Minneapolis, 1887.

Fauchille, Paul. *La Diplomatie française et la lique des neutres de 1780 (1776–1783).* Paris, 1893.

Fay, Bernard. *L'Esprit révolutionnaire en France et aux États-Unis à la fin du XVIIIe siècle.* Paris, 1925.

——. *Louis XVI ou la fin d'un monde.* Paris, 1955.

Fenn, Percy Thomas. *The Origins of the Right of Fishing in Territorial Waters.* Cambridge, Mass., 1926.
Fitzmaurice, E. G. P. *Life of William, earl of Shelbourne*... 3 vols. London, 1875–76.
Flassan, Gaetan de Ruxis de. *Histoire générale et raisonnés de la diplomatie française.* 6 vols. Paris, 1809.
Freeman, Douglas S. *George Washington, Leader of the Revolution.* Vol. 4. New York, 1954.
——. *George Washington, Victory with the Help of France.* New York, 1955.
Geffroy. A. *Gustave III et la cour de France.* 2 vols. Paris, 1867.
Gerhard, Dietrich. *England und der Aufstieg Russlands.* Munich, 1933.
Gibb, Sir Hamilton, and Bowen, Harold. *Islamic Society and the West.* New York, 1950.
Gignoux, Claude J. *Turgot.* Paris, 1945.
Goertz, E.J., Comte de. *Mémoire historique relatif aux négociations qui eurent lieu en 1778 pour la succession de Bavière*... Paris, 1812.
Gomel, Charles. *Les Causes financières de la révolution française.* 2 vols. Paris, 1892–93.
Gottschalk, Louis R. *Lafayette and the Close of the American Revolution.* Chicago, 1942.
——. *Lafayette Joins the American Army.* Chicago, 1937.
Goubert, Pierre. *The Ancien Regime: French Society 1600–1750.* New York, 1969.
Goutel, Henri de. *Vergennes et l'indépendance américain: Vergennes et Wilson.* Paris, 1918.
Graham, Robert A.S.J. *Vatican Diplomacy; A Study of Church and State on the International Plane.* Princeton, 1959.
Green, Vivian H.H. *The Hanoverians, 1714–1815.* London, 1956.
Grosjean, Georges. *La politique Rhénane de Vergennes.* Paris, 1925.
Grunwald, Constantin. *Trois siècles de diplomatie.* Paris, 1945.
Hale, E.E. *Franklin in France.* Boston, 1887.
Hamon, Joseph. *Le Chevalier de Bonvouloir*... Paris, 1953.
Hanotaux, Gabriel. *Histoire de la nation française.* Vol. 9, *Histoire diplomatique,* by René Pinon. Paris, 1929.
Harris, Robert D. *Necker, Reform Statesman of the Ancien Régime.* Berkeley, 1979.
Hassall, Arthur. *The Balance of Power, 1715–1789.* London, 1929.
Henderson, W.O. *The Genesis of the Common Market.* Chicago, 1962.
Horn, D.B. *British Diplomatic Service: 1689–1789.* Oxford, 1961.
——. *Sir Charles Hanbury Williams and European Diplomacy 1747–58.* London, 1930.
Innis, Harold. *The Cod Fisheries.* New Haven, 1940.
Jay, John. *Peace Negotiations of 1782 and 1783.* New York, 1884.
Jolly, Pierre. *Calonne, 1734–1802.* Paris, 1949.
Kaplan, Herbert H. *The First Partition of Poland.* New York, 1962.
Kaplan, Lawrence S. *Colonies into Nation: American Diplomacy 1763–1801.* New York, 1972.
——. *Jefferson and France.* New Haven, 1967.
Kennett, Lee. *The French Forces in America, 1780–1783.* Westport, Conn., 1977.
Kluge, Svetlana. "Vergennes and the Franco-Russian Rapprochement." Master's thesis, Columbia University.
Koser, Reinhold. *König Friedrich der Grosse.* 3 vols. Stuttgard and Berlin, 1893–

1915.
La Croix, René de, duc de Castries. *Le Testament de la monarchie.* Paris, 1958–59.
La Morandière, Charles de. *Histoire de la pèche française de la morue dans l'Amérique septentrionale.* 2 vols. Paris, 1976.
Lavaguéry, Eugene. *Necker, fourrier de la Révolution, 1732–1804.* Paris, 1933.
Lavisse, Ernest, ed. *Histoire de France.* Vol. 9 by H. Carré. Paris, 1910.
LeRoi, J. A. *Histoire de Versailles...* 2 vols. Versailles, 1868.
Lindsay, J.O., ed. *The Old Regime: 1713–1763.* Vol. 7 in *The New Cambridge Modern History.* Cambridge, Eng., 1957.
Lodge, Sir Richard. *Great Britain and Prussia in the 18th Century.* Oxford, 1923.
——. *Studies in Eighteenth-Century Diplomacy, 1740–1748.* London, 1930.
Logette, Aline. *Le Comité contentieux des finances près du conseil du roi 1777–1791.* Nancy, 1964.
Loir M. *La Marine royale en 1789.* Paris, 1892.
Madariaga, Isabel de. *Britain, Russia and the Armed Neutrality of 1780.* New Haven, 1962.
Magnette, F. *Joseph II et la liberté de l'Escaut.* Paris, 1896.
Marsangy, Bonneville de. *Le Chevalier de Vergennes: son ambassade à Constantinople.* 2 vols. Paris, 1894.
——. *Le Comte de Vergennes: son ambassade en Suède, 1771–1775.* Paris, 1898.
Mayer, Charles Joseph de. *La Vie publique et privée de Charles Gravier de Vergennes.* Paris, 1789.
Meng, John J. *The Comte de Vergennes: European Phases of His American Diplomacy, 1774–1780.* Washington, D.C., 1932.
Mercier, S. "Le Service diplomatique pendant le ministère de Vergennes." Mémoire rémis à M. Vaucher, Bibliothèque de Versailles.
Monaghan, Frank. *John Jay: Defender of Liberty.* New York, 1935.
Moore, John Bassett, ed. *A Digest of International Law.* 8 vols. Washington, D.C., 1906.
Morris, Richard B. *The Peacemakers: The Great Powers and American Independence.* New York, 1965.
Muret, Pierre. *La Prépondérance anglaise (1715–1763).* Paris, 1942.
Nicolson, Sir Harold. *The Congress of Vienna: A Study in Allied Unity 1812–1822.* New York, 1961.
——. *Diplomacy.* London, 1963.
Oliva, L. Jay. *Misalliance: A Study of French Policy in Russia during the seven Years' War.* New York, 1964.
Oursel, Paul. *La Diplomatie de la France sous Louis XVI...* Paris, 1921.
Padover, Saul. *The Life and Death of Louis XVI.* New York, 1939.
Palmer, Robert R. *The Age of the Democratic Revolution.* 2 vols. Princton, 1959.
Perkins, J.B. *France in the American Revolution.* Boston and New York, 1911.
Peyssonel, Charles de. *Traité sur le commerce de la Mer Noire.* 2 vols. Paris, 1787.
Peyster, Henry de. *Les Troubles de Hollande... 1780–1795.* Paris, 1905.
Philippes, Paul C. *The West in the Diplomacy of the American Revolution.* New York, 1967.
Porter, Sir James. *Turkey: Its History and Progress.* 2 vols. London, 1854.
Posselt, Ernst Ludwig. *Histoire de Gustave III, roi de Suède.* Genève, 1807.
Rain, Pierre. *La Diplomatie française d'Henri IV à Vergennes.* Paris, 1945.
Renaut, Francis. *La Neutralité hollandaise durant la guerre d'Amérique* 1775–1780. Paris, 1924.

——. *Les Relations diplomatiques entre la Russie et les États-Unis (1776–1825)*. Paris, 1923.

——. *Le Pacte de Famille et l'Amérique*. Paris, 1922.

——. *La Politique de propagande des américains durant la guerre d'indépendance (1776–1783)*. Paris, 1922.

——. *Les Provinces-Unies et la guerre d'Amérique (1775–1789)*. Paris, 1924.

Richmond, Sir Herbert W. *Statesmen and Seapower*. Oxford, 1946.

Rousseau, F. *La Règne de Charles III*. 2 vols. Paris, 1907.

Rulhière, Claude Barloman de. *Le comte de Vergennes; première cause des États-Généraux*. s.i. 1789.

Salomon, Robert. *La Politique orientale de Vergennes (1780–1784)*. Paris, 1935.

Scott, James Brown. *The Armed Neutralities of 1780 and 1800*... New York, 1918.

Segur, L.P. *Politique de tous les cabinets de l'Europe pendant les règnes de Louis XV et de Louis XVI*. 3 vols. Paris, 1801.

Shaw, Peter. *The Character of John Adams*. Chapel Hill, 1976.

Sheridan, Charles Francis. *A History of the Late Revolution in Sweden*. London, 1776.

Smyth, A.H. *The Writings of Benjamin Franklin*. 10 vols. New York, 1907.

Sorel, Albert. *La Question d'Orient au XIIIe siècle*. Paris, 1878.

Stahlberg, George Georgeson. *An History of the Late Revolution in Sweden... Written by a gentleman who was a Swede*. Edinburgh, 1776.

Stinchcomb, William C. *The American Revolution and the French Alliance*. Syracuse, N.Y., 1969.

Stourzh, Gerald. *Benjamin Franklin and American Foreign Policy*. Chicago, 1969.

Tableau historique et politique des révolutions de Genève. Geneva, 1972.

Temperley, H. W. *Frederick the Great and Kaiser Joseph*. London, 1915.

Vallotton, Henri. *Catherine II*. Paris, 1955.

Vandal, Albert. *Louis XV et Elizabeth de Russie*... Paris, 1882.

Vicq-d'Azur, Félix. *Éloge de M. le Comte de Vergennes, lu le 12 février, 1788 dans la séance publique de la Société royale de médicine*. Paris, 1788.

Unzer, Adolf. *Der Friede von Tëschen*... Kiel, 1903.

Waddington, Richard. *Louis XV et le renversement des alliances*. Paris, 1896.

Waliszewski, K. *La Dernière des Romanovs: Elizabeth Ire, 1741–1762*. Paris, 1902.

Wallace, D.D. *The Life of Henry Laurens*. New York, 1915.

Ward, Christopher. *The War of the Revolution*. 2 vols. New York, 1952.

Williams, Basil. *Carteret and Newcastle, a Contrast in Contemporaries*. Cambridge, Eng., 1943.

Yela Utrilla, Juan F. *Espana ante la independencia de los Estados-Unidos*. 2 vols. Lérida, 1925.

Zévort, Edgar. *Le Marquis d'Argenson et la Ministère des affaires étrangères du 18 November, 1744 au 10 janvier, 1747*. Paris, 1880.

Zinkeisen, Johann W. *Geschichte des Osmanischen Reiches in Europa*. Vols. 5-6. Hamburg, 1840–1842.

Secondary Sources: Articles

Abarca, Ramon. "Classical Diplomacy and Bourbon 'Revanche' Strategy, 1763–1770." *Review of Politics* 32 (1970), 313-337.

Aimé, Denise. "L'Année critique: 1776, Vergennes, DuPont et l'Amérique."

Franco-American Review 2 (1937–38), 1–9.

Amonton, C.N. "Biographie — Le Comte de Vergennes." *Annales de la litérature et des arts* 28 (Paris, 1827), 22–25.

Anderson, M.S. "Great Britain and the Russo–Turkish War of 1768–74." *English Historical Review* 69 (1954), 39–58.

——. "The Great Powers and the Russian Annexation of the Crimea, 1783–84." *The Slavonic and East European Review* 37 (1958–59), 17–41.

Antoine, Michel. "Les Conseils des finances sous le règne de Louis XV." *Revue d'historie moderne et contemporaine* 5, no. 3 (1958), 161-200.

Bailyn, Bernard. "Butterfield's Adams: Notes for a Sketch." *The William and Mary Quarterly* 19, 2 (1963), 244-245.

Barthold, Allen J. "French Journalism in the United States, 1780–1800." *Franco-American Review* 1 (1936–37), 215-230.

Bemis, Samuel Flagg. "British Secret Service and the Franco-American Alliance." *American Historical Review* 29 (1924), 474-495.

Boiteux, L.A. "Un mémoire prophétique de Turgot sur la révolution d'Amérique (1776)." *Revue d'histoire diplomatique* 72, no. 3 (1959), 231-239.

Bosher, J.F. "The premiers commis des finances in the Reign of Louis XVI," *French Historical Studies* 3 (1963-64), 475-494.

Bourge, Gaston de. "Le Comte de Vergennes, ses débuts diplomatiques en Allemagne auprès de l'électeur de Trêves et de l'électeur d'Hanovre." *Revue des questions historiques* 44 (1888), 92-166.

Bowden, Witt. "The English Manufacturers and the Commercial Treaty of 1786 with France." *American Historical Review* 25 (1919–20), 18-35.

Brock, W.R. "The Effects of the Loss of American Colonies upon British Policy." *Publication of the [English] Historical Association,* no. 3 (1957), 3-12.

Browning, Oscar. "The Treaty of Commerce between England and France in 1786." *Transactions of the Royal Historical Society* n.s. 2 (1885), 349-364.

——. "The Triple Alliance of 1788." *Transactions of the Royal Historical Society* n.s. 2 (1885), 77-96.

Buron, Edmond, "Statistics on Franco–American Trade, 1778–1806." *Journal of Economic and Business History* 4 (1931–32), 571-580.

Cahen, Léon "Une nouvelle interprétation du traité Franco-anglais de 1786–1787." *Revue historique 185 (1931), 257-285.*

Castries, René de la Croix, duc de. "La Pacte de famille et le querre de l'indépendance américaine." *Revue d'histoire diplomatique* 75 (1964), 294-306.

Charles-Roux, François, "La Monarchie française de l'ancien régime et la question de la Mer Noire." *Revue de la Méditerranée* nos. 25, 26, 27 (1948) pp. 257-270, 394-409, 531-553.

——. François. "La Politique française en Egypte à la fin du XVIIIe siècle." *Revue historique* 91 (1906), 1-20, 225-252.

Chinard, Gilbert. "Notes on the French Translations of the 'Forms of Government and Constitutions of the Several United States'; 1778 and 1783." *Year Book of the American Philosophical Society* (Philadelphia, 1943), 88-106.

Clough, Shephard B. "The Crisis in the French Economy at the Beginning of the Revolution." *Journal of Economic History* 6 (1946) 191-196.

Cole, W.A. "Trends in Eighteenth-Century Smuggling." *Economic History Review,* 2d series, 10 (1957–58), 394-410.

Constantine, A. "Le Corps Rouchambeau face aux difficultés économiques du royaume et des États-Unis d'Amérique 1780–1782." *Revue historique des Armées,* no. 3 (4 special.) (1976), pp. 106-137.

Cottreau, G. "Les Gardes de la Porte du roi et leur dernier Capitaine Colonel, le Vicomte de Vergennes en 1783." *Carnet de la Sabretache: Revue militaire retrospective,* 2d series, 2 (1903).

Davison, Roderic H. "Russian Skill and Turkish Imbecility: The Treaty of Kuchuk Karnardji." *Slavic Review* 35, no. 3 (1976), 463-483.

Del Perugia, Paul. "Le Comte de Vergennes au ministère." *Revue d'histoire diplomatique* 55 (1942), 84-95.

Dollot, Louis "Conclaves et diplomatie françaises au XVIIIe siécle." *Revue d'histoire diplomatique* 76 (avril–juin 1961), 124-135.

Donaghay, Marie, "Calonne and the Anglo-French Commercial Treaty of 1786." *Journal of Modern History* 50, no. 3 (1978) ii (abstract). The entire article can be obtained from University Microfilms International, IJ 00038.

——. "The Maréchal de Castries and the Anglo–French Commercial Negotiations of 1786–87." *Historical Journal* 22, no. 2 (1979), 295-312.

Doniol Henri. "Le Ministère des Affaires Etrangerès de France sous le Comte de Vergennes." *Revue d'histoire diplomatique* 7 (1893), 528-560.

——. "La Première Négotiation de la paix de 1783 entre la France et la Grand Bretagne." *Revue d'histoire diplomatique* 6 (1892), 56-89.

Dore R. P. "The Prestige Factor in International Affairs." *International Affairs* 51, no. 2 (1975), 190-207.

Dorlodot, M. le baron de. "L'Aide belge aux insurgents américains." *Annales du XXXIV Congrès de la Fédération archéologique et historique de Belge.* (July, 1951), 22-25.

Doyle, William. "The *Parlement* of France and the Breakdown of the Old Regime, 1771–1788." *French Historical Studies* 6, no. 4 (1970), 415-458.

Dull, Jonathan R., "France and the American Revolution: Questioning the Myths." *Proceedings of the Annual Meeting of the Western Society for French History* 1 (1973), 110-118.

——. "Franklin in France: a Reappraisal." *Proceedings of the Annual Meeting of the Western Society for French History* 4 (1976), 256-262.

Dumaine, Alfred. "Le Comte de Vergennes et l'indépendance des Etats-Unis." *Revue d'histoire et de diplomatie* 37 (1923), 432-455.

Eheverria, Durand, and Murphy, Orville T. "The American Revolutionary Army: A French Estimate of 1777." *Military Affairs* 27 (1963), 1-7; 153-162.

Erlanger, Philippe. "Louis XVI fondateur des Etats-Unis." *Revue de Paris* 3 (1952), 78-86.

Fagniez, Gustave. "La Politique de Vergennes et la diplomatie de Breteuil, 1774–1787." *Revue Historique*140 (1922), 1-25; 161-127.

Faverie, A. Schalk de la. "La Révolution américaine et la révolution française." *Journal de la Société des Américanistes de Paris.* 11 (1914–19), 385-40.

Fay, Bernard. "Portrait du Comte de Vergennes." *Franco–American Review*1 (1936–37), 143-148.

——. "Une paix sans victoire: la paix de 1783." *Revue d'histoire diplomatique* 44 (1930), 213-220.

Feifer, Eliane. "Vergennes et Talleyrand." *Science Politique* (1937).

Flamant, Albert. "En rêvant dans le Grand Sérail." *Revue des Deux Mondes* 2 (mars–avril, 1931), 666-680.

Fonteneau, Général. "La Periode française de la guerre d'indépendance (1776–1780)." *Revue historique des Armées* 3 (1976), 47-85.

Fox, Frank. "Negotiating with the Russians: Ambassador Ségur's Mission to Saint Petersburg, 1784–1789." *French Historical Studies* 7, no. 1 (1971), 47-71.

Fraguier, Bertrand de. "Le Duc d'Aiguillon et l'Angleterre (juin 1771–avril, 1773)." *Revue d'histoire diplomatique* 26 (1912), 607-627.

Gilbert, Felix. "The New Diplomacy of the Enghteenth Century." *World Politics* 4 (1951–52), 1-38.

Girard, Albert. "Une négotiation commerciale entre la France et l'Espagne en 1782." *Revue historique* 3 (1912), 292-317.

Glachant, Roger. "Croquis de l'Européen Vergennes." *Nouvelle Revue des Deux Mondes* 8 (1979), 354-366.

Godechot, J. "Les Combattants de la guerre de l'indépendance des États-Unis et les troubles agraires en France de 1789 à 1792. *Annales historiques de la Révolution française* 28 (1956), 292-294.

Golden, F.A. "Catherine II and the American Revolution." *American Historical Review* 21 (1915), 92-96.

Gottschalk, Louis. "The American Revolution in the Causal Pattern of the French Revolution." *Publications of the American Friends of Lafayette* (Easton, Pa. 1948), 19-20.

Greenbaum, Louis. "Talleyrand et Vergennes: The Debut of a Diplomat." *Catholic Historical Review* 56, no. 3. (1970), 543-550.

Guéry, Alain, "Les finances de la monarchie françaises sous l'ancien régime, *Annales, economies, sociétés, civilisations* 33, no.2 (1978), 216-239.

Hargreaves, Reginald. "Franklin Had a Word for It." *Army Quarterly and Defense Journal* 101, no. 2. (1971), 178-185.

Harris, Robert D. "French Finances and the American War, *Journal of Modern History* 48, no. 2 (1976), 233-258.

——. "Necher's *Compte rendu* of 1781, A reconsideration," *Journal of Modern History* 42 (1970), 161-163.

Henderson, W. O. "The Anglo–French Commercial Treaty of 1786." *Economic History Review,* 2nd series, 10 (1957–58), 104-112.

Horn, D. B. 'The Cabinet Controversy on Subsidies in Time of Peace, 1749–1750." *The English Historical Review* 45 (1930), 463-466.

——. "The Origins of the Proposed Election of a King of the Romans, 1748–1750." *The English Historical Review* 42 (1927), 361-370.

Irvine, Dallas D. "The Newfoundland Fishery: A French Objective in the War of American Independence." *Canadian Historical Review* 13 (1932), 268-284.

Kadic, Ante. "Rudje Boskovic on American Independence." *Journal of Croatian Studies* 17 (1976), 10-13.

Kennett, Lee. "L'Expédition Rochambeau-Ternay: un succès diplomatique." *Revue historique des Armées* 3; (4 special) (1976), 86-105.

Keyte, V. J. "War of American Independence (The Failure of British Arms)." *Army Quarterly and Defense Journal* 106, no. 2 (1976), 183-188.

Kite, Elizabeth S. "The Continental Congress and France: Secret Aid and the Alliance 1776–78." *Records of the American Catholic Historical Society of Philadelphia* 39 (1928), 166-167.

Kirchner, Walter. "Le Commencement des relations économiques entre la France et la Russie." *Revue historique* 202 (1949), 162-183.

Laigue, Louis de. "Le Comte de Froullay, ambassadeur à Venise, 1733–1743." *Revue d'histoire diplomatique* 27 (1913), 65-138.

Lodge, Sir Richard. "The Continental Policy of Great Britain, 1740–1760." *History*

16 (1931–32), 298-304.

Logette, Aline. "Quelques nouvelles sources pour l'administration des finances à la fin du: XVIIIe siècle." *Revue historique de droit français et étranger* 47, no. 3 (1969), 408-440.

Madariaga Isabel de. "The Secret Austro–Russian Treaty of 1781." *Slavonic and East European Review* 38 (1949), 114-145.

Malet, Albert, "Un ministre des affaires étrangères au XVIIIe siècle." *Revue bleue* 45 no. 10 (March, 1890), 300-305.

Marans, René de. "Le Centenaire de Vergennes." *Revue Universelle,* no. 2 (1920), pp. 92-98.

Mathias, Peter and O'Brien, Patrick. "Taxation in Britain and France, 1715-1810, A comparison of the Social and Economic Incidences of Taxes Collected for the Central Governments, *Journal of European Economic History* 5, no. 3 (1976), 601-650.

Meidan, G.W. van der. "Een Turks plan om nederlands - indie in France handen te doen overgaan." *Nederlands Archivenbland* 8, no. 1 (1976), 26-28.

Mirepoix, Emmanuel de Lévis. "Quelques lettres du Baron de Montesquieu sur la Guerre d'Indépendance Américaine." *Franco-American Review* 2 (1937–38), 192-204.

Meng, John J. "The Comte de Vergennes: Foundations of His American Diplomacy." *Records of the American Catholic Historical society* 40 (1929), 311-346.

——. "A Footnote to Secret Aid in the American Revolution." *American Historical Review* 43 (1938), 791-795.

Meyer, Jean. "Les Difficultes du commerce franco-americain vues de Nantes, 1776–1790." *French Historical Studies* 11, no. 2 (1979), 159-183.

——. "Un problème mal posé: la noblesse pauvre, l'exemple breton au XVIIe siècle." *Revue d'histoire moderne et Contemporaine* 18 (1971), 161-188.

Moore, Anson D. "The Politics of John Adams." *American Historical Review* 4 (1898–99), 292-312.

Moreaux, René "La Situation de la France dans le Levant à la fin du XVIIIe siècle. *Revue d'histoire moderne et Contemporaine* 3 (1901-1902), 137-155.

Morton, Brian N. "Roderique Hortalez to the Secret Committee: An Unpublished French policy Statement of 1777." *The French Review* 50 (1977), 875-890.

Morton, Brian. "Vergennes, Beaumarchais and Roderique Hortalez et Cie." *Proceedings of the Annual Meeting of the Western Society for French Historical Studies,* no. 3 (1975), pp. 256-262.

Mouser, Sylvan L. "France and the American Revolution." *Indiana History Bulletin* 5, no. 10 (1974), 133-135.

Muret, Pierre. "L'Histoire diplomatique du milieu du XVIIIe siècle d'après les travaux de Sir Richard Lodge." *Revue d'histoire moderne* 6–7 (1931-32), 77-83.

Murphy, Orville T. "The Battle of Germantown and the Franco–American alliance of 1778." *Pennsylvania Magazine of History and Biography* 82 (1958), 55-64.

——. "Charles Gravier de Vergennes: Portrait of an Old Régime Diplomat." *Political Science Quarterly* 83 (1968), 400-418.

——. "The Comte de Vergennes, The Newfoundland Fisheries and the Peace Negotiations of 1783." *Canadian Historical Review* 46 (1965), 32-46.

——. "Dupont de Nemours and the Anglo-French Commercial Treaty of 1786." *Economic History Review* 19, no. 3 (1966), 569-580.

Nussbaum, Frederick L. "The Revolutionary Vergennes and Lafayette versus the Farmers Generals." *Journal of Modern History* 3 (1931) 592-604.

Ormesson, Wladimir d'. "L'Ombre de Vergennes." *Le Temps* (13 mai 1933).
Pacha, Salih Munir. "Louis XVI et le Sultan Selim III." *Revue d'histoire diplomatique* 26 (Paris, 1912), 516-548.
Palmer, Robert R. "Turgot, Paragon of the Continental Enlightenment." *Journal of Law and Economics* 19, no. 3 (1976), 607-619.
Pinon, René. "Louis XVI, Vergennes et la grand lutte contre l'Angleterre." *Revue d'histoire diplomatique* 43 (1929), 37-64.
Prelinger, Catherine M. "Less Lucky than Lafayette: A note on the French Applicants to Benjamin Franklin for Commissions in the American Army, 1776–1785." *Proceedings of the Annual Meeting of the Western Society for French History*, no. 4 (1976), pp. 263-271.
Rahbek, K. Schmidt. "Wie ist Panine Plan zu einen Nordischen System enstaden?" *Zeitschrift fur Slawistik* 2, no. 3 (Berlin, 1957), 414-415.
Rakove, Jack N. "French Diplomacy and American Politics: The First Crisis, 1779." *Mid-America* 60 (1978), 27-35.
Regemorter, J.L. Van. "Commerce et politique: préparation et négociation du traité Franco-Russe de 1787." *Cahiers du Monde Russe et Soviétique* 4 (1963), 230-257.
Roberts, Michael. "Great Britain and the Swedish Revolution 1772–1773." *The Historical Journal* 7 no. 1 (1964), 1-46.
Rose, J. Holland. "The Franco–British Commercial Treaty of 1786. *English Historical Review* 23 (1908), 709-724.
——. "Great Britain and the Dutch Question in 1787–1788." *American Historical Review* 14 (1908–9), 262-283.
Roslund-Mercurio, C. L. "The American Colonial Rebellion and Swedish–British Diplomacy, 1775 to 1778." *Historisk Tidskrift* 4 (1974), 475-489.
Savant, Jean. "Louis XVI et l'alliance russe." *Nouvelle Revue des Deux Mondes* no. 8 (1975), pp. 306-324.
——. "Louis XVI et l'alliance russe d'après un document indédit." *Revue d'histoire diplomatique* 61 (1947), 67-89.
Schmidt, K. R. "Problems connected with the Last Polish Election." *Scando-Slavica* 2 (1956), 134-148.
Scott, H. M. "Great Britain, Poland and the Russian alliance of 1763–1764." *Historical Journal* 19, no. 1 (1976), 53-74.
——. "France and the Polish Throne." *Slavonic and East European Revue* 53 (1975), 370-388.
Sorel, Albert, "Vergennes et sa politique." *Revue historique* 15 (1881), 273-282.
Tratchevsky, Alexandre. "La Diplomatie de Vergennes ou la France et l'Allemagne sous Loui XVI," *Revue historique* 14 (1880), 241-285, 15 (1881), 1-46.
——. "Vergennes et ses apologistes." *Revue historique* 16 (1881), 327-332.
Van Tyne, C.H. "Influences Which Determined the French Government to Make the Treaty with America in 1778." *American Historical Review* 21 (1915), 528-541.
Véou, P. "Un chapitre inédit des mémoires de Barthélémy: la révolution suèdoise de 1772." *Revue des Etudes Historiques* 104 (1937), 401-427.
Viner, Jacob. "Power versus Plenty as Objectives of Foreign Policy in the Seventeenth and Eighteenth Centuries." *World Politics* 1 (1948), 1-30.
Wendel, Jacques M. "Turgot and the American Revolution." *Modern Age* 23, no. 2 (1979), 282-289.
Whitridge, Arnold. "Washington's French Volunteers." *History Today* 24, no. 9 (1974), 640-647.
Wolkonskii, G. "La France et la menace d'expansion russe 1756–63." *Revue*

d'histoire diplomatique 70 (1956), 193-199.
Zeller, Gaston. "Le Principe d'equilibre dans la politique internationale avant 1789." *Revue historique* 215 (1956), 25-37.

Index